Women and the Religion of Ancient Israel

THE ANCHOR YALE BIBLE REFERENCE LIBRARY is a project of international and interfaith scope in which Protestant, Catholic, and Jewish scholars from many countries contribute individual volumes. The project is not sponsored by any ecclesiastical organization and is not intended to reflect any particular theological doctrine.

The series is committed to producing volumes in the tradition established half a century ago by the founders of the Anchor Bible, William Foxwell Albright and David Noel Freedman. It aims to present the best contemporary scholarship in a way that is accessible not only to scholars but also to the educated nonspecialist. It is committed to work of sound philological and historical scholarship, supplemented by insight from modern methods, such as sociological and literary criticism.

John J. Collins
General Editor

THE ANCHOR YALE BIBLE REFERENCE LIBRARY

Women and the Religion of Ancient Israel

SUSAN ACKERMAN

YALE AYBRL

Yale UNIVERSITY PRESS

NEW HAVEN AND LONDON

Set in Adobe Caslon type by Newgen North America.
Printed in the United States of America.

Library of Congress Control Number: 2021932831
ISBN 978-0-300-14178-8 (hardcover : alk. paper)

A catalogue record for this book is available from the British Library.

This paper meets the requirements of ANSI/NISO Z39.48-1992 (Permanence of Paper).

10 9 8 7 6 5 4 3 2 1

To Ben, Harry, Kurt, and Nik,
who have taught me more than I would have imagined possible
about ancient Israelite religion,
and to Becky, Emma, James, and Peter,
who managed to teach me a little about Second Temple Judaism
and early Christianity as well

Contents

PART TWO: WHEN? THE CALENDAR OF WOMEN'S RELIGIOUS LIVES

PART THREE: WHO? WOMEN RELIGIOUS FUNCTIONARIES

Illustrations

Acknowledgments

It is somewhat ironic that the title page of this book carries only my name, as I am all too aware—as is any author of a book like this—of the many, many people who have supported and sustained me through the process that has brought this volume to completion. These include the editorial staff members at Yale University Press who have overseen the Anchor Yale Bible Reference Library during the years I have been working on this book, especially Jennifer Banks, Heather Gold, Susan Laity, and Abbie Storch, as well as copyeditor Jessie Dolch, all of whose patience with me has been extraordinary. John J. Collins, the General Editor of the Anchor Yale Bible Reference Library, has likewise been extraordinarily patient and extraordinarily kind, and I in addition owe my deepest thanks to Saul M. Olyan, the member of the Anchor Yale Bible Reference Library editorial board who took responsibility for editing my draft manuscript. Saul did so with meticulous care and exceptional rigor, yet also with remarkable compassion—not always the easiest combination for an editor to deliver but a true gift for an author to receive. I am grateful.

I am also grateful for the support of the many scholarly communities to which I am fortunate enough to belong. The Dartmouth College Department of Religion has now been my intellectual home for three decades, and it has been a nurturing home indeed, thanks to the many wonderful colleagues who have been a part of its ranks over those thirty years. I especially thank Professors Nancy Frankenberry and Ronald M. Green, both recently retired, who were important mentors to me during a much earlier phase of my Dartmouth career, when I was their student while an undergraduate religion major, and who remained stalwart allies and friends during the twenty-five years we served together on the Dartmouth faculty.

The Religion Departmental Administrator, Meredyth Morley, and the department's Administrative Assistant, Marcia Welsh, also deserve special thanks, especially for the way, too many times, they had to rescue me when the various machines that my mere presence seems to jinx—printer, copier, fax machine, scanner—failed to perform whatever task I needed them (usually urgently) to execute. The staff who served over the years in Dartmouth's Arts and Humanities Resource Center—Susan Bibeau, Tom Garbelotti, Anthony Helm, and Robien Wymans—were equally adept and equally undaunted when it came to shepherding me through my many and various computer ordeals. My work also would have been deeply impoverished had I not had the assistance of William Fontaine, who was the Dartmouth College Reference Librarian in Religion from the time I first joined the Dartmouth faculty in 1990 until he retired in 2017. In fact, I almost found myself retiring when Bill did, as he has been such an invaluable asset to my research.

Beyond Dartmouth, collegial communities that have been particularly important to me are the Biblical Colloquium, the Colloquium for Biblical Research, and the Biblical Studies Research Seminar of New College, at the University of Edinburgh. All these bodies have heard me present parts of the materials that made their way into this book, and their wise and considered feedback has made my work—especially in Chapters 1, 4, and 12—considerably stronger. I am grateful as well for the opportunities I have had to present parts of my work at meetings of the American Schools of Oriental Research, the Society of Biblical Literature, the International Organization for the Study of the Old Testament, the European Association of Biblical Studies, and the British and Irish Society for Old Testament Study, as well as at academic institutions such as Baltimore Hebrew University, Boston College, Brown University, the Institute of Biblical Archaeology at Tübingen University, Jewish Theological Seminary, Johns Hopkins University, La Sierra University, Oberlin College, the University of Arizona, the University of North Carolina at Chapel Hill, and Yale Divinity School.

As I have developed and refined my ideas, I have also benefited by publishing preliminary versions of my research and receiving feedback from readers. Portions of Chapter 3 were published previously as "Who Is Sacrificing at Shiloh? The Priesthoods of Ancient Israel's Regional Sanctuaries," in *Levites and Priests in Biblical History and Tradition,* ed. Mark A. Leuchter and Jeremy M. Hutton (Ancient Israel and Its Literature 9. Atlanta: Society of Biblical Literature, 2011), 25–43, and portions of Chapter 4 were published previously as "Hannah's Tears," in *Celebrate Her for the Fruit of Her Hands: Essays in Honor of Carol L. Meyers,* ed. Susan Ackerman, Charles E. Carter, Beth Alpert Nakhai, Karla Bohmbach, and Franzvolker Greigenhagen (Winona Lake, Ind.: Eisenbrauns, 2015), 13–25. Likewise, portions of Chapter 5 were published previously as "Women and the Religious Culture of the State Temples of the Ancient Levant, Or: Priestesses, Purity, and Parturition," in *Temple Building and Temple Cult: Architecture and Cultic Paraphernalia of Temples in the Levant (2.–1. Mill. B.C.E.). Proceedings of a Conference on the Occasion of the 50th Anniversary of the Institute of Biblical Archaeology at the University of Tübingen (28–30 May 2010),* ed. Jens Kamlah (ADPV 41. Wiesbaden: Harrassowitz, 2012), 259–89, and portions of Chapter 12 were published previously as "Mirrors, Drums, and Trees," in *Congress Volume: Helsinki 2010,* ed. Martti Nissinen (VTSup 148. Leiden: Brill, 2012), 537–67. All are reproduced by permission. Portions of Chapter 11 were also published previously as "'I Have Hired You with My Son's Mandrakes': Women's Reproductive Magic in Ancient Israel," in *Sex in Antiquity: Exploring Gender and Sexuality in the Ancient World,* ed. Mark Masterson, Nancy Sorkin Rabinowitz, and James Robson (New York: Routledge, 2015), 15–29, and are reproduced with permission of the licensor through PLSclear; essay copyright © 2015 by Susan Ackerman. In addition, portions of Chapter 10 appeared in a preliminary and abbreviated form in "Why Is Miriam Also Among the Prophets? (And Is Zipporah Among the Priests?)," *JBL* 121 (2002): 47–80.

My personal networks have been as supportive and sustaining to me as have my professional colleagues, and I am grateful to my family—the late George Ackerman, Peggy Ackerman, Laura, Bruce, Jason, and Gabey Smoller, and Rachel Starr. I am also blessed with good friends with whom to share good food and good wine, including Kate Conley, Anna Covici, Sheila Culbert, Mona Domosh, Steve and Elizabeth Dycus, Frank Magilligan, Deborah Nichols, Saul Olyan, Bill Propp, Fred Schockaert, Richard Stamelman, Richard Voos, John Watanabe, and Richard Wright. Likewise, I have been blessed with good friends with whom to share great adventures, especially traveling in the Middle East: Matt Adams, Hanan Charaf, Bill Dever, Steve Falconer, Patricia Fall, Pam Gaber, Rachel Hallote, Tim Harrison, Sharon Herbert, Ann-Marie Knoblauch, Tom and Alina Levy, Mohammad Najjar, and Andy Vaughn.

Finally, I thank my many students over the years, whose comments and questions in classroom discussions and whose exam essays and term papers pushed me over and over to clarify and refine my ideas. I'm especially grateful to the students who stuck with me through course after course, all the way through to honors projects in their senior year and even onward to graduate work after they left my care. I have learned so much from them, and it is an honor to dedicate this book to these superstars—Becky, Ben, Emma, Harry, James, Kurt, Nik, and Peter—in recognition of their hard work and as a small token of my respect and admiration.

Abbreviations

ABD	*Anchor Bible Dictionary.* Edited by David Noel Freedman. 6 vols. New York: Doubleday, 1992.
ADPV	Abhandlungen des Deutschen Palästina-Vereins
AfO	*Archiv für Orientforschung*
ANEM	Ancient Near Eastern Monographs
ANEP	*The Ancient Near East in Pictures Relating to the Old Testament.* Edited by James B. Pritchard. Princeton: Princeton University Press, 1954.
ANET	*Ancient Near Eastern Texts Relating to the Old Testament.* Edited by James B. Pritchard. 3rd ed. with supplement. Princeton: Princeton University Press, 1969.
AOAT	Alter Orient und Altes Testament
ATANT	Abhandlungen zur Theologie des Alten und Neuen Testaments
AYB	Anchor Yale Bible
AYBRL	Anchor Yale Bible Reference Library
BA	*Biblical Archaeologist*
BAR	*Biblical Archaeology Review*
BASOR	*Bulletin of the American Schools of Oriental Research*
BDB	Francis Brown, S. R. Driver, and Charles A. Briggs, *A Hebrew and English Lexicon of the Old Testament.* Oxford: Clarendon, 1907.
BHS	*Biblia Hebraica Stuttgartensia.* Edited by K. Elliger and W. Rudolph. Stuttgart: Deutsche Bibelgesellschaft, 1983.
BJS	Brown Judaic Studies

BN	*Biblische Notizen*
BR	*Biblical Research*
BRev	*Bible Review*
BZAW	Beihefte zur Zeitschrift für die alttestamentliche Wissenschaft
CANE	*Civilizations of the Ancient Near East.* Edited by Jack M. Sasson. 4 vols. New York: Scribner, 1995.
CBC	Cambridge Bible Commentary
CBQ	*Catholic Biblical Quarterly*
CHANE	Culture and History of the Ancient Near East
CIS	*Corpus inscriptionum semiticarum*
DDD	*Dictionary of Deities and Demons in the Bible.* Edited by Karel van der Toorn, Bob Becking, and Pieter W. van der Horst. 2nd ed. Leiden: Brill, 1999.
ER	*The Encyclopedia of Religion.* Edited by Lindsay Jones. 15 vols. 2nd ed. Detroit: Macmillan Reference, 2005.
ErIsr	*Eretz-Israel*
FAT	Forschungen zum Alten Testament
FCB	Feminist Companion to the Bible
GKC	*Gesenius' Hebrew Grammar.* Edited by E. Kautzsch. Translated by A. E. Cowley. 2nd ed. Oxford: Clarendon, 1910.
HeBAI	*Hebrew Bible and Ancient Israel*
HSM	Harvard Semitic Monographs
HTR	*Harvard Theological Review*
HUCA	*Hebrew Union College Annual*
ICC	International Critical Commentary
IEJ	*Israel Exploration Journal*
JANER	*Journal of Ancient Near Eastern Religions*
JAOS	*Journal of the American Oriental Society*
JB	Jerusalem Bible
JBL	*Journal of Biblical Literature*
JHS	*Journal of Hebrew Scriptures*
JNES	*Journal of Near Eastern Studies*

JPS	Jewish Publication Society Bible
JQR	*Jewish Quarterly Review*
JSOT	*Journal for the Study of the Old Testament*
JSOTSup	Journal for the Study of the Old Testament: Supplement Series
KAI	*Kanaanäische und aramäische Inschriften.* Herbert Donner and Wolfgang Röllig. 3 vols. 2nd ed. Wiesbaden: Harrassowitz, 1966–1969.
KJV	King James Version Bible
KTU	*Die keilalphabetischen Texte aus Ugarit, Ras Ibn Hani und anderen Orten.* Edited by Manfried Dietrich, Oswald Loretz, and Joaquín Sanmartín. 3rd ed. Münster: Ugarit-Verlag, 2013.
LHBOTS	Library of Hebrew Bible/Old Testament Studies
LXX	Septuagint
NAB	New American Bible
NABRE	New American Bible, Revised Edition
NCBC	New Cambridge Bible Commentary
NEA	*Near Eastern Archaeology*
NEB	New English Bible
NJB	New Jerusalem Bible
NJPS	New Jewish Publication Society Bible
NRSV	New Revised Standard Version Bible
OBO	Orbis biblicus et orientalis
OEANE	*The Oxford Encyclopedia of Archaeology in the Near East.* Edited by Eric M. Meyers. 5 vols. New York: Oxford University Press, 1997.
OTL	Old Testament Library
OTS	Old Testament Studies
OtSt	Oudtestamentische Studiën
PEQ	*Palestine Exploration Quarterly*
RB	*Revue biblique*
RBS	Resources for Biblical Study
REB	Revised English Bible

RSV	Revised Standard Version Bible
SBLDS	Society of Biblical Literature Dissertation Series
SBLMS	Society of Biblical Literature Monograph Series
SBLSymS	Society of Biblical Literature Symposium Series
SBLWAW	Society of Biblical Literature Writings from the Ancient World
ST	*Studia theologica*
SWBA	Social World of Biblical Antiquity
TA	*Tel Aviv*
TDOT	*Theological Dictionary of the Old Testament.* Edited by G. Johannes Botterweck, Helmer Ringgren, and Heinz-Josef Fabry. 15 vols. Grand Rapids: Eerdmans, 1974–2006.
UF	*Ugarit-Forschungen*
VT	*Vetus Testamentum*
VTSup	Supplements to Vetus Testamentum
WBC	Word Biblical Commentary
WIS	*Women in Scripture: A Dictionary of Named and Unnamed Women in the Hebrew Bible, the Apocryphal/Deuterocanonical Books, and the New Testament.* Edited by Carol Meyers, with Toni Craven and Ross S. Kraemer. Boston: Houghton Mifflin, 2000.
WMANT	Wissenschaftliche Monographien zum Alten und Neuen Testament
WTJ	*Westminster Theological Journal*
ZA	*Zeitschrift für Assyriologie*
ZAW	*Zeitschrift für die alttestamentliche Wissenschaft*
ZDPV	*Zeitschrift des Deutschen Palästina-Vereins*

Introduction

In the autumn of 1979, when I was a senior in college and my undergraduate degree work in religion was almost complete, I had a chance to take as an elective my institution's introductory (and at that point almost brand-new) course in women's studies. Because I was a religion major, and because I also knew by that time that I was applying to graduate school to study the Hebrew Bible, I wrote a final paper for the class titled "Women in the Old Testament." Much to my delight, I received an A, both for the paper and for the course. Still, I joke today that I seem never to have been satisfied with those results, for over the past three decades, I have repeatedly revisited and revised materials that I first considered in that long-ago essay.

This book, *Women and the Religion of Ancient Israel,* might be said to represent yet another effort at revisiting and revising the ideas I explored in that original paper. But even more, it represents both a contraction and an expansion. It represents a contraction, first, because I do not intend to address here all the myriad aspects of women as portrayed in the Hebrew Bible, or the Christian Old Testament, that my long-ago undergraduate essay sought to discuss; the hubris that led my twenty-one-year-old self to believe I could cover everything that might be said about, say, the political, economic, social, and juridical status of biblical women in fifteen pages, and fifteen double-spaced pages at that (!), has long since disappeared. Rather, my goal in this book is to speak only to the issue regarding the biblical world's women to which my undergraduate major should have pointed me in the first place: how I, as a student of religion, might describe and analyze the *religious* lives and *religious* experiences of the biblical world's women, or what the noted biblical scholar and archaeologist of ancient Israel Carol Meyers has called "women's religious culture."

By this, Meyers means not only the "beliefs in supernatural deities or powers recognized by the group or groups to which people belonged" (in this book, the women of ancient Israel), but also—and more crucially—"the appropriate responses to those powers, responses that were meant variously to praise, appease, or somehow manipulate the impact of those divine beings on people's lives."[1] These responses include the religious rituals and practices in which the biblical world's women engaged, the religious events in which they participated, and the religious roles that they assumed—all in order that these women might facilitate their relationships with the superhuman beings that they believed populated their cosmos. Preeminent among these was the ancient Israelite god Yahweh. But many ancient Israelites—including ancient Israelite women—also devoted themselves to other gods, goddesses, and demigods, as well as acknowledging the supernatural abilities of their families' ancestors (who were thought to be able to affect the course of human events from the world beyond the grave).

This book's focus is also constrained chronologically, as rather than address the entire span of biblical history—that is, the biblical story as it stretches from the dawn of creation to ca. 165 BCE (the approximate date of the Hebrew Bible's latest compositions)[2]—I consider here only what scholars call the preexilic period of ancient Israel. This is the era of Israelite history that begins in ca. 1200 BCE, when, according to the biblical books of Joshua and Judges, and according as well to our best understanding of the archaeological record, the people that eventually became the polity of Israel first settled in the highlands of what was then southern Canaan.[3] This era ends approximately six hundred years later, in 586 BCE, when the Babylonian Empire conquered the last remnant of the Israelite commonwealth—the Southern Kingdom of Judah—and exiled a noteworthy part of the conquered Judahites' elites to the Babylonian homeland in southern Mesopotamia.

I focus on this preexilic period because, at least for its core centuries (which I take to be the ninth to seventh centuries BCE), this was the only era during Israel's long history when its peoples lived in relatively cohesive cultural (although not political) unity. Most important for my purposes, these preexilic Israelites understood themselves as the people of a common god, Yahweh. They also spoke a common language, Hebrew (albeit with some significant dialectical variants), and they "appear to have shared similar patterns of social organization and settlement at the local level."[4] These local settlements, moreover, all lay within a fairly circumscribed geographical area: first, the land that the Hebrew Bible describes as running "from Dan to Beersheba" (i.e., a land that stretched about 240 kilometers from the headwaters of the Jordan River, in the north, to the northern Negev, in the south—or what we know today as the northern two-thirds of the state of Israel, plus the Palestinian territories; Fig. I.1). Then, after

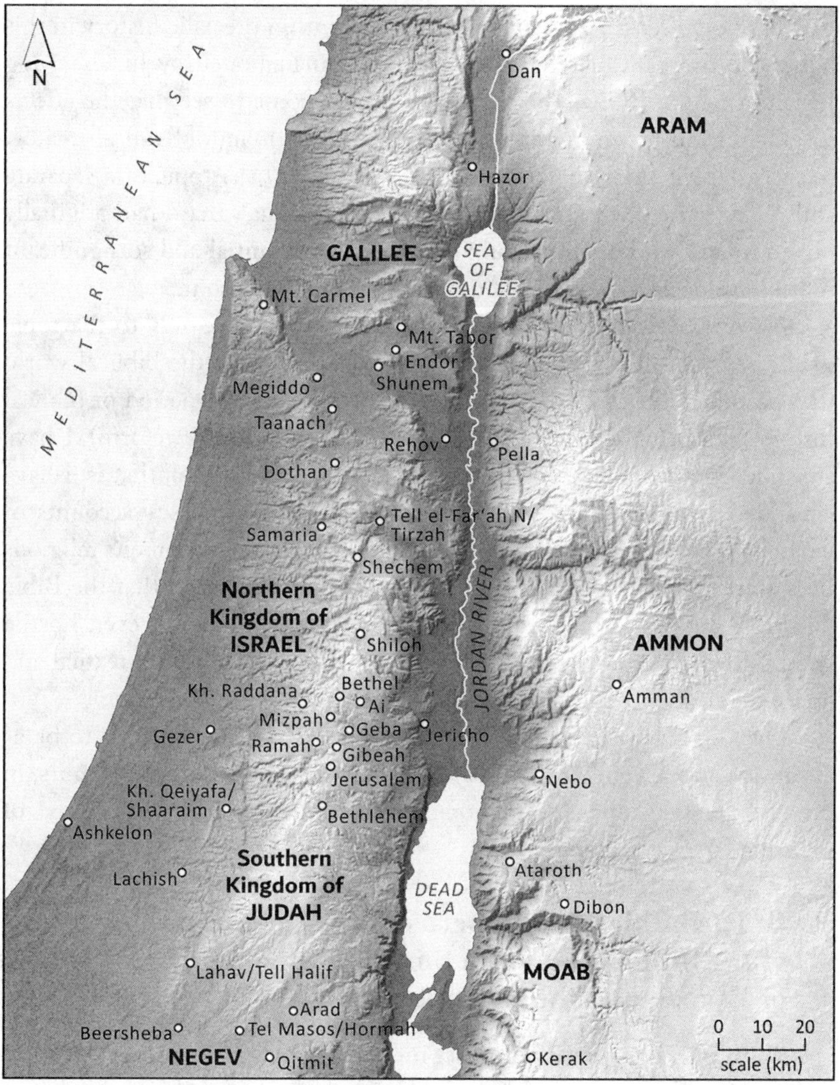

Fig. I.1. Preexilic Israel. Courtesy of Jonathan W. Chipman, Citrin GIS Lab, Dartmouth College.

the Assyrian Empire's takeover of Israel's northern and central regions, in 722/721 BCE, and before the Babylonian conquest of 586 BCE, the ancient Israelites occupied the much more circumscribed territory of Judah (which ran about 80 kilometers from north to south, or, according to the biblical idiom, "from Geba to Beersheba").

Still, even within the context of this preexilic period's six-hundred-year timeframe, I have found it necessary to constrain the scope of my inquiry, as I will not be discussing one particular event within preexilic history in this book: the program of religious reformation inaugurated by Judah's King Josiah in ca. 622 BCE.[5] This is because I have come to see that the effects Josiah's reform program had upon women are so manifold and ultimately so far-reaching that I have decided to make them the topic of a separate study.[6] Likewise, the topic of women's life-cycle rituals that I had originally hoped to address herein has proved to be so substantial and so significant that I have decided to dedicate a separate monograph to it.

Nevertheless, even as I restrict myself in this book only to the topic of the *religious* lives and experiences of the women of the biblical world (less women's life-cycle rituals) and only to the *preexilic* period of biblical history (excepting the events associated with the Josianic reform), I have expanded my scope beyond an analysis that is only biblical; that is, I have expanded beyond an analysis that considers *only* the Bible's accounts of women's preexilic religious culture. Instead, I also explore women's religious lives and experiences within the traditions of ancient Israel that the Bible does not document or documents only in very limited and even hostile ways. I therefore draw on multiple extrabiblical sources—both textual and archaeological—to augment my investigation.

Overall, my goal (but for the exceptions previously noted) is to be as expansive and all-embracing as I am able, and as our evidence permits, in presenting a synthetic examination of the religious lives and experiences of preexilic Israelite women.

Of Partialities and Imperfections: The Limitations of the Biblical Text as a Source for the Study of Women and the Religion of Ancient Israel

With that overview in mind, let me turn to describe in more detail certain aspects of the contractions and expansions that structure this book—in particular, my commitment to move beyond an analysis that examines *only* the Bible's account of women's religious lives and experiences within the preexilic era in order to consider women's religious culture as it was manifest both in the Bible and beyond. Note especially my focus on "the Bible *and* beyond," as opposed to, say, an intent to direct my attention "beyond the Bible," for implicit in my language is a key methodological assumption that undergirds my analysis. To wit: in contradistinction to those who would stress the Bible's literary character and thus understand its production as an act of literary imagination unfettered to a cultural reality, I do take the Bible to be a critical source—and in many cases, *the* critical source—for documenting actual cultural traditions of ancient Israel and especially ancient Israelite religious traditions, including the religious traditions of ancient Israelite women.

To be sure, one cannot deny the Bible's literary character, as the Bible—or at least a significant portion of its contents—must be classified as great literature whose promulgators brought to bear upon their compositions all the skills of narrative and poetic artistry that characterize the world's best literary creations. Nevertheless, the Bible—or at least the parts of the Bible in which my analysis is most interested—presents itself as depicting the Israelite community in which it was promulgated. More important, it is directed (at least in my opinion) toward that community as its primary audience (more on this issue below and on the related issue of the date of our biblical sources). This means the biblical accounts (again in my opinion) must transcend the purely imaginary in order to ground themselves in ancient Israelite cultural reality. To put the matter another way: if a literary production that intends to reflect and is addressed to its promulgators' own community is to succeed in, say, persuading that community regarding the validity of a particular message or agenda (and this is often the goal of biblical texts), then the community needs to recognize itself in that composition—it needs to recognize, for example, its own customs and ways of being. To be clear: this is not to say that in some factual sense, the biblical record is "true." But for the Bible's accounts to speak to an Israelite audience in the ways their authors and/or redactors intended, biblical texts need to have "rung true" to that audience in terms of their basic presentation of ancient Israelite norms of existence.

In short, the biblical text, as Phyllis Bird has written, is a product of the ancient Israelite world, and as such, it is a window into that world. Still, Bird describes the Hebrew Bible as an essential source for reconstructing Israelite religion, including "a woman-centered reconstruction of religion in ancient Israel," "*despite* its [the text's] biases, lacunae, and distance from the recorded 'events'" (emphasis mine).[7] I hold the same reservations; that is, even as I affirm my conviction that actual data regarding Israelite cultural traditions are reflected in the biblical text, I remain aware there are traditions of ancient Israel—most important for my purposes, women's religious traditions—that the Bible fails to document, or documents only inadequately and/or in inaccurate ways. This is because the interests of the Bible's authors and redactors were not all-encompassing when its came to ancient Israel. Rather, these authors and redactors were often interested only in very specific and sometimes idiosyncratic features of Israelite life. As a consequence, the Bible provides a perspective of ancient Israelite experience—and thus a perspective of Israelite women's religious experiences—that suffers from being both partial and imperfect.

Among the biblical text's partialities and imperfections, perhaps most often noted is the frequent disjunction between a text's temporal focus and that text's date. For example, the Bible purports to recount in some detail what we might think of as the prehistory of Israel's preexilic period—the era of the biblical matriarchs and patriarchs as chronicled in the book of Genesis. Yet according to a dominant strain within the Bible's presentation of ancient Israel's chronology, this ancestral age predates the Genesis accounts in which it is described by more than a millennium.[8] As a result, the Genesis narratives cannot be expected to reflect with any accuracy the past of the Israelites' ancestors. This problem of inaccuracy can in addition persist even if our inquiry is confined to events that allegedly took place within the preexilic period that is this volume's focus and to preexilic texts that describe them. For instance, although the narratives of the book of Judges purport to recount events that occurred at the very beginning of the preexilic era (during the twelfth and eleventh centuries BCE), they are recorded, according to many scholars, within a complex called the Deuteronomistic History that dates from a point quite late in the chronology of preexilic Israel—the last decades of the seventh century BCE and the beginning decades of the sixth (again, more on this below). That is, even though the text of Judges and the period this text claims to document both fall within the preexilic period, they are separated chronologically by a span of five hundred years, and it is problematic to take these much later biblical accounts as accurate representations of the happenings they contend to present.

Unfortunately, moreover, one of the theses commonly adduced to argue for the historical reliability of these sorts of later accounts—that they depend on a basically accurate transmission within oral tradition that can span hundreds of years—cannot be sustained. Instead, as students of the two great epics of Homeric tradition, the *Iliad* and the *Odyssey,* have shown, it is methodologically flawed to posit that because of a reliable transmission via oral tradition, these eighth-century BCE poems contain accurate accounts of the Greeks' exploits from the thirteenth to twelfth centuries BCE, the putative period of the Trojan War. The classicist Ian Morris sums up the Homeric case succinctly: "The much-vaunted oral tradition was not in any sense a 'chronicle,' a repository of antiquated institutions and worldviews."[9] The "much-vaunted oral tradition" that, according to some, grants historical credibility to the long-ago events recounted by the authors and/or redactors of books such as Genesis and Judges must be similarly assessed.

All of which is to say: using biblical texts of a later date as historically accurate sources for the events and practices of an earlier era they claim to describe is problematic. An equally problematic consideration is that even biblical texts contemporaneous with the community that they seek to represent—in the case of our inquiry, biblical texts that date from the core centuries of the preexilic period (which as noted above, I take to be the ninth to seventh centuries BCE) and that speak to ninth- to seventh-century BCE religious practices and beliefs—do not necessarily contain as straightforward portrayals of Israelite tradition as one might wish. For instance, what to make of texts from these core centuries that speak to the same matter yet with seemingly contradictory voices? Consider, on one hand, eighth-/seventh-century BCE legal texts from the books of Exodus, Leviticus, Numbers, and Deuteronomy that insist the members of Israel's priestly caste must come from the tribe of Levi, and compare, on the other hand, the late eighth-century BCE narrative account of Samuel's miraculous birth (1 Sam 1:1–2:26) that I consider in Chapters 3–4. There, Samuel is admitted into the priestly community at Shiloh even though he is a member of the tribe of Ephraim or Benjamin.[10] Or, to address an issue of greater relevance to this inquiry: we will also see in Chapters 3–4 that the narrative account of Samuel's birth suggests that the rituals of sacrifice enacted at Shiloh were performed by the family groups that worshipped at the site and involved the participation, at least to some degree, of these family groups' women. According to the Bible's eighth-/seventh-century BCE legal corpora, however, sacrificial rituals, in particular the altar-based components of sacrificial service, are to be performed only by members of Israel's *all-male* priesthood.

This is not, moreover, just a case of law versus story, for even within texts of the same literary genre one can find discrepancies. To illustrate again with an example relevant to our inquiry: Saul M. Olyan has argued that texts from the eighth- and seventh-century BCE prophetic corpora of Isaiah, Jeremiah, and Micah condemn Israelites (including, presumably, Israelite women) who worshipped Asherah, the great mother goddess of the Canaanite world, seemingly alongside the god Yahweh, even as other prophets from this period—for example, the eighth-century BCE prophet Amos—do not seem opposed to Asherah worship.[11] Indicated here is the degree to which any biblical text, even as it claims to present a normative picture of Israelite religion or, indeed, of any given aspect of Israelite society, in fact represents only the particular point of view and perspective of its author(s) and/or redactor(s).

What's more, even if all these authorial and redactional perspectives and points of view are positioned side by side, in an attempt to reveal the spectrum of opinions that can pertain concerning any specific component of Israelite tradition, the resulting picture is still flawed, for however diverse our biblical accounts, they provide only a partial representation of ancient Israel's cultural matrix.[12] For example, significantly more of the Bible's texts come from (and thus document the history and traditions of) the divided Israel's Southern Kingdom of Judah than come from (and thus document the history and traditions of) divided Israel's Northern Kingdom (see Fig. I.1). Yet the Northern Kingdom of Israel was geographically and in terms of population significantly larger than the Judahite South. During the period of the two kingdoms' joint existence (from ca. 931 BCE, when—at least according to biblical tradition—the North and South divided after the death of King Solomon, the last king of Israel's united monarchy, until 722/721 BCE, when the North was conquered by and subsumed into the great Assyrian Empire), the North was arguably also the more prosperous and cosmopolitan of the two polities.[13] Again, though, the Judahite perspective that dominates in our textual sources means we learn disproportionately more from the Bible about the less culturally robust South. Moreover, because the North and South were politically at odds with each other throughout much of their joint history, and because the Bible's southern writers tend to reflect these nations' disagreements, what we learn about both South and North is propagandistically distorted because of our texts' very pro-southern and, simultaneously, anti-northern perspective.

Our southern sources furthermore are really only concerned, within the South's cultural orbit, with Judah's capital city of Jerusalem and so tell us very little about the rest of Judahite society. They barely address, for example, life in Judahite urban centers other than Jerusalem. As a result, the great southern city of Lachish is mentioned only three times in the southern-authored account of Judahite and Israelite history found in 1–2 Kings (2 Kgs 14:19, 18:13–17, 19:8), and the southern fortress city of Beersheba—although the remains revealed by archaeological excavations there have been significant (see Chapter 6)—is not spoken of at all. This is like writing a history of the nineteenth and twentieth centuries in the United States that only mentions New York City three times and ignores Atlanta altogether, while recounting in fulsome, even excessive detail multiple aspects of life in Washington, D.C. We might further imagine that this hypothetical American history, with its obsessive focus on the *city* of Washington, would offer next-to-no comment on that metropolis's nearby rural environs in Maryland and Virginia, although 80 percent of nineteenth-century Americans were country-dwelling agriculturalists.[14] Likewise, life in ancient Judah's rural environs is barely addressed in the Jerusalem-centered account of 1–2 Kings, even as it is estimated that during the part of the preexilic period 1–2 Kings describes, up to 80–90 percent of Judah's population lived in (and off the land of) the Judaean countryside.[15]

It is in addition the case that although our southern sources can be significantly concerned with the general issue of Israelite religion that is my interest in this volume, their Jerusalem-centered focus means these sources are really engaged only with the rather distinctive religious traditions of the great temple in Jerusalem originally built, according to the biblical account, in ca. 950 BCE, during the reign of King Solomon, and destroyed during the Babylonian conquest of 586 BCE. This is especially true of texts that stem from the Bible's various priestly authors, and even more so is it true of the various priestly authors' accounts found in the latter third of the book of Exodus, throughout the book of Leviticus, and in the first ten chapters of the book of Numbers.[16] In these texts, the tent shrine purported to have been used by the Israelites during their forty years of wandering in the Sinai wilderness, just before their settling in the land of Canaan in ca. 1200 BCE, along with all this tent shrine's appurtenances (including both its furnishings and its priestly personnel), is painstakingly construed as both the antecedent to and the prototype of the Jerusalem temple. But such temple-centered accountings by the priestly elite, who were, moreover, closely aligned with the political elites of the Jerusalem monarchy, can hardly represent the religious norm among the larger Judahite, much less the larger ancient Israelite population.

Nor can the perspective of the other major cadre of religious leaders whose work is compiled in the Bible—the prophets—be deemed representative of the religious norm among the larger Judahite and the larger still ancient Israelite population. To be sure, not all the biblical prophets, even those from the Southern Kingdom, come from, or speak from the point of view of Jerusalem's urbanized context (the southern prophet Micah is a "country boy," for example).[17] And even Jerusalem-based prophets are not necessarily supporters of their city's great temple or its priesthood (the Jerusalem-based prophet Jeremiah, for instance, often seems at odds with Jerusalem's temple culture and its priestly administrators, as well as with the Jerusalem monarchs with whom the temple's priests are closely affiliated).[18] Others among the biblical prophets also identify themselves as being "of the people" rather than as allies of their communities' priestly and political elites—for example, the prophet Amos, who during a confrontation with the priest Amaziah at the Northern Kingdom's temple at Bethel describes himself as a "herdsman" and "dresser of sycamore trees" (Amos 7:14). Still, however modest Amos is in terms of his self-presentation, it is clear that both he and all the prophets whose oracles have been preserved for us in the biblical record were at least members of Israel's intellectual elite. This is vividly demonstrated by these prophets' superb mastery of the Hebrew language, of Hebrew rhetoric, and of the various types of literary genres they deploy to articulate their messages.[19]

Moreover, while the Bible does occasionally document the presence of female prophets within Israelite society (see Chapter 10), no book within the Bible's prophetic corpus is attributed to a woman. This means that whatever records we have of women prophets are mediated to us through third-person accounts whose authors I take to be without exception male. In fact, although a case is sometimes made in the scholarly literature for the female authorship of certain biblical texts, I take the entire Hebrew Bible—and thus all the Bible's texts that pertain to women's religious lives and experiences—to be male-authored.[20] Certainly, the priestly authored texts found in the latter third of the book of Exodus, throughout Leviticus, and in the first ten chapters of the book of Numbers mentioned above, as well as the kindred yet distinct priestly authored book of Deuteronomy, must have been written by men, given that the Israelite priesthood, both in and beyond the Jerusalem temple, was a male-only institution.[21] Likewise, I take the books of Joshua, Judges, 1–2 Samuel, and 1–2 Kings, which comprise the Deuteronomistic History (also mentioned above), to be, like the book of Deuteronomy to which the Deuteronomistic History is closely related, male-authored. So too, I maintain, are the so-called epic materials found in books such as Genesis, the first two-thirds of Exodus, and the latter two-thirds of Numbers written by men. These epic texts at least seem to me—given their intricate literary artistry—to be the work of scribal elites who, like almost all the professional elites of the ancient world, are most obviously to be identified as male.[22]

It is not impossible, of course, for male authors to speak to the lives and experiences of women, and thus not impossible for the Bible's male authors to speak to the lives and experiences of Israelite women, including the religious lives and experiences of preexilic women that are my interest. But in fact, the biblical authors, like many other male authors, especially male authors of the ancient world, address such matters only occasionally. For example, John Gould has written of the textual corpus from classical Athens that it is the "product of men and addressed to men in a male-dominated world." Gould then continues regarding the Athenian material that "it takes the assumptions of the masculine order of things for granted."[23] In the same vein, J. Cheryl Exum writes of the Bible: "the Bible was produced by and for men . . . [and] it is the male worldview that finds expression in the biblical literature."[24] It follows that even when biblical texts consider issues pertaining to women, they tend to view their women subjects in terms of only their meaning for and their significance to men. Or, to paraphrase the noted historian of medieval Christianity, Caroline Walker Bynum, the Bible's authors and redactors tend only "to look at women," rather than "to stand *with* women" and consider their point of view as well.[25]

All of which is to say: I take the majority of Israelite women whose religious lives and experiences I wish to speak about in this book to come from a context that is in many respects the antithesis of what the biblical writers represent. They are, obviously, female instead of male; "ordinary folk" as opposed to the Bible's priestly, prophetic, and scribal elites; predominantly denizens of the countryside rather than of urban locales; and, at least until the fall of the Northern Kingdom in 722/721 BCE, just as likely—if not more so—to have lived in the North and not in the Southern Kingdom from whence the bulk of the Bible's texts come. Equally important: I take Israelite religion as it was lived and experienced by the women who are my book's subjects to have been in many respects the antithesis of the religion the Hebrew Bible represents. To be sure, the biblical tradition can present, as we have already seen, some diversity in terms of the religious culture of which it speaks—regarding, for example, the appropriateness of worshipping the goddess Asherah alongside Yahweh. Within this diversity, moreover, there can be manifest, as we have also seen, indications of Israelite women's religious practices: for instance, the possibility that women, at least in some measure and in some contexts, might participate in rituals of sacrifice.

Nonetheless, as I have yet again already documented, the Bible focuses its attention when it comes to religion overwhelmingly on the temple-centered environment of the city of Jerusalem, whereas Israelite religion was undoubtedly practiced in a far more disparate set of venues. Moreover, as Francesca Stavrakopoulou and John Barton have discussed in their tellingly titled 2010 volume *Religious* Diversity *in Ancient Israel and Judah* (emphasis mine), these venues could vary significantly "from place to place—whether temple, tomb, or home." Stavrakopoulou and Barton then go on to say that the practices of Israelite religion could vary significantly "within and among different groups of people—from rural households to royal households, from garrison troops to women's local networks."[26] Note especially here their comment regarding "women's local networks" as a particular site of Israelite religious expression, concerning which Stavrakopoulou elsewhere writes, "As most scholars now recognize, women are the major group for whom male-dominated 'official' religion might have been relatively inaccessible, irrelevant, alien, or even (for the majority) unknown."[27] Yet it is this "male-dominated 'official' religion" that I take to be closely coordinate with—if not for the most part equivalent to—the temple-centered religious world of Jerusalem's priestly, political, and to some degree prophetic elites that is the biblical tradition's predominant focus.

From this conclusion it follows that to speak meaningfully, and in the comprehensive way to which I aspire, about the religious culture of Israelite women, recourse must be made to something more—indeed, something much more—than the partial and imperfect documentation of women's religiosity found in the biblical text. Most obvious is the need to draw heavily on resources other than the Bible to illuminate women's religious lives. Nevertheless, the claims I made earlier about the Bible as a critical, if not *the* critical source for reconstructing many facets of life within the Israelite commonwealth—and even women's religious lives—still hold. Thus, in addition to drawing on resources other than the Bible, we also need to cultivate strategies for reading the Bible that address its partialities and imperfections. By so doing, we can hope to reveal at least some of the information about women's religious culture we seek, even as this information remains something the biblical writers are disinclined to provide.

Of Resources and Recourses: Overcoming the Biblical Text's Limitations as a Source for Israelite Women's Religious Lives and Experiences

Let me speak first to the former and more straightforward of the two points I have just articulated: the need to draw heavily on resources other than the Bible in order to illuminate Israelite women's religious lives. Two bodies of extrabiblical materials are particularly important in our examination: (1) data derived from archaeological excavations of ancient Israelite sites, and (2) comparative data that come from the many peoples of the ancient Near Eastern and eastern Mediterranean world with whom the Israelites interacted and with whom, in many cases, the Israelites shared certain cultural and, more specifically, religious conventions. Preeminently, these are the peoples of Mesopotamia, of Egypt, of Greece, and of the larger West Semitic community of which Israel was a part. This West Semitic community included both the Canaanite peoples of the period archaeologists call the Late Bronze Age (ca. 1550–1200 BCE), from whom the Israelites were descended, and the Late Bronze Age Canaanites' other descendants as represented among polities of the archaeological era known as the Iron Age (ca. 1200–586 BCE): Phoenicia, Ammon, Moab, and Edom. It also included other non-Canaanite Semites, preeminently the Aramaeans of the first millennium BCE (Fig. I.2).

Of course, information derived from extrabiblical sources is, like information derived from the biblical record, not without problems in terms of its usefulness.[28] For example, ever since the beginnings of the modern discipline of archaeology at the end of the nineteenth century, the attention of archaeologists who have excavated ancient Israelite sites, as well as the attention of those who have excavated sites in the greater Syro-Palestinian region in whose southern reaches Israel lies, has been primarily focused on urban tells, which are large, trapezoid-shaped mounds made up of layers of debris that accumulated throughout ancient times as a city's occupants repeatedly built on top of older settlers' remains (Fig. I.3). Israelite examples include the aforementioned tell of the city of Lachish and also tell cities such as Gezer, Hazor, Jericho, and Megiddo (see Fig. I.1). It is furthermore the case that in investigating these tells, archaeologists have predominantly

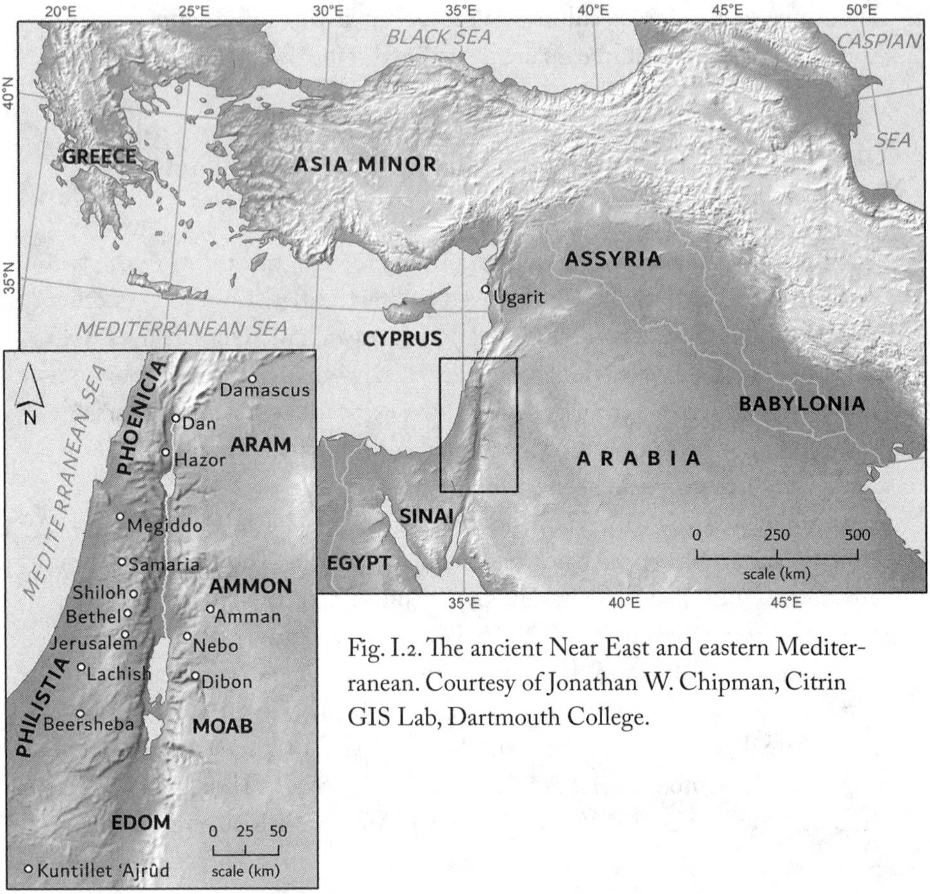

Fig. I.2. The ancient Near East and eastern Mediterranean. Courtesy of Jonathan W. Chipman, Citrin GIS Lab, Dartmouth College.

focused on excavating large-scale architectural remains, such as the remains of administrative centers, military installations, palaces and villas, public storehouses and granaries, water-supply systems, industrial complexes, and city gates.[29] Analysis of such remains can tell us a great deal about the urban life of the Israelites and of their neighbors and also a great deal about the bureaucratic institutions that administered these urban centers' great public works.

Yet such analysis tells us very little about women. While women were surely not absent within ancient Israel's cities, the majority of Israelite women—as well as the majority of Israelite men, as already noted—lived in rural settings. In these rural locations, moreover, patterns of social organization were constituted differently than in urban locales. Within urban locales, economic, political, and juridical affairs were typically dealt with in institutionalized and bureaucratized settings that lay outside the domestic sphere, whereas in rural environments, such matters were managed more within family households. For Israelite women, whose time was most typically spent within domestic space, this means that opportunities to participate in rural communities' economic, political, and juridical affairs could be substantial.[30] Conversely, Israelite women's engagement in urban communities' economic, political, and juridical life was limited, a conclusion that also holds in the sphere of religion, as I have intimated above and as I discuss in much more detail in Chapters 5 and 6.

Fortunately, more recent archaeological excavations of, especially, sites from the centuries designated as the Iron Age I period of Israel's preexilic era (ca. 1200–1000 BCE) can offer more promising results, as these excavations have focused on household-centered villages that proliferated during the twelfth century BCE in the hill country of the southern Levant, where the polity that eventually became Israel first emerged.[31] We will see in Chapter 1, for example, how the archaeological remains from the twelfth-century BCE village of Ai might help illuminate women's roles in ancient Israelite household religion. Still, the primary questions excavators have asked of the Iron Age I data—from what cultural background did

Fig. I.3. Tel Abel Beth Maacah. Photograph by the author.

the highland settlers come, and with which ethnic groups are their material remains most closely parallel?—do not particularly engage issues of women generally or women's religious lives and experiences specifically, and extracting gender-pertinent information from excavation reports driven by different agendas can prove difficult.[32]

Moreover, I should make clear that while I draw extensively on archaeological data (despite their flaws) at certain points in this book, I am not an archaeologist and thus can offer commentary on archaeological materials only from the perspective of a consumer (I hope an informed consumer) of archaeologists' work and not from the perspective of a practitioner. Conversely, I do consider myself able to speak with significant expertise regarding the peoples of the ancient Near East and eastern Mediterranean world with whom the Israelites interacted and whose religious assumptions they sometimes shared. Still, the evidence that can be garnered from these other peoples is not without weaknesses. For example, while textual materials that stem from elsewhere in the ancient Near East and eastern Mediterranean sometimes reflect a more diverse demographic sample than do our Israelite textual remains, these comparative texts more often than not—like the Israelite materials—reflect only the perspective of their communities' elite males (as is indicated in John Gould's quotation cited above regarding the male-dominated focus of the ancient Athenian literary corpus).[33]

It is also the case that while manifold commonalities can be documented between the culture of ancient Israel, on one hand, and the other cultures of the ancient Near Eastern and eastern Mediterranean world, on the other, significant differences can hinder the comparative enterprise. We will see in Chapter 9, for example, that the work of ritual mourning often assumed by Israelite women is helpfully illuminated by evidence concerning women's ritual mourning that comes from Israel's neighboring communities. However, Near Eastern and eastern Mediterranean traditions regarding women religious functionaries may not be well paralleled in the Israelite context. Most notably: although there is a fairly rich body of ancient Near Eastern evidence regarding women priests—including evidence from Phoenicia, one of ancient Israel's closest counterparts in terms of language, culture, chronology, and geography (see Fig. I.2)—the priesthood in Israel, as already noted, was an exclusively male institution.[34]

This brings us back to the Bible itself, and while my reservations about it as a source for ancient Israelite tradition—and especially traditions concerning Israelite women's religious lives and experiences—are, as I have already indicated, profound, I nevertheless do take the Bible, as I have also already indicated, to be a critical, if not *the* critical source for reconstructing many facets of Israelite culture, including ancient Israel's religious culture. Yet using the Bible as a source for reconstructing preexilic women's religious lives and experiences, while simultaneously taking seriously the reservations I have articulated, requires some particular interpretive strategies and skills. We will repeatedly be called upon, for instance, to read the biblical text "against the grain." Consider by way of example biblical texts that concern the religious center of Dan, which was one of the major sanctuary sites of the divided monarchy's Northern Kingdom of Israel. The Bible's southern-based writers, as part of their anti-northern polemic, unanimously condemn the practices used at Dan to worship Yahweh as inappropriate within the religion of ancient Israel. But the Israelites who worshipped at Dan surely did not conceive of themselves as acting inappropriately; no religious practitioner—or at least no serious-minded religious practitioner—acts with the goal of worshipping in ways he or she considers apostate. Rather, the practitioners who worshipped at Dan must have understood their religious observances to be proper within Yahwistic tradition. We, as modern students of Israelite religion, need to take this perspective seriously, by setting ourselves to read against the grain of the southern biblical writers' condemnations in order to accommodate the Danites' point of view as well.

Or, to take an example that pertains more to the religious experiences of Israelite women, consider Jer 7:16–20 and 44:15–19, 25. In these texts, as we will see in Chapter 2, Jeremiah lashes out at some of his community's women (and also men) in the late seventh and early sixth centuries BCE for worshipping a goddess called the Queen of Heaven. The women whom Jeremiah castigates, however, vehemently defend their worship of the Queen of Heaven, staunchly maintaining that they have found their acts of devotion to be meaningful and, more important from their point of view, efficacious (Jer 44:16–18). Although Jeremiah considers these women's religious observances to be inappropriate for practitioners of ancient Israelite religion, the worship of the Queen of Heaven was clearly a significant aspect of the religious experience of some Israelite women—and thus a significant topic for investigation in our study. Indeed, as Philip J. King and Lawrence E. Stager have written in their book *Life in Biblical Israel,* no matter how "self-serving and tendentious" certain biblical accounts are, they all are potentially "grist for the . . . mill" in an examination like ours.[35]

This examination, moreover, will require not only reading the Bible's self-serving and tendentious texts "against the grain," but also reading "between the lines" of these and other texts, with the aim of teasing out important pieces of data regarding the religious culture of Israel's womenfolk embedded within the biblical record, despite the Bible's biased—that is, its overwhelmingly male, elitist, urban, and southern—point of view. The prophet Isaiah's point is satiric, for example, when, in Isa 5:1–7, he appropriates an old song celebrating the wine harvest and reinterprets it in order to describe a failed vintage and so the failure of the nations of Israel and Judah to respond properly to the loving care lavished upon them by God as their vintner. To read against the grain would be, as above, to refuse to accept, without further consideration, the prophet's negative conclusions; to read in addition between the lines would be to note that in the first verse of his condemnatory oracle, in which Isaiah quotes from the appropriated vintage song, the prophet inadvertently reveals that the song on which his satire depends must have originally been sung by a woman. When coupled with other evidence, such a datum suggests, as I consider further in Chapter 9, that women were particularly responsible for music-making at ancient Israel's autumn harvest festival, which preeminently celebrated the pressing of that year's new wine.

An approach related to this sort of endeavor of "reading between the lines" mines the biblical witness for what the classical scholar Ian Morris, whose work I have already mentioned, has called with regard to Homeric epic his sources' "unintended evidence." Regarding, specifically, Homer, Morris writes, "For many purposes Homer is of little use to the historian."[36] This is because, as I have again already noted, the *Iliad* and the *Odyssey,* which date from the eighth century BCE, cannot be presumed to depend on an oral tradition that represents accurately the affairs of the Aegean world of the thirteenth to twelfth centuries BCE that these epics purport to describe. Yet in discrediting the historical accuracy of the Homeric world's "much-vaunted oral tradition," Morris does not mean to claim that no oral traditions underlie the *Iliad* and the *Odyssey* as we have them. Still, he insists the oral tradition on which Homer drew was a constantly changing and evolving phenomenon, "*intimately linked to the present*" (emphasis mine).[37]

Of course, Homer does not intend for us to know of his sources' presentist orientation; his intent is that we take his poems and the oral tradition on which they depend to describe events long ago. But because "the institutions, attitudes, and conditions of action that we find in the *Iliad* and the *Odyssey* must of necessity be derived in some way from those of the functioning societies that Homer himself knew," Morris argues for their "unintended evidence" concerning the eighth century BCE during which they were composed.[38] The *Iliad* and the *Odyssey,* that is, "are scrutinized not for what their authors wished to say [regarding the Greeks' purported exploits against Troy in the thirteenth to twelfth centuries BCE], but for the unarticulated assumptions they carry with them [regarding the Greek world of the eighth century BCE]."[39]

The Hebrew Bible can be treated similarly when looking for information regarding Israelite women's religious lives and experiences. It might seem from my previous comments, for example, that I will make no reference to the Genesis ancestral narratives in this volume, given that these accounts (or at least many parts of these accounts) date, as do the *Iliad* and the *Odyssey,* from the eighth century BCE or so and thus cannot be presumed to represent accurately the earlier period (in Genesis's case, a millennium before) that they purport to describe. Yet even though these Genesis accounts are, like the Homeric epics, "of little use to the historian" with respect to documenting an earlier time, they are nevertheless, again like the Homeric epics, of considerable use for the "unintended evidence" they provide regarding the time during the preexilic period in which they were composed. While we cannot, therefore, take the description found in Gen 30:14–16 of the matriarch Rachel's laying claim to her sister Leah's mandrake roots to be an accurate representation of events that happened in the early second millennium BCE, we can, as I propose in Chapter 11, take this text to suggest that it was a known practice during the preexilic period, when the Genesis 30 account was recorded, for women to use purported aphrodisiacs, like mandrakes, in rituals of reproductive magic. Again, to reveal such information is not the intent of the Genesis account; rather, it is that the text's unintended evidence can be of crucial importance for us in uncovering aspects of the religious lives and experiences of preexilic Israelite women.

This method, of course, applies to texts other than Genesis. Indeed, while Morris, as noted above, focused his attentions on only Homer's *Iliad* and *Odyssey,* other scholars of ancient Greece have made the same point regarding Greek resources in general. King and Stager, for example, quote the nineteenth-century cultural historian Jacob Burckhardt, who writes about the importance within Greek data of "material conveyed in an unintentional, disinterested or even involuntary way by sources and monuments . . . [that] betray their secrets unconsciously and even, paradoxically, through fictitious elaborations, quite apart from the material details they set out to record and glorify."[40] The Hebrew Bible, King and Stager go on to propose, can similarly be read with an eye toward such betrayals, that is, with an eye that looks for incidental data or involuntary disclosures that in turn reveal valuable information about the conceptions, beliefs, attitudes, and worldviews of the Israelite cultural milieu from which these data and disclosures stem. Indeed, King and Stager cite the classicist Oswyn Murray as describing "this principle of unconscious revelation through representation" (or what I again, following Morris, would describe as mining a source for its "unintended evidence") as "being one of the most powerful tools in the modern historian's study of mentalities."[41]

Both Morris and King and Stager further indicate that implicit within this strategy of reading—and implicit as well in the other strategies I have outlined—is the same presumption of verisimilitude I put forward earlier. Which is to say: even as the Homeric or biblical scholar makes no claim for the actual historicity of many of the events and (more important for my purposes) many of the moments of religious practice described or alluded to in his or her sources, he or she should presume that these putative histories must have seemed believable to the ancient audiences for whom they were intended and to whom they were addressed. As Morris writes about the *Iliad* and the *Odyssey,* "Homeric poetry had to be satisfactory to its audience; it had to conform to *their* ideas of the way reality was structured and the way the world worked."[42] King and Stager argue similarly: "It matters little whether the biblical accounts are true in the positivistic sense of some historians and biblical scholars. It is enough to know that the ancient Israelites believed them to be so. The stories must have passed some test of verisimilitude, that is, having the appearance of being true or real."[43]

This means, for example, that whether or not there really was a Hannah who, as 1 Sam 1:9–18 would have it, actually stationed herself in ca. 1050 BCE at the entrance to the sanctuary at Shiloh to pray, to make a vow, and to engage, as I argue in Chapters 3–4, in related rituals concerning her barrenness and its resolution, her story could not have been successful in promoting to its preexilic audience its overall message and agenda (which concern the extraordinary natures both of the son Samuel to whom Hannah eventually gives birth and of Yahweh, the god who made Hannah's pregnancy possible) unless the idea that a woman could undertake significant religious practices at Shiloh and similarly constituted shrines "rang true" within a preexilic context. The text, that is, need not, and indeed, in the words of Marc Zvi Brettler, "does not reflect history," but it does need to reflect "the reality of the author, who could recognize a woman like Hannah offering a prayer," as well as performing other ritual acts.[44] Even though there was (probably) never a Hannah, the author(s) and consumers of the Hannah story must have shared a presumption that a woman like Hannah could act in ritually meaningful and complex ways at a sanctuary such as Shiloh.

Whose Data, Whose Disclosures? The Biblical Texts Most Relevant to This Examination

Still, even with all these strategies for interpreting the biblical text in hand, there are yet more challenges that must be faced: most urgently, which biblical texts should be mined for data and disclosures when applying the various methods of reading identified above? Given that it is my intention to focus only on the preexilic period of Israelite history, beginning in ca. 1200 BCE and ending in 586 BCE, and given as well Ian Morris's point that texts such as the Homeric corpus and, I have added, the Bible's kindred documents reflect best—whatever their intent may be—the period in which they were actually composed, it logically follows that an examination of the preexilic period must depend on biblical texts that date from preexilic times.

Unfortunately, however, many of today's biblical scholars have repudiated the consensus reached by previous generations concerning the biblical texts' dates. Consequently, identifying definitively the Bible's preexilic sources is much less possible than it once seemed. Indeed, some scholars would redate to later periods entire blocks of material previously taken to be preexilic. For example, John Van Seters argued beginning in the 1970s that the Bible's so-called J or Yahwistic writer, whose work is interspersed within the books of Genesis and Exodus and the last two-thirds of the book of Numbers, dates not from the tenth, ninth, or eighth century BCE, as scholars of the late nineteenth century and earlier part of the twentieth century had argued, but rather from the late exilic period: that is, the end of the sixth century BCE.[45] Some European scholars, for example, Hans Heinrich Schmid and his student Martin Rose, concur.[46] Still others question whether there is any J source at all.[47] It is also a group of primarily European scholars that has argued that the so-called Deuteronomistic

History that runs from Joshua through Judges, 1–2 Samuel, and 1–2 Kings was written during the Persian (ca. 539–333 BCE) or Hellenistic (ca. 333–37 BCE) period, and not, as a major strand of American biblical scholarship would posit, rendered in a "first edition" at the end of the seventh century BCE, in ca. 620–610 BCE, and in a "second" or "revised edition" a few decades later, in ca. 580 BCE.[48]

Scholars have also come to express far less certainty than they once did about the dating of the so-called P or Priestly source, whose writings are found interspersed within Exodus, Leviticus, and Numbers, and within Genesis as well. According to the consensus of previous generations, these texts were composed during either the late exilic or early postexilic period. But I heard a colleague at a recent conference compare today's discussions regarding P's date to a dart game, whereby the darts that get littered across a dartboard's spread resemble various scholarly "stabs" at dating P in the mid-eighth, the late eighth, the seventh, the sixth, or the fifth century BCE.[49] Some would even date at least parts of P, and even "P in all its manifestations," as early as the "very beginning of Israel's settlement in the land of Canaan" in ca. 1200 BCE or to the period of the Israelite early monarchy in the tenth century BCE.[50]

What's more, many of the scholars who adhere to the traditional dating of P in the late exilic or early postexilic period (i.e., the late sixth or even early fifth century BCE) have come to think that this "does not mean that its authors spun it out of thin air," which gives P roots, at the least, in the late preexilic period.[51] Ernest W. Nicholson, for example, even as he supports an exilic or postexilic date for P, writes that "the Priestly material . . . embodies more ancient tradition"; it "contain[s] elements of tradition from much earlier periods."[52] Likewise, Victor Hurowitz, while arguing that "P was given its final form in the Persian period," maintains that P "developed out of pre-existent literary sources of a considerably older date . . . its content, language, and style are firmly planted in the literature and customs of the First Temple period [that is, the period that began with Solomon's original building of the Jerusalem temple in ca. 950 BCE and ended with that temple's destruction in 586 BCE]."[53] William H. C. Propp, too, imagines the P materials to have "originated in the late monarchic period [that is, the late eighth and seventh century BCE]," even as they "attain[ed] their final form in the exile or early restoration," as do Baruch A. Levine ("P is a source that most probably took shape over a protracted period of time, beginning in the late preexilic period; it preserved some quite early material and continued to develop during the postexilic period") and the German scholars Jan Christian Gertz, Angelika Berlejung, Konrad Schmid, and Markus Witte ("P reckons with rituals and approaches to ritual that have their roots in the cult of the First Temple," even as "there is no doubt that it [P] should be given a late exilic–early postexilic date").[54]

I similarly understand some core traditions on which P depends to be preexilic and thus consider P materials in my examination of women's religious lives and experiences in preexilic Israel. I also occasionally make use of the related materials of the so-called H or Holiness source found preeminently in Leviticus 17–26, although with significant caution, for while scholarly consensus about the date of H has proved equally as elusive as consensus concerning the date of P, there is considerable agreement that, contrary to an earlier scholarly understanding, H postdates P.[55] It follows that if the final form of P, as suggested above, postdates the preexilic period, then H stands more removed still from a preexilic provenance. Hence my intent to use H only sparingly.

I do, however, agree with Nicholson that "even as some of the conclusions of the earlier consensus" arrived at by biblical scholars need to be "modified," the basic arguments of this consensus regarding the date of the J source still hold.[56] Thus J should be assigned a preexilic date that falls, as previously intimated, somewhere within the ninth or, more probably, the eighth century BCE.[57] I also take the so-called E, or Elohistic source to date from this same period.[58] E is, moreover, like J in many other respects: for example, like J's materials, E's are interspersed in Genesis, Exodus, and the last two-thirds of the book of Numbers; also, E's accounts, like J's, are narrative and even legendary in character. Indeed, like many scholars, I see J and E as so closely kindred that I tend to speak of them as a complex, JE, made up of epic traditions that describe the putative history of Israel's long-ago ancestors.[59]

I further agree with the position that dates the initial compilation of the so-called Deuteronomistic History that runs from Joshua, through Judges, 1–2 Samuel, and 1–2 Kings to the end of the seventh century BCE. This date has traditionally been argued for on textual grounds: because the Deuteronomistic History culminates by lauding the religious reforms of King Josiah, who reigned from ca. 640 to 609 BCE, scholars have presumed that its various narratives came together—at least in a preliminary form—during the closing years of his reign, in ca. 620–610 BCE. Certainly, this complex could not have been compiled much earlier. And to many biblical scholars, it has seemed unlikely that it could have come into existence much later, as it reflects barely any knowledge of the calamitous events of the sixth century BCE. The text in its final, or revised edition thus describes only the initial years after the destruction of Judah and Jerusalem by the Babylonian Empire in 586 BCE and seems to know nothing about the difficulties encountered afterwards, including those encountered fifty years later, when some of the members of the Judahite community who had been exiled to Babylon returned to their homeland and struggled to rebuild both their body politic and their culture's core social institutions. So too, it follows, must the date of the book of Deuteronomy, which serves the Deuteronomistic History as prologue and on whose theology the Deuteronomistic History in large part depends, lie in the preexilic period, and, more specifically, in the same general period during the late seventh century BCE in which the Deuteronomistic History was originally promulgated.[60]

Rounding out this catalogue of the Bible's preexilic writings are the books of the great eighth- and seventh-century BCE prophets—Amos, Habakkuk, Hosea, Isaiah, Jeremiah, Micah, Nahum, and Zephaniah—and also parts of the prophetic book of Ezekiel, whose ministry according to Ezek 1:1–3 begins at the very end of the preexilic period, in ca. 593 BCE.

Of Synchronic Versus Diachronic, of Practice Versus Belief: Methodological Principles That Guide the Study of the Religious Culture of Ancient Israelite Women

The preexilic sources on which my study primarily depends thus are the following:

1. J, or the Yahwistic source, whose writings lie interspersed in Genesis, Exodus, and the last two-thirds of the book of Numbers;
2. E, or the Elohistic source, whose materials, like J, are interspersed in Genesis, Exodus, and the last two-thirds of the book of Numbers;
3. P, or the Priestly source, whose work is found primarily in Exodus 25–31, 35–40, Leviticus 1–16, and Numbers 1–10, as well as being incorporated elsewhere in Genesis, in Exodus 1–24, and in the last two-thirds of the book of Numbers;
4. D, the siglum biblical scholars use to identify the authors and redactors of the book of Deuteronomy;
5. the Deuteronomistic History of Joshua, Judges, 1–2 Samuel, and 1–2 Kings; and

6. the preexilic prophetic books (especially Amos, Hosea, Isaiah, Jeremiah, and parts of Ezekiel).

Despite the fact, however, that just above I assigned Ezekiel's writings—or at least his earliest writings—to a very specific date within preexilic chronology, I should be clear that it is not my intent to pinpoint dates for or, more significantly, to establish a relative chronology among the various preexilic texts that I cite. In part, I resist establishing a relative chronology because it is an impossible task, given the current scholarly disputes regarding dating that I have just described. But more important, I resist here any attempt to establish a relative chronology among my various sources because I do not think that, for the purposes of my inquiry, it matters.

Which is to say: although it is my intent to address the religious lives and experiences of women during the preexilic period of Israelite history, it is not my intent to present a history of preexilic women's religious lives and experiences. By this I mean it is not my intent to present the sort of developmental account that writing a "history" often implies—that is, the sort of rendering that describes "first this happened," "and then this changed," "and next this occurred," "and later there was this." Rather, whatever my optimism regarding our ability to push beyond the limitations of the biblical text in order to recover from it, and from extrabiblical materials, meaningful information about preexilic women's religious experiences and lives, I am not so optimistic as to think we can push enough beyond the limitations of the text and our extrabiblical data to write a chronological account of these experiences and lives. Our sources simply do not contain the sorts of evidence needed to develop this kind of diachronic description.

Moreover, and more crucially: even if we had better data, I do not think they would yield a diachronic account of development and change within women's religious culture. As Victor H. Matthews and Don C. Benjamin write in their study of the institutions of Israelite politics, economics, diplomacy, law, and education, "the world of the Bible is virtually changeless," whereas "ours is ever changing."[61] Israelite religion too, as I see it, was for the most part an unchanging phenomenon throughout the preexilic period, and this was especially true of Israelite religion as it was practiced outside of major temple and urban centers and within the less formally constituted and more rurally situated worship venues (including household venues) in which most women's (and most men's) religious lives primarily were lived. Indeed, in a 2010 study of ancient Israelite household religion, Carol

Meyers argues precisely this, both with regard to religious practices' general "tend[ency] to be very conservative" and with regard to the domestic religious activities on which she specifically focuses: "it is likely that the[se] . . . would have changed little."[62]

For example, as we will see in Chapters 1 and 2, even though trade with the Arabian peninsula would have brought new and exotic incense products into Israel by the eighth and seventh centuries BCE, the burning of aromatic plants, along with making grain and libation offerings, seems to have been a standard part of household ritual practice from the earliest days of the preexilic period until the preexilic era's end. Similarly, as we will see in Chapter 8, even though the names and some of the particulars of the Israelite festival calendar can be presented differently in different preexilic sources, the basic calendrical structure, centered around three annual festivals associated with the three major harvests of the agricultural year, remained basically static throughout the preexilic period. In Chapter 10, I in addition document how women's work as prophets extends throughout the preexilic period and indeed, in the case of the prophet Noadiah (Neh 6:14), into postexilic times. From all this it follows, as already suggested, that the religious culture of preexilic Israel is better studied as a synchronic, as opposed to a diachronic, phenomenon.

To be sure, it has not necessarily been the norm among biblical scholars to study ancient Israelite religion in a synchronic way.[63] Already in 1878 and then in 1883, the great *Geschichte Israels* (later the *Prolegomena zur Geschichte Israels*) of Julius Wellhausen laid out an approach to analyzing Israelite religion that discussed the tradition in terms of a historical trajectory: note particularly in this regard that as Wellhausen traced, according to his book's title, the history of Israel (his *Geschichte Israels*), he called the three major sections of his work (1) "Geschichte des Kultus" ("*History* of the Cult"; emphasis mine), (2) "Geschichte der Tradition" ("*History* of the Tradition"; emphasis again mine), and, as he turned to discuss the postexilic period (during which, we can agree, major religious developments and changes did occur) (3) "Israel und das Judentum" ("Israel and Judaism"). Scholars into the second half of the twentieth century followed suit: Helmer Ringgren's *Israelitische Religion* (1963), for instance, runs from "The Pre-Davidic Period" (Part I), through "The Religion in the Period of the Monarchy" (Part II), to "The Exilic and Post-Exilic Period (Judaism)" (Part III). A similar organizational structure can be found in Georg Fohrer's *Geschichte der israelitischen Religion* (1969), in Frank Moore Cross's *Canaanite Myth and Hebrew Epic: Essays in the History of the Religion of Israel* (1973), and in George Mendenhall's *Ancient Israel's Faith and History* (2001).

The problem with these sorts of diachronically focused examinations for our purposes is, as already intimated, they presume evolution, development, and change, rather than the relatively unchanging or at best slowly changing nature of Israelite religion that I have suggested is characteristic during the preexilic period. Moreover, to create their descriptions of evolution, development, and change, histories of this sort typically find themselves relying on a structure defined in terms of "great events": the establishment of an Israelite monarchy in ca. 1025 BCE; the division of this monarchy in ca. 931 BCE (at least according to the biblical account) into the Northern and Southern Kingdoms; the rise of the powerful dynasty of King Omni in the Northern Kingdom beginning in ca. 876 BCE; the period of Assyrian hegemony over Israel and, eventually, Judah that lasted from ca. 738 to ca. 643 BCE; and, as the signal occurrence of the Assyrians' domination, the fall of the Northern Kingdom to the Assyrian Empire in 722/721 BCE. But "great events" such as these are the affairs, really, of "great men," the "patriarchs, warlords, kings, their armies, and their enemies" who are the primary actors within these sorts of monarchical and military happenings.[64] Not surprisingly, however, to study ancient Israel's "great events" as promulgated by Israel's "great men" is a poor avenue for exploring almost all aspects, including the religious aspects, of the world of Israelite women. Hereby is exposed another reason why a diachronically organized (and thus a "great events"/"great men") historical study is inappropriate to the task I undertake here.

In addition, to study Israelite religion using the rubrics of "great events" and "great men" is often to study "great ideas": the state-sponsored religious ideology established in Jerusalem already in the tenth century BCE; the seeming popularity of the worship of the Canaanite god Baal during the period of the Omride dynasty; the issue of Assyrian influence on Israelite religion during the time of the Assyrians' domination; and the theological posturing of the biblical prophets against these sorts of (from the prophets' point of view) syncretisms. But the careful reader will note I have been extremely deliberate throughout this Introduction to shy away from using the language of religious "ideas," or more specifically, the language of "theology" or "belief," in speaking of the religious culture of Israelite women that I explore in this book. Rather, I began already in my opening comments to speak of women's religious *practices,* women's religious *experiences,* women's religious *roles,* and, more generally, of women's religious *culture* and women's religious *lives.* Indeed, as much as this book is a synchronic, as opposed to a diachronic discussion of the religion of the preexilic period, it is a discussion of the actual *doing* of religion as opposed to a discussion of the theological convictions that motivate religious adherents' actions.[65]

In part, my intention to speak to practice, as opposed to belief, is related to my intent to speak synchronically as opposed to diachronically: that is, it is a response to the quality of our data. Which is to say: just as I suggested earlier that we really do not have the sorts of evidence needed to develop a diachronically based description of Israelite women's religious culture in the preexilic period, we also do not have the sorts of evidence that would be necessary to develop an ideologically based description of preexilic women's theological convictions and beliefs. In particular, as previously noted, we are without any woman-authored, much less autobiographical witness to women's religious culture in preexilic Israel, and we are by and large also without any male-authored descriptions of women's religious culture that take women's point of view into account. We therefore have no, or at best next-to-no, access to what was going on in Israelite women's heads, so to speak. Thus, although we can discuss the theology of the prophet Isaiah (but even here we should have some reservations)[66] or of the biblical prophets (or at least the so-called writing prophets) more generally, we have essentially no way to describe the theological premises held by any one Israelite woman, much less by Israelite women in general.

Furthermore, just as I suggested above that even if we had more fulsome and robust sources than the partial and imperfect materials available to us, we would be poorly advised to try to use these sources to write a diachronic history of preexilic Israelite religion, especially the religion of village-dwelling "ordinary folk," the same point holds here regarding theology or belief: even if we had better and more fulsome evidence regarding preexilic women's religious traditions, we would be ill-advised to try to use this evidence to write an account of women's ideological presuppositions or theological beliefs. This is because the premise that one best understands a particular group's or community's religion by documenting and analyzing its beliefs is a sensibility that poorly describes religion as it is manifest among many cultures of the world, including the culture of ancient Israel. Rather, a belief-centered approach to understanding religion is in large part an idiosyncrasy of the Protestant cultures of Europe, the United States, and Canada and their offshoots in sub-Saharan Africa, the South Pacific, and elsewhere around the globe. It is Protestant tradition, after all, that has so zealously championed "faith," or belief, as the sole path to establishing a right and proper relationship with God (hence the Protestant doctrine of *sola fide,* or "faith alone"), and, concomitantly, it is Protestant tradition that has so zealously championed the primacy of the individual as the agent in whom the proper "faith," or belief, must be manifest.

But for most of the world, as Francesca Stavrakopoulou and John Barton have argued with respect to ancient Israel, religion is about community and "social and cultural *activities*" (emphasis mine) within community. "Put crudely," Stavrakopoulou and Barton continue, "people 'do' religion," and religion cannot be defined in terms of abstract theologies that are "divorced from those 'doing' it."[67] Meyers similarly has written that "focusing on beliefs or doctrinal systems, following the model of Christianity, is inadequate for the study of many ancient peoples, the Israelites included," and Karel van der Toorn speaks also of Israelite religion as a tradition "more . . . of action than of speculation."[68] Meyers moreover notes, on the basis of cross-cultural studies, that "the religious lives of *women in particular* are characterized by non-verbal and non-textual activities" (emphasis mine)—that is, "performative ritual," as well as other "material and behavioral components," as opposed to "beliefs."[69]

It is in this vein that I often speak in this book of "cult": not "cult" in the pejorative way this term is often employed in common parlance—as "a relatively small group of people having (esp. religious) beliefs or practices regarded by others as strange or sinister"—but rather "cult" in its more archaic usage as it pertains, again, to the "doing" of religion.[70] According to the noted biblical scholar Roland de Vaux, cult in this sense refers to "all those acts by which communities or individuals give outward expression to their religious life, by which they seek and achieve contact with God." De Vaux also stresses, as I have above, cultic worship as "essentially a social [as opposed to an individualistic] phenomenon."[71] Indeed, Ziony Zevit, in his magisterial study of ancient Israelite religion, writes of religion as "attested *only* within social groups" (emphasis mine) and "requir[ing] such groups for [its] maintenance."[72]

Of Dogma and Deviation: A Few Remarks About How the Argument of This Book Will Unfold

All this said, almost no methodological principles can be followed absolutely, and therefore on occasion I deviate from the axioms I have heretofore articulated. For example, in Chapter 9, I explore some aspects of women's music-making during the course of life-cycle rituals, even though I have otherwise committed to devoting a separate study to women's life-cycle events. Likewise, with regard to my principle of "synchronic versus diachronic," I have found it necessary in Chapter 11, in discussing women as magical practitioners and especially women as necromancers, to consider the ways attitudes toward necromancy in Israel seemingly changed over time. Indeed, as part of that analysis, I have found it necessary to address briefly changes promulgated in the course of the religious reformation program undertaken by King Josiah, even though I have otherwise determined that the Josianic reform and its effects upon women should be the topic of a separate monograph.

In general, however, my analysis throughout is conceived of synchronically and is also, as already indicated, conceived of in terms of preexilic women's religious practices and activities, as opposed to their beliefs. More specifically, the questions I explore regarding those practices seem to me the basic questions one would ask about all sorts of social activities: *Where* are they enacted? *When* are they enacted? And *who* are the actors and *how* is their participation in said activities manifest?[73] I begin, in Part I of this book (Chapters 1–6), by engaging in a discussion of "where," or the various sites of preexilic women's religious practice.

I next turn, in Part II (Chapters 7–8), to explore the question of "when," through an examination of Israelite women's ritual calendar, addressing the various festivals and religious celebrations the ancient Israelites observed regularly (weekly, monthly, annually). Part III (Chapters 9–13) concerns "who" and "how": women as actors in religious settings and during ritual events and especially the important roles as religious agents that women sometimes assumed within the Israelite cult. The Epilogue offers some concluding reflections on the arguments presented throughout.

PART 1

Where? The Sites of Women's Religious Practice

1 "Micah's Mother Had Made a Cast-Metal Figurine": Women and Ancient Israelite Household Religion, I

In Judg 17:1–4, we find a story describing how the mother of a man from the tribe of Ephraim named Micah (or Micaiah, an expanded form of the same name) had two hundred pieces of silver cast into a religious figurine that then stood in her son's home (*bĕbêt mîkāyĕhû*), most probably (at least as the text as it has come down to us suggests) in the household shrine (*bêt ʾĕlōhîm*) of Micah mentioned in a subsequent verse (Judg 17:5). In 1 Sam 1:1–5, we are told that Hannah and Peninnah, the two wives of another Ephraimite, Elkanah, used to accompany their husband when he traveled annually from their hometown of Ramathaim (or Ramah; the textual tradition is confused) to sacrifice at the sanctuary of the Israelite god Yahweh in Shiloh, a journey of approximately 25–30 kilometers.[1] In Ps 68:25–26 (in most of the Bible's English versions, 68:24–25), young women who play frame drums are listed as being among the musicians who participate in a procession into Yahweh's *qōdeš,* or sanctuary—most likely to be identified, as in v. 30 (English v. 29) of the following stanza, as God's temple in Jerusalem:

> Behold your processions, O God,
> the processions of my God, my king, into the sanctuary (*qōdeš*)—
> the singers go first, the musicians last,
> between [them] frame-drumming young maids.

Together, these texts identify for us three of the most important types of sacred sites at which the biblical writers could imagine ancient Israelite women engaging in religious practice.[2] These are (1) as in the story of Micah's mother, small-scale shrines that stood within these women's own homes or, as I discuss in some detail below, within their larger household compounds; (2) as in the story of Hannah and Peninnah, regional sanctuaries located a relatively short distance from their family's hometowns; and (3) as in the account of young women drumming, the great "temples of the kingdom" (paraphrasing here Amos 7:13), preeminently found in Jerusalem, the capital city of the Israelites' Southern Kingdom of Judah, and in Northern Kingdom cities such as Dan, Bethel, and probably Samaria.[3]

My purpose in this chapter and in the several that follow is to examine each of these religious environments in turn and to consider what might be said about women's religious experiences within them. The thesis that guides this analysis is straightforward and not unique to me: it is that the more localized a site of religious practice and the smaller its scale, the greater the potential for women to act within this venue as significant religious agents.[4] Yet even though several noted students of Israelite religion have made this same claim, I believe the evidence that stands in support of it has not been as fully described as I hope to delineate it here. I also believe that several important nuances concerning this thesis need to be more thoroughly adduced than they have been heretofore, and I intend to consider these both as my discussion of Israelite sacred sites develops through Chapter 6 and also in my later (and related) discussion of the Israelite woman's ritual calendar in Chapters 7–8.

I begin my examination, in this chapter and the next, with a discussion of women's place within the smallest and most localized of Israel's sacred spaces: shrines dedicated to the practice of ancient Israelite household religion. More specifically, in this chapter I begin by explicating several aspects of a biblical text that in my opinion well illuminates ancient Israelite household religion in general and women's roles and responsibilities within the household cult in particular: the aforementioned Judg 17:1–4 story of Micah's mother and the longer account of Judg 17:1–18:31 in which Micah's mother's story is embedded and in which Micah's household and that household's religious accommodations are more extensively described. Yet while Judg 17:1–4 and the larger unit of Judg 17:1–18:31 reveal much about women's place in ancient Israelite household religion, some issues of household ritual are not addressed in these accounts. I thus move, in Chapter 2, to examine two other biblical texts that offer additional detail regarding women's roles and responsibilities in household religion—Jer 7:16–20 and 44:15–19, 25.

For now, though, let us consider Judg 17:1–4 and the longer account of Judg 17:1–18:31, beginning with a survey of some of the major accommodations of household religion these passages describe.

The Religious Accommodations of the House of Micah

As my introductory remarks to this chapter have already indicated, the mother of Micah the Ephraimite is described in Judg 17:1–4 as giving two hundred pieces of silver to a craftsman (more specifically, a metallurgist or a refiner; *ṣôrēp*) and commissioning him to make a religious figurine; as 17:4 puts it, "his [Micah's] mother took two hundred pieces of silver and gave it to the metallurgist, and he made it into a cast-metal figurine [*pesel ûmassēkâ*]."[5] To make a religious figurine is, of course, something generally prohibited by biblical law, and Exod 34:17 more specifically forbids making almost precisely the sort of figurine, a "cast" or "molten" divine image (*'ĕlōhê massēkâ*), that Micah's mother is said to have commissioned. Nevertheless, we are arguably to understand the mother's figurine as somehow representing the Israelite god Yahweh. After all, Yahweh is the only deity mentioned in both the Judg 17:1–4 account that describes the cast-metal figurine's production and the larger Judg 17:1–18:31 narrative of which 17:1–4 (at least in the biblical text as it has come down to us) is a part.[6] Moreover, the mother is explicitly depicted in 17:1–4 as a Yahweh worshipper. She utters a blessing in the name of Yahweh in Judg 17:2 and then declares she is consecrating her silver to Yahweh in Judg 17:3. Note also that the mother's son carries the divine name Yahweh in the form of his name used in 17:1 and 4 (*mîkāyĕhû,* or Micaiah, which means "Who is like Yahweh?"). This is significant because in the Hebrew Bible, mothers are more often said to name their children than are fathers.[7] Therefore, an Israelite audience would likely have understood that the mother had bestowed upon her son a name that identifies Yahweh as the object of her religious devotion. Or to put the matter another way: the use of the name Micaiah to designate the mother's son in turn designates the mother as a Yahweh worshipper.

Arguably as well we are to envision the mother's Yahwistic figurine, despite the text's mention of silver only, as an image cast in bronze, or perhaps carved from wood, and then covered with silver overlay.[8] This is because a statue of solid silver would have been an almost unimaginable luxury in the generally impoverished world of ancient Israel. However, silver- and gold-covered images are attested. For example, Isa 30:22, an oracle from the eighth-century BCE prophet Isaiah that I take to be roughly contemporaneous with Judg 17:1–18:31, speaks of "your silver-covered figurines" (*ṣippûy pĕsîlê kaspekâ*) and "your gold-plated images" (*'ăpuddat massēkat zĕhābekâ*).[9] Habakkuk 2:19, although somewhat later in date (very late seventh or early sixth century BCE), likewise refers to wooden images that were silver- or

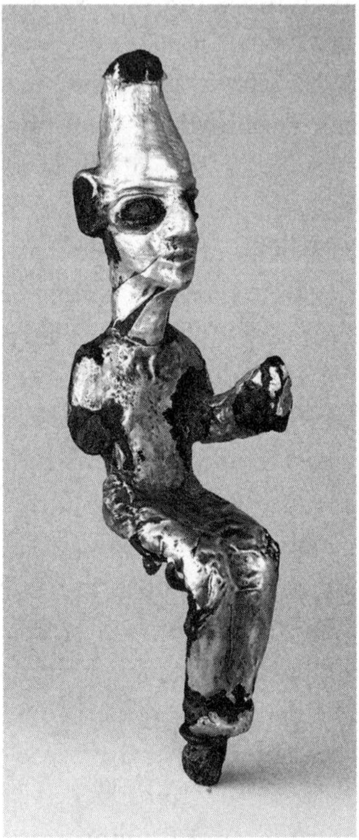

Fig. 1.1. Bronze figurine of an enthroned deity, covered with gold foil. Canaanite; ca. fourteenth to thirteenth century BCE. Height, 12.7 centimeters. From the collection of the Metropolitan Museum of Art, New York, Gift of George D. Pratt, 1932, accession no. 32.161.45.

gold-plated, and Mesopotamian texts similarly speak of cult statues made of wood, which might then be overlaid with precious metals.[10] Small-scale bronze figurines covered with silver and/or gold have in addition been found by archaeologists at several Syro-Palestinian sites that date from the pre-Israelite and early Israelite periods of Levantine history (Fig. 1.1).[11]

It further seems to be the case that the biblical writers mean us to understand that after it had been cast, Micah's mother's figurine stood, as indicated in 17:4, in the "house of Micah" (*bĕbêt mîkāyĕhû*) and more specifically (at least as I interpret the text as it has come down to us) in the household shrine (*bêt 'ĕlōhîm*) of Micah mentioned in Judg 17:5 (more on this below). The text in addition seems to envision that this shrine was presided over, at least initially, by one of Micah's sons whom, according still to v. 5, Micah is said to have installed as his household's priest. Verse 5 also indicates (at least again as I interpret) that this shrine held, alongside the cast-metal figurine commissioned by Micah's mother, other sacred objects—*'ēpôd ûtĕrāpîm*—that Micah, according yet again to v. 5, is said to have made.

But how to understand this phrase *ʾēpôd ûtĕrāpîm?* The specific meaning here can be as, or even more difficult to ascertain as it was to ascertain the Judges text's specific understanding of Micah's mother's cast-metal figurine, and thus scholars disagree, and markedly, in their interpretations. For some, the phrase *ʾēpôd ûtĕrāpîm* refers only to a single object, perhaps a kind of image known as a *tĕrāpîm,* "teraphim," that was "ephoded," that is, covered with an overlay, or *ʾēpôd*/ephod, of silver or gold (the term *ʾēpôd* is used in precisely this way—to describe the gold plating that covers an image—in the Isa 30:22 passage cited above).[12] According to others, however, *ʾēpôd* and *tĕrāpîm* refer to separate objects. *Tĕrāpîm*/teraphim are most likely ancestor figurines used in rituals of necromancy (more on this in Chapters 7 and 11).[13] *ʾĒpôd*/ephod might similarly refer to a representation of some sort of supernatural being, as the term *ʾēpôd* might mean in 1 Sam 21:10 (in most of the Bible's English versions, 21:9) and in Judg 8:27, where Gideon and his family bow down to the *ʾēpôd* he has made.[14] Or *ʾēpôd* possibly refers—as it does most commonly in the Bible—to an overgarment that was part of the priestly vestments and used by priests in the performance of divinatory rites. If so, then *ʾēpôd* in Judg 17:5 might denote a special piece of ritual clothing that Micah's priestly son would have worn when using the *tĕrāpîm* to solicit necromantic oracles. Indeed, whatever the *ʾēpôd* was exactly, it seems probable it was used, either like or along with the *tĕrāpîm* (depending on how one translates), in rituals of divination.[15]

As such, the *ʾēpôd* and *tĕrāpîm* were surely objects of great significance within the religious life of Micah's household (or the "ephoded teraphim" was surely such an object). Nevertheless, they were (or it was) seemingly of less *monetary* value than the mother's cast-metal figurine. After all, no silver is said to have been used in its/their manufacture, and my own sense, based on texts such as Jer 2:27 and Hos 4:12, is that *tĕrāpîm* were made of wood.[16] More significantly, the *ʾēpôd* and *tĕrāpîm* were (or the "ephoded teraphim" was) arguably of less *religious* value than was the figurine the mother had commissioned, for even though the *ʾēpôd* and *tĕrāpîm* were (or the "ephoded teraphim" was) associated with the cult of the ancestors that was extremely important within Israelite household and family religion (see further Chapter 7), the mother's *pesel ûmassēkâ* went further still in somehow representing Yahweh as her household's patron god. Moreover, *tĕrāpîm* texts elsewhere in the Bible—especially Gen 31:19–35—suggest that a household such as Micah's would have had multiple *tĕrāpîm* (representing a household's multiple deceased ancestors),[17] whereas Micah's mother's *pesel ûmassēkâ* appears to have been the *only* representation of Yahweh found in Micah's home.

I will have much more to say about the mother's figurine and its signal importance below, but for the time being, let us follow the story of Micah's household as it continues and we learn still more about its religious accommodations. In Judg 17:7–13, a young Levite—a member, that is, of the tribe of Levi, which is generally depicted in biblical tradition as the tribe from which members of Israel's priestly caste must come—goes forth from the Judahite town of Bethlehem, where he had been a sojourner (*gēr*), in order to find a home and a place for himself, as, in the Bible's understanding, the members of the landless Levitical community were generally expected to do. As Judg 17:8 tells it, this Levite comes in his wanderings to Micah's home (*bêt mîkâ*) in the territory of Ephraim, where Micah offers him room, board, clothing, and ten pieces of silver a year if he will serve him as a priest and as a "father" (v. 10), meaning, perhaps, a divinatory specialist who has the skills requisite to manipulate the *'ēpôd ûtĕrāpîm* (whatever it/they might be).[18] At any rate, the Levite accepts Micah's offer, thereby displacing Micah's less formally qualified son from the priestly office the son had theretofore held in the story. The Levite is then installed, according to 17:12, in the house of Micah (*bĕbêt mîkâ*).

In Judg 18:2, yet more visitors come to the house of Micah (*bêt mîkâ*), men from the tribe of Dan, which in the premonarchic period during which Judges 17–18 is set is understood by the author(s) and redactor(s) of our story as not yet having secured territory of its own in which to dwell. The Danites, as the story goes, have thus sent five of their members north from their tribe's temporary encampments in Israel's southwest to scout out possible land to settle. While staying with Micah, these five scouts are said to overhear the voice of the Levite and to recognize it, probably because this Levite from Bethlehem is to be understood as speaking, like them, with the accent and speech patterns of the Israelite South rather than those of the territories of Israel's North.[19] The scouts then approach the Levite and, after some preliminary conversation, ask him to perform for them one of the same ritual functions he was presumably hired to perform for Micah: to make an oracular inquiry in order to determine whether their quest for territory will be successful. The Levite affirms the Danites will accomplish their goal, and, indeed, according to 18:7, the five scouts soon thereafter identify land in the vicinity of Laish, later known as Dan, suitable for their tribe's settlement. After returning south and reporting this to their tribesmen, six hundred armed Danites march north to secure the site. They basically follow, Judg 18:13 suggests, the same route as did the five initial scouts (who are among them), and so the six hundred warriors of Dan come in the course of their traverse to the house of Micah (*bêt mîkâ*) in Ephraim.

Yet while the previous visit of the five Danites to the house of Micah had passed without incident, the visit of the six hundred warriors does not, as the five scouts make their tribesmen aware that within Micah's house are the *'ēpôd*/ephod and *tĕrāpîm*/teraphim (or the "ephoded teraphim") that Micah had made and the cast-metal figurine his mother had commissioned. The Danites resolve to steal these objects, and the five original visitors to Micah's house then undertake this task. As they go forth with their loot, the young Levite confronts them. But the miscreants rather quickly persuade him to throw in his lot with Dan, suggesting it will profit him more to serve as priest for an entire tribe than it has serving as priest for only Micah's household. The Danites then leave, priest in tow.

Still, these Danites and their newly recruited priest do not make a totally clean getaway, as Micah and some associates discover the theft and give chase. Upon encountering Dan's six hundred armed men, however, Micah's confederates realize they are greatly outnumbered, and so they retreat, leaving their priest and their religious treasures to the Danites. The tribe of Dan is then said in 18:30 to have been served by descendants of Micah's Levite priest until "the time of the Israelite exile," until, that is, either 734–732 BCE, when much of the population of the Northern Kingdom of Israel was deported by the Assyrian conqueror, King Tiglath-Pilesar III (2 Kgs 15:29), or 722/721 BCE, the date of the Assyrians' final destruction of the North. In 18:31, the Danites are also said to have maintained the mother's figurine that the six hundred warriors had stolen as long as "the house of God" was in Shiloh, which perhaps refers to the destruction of Shiloh in the second half of the eighth century BCE by the Assyrians, or perhaps to the destruction of Shiloh some centuries earlier—perhaps, for example, in ca. 1050 BCE, presumably by the Philistines (the inhabitants of the region of today's Gaza Strip; see Fig. I.2). The archaeological evidence has been interpreted in multiple ways.[20]

Thus ends the Bible's story of Micah's mother's cast-metal figurine with which both Judges 17 and my recounting of the Judg 17:1–18:31 narrative began.

Unpacking the Polemic of Judges 17–18

This account in Judg 17:1–18:31 raises many fascinating issues for students of the Hebrew Bible: for example, the text's redactional history, whereby what may have been originally separate stories of the cast-metal figurine commissioned by Micah's mother (Judg 17:1–4) and Micah's installation of a Levitical priest to serve his household (Judg 17:7–13) were eventually stitched together using Judg 17:5–6 and then were further used as a prologue for the account of the establishment of the religious sanctuary at Dan found in Judg 18:1–31.[21] More significant for my purposes, however, is the polemical intent of Judg 17:1–18:31, which seeks to deride, first, Dan's Levitical priesthood (by ridiculing its founder's integrity, as he was easily persuaded to abandon his contractual obligations to Micah for want of greater power and prestige), and, second, the sanctuary the Levite came to serve at Dan (by portraying it as a shrine centered around a figurine that is doubly tainted, because it was originally cast from silver that Micah had stolen from his mother and had only returned when threatened by her curse of the unknown thief and because it then came into the Danites' possession through equally illicit means).[22]

Several scholars in addition argue that the text intends to deride Micah's mother. Michael K. Wilson claims, for example, that "the anomaly of Micah's mother being the one who determines the nature of the cult . . . underscore[s] [its] illegitimacy, given that the mother assumes a role not then appropriate for a woman to exercise."[23] Lillian R. Klein somewhat similarly suggests that Judg 17:2—in which the mother is said to have sworn an oath cursing whoever has stolen her silver and then blesses her son in the name of Yahweh after he confesses he is the thief and makes restitution—pokes fun at the woman for "assum[ing] the right to make oaths and invoke blessings, and to do so on behalf of a worldly tangible—silver."[24] Klein, along with many other interpreters, further proposes that Judg 17:4 indicts the mother as selfish and stingy by having her consecrate only two hundred pieces of her silver cache to Yahweh, although there were said to be eleven hundred pieces in her original hoard.[25]

Biblical polemics, however, whatever their intent to deride, are important sources of information for scholars who would reconstruct aspects of Israelite culture and tradition, including the society's religious aspects, for, like any polemic, the polemical texts of the Bible were generated as a result of very real and live arguments taking place within the Israelite community at the time of these polemics' production. Or, to put the matter somewhat more colloquially: polemics aren't about beating a dead horse. Rather, the compulsion to polemicize against, say, some religious institution or practice stems from a belief on the part of the polemicist(s) that the institution or practice is a true threat to the society of that time. It follows, at a minimum, that we can deduce something about our text's date: that even though Judg 17:1–18:31 is, in the form we have it, part of the Deuteronomistic History that I have dated in the Introduction to ca. 620–610 BCE (with a revised edition dating from ca. 580 BCE), the Judges 17–18 narrative predates this history by approximately one hundred years.[26] This is because our text, although it must (at least as it has come down to us) postdate the Israelites' deportations at the hands of the Assyrians in 734–732 BCE or 722/721 BCE (since these are referred to in Judg 18:30), still seems to come from a time when memories of the Dan sanctuary, which was destroyed as part of the Assyrians' conquests in the second half of the eighth century BCE, loomed large within Israelite tradition. In later Deuteronomistic History texts, conversely, the Israelite sanctuary at Dan virtually disappears.[27]

More important for my interests here, though, are what the polemics of Judges 17–18 tell us about Israelite religion. For example, the fact that the author(s) and/or redactor(s) of Judg 17:1–18:31 felt it necessary to polemicize against the Levitical priesthood at Dan reveals to us not only that this priesthood did exist and was considered legitimate by at least some ancient Israelites, but that Dan's Levitical priesthood was considered legitimate by enough members of the Israelite population that its rivals—perhaps non-Levitical priests at Dan's sister yet competitor sanctuary at Bethel (1 Kgs 12:31–32)?; perhaps southern propagandists intent on denigrating all things northern?[28]—found themselves threatened by Dan's priestly community and compelled to call its credibility into question. Likewise, the fact that the author(s) and/or redactor(s) of Judg 17:1–18:31—along with the authors and redactors of the larger Deuteronomistic History, in texts such as 1 Kgs 12:25–30—felt compelled to offer such a virulent critique of the religious imagery used at Dan indicates that whatever the interdictions against graven and/or molten images found in the Bible's legal corpora, the icon associated with the Dan cult was seen as a wholly appropriate, and even profoundly significant means of worshipping Yahweh by many ancient Israelites.

More important still: if we strip the polemic of Judg 17:1–18:31 of its contemptuous intent, we reveal that the eighth- and later the seventh-century

BCE Israelites who were presumably the intended audience of our text could envision a man like Micah having a household shrine that was furnished with religiously significant items. Indeed, as we will see below and more extensively in Chapter 2, this is precisely what is indicated by a wealth of preexilic archaeological remains, and not just remains from the eighth-century BCE era from which our text (as I have argued) stems, but from the twelfth, eleventh, tenth, and ninth centuries BCE as well. "In this respect," Karel van der Toorn affirms, the Micah story—even though van der Toorn describes it as "polemical" in "intention"—"reflects the religious situation adumbrated by the archaeological . . . record." Van der Toorn continues, moreover, by suggesting that what is more specifically reflected in the Micah story is that religion "was primarily a matter of the joint family or clan."[29]

But "primarily a matter" for *which members* of an Israelite family or clan? This question is most critical for my investigation, for even if we were to agree with Wilson that sarcasm drives the claim of Judg 17:1–4 that a *woman* (gasp!) originally fashioned the Dan sanctuary's figurine (and I have my doubts), we nevertheless would need to admit that underlying such sarcasm is a presumption that the eighth- and later the seventh-century BCE Israelites whom I have presumed to be the audience of our text could imagine a woman having a cult figurine made as an act of religious piety and having that image subsequently erected in her household's shrine. This, I contend below, provides us with important evidence concerning leadership functions women could and did assume within Israelite household religion. In addition, I cannot accept the analyses of Klein and others which suggest that the Judg 17:4 description of Micah's mother consecrating only two hundred of her eleven hundred pieces of silver to have her cult figurine cast represents her as acting parsimoniously. Rather, as C. A. Faraone, B. Garnand, and C. López-Ruiz have definitively shown, the two hundred pieces of silver this woman consecrates for the making of her figurine is a perfectly appropriate and even expected amount within the context of ancient Mediterranean religious traditions.[30] Also flawed is Klein's argument that the mother's swearing of an oath that curses the unknown thief of her silver and then pronouncing a blessing of her son in the name of Yahweh once he confesses his crime are transgressive acts. Instead, as pointed out by Josef Scharbert, the mother's curse in Judg 17:2 should be understood as analogous to the "audible curse oath" that is presented in Lev 5:1 as a perfectly proper mode of legal and religious expression within Israelite tradition. This sort of curse oath, moreover, is by definition conditional, which is to say, revocable, meaning that once Micah has come forward and confessed as Lev 5:1 requires, the mother again acts in a legally and religiously appropriate way to nullify her curse by uttering a blessing.[31]

It is my contention, in short, that whatever its polemical intent, embedded within the story of Micah's mother and her fabrication of a religious icon is a veritable treasure trove of information concerning the roles women could play within the context of Israelite household religion. In order to substantiate this claim, I turn first to consider more thoroughly the household context of Judg 17:1–18:31 and specifically what it means to set this story *bĕbêt mîkâ,* or "in the house of Micah."

Archaeology and Micah's Household Compound

As I have taken some care to mark in my recounting above of Judges 17 and 18, the phrase *bêt mîkâ,* "the house of Micah," or some variation of it, occurs at multiple points in the text: in 17:4, 8, 12 and 18:2, 3, 13, 15, 18, 22, 25, and 26. On several of these occasions, moreover, *bêt mîkâ* seems to refer to the sort of free-standing, single-family dwelling of which many today might most readily think when hearing a reference to someone's house. Yet certain passages within the story make clear that *bêt mîkâ* can also refer to some type of extended compound in which there were numerous structures. This is suggested, for example, in 18:13–14, as the six hundred Danites approach "the house of Micah" (*bêt mîkâ;* v. 13) and the five original scouts in their company tell them that the *'ēpôd*/ephod, *tĕrāpîm*/teraphim (or the "ephoded teraphim"), and the cast-metal figurine Micah's mother had commissioned are *babbāttîm hā'ēlleh* (v. 14), literally "in these *houses*" (plural) or more idiomatically, at least as I interpret, "in these buildings" that make up the extended compound that is called here "the house of Micah."

Among these buildings, surely, are other homes in addition to the home of Micah, as is indicated in 18:22, where "the men who were in the houses that were with the house of Micah" (*hā'ănāšîm 'ăšer babbāttîm 'ăšer 'im-bêt mîkâ*)—or more idiomatically (at least, again, as I interpret), "the men whose homes were within Micah's extended household compound"—went forth to pursue the thieving Danites.[32] Given the kin-based organizational principles that structured Israelite society, these men whose homes were a part of Micah's extended household compound are almost undoubtedly to be taken as somehow related to Micah. Perhaps they were members of Micah's immediate family: his uncle(s) or his brother(s), say, or someone like the son who was appointed as priest in Judg 17:5, who, when he had come of age and married, had continued to live in his father's household compound, but in a home other than Micah's personal domicile.[33] Or perhaps these men were more distant relations: cousins and the like who were members of Micah's extended family or clan.[34] Still, as the Levite's presence within Micah's household indicates, nonfamily members could also be counted among the inhabitants of an ancient Israelite household compound. The text of Judg 17:1–18:31 seems to indicate as well that a wall could surround a compound such as Micah's, as is suggested in 18:16 and 17, where the Levite priest is said to be standing by a *gate* with most of the six hundred Danites while the five original scouts plunder Micah's shrine.[35]

Indeed, the verses in Judg 17:1–18:31 that speak of Micah's shrine are especially significant for my study, in particular the verses that seem to speak of Micah's shrine as being a space within Micah's compound *distinct* from the compound's family homes. The first of these verses I have already mentioned, Judg 17:5, which describes Micah as having a *bêt ʾĕlōhîm,* or a shrine, over which his priestly son and eventually the Levite presumably presided and in which were arguably housed the *ʾēpôd*/ephod and *tĕrāpîm*/ teraphim (or the "ephoded teraphim") that Micah had made and the cast-metal figurine (the *pesel ûmassēkâ*) his mother had commissioned. To be sure, Judg 17:5 does not definitively indicate that the mother's *pesel ûmassēkâ* and the *ʾēpôd* and *tĕrāpîm* (or the "ephoded teraphim") were housed in Micah's *bêt ʾĕlōhîm,* but the juxtaposition of the phrase "and the man Micah had a shrine" (*wĕhāʾîš mîkâ lô bêt ʾĕlōhîm*) in the first half of Judg 17:5 with the notices regarding the fabrication of the mother's figurine in 17:4 and of Micah's *ʾēpôd* and *tĕrāpîm* (or "ephoded teraphim") in the next part of 17:5 strongly suggests that the *pesel ûmassēkâ,* the *ʾēpôd* and *tĕrāpîm* (or "ephoded teraphim"), and the *bêt ʾĕlōhîm* were all affiliated. Likewise, in Judg 18:14, 17, 18, and 20, the fact that the terms *pesel, massēkâ, ʾēpôd,* and *tĕrāpîm* appear together (once rendered in their composite forms, *pesel ûmassēkâ* and *ʾēpôd ûtĕrāpîm* [18:14] and otherwise as up to four seemingly independent items [18:17, 18, and 20])[36] suggests that these objects were envisioned as housed together: more specifically, in the *bêt ʾĕlōhîm,* or shrine.

Still, on the basis of the evidence of Judg 17:5 and 18:14, 17, 18, and 20, why say, as I have proposed, that Micah's *bêt ʾĕlōhîm* was a space distinct from Micah's actual house? Perhaps the *bêt ʾĕlōhîm* should instead be understood as a small shrine corner or a shrine niche—that is, a "part of a room or courtyard" that lay *within* Micah's home, that was designated for religious purposes, and that thus contained Micah's family's collection of religious objects.[37] After all, such shrine corners or shrine niches, as I discuss more fully in the next chapter, are relatively well attested in the ancient Israelite archaeological record. This record in addition attests that an Israelite home might be furnished with a small model shrine meant to represent, in miniature, a shrine building that could hold sacred objects such as the cast-metal figurine and/or the *ʾēpôd ûtĕrāpîm.* Possibly Micah's *bêt ʾĕlōhîm* is therefore to be taken as one of these model shrines (see Figs. 12.1, 12.4–12.10, 12.12). Or maybe, some scholars propose, Micah's *bêt ʾĕlōhîm* was, like the *bêt ʾĕlōhîm* of Gen 28:22, a simple *maṣṣēbâ,* or standing stone.[38]

Two verses in Judges 18 suggest, however, that Micah's *bêt ʾĕlōhîm* or shrine was in fact a building, and a building distinct from Micah's actual house. The first is Judg 18:3, in which the five Danite scouts who were staying in the house of Micah (*bêt mîkâ*) overhear the voice of Micah's Levite priest and then "turn aside" (*sûr*) to speak to him "there" (*šām*), that is, in a space seemingly other than Micah's home. Yet the Levite elsewhere (for example, in Judg 17:12) is said to be in the house of Micah (*bêt mîkâ*). How to explain this apparent contradiction? I suggest that the Levite was indeed in "the house of Micah" in the sense that he was resident in one of the several buildings—more specifically, the shrine building—that made up Micah's multistructure compound, and it was "there" (*šām*) that Micah's Danite visitors encountered him when they "turned aside" (*sûr*) from the actual "house of Micah"—meaning Micah's personal domicile—to speak to him. I interpret similarly the grammatically difficult passage found in 18:15, where the Danites who had determined to steal Micah's religious treasures come to the *bêt-hannaʿar hallēwî bêt mîkâ,* literally "the house of the Levite youth, the house of Micah," in order to carry out the theft. Because this phrase approaches the nonsensical, some commentators delete the second half of it, the reference to "the house of Micah," as a gloss that was secondarily added to the text.[39] A better solution, however, is to note that in biblical Hebrew, the preposition *bĕ,* meaning "in," is often elided before nouns beginning in the letter *b* (like *bayit,* "house"),[40] as, indeed, happens elsewhere in our text (in Judg 18:18, where in a description of how the thieving Danites entered into Micah's household compound, we read *bāʾû bêt mîkâ* [literally, "they came the house of Micah"] instead of the expected *bāʾû bĕbêt mîkâ* ["they came *into* the house of Micah"]). Alternatively, we might imagine a point during the scribal transmission of Judg 18:15 (and also Judg 18:18) when the *bĕ,* meaning "in," that preceded the phrase *bêt mîkâ,* or "house of Micah," was mistakenly dropped.[41] In either case, Judg 18:15 should properly be rendered "the house of the Levite youth that was *in* (*bĕ*) the house of Micah." Most logically, as suggested above, the reference here is to a distinctive shrine building that was part of the larger compound of which Micah was head and in which the Levite was housed.[42]

These texts in Judg 17:1–18:31 that seem to envision the "house of Micah" as an extended compound whose many buildings included several personal domiciles, as well as Micah's household shrine, can be further illuminated by archaeological remains. Indeed, in the past forty or so years, a significant amount of ancient Israelite archaeological evidence has appeared that suggests to many of its interpreters that the extended household compound was a common architectural configuration used throughout the preexilic period of Israel's history, at least in the villages of the Israelite countryside, in which, it is estimated, 80 to 90 percent of the population lived.[43] To be sure, not all agree, and even among those who suggest the household compound was a common architectural configuration in preexilic Israel, there is acknowledgment that the use of such compounds was not universal.[44] Baruch Halpern cautions, "Other factors entered in, such as limitations of space, defense, urban planning, and so on," but he nonetheless concludes, "the compound deserves investigation."[45] In particular, parallels between the archaeological evidence regarding household compounds and the Micah story suggest that "the compound deserves investigation" here.

I begin by noting that within the extended household compound, the basic architectural unit was the single-family house, called by archaeologists the pillared, or the pillar-courtyard, or sometimes the four-room house.[46] All these terms are meant to describe this house's distinctive layout: a central courtyard that served as the entry portal to the space, flanked by pillars that separated it from the three or so rooms arranged in a U-shape around it (Figs. 1.2 and 1.3). The central courtyards of these houses seem to have been used primarily for food processing: archaeologists have found in them querns and millstones for grinding grain, cooking pots, fire pits, and sometimes ovens.[47] The courtyards were in addition used for some food storage; a more substantial space for food storage—for example, space for grain silos—and for storage of other provisions was available in the broadroom located to the rear of the courtyard that often ran the house's entire width (this room forms the base of the house's U-shaped complex of rooms).[48] The rooms set off with pillars (and often a low curtain wall) on the two

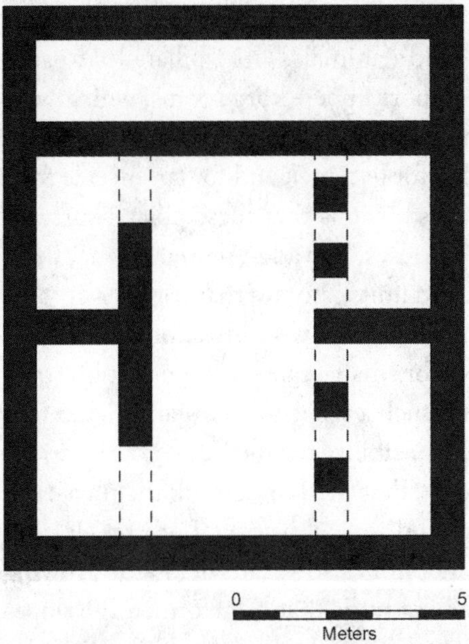

Fig. 1.2. Plan of a representative pillared, or pillar-courtyard, or four-room house. Drawing by Elise J. Laugier.

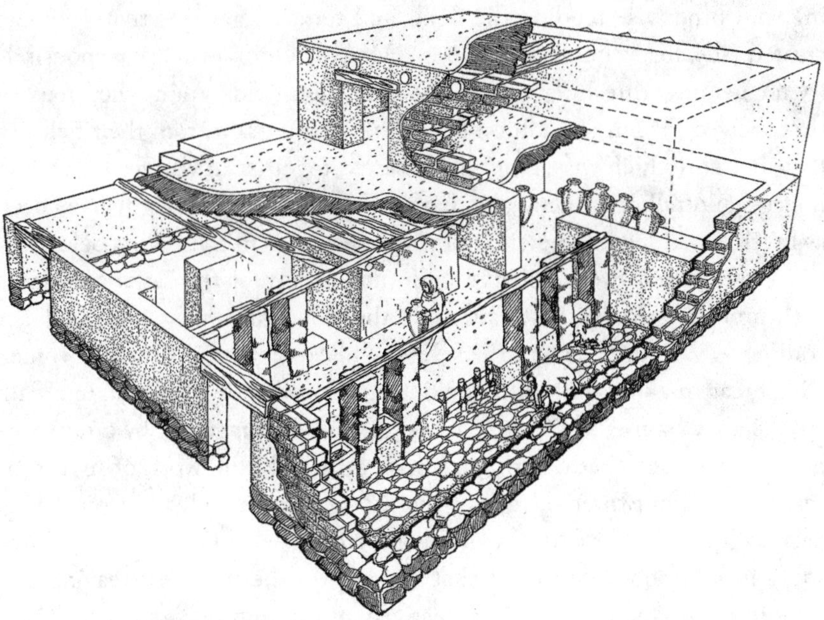

Fig. 1.3. Artist's reconstruction of a representative pillared, or pillar-courtyard, or four-room house. Drawing by Giselle S. Hasel.

sides of the courtyard (the two arms of the U-shaped complex of rooms) functioned as stables for the household's animals.[49] The pillars that partitioned off these stables could also support upper-story rooms, which were used for sleeping, dining, and entertaining.[50]

Because of their accommodations for livestock and for large-scale food storage, William G. Dever writes, "it is obvious that these pillar-courtyard houses . . . would have been ideal farmhouses." He adds, moreover, that these farmhouses are "efficient, self-contained units," homes that could easily sustain a self-sufficient farm family because of their facilities for stabling, for food processing and storage, and also for small-scale craft production (tool, textile, and pottery making).[51] Within such a self-sufficient family, different members surely assumed primary responsibility for the household's various activities. We can imagine, for example, that men undertook the physically demanding task of developing farmland for cultivation, both by clearing previously forested tracts of trees and stones to create fields for growing grain and by building the stone retaining walls that transformed the slopes of the southern Levant's central hill country—the heartland of ancient Israelite settlement—into artificially flat terraces used for cultivating olive trees and grapevines. Men probably did the work as well of plowing, planting, and otherwise tending the fields and terraced gardens that they had created (see, for example, 1 Sam 8:12). Men also took primary responsibility for reaping, threshing, and winnowing their fields' grain when harvest time arrived.[52] Men in addition ferried harvested grain from their fields to their homes (which were typically clustered together in villages located on nonagriculturally productive land, often on hilltops that might have been as much as a three kilometer climb from the fields in the valleys below).[53]

Women, however, probably performed many of the tasks associated with processing harvested grain and other foodstuffs, as is indicated, according to Carol Meyers, by the several biblical texts that associate women with bread-making and with cooking more generally (Lev 26:26; 1 Sam 8:13, 28:24; 2 Sam 13:8; 1 Kgs 17:12–13). This is also suggested by a 1973 ethnographic survey that determined that women do the work of food processing in all but three or four of the 185 societies worldwide from which data on human labor patterns were collected (see also Fig. 2.7).[54] This same study in addition determined that women do the work of weaving and spinning in 84 and 87 percent, respectively, of the cultures surveyed.[55] Many biblical texts—Josh 2:6, Judg 16:13–14, 2 Kgs 23:7, Ezek 13:17–18 (on which see Chapter 10), and, most famously, Prov 31:10–31—associate women with

Fig. 1.4. Limestone statuette of a female burnishing (?) or adding handles to (?) a pot, from New Kingdom Egypt (ca. 1539–1075 BCE). Courtesy of the Petrie Museum, University College London, object no. UC 15706.

textile production as well.[56] Small-scale, domestic pottery production, if ethnographic data from Cyprus and other Mediterranean and Levantine locations are any guide (Crete, the southwestern Peloponnese, the Magreb, Lebanon, northern Syria, and early twentieth-century Ramallah and surrounding villages), was another task women assumed, especially the production of modest-sized pots that were hand-formed or made using a tournette, or a slow-wheel, rather than having been thrown on a fast- or kick-wheel (Fig. 1.4).[57] Children's work may have involved watering and harvesting vegetables grown in small gardens near the home and helping tend to their families' sheep and goats.[58] In addition, boys, as we will see in the next chapter, assumed the task of gathering wood for fuel.

Also in the next chapter, I consider more extensively women's roles within a typical Israelite pillared house and the way in which these roles can help in my quest to describe women's experiences within Israelite household religion. I return to this topic in this chapter as well. Before I conclude my current discussion of the Israelite household environment, however, let me briefly note the evidence archaeologists have produced to show that, sometimes, two to three (or occasionally even more) individual pillared houses could stand clustered together in compounds within Israelite villages, sometimes clustered together so tightly that houses within any given compound might be contiguous, built with shared walls and with doorways all opening onto an open-air yard (Fig. 1.5).[59] This open-air yard, which could be either walled and gated (as is indicated in the Judg 17:1–18:31 story) or more simply demarcated by pathways and passageways, seems

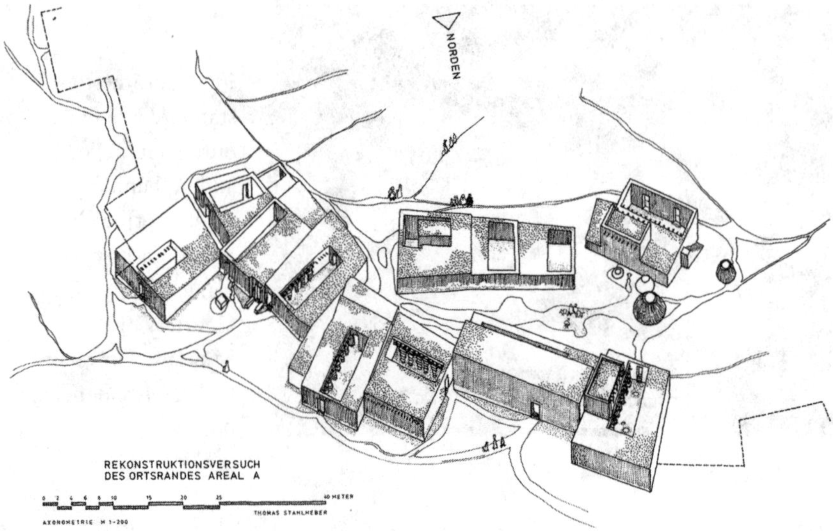

Fig. 1.5. Artist's reconstruction showing several multihouse compounds within a typical ancient Israelite village. From Volkmar Fritz and Aharon Kempinski, *Ergebnisse der Ausgrabungen auf der Hirbet el-Mšaš (Tel Masos) 1972–1975* I: *Textband* (ADPV 6. Wiesbaden: Harrassowitz, 1983), Figure 2. Used by permission.

to have been the locus of certain communal activities undertaken jointly by the occupants of the compound's clustered-together houses.[60] It could contain a baking oven, for example, and perhaps the sort of small vegetable garden I mentioned above.[61]

At the early Israelite village of twelfth- through mid-eleventh-century BCE Ai (see Fig. I.1), there is also evidence of a dedicated shrine room associated with a compound of clustered-together houses. This shrine, like the open-air yard that held a household compound's communal oven and that was the site of other communal enterprises, probably served as a space used jointly by the members of the compound for religious devotion. Amihai Mazar's excavations at Tel Reḥov (see again Fig. I.1) have revealed a similar shrine from the late tenth and ninth centuries BCE, which, in Mazar's words, could have served "an extended family . . . or several extended families living nearby."[62] Aaron J. Brody has somewhat similarly identified a room—Room 513—among the remains of Tell en-Naṣbeh (biblical Mizpah; see, yet again, Fig. I.1) from the Iron Age II period (ca. 1000–586 BCE) that, although it was also used as a storeroom, held a shrine Brody theorizes would have served as a place of religious observance for the members of its family's or clan's five-building household compound.[63]

Archaeology, Micah's Shrine, and Micah's Mother

The dedicated shrine room at Ai—Room 65—sits among the domestic buildings found in Area D of the site, which is in Ai's northeast corner. It was excavated by Judith Marquet-Krause in the 1930s and labeled by her as a cult room ("un lieu saint").[64] Still, its religious character was thoroughly analyzed only recently, by Ziony Zevit in his 2001 study of Israelite religion.[65] In support of the identification of the space as a shrine, Zevit—and also Beth Alpert Nakhai, in her archaeological survey of Canaanite and Israelite cultic sites—cites several factors.[66] First, the room itself, which is 8.5 by 3 meters, is somewhat larger than the others found at Ai, which suggests a special role for it.[67] Unlike any other room at Ai, moreover, two walls of Room 65 (the western and southern) are benched (Fig. 1.6).[68] This

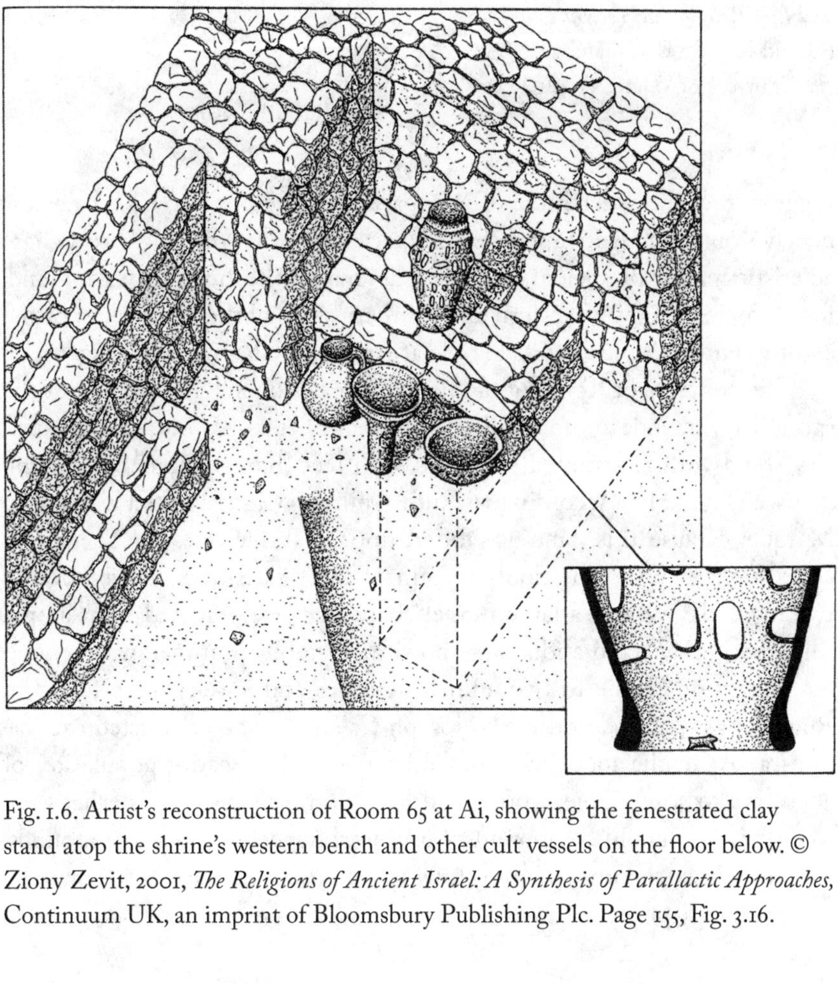

Fig. 1.6. Artist's reconstruction of Room 65 at Ai, showing the fenestrated clay stand atop the shrine's western bench and other cult vessels on the floor below. © Ziony Zevit, 2001, *The Religions of Ancient Israel: A Synthesis of Parallactic Approaches*, Continuum UK, an imprint of Bloomsbury Publishing Plc. Page 155, Fig. 3.16.

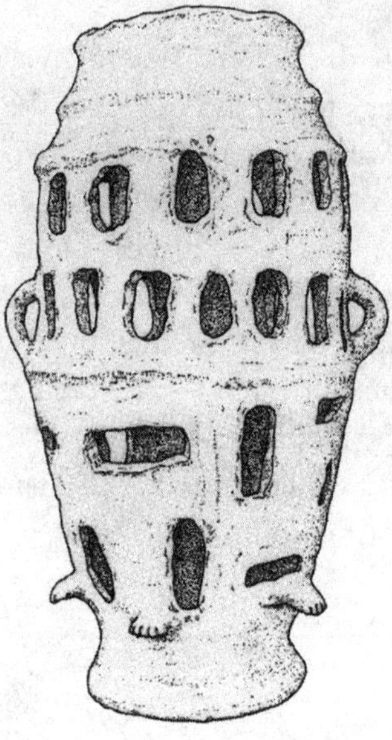

Fig. 1.7. Fenestrated offering stand from Ai. From William G. Dever, *Did God Have a Wife? Archaeology and Folk Religion in Ancient Israel* (Grand Rapids: Eerdmans, 2005), 112. Courtesy of Valerie Woelfel.

suggests that the special role of the space was religious, given that narrow benches on which worshippers could place dedicatory offerings are a characteristic feature of ancient Israelite religious architecture. They are found, for example, along the western and southern walls of the main room of the eighth-century BCE fortress temple at Arad (see Chapter 6 and Fig. 6.3).[69]

The contents of Room 65 at Ai also suggest the religious nature of the space. They include an unusually tall (80 centimeters), cylindrically shaped clay stand with fenestrated sides and with feet (human? lion?) encircling its base (Fig. 1.7).[70] According to Ruth Amiran, who excavated at Ai with Marquet-Krause, this stand was found atop the shrine's western bench (see again Fig. 1.6).[71] On the floor in front of the western bench were found two more clay vessels: a large funnel-shaped chalice designed to fit atop a (different?) clay stand and a large bowl with stubby protuberances around its midsection.[72] One to two animal figurines and jewelry were found in Room 65 as well.[73] According to Joseph Callaway, who conducted excavations at Ai in the 1960s, eleventh-century BCE Ai had a population of about 150 to 300 people, who would have been grouped into perhaps ten to twenty household compounds.[74] Presumably, each of these compounds, as I have discussed in relation to Judg 17:1–18:31, would have been occupied by members of a kinship group, as well as this kinship group's affiliates. Room 65 easily could have served as a shrine for one of these compounds.

More specifically, Room 65 would have been a space within a kinship group's household compound where compound members could stop by and engage in what both archaeological data and biblical texts (such as Jer 7:16–20 and 44:15–19, 25, as we will see in the next chapter) imply are the fundamental rituals of ancient Israelite household religion. These include, first, making grain and similar foodstuff offerings (although not offerings that result from animal sacrifice, a rite that seems—Judg 6:19–21 and 13:15–16, 19 notwithstanding—only to have been a part of sanctuary and temple ritual).[75] In addition, the rituals of household religion include burning aromatic plant materials (woods and herbs) and, perhaps (in the eighth and seventh centuries BCE, subsequent to the establishment of a thriving incense trade with the Arabian peninsula), burning incense.[76] Household ritual also included the pouring out of libations. Indeed, with regard to libations, note that Room 65 has a channel that appears to have drained the floor area in front of the western bench, a feature not found in any of the nearby buildings.[77] Likewise, regarding offerings of food and of aromatic plant materials, note that the fenestrated stand that stood on Room 65's western bench could have been used for making both these sorts of presentations. More specifically, grain and similar foodstuff offerings could have been set in a bowl placed atop the cylindrically shaped stand, and aromatic plant materials could have been burned within the cylinder proper, with smoke issuing forth from the fenestrations.[78]

Would Room 65's worshippers have included the household compound's women? I think the evidence of Judg 17:1–18:31 suggests this, at least to some degree. More specifically: if I am correct in assuming, first, that we are meant to envision the cast-metal figurine Micah's mother is said to have commissioned in Judg 17:4 as standing in the *bêt ʾĕlōhîm,* or the household shrine of Micah, mentioned in 17:5, and if I am further correct in assuming that Judg 18:3 and 15 indicate that this household shrine was a distinct and dedicated space within Micah's household compound, much like Room 65 at Ai, then Judg 17:1–18:31 allows us at a minimum to conclude that just as Micah's mother was able to install her cast-metal figurine as one of the religious furnishings of her family's household shrine, so too could Israelite women more generally have played a role in helping furnish household shrines such as the Ai cult space. Important to recall in this regard is the assemblage of cultic items found in Ai's Room 65—especially the cylindrically shaped clay stand with fenestrated sides, the clay bowl with stubby protuberances around its midsection, and the funnel-shaped clay chalice—and to consider who might have manufactured these objects. Men? It must be admitted that some archaeological evidence and some biblical texts—Jer 18:1–3 and 1 Chr 4:23—might suggest this, as these data point to the presence of pottery workshops in ancient Israel staffed by male professionals.[79] Still, this sort of industrialized pottery production seems to have appeared in Israelite society beginning only in the eighth century BCE and only in urban centers.[80] There, pottery production was part of a larger "economic and commercial system [developed] under the centralized Judean and Israelite states."[81] Who, though, would have been responsible for pottery production in twelfth- and eleventh-century village sites such as Ai and, indeed, throughout Israelite history within household settings, especially households located outside of urban enclaves? I have argued above that women would have made such domiciles' pottery, especially vessels that, like the Ai cylindrical offering stand and the large clay bowl and chalice, are characterized by hand-forming (rather than having been thrown on a fast- or kick-wheel). It is at least possible, therefore, that a woman, or several different women, made the various cultic vessels discovered in Room 65's household shrine.

Recall also the cylindrically shaped stand's significant height (80 centimeters), which suggests that the stand would have commanded a certain prominence within the Room 65 shrine. Also note in this regard that the western bench of Room 65 on which the offering stand was positioned was itself 27 centimeters tall, as opposed to the adjoining southern bench, which was only 15 centimeters high.[82] This architectural layout would obviously work in conjunction with the cylindrically shaped stand's significant height to concentrate the attention of the shrine-room's visitors upon the offering stand. The stand's eye-catching position within Ai's Room 65, and so its focal role, is highlighted even more if we follow Dever in suggesting that the stand is meant to represent a temple of the Israelite god, Yahweh, with the stand's fenestrated column representing a windowed shrine building and the feet that ring the stand's base indicating symbolically that Yahweh, otherwise not depicted, is "at home" in this sanctuary.[83] Indeed, it is tempting to view the elevated western bench in Room 65 as a podium on which the offering stand that could house Yahweh's divine presence sat.[84]

Because it could house Yahweh's divine presence and because of its focal location, this cylindrically shaped offering stand surely would have been understood as the most valuable object housed in Ai's Room 65 shrine. This suggests—if we are to assume, as I argued above, that a woman could have made this vessel—that not only could Israelite women have played a role in helping furnish household shrines such as the Ai cult space, but women also could have contributed to their household shrines the objects that were each sanctuary's *most valuable* furnishing. Indeed, this is just what was indicated in my analysis of Judg 17:1–18:31, wherein I determined that the cult figurine Micah's mother contributed to her household shrine was the *most valuable* object within it. Recall, for example, that this cult figurine was overlaid with silver and perhaps had been cast in bronze, and that both of these materials were, like all metals, relatively scarce in ancient Israel and hence remarkably precious. Recall also that, just as the fenestrated offering stand from twelfth-/eleventh-century BCE Ai arguably signifies Yahweh resident in his temple, the mother's figurine, I proposed in this chapter's opening pages, was somehow meant to represent Yahweh. In addition, just as the Ai stand seems to have served as the focal point of that site's household shrine, so too Micah's mother's figurine—given that it signified Yahweh and given its value—could have served as the focal point of Micah's household shrine. As I have again already indicated, moreover, we are allowed these conclusions about Micah's mother's figurine regardless of the polemical overtones that might characterize Judg 17:1–18:31 as it has come down to us. That is: whatever negative judgment the passage's author(s) and/or redactor(s) may wish to impose about, say, the "tainted" nature of the silver Micah's mother consecrated to make her figurine, the text nevertheless makes clear that among the Israelite community in which this story was generated and recounted, the notion "rang true" that Micah's mother could commission an exceptionally valuable cultic object that served as the focal point of the shrine located within her extended household compound.

Judges 17:1–18:31 thus correlates with our archaeological evidence to suggest that an Israelite woman such as Micah's mother could take responsibility for producing or commissioning a precious icon that signified the god Yahweh who was venerated in her household and could further expect to see that icon revered as the most sacred object of her household's shrine. Such a woman could—and *should*—be readily understood as her household shrine's primary patron, an extraordinary indication of the powerful role women might play within ancient Israelite household religion.

Still, as is often the case, the biblical writers, even when suggesting a powerful role for women within Israelite tradition, refuse to affirm this absolutely. We see this, for example, in the failure of Judg 17:1–4 to assign to Micah's mother a name, instead referring to her only as *'immô*, "his [Micah's] mother," six times in the space of three verses (17:2–4). This is significant, for the giving of a name in the Bible, especially the giving of a name to a woman, is often an important marker of that woman's autonomy and authority. Conversely, to deny a woman a name is often to mark her as powerless and someone easily victimized within a male-dominated culture.[85] This is especially true in the book of Judges, where the text's many powerful women are most typically named—Achsah (Judg 1:11–15), Deborah (Judg 4:4–16, 5:1–23), Jael (Judg 4:17–22, 5:24–27), and Delilah (Judg 16: 4–22)—whereas women who fall victim to androcentric agendas or traditions most often remain nameless: Sisera's mother, who waits helplessly and ultimately in vain for her son to return victorious from battle (Judg 5: 28–30); Jephthah's daughter, who is killed to fulfill her father's rash vow to sacrifice whoever or whatever (the Hebrew *'ăšer* is ambiguous) first comes forth from his house when he returns home from war (Judg 11:29–40); Samson's Timnite wife, who is abandoned by her husband seven days after they were wed and then unjustifiably murdered by her own countrymen as they seek revenge against the equally unjustified rampages of Samson (Judg 14:1–15:6); and the Levite's concubine, who is thrust by her husband out of the house in which they have lodged for the night to be raped and killed by the Benjaminites of Gibeah (Judg 19:1–30). To be sure, there are some exceptions within Judges, as both the woman of Thebez, who crushes the skull of the royal pretender Abimelech and so brings an end to the civil strife that has consumed her land (Judg 9:50–57), and Samson's mother, who outshines her husband Manoah in the story of Samson's birth (Judg 13: 2–24), remain unnamed.[86] Nevertheless, biblical convention would lead us to expect that a woman such as Micah's mother, who plays such a leadership role in her household's cult, would be identified by name. The effect of the biblical writers' failing to do so is to downplay the importance of this otherwise quite powerful woman.

Also in the concluding verses of Judg 17:1–18:31, the redactors who seem to have brought 17:1–4 into association with 17:7–13 and 18:1–31 and so rendered the text in the form we have it today move to obscure any indication of Micah's mother's contribution to her household's shrine. Thus, in 18:31, we are told that the Danites "maintained for themselves Micah's image that he had made" throughout the time that Yahweh's sanctuary stood in Shiloh. As already noted, this reference to Yahweh's sanctuary that stood and then, our text implies, ceased to stand in Shiloh is oblique and can be interpreted in various ways.[87] But "*Micah's image* that *he* had made": What does the narrative refer to here? It might be the *ʾēpôd ûtĕrāpîm,* the "ephoded teraphim" or the *ʾēpôd*/ephod and *tĕrāpîm*/teraphim, that Micah is said to have made in 17:5. Yet as noted above, the *ʾēpôd*/ephod does not necessarily represent any sort of supernatural being; rather, most commonly in the Bible, it refers to some sort of religious garment worn by a priest. And while *tĕrāpîm*/teraphim does seem to refer to some sort of image, the images in question, as also already noted, are most probably representations of family ancestors, and it seems highly unlikely that representations of an *Ephraimite's* family ancestors would interest the *Danites* as the object of their primary religious veneration. More important, the Hebrew term used for Micah's image in 18:31 is *pesel,* a word that elsewhere in Judg 17:1–18:31 is used exclusively to describe the image Micah's mother had commissioned (see Judg 17:3, 4; 18:14, 20; and even 18:17 and 18, in which, although the Hebrew is somewhat ambiguous, the *pesel* is clearly distinguished from the *ʾēpôd* and the *tĕrāpîm* [which are themselves distinguished as separate objects in these two verses]).

One is left to conclude that the *pesel* credited to Micah in 18:31 is the one Micah's mother is said to have commissioned in 17:4, meaning that in 18:31, the text erases Micah's mother from her own story, ignoring her contribution to the furnishing of her household's shrine and assigning that honor to her son instead. I am reminded of Exod 15:1–18, in which the victory hymn that, according to 15:20–21, was sung by Miriam after Yahweh's miraculous triumph over Pharaoh and his Egyptian army at the Reed (more traditionally "Red") Sea was reassigned to Moses in Exod 15:1 (see further Chapter 9).[88] I think also of Judges 4–5, where the role described for Deborah as war leader in the Israelite tribes' holy war against a coalition of Canaanite kings led by Sisera in Judges 5, especially in vv. 7, 12, and 15, was reassigned in the later prose retelling of this tale in Judges 4 to her male counterpart, Barak (see further Chapter 10).

Indeed, the redactors of the Judg 17:1–18:31 story so completely erase Micah's mother from the text that she is not mentioned again after 17:4, immediately following the story of her commissioning the cast-metal figurine. In this way, not only do this passage's editors move to obscure the role that a woman such as Micah's mother could play in furnishing her household's shrine, even serving as that shrine's principal patron, they also deny us information regarding women's continuing roles in the life of such a sanctuary. Did women, for example, after providing some of a shrine's furnishings, continue to visit the objects they had dedicated and venerate the deity or deities to whom their gifts had been consecrated? In particular, did they participate in the ritual events of their households' shrines by making the grain and foodstuff offerings, the libation offerings, and the offerings of aromatic plant materials and even incense that comprised the core rituals, as suggested above, of ancient Israelite household religion? Common sense, it seems to me, suggests women would be engaged in these aspects of the household cult, but Judg 17:1–18:31 is mute. Fortunately, however, we can make up somewhat for this silence by turning to consider two other texts in the Hebrew Bible that illuminate women's role in Israelite household religion: Jer 7:16–20 and the related Jer 44:15–19, 25.

2 "The Women Knead Dough": Women and Ancient Israelite Household Religion, II

Jeremiah 7:16–20 is part of a long diatribe (Jer 7:1–8:3) attributed to the prophet Jeremiah and set in Jerusalem during the waning years of the pre-exilic period (ca. 609–586 BCE).[1] In it, Jeremiah condemns Jerusalem's late seventh- and early sixth-century BCE inhabitants for all sorts of behaviors he considers religiously misguided. In some cases, the acts in question are, in Jeremiah's opinion, theologically misinformed (such as the people's conviction that Yahweh will not allow the foreign powers to which the Southern Kingdom of Judah has become vassal—Egypt and then the Babylonian Empire—to destroy their national temple in Jerusalem). In other cases, Jeremiah deems the people's deeds to be ritually apostate (such as their worship of the sun, the moon, and the host of heaven). Included in this latter harangue is Jeremiah's censure of Judahites who participate in the cult of a goddess known only as the Queen of Heaven. In Jer 44:15–19, 25, Jeremiah similarly denounces his fellow Judahites for their worship of the Queen of Heaven, both the worship of the Queen of Heaven in which these particular Judahites, who were part of a group that had fled to Egypt in the aftermath of the Babylonian destruction of Jerusalem in 586 BCE, were currently engaging and the worship of the Queen of Heaven by these same Judahites, and others, in their homeland during the decades before their nation's fall.[2]

Elsewhere, I have commented in detail on the identity of the Queen of Heaven, and I also have discussed factors that may have motivated Judaeans in the late seventh and early sixth centuries BCE to embrace this goddess's cult.[3] Here, though, in the context of our discussion of women and Israelite household religion, it is more appropriate to concentrate not on questions of *who* the Queen of Heaven was and *why* her adherents were attracted to her cult, but rather to ask *where* this goddess was worshipped. We will want to address as well the specific acts of religious devotion that took place within the Queen of Heaven's worship venues and, of course, consider what role women played in performing these rites. As should be obvious, given my intention to discuss Jeremiah's Queen of Heaven texts at this point in my study, it is my presumption that the *where* of the goddess's worship included (but was not necessarily limited to) ancient Israelite household shrines. It is further my presumption—and this may not be so obvious—that while devotion to the Queen of Heaven as it is presented in the Bible was a part of some Judaeans' religious practice *only* in the late seventh and early sixth centuries BCE, the means by which the Queen of Heaven was worshipped within Judaean households, and the responsibilities assumed for her worship by various household members (including women), were not unique to the ritual traditions of, say, 610–580 BCE. Nor were the means of the Queen of Heaven's worship unique to her cult. Instead, evidence indicates that the modes of cultic practice that characterize the worship of the Queen of Heaven according to Jer 7:18 and 44:15, 17–19, and 25 (making grain offerings, pouring out libations, and burning aromatic plant materials) were—as I suggested in the last chapter—typical of Israelite household religion throughout the preexilic period, regardless of the deity or deities to whom they were directed. A preexilic Israelite household dedicated to the worship of Yahweh, that is (or any other god), would have expressed its dedication in just the same way as did the Queen of Heaven's devotees.

To put the matter another way: while Jeremiah's harangue concerning the Queen of Heaven's worship is no less polemically charged than was the Judg 17:1–18:31 attack on the Danites' religious heritage on which I focused in Chapter 1, the same conclusion I reached in Chapter 1 about the details that underlie such polemical texts holds here: that even though Jer 7:16–20 and 44:15–19, 25 seek forcefully to condemn religious forms of expression that Jeremiah perceives to be apostate (or that the author[s] and/or redactor[s] who are responsible for Jeremiah's oracles in the form that we have them perceive as apostate), these texts cannot be dismissed as useless hyperbole. Rather, in order to compel the response that Jeremiah (and/or his redactor[s]) desired from his late seventh- and early sixth-century BCE audience, Jer 7:16–20 and 44:15–19, 25 must describe the conduct of Israelite household religion in the preexilic period, whoever the deity being worshipped, in ways that "rang true" to the audience these texts were meant to address. Underlying Jeremiah's tendentious accusations, that is to say, are generally accurate details regarding household cult and, moreover, generally accurate indications regarding women and the practices of Israelite household religion that this investigation will need carefully to consider.

Siting the Religious Practices of Jeremiah 7 and 44

In Jer 7:17 and again in Jer 44:17, we find Jeremiah's initial answer to the question I posed above about *where,* according to Jer 7:16–20 and 44:15–19, 25, the Queen of Heaven was worshipped: "in the towns of Judah and in the streets of Jerusalem." We are also told, in Jer 44:17, that the devotees who worshipped the Queen of Heaven in these locales comprised a broad swath of the Judaean population, including the Judaeans who were part of the company that had fled into Egypt after the fall of Jerusalem, these fugitives' ancestors, and their "kings" (*mĕlākîm*) and "princes" or "officials" (*śārîm*). From this last remark, we might deduce that at least one site where the Queen of Heaven was more specifically worshipped was in shrines within palaces and other monumental state buildings that were the domains of these kings and officials. Although they predate the Jeremiah passages by centuries, archaeological analogies might be provided by the ninth-century BCE remains from Building CF at Tel Reḥov and by two sets of remains from tenth-, ninth-, or eighth-century BCE Megiddo: Room 340 in Building 338 and Cult Corner 2081 (Figs. 2.1, 2.2, and 2.3).[4] Reḥov's excavator, Amihai Mazar, hypothesizes that the elaborate Building CF served "elite families and officials," who—given the "particularly rich cultic assemblage" found in the building's remains (including a model shrine and a fragmentary pottery altar that I discuss in Chapter 12)—"had their own cult corners and cult paraphernalia."[5] Room 340 in Building 338 and Cult Corner 2081 at Megiddo are both small installations located within large administrative buildings—in the case of Building 338, perhaps even a "palatial complex."[6] In each, cultic equipment was found that seems clearly to indicate that these spaces were used by the respective administrative buildings' occupants for religious purposes, and in ways analogous, we might suggest, to the cult that Judah's "kings" and "princes" extended to the Queen of Heaven in monumental state buildings in the late seventh and early sixth centuries BCE.

The real emphasis in Jer 7:16–20 and 44:15–19, 25, however, is not on the Queen of Heaven's worshippers among members of the Judaean officialdom,

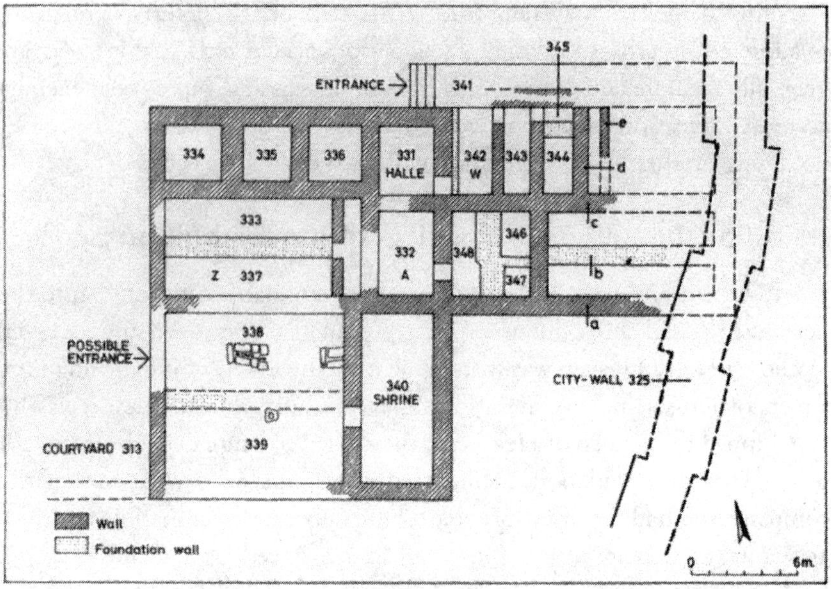

Fig 2.1. Plan showing the location of Room 340 within Building 338 at Megiddo. From David Ussishkin, "Schumacher's Shrine in Building 338 at Megiddo," *IEJ* 39 (1989): 157, Fig. 4. Courtesy of the Israel Exploration Society.

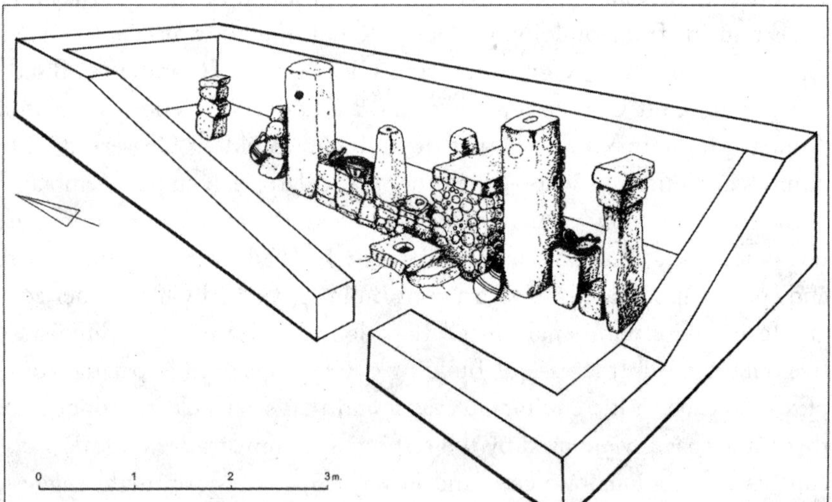

Fig. 2.2. Artist's reconstruction of Room 340 in Building 338 at Megiddo. © Ziony Zevit, 2001, *The Religions of Ancient Israel: A Synthesis of Parallactic Approaches,* Continuum UK, an imprint of Bloomsbury Publishing Plc. Page 229, Fig. 3.60.

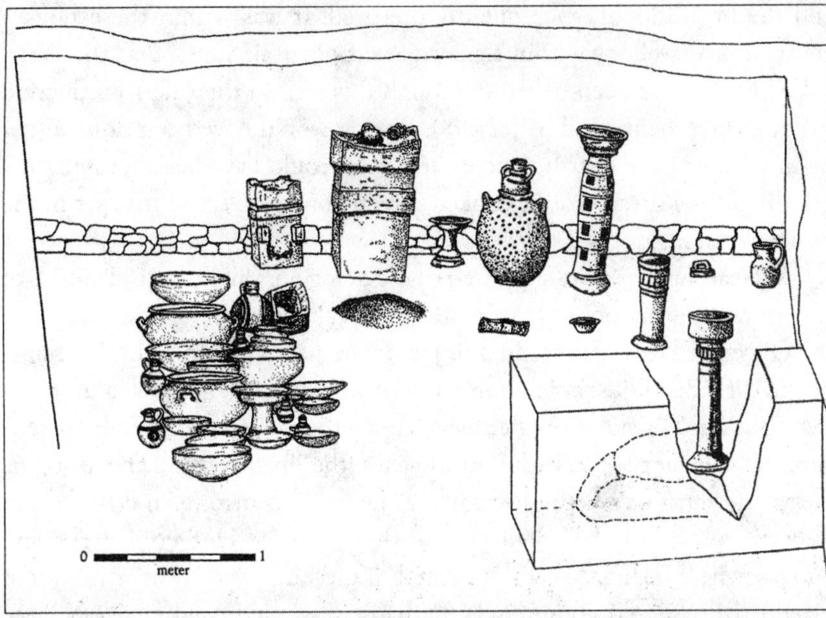

Fig. 2.3. Artist's reconstruction of Cult Corner 2081 at Megiddo. © Ziony Zevit, 2001, *The Religions of Ancient Israel: A Synthesis of Parallactic Approaches,* Continuum UK, an imprint of Bloomsbury Publishing Plc. Page 224, Fig. 3.55.

but on her worshippers among Judah's nonelites. Certainly, in Jer 44:15–19, 25, it is nonelites whom Jeremiah censures for "making bread cakes for" and "burning incense" and "pouring out libations" to the Queen of Heaven, particularly the husbands and wives who are among the company of fugitives who had fled to Egypt in the face of the Babylonians' conquest of Judah. Likewise, in Jer 7:16–20, it is husbands, wives, and also the children of predestruction Judah and Jerusalem who are the object of the prophet's scorn for "mak[ing] bread cakes for the Queen of Heaven": as their contributions to this project, we are told, "the sons gather wood, the fathers kindle fire, and the women knead dough to make bread cakes for the Queen of Heaven" (Jer 7:18).[7] The location, moreover, where these sons', fathers', and women's cake-making activities *must* have taken place is within these individuals' households or within their extended household compounds, for, as we have seen in Chapter 1, it was within individual households that the grain and other foodstuffs that would have been needed to make the Queen of Heaven's bread cakes would have been stored, and it was within these houses' central courtyards that this grain would have been ground into flour and the bread dough subsequently prepared. It was within these houses' courtyards as well, or within their adjacent open-air yards, that the bread cakes would have been baked (although this step in the cakes' production is not in fact mentioned in Jer 7:18). Baking would have been done either in an oven or on a hearth, where the dough could have been toasted on a griddle or in a bread pan or cooked directly on a hot stone that sat in the hearth's ashes.[8]

We can furthermore suppose—there being absolutely no indication to the contrary—that not only were the bread cakes that were to be offered to the Queen of Heaven according to Jer 7:18 prepared within a family's home or the extended household compound of which that home was a part, but that the actual bread cake offerings were presented there as well. By extension, we can suppose that the bread cakes, the libations, and the aromatic burnt offerings that the fugitives whom Jeremiah confronts in Egypt claim that they previously had dedicated to the Queen of Heaven in Jerusalem and elsewhere in Judah were presented in these fugitives' former homes or extended household compounds. Perhaps we should even envision these ritual presentations as taking place within a household compound's distinct and dedicated shrine building, such as Room 65 at Ai that I discussed in the last chapter. Indeed, we should remember that two of the walls of this room were lined with benches on which dedicatory offerings such as bread cakes could be placed; in addition, recall that the cult stand found in Room 65 was designed to hold a bowl on top for foodstuff offerings, while aromatic plant materials could have been burned in the fenestrated cylinder below (see Figs. 1.6 and 1.7). Also, as we have seen, a channel in Room 65's floor seems to have served as a drain to carry away the overflow from libation offerings.

Still, while it seems reasonable to imagine that distinct and dedicated shrine buildings could have been used by devotees who lived in small villages like Ai to offer bread cakes, libations, and aromatic plant materials to the Queen of Heaven, Jer 7:16–20 and 44:15–19, 25 focus on households "in the towns of Judah" and "in the streets of Jerusalem." In these more urban settings, as in all urban locations, space would have been at a premium, lessening the possibility that a household would have had land it could commit for a dedicated shrine room. In fact, we might recall again from Chapter 1 the shrine room belonging to a five-building household compound that Aaron J. Brody has identified within the Iron Age II remains (ca. 1000–586 BCE) of Tel en-Naṣbeh (biblical Mizpah; see Fig. I.1), which was a fairly large (3-hectare) fortified town.[9] This room was not reserved for religious purposes only, but was also used for storage.[10] Somewhat similarly, James W. Hardin has described how an individual dwelling (Dwelling F7) from the eighth-century BCE Judaean town of Lahav (Tell Halif; see again Fig. I.1), 19 kilometers northeast of Beersheba, had a room (Room 2) used both for food preparation and consumption and for domestic religious activities.[11] Because, moreover, the cultic artifacts found in this room were confined to its northern end (Area B), Hardin defines the space associated with their use as a "cult corner": that is, the sort of small shrine corner or shrine niche that I also mentioned in the last chapter, which would have been located *within* an individual home.[12] More specifically, these shrine corners or shrine niches were spaces designated for religious purposes that sat within some room of an ancient Israelite home or within the home's central courtyard.[13] Such corners or niches served both as the place where a household's religious images and/or related objects were located and as a site for the acts of devotion that these images and/or objects might engender.

Our understanding of Israelite shrine corners or shrine niches and their furnishings can be enhanced by considering in greater detail the archaeological record, as materials that arguably come from shrine corners or shrine niches have been identified in the excavations of many Israelite homes. Such materials have been found, for example, in household remains from (1) the twelfth- and eleventh-century BCE village of Khirbet Raddana, (2) twelfth- and eleventh-century BCE (or perhaps eleventh- and tenth-century BCE) Tel Masos (biblical Hormah?), (3) tenth-century BCE Khirbet el-Qeiyafa (biblical Shaaraim?), (4) tenth-century BCE Megiddo, (5) tenth- or ninth-century BCE Tell el-Far'ah North (probably biblical Tirzah), (6) ninth- and eighth-century BCE Beersheba, (7) Level A (ninth- to seventh-century BCE) at Tell Beit Mirsim, (8) eighth-century BCE Hazor, and, as noted just above, (9) late eighth-century BCE Lahav/Tell Halif.[14] For instance, at twelfth- and eleventh-century BCE Khirbet Raddana, several homes within two of that village's household compounds (Sites R and T) produced artifacts that suggest the presence of household shrine corners: offering stands, stone-paved platforms that could have been used for presenting offerings, and (in one home) a large multihandled krater with bullhead spouts probably used for making libation offerings.[15]

The evidence from tenth- or ninth-century BCE Tell el-Far'ah North/Tirzah (see Fig. I.1) is particularly rich, especially the evidence from House 440 (Stratum VIIb).[16] Finds include the foot of a miniature column, about 9.6 centimeters high, which was originally part of the sort of small model shrine that I mentioned briefly in Chapter 1 and will discuss further, and in far more detail, in Chapter 12 (see Figs. 12.1, 12.4–12.10, 12.12). This House 440 model shrine, when it was whole, was presumably box-shaped, albeit with an opening on one of the box's sides, rather than on the top (Ziony Zevit describes such shrines as looking "like up-ended [and, we can add, unlidded] shoe . . . boxes").[17] This is the shape, at least, of a model shrine to which the House 440 shrine fragment is presumably close kin—an almost perfectly preserved shrine model (12.5–13.9 centimeters wide, 20.8 centimeters high, and 10.5 centimeters deep) found elsewhere at Tell el-Far'ah North (see Fig. 12.5).[18] Unfortunately, no associated figurine was found with the more complete Tell el-Far'ah North shrine model, but model shrines discovered at other ancient Near Eastern sites can house an image of a deity, making it clear that these model shrines could serve as installations in which a representation of a god or goddess (or perhaps of more than one god and/or goddess) was lodged.[19]

The excavators of House 440 also discovered two fragmentary terracotta female figurines, one of a woman holding (nursing?) a child and one of a woman holding a disk (often interpreted as a frame drum). They unearthed as well a horse head from a zoomorphic vessel, which, like the bowl with bullhead spouts from Khirbet Raddana described above, is an object scholars generally assume was used for libation offerings (Fig. 2.4). All of the House 440 materials, moreover (the model shrine fragment, the female figurines, and the horse head), came from the home's central courtyard (although the model shrine had fallen over into Room 439, which was adjacent), with the figurine of the disk-holding woman found near a 3-meter stone bench that ran along the courtyard's west wall (Fig. 2.5).[20] In her Ph.D. dissertation that examines these Tell el-Far'ah North materials, as well as evidence from several household shrines found elsewhere (Tel Masos/Hormah, Beersheba, and Lahav/Tell Halif), Elizabeth A. Willett plausibly argues that this House 440 courtyard bench was used for making dedicatory offerings, in the same way benches were used for making dedicatory offerings in shrines such as Room 65 at Ai.[21]

Data pertaining to household shrines from ninth- and eighth-century BCE Beersheba (see Fig. I.1 and Fig. 6.1) are also quite rich and suggest that about 45 percent of the houses there had some sort of remains that are arguably from the homes' shrine niches or shrine corners: female figurines somewhat like those I described in conjunction with the remains from Tell el-Far'ah North; several representations of what scholars call horse-and-

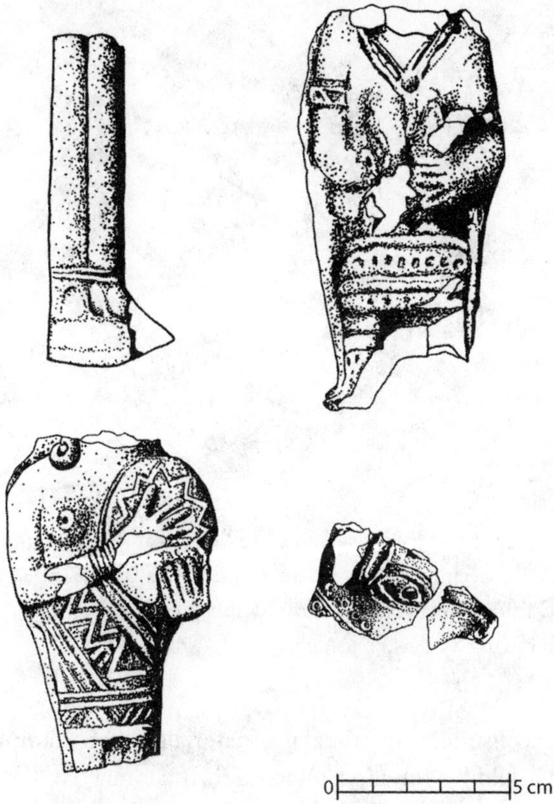

Fig 2.4. Cultic remains from House 440 at Tell el-Far'ah North (foot of a column from a model shrine, a nursing female figurine, female figurine with a disk [possibly a frame drum], and horse head from a zoomorphic vessel). After Alain Chambon, *Tell el-Far'ah* I: *L'âge du fer* (Paris: Éditions Recherche sur les Civilisations, 1984), Pl. 63 (nos. 2 and 4), 65 (nos. 3+5), and 66 (no. 2). Drawing by Dorothea Ulrich.

rider figurines (small, three-dimensional clay objects, between 6 and 12 centimeters tall, whose appearance is pretty much what the name "horse and rider" implies); various sorts of other zoomorphic figurines; anthropomorphic and zoomorphic vessels; representations of model furniture and model chariot wheels; rattles; model lamps; cup-and-saucer vessels (which, like the horse-and-rider figurines, have an appearance that is pretty much what their designation "cup and saucer" suggests); and small limestone altars

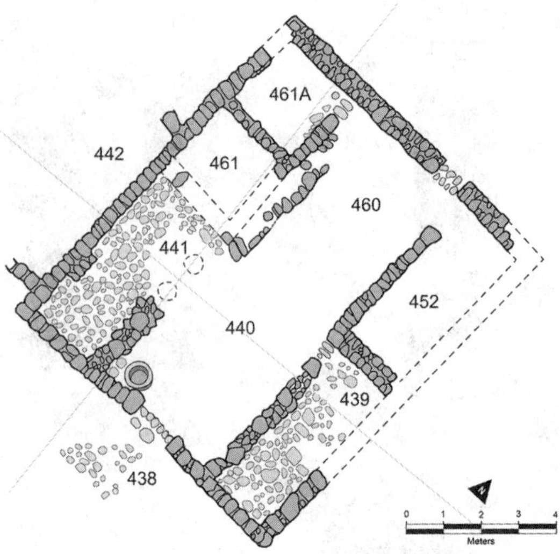

Fig 2.5. Plan of House 440 at Tell el-Far'ah North. After Alain Chambon, *Tell el-Far'ah* I: *L'âge du fer* (Paris: Éditions Recherche sur les Civilisations, 1984), Pl. 11. Drawing by Elise J. Laugier.

for burning incense or aromatic plant materials.[22] For example, in a paved room within Building (or House) 25 (eighth century BCE) at Beersheba were found a miniature lamp that seems to have been used as a burner for incense or other aromatics, a model couch, and an image of the so-called pillar-figurine type (meaning a female figurine with breasts marked on the upper body, while the lower body is rendered in the shape of an unmodeled and featureless pillar or column) (Fig. 2.6). Similarly, in the entrance area of Building (House) 430 at Beersheba (eighth century BCE), a model couch and the heads of a female and a zoomorphic figurine were discovered, and two small stone altars for burning incense or other aromatics were uncovered in an adjoining room.[23]

Women's and Men's Roles in Ancient Israelite Household Religion

In considering what these archaeological data, in conjunction with our biblical materials, suggest regarding women's roles and responsibilities within their households' religious life, we might initially remember that I proposed in Chapter 1, on the basis of the story of Micah's mother,

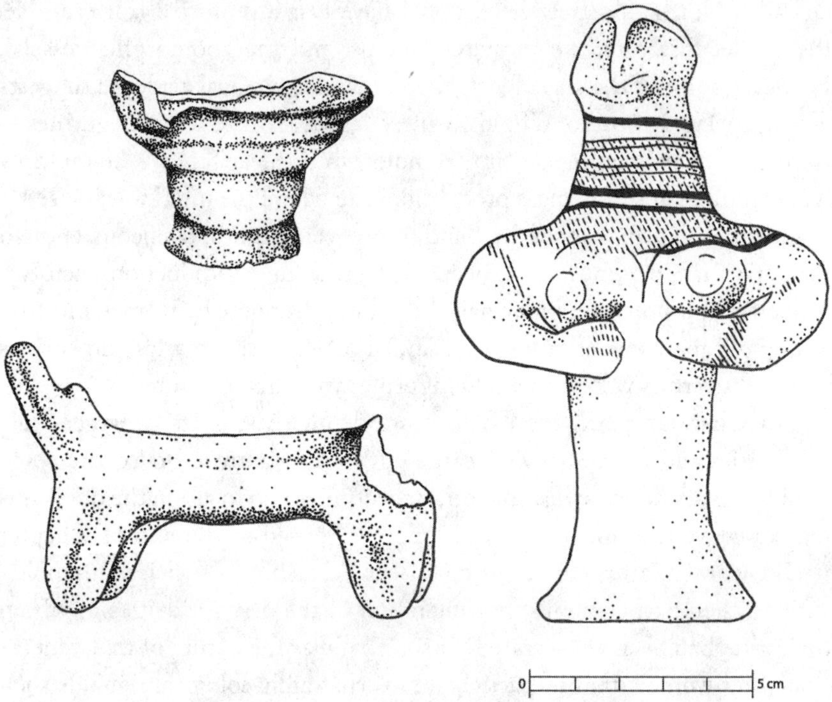

Fig. 2.6. Cultic remains from Beersheba House 25 (a miniature lamp that seems to have been used as an incense burner, a model couch, and a female image of the so-called pillar-figurine type). After Yohanan Aharoni, ed., *Beer-Sheba* I: *Excavations at Tel Beer-Sheba, 1969–1971 Seasons* (Publications of the Institute of Archaeology 2. Tel Aviv: Tel Aviv University, Institute of Archaeology, 1973), Pl. 27.1–3, and Raz Kletter, "Clay Figurines," in Ze'ev Herzog and Lily Singer-Avitz, *Beer-Sheba* III: *The Early Iron IIA Enclosed Settlement and the Late Iron IIA–Iron IIB Cities* (Monograph Series of the Sonia and Marco Nadler Institute of Archaeology, Tel Aviv University 34. Tel Aviv: Emery and Claire Yass Publications in Archaeology; Winona Lake, Ind.: Eisenbrauns, 2016), 1076, Fig. 21.1. Drawing by Dorothea Ulrich.

that Israelite women would have been integrally involved in providing at least some of the objects that furnished their families' household shrines. In particular, we might remind ourselves that women, who were generally responsible for the production of their households' domestic pottery, may have produced a shrine's terra-cotta furnishings, including the cult stand and other pottery vessels found in Room 65 at Ai and, arguably, at least some of the terra-cotta remains from sites such as Khirbet Raddana, Tell el-Far'ah North, and Beersheba that I have just inventoried (for example, the model furniture, the miniature lamps, and the zoomorphic vessels). However, some of the clay objects that our archaeological evidence suggests were associated with household shrines—especially the female figurines—were formed by pressing clay into a mold, which means they were multiply manufactured at some "mass production" site where the mold was housed.[24] Even some figurines made by hand, moreover, are homogeneous enough in shape that they must have been made at a "mass production" facility.[25] These figurines therefore may have been brought home by women or other household members after visits to, say, larger-scale sanctuaries and shrines that had nearby workshops where figurines were manufactured.[26]

In Chapters 3–4, I discuss in more depth these sorts of larger-scale sanctuaries and shrines, as well as the pilgrimage journeys household communities made to them. Let me turn here, though, to focus on the questions regarding women and household religion I posed at the end of Chapter 1: Did women, after participating in the furnishing of their households' shrines, then participate in the veneration of the deity or deities to whom their gifts had been consecrated? If so, what was the nature of that veneration? Did women, that is, participate in what archaeological remains such as Khirbet Raddana's and Tell el-Far'ah North's libation vessels and Beersheba's altars for burning aromatics, along with the textual references in Jer 7:16–20 and 44:15–19, 25, indicate yet again were the fundamental rituals of ancient Israelite household religion?—making grain and other foodstuff offerings, pouring out libations, and burning aromatic plant materials.

More important, *to what degree* did women participate in these rituals? Ancient texts such as Jer 7:16–20 and 44:15–19, 25, as well as all modern scholars of whom I am aware, suggest that women participated in some way in household religion's offering rituals, yet commentators, both ancient and modern, can differ rather markedly regarding the precise nature of women's participation. Within our ancient sources, for example, it is *women alone* who speak of making libation and incense offerings and bread cakes for the Queen of Heaven in Jer 44:19.[27] Somewhat similarly, in Jer 44:15, while it the husbands of the Judahites who have fled to Egypt who are the subject of the verse, it is their *wives* who are specifically identified as having burned incense to other gods. Yet in Jer 44:17–18, it is husbands and wives who dismiss Jeremiah's censure of them by affirming *together* their intent to continue burning incense and pouring out libations to the Queen of Heaven. Then there is Jer 44:25, which is hopelessly confused. The verbs with which

Jeremiah, speaking for God, condemns his audience refer to those who have "spoken" and "vowed" to make offerings and pour out libations to the Queen of Heaven using *feminine* plural forms, suggesting that Jeremiah's subject is the assembly's women. But when it comes to nouns, the "mouths" with which the assembly has articulated its intentions, the "vows" regarding the offerings and libations to which it has committed, and the "hands" with which these commitments have been fulfilled carry *masculine* suffixes. This has driven the Hebrew text as it has come down to us to direct the words of opprobrium in v. 25 to both "you" (masculine plural; presumably the assembly's husbands) and "your wives," even as the ancient Greek translation of the Bible gives priority to the feminine verb forms and so renders the verse as addressed to the assembly's women alone.

Perhaps because they follow these ancient texts' lead, modern scholars can also vary in their assessments of women's precise roles within their households' religious practices, both in their assessment of the degree to which women were involved in Israelite household cult and in their assessment of what might motivate women's engagement. Willett's already-mentioned Ph.D. dissertation on women and household shrines in ancient Israel puts forward what I take to be the most maximal case possible for women's participation in household cultic rites and for the ideological interests that motivate their involvement: her thesis is that Israelite household shrines and the rituals that took place in them were primarily, if not exclusively, the domain of women, who used the rites of household cult preeminently to address female reproductive concerns.[28] In her words, women "supervised [the] religious duties" of the household by "set[ting] up" and "tend[ing]" household shrines "to protect themselves and their families," especially from "child-stealing demons who attempted to enter the houses and sicken mothers and their newborn infants."[29]

More specifically Willett, who focuses predominantly on archaeological data, suggests regarding the courtyard bench in House 440 at Tell el-Far'ah North and the fragmentary female figurine (which Willett takes to be a deity) found near it that "the mistress of the house possibly used the bench for offerings to the family's protective goddess" (see Figs. 2.4 and 2.5).[30] Similarly, she writes of Building (or House) 25 at Beersheba that the pillar-based figurine found there represents a "fertile goddess nurturing her children and lending her protective powers to the mother of the house," that the model couch represents "a miniature offering table symbolizing the lap of the goddess," and that incense or oil was burned in the miniature lamp "to expel demonic influences" that threatened women and their newborn children (see Fig. 2.6).[31] Willett likewise supposes that the model couch found in conjunction with the head of a female figurine in Beersheba Building (or House) 430 "represent[s] the lap of the child-protecting goddess," a protective image positioned by women "near vulnerable entrances to their dwellings," and that the burners used for incense or other aromatics that were found nearby "doubtless served the mother of the house" as she "burned oil and incense" to invoke the aid of the family goddess.[32]

Ziony Zevit, too, in his magisterial study of ancient Israelite religion, suggests that the remains from Beersheba Buildings (or Houses) 25 and 430 may be associated with women's religious activities, in particular, religious activities that concerned reproduction. He differs from Willett, however, regarding the specific interpretation of the model couches and is also significantly more cautious than she in putting forward his proposals. As he writes: "*If* the female figurines may be associated with fertility and/or lactation, and *if* the model couches may be associated with a birth stool or a birthing bed . . . then these artifacts *may* constitute a woman's collection intending to insure her fertility, her ability to give birth, and her continued ability to lactate" (emphases mine).[33] William G. Dever is more restrained still: he suggests that the remains from sites like Tell el-Far'ah North represent "family shrines," and although he believes "women played a significant role" in them, "various members of the *family* probably stopped briefly at these convenient shrines daily . . . as they felt the need" (emphasis mine).[34] Rainer Albertz and Rüdiger Schmitt seem to express a similarly nuanced point of view in their book on family and household religion: while in the book's conclusion they write that "women played an important role in the rituals of everyday life" that are associated with "domestic structures," Schmitt's earlier discussion of domestic cult describes the home as "the primary center of the fundamental religious activities and needs of the *family*" (emphasis again mine).[35]

In my opinion, Dever and Albertz and Schmitt have the best of this argument, for several reasons. First, I find myself unconvinced by the data Willett presents to demonstrate her hypothesis that women were the exclusive or even primary actors within the offerings cult of the Israelite household, especially her attempts to demonstrate that the cultic artifacts found in the household remains from her "four test sites"—Tel Masos/Hormah and Lahav/Tell Halif, as well as Tell el-Far'ah North/Tirzah and Beersheba—are to be taken as objects of *women's* religious culture because they "exist in the context of *women's* work areas and associate with *feminine* implements like food storage and preparation vessels, apotropaic jewelry and accessories, and textile tools" (emphases mine).[36] For example, Willett argues regarding House 314 from Tel Masos (see Fig. I.1), which dates from the twelfth to eleventh century or perhaps the eleventh to tenth century BCE,[37] that the presence of two ovens, numerous pieces of kitchen pottery, and loom weights (weights used to hold yarn taut as it hangs from the top beam of a loom that stood upright, leaned against a wall) suggests women occupied the room in the house, Room 343, that was closest to a courtyard bench that Willett proposes would have provided "a logical location for standing a figurine to protect the house from malevolent spirits." This proximity, she goes on to argue, "illustrates the importance of household religion to Israelite women's daily lives."[38] Somewhat similarly, Willett proposes with regard to Building (or House) 76 at eighth-century BCE Beersheba that the presence of a loom weight, cooking pots, a grinding stone, kernels of wheat and barley, numerous food containers, and a cosmetic stick in rooms proximate to a room that held a krater inscribed *qdš*, or "holy," demonstrates "that the krater inscribed with the *qdš* label belonged to a female domain."[39]

But Willett errs here in assuming that proximity is tantamount to equivalence, in assuming, that is, that finding cultic remains *near* to artifacts arguably associated with women's work—cooking pots and loom weights, for example—means that those cultic remains are *definitively* to be associated with women. Regarding Building (or House) 76 at Beersheba, for example, Zevit has suggested that the house in question may have belonged to a priest and that the *qdš* bowl was a part of the cultic apparatus associated with *his* religious responsibilities.[40] Alternatively, Beersheba's excavators have proposed that Building (or House) 76 was a potter's dwelling and workshop, meaning that the cooking pots, storage vessels, and *qdš* bowl were all part of the workshop's inventory.[41] Also in the case of House 314 from Tel Masos, Willett's argument falters, for however much Room 343 may have been women's space, the adjacent courtyard in which the possibly cultic bench stood was surely—as was the courtyard area of any typical Israelite house—a space shared by *all* of House 314's family members. Indeed, as discussed in the preceding chapter, these sorts of household courtyards served as the entry portals to ancient Israelite homes and as the access routes to all a house's other rooms, meaning that *every* member of a household's family would necessarily pass through them regularly (see Figs. I.2

and 1.3). Similarly, the religious artifacts found in the courtyard of House 440 at Tell el-Far'ah North would have been equally encountered and thus equally honored by *all* of the members of the family who lived there, as opposed to Willett's suggestion that it was "the mistress of the house" who used that home's courtyard-area bench "for offerings to the family's protective goddess."[42] Note again in this regard Zevit, who writes that because three of the four arguably cultic artifacts found in Tell el-Far'ah's House 440 (the horse head, the female figurine holding a disk, and the figurine of a nursing woman) were found in the house's courtyard, "their use was a matter of *family* consent and knowledge" (emphasis mine).[43]

Recall that Willett, however, does offer a second, and more ideologically based reason for associating the cultic remains from Building (House) 25 at Beersheba—the miniature lamp, the model couch, and the pillar-based female figurine—with women's religious activities, by proposing that all these artifacts speak to female reproductive concerns. Recall also that Zevit, albeit more cautiously, makes the same suggestion. Yet while I agree that these objects may speak to reproductive issues (see, for example, my discussion in Chapter 11 on the relation of the model couch to reproduction), I am not convinced that reproduction was as exclusively a women's concern in ancient Israel as are Willett, Zevit, and also Carol Meyers, who in an article on women's household religion writes, "rituals surrounding pregnancy, labor, and birth, along with those securing fertility before pregnancy and those dealing with post-partum lactation, infant care, and circumcision, constitute the religious culture of women more than of men."[44] In support of this claim, Meyers cites biblical texts such as Gen 30:14–16, in which the barren Rachel barters with her sister Leah for some mandrakes, which were thought to bring fertility (more on this also in Chapter 11), and 1 Sam 1:10–12, in which Hannah prays for an end to her barrenness and makes a related vow (more on this in Chapter 4).

Meyers admits, however, that it is *Abram* (later Abraham) who utters a petitionary prayer in Gen 15:2 pleading that he might be granted offspring and that it is *Isaac* who similarly asks in Gen 25:21 that his wife Rebekah's barrenness might be reversed. Elsewhere, Meyers points out that the command to "be fruitful and multiply" is addressed to *both* men and women,[45] and one should note as well that it is *David* who undertakes a series of demanding ritual actions (pleading with God, fasting, weeping, and spending the night on the ground) in an attempt to try to save the life of his first child by Bathsheba (2 Sam 12:15–23, discussed further in Chapter 4). Indeed, Israelite men had good reason to solicit God or the gods for offspring and to secure, after they were born, those offspring's well-being. Sons in particular were important for maintaining a father's lineage within ancient Israel's social system of patrilineal descent, and a son also played a critical role in caring for an aging father and in performing proper death-cult rites for him.[46] In addition, both sons and daughters were an important source of labor on the self-sufficient family farms that were the means of livelihood for most Israelites.[47] Modern population studies in fact show that even in locales that might seem to nonagriculturalists to be vastly overpeopled, farm families seek to bear and raise as many children as possible, to the extent that they will eschew an increased standard of living in favor of an increased family size.[48]

All these data suggest that Israelite men were as interested as were their wives in these women's bearing and rearing healthy children and thus as likely to participate as were their wives in whatever religious rites might help ensure this outcome. We should therefore be wary of arguing that the reproductive rituals of Israelite household cult were more the province of women than of men.[49] Rather, in Israel, as elsewhere in the ancient Near East, fertility was a matter of *family* concern. We should also be wary of giving too much priority to reproductive concerns as an exclusive or predominant focus of household religion. While Willett, for example, argues that incense or oil was burned in miniature lamps "to expel demonic influences" that threatened women and their newborn children,[50] Karel van der Toorn has carefully catalogued evidence from both Israel and Mesopotamia showing that the symbolic use of lamps in domestic settings could speak to many different household matters. Keeping a lamp lit through the night, for instance, could signify economic well-being, whereas someone who woke in the night after having an ominous dream might touch the ground, light a lamp, and importune a household's god(s) and/or goddess(es) to help counteract the dream's foreboding portents. In addition, "in [Babylonian] pictures of therapeutic rites against diseases we often see a portable lamp set up at the head of a bedridden person."[51] The available evidence thus forestalls our concluding that lamps—and, presumably, at least some other items from domestic cultic assemblages—spoke exclusively, or even primarily, to a household's reproductive concerns.

Jeremiah 7:16–20 and 44:15–19, 25, the texts I am exploring in this chapter, are also germane when considering the focus of ancient Israelite household religion, especially Jer 44:16–18. In these verses, the husbands and wives who are among the company of Judaeans that had fled to Egypt to escape the Babylonian onslaught respond to Jeremiah's censure of them for both their past and present worship of the Queen of Heaven by refusing to end their devotions, arguing instead that they find the worship of the Queen *efficacious.* More specifically, they claim that when they worshipped the Queen in the past, in Judah and Jerusalem before the Babylonian destruction, "we had plenty of food, and it went well with us, and we saw no evil." Yet they go on to say that since they have left off worship of the goddess (in response, perhaps, to Jeremiah's earlier castigations?), "we have lacked everything, and we have been consumed by the sword and by famine." Note here that there is *no reference whatsoever* to reproduction as a focus of this household cult; rather the stress is on each family's having enough food to eat and its physical safety in a time of war.

From this, I conclude that Israelite household religion—while surely concerned with issues of human fertility and reproduction—also addressed the many, many other issues that would concern a household's residents: agricultural fecundity and security from enemy attack, as in Jer 44:16–18, as well as the physical health of all household members and the observance of major life-cycle events, such as coming of age, marriage, and death. I further conclude, contra Willett and somewhat Zevit (with regard to his discussion of Beersheba Houses 25 and 430), but in accord with Dever, Albertz and Schmitt, and somewhat with Zevit (with regard to his discussion of Tell el-Far'ah North House 440 and Beersheba House 76), that because all these issues (reproduction included) were of concern to the entirety of a household's residents, and because it is both the wives and husbands who make an argument in support of the Queen of Heaven's worship in Jer 44: 16–18 and husbands, wives, and children who act together to produce bread cakes for the Queen in Jer 7:18, that Israelite household religion involved *all* family members.

Women's Special Responsibilities Within Ancient Israelite Household Religion

From the foregoing discussion, we have therefore reached the following (negative) realizations regarding women's roles and responsibilities in Israelite household religion. First, the ideological agenda of household religion, which addressed both human reproduction and other crucial aspects of household security, was not exclusively, or even primarily, a matter of women's concern. Second, the execution of rituals that sought to secure this ideological agenda was not exclusively, or even primarily, women's responsibility. Rather, these ritual acts, as well as the agenda that motivated them, demanded the attention of *all* a household's members: men, women, and children.

Still, as we have seen, the prophet Jeremiah's witness with regard to all family members' participation in the rituals of Israelite household religion is not unambiguous, as sometimes in Jer 44:15–19, 25, he focuses on husbands and wives in conjunction (44:17–18), yet sometimes he focuses on women alone (44:15, 19). In addition, in Jer 7:18, the prophet specifically identifies women as kneading the dough for the Queen of Heaven's bread cakes and, presumably, also baking them. These acts were surely more integral to a family's fulfilling of this ritual obligation than were its sons' gathering of wood and the father's kindling of fire. Indeed, it is perhaps because their cake-making role was so integral within their household's devotions that Jeremiah, in his tirade against the Queen of Heaven cult in Jer 44:15–19, 25, seems to focus on women as the object of his special scorn.[52]

It follows that the special stress in Jer 7:18 and in 44:15–19, 25 on women's role in the offering rituals of Israelite household religion is a feature of household cult that, given my interests in this chapter, needs to be explained. In order to do so, I propose to return to the data I considered in Chapter 1 regarding gender roles within the typical Israelite pillar-courtyard house and especially Carol Meyers's observation that, in the typical Israelite household, it was women who took responsibility for most aspects of food processing, especially the processes that pertained to making bread. Several biblical texts, for example, speak specifically to women grinding grain (Exod 11:5, Isa 47:2, Job 31:10, Eccl 12:3)[53] or to attempts to feminize men (and consequently, from the Bible's point of view, to humiliate them) by forcing them to grind grain like women (Judg 16:21, Lam 5:13). Iconographical evidence from elsewhere in the ancient Near East—more specifically, from ancient Egypt—similarly represents women as engaged in the work of grinding (Fig. 2.7).[54] Indeed, Meyers estimates that the task of grinding grain was so integral within Israelite women's lives that they would have spent up to two to three hours every day in this endeavor.[55] Other scholars propose women's grinding work took up to four to five hours per day (!).[56] During this time, women rendered wheat and barley into first a rough meal and then the flour (according to Meyers's and other scholars' calculations, about 1 liter [0.5 kilogram] per person per day) that

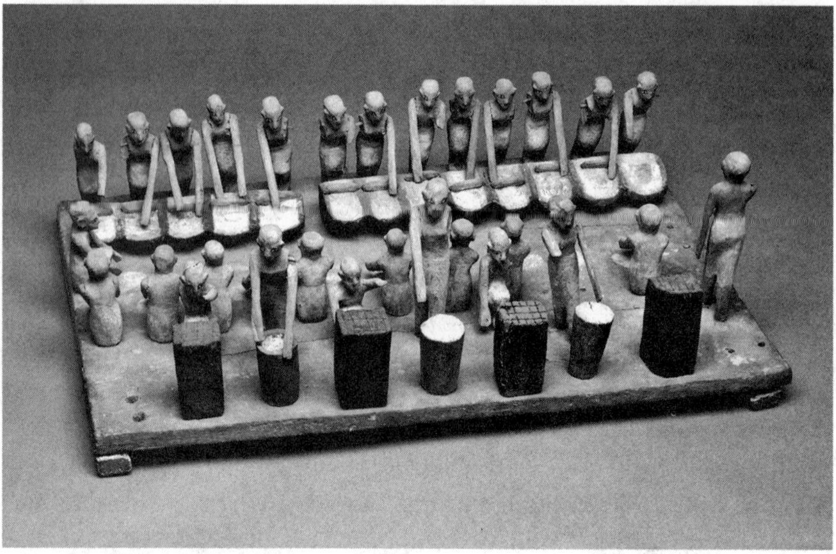

Fig. 2.7. A wooden model from Egypt (Thebes), ca. 2050–2000 BCE, showing thirteen women grinding grain, nine women (originally thirteen) sifting the flour ground by their companions opposite, three women (originally four) crouched before ovens baking bread, and three women sieving mash from the baked bread to be used for brewing beer. Height/width/depth: 25.5 by 79.5 by 48 centimeters. British Museum, London, BM no. EA40915. © Trustees of the British Museum.

would have been used for their families' bread.[57] Meyers has moreover argued that women, having undertaken this labor-intensive responsibility for processing food, especially grain, for their families' consumption, also would have undertaken the responsibility for distributing food, especially bread, within their households: that is, determining how the foodstuffs, especially the bread cakes or bread loaves they had prepared from the flour they had ground, should be allocated to their families.[58] This is also indicated in biblical texts such as Lev 26:26, which speaks of women distributing bread by weight to those on whose behalf they had baked it.[59]

These obligations regarding grain and bread distribution, Meyers has additionally intimated, might reasonably be expected to carry beyond the familial sphere and into the supernatural.[60] This means women would assume not only the tasks of preparing food in general and bread in particular for their households and allocating these foodstuffs to their households' members, but also the tasks of preparing food (and drink) offerings in general and grain and/or bread offerings in particular for their households' god or gods and then apportioning these offerings to their households' deities. Alternatively, they could apportion these offerings to other household members for these household residents to use in their own devotions. Or, in some cases, they might apportion or otherwise make available to other household members the raw ingredients those individuals would need to prepare, say, bread cakes by themselves. After all, who but Gideon's mother or some other women within Gideon's father's household (Judg 6:15) would have ground the ephah of flour (a measure of about 22 liters, or 0.6 of a bushel) that Gideon uses in Judg 6:19 to make offering cakes for the divine messenger who has unexpectedly appeared to him?[61] Lot also seems easily able to access flour in order to make bread cakes for the divine visitors who unexpectedly end up in his home in Sodom (Gen 19:3), and who should be imagined as having ground the grain to make this flour but Lot's wife and/or his two daughters?

Israelite women thus do lay claim, according to this reconstruction, to a special responsibility within their households' religious cult: because of their role as their families' "food processing managers," they facilitate the flow of foodstuffs—especially grain and/or bread offerings—that they and all a household's members dedicate to the deity who is (or the deities who are) the object(s) of their home's ritual observances. The Queen of Heaven texts from Jeremiah thus bear witness not to Israelite household religion and its concerns as women's particular or even exclusive domain—this maximalist view of women's role within the household cult goes too far—but to the special congruence that existed in ancient Israel between the managerial responsibilities that households' women members undertook on behalf of their families and those they undertook on behalf of their families' god(s). In other words: because it is women who generally assumed responsibilities within their households for food processing and food distribution, it is women in Jer 7:16–20 and 44:15–19, 25 who especially took charge of preparing food and drink offerings for the goddess venerated in their households, the Queen of Heaven, and then presenting these foodstuffs to her. Likewise, women in households throughout ancient Israel can be understood as facilitating the making of offerings to whatever deity or deities their families and household affiliates gave cult.

I realize, of course, that for some, my conclusions regarding women's responsibilities as the facilitators of household religion's ritual offerings might seem a far cry from more full-blown reconstructions that see Israelite household cult and its concerns as women's primary or even exclusive domain. Still, even as I minimize claims regarding household religion as women's primary or even sole dominion, I do not mean to minimize the significance of women's contributions as I have described them within their households' religious life. Quite the contrary: as I have noted repeatedly and emphasize again here, making grain and other foodstuff offerings and engaging in the related rites of pouring out libations and burning incense or other aromatics were the rituals *central* to ancient Israelite household religion, as in fact these rituals—what the great historian of Mesopotamian civilization A. Leo Oppenheim has famously described as "the care and feeding of the gods"—were central to ancient Israelite religion generally and to all ancient Near Eastern worship.[62] Let me reiterate, as this ancient stress on the centrality of making grain and libation offerings and burning aromatics (and, within sanctuary settings, the related act of animal sacrifice) can seem quite alien within the relatively dematerialized and etherealized definition of religion to which many today, especially those in the Euro-American West, more commonly subscribe. But in the ancient Near East, including ancient Israel, making food, drink, and related offerings was *the* primary act of religious ritual and devotion. From this it follows that if women are as crucially involved as I have suggested in preparing and apportioning to their households' god or gods the grain and other foodstuff offerings that were the essence of ancient Israelite worship and/or in facilitating the offerings dedicated by others within their homes, then women must be seen as extremely important actors within Israelite household cult. While women, therefore, cannot be said to have been the sole or even the primary worshippers within Israelite household religion, Israelite women nevertheless must be understood as having assumed a critical role in the most fundamental and indeed indispensable acts of domestic ritual.

I asked both earlier in this chapter and at the end of the last: to what degree did women participate in the central rites of ancient Israelite household religion—making grain and other foodstuff offerings, pouring out drink libations, and burning incense and other aromatics—to which the cultic remains from the houses at Khirbet Raddana, Tell el-Far'ah North, Beersheba, and similar sites point? I am now prepared to answer emphatically: as in Jer 7:18 and 44:15, 19, and 25, women would have been active and essential participants in household religion's devotional acts, playing a key role in providing the grain and foodstuff offerings integral to the ritual observances of the household cult and its aim of securing the offspring, the agricultural fecundity, and the security from illness, natural disasters, and human attackers that all a household's residents needed to survive. Likewise, as in Judg 17:4, women could serve as patrons, and even the primary patrons, of their households' shrines, creating or commissioning sacred objects that would have been the focus of worshippers' veneration.

How, though, did this compare to women's involvement in the religious life of Israelite sanctuaries and shrines beyond the household domain? To answer, I turn, in the chapters that follow, to examine, first, women's roles in the religious life of regional shrines that would have been located reasonably close to their hometowns and, then, women's roles and experiences in Israel's great national temples, preeminently Dan and Bethel in the North and Jerusalem in the South.

3 "She Went Up with Her Husband to Offer the Annual Sacrifice": Women and Ancient Israel's Regional Sanctuaries, I

First Samuel 1:1–2:26 is a text that, from the point of view of the biblical narrative, functions only as a prologue: recounting, first, the birth story of Samuel, the great priest-prophet whose presence looms large over the rest of 1 Samuel (and after whom, of course, the book was eventually named), and second, describing how Samuel, while still a toddler, became associated with the shrine at Shiloh whose presence similarly looms large over, at least, the first four chapters of 1 Samuel (until the site was perhaps destroyed by the Philistines, as part of the aftermath of their battle with the Israelites described in 1 Sam 4:1–11).[1] Yet however much 1 Sam 1:1–2:26 serves the larger Samuel account solely as a prologue, the text is, for my purposes, of great significance in its own right, as it illuminates multiple aspects of the religious lives of ancient Israelite women. For example, as I noted in Chapter 1, the role that Samuel's mother, Hannah, assumes in 1 Sam 1:20 of naming her recently delivered son is a responsibility frequently undertaken by women during childbirth rituals.[2] In addition, I will suggest in Chapter 9 that the once-a-year visit to the sanctuary at Shiloh in which Samuel's family is said to participate according to 1 Sam 1:3, 7, 21, and 2:19 was made in celebration of the autumn pilgrimage of the Ingathering, also called Sukkot ("Booths"). That Samuel's mother, Hannah, his father's other wife, Peninnah, and possibly Peninnah's daughters are said to have joined in this journey thus becomes critical evidence regarding women's participation in the Ingathering festival, which not insignificantly is understood within biblical tradition to be the greatest of the pilgrimage feasts of the Israelite ritual calendar.[3] Also in Chapter 9, I will propose that the song Hannah is said to sing in 1 Sam 2:1–10 is evidence of a special role Israelite women played as ritual musicians at the Ingathering/Sukkot festival, and later, in Chapter 12, I will explore another cultic role assigned to women in 1 Sam 2:22 and in its not-so-problematic parallel in Exod 38:8, both of which speak of "the women who served at the entrance to the tent of meeting."

Finally, in this chapter and in the next, as I continue to explore the sites of Israelite women's religious practice, I consider Shiloh's character as a regional sanctuary and the experiences and roles of women in the ritual observances that took place at such shrines. In this chapter, I ask to what degree, if any, were women who worshipped at a shrine like Shiloh engaged in its sacrificial practice? Then, in Chapter 4, I turn to examine other aspects of 1 Sam 1:1–2:26, to ask what might be additionally revealed about women's religious experiences at a regional sanctuary such as Shiloh. Overall, what I hope to demonstrate is that while regional sanctuaries were not as unequivocally productive sites of women's religious agency as were the household settings I explored in Chapters 1 and 2, they nevertheless offered significant opportunities for women to engage in ancient Israelite ritual practice.

Introducing Ancient Israel's Regional Sanctuaries

First Samuel 1:1–2:26 begins, in 1 Sam 1:1–2, by introducing Elkanah, the father of the yet-to-be-born Samuel, and Elkanah's two wives, Hannah and Peninnah. In 1 Sam 1:1, we are also told that this family comes from a village called Ramathaim-zophim, in the hill country of Ephraim. Somewhat later, however, in 1 Sam 1:19 and 2:11, the family is described as coming from Ramah (modern er-Ram), a village located in the tribal territory of Benjamin. Ramah is, moreover, identified as the home of Elkanah's son Samuel at several other points in 1 Samuel—in 1 Sam 7:17, 8:4, 15:34, 16:13, 19:18, 25:1, and 28:3—and in his Anchor Yale Bible commentary on 1 Samuel, P. Kyle McCarter also notes that the place name of Ramathaim-zophim found in 1 Sam 1:1 is "grammatically impossible."[4]

Many scholars therefore suggest that the seemingly geographical designation *ṣôpîm,* "zophim," in the place name Ramathaim-zophim is better read as *ṣûpî,* or "of the Zupi," a reference, that is, to Elkanah's hometown as the dwelling place of a clan called the Zuphites (who are referred to later on in 1:1, in the name of Elkanah's ancestor Zuph, and also in the ancient Greek rendering of Ramathaim-zophim).[5] Some commentators have furthermore argued that the territory of this Zuphite clan lay on the border of Benjamin and Ephraim, proximate to, if not encompassing, Benjaminite

Ramah.[6] According to this reconstruction, the Ramathaim (which means "the double height") of 1 Sam 1:1 is thus identical to the Ramah (which means "height") of 1 Sam 1:19, 2:11, and elsewhere, and there is no contradiction among the various 1 Samuel texts regarding Elkanah's family's hometown. An alternative reconstruction suggests, however, that there was in fact a Zuphite Ramathaim of Ephraim, separate from Ramah of Benjamin and possibly to be identified with New Testament Arimathea/modern Rentis. Or possibly this Zuphite Ramathaim is to be identified with Khirbet Raddana, a site located on the northern perimeter of modern-day Ramallah.[7] But either way, adherents of this line of reasoning hold that one strand of the Samuel tradition understands Ramathaim of Ephraim to be Elkanah's (and Samuel's) hometown, even as the dominant narrative line of 1 Samuel describes Elkanah (and Samuel) as Benjaminites from Ramah.[8]

Fortunately, resolving this conundrum is not essential for my analysis, as it just so happens that it is about a 25–30-kilometer journey from both Benjaminite Ramah (modern er-Ram) and Ephraimite Ramathaim (assuming it indeed existed, and regardless of whether it is identified with New Testament Arimathea/modern Rentis or with Khirbet Raddana) to Shiloh, the site that is my primary interest in this chapter.[9] First Samuel 1:1–2:26 thus describes how Elkanah and his family embark annually, according to 1 Sam 1:3, 7, 21, and 2:19, from either their Benjaminite hometown of Ramah (which according to one group of scholars was also known as Ramathaim) or from their Ephraimite hometown of Ramathaim (if we take Ramathaim to denote a location other than Ramah) to travel approximately 25–30 kilometers, or about one day's walk,[10] to visit what we should arguably understand (given the length of Elkanah's family's travels) to be a regional sanctuary at Shiloh. There, Elkanah's family members engage in ritual observances alongside others (note the communal context implied by 1 Sam 2:12–17), whom we are presumably to envision as traveling to the shrine at Shiloh periodically, as did Elkanah's family, from villages in Ephraim and/or in Benjamin and more generally from sites roundabout Israel's central hill country that were about a day's walk away. Indeed, as Jacob Milgrom writes, "The distance to Shiloh from any point in the central hill-country of Benjamin, Ephraim, and Manasseh is just a one-day's journey."[11] Moreover, Shiloh's position just east of a major highway that led north from Jerusalem through the important center of Bethel to the equally important city of Shechem (Judg 21:19) well positioned it to serve as a religious hub at which central hill-country worshippers might gather (see Fig. I.1).[12]

To be sure, certain biblical sources put forward a different understanding, by suggesting that Shiloh was not a sanctuary of only local or regional importance for the hill-country inhabitants of Ephraim, Benjamin, and other nearby environs. Rather, these sources propose that Shiloh was the premier place of worship for *all* of Israel's tribes during the premonarchic period of Israelite history, before it was destroyed, possibly by the Philistines in ca. 1050 BCE.[13] The sources that promulgate this view, however (Jer 7:12, 26:4–9; Ps 78:60), all come from a date far later in time than the premonarchic era that 1 Sam 1:1–2:26 purports to describe. More important, these sources come from a date quite late within Israel's monarchic period (the late seventh century BCE).[14] They thus reflect a late seventh-century BCE theological ideal particularly associated with the book of Deuteronomy. According to this ideal, Israel had only one "chosen place" for Yahwistic worship (see, preeminently, Deut 12:5), which was, in the late seventh century BCE, the Jerusalem temple and which previously had been, in the premonarchic period of Israelite history, the shrine at Shiloh.[15]

That this "posture of the Deuteronomistic movement in the late 7th century" reflects the actual status of a premonarchic sanctuary at Shiloh seems, though, unlikely, if for no other reason than pragmatic, as "it is absurd to assume," in the words of the noted scholar of Deuteronomic thought Moshe Weinfeld, that worshippers would routinely travel to a sanctuary that was, for those who lived in Israel's farthermost reaches, "some three, or more, days' journey distant."[16] In fact, Weinfeld makes clear that even after "the establishment of the monarchy," when, according to Deuteronomic thought, the "law of cult centralization" came fully into effect (1 Kgs 3:2), the ideal that all Israelite worship would take place at only one "chosen place" still could not, for pragmatic reasons, be realized. Rather, for both the premonarchic and the pre-Deuteronomic monarchic periods, we must posit, to quote again Weinfeld, "the existence of provincial sanctuaries" within a reasonable distance (about a day's walk, I once more suggest) from worshippers' homes.[17] As already indicated, I take 1 Sam 1:1–2:26 to suggest that one of these premonarchic provincial or regional sanctuaries was Shiloh.[18] In the discussion that follows, I propose that the so-called Bull Site of the twelfth century BCE, which was located near biblical Dothan, was a premonarchic provincial or regional sanctuary as well.[19] Provincial or regional sanctuaries of the monarchic era might include Gilgal, Lachish, Nebo, Carmel, Dor, Tel Motza, and Tel Reḥov, as well as the various *bāmâ* sanctuaries that I discuss in more detail below.[20]

But first, can more be said about the nature of the regional sanctuary at Shiloh? With respect to 1 Sam 1:1–2:26, the answer is unfortunately only if we apply due caution concerning issues of date, for 1 Sam 1:1–2:26 certainly cannot be taken to be a text contemporaneous with the premonarchic shrine at Shiloh it purports to describe. Yet as my discussion of the presumptions of 1 Sam 1:1–2:26 as opposed to the Deuteronomic ideal of cult centralization has just intimated, neither can 1 Sam 1:1–2:26 be taken as contemporaneous with the late seventh-century BCE Deuteronomistic History in which it is embedded. Rather, as McCarter has noted, 1 Sam 1:1–2:26 is "pre-Deuteronomistic" in nature and, compared with the Deuteronomistic History, of a fundamentally different thrust.[21] McCarter, moreover, offers a specific date for our text's pre-Deuteronomistic origins: "near the end of the eighth century B.C."[22] Thereby it follows, according to the principles set out in the Introduction, that 1 Sam 1:1–2:26, whatever its claims to describe Shiloh as a regional sanctuary of Israel's premonarchic period, reflects more the traditions of Israel's regional sanctuaries of the late eighth century BCE. Nevertheless, and further in accord with principles set out in the Introduction, factors that define the regional sanctuaries of the late eighth century BCE may not have been significantly different during the premonarchic and monarchic periods because of the relatively unchanging nature of Israel's preexilic religious culture, especially the religious culture of Israel's rural environs. For example, during both the premonarchic and monarchic periods, Israel's regional sanctuaries seem just as likely to have been open-air places of assembly as to have had actual sanctuary buildings on site.

That said, scholars have debated whether Shiloh was primarily an open-air sanctuary or home to a shrine building. Some follow a biblical tradition that insists that Shiloh's sanctuary was only a tent shrine, as is indicated in Ps 78:60, which speaks of Yahweh's "tabernacle" (*miškān*) and "tent" (*ʾōhel*) at Shiloh.[23] Joshua 18:1 and 19:51 similarly describe the shrine at Shiloh as the "*tent* of meeting" (*ʾōhel môʿēd;* emphasis mine), and so too does one verse within 1 Sam 1:1–2:26, to wit, 1 Sam 2:22, which I mentioned in the opening paragraph of this chapter. This 1 Sam 2:22 passage, however, may have been added to the account of 1 Sam 1:1–2:26 at an extremely late date in the history of the Samuel tradition's development (more on this in Chapter 12). Psalm 78:60 somewhat similarly comes, as I noted above, from a late date within Israel's preexilic history (the late seventh century BCE), and Josh 18:1 and 19:51 likewise seem to represent the work of the late seventh-century BCE editors and redactors of the Deuteronomistic History. More important: Josh 18:1, 19:51, and Ps 78:60 represent again a late seventh-century BCE theological ideal regarding Israelite sacred space, which is that before the construction of the temple in Jerusalem in ca. 950 BCE, during the reign of King Solomon (r. 970–931 BCE), Yahweh was worshipped only "in a tent and a tabernacle" and not in any fixed sanctuary building (see, preeminently, 2 Sam 7:6–7).

But just as we saw in our earlier discussions that the pre-Deuteronomistic (late eighth-century BCE) traditions reflected in 1 Sam 1:1–2:26 repudiate the late seventh-century BCE theological ideal of Shiloh as Yahweh's one "chosen place" during the premonarchic era, so too can we affirm that 1 Sam 1:1–2:26 (minus the interpolated 1 Sam 2:22) repudiates the late seventh-century BCE theological ideal that Yahweh, before the building of the Jerusalem temple, was worshipped only in a tent. This ideal is also repudiated in the pre-Deuteronomistic (i.e., late eighth-century BCE) text of Judg 17:1–18:31 discussed in Chapter 1. There, in Judg 18:31, Shiloh's sanctuary space is identified as an actual "*house* of God" (*bêt hā-ʾĕlōhîm;* emphasis mine), just as it is the "*house* of Yahweh" (*bêt yhwh;* emphasis once more mine) at Shiloh that is referred to in 1 Sam 1:7 and 1:24. First Samuel 1:9 similarly speaks of a temple (*hêkāl*) of Yahweh at Shiloh and of its doorpost(s) (*mĕzûzâ* or *mĕzûzôt*).[24] There are further references to a Yahwistic "temple" (*hêkāl*) at Shiloh in 1 Sam 3:3 and its "doors" (*daltôt bêt yhwh*) in 1 Sam 3:15, both texts that McCarter identifies as belonging to a continuation of the pre-Deuteronomistic (late eighth-century BCE) narrative found in 1 Sam 1:1–2:26.[25] The ancient Greek rendering of 1 Sam 1:18, moreover, describes how Hannah, after praying at Yahweh's temple at Shiloh, ate in a *katalyma,* which in Greek means a sort of guest chamber, and several scholars have suggested that in the version of the Bible antecedent to this Greek account (a version that, as we will see, differed in multiple respects from the Hebrew text as it has come down to us), the Hebrew word used for *katalyma* was *liškâ.*[26] Notably, this term *liškâ* refers elsewhere in the Bible to a room or chamber that is part of a sanctuary *building.*[27] For example, in 1 Sam 9:22–24, a sacred meal much like the one Hannah is said to consume in 1 Sam 1:18 is eaten in a *liškâ* that is part of a small-scale sanctuary *structure* (according to 1 Sam 9:22, about thirty people worshipped there).

The archaeological data from premonarchic Shiloh may coordinate with the eighth-century BCE biblical witness regarding the presence of a sanctuary building at the site. More specifically: although the remains from the premonarchic (or Iron Age I) period at Shiloh are difficult to interpret, because of erosion and destruction by later occupation, the evidence that is extant (in particular, remains of large pillared buildings with a rich ceramic assemblage, as well as vessels of an arguably cultic nature found elsewhere at the site) does imply that there was some kind of major, nonresidential complex on Shiloh's summit during the Iron Age I period of Israelite history—possibly a shrine, according to Israel Finkelstein, who excavated at Shiloh from 1981 to 1984.[28] Finkelstein's excavations may intimate, moreover, that just as the eighth-century BCE text of 1 Sam 1:1–2:26 suggests (at least as I have interpreted it), Shiloh served as a *regional* shrine for Israel's central hill-country residents during the Iron Age I era (or at least until the site's destruction, as Finkelstein would have it, toward the end of the Iron Age I period).[29] Indeed, in Finkelstein's estimation, "In the beginning of the Iron Age, Shiloh was the outstanding candidate to become the sacred center of the hill-country population, since it was . . . in an area with . . . a high concentration of 'Israelite' sites."[30] In fact, Finkelstein theorizes that Shiloh's role as a sacred center dates back even to the Canaanite period of the late Middle Bronze Age (sixteenth century BCE), when Shiloh, although it was relatively small, may have served local worshippers as a cultic gathering site that perhaps housed a temple (evidence suggests that some sort of significant building may have stood on the site's summit).[31]

Unfortunately, no architectural remains from the succeeding Canaanite period of the Late Bronze Age (ca. 1550–1200 BCE) were unearthed at Shiloh; instead, archaeologists discovered only a thick deposit (1.5 meters) of earth, ashes, and stones, in which pieces of (deliberately?) broken pottery, animal bones (mostly sheep and goat), and nearly intact vessels containing ashes and more animal bones were found.[32] Still, Finkelstein has proposed this means that the memory of the sixteenth-century BCE temple persisted among Late Bronze Age worshippers who lived in Shiloh's vicinity and who, despite the site's lack of a shrine building in their day, nevertheless came to this sacred location to leave dedicatory offerings and, more important, to participate (as is indicated by the preponderance of animal bones) in the major ritual associated in Near Eastern religions with sanctuary space: animal sacrifice.[33] That Shiloh remained a central gathering place, and perhaps a sacred center, for the Israelites who inhabited the surrounding hill country during the subsequent Iron Age I period is further suggested to Finkelstein by two factors: first, the remarkable number of other Iron Age I Israelite sites surrounding Shiloh (twenty-six sites within a 5–6-kilometer radius), in a density "two and even three times greater," as Finkelstein writes, than is found elsewhere in the Ephraimite hills;[34] second, the evidence noted above that may point to the presence of a sanctuary building at twelfth- and eleventh-century BCE Shiloh. Moreover, just as Finkelstein posits that the memory of a Middle Bronze Age cult site at Shiloh persisted into the Late Bronze Age, so might we theorize that the memory of a shrine at twelfth- and eleventh-century BCE Shiloh persisted among the Israelites into the eighth century BCE—and so influenced the account of Shiloh's sanctuary building found in 1 Sam 1:1–2:26.[35]

Nevertheless, archaeological remains from elsewhere in premonarchic Israel make clear that regional sanctuaries of the Iron Age I period need not have a shrine building associated with them.[36] The crucial materials here come from the so-called Bull Site, which was discovered somewhat accidentally by a young Israeli soldier and then systematically excavated by Amihai Mazar between 1978 and 1981.[37] This site, which dates from the twelfth century BCE, lies on the summit of a high ridge in the northern reaches of the tribal territory of Manasseh, about 9 kilometers east of biblical Dothan and near the road that connected Dothan to the site of biblical Tirzah (see Fig. I.1).[38] The site's layout suggests it was meant to be used for communal gatherings by a reasonably sized, although not an overwhelmingly large group of people: it consists of an open-air, circular space, a little more than 21 meters in diameter, surrounded by a low-lying enclosure wall at least 1 meter and possibly as much as 2 meters in height (Fig. 3.1).[39] Within this enclosed precinct was found a large standing stone, or in the language of the Bible a *maṣṣēbâ,* about 1.30 meters long, 0.97 meter high, and 0.55 meter thick. This sort of stone is often found in religious settings in the Syro-Palestinian world, and its presence at the Bull Site thus suggests that the communal gatherings that apparently took place within the site's enclosed precinct were religious in character.[40] The standing stone was fronted by a paved area that arguably functioned religiously as well, as a place where offerings were left and perhaps also where animal sacrifices were enacted.[41]

The Bull Site takes its name, however, from an even more significant artifact (Fig. 3.2): a bronze bull about 17.5 centimeters long with a maximum height of 12.4 centimeters.[42] Yet despite this object's obvious significance (and we will recall from Chapter 1 how precious, and therefore how rare, this sort of cast-metal figurine was within Israelite tradition), scholars are unsure how, exactly, to interpret it. Both of the principal gods of the

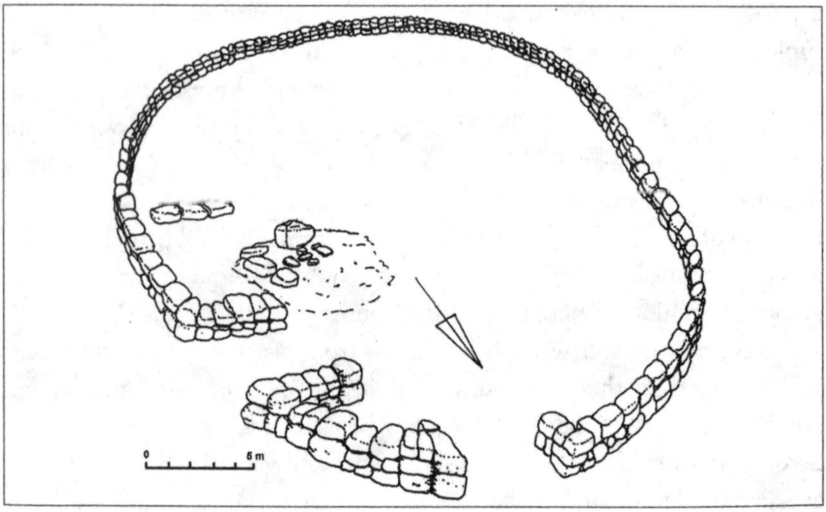

Fig. 3.1. Artist's reconstruction of the "Bull Site" precinct and enclosure wall. © Ziony Zevit, 2001, *The Religions of Ancient Israel: A Synthesis of Parallactic Approaches,* Continuum UK, an imprint of Bloomsbury Publishing Plc. Page 177, Fig. 3.27.

Fig. 3.2. The "Bull Site" bull. From Amihai Mazar, "The 'Bull Site'—An Iron Age I Open Cult Place," *BASOR* 247 (1982): 30, Fig. 2; the complete article is available on the online journal platform of University of Chicago Press. Courtesy of Amihai Mazar, The Hebrew University of Jerusalem.

Canaanite pantheon, the divine patriarch and head of the pantheon El and the storm/warrior god Baal, can be associated with bulls. For example, in fourteenth-/thirteenth-century BCE mythological texts from the northern Levantine city-state of Ugarit (see Fig. I.2), El is repeatedly referred to using the epithet *ṯr*, "Bull," and archaeologists have discovered multiple bull images from the ancient Canaanite world that were arguably a part of the cult of Baal.[43] However, the biblical record makes clear that the Israelite god Yahweh can also be referred to as "Bull": see the epithets "Bull of Jacob" and "Bull of Israel" used of Yahweh in Gen 49:24; Isa 1:24, 49:26, 60:16; and Ps 132:2.[44] Other biblical texts—preeminently 1 Kgs 12:28–29—report that two bull-calf images represented Yahweh in the Northern Kingdom's state sanctuaries in Dan and Bethel. Moreover, a cult stand from tenth-century BCE Taanach, which lies near Megiddo in the southern reaches of the Jezreel Valley (see Fig. I.1), has been interpreted as using a bull image to depict Yahweh.[45] In conjunction with other evidence—for example, a constellation of arguably Israelite villages proximate to the Bull Site (five within a 1-kilometer radius)[46]—this has suggested to most that the Bull Site is indeed Israelite and that the bull found there is a Yahwistic icon.

In short: the twelfth-century BCE Bull Site was arguably a sacred precinct where worshippers could encounter a ritual object they understood to signify the presence of Yahweh. So too at Shiloh, according to biblical texts such as 1 Sam 3:3 (a text that McCarter, as noted above, identifies as belonging to the continuation of the pre-Deuteronomistic [late eighth-century BCE] text of 1 Sam 1:1–2:26), worshippers could encounter a ritual object—the ark of the covenant—that signified Yahweh's presence at that sanctuary. As at Shiloh, moreover, those who worshipped at the Bull Site, as already suggested, were arguably Israelites who lived generally proximate to the Bull Site and who used the shrine as a regional sanctuary. Indeed, as just mentioned, the Bull Site, like Shiloh, was situated in the midst of a constellation of apparently Israelite villages, and it seems reasonable to assume that the residents of these various villages, and perhaps others who traveled the nearby Dothan-Tirzah road, would come periodically to the Bull Site for communal worship, just as central hill-country residents came periodically to Shiloh. One can easily imagine, in fact, the inhabitants of villages within, say, a 25–30-kilometer radius of the Bull Site making the same sort of occasional journey that Elkanah's family is said to have made annually to Shiloh and then gathering within its enclosure wall to participate in religious observances.

We can also readily imagine that at both the Bull Site and Shiloh, the religious observances in which worshippers engaged included, preeminently, animal sacrifice, which was, I again note, the central ritual practice at ancient Israelite sanctuary and temple settings. As previously documented, the paved area in front of the Bull Site's standing stone or *maṣṣēbâ* may have been used for animal sacrifice, and archaeologists have also found at the Bull Site some of the detritus of sacrificial ritual—animal bones and cooking pots.[47] The presence of cooking pots suggests, moreover, that at least some of the animal sacrifices offered at the Bull Site were what the Bible calls *šĕlāmîm* as opposed to *ʿōlâ* offerings, *ʿōlâ* offerings (literally, "an offering of ascent") being those in which the entire animal was burned on an altar to Yahweh, whereas *šĕlāmîm* offerings were those in which only the two kidneys, part of the liver, and the visceral fat of the slaughtered animal (that is, the fat that is beneath the skin and that surrounds the animal's organs) were burned to God.[48] The rest of the meat was boiled (hence the need for cooking pots) and eaten by the ritual's participants.[49] Indeed, it is tempting to suggest that the enclosure wall of the Bull Site demarcated the area in which worshippers ate the communal meals that would have been prepared using the flesh of *šĕlāmîm* offerings.[50]

Likewise at Iron Age I Shiloh, even though the archaeological evidence is meager, we can suggest—on the basis of the remains of ceramic vessels found at the site—that the sacrifice of animals as *šĕlāmîm* offerings was the central ritual. Certainly this is the presumption of the later textual witness of 1 Sam 1:1–2:26. Indeed, in 1 Sam 1:3, 21, and 2:19, we are told explicitly that the reason the household of Elkanah goes annually to Shiloh is *lizbōaḥ*, which means, literally, "to slaughter [an animal for sacrifice]" but more specifically means "to slaughter [an animal as a *šĕlāmîm* offering]."[51] In addition, 1 Sam 1:4–5 reports that Elkanah apportions a sacrificed animal's meat to the members of his family to eat, just as the *šĕlāmîm* ritual requires. A similar tradition is found in 1 Sam 2:13, which describes the larger community of Israelite worshippers at Shiloh as *zōbēaḥ zebaḥ*, which we might most literally translate as "slaughtering a *šĕlāmîm* sacrifice," and then apportioning the sacrificial meat from the pots in which the sacrificial meat is boiled. According also to the text of the succeeding verse, 1 Sam 2:14, as found in the ancient version of 1 Samuel that comes from the Dead Sea Scrolls (the scroll known as 4QSam[a], which dates from the second half of the first century BCE), the Israelites came to Shiloh *lzbḥ*, "to slaughter [an animal as a *šĕlāmîm* offering]," to Yahweh. This understanding is in addition clearly implied in the larger story in which 1 Sam 2:13–14 is embedded, 1 Sam 2:12–17. This account concerns the way in which Hophni and Phinehas, the two sons of Shiloh's presiding priest Eli, abused the system that the Israelites who had come to Shiloh to sacrifice deployed, so that these sons might claim a particularly choice part of the slaughtered animals' meat for their portion of the *šělāmîm* meal.

I will have more to say about this episode involving Hophni and Phinehas below; for the moment, though, it is enough to note the appearance of these two priestly offspring during the *šělāmîm* meal in 1 Sam 2:12–17, as well as their father Eli's appearance in 1 Sam 1:9–18, 25–28, and 2:22–25 as one of the central figures of the 1 Sam 1:1–2:26 account. Yet it is equally important to note that despite these priestly actors' appearances and even these priestly characters' centrality, it is not obvious in 1 Sam 1:1–2:26 that any significant role is played by Shiloh's priests during the *šělāmîm* ritual. Instead, they seem generally removed from most aspects of the sacrificial rite. For example, 1 Sam 1:4–5 speaks of *Elkanah* only in describing the offering of the *šělāmîm* sacrifice and the subsequent apportioning of the slaughtered animal's meat, and 1 Sam 2:13 similarly speaks of a nonpriestly agent—a *kol-'îš,* or "someone," whom the passage clearly differentiates from Shiloh's priests—as making the *šělāmîm* sacrifice at Shiloh and then overseeing the cooked meat's distribution.[52]

Other biblical texts, however, assume that key aspects of the *šělāmîm* rite were priestly responsibilities, especially those parts of the rite that took place at Yahweh's altar after the sacrificial animal had been slaughtered at some nearby location.[53] These altar-based rituals, as already noted, included the burning of the animal's visceral fat and certain organs, which were reserved for the deity, and, according to some biblical passages, dealing with the animal's blood, which, according to these same passages, was also reserved for God and thus was dashed against or sprinkled or daubed upon the altar. That "it was always a priest who presented and who placed upon the altar the[se] part[s] of the sacrifice which belonged to God" is especially (and not surprisingly) attested in texts that stem from priestly communities.[54] These include texts in Leviticus 1–7 attributed to the P or Priestly source and texts in the related Holiness Code (H) of Leviticus 17–26 (see, for example, Lev 1:5, 8–9, 11–12, 15–17; 3:1–16; 17:6; see also, from elsewhere in P and related sources, Num 18:8, 17; Ezek 44:15).[55] In these accounts, "the preliminary rites with the sacrificial animal are performed by the offerer," Jacob Milgrom writes in his magisterial three-volume commentary on Leviticus, including "hand-leaning, slaughtering, flaying, quartering, and washing." But, Milgrom goes on to say, "the priest takes over at the altar."[56] Some late priestly authored texts (Ezek 44:11, from the early sixth century BCE) even go so far as to assign to priests the role of slaughtering the sacrificial animal.[57]

Texts from the book of Deuteronomy, although they are not as overwhelmingly emphatic, similarly suggest that the parts of the sacrificial ritual enacted at Yahweh's altar were a priestly obligation. Thus, according to Deut 10:8, it is the members of Israel's priestly tribe, the Levites, who have been designated by divine decree "to stand before Yahweh and serve him" (see similarly Deut 18:5, 7), and Deut 26:4 specifically speaks of a Levite's taking a basket of vegetative offerings that an Israelite has brought to the sanctuary and placing it beside Yahweh's altar on that worshipper's behalf. Deuteronomy 33:1–29, which is a poetic text embedded in Deuteronomy's prose, furthermore affirms, in 33:10, the Levites' role in presenting burnt offerings on Yahweh's altar. Most significant for my purposes is 1 Sam 2:28, a text that is a part of a fairly heavy-handed editorial addition (1 Sam 2:27–36) made to 1 Samuel 1–2 in the late seventh century BCE by the Deuteronomistic Historians as part of their project of bringing the Samuel narratives into line with the book of Deuteronomy's theological agenda.[58] In this text, the special role of the Levites (or, more specifically, of Moses as the Levites' progenitor) in performing the rites of altar service is articulated: "I chose him [Moses]," Yahweh is said to proclaim, "out of all the tribes of Israel to be my priest [and] to go up to my altar."

Yet just as 1 Sam 1:1–2:26, as noted earlier, stands at odds with the seventh-century BCE Deuteronomistic conviction that Israelite worship should be concentrated at a single, central sanctuary, and just as 1 Sam 1:1–2:26 (minus the interpolated 1 Sam 2:22) stands at odds, as also noted earlier, with the late seventh-century BCE conviction that Yahweh was worshipped at Shiloh only "in a tent and a tabernacle," so too does 1 Sam 1:1–2:26 seem to stand at odds with the conviction of late seventh-century BCE texts such as Deut 10:8, 26:4, 33:10, and even the closely succeeding 1 Sam 2:28 that the parts of the sacrificial ritual that require altar service must be performed by priests. Instead, as I noted above, nonpriestly agents—Elkanah and a generic "someone," or a *kol-'îš*—are described in 1 Sam 1:4–5 and 1 Sam 2:13, respectively, as presiding over the offering of the *šělāmîm* sacrifice and the subsequent distribution of the slaughtered animal's meat. Likewise, 1 Sam 1:25 (although this is a textually confused verse, as I discuss further below) recounts how a bull that had been brought to Shiloh on behalf of Elkanah's household as an offering (presumably as the household's annual *šělāmîm* offering; more on this also below) was slaughtered without there being any mention of a priest's presence, to the extent that no priest is said to be present after the slaughter to attend to the presentation of the animal's visceral fat and organ meat at Shiloh's altar and (if this was included in the Shilonite ritual) its blood (the blood is not specifically mentioned in any of our text's descriptions of Shilonite sacrifice).[59] Nor is any priest on hand to attend to the grain offering of an ephah of flour that 1 Sam 1:24 identifies as having accompanied the sacrifice of the bull, even though other biblical texts (for example, Lev 2:2, 8) require a priest to bring this sort of offering to Yahweh's altar and burn a designated portion of it there. Certainly, the priest Eli is not present to deal with these altar rites according to 1 Sam 1:25, as he is sought out only after the sacrifice and, presumably, its attendant rituals had been completed.

Even more significant is 1 Sam 2:15–16, where within the tale of Hophni's and Phinehas's abuses, we read of how these two sons of Eli are accused of attempting to claim some of the sacrificial meat for themselves before the animal's visceral fat and organ meat had been properly burned. But was it these priests who were supposed to have burned the fat and organ meat? This might be suggested by the third-person masculine plural verb used twice (in both 2:15 and 2:16) to describe the burning (*yaqṭîrû,* "and they burned"). But upon closer inspection, the referent of the "they" of 2:15 and 2:16 seems less than grammatically clear, so much so that interpreters often avoid the pronoun's ambiguities by translating using the passive voice (see, for example, the NRSV rendering of 2:15, "Before the fat had been burned," or McCarter's rendering of 2:16, "Let the fat be burned").[60] McCarter also points out that in the version of 1 Samuel found among the Dead Sea Scrolls, the ambiguity of 2:16 was addressed through expansion, in order to read decisively *yqṭr hkwhn,* "let the priest burn [the fat]."[61] Yet this clarificatory expansion seems almost special pleading within the Dead Sea Scrolls, whose parent community's priestly biases are well known: an admission, that is, on the part of the Dead Sea Scrolls' priestly transmitters that without further elaboration, the ambiguities of 1 Sam 2:15–16 might allow these verses to be interpreted as assigning the responsibility for the burning of the fat of Shiloh's *šĕlāmîm* offerings to nonpriestly worshippers. And in fact, the nearest plural antecedent of *yaqṭîrû* in 1 Sam 2:15 and 16 is *not* the priestly pair Hophni and Phinehas, but *kol-yiśrāʾēl,* or the Israelites. Thus Georg Braulik concludes that 1 Sam 2:15–16 does not "create the impression that it was a priest who usually 'smoked' [i.e., burned the fat and the organ meat] as if it was his right."[62]

In fact, the only point in the entire 1 Sam 1:1–2:26 story where the Shiloh priesthood is explicitly said to play a part in the *šĕlāmîm* ritual is in claiming the portion of the sacrificial animal allotted for priestly consumption: properly, as the text sees it in 1 Sam 2:13–14, by the priest or his attendant coming to someone who had made the *šĕlāmîm* offering and was then boiling the meat for the subsequent meal, in order to stick a fork in the cooking pot and fish out whatever piece providence might provide (but cf. Lev 7:28–36 and Deut 18:3); improperly, according to 1 Sam 2:15, as I have just remarked, by trying to claim a piece of the sacrificial meat immediately after the animal had been slaughtered and before the fat and organs owed to the deity had been burned. According to 1 Sam 2:15, this is because this just-slaughtered and fat-enriched meat could then be roasted, rendering a much tastier meal than was to be had from eating meat that was stripped of its fat and cooked on the boil.

At any rate: whatever the expectations set forward in other biblical texts regarding the priesthood's role during the altar-based rituals of *šĕlāmîm* sacrifices, including the expectations set forward in other texts from the Deuteronomistic tradition into which 1 Sam 1:1–2:26 was eventually incorporated, the *šĕlāmîm* rite that 1 Sam 1:1–2:26 describes seems *not* to depend heavily on the participation of official cult personnel. As Richard D. Nelson writes in his study of the Israelite priesthood, "Eli and his sons . . . played no special role in the sacrificial ritual except to collect their tariff (1 Sam 2:13–14)," and Aelred Cody similarly remarks, "The priesthood at Shiloh . . . had no monopoly on sacrifice, for we know that Samuel's father Elkanah sacrificed as a pilgrim to the sanctuary they frequented."[63] A similar situation could well have pertained at the Bull Site, since its open-air design would require at most only modest priestly oversight. Was a priest or priestly family such as Eli's even resident at the Bull Site? Perhaps the site was serviced only by a priest or priests who lived in the sanctuary's satellite villages (someone like the Levite of Micah described in Judg 17:7–13), who came along with village worshippers on their occasional sacrificial journeys to oversee their ritual devotions. Or perhaps it was only some clan elder or elders, or other clan leader or leaders, who oversaw their families' worship.[64] Or perhaps there was no official oversight at all. Certainly, the Bull Site, as an open-air shrine, would have required, at most, the presence of only a fairly modest and informal cadre of cult personnel.[65]

Some biblical passages in addition suggest that even small-scale shrines that had buildings associated with them required, like the Bull Site, only the occasional presence of a limited number of cultic personnel. Especially noteworthy in this regard are the various notices found in 1 Samuel 9 (vv. 11–14, 19, 22–25) regarding the small-scale shrine that I mentioned briefly above. This shrine is said to have been located somewhere in Benjamin; perhaps, if it is to be equated with the shrine Samuel is said to found in 1 Sam 7:17, it was sited in Ramah (see Fig. I.1), which 1 Sam 7:17 takes to be Samuel's family's hometown.[66] Yet wherever the shrine's location, 1 Samuel 9 reports that Samuel went there only occasionally to render service as a priest. First Samuel 9:12, for example, describes Samuel as coming to the shrine specially on the day of this text's setting because the people were sacrificing, and this despite the fact that the sanctuary is said (as also noted above) to have a permanent *liškâ,* that is, a room or chamber that is part of a sanctuary building. Which is to say: it is not just the open-air Bull Site, but even the sort of multichambered and thus structurally complex sanctuary compound intimated in 1 Sam 9:11–14, 19, 22–25 that seems, according to this strand within Israelite tradition, *not* to require the presence of a resident priest.

Despite William McKane's claim, moreover, that "Samuel is . . . represented as enjoying priestly authority and performing priestly duties" in 1 Samuel 9, and Patrick D. Miller's similar sense that "Samuel is depicted as carrying out priestly responsibilities, specifically sacrifice, at what seems to be a local shrine . . . (1 Sam 9:11–14)," Samuel's role in the sacrificial cult while he is present at the 1 Samuel 9 shrine seems to be negligible.[67] He blesses (*yĕbārēk;* 1 Sam 9:13) the *šĕlāmîm* sacrifices (the use of the noun *zebaḥ* in 1 Sam 9:12, in addition to the notice in 1 Sam 9:13 and 24 that the people subsequently ate of their sacrifices, makes clear that it is *šĕlāmîm* offerings that are referred to), and he also seems able to designate how certain portions of the slaughtered animal's meat are to be distributed at the postsacrificial meal (1 Sam 9:23). Samuel is not said, however, to attend during the slaughter of the sacrifice, nor to have performed ritual manipulations of the sacrificial animal's visceral fat and organs or its blood (if this was a requisite part of the 1 Samuel 9 ritual). Nor does he engage in preparing the animal's flesh for consumption, except for directing that a certain portion of the sacrificial meat be set specially aside (see again 1 Sam 9:23). Rather, this task is assigned to a different (cultic?) agent: the *ṭabbāḥ*, or the "butcher," "cook."

In 1 Samuel 9, then, we seem again to find what I take to be a sanctuary space that is (at best) regional in nature (given that only about thirty people worshipped there) and where, like the other regional or provincial sanctuaries I have surveyed, priestly engagement in the sanctuary's sacrificial ritual is minimal. Note, moreover, that in 1 Sam 9:12, 13, 14, 19, and 25, the shrine in question is called a *bāmâ,* typically translated as a "high place."[68] Note as well that biblical tradition elsewhere suggests that other (although not all) *bāmôt* (the plural form of *bāmâ*) served as regional sanctuaries during the ninth, eighth, seventh, and early sixth centuries BCE.[69] For example, by identifying *bāmôt* that were sites of Israelite worship within fortified settlements (Hebrew *ʿārîm*) located roundabout the Northern and Southern Kingdoms,[70] texts such as 1 Kgs 13:32 and 2 Kgs 17:9, 23:5, 8, and 19 seem to indicate that these *bāmôt* served as provincial or regional sanctuaries scattered throughout Israel and Judah. At least some of the Israelite and Judaean *bāmôt* sanctuaries mentioned in the eighth-, seventh-, and early sixth-century BCE oracles of the prophets Amos, Hosea, Jeremiah, and Ezekiel (Amos 7:9; Hos 10:8; Jer 7:31, 19:5, 32:35; Ezek 6:3, 6; 20:29) might be taken as provincial or regional sanctuaries as well.[71] Thus, although Miller notes that there may have been provincial or regional shrines during the monarchic era that were not called by the designation *bāmâ,* he concludes that "the *bāmôt* or 'high places' . . . served as geographical or regional cult centers."[72]

Biblical tradition furthermore suggests that a situation regarding priestly oversight very similar to that described for the *bāmâ* sanctuary of 1 Samuel 9 (or, more specifically, a lack of priestly oversight at the 1 Samuel 9 *bāmâ*) prevailed at the provincial or regional *bāmôt* sanctuaries of the ninth, eighth, seventh, and early sixth centuries BCE. For example, even though King Jeroboam I of the Northern Kingdom of Israel is said in 1 Kgs 13:33 to have appointed priests to serve at the North's *bāmôt* shrines already at the beginning of his reign (ca. 931 BCE), 2 Kgs 17:9–11, which purports to describe the general history of Israel's Northern Kingdom from its establishment to its fall (ca. 931–722/721 BCE), describes only *the people* of Israel as worshipping and making offerings at *bāmôt* sanctuaries. To be sure, these verses do not specifically refer to the people (as opposed to the priests) performing the *šĕlāmîm* sacrifices that are my particular interest here, but this point is explicitly (and repeatedly) made in texts that purport to describe the religious practices of the *bāmôt* of the Southern Kingdom of Judah in the ninth and eighth centuries BCE. Thus, it is the Judaean *people* (*hāʿām*) who are described as conducting *šĕlāmîm* sacrifices (*mĕzabbĕḥîm*) and making offerings at the *bāmôt* in the following:

1. 1 Kgs 22:44 (in most of the Bible's English versions, 22:43), which purports to date from the first half of the ninth century BCE;
2. 2 Kgs 12:4 (in most of the Bible's English versions, 12:3), which purports to date from the second half of the ninth century BCE;
3. 2 Kgs 14:4, which purports to date from the first half of the eighth century BCE;
4. 2 Kgs 15:4, which also purports to date from the first half of the eighth century BCE; and
5. 2 Kgs 15:35, which purports to date from the second half of the eighth century BCE.

Even in the seventh and early sixth centuries BCE, the people's role in offering sacrifice at *bāmôt* sanctuaries may have persisted, and this even though by the late seventh century BCE, the Deuteronomistic redactors of 1–2 Kings were forcefully putting forward the view that Levitical priests, rather than the populace more generally, had been responsible for sacrifices at the *bāmôt* of both the Northern Kingdom of Israel and the Southern Kingdom of Judah throughout these kingdoms' respective histories (see in this regard the late seventh-century BCE texts found in 1 Kgs 13:2 and 2 Kgs 23:8–9). Nevertheless, Ezek 20:28–29, which dates from ca. 591 BCE, echoes 1 Kgs 22:44 (English 22:43) and 2 Kgs 12:4 (English 12:3), 14:4, 15:4, and 15:15 in identifying *the people* of Israel as those who had, throughout their history, offered sacrifice—and specifically, as Ezekiel's use of the verb *zābaḥ* indicates, *šĕlāmîm* sacrifices—at a sanctuary that "is called Bamah to this day."

Of course, one must grant that Ezekiel's intent in his description of the people's *bāmâ* worship is to speak polemically, and even more one must grant that the Deuteronomistic passages from 1–2 Kings cited above regarding the *bāmôt* are some of the most polemically laden texts in the Bible, given the challenge that the *bāmôt* present to the Deuteronomists' core theology of centralized worship. It is thus difficult, as we saw in discussing the similarly polemical passages I considered in Chapters 1 and 2, indisputably to assign to these texts historical reliability. Yet I have also suggested in Chapters 1 and 2 that while polemically laden texts can hardly be taken as straightforward depictions of Israel's religious history (we should not, for example, maintain that the Danites of Judg 17:1–18:31 actually founded a sanctuary centered on the worship of a stolen icon), the Bible's polemics nevertheless must, in terms of their underlying portrayal of Israelite religious practice, present a picture that was generally believable to their ancient Israelite audiences (however dubious the story of the Danites' theft, the idea that a cast-metal figurine of some value could have sat, ripe for the taking, within an Israelite household shrine must have been a plausible conceit for the audience of the Judges 17–18 narrative). It follows, therefore, that whatever the polemic against *bāmôt* worship that the Deuteronomists and Ezekiel sought to unleash, these authors' intimations that priests were significantly detached from the sacrificial rites of these regional sanctuaries would have needed to "ring true" to their Israelite audiences, presumably because these intimations reflected an experience of priestly detachment at regional sanctuaries similar to these audiences' own. Thus Baruch Halpern rather flippantly describes regional shrines as sites of "back-yard-barbeque cult," characterized by a "rejection of the absolute need for ritual specialists to execute offerings."[73] Erhard S. Gerstenberger makes the same point, albeit in more sober terms: "the small town has its own sanctuary, but needs very few personnel, if any."[74]

These data regarding the priesthood's (non)participation in sacrificial ritual at Shiloh and the other premonarchic and monarchic-era regional sanctuaries I have surveyed hold important implications for addressing the issue that concerns us for the rest of this chapter and the next—preexilic women's religious experiences at regional sanctuaries—and for evaluating specifically the topic I wish to address in my comments that immediately follow: preexilic women's role in the offering of the *šĕlāmîm* sacrifice at regional shrines. My hypothesis is that because the priests at Israel's regional sanctuaries were significantly divorced from the execution of these sanctuaries' key ritual of the *šĕlāmîm* sacrifice, more opportunities were available for the worshipping community's nonelites, or ordinary folk, including women, to be involved.

That said, I must quickly admit that an increased opportunity for a worshipping community's nonelites to be involved in a regional sanctuary's sacrificial rites need not mean that *all* the community's members would be equally involved, and given the male-dominated nature of Israelite society, we can easily imagine a scenario whereby only a community's men would actually offer the *šĕlāmîm* sacrifices. In fact, this is precisely what is suggested by 1 Sam 2:13, where the nonpriestly "someone" who makes the *šĕlāmîm* sacrifice at Shiloh and then oversees the cooked meat's distribution is specifically gendered as male (*'îš*). Likewise, in 1 Sam 1:4, Elkanah alone is described as offering up an animal for slaughter. Elkanah is also described in 1 Sam 1:4 and in the subsequent verse as taking sole responsibility for the distribution of the meat consumed at the *šělāmîm* meal, and we perhaps should also envision Elkanah as cooking that meat as well, as in ancient Israel (as in many households today, especially within the Euro-American orbit), "the cooking of meat" is "the aspect of food production men are most likely to take on."[75] This is especially the case in sacrificial contexts: thus, in Gen 18:7, it is Abraham's male servant, or *naʿar,* who prepares the calf that Abraham serves to Yahweh and the deity's two divine attendants when they visit him at the oaks at Mamre that were near his and Sarah's tent; in Judg 6:19, it is Gideon who prepares a kid for the divine messenger who appears to him at the terebinth at Ophrah; and in 1 Sam 9:23–24, it is a male cook (*ṭabbāḥ*), as noted above, who is described as having prepared at least one portion of the *šělāmîm* sacrifice described in that text (contrast the traditions of the royal palace, where it is women *ṭabbāḥôt* who, according to 1 Sam 8:13, serve as cooks).[76]

Still, according to 1 Sam 1:4–5, Elkanah distributes portions of the sacrificial meat to his two wives, Hannah and Peninnah, and to Peninnah's sons and possibly her daughters,[77] showing that this text's author(s) and/or redactor(s) envisioned women as engaged participants in at least the ritual meal that followed the offering of the *šělāmîm* sacrifice. The role of Hannah as a significantly engaged participant in the ritual described in 1 Sam 1:24–25—which, as already intimated, is best understood as a *šělāmîm* sacrifice that takes place after the previously barren Hannah has born Samuel, her miracle child—should give us further pause.

Women's Roles in the Sacrificial Rituals of Israel's Regional Sanctuaries

In turning to focus on the role of Hannah in 1 Sam 1:24–25, we unfortunately find that these verses raise interpretive challenges. For example, although I maintain, as just indicated, that the sacrifice described in this text is a *šělāmîm* offering, the Hebrew of 1:24–25 as it has come down to us (what scholars refer to as the Masoretic Text, after its medieval editors, who were called the Masoretes) does not in fact include the usual form *lizbōaḥ* otherwise used in 1 Sam 1:1–2:26 to describe the *šělāmîm* sacrifices made by Elkanah's family during their yearly visits to Shiloh (1:3, 21, and 2:19). Nor does the Masoretic Text of 1 Sam 1:24–25 invoke other terminology that might refer to Elkanah's family's characteristic slaughtering of an animal as a *šělāmîm* offering (*zebaḥ, zebaḥ šělāmîm, zibḥê-šělāmîm,* or just plain *šělāmîm*).[78] However, in the Dead Sea Scrolls rendering of 1 Sam 1:25, the noun *zebaḥ* is clearly present.[79] The 1 Samuel 1 story as found in one of our ancient Greek Bible manuscripts, the Codex Vaticanus (fourth century CE), similarly suggests that the sacrifice of vv. 24–25 was at one with the *šělāmîm* sacrifice made during the yearly trip that Elkanah's family customarily made to Shiloh. More specifically, in Vaticanus, Elkanah is said to slaughter a sacrificial animal in 1 Sam 1:24–25 as "he did regularly," that is, as he did on his family's regular, or annual journeys to Shiloh. This is suggested as well in the ancient Greek rendering of 1 Samuel 1 found in the so-called Lucianic group of minuscules (thought to date back to the third century CE and based on older traditions still). Which is to say: in the Dead Sea Scrolls, in Vaticanus, and in the Lucianic minuscules, there is a clear enough reference in 1 Sam 1:24–25 to the annual *šělāmîm* sacrifice of Elkanah's family. Most commentators think such a reference was also originally present in (but subsequently dropped out of) the Masoretic account.[80]

Let me turn, then, to look at Hannah's role during the *šělāmîm* ritual as depicted in 1 Sam 1:24–25, beginning with the description found in the Masoretic account. There, in 1 Sam 1:24, we read, "She [that is, Hannah] took him [that is, Samuel] up with her after she had weaned him, along with three bulls, one ephah of flour, and a skin [or 'vessel'] of wine, and she brought him to the house of Yahweh at Shiloh."[81] Again, however, the Greek and Dead Sea Scrolls materials are somewhat different, as the Greek (and seemingly the Dead Sea Scrolls text, although it is fragmentary at this crucial point) has Hannah bringing "a three-year-old bull" to Shiloh, as opposed to the Masoretic Text's "three bulls." Since according to the Masoretes, the Greek, and the Dead Sea Scrolls text, only one bull is killed in v. 25, "a three-year-old bull" is surely the correct reading.[82]

More important for my purposes, though, are the Greek (and, seemingly, the Dead Sea Scrolls) renderings of the first half of v. 25 (or v. 25a), which are more constrained than the Masoretic Text with regard to Hannah's agency. Consider vv. 24 and 25a as presented in Table 3.1. Note that at the end of v. 24, the Greek tradition (as well as, seemingly, the fragmentary text from the Dead Sea Scrolls) asserts that Elkanah was present along with Hannah at Shiloh (a point on which the Masoretic Text is silent; in the Masoretic tradition, Elkanah appears together with Hannah only at the beginning of v. 25 at the point at which the bull is slaughtered).[83] More significantly, in v. 25 of the Masoretic tradition, Hannah seems to be envisioned

Table 3.1. Different renderings of 1 Sam 1:24–25a

Masoretic Text	Greek (Codex Vaticanus)[a]	Dead Sea Scrolls (4QSam[a])[b]
[24]And she [Hannah] took him [Samuel] up with her after she had weaned him, along with three bulls, one ephah of flour, and a skin [or "vessel"] of wine, and she brought him to the house of Yahweh at Shiloh, and the boy was a boy. [25]And they [presumably Hannah and Elkanah] slaughtered the bull.	[24]And she [Hannah] went up with him [Samuel] to Shiloh, with a three-year-old bull, and bread, and an ephah of flour, and a skin of wine, and she came into the house of Yahweh in Shiloh, and the child [Samuel] was with them [Hannah and Elkanah]. [25]And they went before Yahweh, and his father slaughtered the sacrifice as he did regularly to Yahweh. And she took the child, and he slaughtered the bull.	[24]And she [Hannah] took him [Samuel] up to Shiloh when <Elkanah went up to sacrifice to Yahweh, along with a bull from> the herd [that was] three years old, and bread <and one ephah of flour, and a skin [or "vessel"] of wine, and she brought him to the house> of Yahweh at Shiloh, and the boy [Samuel] was <with them [Hannah and Elkanah]. [25]And they went before Yahweh, and his father slaughtered the> sacrifice as <he did regularly before Yahweh, and he> slaughtered <the bull>.

Note: Materials in square brackets are my glosses; material in angle brackets is reconstructed.

a. This translation is from McCarter, *I Samuel,* 56–57; note that the last line, however, could as easily be translated, "And *he* took the child [or "brought the child near," or even "presented the child"] and slaughtered the bull." See, e.g., Walters, "Hannah and Anna," 398.

b. Following Ulrich, ed., *Biblical Qumran Scrolls,* 260.

as standing alongside her husband Elkanah and acting in tandem with him while a sacrificial animal is killed. Conversely, the Greek Codex Vaticanus (as well as, seemingly, the fragmentary text from the Dead Sea Scrolls) describes Elkanah alone (as opposed to both Elkanah and Hannah) as killing the sacrificial animal in v. 25a.

I suggest that the Greek Vaticanus text (and, seemingly, also the fragmentary manuscript from the Dead Sea Scrolls) is more reliable than the Masoretic Text in envisioning Elkanah alone as actually performing the slaughter, this as opposed to the arguments of some other scholars that the Greek shows "'patriarchalizing' of the text in removing Hannah's agency in performing the sacrifice."[84] The Greek rendering, though, seems to me the more probable, for several reasons. First, Emanuel Tov has shown that if there is any "patriarchalizing" at play in the various renditions of 1 Samuel 1–2, it is not on the part of the Greek, but on the part of the Masoretic Text, where we can note the "removal or change of some of Hannah's cultic actions in 1 Samuel 1–2 considered inappropriate for a woman."[85] Under the terms of this understanding, the Greek (and also the fragmentary Samuel manuscript from the Dead Sea Scrolls) reflects an older, a more reliable, and a more "Hannah-friendly" text (the Greek and Dead Sea Scroll renderings of v. 25a notwithstanding).[86] In 1 Sam 1:25a, the Greek (and seemingly the Dead Sea Scrolls Samuel manuscript) also reflects a more logistically sensible text (for two people jointly to wield a knife and slaughter a bull, as the Masoretic Text would have it, seems awkward).[87]

More important, understanding the man Elkanah as solely executing the slaughter, as in the Greek (and presumably the Samuel materials from the Dead Sea Scrolls), seems consistent with the description of Elkanah alone sacrificing in 1 Sam 1:4 and of a single male agent (*kol-'îš*) sacrificing in 1 Sam 2:13. It is furthermore consistent with narrative traditions elsewhere in the Bible that depict only men as killing sacrificial animals (for example, Gen 31:54, 46:1; Judg 6:19; 1 Sam 9:23–24)[88]—although the biblical writers certainly thought that women were capable of slaughtering bulls and similar animals in other contexts if the situation required it (1 Sam 28:24). In addition, to understand Elkanah alone as performing sacrificial slaughter in 1 Sam 1:25a is consistent with our evidence from elsewhere in the eastern Mediterranean and ancient Near East that treats sacrifice as a male prerogative.[89] It is consistent as well with the anthropological/sociological analysis famously put forward by Nancy Jay.[90] As Jay writes, "*around the world*" (emphasis mine), "ordinarily only adult males (fathers, real and metaphorical) may perform sacrifice," and while there are, to be sure, exceptions, the exceptions are quite particular in nature: "where women do so [i.e., perform sacrifice]," according to Jay, "it is as virgins or in some other specifically nonchildbearing role." Conversely, "women as childbearers or as potential childbearers"—that is, women who are precisely in the same position as Hannah in 1 Sam 1:25a—"are regularly prohibited from sacrificing."[91]

Yet despite Elkanah's exclusive role at the moment the sacrificial animal is slaughtered in the Greek and Dead Sea Scrolls renderings of 1 Sam 1:25a, Hannah is still said to stand alongside him as he kills the three-year-old bull, suggesting that even as the Greek and Dead Sea Scroll texts would have it, she is significantly engaged in this aspect of the sacrificial rite. This is intimated as well in 1 Sam 2:19, in which Hannah is described in the Masoretic, Dead Sea Scrolls, and Greek traditions as coming annually to Shiloh to, in the words of the Masoretic Text, "slaughter the annual sacrifice" (*lizbōaḥ 'et-zebaḥ hayyāmîm*). Granted, across the Masoretic, Dead Sea Scrolls, and Greek accounts of 1 Sam 2:19, Hannah is said to come with her husband to make this offering, and as in 1 Sam 1:4 and 1:25a, we should envision him as doing the actual killing. Still, in the Masoretic Text, the Dead Sea Scrolls materials, and the Greek, it is *Hannah* who is the subject of the verbs in 1 Sam 2:19, suggesting again that although she is not the agent who slaughters the sacrificial animal, all three textual witnesses understand her to be a significant participant in this component of the sacrificial rite.

In addition, it seems possible in both 1 Sam 1:25a and 2:19 to envision Hannah joining together with Elkanah after the sacrificial animal has been slaughtered to approach Yahweh's altar and dedicate the deity's assigned portion of the *šělāmîm* offering: the fat, the organ meat, and (if this is a part of Shilonite ritual) the blood. After all, as already noted, no priest seems present in 1:25 to assume responsibility for this altar service, and we have also already seen that 1 Sam 2:15–16 suggests the altar rites were performed by the same nonelites who slaughtered sacrificial animals and cooked their meat. Of course, this could well mean that Elkanah alone enacts the altar rituals, just as Elkanah alone killed the three-year-old bull. Nevertheless, it is plausible that the man Elkanah and the woman Hannah, having been jointly present for the slaughter, even though Elkanah wielded the knife, might also have been jointly present for the subsequent altar ritual, even though Elkanah took on the responsibility for dedicating the necessary offerings to God. Note in this regard Judg 13:23, where Manoah's wife says to her husband regarding the sacrifice of a kid and grain offered to the divine messenger who had appeared to them, "Yahweh . . . took an *'ōlâ* offering and a grain offering from *our* hands" (emphasis mine)—and this even though Judg 13:19 clearly states that *only Manoah* performed the actual dedicatory rites at a near-to-hand rock-cum-altar.[92] So too might Hannah be said to have joined with Elkanah to give God "our" offering at Shiloh's altar, even as only Elkanah enacted first the slaughter and then the rituals of altar service.

Moreover, it is Hannah alone who is said in both the Masoretic Text and the Greek of 1 Sam 1:24, as well as in the fragmentary Dead Sea Scrolls materials, to bring to Shiloh the bull, along with the flour and wine offerings that are represented as the norm for Yahwistic sacrifice elsewhere in biblical tradition (see, for example, in the P source, Exod 29:38–42, or, within the narrative accounts of the Deuteronomistic History, 1 Sam 10:3). Presumably, Hannah is to be envisioned as having brought the same, or similar offerings in other years as well. Of course, Hannah's family's annual food offerings can be delivered to Shiloh without her being present (given that after she had given birth to Samuel, she is said in 1 Sam 1:21–23 to have stayed home from the annual pilgrimage to Shiloh until she had weaned the boy, a period that may have lasted as long as three years).[93] Still, we should remember, as I discussed in Chapter 2, that what we know about Israelite household life, especially household life in rural environments such as the villages of the Ephraimite hill country that surrounded Shiloh, suggests that women would have had primary responsibility for the allocation of a family's food resources, including food resources that were to be allocated to some god or gods. Thus it makes perfect sense for Hannah in her role as a manager of her household's foodstuffs to take on the obligation for delivering her family's sacrificial offerings to Shiloh in 1 Sam 1:24. And in the years Hannah stayed home and was unable to fulfill her duty in this regard, Elkanah's other wife, Peninnah, may be envisioned as taking on this womanly task. Certainly, 1 Sam 1:21–22, which speaks of Elkanah and "all his household" minus Hannah going to Shiloh while Samuel was still nursing, suggests Peninnah would have made this trip and thus could have assumed the responsibility of conveying the foodstuffs for her family's offerings to the Shiloh shrine.

Hannah and Peninnah should also be envisioned as assuming the responsibility for manufacturing the ephah of flour that was a part of the offerings described in 1 Sam 1:24,[94] for, as I discussed also in Chapter 2, women within Israelite households not only took charge of the allocation of foodstuffs, both to their family members and to their families' gods, but also undertook the work that immediately preceded allocation: the tasks of food processing generally and the tasks associated with bread-making more specifically. More specifically still, as we again saw in Chapter 2, women assumed the task of grinding grain to make flour, such as the ephah of flour that Hannah brought to Shiloh. And what role might women have had in the production of the skin (or "vessel") of wine included in the dedicatory foodstuffs? Textual evidence from ancient Israel and iconographic evidence from ancient Egypt suggest men undertook responsibility for planting vineyards (Isa 5:1–2, but cf. Prov 31:16), pruning the vines (Lev 25:3, Isa 18:5, but cf. Cant 1:6), harvesting the grapes (Lev 25:5; Deut 24:21; Judg 9:27; Jer 6:9, 49:9; Obad 5), and treading them (Judg 9:27; Isa 16:10, 63:2; Amos 9:13).

Given the physical labor involved, men probably also "bottled" the fresh grape juice in the large jars used for fermentation (their capacity was about 37 liters), and it was probably men again who saw to these jars' storage in rock-cut cellars.[95] When the wine was to be drunk, however, women may have had a role, given their role as managers of their homes' foodstuffs. For example, it may have been women who decanted the finished product into the sort of smaller vessel or wineskin (*nēbel*) mentioned in 1 Sam 1:24.

Another task for which women assumed primary responsibility within Israelite households, we will recall from Chapter 1, was the production of textiles, and it is significant in this regard that in 1 Sam 2:19, Hannah is said to make for Samuel a "little robe" every year, which she delivers to him during her family's annual visit to Shiloh (Samuel by this point in the story having been given over to Yahweh's service and thus having taken up residence at the shrine at Shiloh to attend the deity there). Moreover, I would argue that, like the animal for sacrifice, the flour, and the wine that Hannah takes charge of bringing to Shiloh on her yearly journeys, this robe she makes annually for Samuel should be seen as dedicated for *religious* purposes.[96] Crucial to note here is 1 Sam 2:18 and its indication that Samuel is "rendering service before Yahweh" and wearing in this capacity a linen ephod, which we will remember yet again from Chapter 1 is a part of the priestly vestments. The robe Hannah brings to Shiloh for Samuel each year is, by implication, also a part of his priestly apparel and hence an item that she should be seen as offering in service of Shiloh's religious community.

In moving from the venue of household religion, which I discussed in Chapters 1 and 2, to consider ancient Israel's regional sanctuaries in this chapter, we have not surprisingly encountered several differences in terms of religious practice. Most obviously, we have encountered a difference in scale, as regional sanctuaries—especially regional sanctuaries such as Shiloh, which seem to have dedicated shrine buildings—are clearly larger and more complex sites of Yahwistic worship than household shrines, even household shrines that are distinct and dedicated worship spaces within a household compound (such as Room 65 at Ai). This issue of scale in turn affects another difference significant for our analysis, as regional sanctuaries' central ritual event—the offering of animal sacrifice—is alien within the more modest household context.

Still, within both household shrines and regional sanctuaries, the basic ritual imperative—"the care and feeding of the gods," to cite again A. Leo

Oppenheim's famous formulation—is ultimately the same,[97] and also surprisingly similar is the negligible role that members of Israel's priestly community play in that feeding and care, both in household and in regional sanctuary settings. Rather, it seems to be the "ordinary" members of Israelite families who undertake the "care and feeding" rituals that cater to a deity's well-being, whether at home or on a visit to a regional sanctuary. Because, moreover, feeding—or, more specifically, the processing of foodstuffs and the apportioning of that which has been processed—is primarily a female responsibility within Israelite tradition, it is women, whether in household shrines or at regional sanctuaries, who play a major role in processing foods for and apportioning food to the divine.

To be sure, in both household shrines and regional sanctuaries, men can take possession of that which women process, in order, for example, to make grain offerings (Judg 13:19) or even to make their own bread cakes (Judg 6:19). Even when women are identified as having delivered an animal for sacrifice (as in 1 Sam 1:24), men also seem to take on the responsibility of performing the actual slaughter of that animal within regional sanctuaries and enacting the subsequent dedication rites at Yahweh's altar. Because, moreover, the slaughter of a sacrificial animal and the dedication of its fat, its organ meat, and (according to certain dicta) its blood are the central rituals of regional shrines, men can become foregrounded as regional shrines' primary ritual agents, as they also seem foregrounded in the primary rituals that follow an animal's slaughter and the subsequent altar rites, the cooking and the apportioning of the slaughtered animal's meat during the postsacrificial meal. Indeed, if 1 Sam 1:4–5 is any guide, the male head of household assumes the otherwise female roles of cooking the meat of the *šĕlāmîm* sacrifice and apportioning it to other family members.

In these ways, male agency does stand more to the fore in regional sanctuary locations than within household cult. Nevertheless, I hope I have demonstrated in this chapter that 1 Sam 1:1–2:26 suggests multiple ways in which Israelite women still functioned as significant ritual actors within regional shrines. In Chapter 4, I consider further women's experiences within regional sanctuaries.

4 "She Prayed to Yahweh, She Wept . . . and She Made a Vow": Women and Ancient Israel's Regional Sanctuaries, II

In the previous chapter, I discussed—among other things—the various religious offerings that Hannah takes responsibility for bringing to the regional sanctuary at Shiloh: the three-year-old bull,[1] the ephah of flour, and the skin (or vessel) of wine listed in 1 Sam 1:24 and the vestments for her priest-son Samuel described in 1 Sam 2:19. The greatest gift that Hannah offers to the religious community at Shiloh, however, is Samuel himself. In this chapter, I consider the passages in 1 Sam 1:1–2:26 that concern this dedication: first, the ritual acts in which Hannah engages in order to overcome her barrenness so that she might give birth; then, the events that surround the actual handing over of her son to Yahweh's service. The crucial texts I examine are 1 Sam 1:9–18 and 25–28.

Hannah's Ritual Acts Soliciting Yahweh for a Son

First Samuel 1:9–18 immediately follows the description of the annual sacrificial meals I discussed in Chapter 3, of which Elkanah's two wives, Hannah and Peninnah, seem invited to partake as equals or near-equals of their husband (1 Sam 1:4–5). According to 1 Sam 1:7, though, Hannah refuses to share in these yearly meals. This is because, as interpreters typically have it, she was grieved because she was childless and/or because Elkanah's other wife, Peninnah, who had children, provoked Hannah on account of her barrenness.[2]

Note, however, that the ancient Greek rendering of the Hannah story (the LXX) does not include the tradition of Peninnah provoking Hannah; rather, according to the Greek, Hannah "was in depression" solely because of her barrenness. The Greek and the Hebrew text as it has come down to us (the so-called Masoretic Text) also differ in their descriptions of what happens during the particular year in which 1 Sam 1:9–18 is set. The Greek account begins the story, in 1 Sam 1:9, by describing how Hannah leaves her family after "they" (the family) had eaten their ritual meal, "to present herself," still according to the Greek text, "before the Lord." The Masoretic version reads only that "Hannah arose" (but to go where?), seemingly "after she [as opposed to "they"] had eaten" and after she had also drunk.[3] However, the Masoretic Text's grammar here is unclear, as the form *ʾoklâ,* most commonly taken as an infinitive construct of the verb *ʾākal,* "to eat," plus a third-person feminine singular suffix, is missing the *mappîq* mark that would make it certain that a third-person feminine singular suffix, and so a reference to "her [Hannah's] eating," is truly intended.[4] What's more, the form *šātô* is an infinitive absolute of the verb *šātâ,* "to drink," rather than a conjugated form that would definitively indicate whether Hannah is the intended subject.

The Masoretic Text's logic also seems confused, as we have already seen that according to v. 7, Hannah routinely refused to join in her family's annual sacrificial feast. Thus it is a bit of a problem to explain why the Masoretic account would describe her as having eaten and drunk in v. 9. To be sure, one could perhaps suggest—although I would not (more on this below)—that in the year in which 1 Sam 1:9–18 is set, Hannah had been persuaded to eat in v. 9 as a result of Elkanah's attempts to comfort her in v. 8. But those who adopt this explanation must immediately confront another logical problem, for why does Hannah eat in v. 18, presumably because she has been encouraged by the priest Eli's oracular pronouncement in v. 17 that her barrenness will be ended (more on this also below), if she had already eaten a short time before, in v. 9? Moreover, in v. 15, when queried, Hannah forcefully denies that she has been drinking, meaning either that she lies in that verse or that the notice in v. 9 regarding her drinking does not actually belong in the text. Almost all commentators assume that the latter explanation is correct—that the reference to Hannah's drinking in v. 9 should be deleted—given Hannah's claims of abstinence in v. 15 and given that the Masoretic Text's description of drinking is not found in the Greek rendering of 1 Sam 1:9.[5] I also would prefer to follow the more logically consistent Greek text in assuming that those who ate according to v. 9 were the "they" of Hannah's family, but not Hannah herself, who rather abstains from eating from (at least) the time she forgoes joining her family for their sacrificial meal (as in 1 Sam 1:7) until the time she eats in v. 18, after the priest Eli declares in God's name that her barrenness is to be ended.[6] Which is to say: despite the ancient Israelite assumption that participants in a sacrificial ritual *must* partake of the attendant feast, Hannah, as the Greek text would have it, fasts.

The Greek text of v. 9 is also surely right to suggest that Hannah presented herself "before the Lord" after leaving her family's repast (by which the text means that Hannah presented herself at or near the entrance to Yahweh's sanctuary at Shiloh). Indeed, although the Masoretic tradition lacks any notice of where Hannah went after she "arose," the same destination as found in the Greek is undoubtedly meant, as the next verses in both the Masoretic and Greek accounts are set at the Shiloh temple (clearly envisioned in this episode as a building, not a tent). There, Eli the priest is said to be sitting at the shrine's doorpost(s),[7] as Hannah, seemingly oblivious to his presence, prays and makes a vow. This is a ritual action whereby the individual in question promises to give to a deity some gift or service in exchange for that deity's providing the boon or favor for which the petitioner has asked.[8] In this case, Hannah promises (according to the Masoretic Text) that if Yahweh will give her a son, she will "give him to Yahweh all the days of his life" and "no razor shall touch his head" (v. 11).

Elsewhere in the Hebrew Bible, the second part of this promise—that the hoped-for son's hair will remain uncut all his life—is a component of the commitment undertaken by individuals known as Nazirites as part of their special dedication to God (the most famous example is the story of the long-haired Samson found in Judges 13–16; see also Num 6:5). Indeed, the rendering of 1 Sam 1:11 found in the ancient Greek Codex Vaticanus makes the Nazirite connection explicit, quoting Hannah as saying to Yahweh, "I will set him before you *as a Nazirite* until the day of his death" (emphasis mine). In this Greek account, Hannah promises as well that the child will drink neither wine nor other strong drink, which, as indicated explicitly in Num 6:3 and implicitly in Judg 13:4, 7, and 14, is another requirement incumbent on Nazirites.[9] In his Anchor Yale Bible commentary on 1 Samuel, P. Kyle McCarter theorizes that although fragmentary at this point, the Samuel text known as 4QSam[a], from the Dead Sea Scrolls, also included a notice that Hannah promised her son's abstinence.[10]

I take this all to be of great significance for our study. Of initial note is the fact that Hannah is said to pray to Yahweh (*wattitpallēl*) after she comes to the deity's sanctuary building in 1 Sam 1:10 and to continue praying in

1:12. She then alludes back to this prayer in 1 Sam 1:26–27, and in 1 Sam 2:1, she is said to pray again. Rather astonishingly, these are the *only times* in the entire Hebrew Bible that the common verb "to pray," *hitpallēl,* is used of a woman. Furthermore, the other verb most commonly associated with prayer in the Bible—*ʿātar,* "to make an entreaty, plead, supplicate"—is never used of a woman.[11] To be sure, scholars have sought to identify biblical women other than Hannah who pray.[12] For example, Marc Zvi Brettler has argued that Ps 113:4–9 so closely parallels the text of Hannah's prayer in 1 Sam 2:1–10 that it must be understood, like Hannah's utterance, as a newly delivered mother's "prayer of thanksgiving."[13] Rebekah's "inquiring" of Yahweh—*dāraš*—in Gen 25:22 and Micah's mother's curse in Judg 17:2 have also been interpreted as prayers.[14] In none of these instances, though, is the woman explicitly identified as praying.[15] In addition, while the prayer addressed to Yahweh in Psalm 131 may be uttered by a woman, this is not necessarily clear.[16] Psalm 113:4–9, moreover, dates from the postexilic period rather than the preexilic period that is this book's focus.[17]

Yet however sui generis Hannah's prayers may be, the author(s) and/or redactor(s) of 1 Sam 1:1–2:26 do nothing to indicate that female prayer is anything out of the ordinary. Even the priest Eli, who chides Hannah in 1 Sam 1:14, rebukes her only for praying in what was regarded in the ancient world as a curious manner—silently, but with her lips moving—rather than for the act of praying itself.[18] This suggests that it was fully the norm for Israelite women to pray as part of their religious devotions, including their ritual devotions at regional sanctuaries, and that it is simply a coincidence (albeit one that reveals the characteristically male focus of the biblical text) that Hannah is the only woman in the Hebrew Bible who is specifically identified as doing so.[19]

Indeed, women's prayers are relatively well attested elsewhere in the eastern Mediterranean and Near Eastern world—in late third- and second-millennium BCE Mesopotamian, Hittite, and Egyptian iconographic and textual sources and in first-millennium BCE Punic and Neo-Punic inscriptions.[20] Later biblical tradition, moreover, treats female prayer as a given, as can be seen in both apocryphal/deuterocanonical and New Testament texts. The heroine Judith prays to God at several points in the second-century BCE apocryphal/deuterocanonical book that bears her name before she undertakes to kill her people's enemy, the Assyrian general Holofernes (Jdt 9:2–14; 12:5–6, 8; 13:4–7). Likewise, Esther prays in the so-called Greek Additions to Esther (second or first century BCE) found in the LXX version of that book (Esth 14:1–19), and in Theodotion's version of the story of Susannah (a text from the second century CE, although it depends on earlier traditions, probably from the second century BCE), Susannah cries out to God to deliver her from execution after she has been unjustly found guilty of sexual impropriety (Susannah 42–43).[21] So, too, in the fourth- or third-century BCE apocryphal/deuterocanonical book of Tobit, Sarah, the future wife of Tobit's son Tobias, prays to God that she might die rather than face the reproach to which she has been subject, which is the result of circumstances beyond her control (Tob 3:10– 11). She is then exhorted to pray again in 6:18 and 8:4, and in 8:5, she does in fact pray as she has been urged.[22] New Testament references to women's prayer include Acts 1:14, where the eleven disciples who remain after Jesus's death are said to be constantly devoting themselves to prayer, along with "certain women," including Jesus's mother, Mary. Also note 1 Cor 11:13, in which, although women are forbidden to pray with their heads uncovered, no other strictures on women's ability or right to pray are presumed.

Hannah is furthermore described as making a vow to Yahweh in 1 Sam 1:11 (*wattiddōr neder*), one of only three times in the Hebrew Bible that an individual woman is identified as making such a pledge (the others are cited in Prov 7:14 and 31:2).[23] Certain issues regarding women's vows are, however, the subject of legal materials found in Num 6:2 and Num 30:4–16 (in most of the Bible's English versions, 30:3–15; to be discussed more thoroughly below).[24] Legal issues regarding vows made by women prostitutes are also addressed in Deut 23:19 (English 23:18).[25] Vows made by women (along with their husbands) are in addition described in Jer 44:15–19, 25, where, as we saw in Chapter 2, the women among the assembly of fugitives that Jeremiah harangues in Egypt are said to have "vowed" to burn incense to the Queen of Heaven and to pour out libations to her. Yet even though Jeremiah objects to the deity to whom these women's vows were directed, he does not indicate that the practice of women making vows is in any way exceptional. Nor do any of the Bible's other accounts of women's vows indicate this. This suggests, as I argued above concerning Hannah's prayer, that Hannah's making of a vow, despite this act's relative distinctiveness in the annals of biblical tradition, was a perfectly acceptable and even expected aspect of Israelite women's piety.[26]

In fact, like women's prayers, women's vows are relatively well attested elsewhere in Near Eastern sources. In his book *Vows in the Hebrew Bible and the Ancient Near East,* Tony W. Cartledge cites Mesopotamian examples that come from as early as the Neo-Sumerian period (ca. 2100–2000 BCE): for instance, a vow made by a woman, Inannakam, that she will render temple service to the goddess Nintinugga, as well as bestow on her public praise, if Nintinugga delivers Inannakam from the Azag-demon that is said to afflict her.[27] Cartledge also notes the many vows of Queen Puduhepa, wife of King Hattusili III (r. 1264–1239 BCE), that are attested in Hittite tradition, most promising gifts that the queen will give to various deities in exchange for their guarantee of Hattusili's good health.[28] Inannakam's and Puduhepa's vows, moreover, are, like Hannah's, coupled with prayer.[29] Evidence for women's vows—again coupled, in at least two instances, with prayer—also comes from first-millennium BCE Phoenician, Punic, and Neo-Punic tradition.[30] For example, a short Punic text records how the woman 'KBRT made a sacrifice to the god Baal-Ḥamon in payment for a vow she had made.[31]

Thus, in making a vow to dedicate her son to a life of Nazirite service, Hannah is depicted as following upon a path otherwise well trodden by female supplicants. Of further note is that Hannah may herself assume the Nazirite obligations entailed by her vow regarding her unborn son. Or, more specifically, Hannah might be understood as assuming the dietary obligations incumbent upon a Nazirite, at least temporarily. This is suggested at two points in 1 Sam 1:9–18: first, in 1 Sam 1:12–15, when the priest Eli, as he watches Hannah pray silently, yet with her mouth moving, assumes Hannah is drunk and chides her to put away her wine (*yayin*). This accusation Hannah vigorously denies, insisting (consistent with my interpretation of 1 Sam 1:9) that she has consumed neither wine nor strong drink (*yayin wĕšēkār*). Note Eli's and Hannah's precise words here, as it is significant that Hannah takes Eli's censure regarding the drinking of wine and elaborates upon it by using the exact phrase to describe the intoxicants from which she abstains, *yayin wĕšēkār,* that, as discussed above, is used elsewhere in the Bible (Num 6:3; Judg 13:4, 7, and 14) and in the Greek text of 1 Sam 1:11 to describe the nature of the abstinence required of Nazirites. That is, as the Nazirites refrain from drinking wine and strong drink (*yayin wĕšēkār*), so too does Hannah claim to have refrained. Furthermore, in 1 Sam 1:18, once Hannah, who has been reassured by Eli, leaves off from her vigil of prayer, she eats (which, as I interpret 1 Sam 1:7 and 9, she had refused to do previously; see again my discussion above), and, according to the Greek version of 1 Samuel, she drinks. But there is no mention of her drinking in v. 18 of the Masoretic Text, and McCarter argues that this is the original reading (the Greek represents a secondary expansion).[32] It becomes tempting, then, to propose that Hannah is *not* described as drinking in conjunction with her eating in 1 Sam 1:18 because, as in v. 15, she imposes upon herself, at least temporarily, the abstinence from alcoholic beverages that will someday be required of her Nazirite son.

To be sure, to make an argument based on the silence of the Masoretic Text in 1:18 is precarious, not only because arguments from silence are always precarious, but also because as we have now repeatedly seen, the Masoretic Text of 1 Sam 1:1–2:26 can be so unreliable. Yet evidence from elsewhere in the Hebrew Bible supports my interpretation. First, we can note that according to the terms of Nazirite service as articulated in Num 6:1–21, women can dedicate themselves as Nazirites (Num 6:2): there is thus nothing that would prevent Hannah from taking on the Nazirite obligation of abstinence in 1 Samuel 1.[33] Also according to this Numbers text, Nazirite service can be temporary (Samuel's lifelong dedication as a Nazirite notwithstanding), just as I have suggested Hannah's avoiding *yayin wĕšēkār* may be temporary, lasting, say, through the course of her pregnancy or perhaps until the time Samuel is weaned (as Cynthia R. Chapman has provocatively argued).[34]

That said, Num 6:1–21 comes from a different ideological tradition (the P, or Priestly source) than does 1 Sam 1:1–2:26, and so this text alone cannot drive our interpretation of the Hannah story. More significant is the tale of Samson's mother recounted elsewhere in the Deuteronomistic History, in Judges 13. As that narrative begins, we learn that Samson's mother, like Hannah, is barren (Judg 13:2). In Judg 13:3–5, however, a messenger from Yahweh appears and promises her that she will bear a son. She is also told that this son will be consecrated as a Nazirite, and that, like Hannah's son Samuel, "no razor shall touch his head." The messenger in addition articulates the requirement to abstain from wine and strong drink (*yayin wĕšēkār*) that according to Num 6:3 is imposed upon Nazirites. But in the Judges 13 text, this need to abstain is *not* set forth as something that will eventually be asked of the Nazirite Samson. Rather, it is something demanded of his mother (Judg 13:4, 7, and 14), presumably throughout her pregnancy or perhaps, again, until Samson has been weaned.[35] Likewise, I would argue, the Nazirite obligation to abstain from wine and strong drink (*yayin wĕšēkār*) is assumed by Hannah in 1 Samuel 1 as she seeks to bear her Nazirite son. Thus, she truthfully denies having drunk intoxicating beverages in 1 Sam 1:15 (assuming, as I have argued, there is no reference to her drinking in

1 Sam 1:9), and, presuming the Masoretic Text's silence is significant, eats without drinking in 1:18 when she breaks her fast after praying and making her vow before Yahweh at the sanctuary of Shiloh.

Let me consider in greater detail, moreover, Hannah's fast and her breaking of it, especially the notice in 1 Sam 1:7 that typically when the sacrificial meal was served at Shiloh, Hannah "wept and did not eat" and the concomitant indication in 1:9, at least as I interpret, that in the particular year in which 1 Sam 1:9–18 is set, Hannah did not join her family for their ritual feast. As already noted, commentators overwhelmingly take Hannah's fasting in 1 Sam 1:7 and 9, along with her weeping in 1 Sam 1:7 (and also vv. 8 and 10), as *emotional responses* to her barrenness and/or to Peninnah's words of torment that Hannah has had to endure. Regarding Hannah's fast, for example, Adele Berlin writes, "not eating is a common *sign of depression* in the Bible."[36] Regarding her tears, Mayer I. Gruber lists 1 Sam 1:7, 8, and 10 as three among "twenty instances [in the Bible] where crying or weeping [is] an expression of *sadness or depression.*"[37] In a 2014 article about the Hannah story, Rodney A. Werline similarly comments about both fasting and weeping, "This [Peninnah's provoking Hannah about her barrenness] caused *great hurt to Hannah,* to the point that she would weep and not eat" (emphases in all cases mine).[38]

I agree that Hannah is portrayed in 1 Sam 1:9–18 and the related vv. 7–8 as emotionally on edge (indeed, in 1:16, she describes herself to Eli as "anxious" [*śîaḥ*] and "vexed" [*ka'as*]).[39] Nevertheless, we must acknowledge that frequently in the ancient Near East and eastern Mediterranean, weeping and fasting were undertaken as *ritual acts,* deliberately engaged in by petitioners who seek to receive some sort of divine oracle from a god.[40] Concerning weeping, note the Hittite version of the legend of the Mesopotamian king Naram-Sin, which dates to the fifteenth century BCE. In it, Naram-Sin is said to have sought a divine revelation during a military emergency by "cry[ing] out" and "wail[ing] to his gods"; he then received an oracle as he slept on a "sacred" or a "purified bed."[41] Elsewhere in the Near East and eastern Mediterranean, oracles induced by weeping can likewise be revealed in dreams.[42] For instance, an inscription of King Ashurbanipal of Assyria (r. 669–627 BCE) describes how Ashurbanipal came to the sanctuary of Ishtar of Arbela in a time of war to pray and weep at the feet of the cult statue of the goddess, who later that night responded by appearing in a dream to one of Ashurbanipal's priests.[43]

Weeping also seems to invoke a dream theophany in the Canaanite legend of King Kirta, part of a fourteenth-/thirteenth-century BCE textual archive from the northern Levantine city-state of Ugarit (see Fig. I.2). As that story begins, we find Kirta facing a desperate situation: he has lost his wife (to death? because she has deserted him?), and his many children have likewise perished because of various calamities (for example, plague and drowning at sea). Left without an heir and royal successor, Kirta weeps, and, as in the stories of Naram-Sin and Ashurbanipal, crying induces a god to appear (*KTU* 1.14.1.31–32, 35–37):[44]

> And as he wept he fell asleep,
> as he cried, he slumbered . . .
> and in his dream [the god] El came down,
> in his vision the Father of Men [an epithet of El].

Upon ascertaining the cause of Kirta's tears, El responds with detailed instructions on how Kirta is to procure a wife and eventually a son, just as the gods of Naram-Sin and Ashurbanipal responded to those kings' petitions. However, in Kirta's case, the dream revelation takes place in his own bedchamber, rather than in a specially sanctified bed (Naram-Sin) or in sanctuary space (Ashurbanipal).[45]

As we turn to the Bible, we find that the specifics there can also vary, even as the general principle of weeping as a means of invoking some kind of divine response is well attested.[46] For example, in Ps 6:7 (in most of the Bible's English versions, 6:6), the anonymous psalmist, much like Kirta, speaks of drenching his bed with tears every night in the hopes that God will respond, although the psalmist's specific hope—that God will deliver him from the enemies and illness that he faces (vv. 3 and 11 [English vv. 2 and 10])—are different from Kirta's.[47] Also different is the fact that no dream is mentioned. Indeed, although the psalmist does make clear that Yahweh did somehow react to his weeping and relieve him from his woes (vv. 9–11 [English vv. 8–10]), he does not report receiving a direct visitation or revelation from God.[48] Conversely, in Ps 42:3–4 (in most of the Bible's English versions, 42:2–3), the weeping psalmist does aspire to see the face of God (i.e., to receive a divine revelation). However, this psalmist sheds tears "day and night" in supplicating the deity, instead of engaging in a ritual of only nighttime weeping that would presumably provoke a visit from Yahweh in a dream.

Daytime is also the setting of Judg 20:23, a text in which the Israelite army is described as weeping "until the evening" as they sought an oracle from Yahweh about whether to continue their civil war against the renegade tribe of Benjamin. Judges 20:23 is in addition noteworthy because the

Israelites' weeping is said to take place "before Yahweh," meaning, presumably, within the sanctuary precinct of Bethel that, according to Judg 20:18 and 26–28, was the site of the army's previous and subsequent attempts to solicit a divine oracle regarding the civil war. Judges 20:18, 23, and 26–28 state as well that the Israelites' aim at Bethel was to "inquire" (*šā'al*) of Yahweh, vocabulary that is significant because *šā'al* can be used in the Bible as a technical term that refers to the soliciting of cultic oracles.[49] Similarly, in Jer 50:4, the "people of Israel" and the "people of Judah" are described as "weeping" as they "seek" (*biqqēš*) Yahweh, with *biqqēš,* like *šā'al,* functioning as a technical term that indicates God is specifically being asked to deliver an oracular revelation.[50]

Judges 20:26–28, moreover, indicates that the Israelites fasted along with weeping as they sought an oracle from God at Bethel, for fasting, like weeping, is a ritual behavior that can help induce a divine oracle.[51] As with weeping, the oracle can be revealed in a dream—for example, in 1 Kgs 3:4–15 (2 Chr 1:1–13). This is the story of how King Solomon went to the *bāmâ* sanctuary at Gibeon to sacrifice; then, when Yahweh subsequently appeared to him in a dream, Solomon requested and received a grant of wisdom. Notably for my purposes, Solomon, according to 2 Chr 1:5, deliberately sought (*dāraš*) this dream, with *dāraš,* like *biqqēš* and *šā'al,* functioning as a technical term used in the Bible to refer to the soliciting of cultic oracles.[52] Equally notable is the fact that Solomon's sacrifices before he slept and dreamt are explicitly described as *'ôlâ* offerings, offerings, that is, that were burned in their entirety to the deity and thus (unlike the *šělāmîm* offerings I discussed in Chapter 3) were not partaken of by the sacrificer in a ritual meal after the offering had been made. Solomon, that is to say, *fasted* before lying down to sleep in a sacred place (Gibeon's *bāmâ* sanctuary) with the explicit goal (at least according to the Chronicles text) of seeking Yahweh in a dream.

But as in Judg 20:26–28, fasting can induce divine oracles that are delivered by means other than dreams—for example, in 2 Chr 20:3–4. There, King Jehoshaphat of Judah (r. 870–848 BCE) finds himself threatened by a coalition of the Moabite, Ammonite, and Edomite armies. In response, Jehoshaphat proclaims a fast throughout all of Judah as he sets himself and his countrymen to "seek" (*dāraš,* v. 3; *biqqēš,* v. 4 [twice]) Yahweh. Jehoshaphat is then said, in vv. 5–12, to come with his people to the Jerusalem temple, where the king offers up a long prayer petitioning Yahweh for help. In this prayer, Jehoshaphat mentions that throughout its history, the temple has been a place where the Israelites have come to "cry out" (*zāʿaq*) to God and seek a divine response. And, indeed, in vv. 14–17, such a response is given, as the "spirit of Yahweh" is said to come on a Levite named Jahaziel, who utters an oracle promising that God will deliver Jehoshaphat and the Judahites from the military threat they are facing.

Multiple elements of the ritual complex I have been exploring come together in this passage: fasting, an allusion to weeping (through reference to previous occasions of "crying out"), a sanctuary setting, vocabulary indicating a deliberate attempt to solicit an oracle (*dāraš, biqqēš*), and that oracle's delivery. Many of these same elements also come together in 2 Sam 12:15–23, which describes how King David sought (*biqqēš*) God in an attempt to save the life of his first child by Bathsheba. The use of the term *biqqēš* is yet again noteworthy; equally of note is the fact that, according to v. 16, David fasted before seeking Yahweh. According to 2 Sam 12:21, David may too have wept as well as fasted in order to solicit an oracle.[53] In this verse, which is set after Bathsheba's ailing child had died (meaning that David's attempts to induce a divine oracle and receive a favorable response to his petition had failed), David's servants describe the behaviors in which the king had earlier engaged by saying "you fasted and wept" (*ṣamtā wattēbk*). Also, according to v. 16, David, after preparing himself through the rituals of fasting (and weeping?) to seek Yahweh, "went in, lay down, and spent the night" (*ûbāʾ wělān wěšākab*). Where, exactly, David went "into" to spend the night is unspecified in the text, but since he is said to have lain "on the ground," it was surely not his regular sleeping chamber (which typically would have been located in his dwelling place's upper story).[54] Rather, I suggest that as in Judg 20:18, 23, 26–28; 1 Kgs 3:4–15 (2 Chr 1:1–13); 2 Chr 20:1–17; and the Mesopotamian and Hittite examples cited above, some kind of special or even sacred precinct is indicated.[55] There, David slept with the intent to induce a divine visitation in a dream. Indeed, in several Canaanite and biblical texts, the verbs that describe David's repose in 2 Sam 12:16, *lûn* and *šākab,* are explicitly used, either alone or in conjunction, to denote an attempt to induce a dream visitation.[56]

Many parallels to the Hannah story suggest themselves here. To be sure, Hannah, unlike David, did not seek a divine visitation in a dream,[57] and while David sought to save the life of a child that had already been born, Hannah sought to end her barrenness and give birth. Still, both David and Hannah (as I interpret 1 Sam 1:7 and 9) fast; both David (arguably) and Hannah weep; both David and Hannah, having fasted and wept, go to some special precinct, one that is surely, in Hannah's case, sacred (the temple at Shiloh) and one that, in David's case, may well be. David's avowed intent in undertaking all these actions is to solicit (*biqqēš*) a divine oracle concerning a child. I propose this is Hannah's goal as well.

Indeed, at several points in 1 Sam 1:1–2:26 Hannah is said to have "asked" (*šā'al*) Yahweh for her son (1 Sam 1:17, 20, 27 [twice]; note also 1:28 [twice] and 2:20, where the verb *šā'al* occurs in the Hiphil conjugation, with the meaning "to dedicate").[58] Hebrew *šā'al,* however, although it can be used, as noted above, to refer to soliciting cultic oracles, need not mean this, and at least part of the word's significance in 1 Samuel 1 is not due to a reference to oracular solicitation but due to a now obscured wordplay having to do with the naming of Hannah's child.[59] Still, given all the other indications I have located in 1 Samuel 1 which suggest that Hannah deliberately sought to solicit a divine oracle at Shiloh, it is tempting—in fact, more than tempting—to propose that the text's repeated use of *šā'al* to describe Hannah's petitioning God for her child is meant to indicate that Hannah, through her fasting and weeping in a sacred space, *intended* to induce an oracle promising her the son she so earnestly desired. Hannah, moreover, is fortunate enough to receive her hoped-for oracle, mediated through Eli once Hannah explains to the priest that her behavior that had originally so concerned him—when her mouth moved but no sound came forth—was not because of drunkenness but was an act of fervent although silent prayer. More specifically: while many translations—including some ancient sources (the fourth-century CE Latin Vulgate)—render Eli's response to Hannah's explanation regarding her prayer as a wish ("May the God of Israel grant your request"), it is grammatically just as possible, and given the evidence cited here much more probable, to read his utterance as a divine promise.[60] "Go in peace," Eli says, "and the God of Israel will grant (*yittēn*) the request that you have asked (*šā'alt*) of him" (1 Sam 1:17).[61] In fact, the promise to which Eli (in my interpretation) gives voice in 1 Sam 1:17 is virtually the same as God's promise to Solomon when Solomon petitions the deity for wisdom in 1 Kgs 3:5 (2 Chr 1:7): "Ask (*šĕ'al*) for that which I should grant (*'etten*) to you."

All of which is to say: while Hannah's acts of fasting and weeping before she approaches the Shiloh temple to pray have typically been taken as the emotional responses of a distraught woman in a difficult situation, there are good reasons for understanding them instead as ritual actions that Hannah deliberately undertakes within a sacred precinct in an attempt to induce a divine oracle. In fact, understanding them as ritual acts helps address a nagging question raised by Yairah Amit and by certain other commentators: Why does Hannah, who according to 1 Sam 1:7 routinely fasts and weeps during her family's annual visits to Shiloh, not leave off her fasting and weeping after being consoled by the words of comfort that Elkanah speaks in v. 8?[62] Here, I have suggested it is because Hannah's weeping and fasting are more ritual acts than they are expressions of grief, and as ritual acts they are *not* satisfactorily answered by her husband's words of consolation. Rather, their desired response lies in the divine oracle they seek to solicit, and this is why Hannah does not eat and leave off crying until v. 18, after the priest Eli delivers Yahweh's promise in v. 17 that her petition for a child will be answered.[63] Her ritual acts of fasting and weeping must be rejoined by the ritual response of Eli's oracle—as opposed to Elkanah's consoling words—before she will desist from them.

We have already seen in 1 Sam 1:9–18 many aspects of Hannah's role as a ritual agent: she prays (the only woman in the Hebrew Bible explicitly identified as doing so), she makes a vow (one of only three specific women said to do this in the Bible), and she arguably dedicates herself to following the Nazirites' dietary obligations for the duration of her hoped-for pregnancy and perhaps even for the duration of the breastfeeding period that follows. Now we can add that she engages in a specific sequence of ritual actions—fasting, weeping, and approaching a sacred space—all in an attempt to solicit a divine oracle. This is an extraordinary collocation of female religious behavior.

The Dedication of Samuel to a Life of Divine Service

However extraordinary the collocation of religious behaviors undertaken by Hannah that I have just described—her prayer, her making of a vow, her taking on, at least temporarily, the dietary obligations of a Nazirite, and her fasting and weeping within a sacred precinct in order to solicit a divine oracle—there are yet more matters concerning Hannah's ritual actions that we must consider. First is a locution used by the Greek text in 1 Sam 1:9 that I have briefly mentioned already: that when Hannah leaves her family to approach the temple at Shiloh, she is said to present herself *enōpion kyriou,* "before the Lord." Likewise, according to both the Greek text and the Masoretic Text, plus the 4QSam[a] manuscript from the Dead Sea Scrolls, Hannah is said to pray *enōpion kyriou,* "before the Lord," or *lipnê yhwh,* "before Yahweh," in 1 Sam 1:12 and to have been pouring out her heart "before the Lord" (*enōpion kyriou*) or "before Yahweh" (*lipnê yhwh*) in 1:15. Hannah similarly should be understood as part of the "they" of Elkanah's family who worshipped "before Yahweh" (*lipnê yhwh*) according to the Masoretic Text of 1 Sam 1:19, and in 1 Sam 1:25, according to the Greek and the Dead Sea Scrolls tradition, Hannah was with Elkanah and Samuel "before the Lord" (*enōpion kyriou*) or "before Yahweh" (*lipnê yhwh*) at the time of Samuel's being given over to Yahweh's service (see Table 3.1). The Greek text in addition describes Hannah as being "before the Lord" (*enōpion kyriou*) in 1 Sam 2:11.[64]

Several points here are worthy of note. Most significantly: Hannah's presence "before the Lord" or "before Yahweh" at multiple points in 1 Sam 1:1–2:26 is analogous to her uttering prayers in 1:10, 12, and 2:1 and to her making a vow in 1:11, in that being "before the Lord" or "before Yahweh" is a fairly distinctive position for a woman to occupy according to biblical tradition. Indeed, we will see in Chapter 6 that in P texts found in Leviticus—the book in the Bible where we find by far and away the greatest concentration of the phrase "before Yahweh" (about 58 of 230 total citations)—women are resolutely excluded from a position "before Yahweh."[65] Elsewhere within the P corpus, moreover, a woman is described as being "before Yahweh" only once, and only when brought there forcibly—by a husband possessed of a "spirit of jealousy" (Num 5:30) who wishes to put his wife on trial "before Yahweh" (Num 5:16, 18, 30) for adultery.[66] Conversely, Deuteronomic law in Deut 12:12 and 18 does include women—a household's daughters and female slaves—among those who should rejoice *lipnê yhwh,* "before Yahweh," on occasions of sacrificial feasting. Deuteronomy 16:11 adds that widows should join with these daughters and female slaves to rejoice *lipnê yhwh* at the annual pilgrimage feasts of Shavu'ot ("Weeks"), and Deut 31:10–13 includes all Israel's women among the congregation that is supposed to come *lipnê yhwh* every seven years, at the time of the annual Ingathering festival, or Sukkot.

The Hannah story's use of the phrases *enōpion kyriou* and *lipnê yhwh* to describe a woman's ability to come "before the Lord" or "before Yahweh," and without censure, thus appears to be a motif that, although not unique, is only occasionally paralleled in biblical tradition—and thus one worthy of examination and, if possible, explanation. Given the data concerning *lipnê yhwh* I have just catalogued, moreover, a seemingly obvious explanation is at hand. To wit: despite the fact that, as discussed in Chapter 3, 1 Sam 1:1–

2:26 both predates the Deuteronomistic History and differs significantly from Deuteronomistic ideology regarding certain key issues, the Hannah story nevertheless shares the assumption of the book of Deuteronomy that women can come *lipnê yhwh,* or "before Yahweh," whereas texts that stem from the Bible's P source reject this possibility.

That said, there is a superabundance of the phrase *enōpion kyriou*/*lipnê yhwh* in the Hannah story (up to six occurrences across the Masoretic, Dead Sea Scrolls, and Greek traditions), whereas there are *no* references to a woman *lipnê yhwh,* "before Yahweh," among the other forty-four instances of *lipnê yhwh* that appear in the six books of the Deuteronomistic History. What's more, the references in the book of Deuteronomy to women *lipnê yhwh* concern women in general, not a specific woman. Again, that is, there is something "above and beyond" about Hannah, for just as Hannah is the only woman described as praying in the Hebrew Bible, and just as she is one of only three specific females who are said to make vows, so too is she the only woman to come *lipnê yhwh* who is identified by name or otherwise individuated within Deuteronomy or the Deuteronomistic History. She is also the only individual woman lauded for coming "before Yahweh" within the entire biblical corpus (recall that the woman who comes "before Yahweh" in Num 5:16, 18, and 30 does so to be put on trial).

Hannah, too, is depicted as freely interacting with the priest Eli on the various occasions when she comes to Shiloh's temple. As we have seen, Hannah and Eli readily engage in a conversation—albeit, a confrontational one—about her behavior during prayer in 1 Sam 1:14–16; then in 1 Sam 1:17–18, they continue to speak, now in a more conciliatory manner, as Eli delivers the oracle promising that Yahweh will give Hannah the son for whom she has asked. Equally striking is the subsequent account in 1 Sam 1:25–28, of Hannah fulfilling the vow that she had made in 1 Sam 1:11 by giving the newly weaned Samuel over to Eli and thus over to Yahweh's service. In particular, the Greek and Dead Sea Scroll renderings of this account are striking; the Masoretic version, as it is elsewhere, is less emphatic regarding Hannah's cultic actions.[67] Thus, in the Masoretic Text, as v. 25 concludes, we read, "And they [presumably, Hannah and Elkanah] brought the boy [that is, Samuel] to Eli."[68] The ancient Greek rendering, conversely, describes Hannah alone as delivering Samuel into Eli's hands: "And Hannah, the mother of the child, went to Eli."[69]

The Greek text is surely to be taken as presenting the preferred reading of this "b" or second half of v. 25, as the Greek account makes much better sense of the materials that follow in vv. 26–28, in both the Greek and Masoretic traditions, in which only Hannah is described as speaking to Eli and declaring the boy Samuel to be dedicated to Yahweh's service. The 4QSam[a] manuscript from the Dead Sea Scrolls is fragmentary at this point, but McCarter writes in his Anchor Yale Bible commentary on 1 Samuel that "enough is preserved" to ensure that in v. 25, the Dead Sea Scrolls manuscript—like the Greek—describes Hannah alone as taking the child Samuel to present him to Eli.[70] McCarter also suggests that the Dead Sea Scrolls tradition preserves the best reading at the end of v. 28: "And *she* [Hannah] left him there, and *she* worshipped [literally, "bowed down to"] Yahweh" (emphases mine).[71] This is as opposed to the last few words of v. 28 of the Masoretic Text, where Elkanah, who goes unmentioned in vv. 26–27 and the first half of v. 28, rather curiously reappears: "And he [most likely Elkanah; perhaps Eli; much less probably, in my opinion, the toddler Samuel] worshipped [literally, "bowed down to"] Yahweh there."[72]

Still, even though the Greek and Dead Sea Scrolls renditions of 1 Sam 1:25b–28 foreground Hannah's role in presenting her miracle son to Eli and dedicating him to Yahweh's service, no stricture against Hannah coming into contact with the priest is presumed in any version of these verses (Greek, Dead Sea Scrolls, Masoretic). This is not, however, the norm throughout biblical tradition: again we will see in Chapter 6 that women's access to priestly functionaries is constrained in significant ways in materials that come from the P source. Within Deuteronomy and Deuteronomistic tradition, moreover, only the Hannah story and one other text—the story of the woman prophet Hulda in 2 Kgs 22:14–20 (see Chapter 10)—describe a specific woman interacting with a priest; even in 2 Kgs 11:13–16, at a point when Queen Athaliah has come to the Jerusalem temple compound (see Chapter 5), the priest Jehoiada speaks to the army captains *about her* and only these captains are said to engage with her directly. What's more, the Deuteronomistic accounts of Hannah and Hulda engaging with priestly functionaries come close to being the only texts in the entire Hebrew Bible where a specific woman and a priest interact. One exception in the preexilic corpus is Isa 8:3, where the priest-prophet Isaiah fathers a child with a female prophet who is in all likelihood his wife (again, see Chapter 10), just as all priests would have had sexual relationships with their wives.

In addition, while women in the Bible are frequently described as "bowing down" to show obeisance, as does Hannah before Yahweh in 1 Sam

1:28 (reading, as above, with the Dead Sea Scrolls tradition), Hannah is the only woman in the Bible who is specifically identified as bowing down to show obeisance to *God.* More typically, women bow down to human males, to indicate that these males are somehow superior to them (Gen 33:6; 1 Sam 25:23, 41; 2 Sam 14:4; 1 Kgs 1:16, 31; 2 Kgs 4:37; Ruth 2:10). Or we must presume women's presence within larger groups that "bow down" to worship the deity. For example, we must presume women's presence among the Israelite people, or *ʿām,* who "bow down" in texts such as Exod 4:31 and 12:27 (Exod 19:15 notwithstanding),[73] and we must presume Hannah's presence among Elkanah's entourage when "they bow down" in 1 Sam 1:19. The fact that Hannah as an independent ritual actor is depicted as "bowing down" to worship Yahweh in 1 Sam 1:28 thus demonstrates yet again—as with her prayer, her vow, her taking on the Nazirites' dietary obligations, her ritual soliciting of a divine oracle, her presence "before Yahweh," and her ability to interact freely with the priest Eli—the many ways in which a regional sanctuary such as Shiloh could facilitate women's ability to engage in significant ways in the practice of ancient Israelite religion. This will be much less the case in the Israelite and Judaean state-sponsored temples of the preexilic era that I now turn to examine.

5 "This Is the King's Sanctuary and a Temple of the Kingdom": Women and Ancient Israel's State Temples, I

In his *Antiquities* (15.380–425), the Jewish historian Josephus describes in some detail the renovations to the temple in Jerusalem (indeed, its almost total rebuilding) undertaken by Judaea's King Herod beginning in ca. 20 BCE and lasting for at least forty to forty-six years (John 2:20) and in some respects even longer (a few finishing touches were still being attended to at the time of the temple's destruction by the Romans in 70 CE).[1] Scholars have long marveled over Josephus's accounts of this temple's elaborate furnishings and decorations, as well as those set forth in other ancient sources. In *The Jewish War* (5.5.6), for example, Josephus claims that the gold that adorned the temple's outer walls virtually blinded those who looked upon the edifice, even in the early morning light of the rising sun, and according to the Jewish Talmud, "no one has seen a truly beautiful building unless he has seen the temple" (b. Sukkah 51b).[2] Also of note is the enormous size of Herod's temple precinct as presented in Josephus and in other ancient sources (in particular the rabbinic-era Mishnah, tractate Middot) and as indicated by archaeological remains, especially the hugely enlarged temple platform that Herod had built to hold his sanctuary complex (approximately 280 by 488 meters, an area of 18 hectares).[3] Indeed, Carol Meyers, citing Meir Ben-Dov, observes that Herod's temple platform was the largest structure of its kind built in the ancient world, "twice as large as the monumental Forum Romanum built by Trajan, and three and a half times more extensive than the combined temples of Jupiter and Astarte-Venus at Baalbek."[4] Brian Lalor similarly describes this platform as "one of the most ambitious public works building projects of the classical world" and "among the most spectacular building projects of antiquity."[5]

In his analysis, Lalor goes on to suggest that "perhaps the most remarkable" aspect of the temple's massive platform was the sophisticated way in which the precinct's engineers handled the complexity of the circulation problems in the compound's southwest corner. He refers in particular to the various planes, or courtyards, that stood "parallel, at right angles . . . and on top of one another" and were used to "separate people" and thereby control the "comings and goings" of worshippers, especially when large groups of people flocked to Jerusalem and its temple during the three great pilgrimage festivals of the Jewish year.[6] But for scholars interested in women's religious culture during the Herodian period, the engineering skills required to design and build these various planes or courtyards are less significant than is the fact that, as the plaza/courtyard design of the complex's southwest corner was extended inward, toward the temple itself, there was, for at least the last several decades before the temple was destroyed, a courtyard designated as a gathering place for women (although men could be present there as well).[7] This courtyard, moreover, was positioned fifteen steps below the temple and its main courts, and it was further set apart from the temple's main courts by a wall.[8] Women, that is, were apparently not allowed to ascend to, or even to see, the courtyards immediately proximate to the temple, including the temple's central area of assembly and main sacrificial court, the so-called Courtyard of the Israelites—a rather pointed indication of how men were categorized as "real" Israelites within the thought world of the Herodian temple compound while women were not. Although her focus is not the Herodian temple, Phyllis Bird captures its governing principles aptly when she writes, "Women possessed dual status in the . . . cultic realm, being members of the outer circle governed by the community's norms but restricted in varying degrees from the inner circle where the norms were formulated, inculcated, and rationalized."[9]

How different was the situation in earlier centuries of ancient Israel's history, especially the preexilic period that is this book's focus? As I discuss in the pages that follow, women's access to the main areas of assembly within the preexilic temple compound in Jerusalem, the capital city of King David (r. 1005–970 BCE) and King Solomon (r. 970–931 BCE), and then, in the era of the divided monarchy, the capital of the Southern Kingdom of Judah, does not seem to have been restricted to nearly the same degree as was women's access to the central courtyards of the Herodian temple of the first century CE.[10] Nor do there appear to have been any particular limitations placed on women's access to the major public spaces of the two national temples of the Northern Kingdom of Israel that stood during the time of the divided monarchy in Bethel and Dan.[11]

Still, relatively little evidence points to *significant participation* on the part of women in the religious life of the temples of preexilic Jerusalem, Dan, and Bethel or to women's participation in the religious life of other Israelite and Judaean state-sponsored temples of the preexilic era (for example, the temple that in all probability stood in the Northern Kingdom capital city of Samaria and the Judaean fortress temple at Arad; see Fig. I.1). To be sure, this may indicate only the vagaries of our ancient sources, and especially the tendency of our primary source—the biblical text—to focus its attention almost exclusively on the experiences (both religious and otherwise) of men. But in my opinion, it is more likely that our sources say little about preexilic women's participation in the religious life of Israel's and Judah's great "temples of the kingdom" (paraphrasing here Amos 7:13) because there is little to say, and this because the Northern and Southern Kingdoms' state-sponsored temples were not particularly productive forums for preexilic women's exercise of religious agency. Indeed, I argue in the discussion of Israel's and Judah's state-sponsored temples that follows that these venues were significantly less productive forums for preexilic women's religious practice than were the Israelite household shrines I discussed in Chapters 1 and 2 and were also less productive, although not as overwhelmingly so, than the Israelite regional sanctuaries that were the subject of Chapters 3 and 4.

Introducing Ancient Israel's State Temples

To begin, a brief survey of ancient Israel's national temples—and especially the reason they are properly designated as "national," or similarly "state" or "state-sponsored" temples—is in order. It would in addition be helpful to know just how many of these temples there were in ancient Israel. Unfortunately, the answer to this latter question is unclear, although archaeological and some textual evidence suggests that there may have been as many as a half-dozen, or even more, including (as noted just above) a Northern Kingdom temple located in Israel's capital city of Samaria and several Israelite and Judaean state-sponsored sanctuaries located within border fortresses and/or in border towns such as Arad, Beersheba, Benjaminite Mizpah, Ramah, and, possibly, Geba (see Fig. I.1). For the time being, though, let us concentrate on the three state temples on which the biblical text focuses. Again, these are the Jerusalem temple and, during the period of Israel's divided monarchy (ca. 931–722/721 BCE), the Northern Kingdom's state temples of Dan and Bethel (see again Fig. I.1).

According to biblical tradition, which I see no reason to doubt, the oldest of these is the Jerusalem temple, which is said to have been built in ca. 950 BCE, during the reign of King Solomon. Also according to biblical tradition, certain preparatory work was undertaken by Solomon's father, King David, albeit here, the tradition is less clearly reliable. As the David story recounted in 2 Samuel would have it, David, after he began his reign by spending a prolonged period of time securing his throne (2 Sam 2:1–5:5), moved to consolidate his nascent monarchy: first, by subduing many of the nations that surrounded his kingdom (Philistia, Edom, Moab, Ammon, and Aram), and second, by conquering Jerusalem, a previously non-Israelite city that nevertheless lay within Israelite territory, and establishing it as his capital. Then he secured Jerusalem's new status as capital (and concomitantly his new status as its king) by bringing into the city a central cult object of Israelite tradition, the ark of the covenant. According to the biblical story, however, the ark was housed in David's Jerusalem only in the sort of tent shrine that had served, according to a dominant strand of thought within biblical tradition, as the ark's dwelling place throughout its earlier history (see further my discussion in Chapter 3).[12] The temple as the ark's more permanent residence was built, under the terms of this account, later on, by Solomon.

The amount of credence that should be ascribed to this David story has been a matter of considerable debate among biblical scholars, as it seems clear that much of it is hyperbole—for example, the passages that portray David as a mighty emperor who ruled over a kingdom that extended well beyond Israel's traditional borders to encompass the lands of Edom, Moab, and Ammon in the east and Aramaean territories reaching as far as Damascus in the north.[13] Indeed, according to some scholars, so grossly exaggerated are these and other parts of the David story that the narrative as a whole should be taken as nothing more than a late legend, developed during the Persian period of the late sixth, fifth, and fourth centuries BCE, or even during the Hellenistic era of the third and second centuries BCE, in an attempt to hearken back, during these times of hardship, to some "golden age" of Israelite glory that never was.[14]

But as I have discussed in greater length elsewhere, I would not assume such a minimalist position.[15] Rather, I prefer to side with those who understand that there was in fact some historical David, albeit a David who was just a small-scale chieftain who ruled over only his own tribal community of Judah and the Israelite tribal communities of Benjamin and Ephraim located to Judah's north. David may also have exercised some measure of control over territories congruent to these various tribes' lands farther to the north, in the Galilee; to the east, in Transjordan; and to the south, in the Negev (see Fig. I.1).[16] This is obviously a far less powerful David than the mighty potentate the Bible makes him out to be. Still, it seems reasonable to assume that even this more modestly imagined David would have needed a royal seat—or, as Baruch Halpern writes in his study of the David story, really a "stronghold" or a "den"—from which to rule over his fief in the Judaean hills.[17] Ancient Jerusalem fit the bill perfectly: first, because in David's day it was probably nothing more than a relatively small (and thus easily conquerable) hilltop fortress; second, and even more so, because Jerusalem was strategically located between the Israelite territories of Benjamin and Ephraim that were the domain of David's predecessor and rival, Saul, and the Judahite territories that were the region of David's core support.[18]

It further seems reasonable to assume that in order to lend stature to his newly conquered "stronghold" or "den" in Jerusalem, David would seek to associate the city with Israel's divine patron, Yahweh, by bringing into Jerusalem a cult object such as the ark of the covenant. Indeed, as Halpern points out, to establish one's capital and then ensconce one's god or gods there was a standard way for an ancient Near Eastern king to assert his and his fiefdom's power. Yet in Halpern's understanding, David does not further promote his royal authority by building a temple for Yahweh and the ark in his newly acquired capital city because David was constrained by a crippling poverty that prohibited large-scale building projects.[19] Instead, Solomon is credited in the Bible with building a Jerusalemite temple, and, while the Bible's grandiose descriptions of Solomon's temple decorations and furnishings must be dismissed as exaggeration, I see no reason, as noted above, to query the basic biblical account.

Granted, there are again some who have raised doubts regarding this reliability of the Solomon narratives, especially those who, as above, deny the existence of a historical David—and hence the existence of Solomon, his son. But the noted archaeologist of ancient Israel William G. Dever has worked carefully through the description of Solomon's temple found in 1 Kings 6–8 and pointed out the striking degree to which that text's "lengthy description of the building's plan, construction, and furnishings" correlates with what is known through excavations about the plans, construction methods, and furnishings of temples elsewhere in the Syro-Palestinian world. More important, Dever demonstrates that temples excavated elsewhere in the Syro-Palestinian world that combine "*all* the details in 1 Kings 6–8" are "found in the tenth/ninth century B.C.E.—and only there."[20] Dever therefore concludes that the Jerusalem temple must actually have been built, like its Syro-Palestinian counterparts, in the tenth or ninth century BCE, and most plausibly in the tenth century BCE during the reign of Solomon, just as the Bible asserts. Solomon's point in constructing the temple, and also in building his own palace nearby, was certainly the same as was David's point in bringing the ark to Jerusalem and housing it within his fief: to assert royal power, especially by suggesting that the king now lived in neighborly intimacy with his god. In Yahweh's words, according to the prophet Ezekiel (Ezek 43:8), "They [Jerusalem's kings] set their threshold at my threshold, and their doorpost beside my doorpost; [there was just] a wall between me and them." As a result of this neighborly intimacy, so this assertion of royal power continues, the king enjoyed divine succor, which he, moreover, was positioned to mediate to his kingdom on Yahweh's behalf. In this way, as Patrick D. Miller writes, Solomon's temple "served to tie the divine order to the human order, the eternal kingship of the deity and the eternal human kingship reflected in the dynasty."[21]

It is this close association between Solomon's temple and Solomon's kingship that explains the urgency with which King Jeroboam I of Israel (r. 931–909 BCE) is said to speak in 1 Kgs 12:27. This passage is set very shortly after Solomon's death in ca. 931 BCE and thus very shortly after the point when the biblical narrative describes the peoples of the North (the tribes of Benjamin, Ephraim, and their affiliates) and the South (the clans and tribe of Judah) constituting themselves as two separate monarchies. In the Southern Kingdom, or Judah, Solomon's son Rehoboam assumed the throne after his father's death and continued to rule from Jerusalem; Jeroboam became king over the Northern Kingdom, or Israel, and established his own capital, initially at Shechem (1 Kgs 12:25). But Jeroboam's royal authority in Shechem was apparently compromised, for the city was seemingly without a temple that symbolized the presence of Israel's patron god and indicated Yahweh's support of the king.[22] Thus Jeroboam, in 1 Kgs 12:27, legitimately worries that if his people continue to worship Yahweh at the only state-sponsored temple available to them, the temple of Jerusalem, "the heart of this people will return to their liege lord, Rehoboam, king of Judah; they will kill me and return to Rehoboam, king of Judah."

Consequently, Jeroboam, as the story goes, resolves to build his own temples for Yahweh, one in the city of Dan and one in the city of Bethel. Why these cities is not necessarily clear, but geography seems likely to have played a major role, given that Dan stood near the northernmost reaches of Jeroboam's kingdom and Bethel near its southern boundary. Bethel in addition offered the strategic advantage of being on the road that led to Jerusalem from points north (see Judg 20:31, 21:19, and Fig. I.1). Thus it was perfectly positioned to service northern worshippers who might otherwise have journeyed southward to Jerusalem. By Jeroboam's day, moreover, Bethel had arguably developed (or at least had begun to develop) a distinguished religious pedigree within Israelite tradition, as is reflected in later written accounts that associate the site with the stories of legendary ancestors such as Abraham, who is said to have built an altar there (Gen 12:8), and Jacob, who received there his famous dream vision of angels ascending and descending from heaven (Gen 28:10–19). Dan, as we have seen in Chapter 1, is also the subject of traditions that accord its shrine a pedigree that dated back to, at least, Israel's premonarchic period, when, according to Judg 17:1–18:31, the Danites who moved north to settle the site erected a sanctuary there that housed a valuable religious figurine and that was serviced by a Levitical priest—and a priest whom Judg 18:30 identifies as the grandson of Moses, no less![23]

After establishing his temples at Dan and Bethel, Jeroboam is said to host a feast (1 Kgs 12:32), as had David upon bringing the ark into Jerusalem and as had Solomon at the occasion of the Jerusalem temple's dedication (2 Sam 6:19, 1 Kgs 8:62–66). Jeroboam's aim, as was David's and Solomon's, was to assert his royal authority by demonstrating his intimacy with his patron god and also his ability, concomitant with the god's ability, to see to his people's well-being. Jeroboam is said as well to have designated a priesthood to serve, at least, the Bethel shrine (1 Kgs 12:32), as is said of David regarding the ark (2 Sam 8:17, 20:25) and of Solomon even before his building of the Jerusalem temple (1 Kgs 2:26–27, 35). In asserting his right to appoint this sanctuary's priestly personnel, moreover, and also his right to determine, as did David, his sanctuaries' appropriate furnishings (by stationing in Dan and Bethel two bull-calf images that were somehow meant to represent Yahweh [1 Kgs 12:28–29]), Jeroboam effectively claimed for himself the same position of titular head of the shrines he had founded as had David and Solomon. Indeed, so closely tied are the Jerusalem, Dan, and Bethel shrines to their nations' kings and to affairs of state that in the eighth century BCE, Amaziah, "the [chief] priest of Bethel," can refer to that sanctum both as a "temple of the *kingdom*" and as "the *king's* sanctuary" (Amos 7:10, 13; emphases mine).

Women's Engagement in the Religious Life of Ancient Israel's State Temples

Given the close relationship I have just described between the state temples of Jerusalem, Dan, and Bethel, on one hand, and the Judahite and Israelite monarchies, on the other, it should come as no surprise that the only biblical texts that associate these temples with the acts of specific women (by which I mean women who are named or otherwise designated in the Bible in ways that mark them as identifiable individuals) concern women who either were members of or served the royal family. In 2 Kings 11, for example, Jehosheba, the daughter of King Joram of Judah (r. 851–843/842 BCE) and the sister of Joram's successor, King Ahaziah (r. 843/842 BCE), is described as spiriting away the baby Jehoash (also called Joash), her nephew and the infant son of the recently killed Ahaziah, and hiding him, along with his wet nurse, in the "house of Yahweh," or the Jerusalem temple (2 Kgs 11:3). More specifically, Mordechai Cogan and Hayim Tadmor suggest that Jehoash/Joash was hidden in the "lodgings of the high priest within the Temple precinct."[24] This was done to spare Jehoash/Joash from the murderous purge of his grandmother Athaliah, who sought to destroy all of Ahaziah's male relatives in order to claim Judah's throne for herself.

And indeed, Athaliah is said in 2 Kgs 11:3 to have claimed the Judaean throne for some six years (ca. 843/842–837 BCE), until, in the seventh year, Jehoiada, a priest of the temple, rallied supporters in favor of Jehoash/Joash. These advocates gathered throughout the temple courtyard according to 2 Kgs 11:12 to watch as the boy was crowned and anointed "by the pillar" (meaning perhaps, as 2 Chr 23:13 would have it, by one of the two columns, Jachin and Boaz, that stood at the temple's entry). The crowd then cried out, "Long live the king." Once she heard them, these shouts brought Queen Athaliah to the temple compound to investigate (2 Kgs 11:13), and one notes here—in addition to the narrative's evidence regarding this royal woman's presence in the Jerusalem temple precinct—the many other ways in which this text suggests the close affiliation between the Jerusalem temple and the Judahite monarchy: its presumption, for example, that the temple was the appropriate hiding place for the legitimate royal heir, as well as the appropriate setting for this royal heir's eventual coronation. This text also demonstrates that the Jerusalem temple compound was within earshot of Jerusalem's royal palace, connoting the neighborly intimacy of the kingdom's monarch and the kingdom's god.

Another story that demonstrates the close association between the Judahite royal family and the Jerusalem temple complex, and more specifically a close association between a woman of the Judahite royal family and the Jerusalem temple complex, is the story of Ma'acah found in 1 Kgs 15:9–15. Ma'acah is identified in 1 Kgs 15:2 as the "mother" (*'ēm*) of King Abijam (r. 914–911 BCE). Also, in 1 Kgs 15:10, she is identified as the "mother" (*'ēm*) of Abijam's son, King Asa (r. 911–870 BCE). Obviously, the designation of Ma'acah as both her son's and her grandson's "mother" cannot be taken as biologically accurate; rather, 1 Kgs 15:10 uses *'ēm*, "mother," more metaphorically to indicate that Ma'acah served in her grandson Asa's court, as she did in the court of her son Abijam, as the king's queen mother, or *gĕbîrâ* (1 Kgs 15:13). This is a title given to women who, like Ma'acah, had begotten the current king or who served as the surrogate of the current king's biological mother. More important, *gĕbîrâ* is a title that indicates that the women who held it were official functionaries within the monarchies of ancient Israel and, especially, Judah. In our text, the official role of the Judahite queen mother is demonstrated by the fact that Asa, angered by one of Ma'acah's undertakings, eventually deposed her from her post (1 Kgs 15:13). It is demonstrated more generally in the biblical account by the archival notices embedded within the books of 1–2 Kings that carefully record the names of the queen mothers of all but two of the nineteen kings of Judah (although never the name of a queen).[25] Jeremiah 13:18 also describes how, when Judah's King Jehoiachin was taken into exile by the Babylonians in 597 BCE, it was his queen mother who was deposed along with him. Similarly, 1 Kgs 2:19 recounts how it was Solomon's queen mother Bathsheba who sat in the royal court at her son's right hand. A comparison with Pss 80:18 (in most of the Bible's English versions, 80:17) and 110:1, where the king is described as sitting at the right hand of God, suggests that after the throne of the monarch himself, this is the seat of highest honor on the royal dais.

Throughout the ancient Near East, queen mothers performed many important political functions within their sons' courts: they helped determine the royal succession, for example, and they also served as regents for their sons when those sons were unable to rule (because, say, a king came to the throne as a boy or because he was temporarily absent from court, engaged in diplomatic or military endeavors).[26] Moreover, as I have argued elsewhere, the queen mothers of Judah played a special religious role within their sons' courts.[27] This role stems from the fact that in the royal ideology of the Southern Kingdom, the king was viewed both as the biological son of the previous king, his earthly father, and also as the adopted son of Yahweh, his divine father (2 Sam 7:14; Isa 9:5 [in most of the Bible's English versions, 9:6]; Pss 2:7, 89:20–38 [in most of the Bible's English versions, 89:19–37], 110:1–7).[28] It further seems to be the case that at many points in its history, the royal cult in Jerusalem subscribed to the belief that the father god Yahweh should be worshipped alongside a consort, Asherah, the great mother goddess of the Canaanite world. I will have more to say about Asherah worship in ancient Israel in Chapter 13, but for now, I note only that within a Jerusalem royal court that held both that the king was the adopted son of Yahweh, the divine father, and that Yahweh had as a consort Asherah, the divine mother, an understanding readily would have developed that the king was not only the adopted son of Yahweh as father, but also of Asherah as mother. Yet while the king had by definition no living biological father at the point when he became the adopted son of Yahweh and Asherah (since his biological father, the old king, must necessarily have died in order for the son to assume the throne), Judahite kings typically did have within their courts a biological mother or someone who fulfilled this role as queen mother (as did Maʿacah for her grandson Asa). This biological or queen mother, I suggest, easily would have become identified with Asherah, the king's divine mother, so much so that the queen mother would have been perceived as the human representative or even the earthly counterpart of Asherah within the royal court.

All of this helps illuminate 1 Kgs 15:13, in which the queen mother Maʿacah is said to have made an image for her patron goddess, Asherah, probably an icon that was called, after the goddess, an *ʾăšērâ* or "asherah."[29] It is probable, too, that this Asherah icon was in the shape of a stylized wooden pole or tree (tree imagery was commonly associated with Asherah in both Canaanite and Israelite tradition).[30] More germane here than the image's probable name and probable form, however, is the probability that Maʿacah had this Asherah icon erected at some location *within* the Jerusalem temple precinct, perhaps even within the temple itself. I propose this for several reasons. First, in 2 Kgs 23:6, we are told explicitly that in the seventh century BCE, during the reign of King Josiah (r. 640–609 BCE), an Asherah icon stood within the Jerusalem temple compound, and perhaps within the temple proper, seemingly because the seventh century BCE was one of the points in Israelite history when the Jerusalem royal cult subscribed to the belief that Yahweh should be worshipped in conjunction with Asherah. The fact that Ma'acah commissioned an Asherah icon in the ninth century BCE suggests that this era, too, was a time in Israelite history when the belief pertained among the royal family that Yahweh should be worshipped in conjunction with Asherah. If, moreover, this belief manifested itself physically in the seventh century BCE through the erecting of an Asherah icon in the temple compound and perhaps within the temple itself, then we might well expect it to manifest itself similarly during the time of Ma'acah.

More important, we should recall, as noted above, that the palace in Jerusalem stood essentially next door to the Jerusalem temple ("[there was just] a wall between"; Ezek 43:8). Given this proximity, a temple location seems the most logical place for a member of the royal family such as Ma'acah to place a cult image. We should in addition recall the degree to which state temples such as the Jerusalem temple complex really functioned as "kings' sanctuaries" (paraphrasing yet again Amos 7:13); indeed, as noted above, Israelite and Judaean kings—and, by extension, I would argue, members of the Israelite and Judaean royal families—often assumed for themselves the right to appoint their state temples' personnel and determine these temple complexes' appropriate furnishings. It follows that Ma'acah, as a member of the Judaean royal family, would have assumed the right to erect the cult image she had made in Asherah's honor somewhere within the Jerusalem temple compound.

Given the Judaean queen mother's close association with Asherah worship, and given also the right assumed by Judaean royal family members to appoint their state temple's personnel, it may follow that it was a queen mother who, in the seventh century BCE, stationed a group of women in the *bāttê haqqĕdēšîm,* the "houses of the cult functionaries" that stood within the Jerusalem temple's enclave (more on these functionaries in Chapter 13), in order that these women might weave "garments" for Asherah (2 Kgs 23:7). Most probably, these "garments" were wraps that were somehow to be draped over the pole- or tree-shaped icon of the goddess that stood, as previously noted, somewhere within the temple compound at that time (2 Kgs 23:6).[31] But even if the product of the women's weaving is to be differently interpreted, and even if it was not a royal woman who appointed these women to serve as weavers within the temple compound, their presence there is still highly significant for my purposes: first, because, in conjunction with the texts I have already catalogued that locate women such as Jehosheba, the unnamed wet nurse of Jehoash/Joash, and Athaliah within the Jerusalem temple enclave, we find in 2 Kgs 23:7 additional evidence for women's ability to enter into the precincts of Judah's state sanctuary and even, like the wet nurse of Joash/Jehoash, to take up residence inside the temple compound's walls. More important, just as Ma'acah (I have argued) performed the important religious function of erecting a cult icon of Asherah within the Jerusalem temple precinct, so too does 2 Kgs 23:7 suggest women's ability to perform an important religious role within the Jerusalem temple complex—in this case, the weaving of cult fabrics.

Other biblical evidence may indicate women could assume still another important religious role within the precinct of the Jerusalem temple: serving as cult musicians. The text that perhaps illustrates this best is the one I quoted in the opening paragraph of Chapter 1, Ps 68:25–26 (in most of the Bible's English versions, 68:24–25). In it, young women who play frame drums are listed as being among the musicians who participate in a procession into Yahweh's *qōdeš,* or sanctuary:

> Behold your processions, O God,
> the processions of my God, my king, into the sanctuary (*qōdeš*)—
> the singers in front, the musicians last,
> between [them] frame-drumming young maids (*'ălāmôt tôpēpôt*).[32]

It is not possible definitively to say, however, that Ps 68:25–26 (English 68:24–25) is set in the Jerusalem temple compound, for, while Yahweh's *qōdeš,* or sanctuary, could well be the Jerusalem temple, *qōdeš* could also refer to some other sanctuary location.[33] To be sure, the temple is specifically mentioned in a subsequent verse of Psalm 68, v. 30 (English v. 29), but that verse is part of a stanza that may not have been originally associated with vv. 25–26 (English vv. 24–25).[34] As is well known, moreover, the Psalms are notoriously difficult to date, meaning that even if Psalm 68 were taken to be evidence for women's musicianship within the Jerusalem temple, it cannot necessarily be said to represent the sorts of *preexilic* religious practices that are the subject of my examination.

It is also unclear what to make of a text from the book of 1 Chronicles, 1 Chr 25:5–6, which mentions the fourteen sons and three daughters of Heman and then continues by saying that "all of these" were under the direction of their father "for the music in the house of Yahweh," that is, for producing the music of the Jerusalem temple. Again, there is a problem here with date, for while 1 Chr 25:5–6 purports to describe the temple personnel of King David's day (the early tenth century BCE), 1–2 Chronicles is in fact a fourth-century BCE composition that cannot easily be said to reflect preexilic tradition. There is in addition a problem of translation, as 1 Chr 25:5–6 might be said to imply that Heman's daughters and sons together were among the temple complex's musicians, although preceding verses, which list by name those who were to do the work of making the temple's music (and also prophesying), specify only Heman's fourteen sons (1 Chr 25:1, 4). Likewise, 1 Chr 25:9–31, in subdividing the musicians catalogued in 25:1–6 into twenty-four groups, names Heman's sons alone. Despite its mention of Heman's three daughters, therefore, 1 Chr 25:5–6 most likely does *not* refer to a tradition of women's musicianship either within the preexilic Jerusalem temple that the text purports to describe or within the postexilic temple with which this text is contemporaneous.[35]

It is equally unlikely that a tradition of female temple musicians is documented in 1 Kgs 5:11 (in most of the Bible's English versions, 4:31), where Solomon is said to be wiser than anyone, including one Calcol. William F. Albright has argued that this name is to be compared to the name Kurkur/Kulkul, which appears on four ivory tablets written in Egyptian hieroglyphics from fourteenth- to thirteenth-century BCE Megiddo. There, Kurkur/Kulkul is identified as a female musician who served the Egyptian god Ptah, whose cult was centered in Memphis, just south of the Nile Delta, but who also had a shrine—where Kurkur/Kulkul served—in Ashkelon, on the southern Levantine coast (see Fig. I.1).[36] That Calcol in 1 Kgs 5:11 (English 4:31) should also be taken as a musician and, indeed, a cult musician is suggested by the appearance in the same verse of Ethan and Heman, who are elsewhere (in 1 Chr 6:33, 44) identified as heads of families of Yahweh's temple singers.[37] Yet Ethan and Heman are male names, and so too is Calcol in 1 Kgs 5:11 (English 4:31) best taken as a male, as in 1 Chr 2:6 (the only other place in the Bible where the name Calcol appears). This means there is no good case to be made for Calcol, a female cult musician, in 1 Kgs 5:11 (English 4:31). Likewise, there is no compelling reason, whatever some commentators have argued, to see Amos 8:3 as referring to a tradition of women's musicianship within a Northern Kingdom temple, either Dan or Bethel or even Samaria. Indeed, to make such a claim requires, with no supporting evidence, that we emend the Amos 8:3 text that mentions the *šîrôt hêkāl,* or the "songs of the temple/palace," to *šārôt hêkāl* and then interpret these *šārôt hêkāl* as the "female singers of the temple [Dan, Bethel, or Samaria]."[38]

Still, even if 1 Kgs 5:11 (English 4:31), Amos 8:3, Ps 68:25–26 (English 68:24–25), and 1 Chr 25:5–6 were all excluded from a catalogue documenting women's music-making within Judahite and Israelite state temple compounds, we could note Ezek 8:14, which describes how, in ca. 592 BCE, at the midpoint between the two Babylonian invasions of Judah in 597 and 586 BCE, the prophet Ezekiel, who had been transported back to Jerusalem in a divine vision after being taken to Babylon during the Babylonians' initial incursions, saw women sitting at the entrance of the north gate of the temple precinct of Yahweh, "wailing over Tammuz."[39] Tammuz is a young fertility god well known from Mesopotamian sources, and those sources also make clear that ritual mourning performed by women was a crucial element of the Tammuz cult. As the Mesopotamian story goes, Tammuz (or, in older Sumerian sources, Dumuzi) first courted and then wed the goddess Ishtar (Sumerian Inanna), who, like him, was associated with fertility and especially represented the communal storehouse in which harvested foodstuffs were kept. The sexual union of Tammuz and Ishtar thus helped guarantee fruitfulness in the land and bounty in the storehouse, but this fertility was abruptly arrested, as Mesopotamian mythology would have it, when Tammuz suffered an untimely death (associated in the Mesopotamian calendar with the onset of the blisteringly hot summer months). His passing was mourned, according to the mythological tradition, by women: his young bride Ishtar (Inanna), his sister Geshtinanna, and his mother Ninsun.

Tammuz's death was likewise mourned commemoratively in Mesopotamian ritual by women, and appropriately so, for as we will see in Chapter 9, the task of mourning was one predominantly (although not exclusively) assumed by women throughout the ancient Near East and the eastern Mediterranean. Women's work in mourning, moreover, characteristically involved the *singing* of lamentations, and Mesopotamian tradition has in fact preserved the texts of several dirges sung as part of Tammuz mourning rituals.[40] These include a large corpus of liturgical laments from the first millennium BCE (and so roughly contemporary with Ezek 8:14).[41] We thus can reasonably conclude that the mourning done by the women whom Ezekiel sees in his vision in Ezek 8:14 would have included sung laments, meaning that, whatever doubts I have raised about 1 Kgs 5:11 (English 4:31), Amos 8:3, Ps 68:25–26 (English 68:24–25), and 1 Chr 25:5–6, Ezek 8:14 does provide evidence of women's ritual music-making within the Jerusalem temple precinct, or at least at one of that precinct's entry gates (presuming, that is, as in the previous chapters of this book, that the polemical harangue of Ezek 8:14 has underlying it a basically accurate description of early sixth-century BCE temple practices).

Women are also counted as members of the Israelite ritual community in various texts that describe worship at the premonarchic and early monarchic tent shrine(s) that biblical tradition understood to serve as the antecedent(s) to the Jerusalem temple. According to a Deuteronomistic account in 2 Sam 6:19, for example, women were among the congregation that gathered at the tent shrine of the ark when David hosted the festival that installed this religious icon in Jerusalem.[42] Likewise, women can be present at the wilderness-era tent of meeting (*'ōhel mô'ēd*) that the Pentateuchal sources J, E, P, and H construe as the Israelites' central place of worship before their entry into the "promised land." In Num 12:5, for example, the JE tradition describes Miriam as standing at the entrance of the tent of meeting, along with her brother Aaron, as Yahweh appeared to them in a pillar of cloud (more on this in Chapter 10). In Num 27:2, a text from the Holiness Code, the five daughters of a man named Zelophehad somewhat similarly appear at the entrance to the tent of meeting to bring an inquiry about their inheritance rights, given that their father has died with no male heir.[43] As I noted briefly in Chapter 3, women functionaries are described as serving at the entrance of the wilderness-era tent of meeting in Exod 38:8, a text that comes from the P, or Priestly source, and also in a related text in 1 Sam 2:22, which is dependent upon, and derived from, Exod 38:8.[44] In addition, in Num 6:9–20, Nazirites, including women Nazirites, are commanded to bring offerings to the entrance of the P tent of meeting when their time of consecration has ended, and in Lev 12:6 and 8, women whose period of impurity following childbirth is completed are commanded to come to the entrance of the P tent of meeting and bring offerings as well. Leviticus 15:29 similarly requires women to bring sacrificial offerings to the entrance of the P tent of meeting after the end of a period of impurity brought on by an irregular discharge of vaginal blood.

Presumably, moreover, the P tradition intends its rules about women's impurity to apply not only to the wilderness tent of meeting but also to the national temple in Jerusalem that, according to Leviticus's P and H authors, eventually succeeded the tent of meeting and with which these same authors were closely associated. Certainly, much later, during the time of the Herodian temple, the P dicta about women's observances at the tent of meeting appear to be a part of Jerusalem temple ritual, at least according to Luke 2:24. There, Jesus's mother, although not mentioned specifically, seems to be among the "they" who bring a pair of turtledoves or a pair of pigeons to the temple compound in Jerusalem after Jesus's birth, just as Lev 12:8 requires women who cannot afford the more generous offering of a lamb and a bird to bring an offering of two turtledoves or two pigeons to the tent of meeting once the period of impurity that follows childbirth has come to an end.

Numerous Leviticus passages also speak of a generic "anyone" as coming to present an offering in the precinct of the wilderness tent of meeting and, by implication (if the arguments I just presented hold), in the precinct of the Jerusalem temple that supersedes the wilderness tent (Lev 2:1–2; 4:27–31; 5:15, 17–18, 21–25 [in most of the Bible's English versions, 6:2–6]; see also Num 15:27). Because, moreover, the Hebrew term used in these Leviticus texts, *nepeš,* is glossed by the phrase "a man or a woman" in a related passage, Num 5:6–7, Mayer I. Gruber, Carol Meyers, and Jacob Milgrom (among others) have determined that *nepeš* must be taken in each of the Leviticus passages where it is used "explicitly [to] denote both genders."[45] Gruber also, as well as Milgrom, argues that in Leviticus, the term *'ādām,* although typically taken as referring to men only, should be understood as referring to both men and women.[46] So, for example, in Lev 1:2–9, as Gruber would have it, the instructions detailing how an *'ādām* is to bring a livestock offering to Yahweh apply to both male and female worshippers. This includes the command that this *'ādām* "shall slaughter" (*wĕšāḥaṭ*) the offering before Yahweh, "proof," Gruber writes, "that the slaughter of animals . . . for sacrifice . . . should be performed by women as well as men."[47]

Georg Braulik has likewise argued that in Deut 18:3, "the people" (*'ām*) of the Israelite cultic assembly who are said to slaughter an ox or a sheep as a *šĕlāmîm* offering include women. Braulik makes this claim, at least in part (Braulik's argument is complex, and I will not attempt to reproduce it fully here), because women are listed in Deut 29:9–10 (in most of the Bible's English versions, 29:10–11) along with tribal leaders, elders, officials, children, resident aliens, and all the men of Israel in a catalogue of Israel's covenant community. Thus, for Braulik, women are similarly to be counted among the covenant community, or *'ām,* of Deut 18:3 when this cultic assembly slaughters the *šĕlāmîm* sacrifice.[48] By extension, it could be suggested that texts within the kindred Deuteronomistic History and its related corpora that locate "the people" (*hā'ām*) or "all the people" (*kol-hā'ām*) within the Jerusalem temple enclave (for example, 2 Kgs 23:2; Jer 26:7, 9, 12; 36:6, 10; 2 Chr 7:5, 23:5, 34:30) and, analogously, within the bounds of the Northern Kingdom's national temples at Dan and Bethel (for example, 1 Kgs 12:30) indicate that women participated in sacrificial ritual at these sanctuary complexes alongside men. Indeed, regarding the Stratum III archaeological evidence from what are generally taken to be the remains of the Northern Kingdom's state temple at Dan, Jonathan S. Greer has specifically proposed that "the entire precinct shows evidence of wide-scale feasts in close vicinity to the central altar" (faunal remains of sheep, goats, and cattle, as well as various styles of cooking pots, jugs, and bowls). This Greer interprets to mean that offerings such as the *šĕlāmîm* sacrifice were "consumed within the sanctuary complex in family groups," including males and females.[49]

Greer's analysis regarding women's presence during *šĕlāmîm* feasts celebrated at the Israelite national temple in Dan is certainly plausible and, in fact, coordinates well (the specifics of the location notwithstanding) with the texts in Deuteronomy that I cited in Chapter 4, where women are commanded to present themselves among groups of worshippers who come to "the place that Yahweh your God will choose," the common locution used in Deuteronomy for the Judahite national temple in Jerusalem, to participate in sacrificial feasting (Deut 12:12, 18).[50] In Deut 16:11, 14, and 31:10–13, women are also commanded to be present at the Jerusalem temple for the ritual observance of Israel's pilgrimage festivals of the early summer harvest, called in Deuteronomy Shavu'ot ("Weeks"), and the fall feast of the Ingathering, called in Deuteronomy Sukkot ("Booths")—and thus, presumably, to join in the sacrificial feasting that Deuteronomy mandates as a part of these celebrations (more on this in Chapter 8).

Yet where, according to Deuteronomy, are the women when sacrifice is offered at "the place that Yahweh your God will choose" during the other major pilgrimage festival of Deuteronomy's ritual calendar, the spring pilgrimage feast of Pesaḥ (Passover)? No mention is made of their presence (see Deut 16:1–8). In addition, I cannot agree with Braulik that women are to be counted among the members of the Deuteronomic community, or the *'ām,* that actually conducts sacrificial slaughter at the Jerusalem temple in Deut 18:3. Nor do I think that Gruber is right to suggest that the *'ādām* who is to slaughter a livestock offering in Lev 1:2–9 could be a woman. After all, as we saw in Chapter 3, biblical traditions elsewhere, as well as traditions from throughout the eastern Mediterranean and the ancient Near East, resolutely depict only *men* as killing sacrificial animals. Exodus 19:15, where Moses commands "the people" (*hā'ām*) not to "go near a woman," and Jer 44:24, where Jeremiah speaks to "all the people (*kol-hāʿām*) *and* all the women" (emphasis mine), might also give one pause regarding just who constitutes the "people" (*ʿām*) that slaughter the *šĕlāmîm* offering in Deut 18:3.[51]

In fact, our evidence overall for women's participation in the religious life of the national temple compounds of Israel and Judah might give us pause. Noteworthy data surely attest to women making ritual music at the temple's gateways (Ezek 8:14) and to women resident in the Jerusalem temple precinct weaving cultic cloth (2 Kgs 23:7). Women of at least some of the Jerusalem temple's priestly families—that is, the temple priests' wives and daughters—were also presumably resident within the temple precinct, living, more specifically, within the temple apartments designated for the sanctuary's priestly personnel.[52] Likewise, I have followed Cogan and Tadmor above in suggesting that during her charge's stay in the temple precinct, the wet nurse of Jehoash lived within "lodgings of the high priest within the Temple precinct."[53] This wet nurse's presence in the temple enclave, moreover, is the result of the acts of a royal woman, Jehosheba, who, like other royal women (Maʿacah), seems to have been able to pursue her political and religious agendas within the Jerusalem temple complex. Various texts in Leviticus, Numbers, and Deuteronomy (Lev 12:1–8, 15:19–30; Num 6:9–20; Deut 12:12, 18; 16:11, 14; and 31:10–13) in addition seem to compel preexilic women to bring offerings to the Jerusalem temple in conjunction with certain life-cycle events (childbirth) and to be present within the temple's compound on various festival occasions.

Still, *not one biblical text* speaks definitively to women's presence at the Northern Kingdom's temple complexes at Dan and Bethel, and while this might be explained as a product of the Bible's anti-northern bias, it must be stressed that only 2 Kgs 23:7, Ezek 8:14, and possibly Ps 68:25–26 (English 68:24–25) among all the texts I have surveyed—and among the rather voluminous corpus of biblical texts devoted to Jerusalem temple worship—demonstrate *clearly* a place for women in the religious activities of the Jerusalem temple of the preexilic period. To make this claim about all the other passages I have cited requires, say, a certain latitude about dating: even if 1 Chr 25:5–6, for example, were taken as evidence of women's temple musicianship, what bearing would this postexilic text have on a reconstruction of the preexilic cult? Or there is required either supposition (regarding, say, the meaning of *ʾādām* in Lev 1:2–9 as referring to both men and women) and/or a conviction that the Leviticus, Numbers, and Deuteronomy dicta commanding women to participate in certain rituals at the wilderness tent of meeting (Leviticus and Numbers) or "the place that Yahweh your God will choose" (Deuteronomy) can be taken to represent actual practices of the Jerusalem temple that date from at least some periods of preexilic history.

Furthermore, even if we accept that the Leviticus, Numbers, and Deuteronomy dicta that explicitly pertain to women or that seemingly refer to them (the *nepeš* texts) represent the actual Jerusalem temple practices of at least some periods of preexilic history (and I do), these texts, as I noted already in Chapter 4 and will discuss more fully in Chapter 6, constrain, sometimes in quite significant ways, the extent to which women worshippers were allowed to engage in temple ritual. Likewise, even if we agree (as I have proposed) that according to 1 Kgs 15:9–15, Ma'acah erected her Asherah icon somewhere within the Jerusalem temple compound, it seems clear that this *Asherah* image could not have been the focal point of *Yahwistic* temple worship, this as opposed to, say, the data I surveyed in Chapter 1 which indicated that women such as Micah's mother or the arguably female potters of Ai could have been responsible for the fabrication of the *Yahwistic* images that were the most important objects within their households' shrines.

Indeed, while my discussion in Chapters 1–4 sought to demonstrate the significant role women might play within the religious communities of Israelite household shrines and in regional sanctuaries (albeit less so), I have been able to identify relatively little evidence in this chapter that speaks to the Jerusalem, Dan, and Bethel temple precincts as notable sites of preexilic women's religious practice. And although, as I have previously suggested, this paucity might be explained by the Bible's general tendency to ignore women's lives and experiences in order to focus primarily on the lives and experiences of men, it is in my opinion more probable that women's religious acts are infrequently mentioned in biblical accounts of Judah's and Israel's state temples because these sorts of temple complexes were not particularly conducive to the exercise of women's religious agency and thus not well positioned to serve as meaningful locations for women's religious expression.

But what made Judah's and Israel's state temples such unproductive spaces for women's religious engagement? In the chapter that follows, I turn to explore possible answers to this question.

6 "At the Time of Her Menstruation, She Shall Be Unclean": Women and Ancient Israel's State Temples, II

In Chapter 3, I described how the making of *šĕlāmîm* offerings—that is, offerings in which only the visceral fat and certain organ meat from a sacrificial animal were burned to God, while the rest of the meat was boiled and eaten by the ritual's participants—served as the main act of religious devotion at Israelite regional sanctuaries. I further suggested that because regional sanctuaries were only minimally administered by, at most, a loosely constituted cadre of priests, and priests, moreover, who seem to have been significantly divorced from key aspects of the *šĕlāmîm* rite, nonelites among these shrines' worshippers, including women, were afforded important opportunities to be involved in regional sanctuaries' sacrificial observances. Here, as I seek to explain the antithetical situation that I described in the last chapter—the lack of women's engagement in ancient Israel's state or national temples—I begin by exploring the converse of Chapter 3's thesis: that because of state temples' highly institutionalized and bureaucratized character, and, in particular, because these temples were administered by professionally credentialed, officially sanctioned, and hierarchically organized priestly communities, Israelite women's ability to participate in state temples' religious culture was constrained. Then I turn to explore two other factors that I propose limited women's participation in the religious life of Judah's and Israel's state or national temples: first, the association of at least some of these temples and related shrines with military installations, which were male-dominated spaces where women, if present at all, were only minimally at hand; then, the ways in which ancient Israelite traditions of ritual impurity may have limited women's access to Judah's and Israel's state temples, especially during a woman's reproductive years.

Priestly Institutionalization and Bureaucratization and Their Effects on Women's Participation in the Religious Life of Ancient Israel's State Temples

Our discussion of the highly institutionalized and bureaucratized character of ancient Israel's state temples and of these temples' priesthoods, and the effect such institutionalization and bureaucratization may have had on women's ability to participate in state sanctuaries' religious culture, begins by considering important studies that both Jo Ann Hackett and Carol Meyers published in the 1980s. In these works, Hackett and Meyers demonstrated that women's experiences generally within ancient Israelite society, and especially Israelite women's ability to act as forceful and even autonomous agents within their communities, varied significantly in relation to the degree of social and political organization that distinguished their environment. Originally, both Hackett and Meyers analyzed this variation in terms of time, arguing that in historical periods when Israelite social and political organizations were relatively unstructured, women were accorded greater power and status than they were in times when social and political institutions were more formally constituted. For example, in her book-length study *Discovering Eve: Ancient Israelite Women in Context* (1988), Meyers argued that throughout Israel's premonarchic period (ca. 1200–1025 BCE), women experienced relatively high status and an increased potential for the exercise of power—first, because during this era the household (as opposed to some larger and more formally established organizational unit) was "the central institution for most economic, social, political, and cultural aspects of human existence"; second, because "ethnographic evidence specifically indicates the vital and active roles that females play in societies in which the household is the base unit of production and consumption."[1] Similarly, in a 1985 article, Hackett wrote that "studies have shown that women tend to have more status within a society when the public and domestic spheres are not widely separated, that is, when important decision making is done within or near the home."[2] More specifically, Hackett suggested, like Meyers, that Israelite women would have been accorded high status and attained positions of community power within the domestically based system of social and political organization that dominated during Israel's premonarchic days.

Conversely, Hackett stated in the same article that "an increase in the centralization of a society's institutions will often coincide with a decline in participation by women within those institutions."[3] At what point, if any, such a decline might have occurred in ancient Israel is an issue on which Hackett did not offer further comment, but in *Discovering Eve,* Meyers opined it was with the emergence of the monarchy in the late eleventh and, especially, tenth century BCE. "State formation created hierarchical relationships and robbed females of their customary equality and interdependence with men," Meyers wrote; "the rise of a public world dichotomized the social structure and led to male preeminence."[4] Nevertheless, in the Epilogue of *Discovering Eve,* Meyers suggested there were still opportunities for women of the monarchic period to experience some of the same elevated status and increased potential for the exercise of power that she had argued characterized the lives of their premonarchic foremothers. She proposed, for example, that monarchic-era women who lived in rural as opposed to urban settings would have had more opportunities for status elevation and the exercise of power, given that the self-sufficient household, in which, according to Meyers, the amount of status conferred upon women was relatively high, remained typical of Israel's village landscape throughout much of the monarchic period.[5]

In her concluding remarks of *Discovering Eve,* that is, Meyers modified her book's temporally based analysis to include a more spatially focused hypothesis that argued for the enhanced potential for women to exercise power and be assigned status during *any* period of Israelite history if they were resident in an environment that was rural and household-centered.[6] In subsequent publications, moreover, Meyers pursued this line of thought aggressively, especially in the light of the demographic studies I noted in Chapter 1 which indicate that even during the monarchic period, the vast majority of the Israelite population—up to 80 to 90 percent, according to most estimates[7]—continued to live in the sort of village and household-based setting Meyers finds so critical to women's assumption of important social roles. For example, in a 2003 article, Meyers outlined the evidence I cited in Chapter 1 (and again in Chapters 2 and 3) concerning the crucial responsibilities that women undertook for producing and distributing foodstuffs (particularly bread) and manufacturing crafts (particularly textiles) within the self-sufficient households that characterized Israelite village life and then went on to argue that within this sort of household-based social setting, the "major economic value" of these "productive activities" would result in women's "social power and prestige."[8] In this article, Meyers also suggested that because food processing (especially bread-making) and textile production "involved women working in groups," "the existence of women's networks" was indicated. This could lead in turn to "a sense of solidarity."[9]

None of this, however, necessarily concerns women's participation in the practices of ancient Israelite *religion.* Still, in a 2002 essay and a subsequent 2005 book, Meyers expressed similar convictions about women's ability to experience status and prestige as religious leaders within household settings. "Indeed," she writes, because women were "officiants and practitioners of household [cultic] praxis," their lives within the household context "were replete with opportunities for religious expression and experience."[10] I certainly agree, as my discussion in Chapters 1 and 2 should indicate. I differ from Meyers, though, in my assessment of the opportunities for religious expression available to women in Israel's and Judah's great national temples, and especially the temple in Jerusalem, for while Meyers does suggest—as would I—that these sanctuaries were not as prominent venues for Israelite women's cultic activities as were household-based shrines, she nevertheless lists in her 2002 and 2005 essays some of the same passages I have cited in the previous chapter (Lev 2:1–2; 4:27–31; 5:15, 17–18, 21–25 [in most of the Bible's English versions, 6:2–6]; Ezek 8:14) as "important" evidence "that women were participants in cultic activities at . . . the Jerusalem temple."[11] She sounded this same theme, moreover, in several of the articles she authored in her 2000 edited volume *Women in Scripture: A Dictionary of Named and Unnamed Women in the Hebrew Bible, the Apocryphal/Deuterocanonical Books, and the New Testament.*[12]

In Chapter 5, however, I argued much the opposite: that what strikes me when I survey the biblical text is not a trove of important evidence attesting to women's participation in the religious life of the Jerusalem temple, and also the national temples of Dan and Bethel, but the *paucity* of passages that refer definitively to these sanctuaries as sites of women's religious agency. This I have taken to indicate that women's engagement in the religious life of Judah's and Israel's national temples was relatively infrequent. Indeed, it is curious to me that in making her claims about women's ability to participate in the religious activities of the Jerusalem temple, Meyers seems to back away from her earlier insights about structure and organization and the degree to which increases in organizations' structural complexity compromise rather than facilitate women's agency. As intimated above, I prefer to credit these insights as continuing to have import, and therefore I argue that among the factors that worked to *limit* women's opportunities for religious expression within the Judaean and Israelite state temples of Jerusalem, Dan, Bethel, and (presumably) Samaria were the highly developed systems of institutionalization and bureaucratization that characterized these sanctuaries.

Certainly, there can be no doubt that these state temples were highly institutionalized and bureaucratized sacred spaces. The priesthoods associated with the state temples of Jerusalem, Dan, and Bethel, for example, were hierarchically organized, both in terms of these priesthoods' status vis-à-vis the nonpriestly community and in terms of various priests' status vis-à-vis one another. With regard to the former point, consider Jonathan S. Greer's interpretation of the archaeological evidence at Dan, which suggests the priests at that site were marked as hierarchically superior to the laity in many ways. In analyzing animal bones from the chambers that lie on the western side of Dan's sacred precinct, for instance, Greer notes that right-sided portions of the animals' remains are significantly more common than are left-sided portions, whereas in remains from the main courtyard of the precinct, the ratio is reversed. Moreover, in the western chambers, painted pottery was more abundantly represented than it was in the courtyard remains.[13] Not unreasonably, Greer theorizes that these data "may indicate an elevated social status" for those who cooked and ate their sacrificial meals in the western chambers, as opposed to those who ate in the courtyard, and he further notes that "bear bones . . . notably almost all from paws, and thus indicative of skins . . . [were] also found in the vicinity of the western chambers [and] may perhaps reinforce the idea of an elite presence."[14] Greer, moreover, proposes a wholly plausible identity for the western chambers' elites—"the western chamber area was the domain of priests"—as opposed to the domain of the laity, who celebrated their sacrificial feasts in the courtyard of the Dan sacred precinct. Note in this regard (as does Greer) biblical texts that specify it is the *right* "hindlimb" and "breast" of a sacrificial animal that are designated as priestly portions, as well as biblical texts that direct that the *skins* of sacrificial animals should be apportioned to priests.[15]

Andrew R. Davis has in addition suggested that Dan's priests increased their control of the site's courtyard space over time, for example, during the eighth century BCE, when a wall was built around the precinct's central altar so that accessibility to it was limited.[16] As to whose altar access was limited, Davis reasonably suggests it was nonelite participants and observers, as opposed to "authorized religious specialists" (by which Davis means, as he indicates elsewhere, priests). Indeed, Davis suggests that the "limited participation" of nonpriestly observers in eighth-century BCE Dan "underscores the hierarchical distinctions encoded in the [sacrificial] ritual," in order to "accentuate the elevated status of the religious specialists"—and, we can add, the increase in elevated status these religious specialists seem to have assumed over time.[17]

In Jerusalem too, according to textual evidence, the temple's system of hierarchical organization became increasingly stratified over time, both the stratification systems that distinguished the priesthood from the laity and those that defined status divisions within the priestly ranks. I noted in Chapter 3, for example, that while older materials can describe lay male Israelites as slaughtering animals that priests later presented, either in part or in toto, on Yahweh's altar at the P and H tent of meeting (and presumably at the Jerusalem temple that, according to Priestly and Holiness tradition, succeeded this tent shrine), Ezek 44:11, from the early sixth century BCE, assigns priests the role of slaughtering *all* sacrificial animals before offerings from their flesh were brought to the Jerusalem temple's altar. Likewise, by the sixth century BCE, a clear distinction was drawn within the priestly ranks of the Jerusalem temple between priests who were allowed to officiate at the altar and priests who assumed secondary positions (Num 3:5–10; 8:19, 22; Ezek 44:10–16; 1 Chr 23:2–6). Indeed, both Baruch A. Levine and Steven Tuell have suggested that by the latter half of the preexilic period, an extremely complex categorization of priestly rank was operative within the Jerusalem temple, headed by "*the* priest" (Deut 17:12, 26:3; 2 Kgs 11:9–10, 15; 16:10–11; 22:10, 12, 14), that is, the chief or high priest (*hakkōhēn haggādôl* or *kōhēn hārōʾš;* Lev 21:10; Num 35:25, 28; Josh 20:6; 2 Kgs 12:11 [in most of the Bible's English versions, 12:10]; 22:4, 8; 25:18; Jer 52:24), and the second priest in charge (*kōhēn mišneh;* 2 Kgs 25:18). Under these officers served other senior priests, the so-called elders of the priests or *ziqnê hakkōhănîm* (2 Kgs 19:2). Underlings included as well the "guardians of the threshold" (2 Kgs 12:10 [English 12:9], 22:4, 23:4, 25:18), the "second order of priests" (2 Kgs 23:4, 25:18), and the Levites assigned to bear the ark in procession (Deut 10:8; 31:9, 25; possibly 1 Sam 6:15; 2 Sam 15:24; 1 Kgs 8:3–4, 6).[18]

Biblical tradition moreover suggests that some degree of hierarchy was already in place at the time of the Jerusalem sanctuary's origins. For example, King David is said to appoint two main priests, Zadok and Abiathar, to preside over Jerusalem's ark shrine at the beginning of Israel's monarchic period (2 Sam 8:17, 20:25), prefiguring the office of the chief or high priest that is attested for the Northern Kingdom temple at Bethel by at least ca. 760 BCE (when Amos, according to Amos 7:10–17, had a confrontation with Amaziah, the chief or high priest of Bethel). In addition, the tradition of David's appointing Zadok and Abiathar as the two main priests of the Jerusalem ark shrine, as well as the account of Jeroboam I's appointing a priesthood at Bethel (1 Kgs 12:32), reminds us that Israel's and Judah's national temples were all served by a royally designated and thus a *professional* priesthood. Contrast the Judg 17:5 text I discussed in Chapter 1, where Micah's son rather casually took on the role of priest within his father's household shrine, or even the situation that prevailed at regional sanctuaries such as the Bull Site I described in Chapter 3. This sort of modest open-air shrine would have required (I argued) only an informally designated cadre of cult personnel: perhaps just some village elder or elders who, when visiting the site with worshippers, took on some oversight role.

In addition, we saw in Chapter 3 that even at regional sanctuaries that do seem to have had more clearly designated priestly overseers, such as Shiloh, the priests performed virtually no ritual functions on behalf of the worshippers at these sites—not even the altar rituals associated with sacrificial offerings. Conversely, biblical texts that speak to ritual observances within Israel's and Judah's state temples indicate that it is typically those temples' priests who are to burn upon the altar whatever part of a sacrificial animal was designated as Yahweh's (the entire animal in the case of the *ʿôlâ*, or whole burnt offering, or the visceral fat and organ meat in the case of the *šĕlāmîm* sacrifice) and to attend as required to the animal's blood, by dashing it against or somehow sprinkling or daubing it upon the altar. Likewise, it is state temples' priests who are mandated to attend to grain offerings and drink offerings at Yahweh's altar. As I again noted in Chapter 3, this is especially indicated in texts from P and related materials from H that detail the various sacrificial offerings that are to be made at the wilderness tent of meeting that P and H construe as the Israelites' primary place of worship during their forty years of wandering in the Sinai and are (presumably) to be made as well at the temple in Jerusalem that P and H construe as the tent of meeting's eventual successor.

With all this in mind, let us consider women's specific roles in sacrificial ritual according to some of the P texts I introduced in Chapter 5: for example, Lev 2:1–2, where a *nepeš*—that is, according to Mayer I. Gruber's, Meyers's, and Jacob Milgrom's interpretation, a generic anyone, either man or women[19]—brings a grain offering to the tent of meeting, and, presumably, to the Jerusalem temple that succeeded it. Notably, this *nepeš* only prepares the grain offering for burning by pouring oil and putting incense or some other aromatic plant material upon it; it is *the priest* who takes the offering to Yahweh's altar and burns it. It is likewise *the priest* who deals with the fat and the blood of the goat that a *nepeš* brings as purification offering in Lev 4:27–31 (no organ meat is mentioned in this text), even though this *nepeš* perhaps performs the slaughter of the animal (the meaning of the crucial v. 29 is not totally clear). According to Num 6:13–20, moreover, Nazirites—including women Nazirites—whose term of consecration has ended convey to *the priest* the various sacrificial offerings they are required to make to mark this occasion, in order that this priest might present them as required on Yahweh's altar. So too, according to Lev 12:6–7 and 15:29–30, women whose periods of impurity occasioned by childbirth or an irregular discharge of vaginal blood have ended are to give over to *a priest* the *'ōlâ* and purification offerings they are commanded to bring to the Israelite tent of meeting (and, presumably, in later times, to the Jerusalem temple) for the priest to attend to them as required.

In short: even in texts where the P source possibly (if we are to take *nepeš* as designating a man or a woman) or explicitly (as in Lev 12:6–7, 15:29–30; Num 6:13–20) accords women a role in presenting sacrificial and other offerings at the tent of meeting and (presumably) the Jerusalem temple that succeeded it, P remains resolute in the conviction that altar service at the tent of meeting and the later Jerusalem temple is to be performed by priests alone. As for the Deuteronomic laws governing the sacrificial rituals at "the place that Yahweh your God will choose" (the locution, as already noted, used in Deuteronomy to refer to the Jerusalem temple), the situation is somewhat different, in that Deuteronomy does not seem so stringently to insist on an exclusive role for *priests* within the Jerusalem offerings cult. Still, Deuteronomy does not necessarily allow any greater opportunity for *women* to engage in the sacrificial cult of the Jerusalem temple than do the P materials in Leviticus and Numbers. For example, even were we to follow the argument put forward by Georg Braulik that I mentioned in the last chapter and agree that "the people" of Deut 18:3 who slaughter an ox and a sheep for a *šělāmîm* sacrifice at the Jerusalem temple include women (and, as indicated in my earlier discussion, there are problems here),[20] no mention is made of these "people" approaching Yahweh's altar to dedicate the slaughtered animal's visceral fat, organ meat, and blood. Rather, the almost immediately subsequent verse, Deut 18:5, identifies priestly authorities, and more specifically Deuteronomy's favorite priestly designates, the

Levites, as those who are chosen "to stand and render service in the name of Yahweh" (see similarly Deut 10:8, 18:7). Presumably, this means it is they who are to perform the altar rites of fat and organ immolation and blood manipulation.

Nor is it clear to me that Braulik is right to claim that the less restrictive command found in Deut 12:27 that allows a generic "you" (masculine singular) to offer both the meat and blood of *ʿōlâ* offerings on Yahweh's altar in "the place where Yahweh your God will choose" (i.e., the Jerusalem temple) refers to both men and women and, more specifically, to the male head-of-household and his wife. Braulik bases this argument on the assumption that wives must be implicitly included in the masculine singular "you," given that in Deut 12:18, where an extended list of participants who are required to partake of a postsacrificial meal at the Jerusalem temple is found, those designated include "you" (masculine singular), plus "your [masculine singular] son," "your [masculine singular] daughter," "your [masculine singular] male slave," "your [masculine singular] female slave," and Levites resident in "your [masculine singular] gates."

This Deut 12:18 list obviously includes multiple members of a head-of-household's immediate family, plus some nonbiological affiliates who would have been resident in this paterfamilias's household compound (see further Chapter 1). It does not, however, specifically mention the head-of-household's wife. Yet Braulik finds it "hardly conceivable" that the wife is not among those who are to join in the postsacrificial meal enjoyed by this otherwise quite compendious gathering.[21] Consequently, he argues, she must be subsumed within the masculine singular "you" of Deut 12:18, and thus, by extension, she must be subsumed within the masculine singular "you" who offers meat and blood on Yahweh's altar in the Jerusalem temple according to Deut 12:27.[22] Braulik also posits that to understand Deut 12:27 in this way renders Deuteronomic law consistent with traditions found in the closely related Deuteronomistic History, and especially the traditions found in 1 Samuel, where Hannah not only is present during the slaughter of a bull in Shiloh (1 Sam 1:25), but also plausibly stands alongside Elkanah for the subsequent burning of the fat and organs of this *šĕlāmîm* offering on Yahweh's altar, as well as for the altar rituals of the grain offering and the pouring out of libations (and, perhaps, if this was a part of Shilonite rite, the swabbing or dousing of the altar with the bull's blood).

Yet, as I have indicated, I have reservations.[23] Certainly elsewhere in biblical tradition, a man's wife can be excluded from a list of a household's women with whom that man is otherwise ritually affiliated. For example,

Lev 21:1–6, from H, allows a priest—who according to H should otherwise avoid the contaminating pollution incurred through contact with a corpse (see further below)—to participate in the mortuary rites of his mother, his daughter, and his unmarried sister, but "his wife finds no place in the list of exceptions."[24] Rather, Lev 21:4 may explicitly state that a priest *cannot* have contact with his dead wife's corpse. To be sure, the interpretation of Lev 21:4 is fraught (it contains an expression so enigmatic that it is "said to be the most difficult . . . in the entire book of Leviticus").[25] Thus, the occasional commentator assumes that a priest's wife's corpse must, by implication, be counted among the bodies of women family members with which a priest is allowed contact.[26] But noted scholars of Leviticus such as Levine and Milgrom disagree.[27] Likewise, there are verses in Deuteronomy which make clear that masculine singular "you" in Deuteronomy need not include a man's wife. Most famous of these, perhaps, is the command in Deut 5:21 (part of Deuteronomy's rendition of the Ten Commandments) that "you" (masculine singular) should not covet your neighbor's wife.[28] Moreover, there may be good reasons for Deuteronomy *not* to count a man's wife as part of a collective "you" in verses such as 12:18 and 27 and thereby compel her presence on occasions of Jerusalem temple ritual. Perhaps, for example, a recently delivered mother might prefer—and be better off—staying home with her newborn child (as, according to 1 Sam 1:21–23, Hannah stays home with the unweaned Samuel for up to three years while her family makes its annual journey to sacrifice at Shiloh).[29]

But most important, I would not follow Braulik in seeking *consistency* between Deuteronomy's laws that pertain to sacrificial acts at the Jerusalem temple and Deuteronomistic narratives such as 1 Sam 1:1–2:26 that describe sacrificial rituals that took place at less formally constituted religious venues (the possible parallels regarding newly delivered mothers' participation notwithstanding). Rather, I expect *inconsistency,* given the hypothesis posited here: that at more localized and less institutionalized settings such as the Shiloh sanctuary, nonelites, including women, were able to participate more fully in sacrificial observances than they were at the highly bureaucratized and professionalized state temples of Jerusalem, Dan, Bethel, and (presumably) Samaria. In 1 Samuel, that is, Hannah is readily affirmed as able to stand with her husband at Shiloh during the slaughter of a bull, and she is plausibly to be envisioned as joining her husband at Yahweh's altar when he makes the subsequent fat, organ meat, grain, and libation offerings. Women at the Jerusalem temple, however (and presumably also, women at the national temples of Dan, Bethel, and Samaria), are not able to exercise the same sort of religious agency, due to the fact that Hannah worships in a regional sanctuary conductive to women's engagement in its ritual life in ways that Judah's and Israel's great national temples are not.

Indeed, this is exactly the conclusion reached by Phyllis Bird in her programmatic 1987 article "The Place of Women in the Israelite Cultus": "the extent of professionalization or specialization of cultic maintenance roles" and "the status and affiliation of cultic personnel" affected women's ability to exercise religious agency within ancient Israel's sacred spaces.[30] Or as Patrick D. Miller writes, summarizing Bird's analysis, "there seems to have been an increasing level of restriction [regarding women's exclusion from cultic service], correlating with increasing . . . specialization and power."[31]

Women's Religious Engagement Within the State-Sponsored Temples of Israel's Border Fortresses

When it comes to state-sponsored temples, the biblical account, as documented in Chapter 5, focuses its attention almost exclusively on Jerusalem, Dan, and Bethel. We have both textual and archaeological evidence, however, that points to the existence of other sanctuaries either founded by Judaean and Israelite kings or brought under these kings' administrative control. Many of these were located along Israel's and especially Judah's borders, where they were associated with fortress complexes built to safeguard the boundaries of the Israelite and Judaean states.

For example, at Vered Jericho, a site located some 5 to 6 kilometers south of Jericho proper (see Fig. I.1), archaeologists discovered two stepped platforms that the excavation's director, Avraham Eitan, tentatively identified as cultic installations. These installations stood within a rectangular building, 24 by 20 meters, that Eitan further suggested was a fort.[32] This possible fortress-shrine dates from the end of the seventh/beginning of the sixth century BCE.[33] More specifically, Ephraim Stern understands Vered Jericho to be one among a "dense line of settlements, agriculture estates, and fortresses" that ran from Jericho south to Ein Gedi and that were established during the time of King Josiah (r. 640–609 BCE) to promote and protect commercial enterprises newly in development in this previously uninhabited region on Judah's eastern frontier (for example, the cultivating of date palms and aromatic plants, especially balsam).[34] That is:

Stern understands Vered Jericho to be a state-sponsored fortress that stood on Judah's eastern border, meaning that its two cultic platforms presumably represent border-fortress sanctuary installations that were also under state control.

More (and richer) evidence for this sort of royally sponsored fortress-shrine complex comes from locations along the ninth- and eighth-century BCE border between Israel and Judah and then, after the Northern Kingdom's fall, along the seventh-century BCE border that separated Judah from the Assyrian province of Samaria. Archaeologically, we can note the late seventh-century BCE fortress of Meṣad Michmash, located about 12 kilometers northeast of Jerusalem, on a east-west roadway that ran along Judah's northern border. This fortress's remains include a stepped platform very like the stepped platforms of Vered Jericho and so, like the platforms of Vered Jericho, arguably of cultic significance.[35]

What is not so obviously indicated, however, is that the Meṣad Michmash fortress-shrine complex was royally sponsored and/or under royal control. For evidence of this sort of shrine from Judah's northern border, I turn to a textual account, 1 Kgs 15:16–17, which describes how Israel's King Baasha (r. 908–885 BCE) made incursions into Judah a few decades after the division of the Northern and Southern Kingdoms and built a fortress just south of the Northern Kingdom's border, in Ramah (see Fig. I.1). Baasha's objective was to barricade the so-called Hill Road or Watershed Highway, a major roadway that led from the north, through Ramah and into Judah,[36] thereby preventing comings and goings across the border that might abet his enemy, King Asa of Judah (r. 911–870 BCE). But Ramah, as noted in Chapter 3, is presented in the Bible as an important cultic site of the premonarchic period, on account of the shrine said to have stood there in Samuel's day (1 Sam 7:17; also, perhaps, 1 Sam 9:11–14, 19, 22–25).[37] Of course, the historical reliability of this Samuel tradition is open to question, and even if accepted, biblical tradition is mute on the issue of whether a shrine at Ramah existed in the time of King Baasha. Still, if a Ramah sanctuary was extant in the ninth century BCE, we might well imagine that Baasha incorporated it into his fortress complex, motivated by the same ideology that had previously motivated David and Solomon to associate their capital city of Jerusalem with the tent shrine(s) and subsequent temple of the ark of the covenant and that likewise motivated Jeroboam to associate his kingship with the temples of Dan and Bethel. This ideology is the conviction that Yahweh's presence within a king's stronghold promotes that king's authority by establishing him as a ruler who is under the protection of, favored by, and in alliance with his god.

As the 1 Kings 15 story of Kings Baasha and Asa continues, Asa is said to send tribute to, and thus purchase the aid of King Ben-Hadad of Aram (Syria), who consequently invades Israel from the north and so forces Baasha to withdraw his attentions from his kingdom's southern border. At that point, Asa reclaims Ramah and orders that Baasha's fortress be torn down. According to 1 Kgs 15:22, its stones and timbers are then used to build new fortresses at two different but nearby border locations, Geba and Mizpah (see Fig. I.1). Second Kings 23:8 in addition suggests that Geba may have been the site of a shrine, although this passage dates from a time (the late seventh or early sixth century BCE) that is significantly later than the time of Asa.[38] Also, 2 Kgs 23:8 does not definitively locate a shrine at Geba.[39] Nevertheless, several scholars have connected this verse with the story of Asa's fortresses found in 1 Kgs 15:22 in order to argue that a shrine was in fact erected at Geba during the time of Asa, as part of Asa's border fortress compound.[40]

Asa's other border fortress, located at Mizpah, stood just north of Baasha's old Ramah fortress, on the same major highway that led from the Northern Kingdom into the south (Geba stood slightly to the south and east, on a second and less easily transversed north-south road).[41] Mizpah is in addition represented in several biblical texts as a site of religious assembly in the premonarchic period (Judg 20:1; 1 Sam 7:5–6, 10:17). Samuel, moreover, according to 1 Sam 7:16, included Mizpah, along with Bethel and Gilgal, in a yearly circuit he made among shrines, "judging Israel." If these passages are to be taken as historically reliable, then we might surmise that at the time of Asa's fortress-building endeavors, there was already an established sanctuary in Mizpah that Asa could have subsumed into his military compound. Patrick M. Arnold has argued, however, that the Judges and Samuel Mizpah passages were inserted into accounts of Israel's earlier history by exilic-era and postexilic editors influenced by the presence of a "house of Yahweh" at Mizpah in their day.[42] If so, then we might propose that Asa *founded* a sanctuary at Mizpah in the early ninth century BCE in conjunction with his building of a fortress there, or that the shrine postdates the fortress but nevertheless became associated with it subsequent to Asa's reign. Unfortunately, although about two-thirds of the site of Mizpah was excavated by William F. Badè in the 1920s and 1930s (assuming Mizpah is to be identified with Tell en-Naṣbeh), the archaeological data cannot clarify questions regarding the Mizpah shrine. Still, they do make clear the site's identity as a fortress during the Iron Age II period (ca. 1000–586 BCE).[43] Likewise, Jer 41:5 and, perhaps, Hos 5:1 make clear that a shrine existed at least at some point in Iron Age II Mizpah. Therefore, whatever the specifics of Mizpah's construction history (shrine first, and then fortress; fortress first, and then shrine; shrine and fortress built simultaneously), our evidence may point to a connection between Mizpah's shrine and Mizpah's fortress during the time of Israel's divided monarchy.

All of which is to say: Meṣad Michmash, Ramah, Mizpah, and possibly Geba may represent fortress-shrine complexes of the Iron Age II period that stood on the border between Judah and, first, Israel and then Judah and the Assyrian province of Samaria. Other fortress-shrine complexes were, conversely, located on Judah's southern border with Edom. These include the small, late seventh-century BCE fortress-shrine installations of Ḥorvat 'Uza and Ḥorvat Radum,[44] as well as the earlier and much more significant fortress-shrine complexes found at Arad and Beersheba (see Fig. I.1). Indeed, in biblical tradition, the importance of Beersheba's location at Judah's southernmost extreme is repeatedly signaled by the catchphrase "from Dan to Beersheba," used by the biblical writers to describe their idealized vision of the northern and southern boundaries of Israel during the late premonarchic and early monarchic periods (Judg 20:1; 1 Sam 3:20; 2 Sam 3:10; 17:11; 24:2, 15).

Ironically, though, the Bible has little to say about the Beersheba of the late premonarchic and early monarchic periods other than to refer to it by this catchphrase, nor does the Bible say much about Beersheba in its accounts of the subsequent era of the divided monarchy. Nevertheless, archaeological data indicate that Beersheba thrived during the tenth to the eighth centuries BCE and especially during the ninth and eighth centuries BCE (Fig. 6.1). It thrived, moreover, as a well-secured administrative center, with, initially, a solid fortification wall and an elaborate inner and outer gateway system (Strata V and IV). Then, after these fortifications were destroyed, Beersheba was protected by a casemate wall and a new gate with imposing front walls (Strata III and II). The defensive structures within the Strata III–II city, moreover, were quite meticulously planned: the fortification wall carefully followed the topography of the hill atop which the city sat, and a colossal earthen rampart extended down the hill's eastern side to protect the city's water-supply system.[45] In addition, among the city's buildings were large storehouses and a complex with residential, ceremonial, and

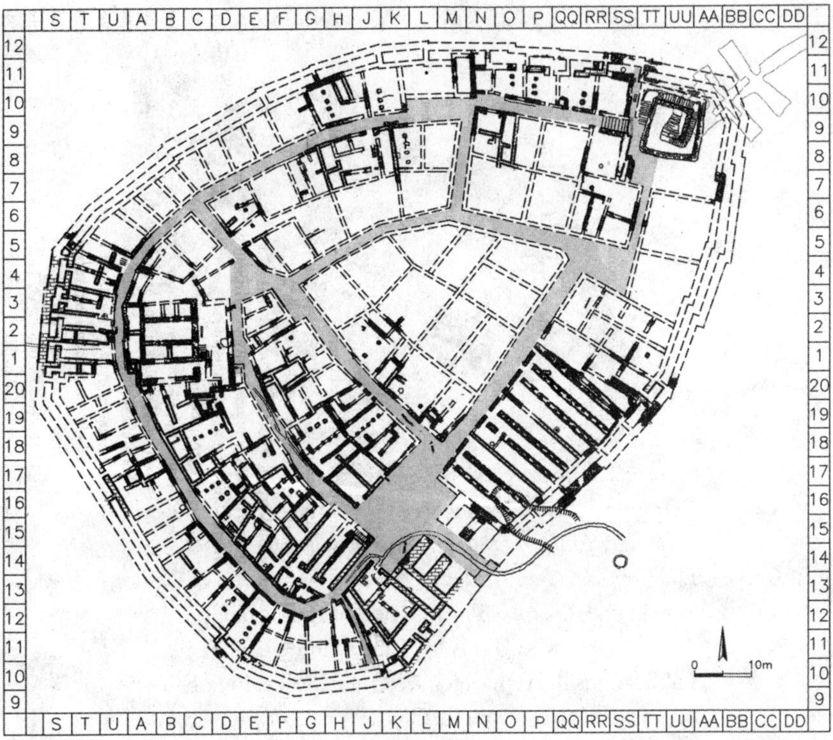

Fig. 6.1. Plan of eighth-century BCE Beersheba. From Ze'ev Herzog, "Social, Historical, and Cultural Ramifications," in Ze'ev Herzog and Lily Singer-Avitz, *Beer-Sheba* III: *The Early Iron IIA Enclosed Settlement and the Late Iron IIA–Iron IIB Cities* (Monograph Series of the Sonia and Marco Nadler Institute of Archaeology, Tel Aviv University 34. Tel Aviv: Emery and Claire Yass Publications in Archaeology; Winona Lake, Ind.: Eisenbrauns, 2016), 1473, Fig. 36.9. Courtesy of Ze'ev Herzog, Tel Aviv University.

service wings that Ze'ev Herzog, who took over the excavations of Beersheba after the death of Yohanan Aharoni, the original director, has labeled the "governor's palace" or "governor's residence." The presence of such a residence along with the "high standard of city planning and "the vast resources and effort invested in . . . fortifications . . . water system, and storehouses" that Herzog has described "clearly point to an administrative role" for ninth- and eighth-century BCE Beersheba, effected under the auspices of royal sponsorship and dependent upon royal support.[46]

Beersheba was also a cultic center during this point in its history, as indicated by both archaeological and textual evidence. Textually, Beersheba's

Fig. 6.2. Reconstruction of the Beersheba Stratum III altar. From Ze'ev Herzog and Lily Singer-Avitz, *Beer-Sheba* III: *The Early Iron IIA Enclosed Settlement and the Late Iron IIA–Iron IIB Cities* (Monograph Series of the Sonia and Marco Nadler Institute of Archaeology, Tel Aviv University 34. Tel Aviv: Emery and Claire Yass Publications in Archaeology; Winona Lake, Ind.: Eisenbrauns, 2016), frontispiece. Courtesy of Ze'ev Herzog, Tel Aviv University.

identity as a cultic site is suggested by the mid-eighth-century BCE texts of Amos 5:5 and 8:14, where it is listed alongside other Israelite cult sites, including Bethel, Dan, and Gilgal.[47] Archaeologically, important cultic remains were found at Beersheba—most significantly, stones that made up a large altar measuring 1.6 by 1.6 by 0.8 meters in height (Fig. 6.2).[48] This altar's impressive scale suggests it once stood in a courtyard that was also impressively sized. The original excavator, Aharoni, and many others have "not unreasonably" associated this altar-courtyard complex with a temple—although no Beersheba temple has definitively been found.[49] Instead, Beersheba's excavators propose that at some point during the waning decades of the eighth century BCE, the city's presumed temple was razed and its altar dismantled: indeed, some of the altar's stones were reused to build a wall of a late eighth-century BCE storehouse. The excavation team has been followed by many in suggesting that the razing of Beersheba's presumed temple and the dismantling of the altar are to be associated with the religious reform efforts promulgated by Judah's King Hezekiah in ca. 715

BCE and especially Hezekiah's attempts to centralize worship in Jerusalem (see 2 Kgs 18:4, 22; Isa 36:7; 2 Chr 31:1, 32:12).[50] If correct, this hypothesis provides evidence that Beersheba's temple, like (presumably) the temples of other royally constructed and royally administered fortress sites, was a state-sponsored enterprise, under the king's control and subject to the dictates of the king's political and religious agendas.

Finally, I turn to Arad, the most richly documented, although perhaps the most difficult to interpret of the border sanctuary/border fortress complexes I have considered. Or at least Arad is richly documented in the archaeological record; it is barely mentioned in the Bible (see only Num 21:1, 33:40; Josh 12:14 and possibly 15:21; Judg 1:16).[51] Archaeologically, the site is divided into two main areas, one from the Early Bronze Age (ca. 3200–2650 BCE) and one from the Israelite period. Israelite-era Arad was excavated between 1962 and 1965 and again in 1967 by Aharoni and, once more, in the second half of the 1970s by Herzog.[52] Unfortunately, the results of these excavations have never been fully published. Still, it seems clear that at about the same time Beersheba was being developed as a meticulously planned and well-secured royal stronghold, another carefully designed although relatively small (about 50 by 50 meters) fortified outpost was being built about 29 kilometers to the east, in Arad—presumably so that these two fortress compounds might function as part of a coordinated defense network that ran along Judah's Edomite border.[53]

Yet while it seems certain that the Arad fortified outpost was built at *approximately* the same time that Beersheba was being developed as a royal stronghold, the specifics are debated.[54] This means there has also been debate about the date of the Arad temple, which stood—along with an associated courtyard and a sacrificial altar—in the northwest corner of Arad's fortress compound (Fig. 6.3).[55] Here, I follow Herzog's most recent assessments, which assign the temple and its associated courtyard and altar only to Strata X and IX, which Herzog dates, respectively, to the mid- and second half of the eighth century BCE.[56] Then, in Stratum VIII, which Herzog dates to the late eighth century BCE, the temple was intentionally dismantled. This is approximately the same time that the altar and hypothesized temple in Beersheba are thought to have been dismantled, and arguably, Herzog theorizes, the Arad and Beersheba cult centers were decommissioned for the same reason: as part of King Hezekiah's attempts to centralize worship in Jerusalem.[57] If so, we can conclude that Arad, like Beersheba, was the site of a state-sponsored fortress-shrine complex that

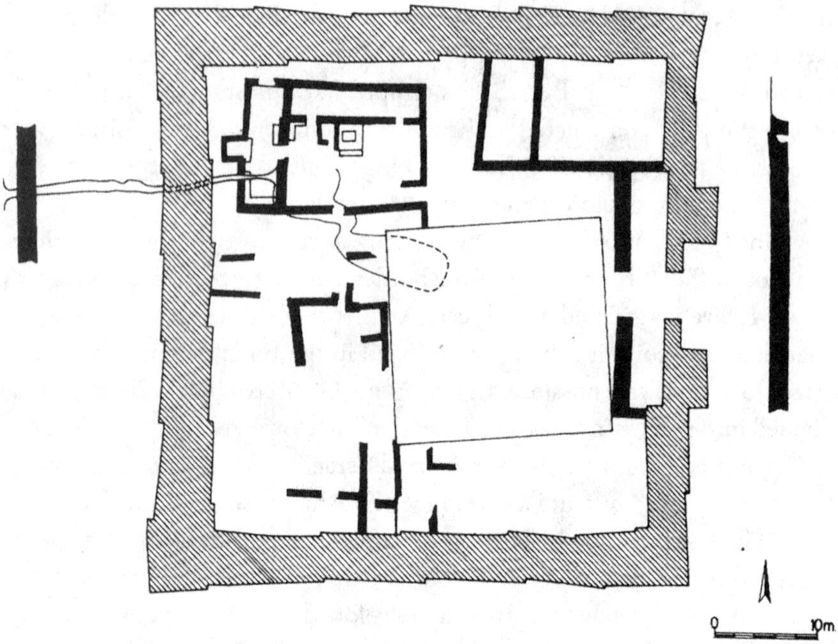

Fig. 6.3. Plan of the Stratum X Arad fortress, with the temple and its associated courtyard and altar in the northwest corner. From Ze'ev Herzog, Miriam Aharoni, Anson F. Rainey, and Shmuel Moshkovitz, "The Israelite Fortress at Arad," *BASOR* 254 (1984): 10, Fig. 10; the complete article is available on the online journal platform of University of Chicago Press. Courtesy of Ze'ev Herzog, Tel Aviv University.

was under royal control and subject to royally promulgated dicta regarding its religious fortunes.

More important for my purposes: we can conclude that because Arad was a relatively isolated military outpost, its fortress complex must have been a space whose inhabitants were almost exclusively male, or at least a space that was heavily male-dominated. This includes the sanctuary that was part of Arad's fortress compound. Women, that is, would have been only minimally represented among this royally sponsored temple's religious practitioners, simply because our evidence suggests there would have been next-to-no women resident at the site. At the state-sponsored fortress-shrine complexes of Ramah and Geba (if we accept the reconstructions that place shrines at these locales), a similar situation may have pertained. For example, Ramah and Geba may have been sites of significant military contestation in the early ninth century BCE, as the biblical account of these fortresses' construction indicates. As such, they most naturally would have housed all-male garrison forces. Geba is also said to have been in the line of attack when Aramaean (Syrian) and Israelite forces marched on Judah in ca. 735–732 BCE, at the time of the Syro-Ephraimite war (Isa 10:29).[58] Again, this means this fortress may well have been occupied, at least during this period, by an all-male garrison force. As at Arad, therefore, Ramah's and Geba's shrines (if these sites in fact had shrine installations), at least at some point during their histories, would have been essentially devoid of female religious practitioners.

There was a civilian settlement proximate to Vered Jericho, however,[59] and some of this settlement's women may have come on occasion to their neighborhood's fortress compound—even to worship at its cultic installations. Indeed, the excavators of the seventh-century BCE fortress-shrine complex at Ḥorvat 'Uza, which lies just south and east of Arad, suggest that when necessary, inhabitants of the civilian settlement near this site would have taken refuge within the fortress's walls—including, surely, the civilian settlement's women.[60] Moreover, artifacts typically associated with women—for example, grinding stones and loom weights—were found in domestic installations located *within* the Ḥorvat 'Uza fortress compound, which may indicate that some of the complex's permanent inhabitants were women.[61] This in turn could suggest that some of the regular worshippers at the cultic installation found at Ḥorvat 'Uza were women as well.

The archaeological excavations at Mizpah have somewhat similarly indicated that a town proper was associated with the fortress, with typical Israelite pillar-courtyard houses. At Beersheba, too, a town was associated with the site's military, administrative, and religious installations (see again Fig. 6.1), with about seventy-five houses, according to the excavators' estimates, during the eighth century BCE (Stratum II).[62] Women surely lived in the houses of both of these fortress towns: see, for example, my discussion in Chapter 2 of the implements of women's culture—a loom weight, a grinding stone, and a cosmetic stick—found in the remains of Beersheba's Building (or House) 76. Still, as William G. Dever writes of Beersheba, the fact that the houses were "actually built into the city walls" means they "cannot have been designed for any other than barracks troops" (and only secondarily, and occasionally, their families).[63] Indeed, a number of small domestic units in the Northern Quarter of eighth-century BCE Beersheba lack evidence that women's most characteristic household activities—food processing and textile production—took place in these spaces, suggesting that these units were not family residences but rather used to billet (male) administrative functionaries and (male) soldiers.[64]

Overall, then, what we see at Beersheba is what I have proposed as a more general theory about the sanctuary spaces sited in border fortresses and their associated border towns: that because strategic considerations generated a population base in border fortresses and towns that was predominantly male, women tended to be *separated* from the religious culture of the state-sponsored sanctuaries found in these locales.

Purity Regulations and Their Effect on Women's Ability to Access Ancient Israel's State Temples

Another factor that Phyllis Bird suggests must be taken into account when considering women's access to state-sponsored sanctuaries is "the periodic impurity of women during their reproductive years."[65] Bird refers here to the laws of purity articulated in the P texts found in Lev 12:1–8 and 15:19–30 that I have now mentioned several times. Leviticus 15:19–30 deems a woman to be impure during the time of her menses and, in addition, during times other than her menstrual period when a vaginal discharge of blood takes place and at times when a menstrual discharge extends beyond the term of the woman's normal menstruation. According to Lev 12:1–8, postpartum discharges from the uterus in addition rendered women who had recently given birth impure, or, as some translators would have it, "unclean" (*ṭāmēʾ*).[66]

As these translators' use of the word "unclean" as a synonym for "impure" suggests, there is an important consideration regarding the ancient Israelite concept of purity that is often hard for those who are familiar only with today's biblically based communities of faith, especially Christian communities, to understand: for the Bible, to be pure (*ṭāhôr*) is *not* an idea conceptualized exclusively or even primarily in moral terms (as in the notion, say, of the "pure" virgin who is "without sin" or the young child categorized as "innocent" and therefore "pure").[67] To be sure, the Bible does recognize the existence of morally based impurities, so that ethically reprehensible acts such as homicide and culturally shunned acts such as incest can render one impure (Lev 18:6–16, 24–30; 19:31; 20:1–3; Num 35:30–34).[68] Still, biblical tradition tends to focus equally, if not more, on naturally occurring and thus unavoidable impurities, such as those just cited that are caused by bodily discharges or impurities otherwise contracted in the course of day-to-day life: for example, impurities brought about by the skin disease known in biblical tradition as *ṣāraʿat* (as in Lev 13:1–14:57, Num 5:2–3) or impurities brought about by contact with a corpse (Num 5:2–3, 9:6–12, 19:11–22, 31:19–20; 2 Kgs 23:14, 16). To incur such impurities in no way implies a moral failing; on the contrary, to be a righteous Israelite, "some ritual impurity was *required*."[69] Giving birth, whatever the impurities incurred, was an act that fulfilled the divine command to "be fruitful and multiply" (Gen 1:28; 9:1, 7; 35:11), and it was generally considered meritorious to shepherd a corpse properly to its grave, especially the corpse of a deceased relative or close confederate, even though impurity ensued. The naturally occurring and unavoidable impurities of the biblical world also differ from more modern notions of moral impurity in that some not only could affect the person contaminated by, say, bodily discharge or *ṣāraʿat* but could be contagious and spread to individuals otherwise considered clean or pure (*ṭāhôr*).

The period and severity of impurity varied depending on the nature of the contagion. According to Lev 15:19–24, a menstruating woman was considered impure for seven days, and her impurity could be communicated for one day to anyone who touched her or who touched a piece of furniture on which she had sat or lain. However, a man who had intercourse with a menstruating woman was rendered impure for seven days. A woman who suffered an abnormal vaginal discharge was considered impure for the duration of the discharge and then for seven days afterwards; as during her regular menstrual period, this woman's impurity was communicated for one day to anything on which she sat or lay and to anyone who then touched those objects (Lev 15:25–28). A woman's period of impurity following childbirth lasted, initially, seven days, if the woman had born a male child, and fourteen days, if the child was female; the nature of this impurity is said to have been identical to the impurity associated with menstruation, meaning, presumably, that anyone who touched the postpartum woman or touched anything on which she had sat or lain was rendered impure for one day (Lev 12:2, 5). There then followed for the postpartum woman a second period of impurity, thirty-three days long if her newborn child was male and sixty-six days if the child was female. During this time, the woman's impurity was no longer considered communicable, although constraints on her activities within her community still applied.

The constraints imposed on the postpartum woman, as well as constraints imposed on the menstruant, moreover, were quite specific: according to Lev 12:4, the parturient was not allowed to touch anything "holy" (*běkol-qōdeš lōʾ tiggāʿ*), nor was she allowed to enter "holy" space (*ʾel-hammiqdāš lōʾ tābōʾ*). Clearly intimated here is the degree to which Israelite concepts of purity were closely related (albeit not identical) to the Israelite concept of the "holy" (*qōdeš*), to the extent that, while "holiness had its *opposite* in the common or the profane (*ḥōl*), it encountered its *opposition* in the presence of impurity (*ṭāmēʾ*)."[70] Impurity, in other words, "is a threat to the holy."[71] Indeed, "biblical sources understand pollution [or impurity] to be the *ultimate threat* to what is holy" (emphasis mine).[72] As a result, that which was impure had to be rigorously separated for the duration of the impurity from that which was holy: "the essence of holiness is separation."[73]

As indicated above with respect to Lev 12:4, this means that anyone deemed to be impure had to be kept separate from holy objects—for example, any item consecrated to Yahweh's cultic service, such as an offering bowl, a libation vessel, or a sacrificial implement.[74] "Holy" can also denote an individual who has been dedicated to service within Yahweh's cult (for example, Exod 28:41; Lev 21:6–8, 15, 23; Ps 106:16).[75] It thereby follows—given the close relationship between holiness and purity—that God's cultic servitors "must be in a state of purity."[76] Preeminently, this meant priests, as those charged with altar service and related responsibilities, had to be in a purified state. This is why the kinds of contact a priest can have with a corpse are so carefully delimited in the Lev 21:1–6 passage from the Holiness Code that I cited earlier in this chapter: especially in the face of an impurity as virulent as corpse pollution, "the holy [priest] needed . . . to be [kept] pure or clean."[77]

Primarily, however, the imperative that impurity had to be kept separate from that which was holy meant that impurity had to be kept separate from God, the ultimate "Holy One." God, that is, was the "source and quintessence of holiness,"[78] an ideology particularly articulated in texts such as "I, Yahweh your God, am holy" (Lev 19:2; see similarly Lev 11:44–45, 20:26, and 21:8) and "Holy, holy, holy is Yahweh of Hosts" (Isa 6:3; see also Ezek 20:39, 36:21; Amos 2:7). This explains why Lev 12:4 takes such care to separate the postparturient woman from "holy" or sanctuary space, since, according to the Israelites' understanding, sanctuary space was not thought of in the way in which we typically construe sanctuary spaces today—as gathering places where religious communities meet for liturgical purposes—but as a place where God as the ultimate holy being was considered actually to dwell. Preeminently, this divine dwelling was identified in Israelite tradition as the temple in Jerusalem and, by extension, as the state-sponsored temples of Dan, Bethel, and (presumably) Samaria. Indeed, the Jerusalem temple is even referred to in the Bible as God's *bayit,* literally "house," or *hêkāl,* literally "palace," and the name of the antecedent tent of meeting (*ʾōhel môʿēd*) likewise may refer to this shrine as a place where the Israelite community came to "meet" or "encounter" the God who dwelt within. So too, the related term *miškān,* or "tabernacle," that the P authors and related sources can use in conjunction with or as a synonym for the phrase "tent of meeting" means, literally, the "tabernacling [i.e., dwelling] place" of Yahweh, or the place where the deity tabernacles/dwells (*šākan*) within the Israelites' midst.[79] Note in this regard Exod 25:8 and 29:45 (both P texts), where Yahweh is said explicitly to designate the tent of meeting as the place where "I dwell" (*šākantî*) among the Israelites.

What it at root means, therefore, to define someone as impure or unclean within the ancient Israelite purity system is to denote that individual as unfit to enter into a "holy" space understood to be the dwelling place of Yahweh, the "Holy God." As Saul M. Olyan writes, "*The primary objective* of purity systems in the Syro-Canaanite cultural context is to protect the sanctity of a deity's space from any sort of defilement . . . that which is polluted is kept out" (emphasis mine), for, as Olyan adds, "a polluted sanctuary is not fit for a deity's continuing residence and cult."[80] Rather, only by rigorously separating the impure from the divine's dwelling place can God's *bêt hammiqdāš,* "the house [or temple] of holiness" (as in 1 Chr 28:10 and 2 Chr 36:17), be preserved and "the abiding presence of God in Israel's midst" be sustained.[81] "The sanctuary . . . must at all times remain pure,"[82] and consequently, Israelite women who suffered impurity were, as in Lev 12:4, forbidden from entering into "holy" space—as, likewise, were impure men.

However, unlike many men—husbands, say, who could avoid touching their menstruating wives, or priests who could steer clear of contact with a corpse—women, especially women of childbearing age, could not safeguard against regularly incurring impurity. These impurities, moreover, were manifest for fairly significant periods of time, either because a woman was menstruating or because she had borne a child within the previous forty or eighty days. To be sure, menstruation may have occurred less often among ancient Israelite women than it does within many highly developed societies today because of less adequate standards of nutrition and poorer health overall.[83] Israelite women's menstrual flow also would have been suppressed during their frequent pregnancies and during at least part of the subsequent period of nursing (which, as noted in Chapter 3, may have lasted as long as three years).[84] Still, women must have contracted impurity on account of menstruation and childbirth relatively frequently. Karel van der Toorn has also noted that midwives, as well as other women who may have attended a woman at birth (1 Sam 4:20, Ruth 4:14), would frequently be rendered impure.[85] Men, conversely—or at least fathers—appear not to have been present when children were born and so, unlike midwives and other women who assembled at childbirth, did not risk contracting impurity through contact with the parturient (note in this regard Jer 20:15, where word must be brought after delivery to Jeremiah's father that a son has been born to him).[86] Men likewise do not experience regular discharges as part of their normal biological functioning. The discharge of semen, moreover, rendered a man impure for only one day, as opposed to, say, the seven days of impurity incurred by a menstruating woman. A man also experienced only a day's impurity if he accidentally came into contact with a menstruant or with a stool or bed on which she had sat or lain.

Which is to say: Israelite women seem more likely to have found themselves in a state of ritual impurity, and often a *sustained* state of ritual impurity, than did their male counterparts. This leads Olyan to conclude that "menstruation and parturition . . . stigmatize and marginalize women in ways that have no parallel among men."[87] Or, as Olyan elsewhere writes, "the opposition of clean and unclean in the biblical text differentiates men from women, and it disadvantages women in a number of respects."[88] Here, in the context of our examination of religious venues, the most significant among these disadvantages concerns, as I noted above, women's access to "holy" space, as women, because of their relatively common experiences of impurity, would have been frequently—and more frequently than men—obligated to absent themselves from sanctuaries where God was considered to dwell and where God's holiness was manifest. Again, this was preeminently the temple in Jerusalem, "*the* place where Yahweh dwells among his people Israel,"[89] and also the state-sponsored temples of Dan, Bethel, and (presumably) Samaria. At these sites, as we saw in Chapter 5, the ideology of Yahweh being resident was of essential significance, in order that their royal founders could promote their claims that they and the deity were neighborly intimates and, more important, confederates in the arenas of power, authority, and political dominion.

Overall: women subject to the purity rules of Leviticus (presumably at least some women at some points in ancient Israelite history; more on this below) may have found their access to the Jerusalem temple and the kindred northern temples of Dan, Bethel, and (presumably) Samaria especially constrained because of purity restrictions. Moreover, even within the Jerusalem temple, and arguably within the kindred northern temples, there were clearly defined gradations of holiness, with the Jerusalem temple's inner sanctum (tellingly called the "Holy of Holies" or "the most holy place"; 1 Kgs 6:16, 7:50, 8:6; 2 Chr 3:8, 10; 4:22; 5:7) representing the most sacred part of the temple, whereas the adjacent central hall of the temple was somewhat less holy ("the holy place"; 1 Kgs 8:8, 10; 2 Chr 5:11), and the courtyard outside less holy still.[90] Access to these various zones of holiness was dictated by one's own degree of holiness: only priests were allowed to enter the temple proper, and only the high priest, the most holy member of the Israelite community, was allowed to enter the Holy of Holies, and this only (according, at least, to the P source; Lev 16:2–34 and see also Heb 9:7) on one day a year (the so-called Day of Purgation or Expiation).[91]

Women, conversely, along with other nonpriestly members of the Israelite community, had access only to the courtyard outside the temple, although women, as we have seen, because they were particularly susceptible to a state of ritual impurity, probably had the least access of all Israelites to even this space. Interesting to consider in this regard is the way in which the few biblical texts we have that do speak (or in the case of Ps 68:25–26 [in most of the Bible's English versions, 68:24–25] possibly speak) to women engaging in religious activities in the preexilic Jerusalem temple suggest the temple's holiness must be safeguarded from these women's potential impurities. Psalm 68:25–26 (English 68:24–25), for example, even though it apparently allows its drum-playing women access to Yahweh's sanctuary—tellingly identified in v. 25 (English v. 24) as *qōdeš,* "holy"—specifically describes these women as *ʿălāmôt,* "young maids." At a minimum, this suggests that these women are unmarried (as in Gen 24:43 and Exod 2:8, although cf. Isa 7:14) and so immune from the impurities that result from childbirth. Given that marriage in ancient Israel followed quickly on the heels of a young woman's entry into puberty,[92] we might also plausibly suggest that the *ʿălāmôt* of Psalm 68 are prepubescent. If so, then they can safely engage in musical performance at God's holy sanctuary without introducing the threat of either menstrual or childbirth impurity. Somewhat similarly, we might suggest that Maʿacah, the queen mother of King Abijam and then of King Asa, was immune from menstrual and childbirth impurities at the point during King Asa's reign when she had an image of the mother goddess Asherah erected at some location within the Jerusalem temple precinct, perhaps within the temple itself (1 Kgs 15:13). Chronologically at least, it seems reasonable to assume that Ma'acah was postmenopausal by the time she served as queen mother during her grandson Asa's reign.[93]

As for 2 Kgs 23:7 and Ezek 8:14, each specifically locates its women actors *elsewhere* than in the heart of the temple compound. Thus, the weaving women of 2 Kgs 23:7 are said to work within houses somewhere within the temple grounds, but not within the temple itself nor necessarily in close proximity to it. Likewise, the wailing women of Ezek 8:14 sit at a site in the complex removed from the temple proper, at the temple precinct's northern gate.[94] Patrick D. Miller tellingly contrasts the male religious practitioners who are described in a succeeding verse (Ezek 8:16), who stand in the temple's inner court and, indeed, right next to its entrance, between the temple's front porch, or *dĕbîr,* and its courtyard altar. In fact, Miller entertains the possibility, along with Walther Zimmerli, that "the entrance to the (inner) temple forecourt, which was later, according to Ezekiel 40ff, firmly reserved for the priests, [was] already prohibited to women in the late preexilic period" during which Ezek 8:14 and 8:16 are set.[95]

Judith Romney Wegner has suggested, moreover, that the special need to protect the holiness of the priesthood of the Jerusalem temple (and its antecedent tent shrine) from women's periodic impurities may explain some peculiar aspects of the wording of Lev 15:2–15 and 25–30, which concern, respectively, irregular male and female genital discharges. According to Lev 15:14–15, a man, at the end of a period of impurity brought on by some sort of genital excretion (generally thought to be "an inordinate secretion of mucus" due to his having contracted gonorrhea),[96] presents the *'ôlâ* and purification offerings required of him at God's sanctuary by "giving" (*nātan*) his offerings to the priest. That is, he "hand[s] the birds [the two turtledoves or two pigeons required] over directly," Wegner writes, "thereby making a meaningful physical contact with the priest as his intermediary to God." The woman whose period of irregular vaginal discharge has ended, though, is commanded in Lev 15:29 only to "bring" (*hēbî'â*) the requisite *'ôlâ* and purification offerings to the entrance of the tent of meeting, but, "unlike her male counterpart, she does not place the birds [once more, either two turtledoves or two pigeons] directly into the hands of the priest." Rather, she "presumably sets her offering down somewhere outside" the entrance for the priest then to pick up.[97]

Why this discrepancy? Wegner proposes that the concern here is to protect the priest from the dangers of women's impurities, which perhaps were conceived as unrelentingly omnipresent (this is the interpretation Wegner prefers). Or perhaps a woman's impurity—or at least the potential of impurity—was thought to linger even though her period of irregular genital discharge was allegedly complete (this is how I interpret). Van der Toorn makes a similar point, "Women . . . were always potentially impure," as does Olyan about, specifically, the menstruant and the parturient: "Even when such women are not menstruating or giving birth, their potential to pollute and the consequent need to restrict their contact with others at regular intervals is presumably never forgotten."[98] According to the terms of these analyses, Lev 15:29, by making sure the recently impure woman has no physical contact with the priest, ensures that he cannot be rendered unfit for cultic service as a result of the woman's never forgotten "potential to pollute."

Wegner also suggests that Leviticus's urgent need to protect the holiness of Yahweh's priests and also Yahweh's sanctuary from either the omnipresent dangers or the lingering potential of women's impurities drives a second and even more significant discrepancy in Lev 15:2–15 and 25–30, regarding the use of the phrase *lipnê yhwh.* This expression, as I noted in Chapter 4, is usually translated "before Yahweh"; however, Wegner points out that within Leviticus, "this translation obscures its [the idiom's] technical significance in the rites of the priestly cult." Rather, she writes that in Leviticus, *lipnê yhwh* "more strictly denotes 'in/into the presence of YHWH [Yahweh].'" Indeed, Wegner suggests that implicit in the phrase *lipnê yhwh* is "a crucial aspect of human relationship to the divine, namely the capacity to approach close enough to communicate with the Deity or at least perceive oneself as being in the Presence of God."[99]

More important, Wegner argues that for Leviticus, the capacity to be in the presence of God at the tent of meeting and, presumably, the Jerusalem temple that succeeded it was differently realized for men as opposed to women. In Lev 15:29–30, for example, it is the priest who takes the *ʿōlâ* and purification offerings of women whose periods of impurity have ended and brings them *lipnê yhwh,* or into the presence of Yahweh at Yahweh's altar. Conversely, according to Lev 15:14–15, although a man who has suffered a period of ritual impurity because of a genital discharge similarly brings *ʿōlâ* and purification sacrifices to the tent of meeting (and presumably, in later times, to the Jerusalem temple) and hands them over to the priest, the man, unlike a woman, is said to come *lipnê yhwh* during this moment of presentation. As Wegner puts it, "the inclusion of *lpny yhwh* [*lipnê yhwh*] in the man's case distinguishes him from the woman in an otherwise identical situation *by according him a symbolic location that brings him much closer to God*." However, "by omitting the crucial words *lpny yhwh* [*lipnê yhwh*] the text purposefully avoids placing the woman in the Divine Presence."[100]

Wegner further notes that Jacob Milgrom, surely the most thorough commentator on Leviticus, discounts this discrepancy, claiming that Lev 15:29 articulates an identical theological understanding to Lev 15:14 but expresses it in a "condensed form" whereby the phrase *lipnê yhwh* is left out.[101] Shaye J. D. Cohen also writes that while Wegner "astutely observes" that a man brings "his atonement offering 'before the Lord' (Leviticus 15:14)," whereas a woman does not (Lev 15:29), "the parallel phraseology in Leviticus 15:15 and 30 implies that this difference is not significant."[102] Wegner, though, obviously disagrees, and evidence from elsewhere in Leviticus supports her case—for example, the numerous other Leviticus passages that specifically describe a man who is required to bring an offering to the tent of meeting (and, presumably again, to the Jerusalem temple), in which that man is said to come *lipnê yhwh* with this offering. See:

1. Lev 4:4, 6, and 7, which concern the purification offerings an "anointed priest" who has incurred guilt is to bring *lipnê yhwh;*
2. Lev 4:15, which describes how the elders (male) of the congregation bring an offering *lipnê yhwh* on behalf all Israel if the community has somehow erred in its keeping of Yahweh's commandments;
3. Lev 4:24, which addresses the offering required *lipnê yhwh* of a (male) tribal leader (*nāśîʾ*) who has committed an offense; and
4. Lev 14:11, 18, 23, and 29, which concern the purification *lipnê yhwh* of an *ʾîš* (v. 11), or "man," who has suffered from *ṣāraʿat,* or skin disease.[103]

Members of the all-male priesthood, moreover, are said to come *lipnê yhwh,* or into the presence of Yahweh, repeatedly upon occasions of sacrificial offering: see Lev 4:17, 18; 5:26 (in most of the Bible's English versions, 6:7); 6:7 (English 6:14); 8:26, 27, 29; 9:2, 21; 10:1, 2, 15, 17; 16:1, 7, 10, 12, 13, and 18.

Rather strikingly, though, in Lev 12:6–7, as in the Lev 15:29–30 passage I just discussed, the woman who is to bring an *ʿôlâ* and purification offering after childbirth is *not* said to come *lipnê yhwh,* or into the presence of Yahweh. Moreover, in *none* of the Leviticus or Numbers passages in which a generic "anyone" (*nepeš*) is commanded to present an offering at the tent of meeting (for example, Lev 2:1–2; 4:27–31; 5:15, 17–18, 21–25 [English 6:2–6]; see also Num 15:27) is that "anyone"—which according to Mayer I. Gruber, Carol Meyers, and Milgrom, recall, is a reference that "explicitly denotes both genders"[104]—said to come *lipnê yhwh*. Especially noteworthy here are the instructions found in Lev 4:27–31 regarding the *nepeš* who is to bring a purification offering after committing some sin. These instructions are part of a larger, four-part catalogue in Leviticus 4 that deals with similar purification offerings; in Parts 1, 2, and 3 of this catalogue, as pointed out in the paragraph just above, the *males* who have sinned, or who represent the sinful Israelite community, come *lipnê yhwh* (the high priest in Lev 4:4, 6, and 7; the male elders in Lev 4:15; and the tribal leader in Lev 4:24). But in the otherwise parallel scenario of the catalogue's Part 4 (Lev 4:27–31), the potentially female *nepeš* does not. The same discrimination that Wegner posits for the man's sacrificial offering in Lev 15:14–15 versus the woman's in Lev 15:29–30 seems, that is, to hold in Lev 4:4, 6, 7, 15, and 24 versus 4:27–31 and also in Lev 12:6–7: "by omitting the crucial words *lpny yhwh* [*lipnê yhwh*] the text purposefully avoids placing the woman in the Divine Presence."[105]

Substantial evidence suggests, therefore, that women subject to the purity rules of Leviticus were significantly inhibited in their ability to access the Jerusalem temple, and arguably also the northern state temples of Dan, Bethel, and (presumably) Samaria, and that women were significantly inhibited as well in their ability to access the priests who served within these sanctuaries and the deity that dwelt therein. Or, I should say: women's access to the Jerusalem, Dan, Bethel, and (presumably) Samaria temples, their priests, and their God would have been significantly inhibited presuming I am right about a supposition that underlies my analysis—that the purity dictates articulated in Leviticus and related biblical texts were actually operative at some point in preexilic Israelite history and within some circles of preexilic Israelite society. I do think, though, that this supposition can be sustained. Certainly, we have substantial evidence from throughout the eastern Mediterranean and ancient Near East—from Mesopotamia, Egypt, Hittite culture, and Greece—that strictures regarding childbirth impurity were widely observed,[106] which strongly suggests these strictures were normative in Israel as well. As for menstruation: the Gen 31:19–35 story of Rachel's theft of her father Laban's *tĕrāpîm*/teraphim, most likely ancestor figurines used in rituals of necromancy,[107] indicates that concerns regarding menstrual impurity were held not only by the P authors of Lev 15:19–24, but also by the nonpriestly author(s), redactor(s), and audience of this Genesis account (Gen 31:19–35 is ascribed by biblical scholars to the epic traditions of JE). After all, it is only the conviction that menstrual discharges were both impure and potentially contaminating that can explain why, in the Gen 31:19–35 narrative, Laban refuses to approach Rachel and search her belongings for his missing *tĕrāpîm* once she has told him she is menstruating. The notion of menstrual discharges as impure also seems to be alluded to in a condemnation of defiled idols, to whom menstrual blood is compared, found in Isa 30:22—although the Hebrew here is difficult and potentially corrupt. Clearer examples of this understanding of menstrual blood as impure, however, are found elsewhere in the prophetic corpus: in Ezek 18:6, 22:10, and 36:17, as well as in Lamentations 1, especially in vv. 8–9 and 17.

Scholars have in addition suggested that the story of David's initial encounter with Bathsheba in 2 Sam 11:2–5, which stems from Deuteronomistic tradition, shares presumptions regarding menstrual impurity with Lamentations; the prophetic tradition reflected in Isa 30:22; Ezek 18:6, 22:10, and 36:17; and Leviticus's P and Genesis's epic (JE) authors.[108] It seems, at least, that the most logical interpretation of v. 4 of that text is to understand Bathsheba as "sanctifying" or "purifying" herself (*hî' mitqaddešet*) from the impurity brought on by her menses,[109] given that shortly afterwards, she ovulates and becomes pregnant by David. Interestingly, however, 2 Sam 11:4—assuming Bathsheba's purificatory rite is a response to menstrual uncleanliness—does not seem to share with Leviticus the notion that a woman's time of menstrual impurity comes to an end after seven days have passed. Rather, Bathsheba's purification apparently comes about by immersion (assuming here that the famous scene in 11:2, where David espies her bathing, is the purificatory ritual alluded to in 11:4). This text therefore suggests that the specific details concerning menstrual impurity and how it is to be handled may have differed among preexilic communities.[110] Nevertheless, "the train of thought" that lay behind various ideologies of menstrual impurity "is deeply rooted in the Israelite experience."[111]

Indeed, 2 Samuel 11, in addition to the other textual sources I have surveyed, indicates that "the ideas of pollution, purity, and purification were fundamental concepts in biblical Israel."[112] Here, I have proposed that "the ideas of pollution, purity, and purification" were particularly of concern with regard to Israelite women, and especially with regard to women's ability to participate in the religious life of Judah's and Israel's national temples. Because the ideological precepts that governed those temple complexes required zealous protection of their sanctuaries, in which God was presumed to dwell, and of the holiness of the priests who served God in these shrines, women's regularly occurring periods of ritual impurity—and perhaps also a perception that the dangers of women's impurity were always or at least potentially present—limited female access to these state-sponsored temples and women's engagement in these temples' rituals.

When I began my examination of the various sites of women's religious practice, in Chapter 1, my focus was women's religious *agency:* what role might a woman play in helping furnish her household's shrine and then (as discussed in Chapter 2) engage in the key rituals of household cult? Here, in Chapter 6, as my review of women's participation in ancient Israelite sacred spaces approached its conclusion, I also initially addressed issues of women's religious agency, asking how the highly institutionalized and bureaucratized organizational structures of ancient Israel's and Judah's state-sponsored temples would have limited women's ability to engage as significant religious actors within these sanctuary settings. Yet my subsequent discussions in this chapter—regarding, first, women's participation in the ritual life of state-sponsored sanctuaries sited in border fortresses and their associated border towns and, second, the effect of Israelite purity laws on women's participation in the religious life of Israel's and Judah's great national temples—concerned not so much issues of women's religious *agency* as they did the even more fundamental issue of women's *access* to sanctuary spaces where agency might (or might not) be enacted. As we have seen, in the case of both border fortress–shrine complexes and the great temple complex of Jerusalem (and, presumably, the national temples of Dan, Bethel, and also Samaria), access could be significantly constrained. These constraints could have been the result of logistical factors, as I have argued regarding the border fortress–shrine complexes, given that in many cases, women would have been only minimally represented among the inhabitants of these male-dominated spaces. Or the constraints imposed upon women could have been the result of ideologies of purity and pollution promulgated in state-sponsored temples such as those in Jerusalem and arguably also Bethel, Dan, and (presumably) Samaria and the concerns that these ideologies generated about safeguarding the holiness of God's dwellings and God's priests.

I have moreover considered, especially in relation to the constraints imposed upon women by ideologies of purity and pollution, the ways in which these constraints regarding access to state-sponsored temples had the effect of constraining women's access to the presence of God. Saul M. Olyan has similarly noted how access to the deity is cut off to those excluded from cultic settings. In his words, "Exclusion from the sanctuary represents a very serious . . . religious disadvantage in the Hebrew Bible's cultural context . . . for the sanctuary is the locus par excellence for encounters with the deity."[113] More specifically, as Olyan elsewhere writes, "to be cut off from the sanctuary means to lose access to . . . the place of prostration and prayer, where vows are fulfilled, and where transgressions are expiated." Yet there is more, for Olyan also notes that on a very pragmatic level, "to be cut off from the sanctuary means to lose access to the primary context of meat consumption."[114] To be sure, recent studies have tended to modify older notions that ancient Israelites ate meat only on feast days and holidays,[115] as is suggested in texts such as Deut 12:15, 20–22, and 15:21–22. Nevertheless, it remains the case that sacrificial occasions "are represented [in the Bible] as the primary loci for the slaughter, processing, and distribution of meat."[116] I estimate that, at most, such sacrifices took place fifteen to eighteen times per year.[117]

The importance of meat consumption, however, goes further than just access to protein, as Carol Meyers has reminded us by quoting the Semitic scholar and social anthropologist William Robertson Smith. He asserted some 125 years ago that "the sacrificial meal . . . was a social act . . . the very act of eating and drinking [together] was a symbol and a confirmation of fellowship and mutual social obligation . . . those who sit at meat together are united for all social effects."[118] Meyers, moreover, reports that similar assessments have been reached by more recent theorists: "feasting . . . is a powerful form of ritual activity" and "a central cultural practice," as "feasts were powerful arenas for establishing, maintaining, or even changing cultural identities."[119] Thus, "taking part in a feast," as Meyers writes, "fosters and maintains a sense of identity" and "provided individuals with a sense of belonging to the commensal group."[120] Karel van der Toorn makes much the same point—"to partake of the [sacrificial] meal is to be part of the community"—meaning, to quote again one of the experts cited by Meyers, commensality "plays a central role in constructing and reinforcing social bonds."[121]

Consequently, for an ancient Israelite to have been cut off from sacrificial occasions would have profoundly compromised that individual's sense of community and social solidarity. Once more, we can cite Olyan: "to be cut off from the sanctuary means to lose access to . . . the major locus for the shaping of social relations," which in turn "effectively denies the excluded individual a place in the social order."[122] Yet while the language

Olyan deploys here regarding an "excluded individual" is gender neutral, we can also note Olyan's words elsewhere: "Women subject to [purity rules] would have spent a substantial amount of time cut off from cultic . . . settings."[123] Thereby we can suggest that women, lacking access to Israel's state-sponsored temples and the sacrificial rites enacted therein, would have found their sense of social identity and solidarity as fostered at such sanctuaries significantly constrained.[124] To put the matter another way: if, as argued by contemporary ritual theorists, "ritual produces social cohesion,"[125] then cohesion can be denied—or, at best, come less easily—to those, like Israelite women, who are cut off from state-sponsored temples and their ritual activities.

Of course, as we have seen in Chapters 3 and 4, Israel's regional sanctuaries were in a position to compensate for the marginalization suffered by women on the national level. Certainly the account in 1 Sam 2:12–17 of other Israelites who come to Shiloh to sacrifice at the same time that Hannah and her family annually visit indicates that this regional sanctuary is envisioned as a space where social relations beyond the individual family unit can be forged. Likewise, Shiloh, according to 1 Sam 1:4–5, functioned as a site where Hannah (and also Elkanah's other wife, Peninnah, and maybe Peninnah's daughters) engaged in the consumption of meat—and seemingly without much concern regarding issues of purity and pollution, which, in the words of Patrick D. Miller, appear only to be "tangentially" of account in the Hannah story.[126] Moreover, 1 Sam 1:1–2:26 indicates at multiple points that the regional sanctuary of Shiloh could serve a woman such as Hannah as a place of "prostration and prayer," a place "where vows are fulfilled," and, more generally, a place where Hannah could engage, by coming *lipnê yhwh,* in "encounters with the deity."[127] Equally, I presume, spaces such as Micah's household shrine and the household shrine of twelfth- and eleventh-century BCE Ai served the women resident in these shrines' household compounds as places where prayer could be offered, where vows could be made, and where the deity—represented symbolically by a cast-metal figurine or by a fenestrated offering stand that symbolized Yahweh "at home" in his temple—would be (at least occasionally) manifest and so could be (at least occasionally) encountered.

Still, household-based shrines did not offer their women worshippers opportunities for meat consumption (given that animal sacrifice was a part of only sanctuary and temple ritual in the ancient Near East).[128] Nor, obviously, did household-based shrines offer opportunities for fostering social relations beyond the household compound's inhabitants. We should remember, moreover, that according to 1 Sam 1:21–23, Hannah did not go on her family's annual journeys to Shiloh after she had given birth to Samuel and until he was weaned, a process that—as I have now noted several times—may have taken as long as three years. Hannah, that is, might be envisioned as suffering prolonged separation from the opportunities for meat consumption and the fostering of social relations that regional sanctuaries afford and that household shrines could not provide.

In short, neither household-based shrines nor regional sanctuaries were fully the recourse they might seem for women coping with the constraints that limited their access to Judah's and Israel's state-sponsored temples. In this regard, we might evoke once again Phyllis Bird's quotation that I cited at the very beginning of my analysis of Israelite state temples, in Chapter 5. In it, Bird speaks of women's "dual status" in the cultic realm, given that, on one hand, they are subject to their community's religious expectations and governed by its religious norms, yet on the other, "they are restricted in varying degrees from the inner circle where the norms were formulated, inculcated, and rationalized."[129] As we have now seen, Israel's state-sponsored temples were a key locus where Bird's "inner circle" did its work. The restrictions imposed on women's agency in and their access to such venues thus constitute a significant barrier to women's ability fully to engage in ancient Israel's religious life.

PART 2

When? The Calendar of Women's Religious Lives

7 "There Is a Yearly Sacrifice . . . for All the Family": The Israelite Woman's Ritual Year, I

In this chapter and the next, I turn from exploring the *where* of Israelite women's religious lives—household shrines, regional sanctuaries, and Israel's state-sponsored temples—to consider the *when:* that is, women's roles and experiences during the various festivals and religious observances that constituted ancient Israel's weekly, monthly, and yearly ritual calendar. In this chapter I consider the following three instances of ritual observance: the weekly rituals of the Sabbath, or Shabbat; the monthly festival of the *ḥōdeš,* or the new moon; and the family or clan sacrificial banquet that kin groups seem to have celebrated annually. Then, in Chapter 8, I take up the festivals identified at several points in the Bible as the three great pilgrimage feasts of the Israelite year: Maṣṣot, or the festival of Unleavened Bread; Harvest, also called Firstfruits and Shavu'ot ("Weeks"); and Ingathering, or Sukkot ("Booths").

Women and Ancient Israelite Sabbath Traditions

In modern Judaism, the weekly observance of the Sabbath, or Shabbat, has sometimes been touted as a primary moment when women experience and express their religiosity. This is because, beginning in the nineteenth century, the Jewish Sabbath shifted from being a primarily synagogue-based ritual to a home-based observance, whose central event is a festive and often lavish evening meal that, typically, the woman of the house is enjoined to prepare. It is also in conjunction with modern-day Shabbat that at least one and frequently two of the three commandments reserved for women according to rabbinic law are observed: first, the lighting of candles to denote the beginning of the Sabbath and, second, the so-called taking of challah.[1] In this ritual, a small piece of dough is pinched off and burned before a batch of bread is baked, in commemoration of the bread loaves the ancient Israelites used to offer to their community's priests (Num 15:20).[2] To be sure, many have raised concerns about whether these Shabbat exercises are really markers of significant religious responsibilities for women: Judith Plaskow follows Cynthia Ozick, for example, in observing that the two women's commandments just described, focused as they are on domestic matters, attest to "the limited religious space offered to women" within traditional Judaism and "the confines of [women's] lives."[3] Nevertheless, commentators have often cited modern Sabbath observance as a special moment in Jewish women's religious experience. In their 1952 study of New York Jews who had emigrated from the shtetls of Eastern Europe, for example, Mark Zborowski and Elizabeth Herzog note how the Sabbath prayers of shtetl communities extolled the woman of the house, and they also quote one of their informant's memories of his mother's response to this praise: "On Friday night, on Sabbath Eve," she is said to have told her son, "I am a queen, like every Jewish woman. On weekdays, I am just a woman."[4]

When we turn to look at Sabbath traditions from ancient Israel, however, the preeminent position that some would claim for women within modern Jewish practice is less readily found. Indeed, scholars have debated whether there even was a tradition of weekly Sabbath observance in Israel's preexilic era.[5] To be sure, many of the source materials that I dated to the preexilic period in the Introduction, representing many textual genres (law, poetry, narrative) and many authorial perspectives (priestly, prophetic, Deuteronomic, Deuteronomistic, and epic [JE]), in some way or another mention the observance of *šabbāt* (the Hebrew noun rendered in an anglicized form as "Shabbat" or "Sabbath").[6] Still, it is sometimes uncertain to what, precisely, these citations refer. In several instances, preeminently in texts from the eighth-century BCE prophets, *šabbāt* is associated with the celebration of the *ḥōdeš,* or new moon (Isa 1:13, Hos 2:13 [in most of the Bible's English versions, 2:11], Amos 8:5; see also 2 Kgs 4:23). This has led some commentators to suggest that in the preexilic period of Israelite history, *šabbāt* was in fact the counterpart of the new moon festival—that is, a full moon festival whose name derives from the Mesopotamian day of the full moon, which was called *šabattu* or *šapattu.*[7]

Obviously, under the terms of this reconstruction, preexilic *šabbāt* was a monthly, rather than today's weekly affair; moreover, as was the case with the new moon festival, the rituals that formally celebrated this purported full moon *šabbāt* would have been temple-based, as opposed to today's home-based *šabbāt* rites (see 2 Kgs 11:5–9, 16:18; Isa 1:13; Hos 2:13 [English 2:11]; Lam 2:6). According to this "*šabbāt* = full moon" hypothesis, however, there was also a home-based tradition in preexilic Israel—albeit one without religious significance—of suspending certain customary labors on every seventh day (the *yôm haššĕbîʿî* of the fourth commandment as presented in Exod 20:10). This day, as the reconstruction goes, was described using the verb *šābat* (Exod 23:12; possibly 34:21), which most literally means "to cease, come to an end" and secondarily "to stop, have a break, rest."[8] Only in the time of the exile, it is posited, did the two originally disparate institutions of the full moon *šabbāt* and the seventh day of *šābat,* "rest," merge (a process perhaps expedited by the linguistic similarities of the terms *šabbāt* and *šābat*), to give rise to the notion of a sanctified Sabbath observance once a week (*yôm haššabbāt*).[9] This is reflected in exilic-era texts such as Ezek 46:1, 4.

Other commentators, though, reject this interpretation in favor of a more traditional understanding that *šabbāt* observance every seventh day was "at a very early period . . . a genuine institution of the Yahweh faith."[10] "No passage suggests that the Sabbath . . . was observed only once a month," E. Haag writes; rather, "the preexilic Sabbath in Israel . . . was identical with the seventh day . . . with the designations 'Sabbath' and 'seventh day' merely referring to two different stages in the development of this holiday."[11] Further critiques of the "*šabbāt* = full moon" hypothesis have been offered by Daniel E. Fleming, William H. C. Propp, and J. Alberto Soggin. Fleming points out, for example, that Mesopotamian *šabattu*/*šapattu* is not mentioned in the thirteenth/early twelfth-century BCE texts from the city of Emar, in northwestern Syria, nor in the roughly contemporaneous textual corpus from the city-state of Ugarit, on the northern Levantine coast (see Fig. I.2). Thus he concludes that *šabattu*/*šapattu* was a distinctively southern Mesopotamian word and not a part of north or northwest Semitic lexicons from whence the term could have been borrowed into Hebrew.[12]

Indeed, scholars have detailed enough flaws in the "*šabbāt* = full moon" hypothesis to indicate that its converse is more likely to be true: that a weekly rather than a monthly *šabbāt* observance was a part of Israel's preexilic ritual calendar. Yet what did this weekly *šabbāt* observance look like? As noted above, it was, at least in part, temple-based.[13] According to the eighth-century BCE prophetic oracle found in Isa 1:13, for example, *šabbāt* observance entails bringing offerings and incense to Yahweh, presumably, given Isaiah's Jerusalem provenance, to Yahweh's Jerusalem temple.[14] The dictum in Exod 35:3 that *šabbāt* is to be observed "throughout your settlements" and not just in a sanctuary setting suggests, however, that some rituals outside of temple purview were also a feature of preexilic *šabbāt* observance.[15] These rituals include the cessation of certain customary labors (albeit not all; more on this below).

To be sure, concerning this issue there is again disagreement: interpreters who accept the general notion that some respite from work is attested within preexilic *šabbāt* texts can question, for example, whether this tradition is universal across biblical sources.[16] Scholars also debate whether the references to the seventh-day suspension of agricultural work found in Exod 34:21 and Deut 5:14 (cf. Exod 23:12) belong within a discussion of *šabbāt* traditions or speak rather to customs associated with the annual feast of Maṣṣot, or Unleavened Bread. This is because Exod 34:21 follows upon a description of the weeklong festival of Maṣṣot found in 34:18, which may suggest that 34:21 intends not to refer to a cessation of agricultural labor that occurs every seventh day throughout the year, but to describe only the day of rest that other texts mandate is to be observed annually on the seventh and last day of the Maṣṣot celebration (Exod 12:16, 13:6; Lev 23:8; Num 28:25).[17] Likewise, the exodus event that Maṣṣot commemorates is the subject of the verse that immediately succeeds Deut 5:14, which could again suggest that Deut 5:14 originally referred not to a weekly Sabbath day, but only to an annual day of rest on the seventh day of the Maṣṣot festival. This interpretation is strengthened by the fact that no references to *šabbāt* appear elsewhere in Deuteronomy.[18]

Still, as already indicated, I contend that overall, our sources do suggest that the cessation of some customary labors was a feature of preexilic *šabbāt* ritual. Amos 8:5 indicates, for example, that on *šabbāt,* as on the day of the new moon, commerce must halt (much to the disgust of Amos's eighth-century BCE audience, which includes merchants eager to maximize their time in the marketplace and thus maximize their profits).[19] Jeremiah 17:19–27 and Neh 13:15–22, although postexilic in date, likewise indicate that especially in Jerusalem, commercial activities ("bearing a burden," i.e., bringing goods to sell at market) must be suspended on *šabbāt.*[20] Exodus 16:4–5,

22–30 somewhat similarly describes how the Israelites who wandered in the wilderness after coming out of Egypt were to collect a double portion of the heavenly manna that sustained them on the sixth day of the week and then refrain from the work of gathering manna on the seventh.[21] According to Exod 35:3 and Num 15:32–36, tasks related to building a fire (gathering wood and kindling a flame) are also to be avoided on *šabbāt,* although the preexilic dating of these two texts, and so their relevance for this study, is debated.[22] Exodus 34:21—if one chooses to interpret it as a *šabbāt* versus a Maṣṣot text—adds that plowing and the reaping of grain are to be abstained from every seventh day.[23] The kindred Deut 5:14—were it likewise to be interpreted as a *šabbāt* versus a Maṣṣot text—mandates a rest every seventh day for the animals who bear the greatest burdens of fieldwork, the ox and the donkey.

In sum, several biblical texts from the preexilic period (some more secure in their interpretation and/or in their date than others) attest that *šabbāt* observance entails the temporary cessation of (1) gathering manna (Exod 16:4–5, 22–30), (2) plowing and reaping grain (depending on how one interprets Exod 34:21 and Deut 5:14), (3) gathering wood and kindling fire (depending on how one dates Exod 35:3 and Num 15:32–36), and (4) commercial activities within the marketplace (Amos 8:5). Yet what do these texts indicate regarding the nature of the *šabbāt* experience for Israelite women? Only the debated Deut 5:14 among the texts I have surveyed cites women explicitly (although cf. Exod 20:10), decreeing a day of rest for not only the ox and the donkey, but also "your (masculine singular) daughter" and "your (masculine singular) female slave" alongside other household members: "your (masculine singular) son," "your (masculine singular) male slave," and "you" (again a masculine singular form that Georg Braulik has nevertheless argued refers both to a household's paterfamilias and his wife).[24] Although not specifically mentioned, the women of the exodus generation are also presumably to be counted among "the congregation" (*hāʿēdâ*) and "the people" (*hāʿām*) that Exod 16:4–5, 22–30 envisions as refraining from the gathering of manna on the seventh day/*šabbāt.*[25] However, even if Exod 16:4–5, 22–30 does include women among those who abstain from gathering manna on the seventh day/*šabbāt,* neither these verses nor texts elsewhere in the Bible suggest that abstaining from the gathering of manna during the exodus from Egypt had any implications for specific *šabbāt* activities from which women (or men, for that matter) were to abstain within the postexodus (i.e., the postmanna) Israelite community.[26]

Furthermore, regarding the texts that do delineate specific activities from which the postexodus community was to abstain, we should note that the work of plowing fields and reaping the grain that these fields produced was, as discussed in Chapter 1, typically assumed by men in ancient Israel.[27] Thus, if Exod 34:21 and Deut 5:14 are to be taken as mandating abstention from this sort of agricultural work every seventh day (which, as we have again seen, is open to question), this decree is most readily seen as affecting males rather than females.

Like the grain fields of Exod 34:21 and Deut 5:14, the marketplace of Amos 8:5 is not a woman's customary domain, meaning that this verse's requirement that the Israelites refrain from commerce on *šabbāt* would seem to concern preexilic women little (although see, among chronologically later texts, Prov 31:18, 24).[28] Similarly, in Num 15:32–36, it is a man (*'îš*) who is castigated for gathering wood on *šabbāt*, and other biblical texts also describe men as responsible for wood gathering and the related kindling of fire prohibited on *šabbāt* according to Exod 35:3. In Gen 22:3, for example, Abraham cuts the wood required for offering up his son Isaac, and while his wood-gathering role in this passage could be seen only as a function of the sacrificial content of Genesis 22 (similar to the way priests assume the responsibility for caring for the fires on Yahweh's altars; Lev 6:2, 5–6 [in most of the Bible's English versions, 6:9, 12–13]), the fact of the matter is that the "secular" woodchoppers of Deut 19:5, 29:10 (in most of the Bible's English versions, 29:11), and Josh 9:16–27 are also gendered grammatically as male. Likewise, in Jer 7:18, as we saw in Chapter 2, it is the "boys" of Jerusalem's and Judah's households who are said to gather wood (see similarly Lam 5:13), and it is in addition the "fathers" of Jer 7:18 who kindle fire. Isaiah 44:15 describes a male as kindling fire as well. Indeed, only two biblical texts of which I know, 1 Kgs 17:8–16 and Isa 27:11, describe women as engaged in gathering wood or in any of the tasks associated with fire-building.[29] Both these texts, moreover, concern a situation of crisis. The woman of 1 Kgs 17:8–16, for example, is a widow whose son, if 17:17–24 is to be taken as any guide, is sickly. Thus she may be out gathering firewood because she has no husband or able-bodied boy in her home who can assume this traditionally male responsibility.

Overall: of the specific activities that our various biblical texts identify as labors suspended on the Sabbath, none seems to be work in which women customarily engaged. Indeed, Exod 12:16 may hint that on *šabbāt*, women were expected to *continue* their most customary work—food preparation—unabated. In that text, the task of food preparation is specifically enjoined on the first and seventh days of the Maṣṣot festival, even though otherwise *kol-mĕlā'kâ lō'-yē'āśeh,* "no work is to be done." Might this injunction analogously suggest that women's task of food preparation is to continue on *šabbāt,* even as other activities are suspended?[30] Without doubt, tasks assigned to certain other members of the Israelite community continued, and their demands were even intensified on *šabbāt:* I think here of temple priests for whom it would have been incumbent to offer the special sacrifices that it seems were required on *šabbāt,* at least by the eighth century BCE (see again, for example, Isa 1:13).[31] With regard to these sacrifices, moreover, it is at this point worth reiterating for the purposes of this inquiry that they "largely excluded the public."[32] Thus, as my analysis of temple culture in Chapters 5–6 indicates, they would have especially excluded women.

In short, the biblical record as we have surveyed it so far offers little to confirm the modern tendency to extol women as central agents in *šabbāt* observances, either in household-based observances that required abstinence from certain activities or in sanctuary-based activities added to customary temple routine. Nevertheless, three texts from the Priestly (P) and Holiness (H) traditions, Exod 31:15, 35:2, and Lev 23:3, and one text from the Deuteronomistic History, 2 Kgs 4:8–37, offer intriguing glimpses into a religiously salutary effect that *šabbāt* rituals may have had upon Israelite women.[33] In Exod 31:15, 35:2, and Lev 23:3 (see also Exod 16:23), although there is language forbidding "work," *mĕlā'kâ,* that in large part parallels the language I have previously discussed that requires abstinence on *šabbāt* from only certain types of work, *šabbāt* is also described using the phrase *šabbat šabbātôn,* usually translated as "a sabbath of solemn [or 'complete'] rest." In the view of many commentators, this "ups the ante," so to speak, in terms of the restrictions placed upon an ancient Israelite's labors, so that while the frequently attested language forbidding "work," *mĕlā'kâ,* refers to what Jacob Milgrom describes as "laborious work," or "work related to one's livelihood" (for example, the work of the marketplace, or the work of plowing and reaping grain, or the work of those designated as "woodcutters" [as in Deut 29:10; English 29:11]), the phrase *šabbat šabbātôn* forbids, to quote again Milgrom, "any manner of work."[34] Hence, for Israelite women who followed the priestly dicta of Exod 31:15, 35:2, and Lev 23:3, there may have been respite from customary tasks such as food preparation on *šabbāt,* even as other *šabbāt* texts may presume this obligation fell to women on *šabbāt* just as on all other days.

Second Kings 4:8–37 approaches the question of women's *šabbāt* rest from a somewhat different perspective. In this passage, an unnamed woman from Shunem (see Fig. I.1) befriends the prophet Elisha (typically called in this narrative a "man of God" [*ʾîš hāʾĕlōhîm*]). He in return gives this Shunammite woman a precious gift: an annunciation that she, who has no son and whose husband is elderly, will miraculously give birth to a baby boy. This indeed happens, but one day, after the child had become older, he is suddenly stricken ill and dies. The woman then asks her husband for the use one of their household's servitors and a donkey, so that she might go to Elisha. Her aim, presumably, is to see whether the prophet might again work his life-giving magic on her behalf. The husband, however, although he knows the child had sickened, does not necessarily know his son has died; the woman also, when she tells her husband that she intends to go see Elisha, does not mention the child's death. Understanding the husband to be ignorant of the matter's urgency helps illuminate his bewildered response to his wife. "Why would you go to him [Elisha] today?" he asks her; "it is neither the new moon nor the Sabbath" (2 Kgs 4:23). Yet more illuminating for my purposes is the assumption implicit here: that while a visit to Elisha or some other "man of God" is an unexpected undertaking for the Shunammite woman within her normal day's routine, it is *not* unusual for her husband to think she would seek to make such a journey on the day of the new moon or on *šabbāt*.

Unfortunately, the text gives no further hint of *why* a *šabbāt* visit to a "man of God" might be thought appropriate, although one could suggest, for example, that *šabbāt* was considered a propitious day on which to travel, or, similarly, that "New Moon and Sabbath were considered propitious days for consultation with a prophet."[35] Or it might be that "the sabbath is a day worth visiting a shrine in search of a holy man [because it is] a day when he would be there."[36] Or perhaps it was considered appropriate to undertake a *šabbāt* visit to see Elisha, a "man of God" who, as the quotation just above suggests, is also designated in 2 Kgs 4:9 as "holy" (*qādôš*), because *šabbāt* is likewise a day biblical tradition can designate as "holy" or as a "holy proclamation" (*qōdeš, miqrāʾ-qōdeš;* see, for example, Exod 16:23, 20:8, 31:14–15, 35:2; Lev 23:3; Isa 58:13; Jer 17:22, 24; Ezek 20:20, 44:24; Neh 13:22).[37] Yet because this designation of *šabbāt* as "holy" is predominantly a feature of chronologically later texts, and because enough chronologically disparate texts, as we have seen, attest that *šabbāt* involves some cessation of one's regular routine, I maintain (along with several other commentators)[38] that underlying 2 Kgs 4:23 is an understanding that although the specific labors (manna collection, agricultural work, fire-building tasks, and mercantile activities) that texts such as Exod 16:4–5, 22–30, 34:21, 35:3; Num 15:32–36; Deut 5:14; and Amos 8:5 mandate must be stopped on *šabbāt* do not pertain explicitly to women, women did at least to some degree suspend work on *šabbāt,* as Exod 31:15, 35:2, and Lev 23:3 might indicate. Yet whereas Exod 31:15, 35:2, and Lev 23:3 might be interpreted to mean that the exertions of travel were among the labors to be suspended on *šabbāt* (certainly, this is how later Jewish tradition, basing itself on Exod 16:29, understood the *šabbāt* prohibitions), 2 Kgs 4:23 seems to assume just the opposite: that the suspension of at least some of women's customary labors on *šabbāt* freed up their time for travel. Thus they were able, like the Shunammite woman, to visit prophets like Elisha and other "men of God."

It seems possible, moreover, that these *šabbāt* visits to "men of God" were an important part of Israelite women's religious experience. We might suppose, for example, that Rebekah's going "to inquire (*dāraš*) of Yahweh" in Gen 25:22, concerning the strivings going on in her womb, was a journey to an oracular specialist that the biblical writers and their ancient Israelite audience envisioned her undertaking on a *šabbāt* day, when she had some respite from other obligations.[39] Likewise, we might suppose that the story in 1 Kgs 14:1–18 of King Jeroboam's wife, who was sent by her husband to the prophet Ahijah at Shiloh to inquire (*dāraš*) about the health of their ailing son, imagines this woman as traveling on a *šabbāt.* To be sure, neither the Genesis 25 nor 1 Kings 14 text has any mention of *šabbāt,* and the 2 Kings 4 pericope describes the Shunammite woman's mission as so urgent that she ultimately travels on some day other than the Sabbath. Nevertheless, the stories of Gen 25:19–26, 1 Kgs 14:1–18, and 2 Kgs 4:8–37 bear some marked similarities—both the sense that it is children's mothers who need to seek divine assistance when the health of their offspring seems threatened and the sense that these mothers go to seek this divine assistance independent of their husbands' company and even, in Gen 25:19–26 and 2 Kgs 4:22–25, independent of their husbands' counsel.[40] This could indicate that just as the husband of the Shunammite woman presumes his wife would most obviously make her proposed journey on *šabbāt,* there was a general presumption in Israel that on *šabbāt* days, women had respite from at least some of their normal household obligations in order to make journeys to visit religious specialists to seek help for children, both born and unborn, who ailed.

If this analysis has any merit, then another point regarding women's religious experiences must quickly follow, for 2 Kgs 4:23 suggests there is another occasion on which women might have respite from their normal labors in order to make journeys to seek help from religious specialists for their ailing children: during the monthly celebration of the new moon (*ḥōdeš*).[41]

Women and the Monthly Festival of the New Moon

Like *šabbāt,* the new moon holiday—observed on "the day on which the lunar crescent becomes visible again"[42]—was celebrated, at least by the eighth century BCE, at a temple, such as the state-sponsored temple complexes of Jerusalem, Dan, and Bethel, or at a regional sanctuary, such as narratives set earlier in Israelite history locate at Shiloh. A temple setting for the new moon festival is indicated, for example, in the oracles of the eighth-century BCE prophet Isaiah (Isa 1:13) and in a P text found in Num 10:10.[43] There, and in similar, although not identical, mandates found in Num 28:11–15, 29:6, and Ezek 46:6, it is specifically prescribed that the new moon festival be marked by the sorts of *ʿōlâ* and *šĕlāmîm* sacrifices that are the centerpieces of the cult of large state temples and regional sanctuaries but are not generally offered in household-based shrines.

Determining the setting of 1 Samuel 20, which is another text describing a new moon celebration, is more challenging. Most typically, commentators, if they address this issue (and many do not), take the setting to be domestic, although the domicile in question could hardly be called a normal Israelite home. Rather, it is understood to be King Saul's royal dwelling, located at Saul's fief in Gibeah (see Fig. I.1).[44] Within this royal dwelling, as interpreters would have it, certain members of Saul's household were expected to gather for a meal at the time of the new moon. Verses within 1 Samuel 20 that lend credence to this analysis include 1 Sam 20:29 and its reference to the "table of the king," or more idiomatically, the "royal table" (*šulḥan hammelek*), which can readily be understood as one of the furnishings in Saul's home (see 2 Sam 9:11, 1 Kgs 5:7 [in most of the Bible's English versions, 4:27]). Nevertheless, the texts describing the sacrifices of the new moon festival cited above, including texts to some degree contemporaneous with 1 Samuel 20 (at least in the form in which these texts have come down to us), suggest that Saul's new moon meal should be the ritual feast that one would expect to follow the *šĕlāmîm* offerings of the new moon celebration. This ritual feast, as we saw in Chapter 3, should be eaten within the sanctuary compound where the sacrifice was made.[45] I thus propose we envision the meal of 1 Samuel 20 as taking place not within Saul's home, but in a *liškâ,* which, as also noted in Chapter 3, is a chamber that is part of a sanctuary complex in which ritual feasts can be consumed (1 Sam 1:18, according to the Greek version of the biblical text, 9:22–24; Jer 35:2–4; Ezek 42:13).[46]

As to what sanctuary complex is the subject of 1 Samuel 20: I further suggest that we are to imagine that Saul ate in a *liškâ* that was part of the *bāmâ* sanctuary (or, as it is typically translated, the "high place")[47] that 1 Sam 10:5, 10–12, and 13 intimate was located within the king's fief at Gibeah. Granted, this proposal requires that we assume that Gibeath-elohim, the "Hill of God," in 1 Sam 10:5, where there is said to be a *bāmâ* and where Samuel predicts that Saul will encounter a band of prophets, is the same as Gibeah (*gib'â*) as cited in 1 Sam 10:10–12, which is the place where Saul does in fact meet a prophetic band.[48] More crucially, we must assume that the Gibeath-elohim of 10:5 and the Gibeah of 10:10–12 are one and the same as the "Gibeah of Saul" (1 Sam 11:4, 15:34), which is the king's hometown, his royal fief, and (according to my interpretation) the site of a *bāmâ-liškâ* complex.[49]

Some commentators, though, have questioned these suppositions.[50] They argue, for example, that *gib'â* in 1 Sam 10:10–12 is just a common noun meaning "hill" and not a reference to the town of Gibeah, much less to the specific Gibeah (which was a popular place name)[51] that was home to Saul. But several pieces of evidence converge to argue otherwise. For example, although this is obscured in many modern translations, the Masoretic Text indicates that after Saul finished his encounter with the prophets in 1 Sam 10:10–12, he adjourned to a nearby *bāmâ* in 1 Sam 10:13, and it defies common sense to propose that this *bāmâ* that was near the site of Saul's prophetic encounter in Gibeah (*gib'â*) would be any other than the *bāmâ* of Gibeath-elohim of 1 Sam 10:5 at which it was predicted this encounter would take place. The Gibeath-elohim of 1 Sam 10:5 and its *bāmâ,* that is to say, must be identical to the Gibeah (*gib'â*) of 1 Sam 10:10–13 and its *bāmâ.*

Moreover, both the Greek Codex Vaticanus and the Greek rendering of the Hebrew Bible found in the Lucianic group of minuscules—manuscript traditions that, as we saw in Chapters 3–4, are often better witnesses to the ancient recension of Samuel than is the Masoretic Text—explicitly speak in 1 Sam 22:6 of a *bāmâ* in Saul's royal fief of Gibeah.[52] Common sense would once more suggest that this *bāmâ* is best taken as equivalent to the 1 Sam 10:5 *bāmâ* of Gibeath-elohim and the 1 Sam 10:10–13 *bāmâ* of Gibeah (*gibʿâ*), as the evocation of a different Gibeah *bāmâ* within such a short span of textual tradition seems improbable. What's more, in 1 Sam 10:10–13, Saul is said to have been observed during his encounter with the prophetic band near the *bāmâ* of Gibeah (*gibʿâ*) by those who had "known him previously" (1 Sam 10:11), and who would those "previous" acquaintances of the still young and unworldly Saul most logically be but the people who had known him in his hometown, the "Gibeah of Saul," during his childhood and adolescence? That Saul's paternal uncle (*dôd*) is identified in 1 Sam 10:14 as being part of the group of Saul's previous acquaintances makes this interpretation—that the Gibeah *bāmâ* of 1 Sam 10:13 is in Saul's hometown, the "Gibeah of Saul"—more likely still. By this means, therefore, the Gibeah (*gibʿâ*) of 1 Sam 10:10–13 and its *bāmâ,* which I have previously established is identical to the Gibeath-elohim of 1 Sam 10:5 and its *bāmâ,* is identified also with a *bāmâ* located in the "Gibeah of Saul," the king's hometown as well as his royal seat. Or, more specifically, the *bāmâ* of Gibeath-elohim (1 Sam 10:5) and the *bāmâ* of Gibeah (1 Sam 10:10–13) are established as one and the same as the *bāmâ-liškâ* sanctuary complex in the "Gibeah of Saul" that I have suggested the author(s) and/or redactor(s) of 1 Samuel 20 mean for us to envision as the setting of Saul's new moon feast.

Positing a sanctuary setting for Saul's new moon feast also explains why Saul, in 1 Sam 20:25, is said to sit "in his seat" at the festive meal "as [from] time to time" or, more idiomatically, "as upon other occasions" (*kĕpaʿam bĕpaʿam;* see Num 24:1 and Judg 16:20). That is, as I interpret, Saul sat *periodically,* at, say, the celebration of the new moon feast and during other ritual observances, in the seat customarily assigned to him in the *liškâ* of his fiefdom's *bāmâ* complex, rather than occupying the seat in his royal palace in which he sat *routinely* for every other meal (the Hebrew describing this would be something like *kĕyôm bĕyôm,* "day by day" [see 1 Sam 18:10]). Saul's *liškâ* seat, whose location in 1 Sam 20:25 is carefully described, is surely, moreover, a seat of honor, much like the seat that, according to 1 Sam 9:22–24, Saul was given when he sat at the head of the *liškâ*'s assembled guests during the festal meal celebrated at a different *bāmâ-liškâ* sanctuary complex (in Ramah?).[53] Ancient Near Eastern parallels furthermore suggest that the "head man" at such a sanctified banquet is attended by his "crown prince," who stands beside him.[54] For example, in a scene from the Late Bronze Age mythological texts concerning the god Baal that come from the northern Levantine city-state of Ugarit (see Fig. I.2), Baal, the warrior god who is the "king" of the pantheon's younger generation, stands beside the patriarch of the gods El at a feast of El's divine council (*KTU* 1.1.2.20–21). Just so does Saul's son Jonathan stand beside his father in 1 Sam 20:25, and note as well how Saul's servant boy perhaps stands by Saul at the meal Saul ate at the *bāmâ-liškâ* sanctuary complex described in 1 Sam 9:11–14, 19, 22–25.

Yet unlike the *bāmâ-liškâ* complex of 1 Sam 9:11–14, 19, 22–25, which I have described in Chapter 3 as a local or regional sanctuary, I take Saul's *bāmâ-liškâ* sanctuary at Gibeah to be more analogous to the state-sponsored temple complexes I discussed in Chapters 5 and 6. Which is not to say, let me quickly add, that we should envision the *bāmâ-liškâ* complex at Gibeah as being of nearly the scale of the (still quite modest) Solomonic temple compound in Jerusalem, or of the (also quite modest) scale of the Northern Kingdom's temple complexes at Dan and Bethel. Nor should we take Saul's "state" to be a nation in anything like the (again quite modest) sense that the later kingdoms of Israel and Judah were "nations." Indeed, I make no presumption that there was a Saul, or a Saulide royal house, or a Saulide *bāmâ-liškâ* at Gibeah. Nevertheless, I presume that the biblical writers who promulgated the 1 Samuel accounts of Saul as king would have imagined Saul as seeking to secure his unassuming highland fief (consisting of nothing more, surely, than the territories of Benjamin and Ephraim, and maybe only southern Ephraim, at that)[55] by promoting the same ideology of kingly intimacy with the divine that characterized the later and more monumental royal sanctuaries of tenth- to seventh-century BCE Israel and Judah. That is, I presume Saul would have been imagined by the biblical writers to have promoted an ideology at Gibeah that claimed Yahweh was resident in the *bāmâ-liškâ* sanctuary complex associated with (even adjacent to?) Saul's royal residence, thereby to propose that Yahweh supported Saul's monarchical undertakings and that Yahweh's presence alongside the king gave succor to Saul (who is, after all, called the "anointed of Yahweh" in 1 Sam 24:7, 11 [in most of the Bible's English versions, 24:6, 10]; 26:9, 11, 16, and 23).[56]

Yet if Saul's *bāmâ-liškâ* sanctuary at the "Gibeah of Saul" is to be understood—at least to some degree—as an analogue (even if only an imagined analogue) to the state-sponsored temple complexes of Jerusalem, Dan, and Bethel, then one must ask whether the same consequence we see in especially Jerusalem of the ideology of Yahweh as resident within that king's royal sanctuary manifests itself: namely, a heightened concern about protecting the holy God and that God's holy dwelling from disabling pollutions. Arguably, according to 1 Sam 20:26 and 21:2–7 (in most of the Bible's English versions, 21:1–6), the answer is "yes." For example, as the former text would have it, David—at this point in the story, the king's son-in-law and also a courtier to Saul—deliberately absents himself from Saul's new moon feast, although his presence was expected, in order that he might determine how great Saul's ever-growing animosity toward him had become.[57] Although he certainly notices David's absence, Saul initially seems basically nonplussed by it, assuming that "he [David] is not clean" (*ṭāhôr*), which is to say: Saul assumes that David had contracted some impurity that kept him from the celebration of the new moon feast. Saul thereby gives voice to the heightened concern for purity that I have posited above we should expect as part of the "Yahweh in residence" ideology that attends a royally affiliated sacred space. Note furthermore that Saul's statement demonstrates my greater hypothesis that the setting of the new moon feast of 1 Samuel 20 *must* be a sanctuary location and not a domestic one, for, as we have yet again seen in Chapter 6, what it means at root to define someone like David as unclean is to require that the individual contaminated by impurity separate himself or herself from a space understood to be sanctified as a dwelling place of Yahweh.

But ultimately, David is not our concern: rather, our question is what all this means for the women who are the subject of our study. The answer is one we well know, once more from Chapter 6: attention to purity regulations "disadvantages women in a number of respects," and one of the most significant of these disadvantages concerns women's access to spaces where Yahweh was considered to dwell.[58] To be sure, this position is more typical of the P source than it is of other biblical authors. Nevertheless, in the Deuteronomistic History's story of Saul's new moon feast, attention to purity regulations is surely a factor. I thus take it to be significant that no women are mentioned as joining Saul within Yahweh's *bāmâ-liškâ* residence in Gibeah to partake of the new moon meal, not even David's wife and Saul's daughter, Michal, and this even though Saul's son Jonathan is identified as being present (1 Sam 20:25). Moreover, no women are mentioned as joining in a subsequent new moon meal celebrated, according to 1 Sam 20:27, a day after the first, as the new moon festival described in 1 Sam 20:24–26 carries over into a second day.[59]

Of course, it is possible to imagine that women are to be understood as joining in both of the new moon feasts of 1 Samuel 20 but that their presence goes unnoted in the text, given the Bible's male-centered focus. But my inclination, as intimated already, is to suggest that the purity concerns articulated in 1 Sam 20:26 have led the author(s) and/or redactor(s) of the 1 Samuel 20 account to resist describing women as participating in the two new moon feasts that take place within the *bāmâ-liškâ* complex in Gibeah in which this text envisions Yahweh to be resident. Indeed, I propose that the author(s) and/or redactor(s) of 1 Samuel 20 indicate explicitly in the subsequent episode of the David story, 1 Sam 21:2–7 (English 21:1–6), that women were absent during the two new moon feasts. In this subsequent episode, David has determined that Saul's animosity toward him was in fact so significant that he must flee from court (this is because Saul, who had initially assumed that David's impurity was of the minor sort that would have passed within a day, does become angered by David's absence at the second new moon meal). As he takes flight, David stops first at the shrine complex in Nob, where he asks the priest there, Ahimelek, to give him five bread loaves as provisions. It turns out, though, that the only bread available has been specially consecrated to Yahweh. Ahimelek agrees, however, that he will give David this bread, but only if David and the entourage that he (falsely) claims he goes to join are in the state of ritual purity required for eating the consecrated loaves. By this, Ahimelek more specifically means that none of the men has lain with a woman and as a consequence has had a seminal emission that would render him ritually impure. The priest therefore asks whether David and his men have kept themselves away from women.

Yet David's response addresses the matter slightly differently, as he says, "women have been kept from us" (1 Sam 21:6 [English 21:5]). "Women have been kept from us" because, in the conceit of David's fabricated story, they were kept from the men of Saul's court in response to purity concerns, when those men convened in 1 Sam 20:24–26 and again in 1 Sam 20:27 in the *liškâ* of the Gibeah *bāmâ* to celebrate the new moon feast? Mutatis mutandis, we can suggest that women were kept separate from men at new moon celebrations in other sanctuary settings where purity was a concern, and thus were women rendered unable to participate in those sanctuaries' new moon observances.

Still, what are we to make of 2 Kgs 4:23? That text, we will recall, raises no concerns about the possibility that its protagonist, the woman of

Shunem, might go to see Elisha on the day of the new moon, and this even though the Shunammite woman was, according to many of our sources' articulation of purity laws, contaminated at that time with the particularly virulent impurity that comes from having had contact with a corpse (her ailing son had died in her arms and she had then laid him out on a bed; 2 Kgs 4:20–21).[60] One might thus think that a visit to Elisha, called specifically in 2 Kgs 4:9 a "*holy* man of God" (*'îš 'ĕlōhîm qādôš;* emphasis mine), would be off-limits to her. We might in addition recall the suggestion of Heather A. McKay that I quoted above in my discussion of *šabbāt:* that the Shunammite's husband thought his wife would most logically seek out Elisha on the Sabbath or the day of the new moon because those were the days "worth visiting a shrine in search of a holy man . . . [because they are] day[s] when he would be there."[61] Note specifically here McKay's assumption that on the occasion of *šabbāt* or the new moon, the place one goes to find a man of God like Elisha is a *shrine;* the same premise is articulated by Baruch A. Levine, who writes of the "custom of visiting *cult sites* on Sabbaths and New Moons [that] is to be found in 2 Kings 4:23" (emphasis mine), and Karel van der Toorn, who speaks of visiting the "*sanctuary*" of the "man of God" on the "sacred days" of the new moon and Sabbath (emphasis again mine).[62] Given that the woman of Shunem found Elisha so expeditiously according to 2 Kgs 4:25, I propose she is envisioned by the author(s) and/or redactor(s) of 2 Kings 4 as sharing this presumption, and not just about *šabbāt* and the new moon (since the Shunammite woman in fact made her journey on a different day altogether). Thus, even though Elisha clearly traveled, at least occasionally, according to the conceit of the 2 Kgs 4:8–37 story (indeed, he had the equivalent of a pied-à-terre in the Shunammite woman's home; 2 Kgs 4:10), the place where he was most likely to be found was a shrine. As a result, the Shunammite woman came readily to Elisha at a sanctuary at Mount Carmel (2 Kgs 4:25; see also Fig. I.1).[63]

Yet would we not think that this shrine would be, like Elisha himself, off-limits to the polluted Shunammite? The answer must be that, unlike 1 Samuel 20, "symbols of holiness and purity" are only "tangentially" operative in the Shunammite's story.[64] Perhaps this is because the Elijah-Elisha cycle of stories in which the Shunammite account is found, which predates the Deuteronomistic History and was only secondarily incorporated into it, was generally unconcerned (or little concerned) with concepts of ritual purity. Or perhaps the pre-Deuteronomistic Elijah-Elisha cycle did not share the particular concerns regarding corpse impurity that are found elsewhere in the Deuteronomistic History (2 Kgs 23:14, 16) and in the Hebrew Bible. Yet whatever the motivations that helped shape the Shunammite's story, the fact remains that its lack of attention to purity regulations opens up opportunities for the Shunammite woman's participation in new moon rituals that might otherwise be precluded. More specifically: by presuming that the woman of Shunem could make her journey on the day of the Sabbath or the new moon, 2 Kgs 4:23 suggests that the woman—had she in fact made her journey on *šabbāt* or the new moon day, and in happier circumstances—could have participated in the *šabbāt* or new moon observances that should have been taking place within the Carmel sanctuary precinct, even though 1 Samuel 20 suggests the women of Saul's court were excluded from the new moon feast held in the king's purity-conscious *bāmâ-liškâ* complex in the "Gibeah of Saul."

The Deuteronomistic tradition, in short, offers two rather different visions of women's participation in the new moon festival, and I have argued these differences depend on the degree that purity concerns were in play in the Deuteronomistic accounts of new moon celebrations. Women engaged only peripherally in the rituals of the new moon imagined to be observed at temples where purity regulations were in force yet could participate more fully in ritual activities that took place in sanctuary contexts where concerns with purity were envisioned to be less stringently observed. Given my sense, moreover, that the biblical accounts needed generally to ring true to their ancient Israelite audience (see the Introduction), we might hypothesize that the Deuteronomists' differing perspectives on women's participation in the monthly celebrations of the new moon reflect the actual situation for women in preexilic Israel, with women able to join more fully in the observances of the new moon festival in ritual communities that were less purity-conscious, while engaging only minimally or not at all in settings where purity concerns stood more to the fore.

Women and Ancient Israelite Clan Festivals

In 1 Samuel 20, as part of his scheme to determine the depth of Saul's antipathy toward him, David asks his ally, Saul's son Jonathan, to tell his father, when Saul inquires after David's absence at the new moon feast, that Jonathan has given David permission to miss the meal with Saul and others of the king's household. The alleged reason is so that David can return to his hometown of Bethlehem to participate in a *zebaḥ mišpāḥâ*, meaning a "sacrifice" (*zebaḥ*, or, more literally, as we saw in Chapter 3, the slaughtering of an animal as a *šĕlāmîm* offering), which would then be followed, as is any *šĕlāmîm* offering, by a meal—in this instance, for the Davidic "family" or "clan" (*mišpāḥâ*). Unlike the royal court's new moon celebration, however, this sacrificial meal, according to 1 Sam 20:6 (the other mention of this sacrifice, in 1 Sam 20:29 is less clear), is said to take place only yearly (*zebaḥ hayyāmîm*).[65] Perhaps it always took place in conjunction with a day of the new moon.[66] Or perhaps the conjunction posited in the 1 Samuel 20 story is only coincidental.[67] We can be more definitive, though, in suggesting that David's claim that his brother has commanded him to join his family for this occasion indicates that a family's yearly sacrifices were presided over by the male clan head (presuming that by this point in the David story, David's father, Jesse, who is said already in 1 Sam 17:12 to be elderly, is understood to have died [but cf. 1 Sam 22:3–4]).[68]

The venue of these clan sacrifices is presumably some family shrine or sanctuary.[69] Perhaps we should envision the sort of family shrine that seems indicated in the archaeological record by Room 65 at Ai and in the biblical record in the account of Micah's shrine in Judges 17–18 (see Chapter 1). Perhaps too, in the case of 1 Samuel 20, the reference is to the same shrine or sanctuary at which Samuel offered sacrifice in the company of Jesse and David's brothers when he came to Bethlehem in 1 Samuel 16 to anoint David as Israel's future king.[70] No women, note, are mentioned as being present at that 1 Samuel 16 meeting of David's clansmen. Would women also have been excluded from the Davidic clan's *zebaḥ mišpāḥâ* of 1 Samuel 20 and more generally from clans' annual sacrificial gatherings and ritual meals?[71]

To some degree, we can certainly answer "yes," in the sense that married women did not necessarily participate in the annual sacrifices of their natal clans. Or more specifically, we should take it as a given that a married woman whose natal clan lived at a geographical remove from her husband's family or was not of the same kinship group as her husband's clan did not participate in the annual sacrifices of her birth family. Given the ideological force of ancient Israel's systems of *patri*local marriage and *patri*lineal descent, it would be unthinkable for the tradition to have such a woman annually take leave of her husband's household to return to the home of her birth family in order to participate in a ritual that would have affirmed (as we will see below) her membership in and solidarity with her natal clan, as opposed to the clan into which she had married. Conversely, 1 Sam 20:29

takes it as a given that the *men* of a clan should be present for their family's annual sacrifice, to the extent that David, although not at the time resident in his hometown, can be commanded (*ṣiwwâ*) by his brother(s) to journey some 14 or so kilometers from Saul's royal fief in Gibeah to the Davidic clan's cult center in Bethlehem (see Fig. I.1), in order to participate in the sacrificial ritual his family is to enact there.[72]

Many scholars have suggested, moreover, that because in Israel, as "in many traditional cultures," "a 'household' is made up of the dead, the living, and the unborn,"[73] a clan's annual sacrificial gathering brought together not just the family's living members. Rather, its deceased ancestors were thought to be present as well. Joseph Blenkinsopp writes of a clan's annual sacrifice, for example, that "it was . . . taken for granted that forebears or ancestors, those already 'gathered to their people,' participated," and Abraham Malamat similarly describes the clan sacrifice as "the occasion on which genealogical accounts were employed to invoke the names of dead ancestors" and so evoke their presence.[74] Baruch Halpern's evaluation is more emphatic still regarding the ancestors' engagement: "the . . . sacrifice around which the patrilineal clan sectors gathered was one *directed toward* the ancestors" (emphasis mine).[75] Yet whether more emphatic or less, these scholars agree: the annual clan sacrifice should be understood as part of the larger tradition of the Israelite ancestor cult, which in addition to a clan's annual sacrificial gathering included rituals such as the proper burial of a corpse in the family tomb, the periodic provisioning of the deceased's ghost with food and drink offerings, the commemoration and regular invocation of the deceased through the evoking of the dead person's name, and the manufacture and use of the ancestor figurines known as the *tĕrāpîm*/teraphim. All of these acts, according to the ancestor cult's underlying tenets, were integral to Israelites' family identity and solidarity across generations.[76]

Yet women—given again the centrality in Israel of *patri*local and *patri*lineal ideologies—do not seem to be fundamental participants within the rituals of this ancestor cult. It seems to be less imperative that women, for example, be buried in their family's tomb, especially if there are compelling reasons (like a pollution-filled death in childbirth) to exclude their corpses. Think here of Rachel, who, according to Gen 35:16–20, was buried in a roadside grave rather than being transported from the site of her demise to her family's burial cave in Machpelah, even though Machpelah was no more than 32 kilometers away.[77] Then contrast the traditions regarding Rachel's husband, Jacob, who in Gen 49:29–30 requests that his body be interred at Machpelah, even though he is about to die at least 300 kilometers to the south and west, in Egypt!

To be sure, the transportation of Jacob's body from Egypt to the cave at Machpelah would have been facilitated in the minds of the biblical authors by the Egyptian process of mummification (or, in the Bible's words, "embalming"; *ḥanūṭîm*). Still, at least two biblical passages describe occasions when the bodies of newly deceased men are transported some distance in order that they be buried in their families' tombs.[78] In Judg 16:31, Samson's body is moved about 60 kilometers from the place of his death in Philistia to his family's tomb in the southwest of Israel, and in 2 Sam 2:32, the body of David's nephew Asahel is moved after his death in battle about 18 kilometers, to his family's tomb in Bethlehem.[79] Israelite custom even permitted previously interred male bodies to be exhumed for transport and reburial so that the bones could be placed in the family's tomb. In 2 Sam 21:12–14, for example, David moves the bones of Saul and Jonathan from their previous resting place in Jabesh-Gilead to their family's tomb in Benjamin.[80]

Overall, Israelite tradition reflects a decided preference that men be buried in their family's tomb, even if considerable efforts were required to relocate their bodies. But as the case of Rachel's demise in childbirth makes clear, there is not the same urgency for women. Similarly, while in Chapter 1, I noted my general agreement with the assessment put forward most recently and thoroughly by Karel van der Toorn and Theodore J. Lewis that takes the *tĕrāpîm*/teraphim figurines mentioned in some eight passages in the Hebrew Bible to be representations of a family's deceased ancestors, it is not clear whether Israelite tradition deemed it necessary to make a *tĕrāpîm* figurine to represent a woman after her death, although this was apparently an expected part of male mortuary practice.[81] Note likewise that if biblical genealogies are any guide, women are normally absent from the "genealogical accounts" that were "employed" on the occasions of clan sacrifices, according to Malamat, in order "to invoke the names of dead ancestors."[82] Memorial stones that invoke the names of dead ancestors are likewise erected on behalf of only males, as is made obvious by two of the Hebrew terms used to describe these memorial stele—*zikkārôn* and *yād* (1 Sam 15:12, 2 Sam 18:18, Isa 57:8)—and these terms' etymological ties to the terms for male (*zākār*) and (euphemistically) phallus (*yād*).[83]

Indeed, as van der Toorn states, the ancestor cult in all its aspects "was addressed predominantly to male ancestors."[84] Van der Toorn supports this conclusion, moreover, by a careful look at both Israelite and comparative evidence. With regard to the latter, he cites, for example, an Old Babylonian prayer to the moon god that "enumerates the names of the dead addressed by the living."[85] Women are included in this list of ancestors and are invited alongside their male counterparts to partake of the food and drink offerings that according to ancestor cult ritual should be made to the deceased. Some women, moreover, are explicitly cited by name.[86] These include two of the male ancestors' wives and five *nadītu* women (women from elite families who were dedicated to some god and who, as part of their service to the god, practiced sexual chastity).[87] Still, these women "are mentioned only as 'wife of' one of the [male] ancestors, or . . . as 'daughter' of an ancestor."[88] In fact, in both this prayer to the moon god and similar incantations, women are often *only* the "wife of" or the "daughter of" a male ancestor; they are not typically given a name.[89] Somewhat similarly, in the so-called Genealogy of the Hammurapi Dynasty, while deceased women from Hammurapi's lineage are included in the list of those who are invited to share in the food and drink offerings made to the dead, these women are identified only as "the daughters of kings" (as opposed to the twenty-eight male ancestors that this text carefully lists by name).[90] Within Old Babylonian tradition, van der Toorn concludes, "women were apparently not regarded as ancestors themselves."[91]

In considering Israelite evidence, van der Toorn also turns to names, more specifically, the so-called theophoric names from ancient Israelite tradition. These are names that have within them terms such as *'āb,* "father," *'āh.*, "brother," and *'ām,* meaning something like "paternal uncle." Most typically, these names' kinship terms have been taken as references to a god (Greek *theos;* hence the names' common designation as "theophoric") that their bearer and/or the name's bestower were thought to have worshipped. For example, an Israelite such as Abiel, a name that means "my father (*'ābî*) is *'ēl,*" is understood to have come from a family that worshipped Israel's god, or *'ēl* (i.e., Yahweh), as a divine *'āb,* or father. Van der Toorn suggests, however, that these names' kinship terms be taken not as references to some metaphorical familiarity with a deity, but much more literally: as references to deceased ancestors who have been deified upon their demise. Abiel thus refers to "my [ancestral] father" who is (or, more specifically, has become upon his death) a deified spirit known as an *'ēl* or an *'ĕlōhîm.*[92]

As van der Toorn explains, his hypothesis—that "the gods referred to in these theophoric names are not gods in the usual sense of the term, but deified ancestors"—accounts well for the fact that the names in question can use kinship terms such as *'āḫ*, "brother," or *'ām*, "paternal uncle," which otherwise are not epithets used of known divinities. More important for my purposes: "the interpretation of the theophoric kinship names as evidence of an . . . ancestor cult" reveals that "the cult was addressed to male ancestors only."[93] This is because all the kinship terms used in the names in question are *male* in their referent (such as the previously cited terms *'āb,* "father," *'āḫ*, "brother," and *'ām*, "paternal uncle," and also terms such as *dôd,* "father's senior brother," and *lĕmû,* "clan"). Conversely, van der Toorn writes, "in Hebrew anthroponymics there is not one feminine kinship term used as a theophoric element." Once more, van der Toorn concludes, "The ancestor cult was apparently concerned primarily with patrilineal ancestors."[94]

As with the dead, so too with the living? Here, the Mesopotamian evidence is somewhat ambiguous, as women could be "obliged to bring offerings to the dead" as ancestor cult ritual requires: daughters can be called upon to make food and drink offerings for their deceased fathers, for example.[95] Similarly, on a stele from Harran, the Neo-Babylonian king Nabonidus (r. 556–539 BCE) quotes his mother as listing the funerary offerings she provided for previous kings.[96] Nevertheless, in Mesopotamia, women seem to make ancestor cult offerings only in exceptional situations; normally, this obligation was undertaken by a man's sons.[97] Likewise, while Late Bronze Age ritual texts from the northern Levantine city-state of Ugarit may attest to Queen T̠ryl making offerings on behalf of the deceased, the evidence is very uncertain.[98] Generally, at Ugarit, "it . . . seems that women seldom performed the cult of the dead."[99]

The Israelite ancestor cult celebration enacted at a clan's annual sacrificial feast may also have been an event during which a clan's living women played little to no part. Note again in this regard the comments of Blenkinsopp: "Annual sacrifices of this kind [the clan sacrifice and meal] served to legitimate and sustain a social order *based on patrilineal descent*" (emphasis mine). Even more significantly: "as an important affirmation of solidarity among living and dead members of the clan (*mišpāḥāh*), presence at this event [the annual clan sacrifice and meal] was mandatory, *at least for adult males*" (emphasis again mine).[100] Van der Toorn is more definitive still: "Women never participate . . . they remain outsiders to the community of . . . the ancestors and the male adults. Or, to put it more mildly, they belong to that community by virtue of their ties, either by blood or marriage, to the men. They participate in the second degree, so to speak."[101] Alan M. Cooper and Bernard R. Goldstein articulate basically the same conclusion, but from a woman's—more specifically, a married woman's—point of view: "In a marital relationship, the wife has a right to ask her husband to intervene with the clan deities, but her contact is with her husband, not with those deities."[102]

Ironically, therefore: although David's family gathering is called in 1 Sam 20:29 a *zebaḥ mišpāḥâ*, or a "family" or "clan sacrifice," a clan's annual sacrificial meal may not really have been an occasion celebrated by the *mišpāḥâ*, the "family," writ large, as a clan's women members are pushed to its periphery. Women's experience of their family's or clan's annual sacrifice thus mirrors in critical respects their experiences of the other two calendrical events I have discussed in this chapter, *šabbāt* and the new moon festival, as women are not fully able to engage in the observances of either of these ritual events. Women's full engagement is likewise compromised in the celebration of the three great pilgrimage festivals of the Israelite calendar, and it is to a study of these that I now turn.

8 "You Will Make Three Pilgrimage Journeys to Me": The Israelite Woman's Ritual Year, II

A clan's annual sacrifice and associated feast are not the only once-a-year event of the Israelite ritual calendar. Rather, several biblical texts speak of three great pilgrimage festivals that were observed annually.[1] The first is the festival of Maṣṣot, or Unleavened Bread, celebrated for seven days in the spring—more specifically, according to both the Priestly (P) and Holiness (H) traditions (Lev 23:6, Num 28:17), for seven days beginning on the full moon day of the month of Abib, which itself would have begun fifteen days earlier, on the new moon day closest to the vernal equinox (which falls on about March 20 on modern calendars).[2] The second pilgrimage festival is the feast of the Harvest, also called Firstfruits and Shavu'ot ("Weeks"), which was celebrated in early summer, about seven weeks after Maṣṣot. The third is the seven-day feast of the Ingathering, or Sukkot ("Booths"), which was celebrated in the fall—more specifically, according, again, to both P and H and also to related priestly sources (Lev 23:34, Num 29:12, Ezek 45:25), for seven days beginning on the full moon day of the Israelite calendar's seventh month (counting from a new year's date in the spring).[3] Thus Ingathering/Sukkot roughly coincided with the autumn equinox, which occurs on about September 23 according to our system of date reckoning. This is when the harvest of late-ripening fruits was coming to its end: preeminently grapes and olives, but also figs, pomegranates, and various types of nuts (see Deut 16:13, and, among later sources, Jer 40:10, Tob 1:7).

In this chapter, I discuss Israelite women's roles and experiences during these three pilgrimage festivals. However, some matters require our attention before this discussion can begin. For example, as may have been suggested by the plethora of biblical references cited in the previous paragraph, the pilgrimage festivals were a matter of interest to many of the Bible's authors and redactors, especially those who had close ties to priestly and temple tradition (for, as we will see, it was in temple venues that the pilgrimage feasts were primarily celebrated). Indeed, the Bible contains no fewer than four calendrical statements regarding the pilgrimage festivals that stem from priestly and/or temple sources. These are the calendar of the P source found in Numbers 28–29; the calendar of the P source's close affiliate, the prophet Ezekiel, found in Ezek 45:18–25; the calendar of Deut 16:1–17, which, like Deuteronomy in general, I ascribe to a school of Levitical priests; and the calendar of the so-called H source found in Lev 23:4–44 (or, better, Lev 23:4–38, as these verses comprise the core of the Leviticus 23 calendar, with an addendum on the festival of Ingathering/Sukkot found in vv. 39–43).[4] Yet even though all these sources' perspectives are, in some sense, priestly, the ways in which they construe Israel's ritual calendar need not agree, and further variations can be found in two other festal calendars, Exod 23:14–17 and Exod 34:18–23. These have traditionally been understood to stem from, respectively, the Pentateuch's E, or Elohistic, and J, or Yahwistic, authors (although in recent scholarship, the attribution of Exod 34:18–23 to J—and, as we saw in the Introduction, even the existence of J—has been debated).[5]

Among these calendars' variations are the different nomenclatures our texts use, as can be seen in the language I used above to describe the second and third of the Israelites' pilgrimage festivals. Some sources call the fall feast Ingathering (*hā'āsīp*, from the verb *'āsap*, "to gather"; Exod 23:16, 34:22), while others use the name Sukkot ("Booths"; Lev 23:34; Deut 16:13, 16; 31:10). Likewise, some texts (Exod 23:16) call the summer festival both Harvest (*haqqāṣîr*) and Firstfruits (*habbikkûrîm*); others call it both Shavu'ot ("Weeks") and Firstfruits (Exod 34:22, Num 28:26); still others (Deut 16:10, 16) call it just Shavu'ot; and others still (Lev 23:17) call it only Firstfruits. According to many scholars, at least some of these terminological differentiations have their roots in these feasts' evolution from an originally agricultural focus (reflected in names such as Harvest and Ingathering) to one that is more historically oriented. The renaming of Ingathering as Sukkot ("Booths"), for example, is theorized to have occurred as the festival came to be associated over time less with the fall harvest at the end of the agricultural year and more with the tradition's accounts of the Israelites' wilderness wanderings during the exodus from Egypt, when it is said that the people lived in tents, or "booths" (see, for example, Lev 23:42–43).[6]

In addition, while it is just the festivals of Maṣṣot, Harvest/Firstfruits/Shavu'ot, and Ingathering/Sukkot that are described in the Bible (with only a few exceptions) using the term *ḥag*, "pilgrimage" (a cognate of Arabic *ḥajj*, the term that designates the annual Islamic pilgrimage to Mecca), not all of our calendrical sources characterize all three festivals as *ḥaggîm* (the plural form of *ḥag*).[7] For example, the H and P calendars of Lev 23:15–21 and Num 28:26–31 do not designate Harvest/Firstfruits/Shavu'ot as a *ḥag*, even though they do include it in their catalogue of Israelite ritual observances and presume (as we would expect of priestly literature) that it should be celebrated within a temple setting. The related priestly calendar found in Ezek 45:18–25, however, does not mention Harvest/Firstfruits/Shavu'ot at all.[8]

More important for my purposes are the ways the Bible's various calendrical sources differ regarding the relationship of Pesaḥ (or what is generally rendered in English Bibles as Passover, following the ancient Greek translation of Exod 12:23) and the feast of Maṣṣot.[9] For example, in the (arguably older) ritual calendar of Exod 23:14–17 and the somehow kindred 34:18–23, only a seven-day Maṣṣot pilgrimage, or *ḥag*, is cited (23:15 and 34:18), while Pesaḥ goes unmentioned.[10] However, the sacrificial offering that is a key part of Pesaḥ ritual appears, somewhat obliquely, in Exod 34:25, a verse that follows almost directly upon the ritual calendar of 34:18–23.[11] This Pesaḥ offering perhaps also appears, albeit even more obliquely, in Exod 23:18, just subsequent to the festal calendar of 23:14–17.[12] Moreover, in Exod 34:25, Pesaḥ is called a *ḥag*. In two other (and arguably later) ritual calendars, however, while both a one-day Pesaḥ celebration and a seven-day festival of Maṣṣot are included, only Maṣṣot is designated as a *ḥag* (Lev 23:4–8, Num 28:16–25; see also Exod 12:1–28, 43–51).[13] Also in these calendars, Pesaḥ and Maṣṣot are treated as discrete (although chronologically sequential) events. Yet in the seventh-century BCE calendar of Deut 16:1–8, the one-day feast of Pesaḥ and the seven-day festival of Maṣṣot coalesce, so that Pesaḥ becomes the first of the seven days of Maṣṣot. In Ezek 45:18–25, a sixth-century BCE composition, Pesaḥ and Maṣṣot are similarly fused, to the extent that Pesaḥ, and not Maṣṣot, apparently assumes the label "pilgrimage," or *ḥag*.[14] Thus by the exilic period, as William H. C. Propp writes, "The name *Pesaḥ* . . . entirely displace[s] *Maṣṣôt* to denote the weeklong observance."[15]

Furthermore, while biblical tradition is in general adamant that at some point during all *ḥaggîm*, celebrants were required to journey to a sanctuary or temple compound to appear before Yahweh, different texts present different pictures of just when, in the course of the Pesaḥ-Maṣṣot festival complex, this journey was supposed to take place.[16] Leviticus 23:7–8 and Num 28:17–25, for example, enjoin the Israelites to appear before Yahweh on both the first and the seventh days of the *ḥag,* or pilgrimage, of Maṣṣot for a *miqrāʾ-qōdeš,* a "holy proclamation" (or, according to some translations, "a holy convocation," or "a sacred assembly," or even just "a sacred occasion").[17] Deuteronomy 16:1–7a, however, although it does not use the term *ḥag,* describes the one-day feast of Pesaḥ as being the occasion when the Israelites should come, as during a pilgrimage, to make a sacrifice at the habitation that Yahweh has chosen, Deuteronomy's circumlocution for the temple in Jerusalem. They then are to return to their homes, according to Deut 16:7b–8, for the remaining six days of Maṣṣot.[18] Exodus 13:6 presents a different tradition still: this text identifies the festival *ḥag,* or pilgrimage, as taking place on the seventh day and last day of the Maṣṣot feast.

As Jacob Milgrom writes, "There can only be one reason why the pilgrimage [in Exod 13:6] takes place on the seventh day": that "in keeping with the regulations of Exod 12:1–13, 22–27a, 28" (but in contrast to the requirements of Deut 16:1–7a, and also Lev 23:5 and Num 28:16), the preceding Pesaḥ celebration was "observed at home."[19] Indeed, Exod 12:1–13, 22–27a, and 28, and especially Exod 12:1–13, differ dramatically from Lev 23:5, Num 28:16, and Deut 16:1–7a in their construal of the Pesaḥ celebration as a home-based observance. Or, at most, the Pesaḥ of Exod 12:1–13 is construed as a neighborhood rite, as smaller households are instructed in 12:4 to band together with those living nearby—who, given Israelite settlement patterns, would almost inevitably have been their kin—to procure the lamb (or young goat; Hebrew *śeh*)[20] that was slaughtered for consumption at a ritual meal.

Most of the scholarly discussions concerning the Exod 12:1–13, 22–27a, and 28 depiction of Pesaḥ as a home-based, or, at most, a neighborhood-based ritual, as opposed to the sense of Lev 23:5, Num 28:16, and Deut 16:1–7a that Pesaḥ was a sanctuary-based rite, have concerned themselves with trying to construct an account of Pesaḥ's changing character. Some have suggested, for example, that Pesaḥ and the festival of Maṣṣot were originally separate and distinct types of ritual observances: Pesaḥ a family-based and pastorally based rite and Maṣṣot a communal pilgrimage festival associated generally with field crops and more specifically with the spring barley harvest. Under the terms of this interpretation, these two rituals were then secondarily brought together—as most would have it, in the Deuteronomic ideologies of the seventh century BCE (reflected, for example, in Deut 16:1–8 and in the kindred Deuteronomistic History in Josh 5:10–12).[21]

Others, however, have proposed that Pesaḥ and Maṣṣot traditions both may have been a part of an old (premonarchic) spring pilgrimage festival; this has been especially suggested by scholars who take the ritual calendar preserved in Exod 34:18–23 to be relatively early and who in turn ascribe significance to the fact that in this allegedly early text and in the adjacent 34:25, both Pesaḥ (in 34:25) and Maṣṣot (in 34:18) are designated as *ḥaggîm*.[22] This theory then goes on to propose that these originally conjoined pilgrimage rites were separated for much of the preexilic period, as "Passover moved into the context of family religion" and Maṣṣot "became the center of a major pilgrimage festival in the spring."[23] Only again in seventh-century BCE Deuteronomic ideologies, according to this reconstruction, were the two reconnected, as Pesaḥ was reconceptualized as a temple-based ritual prefixed to the Maṣṣot feast.[24] This reconceptualization of Pesaḥ is reflected both in Deut 16:1–7a and in 2 Kgs 23:21–23, the story of the nationwide Pesaḥ celebration held at the Jerusalem temple during the reign of King Josiah (r. 640–609 BCE).[25] Still another proposal suggests that throughout the early preexilic period, family groups observed Pesaḥ rites at home on the first evening of the festival and then participated in the communal ritual of Maṣṣot at a local sanctuary the next morning. This changed only when worship became centralized in the seventh century BCE, yet again under the terms of the Deuteronomic reformation, at which point both the home-based Pesaḥ and the locally situated Maṣṣot celebrations were moved to the national temple in Jerusalem.[26]

Whatever these theories' differences, however, I find it is their similarities that are more critical for my purposes, and in particular, their shared sense that for at least some part of Israel's preexilic history, Pesaḥ was a home-based ritual. In what follows, I consider this home-based Pesaḥ as it pertains to women. My argument might be described, like my arguments in the last chapter, as being "on one hand"/"on the other hand" in nature. On one hand, we have come to expect that with only some exceptions—for example, the ideologically male-centered rites of the annual clan sacrifice—ritual events that take place in a domestic context are extremely productive forums for women's religious agency. We would thus expect a home-based Pesaḥ celebration to be a major arena for facilitating women's religious expression. And indeed, as we will see, significant evidence suggests this. On the other hand, the evidence that can be offered regarding women's religious experiences within a home-based Pesaḥ tradition is not necessarily as secure as our sources might initially lead us to think.

Women and the Spring Festival(s) of Pesaḥ and Maṣṣot

Let us first catalogue the ways in which women's religious agency might have been productively realized within home-based Pesaḥ celebrations, especially with respect to the centerpiece of those celebrations' observance: their carefully scripted ritual meal. We can well imagine by this point in our analysis that because a meal is involved, women should have played an important role both in processing the foodstuffs needed to assemble the Pesaḥ feast and in preparing the actual foods that were served. Women would surely, for example, have ground grain into the flour needed for the unleavened bread that Exod 12:8, Num 9:11, and Deut 16:3 identify as one of the Pesaḥ meal's crucial foods.[27] In addition, even though men, as we saw in Chapter 2, sometimes used the flour women produced to make unleavened cakes that are served at ritual and ritual-like meals (Lot makes unleavened bread for his divine visitors in Gen 19:3, and in Judg 6:19 Gideon makes unleavened cakes for the divine messenger who has appeared to him), it is equally possible, given the evidence of other biblical texts, that women would have baked the Pesaḥ meal's cakes of unleavened bread. In addition to Jer 7:18, in which women bake cakes (albeit not said to be unleavened) for the Queen of Heaven, note (1) Gen 18:6, in which Sarah makes *ʿūgôt*, "bread cakes" (which because they are made hurriedly, must have been unleavened, even though this is not specified) for the triad of divine visitors (Yahweh and the deity's two attendants) who came to visit Abraham at the oaks at Mamre that were near the couple's tent;[28] and (2) 1 Sam 28:24, in which the medium at Endor who summons up Samuel's ghost on Saul's behalf makes unleavened cakes to sustain Saul as he breaks his fast at the end of this necromantic ritual (see further Chapter 11). Likewise, if the "bitter herbs" (or "bitter lettuces") that according to Exod 12:8 and Num 9:11 were served alongside these unleavened bread cakes were grown in the sorts of small gardening plots that seem to have been located near the typical Israelite home (see Chapter 1), then a household's women may have raised this crop.[29] Or at least, in their roles as their families' primary childcare providers, women would have supervised the children who otherwise would have undertaken the responsibility for watering and harvesting the produce grown in their homes' "cottage" gardens.[30]

Other aspects of the home-based Pesaḥ ritual potentially significant for women are perhaps less immediately obvious. Most important, as many scholars have pointed out (for example, T. Desmond Alexander, Menahem Haran, Carol Meyers, and William H. C. Propp), the Bible's preeminent description of a home-based Pesaḥ, in Exod 12:1–13, has multiple features more characteristic of a sanctuary setting than of a domestic location.[31] For example, in Exod 12:6, although the slaughter of the sheep/goat whose meat becomes the main dish of the Pesaḥ meal is not described using any of the technical terminology of sacrifice, the act is nonetheless, for all intents and purposes, sacrificial in nature. The animal must be without blemish and a year in age, as should the typical animal offered up in sacrifice (see Exod 29:1; Lev 1:3, 10; 3:1, 6; 9:3; 12:6; 14:10; 23:18; Num 6:14; numerous verses in Numbers 7, 28–29; and Ezek 46:13).[32] According to Exod 12:8 (see also Exod 12:10), all the meat of the Pesaḥ animal must also be eaten during the same night that it is prepared.[33] So too must meat prepared for consumption in sanctuary settings be eaten within a set time after the sacrificial animal has been slaughtered (Exod 29:34; Lev 7:15, 16–18; 8:32; 19:6–7; 22:30; 23:18).[34] Furthermore, according to Exod 12:9, the meat of the Pesaḥ sheep (or goat) is eaten roasted, which is wholly atypical within Israelite tradition (meat is normally cooked by being boiled), and this meat also is said to be eaten along with its fat, which is atypical in Israel as well (see 1 Sam 2:16 and my discussion of this passage in Chapter 3). Yet it is standard that the meat of an *ʿōlâ* sacrifice, that is, a "whole burnt offering," be roasted when dedicated to Yahweh upon a sanctuary altar, and this meat, moreover, is standardly roasted together with its fat.[35]

In addition, even though the smearing of the blood from the Pesaḥ animal on a home's doorposts and lintel has an idiosyncratic purpose within the Exod 12:7 text in which it is depicted (see also Exod 12:22)—it signals to Yahweh that the deity (or the deity's "Destroyer"; Exod 12:23) is to "pass over" the Israelite houses so marked and thus spare their firstborn from the slaughter of the tenth plague that otherwise is to decimate the Egyptians, in whose midst the enslaved Israelites live—this smearing act is nevertheless reminiscent of the standard sanctuary rites of blood manipulation that require dashing, sprinkling, or daubing a sacrificed animal's blood upon Yahweh's altar. And just as it is unleavened bread that must be served at the Pesaḥ meal, so too must cereal offerings presented to Yahweh be unleavened: "No grain offering that you bring to Yahweh shall be made with leaven," Lev 2:11 proclaims.[36]

As Meyers summarizes, "The Passover meal . . . is conceptualized here [in Exod 12:1–13] as a sacrificial meal carried out in the home rather than at a sanctuary."[37] Indeed, one could argue that entailed in Exod 12:1–13 is a reconceptualization of household space during the Pesaḥ celebration so that the home is construed as a shrine. For women, the implications are potentially quite significant. We can envision, for example, that women's work in preparing and perhaps serving at least some of the food of their household-cum-sanctuary's Pesaḥ repast could position them symbolically as agents who make presentation offerings for and even at Yahweh's altar. More generally, it seems reasonable to think that within the household-cum-sanctuary space created at Pesaḥ according to Exod 12:1–13, women could be considered symbolically or metaphorically to be "in the presence of Yahweh" (*lipnê yhwh*), as worshippers were understood to be in temple settings. Yet as we have seen, especially in Chapters 4 and 6, this sort of positioning within cultic space, while not interdicted absolutely for women (Deut 12:12, 18; 16:11; 31:10–13; and Hannah's story in 1 Sam 1:1–2:26), is often not readily available to them. Significant advantages for women therefore can accrue when the Pesaḥ ritual allows sanctuary space to penetrate the less formally construed domestic spaces that women easily inhabit, rather than requiring women to seek access to a more formally constituted Israelite sanctuary. As the whole home becomes a shrine of sorts during the Pesaḥ rite, women can be integrated in this "sanctuary's" ritual life and thus be perceived as being in the deity's symbolic presence.

Still, a number of caveats need to be raised (and so begins the "on the other hand" component of the argument). First, while the case can definitely be made that Israelite women would have performed significant ritual roles and been part of a significant religious experience during a home-based Pesaḥ celebration, the biblical text that preeminently outlines the components of the home-based Pesaḥ rite, Exod 12:1–13, does not mention women once.[38] Rather, women's presence can be inferred only from words in vv. 3–4, 7, and 13 (see also Exod 12:21–23, 27, and 46) such as "family" (*bêt ʾāb*), "clan" (*mišpāḥâ*), "household" (*bayit*), and perhaps most significantly (in 12:4) *nepeš*.[39] Most literally, *nepeš* means "person" (and also "soul," or a person's life force), but as we have seen in Chapters 5 and 6, it is a term that Meyers, Mayer I. Gruber, and Jacob Milgrom argue (I believe correctly) refers within the P corpus (of which Exod 12:1–13 is a part) to both men and women.[40] Still, as we saw at the end of Chapter 7, some of the other vocabulary deployed in Exod 12:1–13—for example, the term *mišpāḥâ*—need not include women. Indeed, in his book-length study *The Hebrew Passover,* J. B. Segal writes that "'Households' and 'families' in this context [Pesaḥ] implies male adults only," and while he is not so emphatic regarding women's exclusion, Clarence J. Vos similarly notes that "there is a rather strong emphasis on the male in . . . matters . . . connected with the Passover."[41] At best, then, we can conclude that the terminology used in Exod 12:1–13 is such that women's presence at the Pesaḥ celebration this text describes is indicated only obliquely (through the use of the term *nepeš*). At worst (through the lack of gender-inclusive language), women's presence in Exod 12:1–13 is wholly obscured.

Moreover, no other Hebrew Bible text of which I am aware explicitly mentions women in conjunction with the Pesaḥ celebration, either in its home-based or temple-based manifestation. We do, conversely, find repeated injunctions across multiple texts requiring circumcision of those who are to join in the Pesaḥ ritual meal: "The uncircumcised shall not eat of it," Exod 12:48 proclaims, and only after Joshua had circumcised "all the nation [*gôy*]" in Josh 5:8 do the Israelites who have just entered into the "promised land" keep Pesaḥ at the site of Gilgal. Obviously, if we presume women's participation in at least home-based Pesaḥ ritual, these verses cannot be taken as literally prescriptive. Still, women's invisibility among the "circumcised" who are specifically enjoined to observe Pesaḥ is disconcerting. Even more disconcerting is the fact that both the Exod 12:48 and Josh 5:8 texts that mandate circumcision as a prerequisite for Pesaḥ observance concern issues of "citizenship," so to speak. More specifically, Exod 12:48 addresses the matter of the *gēr,* or "resident alien," who must be circumcised to participate in the Pesaḥ ritual, and Josh 5:8, as indicated in the quotation I cited above, equates circumcision with being "of the nation." The effect of this terminology on women, who are by definition uncircumcised, is to construe them as less than fully Israelite, and instead, as Exod 12:48 would have it, as "aliens" or "foreigners." Moreover, Josh 5:5 explains that the mass circumcision of 5:8 is necessary because, while all the people (*ʿām*) that came out of Egypt were circumcised, the *ʿām,* "people," born in the Sinai wilderness had never undergone this procedure. Which is to say: in the logic of these verses, women are not only excluded from the "nation" of Israel; they are not even considered to be "people"![42]

A similar caveat about inclusivity: within the Exod 12:1–13 description of a home-based Pesaḥ ritual, it is assumed that the meal's sheep or goat is slaughtered elsewhere than in a household's precincts, at some site where "the community of the congregation of Israel" (*kol qĕhal ʿădat-yiśrāʾēl*) is to gather (Exod 12:6).[43] But does this gathering include the community's women? Meyers, on the basis of the general family and household context assumed in Exod 12:1–13, answers in the affirmative: "the Hebrew *ʿēdâ* . . . ordinarily refers to an assembly of adult males, but . . . here, it functions as an age- and gender-inclusive term."[44] Phyllis Bird, however, is less certain: "We cannot assume without further evidence that such designations as . . . 'the congregation' (*haqqāhāl* or *hāʿēdâ*) or 'Israel' include, or exclude, women."[45] And then there are scholars such as Segal, who writes, "*Qahal* [the 'congregation'] is regularly used to denote . . . adult *male* members of the community" (emphasis mine), suggesting, as already in his description of "households" and "families" cited above, that women were excluded in Exod 12:6 from the gathering at which the Pesaḥ animal was slaughtered.[46]

Yet even if Meyers is right and women do join the congregation gathered for the slaughter of the Pesaḥ animal in Exod 12:6, who wields the knife? Despite the text's language, it surely cannot be "all" (*kol*) within the "community of the congregation of Israel" that actually put the animal to death, if for no other reason than "not everyone had a lamb [or kid] to slaughter"—especially those neighboring households that had banded together to share a sheep or goat.[47] In Chapter 3, moreover, I suggested that even within contexts where women were deeply involved in ritual performance (Hannah at Shiloh), animal slaughter during sacrificial or sacrificially inflected contexts is a male prerogative. Indeed, in Exod 12:21, it is Israel's male elders (*ziqnê yiśrāʾēl*) who are explicitly commanded to enact the Pesaḥ slaughter.[48] Dianne Bergant likewise writes of Exod 12:6: "Perhaps the entire congregation (including women and children) was expected to . . . gather for the [Pesaḥ slaughtering] ritual, but only the heads of households (or clusters of households) would 'kill their lambs.'"[49]

Bergant also envisions it was "those men who killed a lamb [or goat] [who] participated in sprinkling the blood" (that is, the smearing of the blood on their homes' doorposts and lintels), "thus acting on behalf of their households," Bergant goes on to state, "as jural or moral leaders."[50] Or, we might say rather, given the act of smearing's sacrificial qualities, that these men acted as their household-cum-sanctuary's priests. Just as it was priests, too, who roasted the meat of an *ʿōlâ* offering on Yahweh's altar, so might we suggest that a household's male head undertook the responsibility for cooking the animal consumed at the Pesaḥ repast. Recall in this regard the texts I cited in Chapter 3—Gen 18:7, Judg 6:19, and 1 Sam 9:23–24—which clearly identify men as cooking the meat in sacrificial or sacrificial-like contexts, and recall also Meyers's observation, which I also cited in Chapter 3, that "the cooking of meat" is "the aspect of food production men are most likely to take on."[51] The result of such male preeminence, though, is that women in Exod 12:1–13, whose presence, as we have already seen, is at best only obliquely indicated, are obscured all the more.

The most problematic caveat of all, however, as we assess women's ritual obligations and religious experiences within Israel's home-based Pesaḥ traditions, derives from the analyses of scholars such as Haran and Propp, who raise fundamental questions (in somewhat different ways; more on this presently) about the degree to which Exod 12:1–13—which is not just the preeminent but in fact the only text we have that speaks in any significant way to a domestically centered Pesaḥ—can be taken as presenting historically "real" information about household Pesaḥ rites.[52] More specifically, both Haran and Propp identify Exod 12:1–13 as stemming from the P source, as I have above, and argue that for this text's P authors, the idea that the sanctified rites of Pesaḥ, and especially the sacrificial slaughter of some animal, could occur at any site other than Yahweh's temple compound in Jerusalem, or in the precincts of the temple's antecedent tent of meeting, is patently absurd.[53] Yet the P source has somehow to deal with Pesaḥ's historical origins as enshrined in Israelite tradition: that is, the notion that the rite's beginnings lie in Egypt, immediately before the commencing of the exodus and, more important, before the fabricating of the tent of meeting during the Israelites' forty-year wanderings in the Sinai wilderness and the subsequent building of the Jerusalem temple during the reign of King Solomon.

So how to negotiate this Israelite cultural memory of a non-tent and non-temple Pesaḥ? According to both Haran and Propp, P posits a one-time-only "Pesaḥ of Egypt," to use the terminology of the rabbinic-era Mishnah, that anticipates the forever-after "Pesaḥ of the Generations" (the Mishnah's language again) that the P writers advocate.[54] This forever-after "Pesaḥ of the Generations," which begins already in the year following the exodus from Egypt (Num 9:1–5), should *always*, the P writers maintain, be held in the sanctified location where they considered Yahweh to dwell: the wilderness tent of meeting or the succeeding Jerusalem temple. Thus, in Num 9:1–5, the Israelites' second Pesaḥ (that is, the Pesaḥ celebrated in the spring of the year after the escape from Egypt) is said to be held at Mount

Sinai in the compound of the tent of meeting, which according to Exod 40:2, 17 had just been erected two weeks earlier.

As for the first Pesaḥ: even though the circumstances posited by the exodus story dictate that it had to be conducted in individual homes, rather than the communal worship space of the wilderness tent or the Jerusalem temple, this is, to use Haran's language, "anachronistic." As he elaborates, "This particular offering [the Pesaḥ slaughter of Exod 12:1–13] . . . was momentarily removed from its real setting and portrayed as if it were by itself, totally unconnected with the temple."[55] Still, the slaughter anticipates as much as possible what the tent-based/temple-based ritual should look like, with, say, a proper (unblemished, year-old) sacrificial animal and the unleavened bread appropriate to a sacrificial setting. The roasting of the meat along with its fat, the requirement that this meat all be consumed on the very night that the animal was slaughtered, and the special manipulation of the blood also adumbrate proper sanctuary offerings (note in particular in regard to this last point, 2 Chr 30:16 and 2 Chr 35:11, where the Jerusalem temple's priests dash the sacrificed lamb's blood against the altar during the great Pesaḥ celebrations of Kings Hezekiah and Josiah). To be sure, the "Pesaḥ of Egypt" cannot be a real sacrifice for the P tradition, given the absence of sanctified space, and this is why no actual sacrificial terminology is used in Exod 12:1–13. As Haran states, "The projection of the regular paschal observance, customary and familiar, on the image of 'the Passover of Egypt, [*sic*]' thus somewhat distorted the true nature of the sacrifice."[56] Propp reiterates and elaborates: "P's dilemma [was] to describe the '*Pesaḥ* of Egypt' as a sacral meal *sans* Tabernacle and priesthood. The solution was to describe a ritual meal like and yet unlike a burnt offering."[57]

Can Exod 12:1–13 therefore tell us much about a home-based Pesaḥ—what it would have entailed and the nature of its fundamental rituals? The answer that especially Haran offers is "no." Indeed, Haran goes so far as to declare that "according to *all* the biblical evidence the Passover is regarded as a temple sacrifice" (emphasis mine), thus denying that at any point "in the ancient Israelite times the Passover was a family sacrifice."[58] The exodus accounts that "involve the appearance of a non-temple sacrifice, even of a sacrifice made in the home," are "only an 'optical' illusion."[59] As Terence E. Fretheim writes, "Liturgy has shaped literature,"[60] and has so shaped Exod 12:1–13, according to Haran, that the liturgy of the temple is all we should ultimately see in the text. Propp is somewhat more generous, suggesting that "the Priestly Writer" did know of a tradition of "the domestic *Pesaḥ*." Yet "while this was a rite with which he [P] was familiar . . . he did not approve," and P was especially disparaging of what Propp hypothesizes was an older Pesaḥ tradition of domestic sacrifice and an associated rite of blood manipulation (the smearing of blood on a home's doorposts and lintel).[61] If this is so, then we could still imagine that in the home-based Pesaḥ that Propp reconstructs, women would have had some of the opportunities for religiously meaningful experiences described above: for example, the experience of having one's home temporarily transformed into a sanctuary space.

On one hand, we might summarize by saying that the domestic location we can posit for Pesaḥ during at least some part of the preexilic period may have generated for women who were participating in the Pesaḥ rites some significant religious experiences. On the other hand, we have practically no evidence about women's actual roles and responsibilities in home-based Pesaḥ celebrations, given that our primary source, Exod 12:1–13, has so overwritten its narrative's domestic context with its temple-centered concerns. Indeed, I began my discussion of caveats regarding women's religious experiences within ancient Israel's home-based Pesaḥ traditions by noting how Exod 12:1–13 lacks any explicit mention of women within its Pesaḥ account. Perhaps now we see the reason why: despite its ostensibly domestic setting, what Exod 12:1–13 really reflects is the sort of sanctuary location in which Pesaḥ, for this text's P authors, legitimately took place. Thus this text reflects the way in which women are often peripheral in the ritual observances of temple complexes, especially the Jerusalem temple compound that is the P authors' primary concern.

Yet what of the Maṣṣot traditions associated with Pesaḥ? Here, a consideration of women's religious agency offers more promise. This is especially the case regarding the Maṣṣot traditions having to do with the barring of leaven within Israelites homes as analyzed, again, by Propp (Exod 12:15, 19; see also 13:7; Deut 16:4).[62] For example, Propp perceptively points out that while it is the eating of bread made without leaven that gives the Maṣṣot festival its name, this act is not in and of itself so extraordinary within Israelite tradition.[63] Rather, unleavened bread was a standard part of the Israelite diet, especially when preparation time was scarce (see, for example, 1 Sam 28:24).[64] But purging a home of all leaven was another matter altogether and distinctive to Maṣṣot observance. Propp suspects this ritual may have to do with leaven's nature as a facilitating agent of fermentation and, ultimately, putrefaction, which in turn stand symbolically for impurities from which a household should be purged annually.[65] This chain of reasoning may overreach (and, in any case, it cannot be proved); nevertheless, it is indisputable that like anything impure, leaven is, according to biblical tradition, incompatible with holiness, especially the holiness of God as the ultimate holy being.[66] While the Israelites (even priests) may eat both leavened and unleavened bread, for example, cereal offerings presented to Yahweh, as noted above, must always be unleavened. To this extent, the unleavened bread eaten during Maṣṣot is not the stock unleavened bread of the Israelite "fast food" diet but the sanctified unleavened bread of an altar presentation. The effect of "unleavening" one's house during Maṣṣot is thus that "the home . . . becomes like a vast altar to Yahweh, leaven-free."[67]

The agents, moreover, who would have been responsible for this Maṣṣot "unleavening" that transforms a home symbolically into an altar are most logically women. After all, who but women, in their roles as the managers of their households' foodstuffs, would have been in a position to cleanse their homes of all leavened and leavening food products? Let me reiterate, as I consider this point to be of crucial importance for our analysis. When (and if—a caveat again necessitated by the problematic nature of our evidence) the nature of domestic space is reconceptualized during the Pesaḥ observance described in Exod 12:1–13 through a sacrificial-like slaughter and a sacrificial-like rite of blood manipulation, *men* are the critical actors in constructing the celebration's household-cum-sanctuary setting. I have argued above, for example, that in the "Pesaḥ of Egypt" that Exod 12:1–13, envisions, *men* would have carried out the slaughter of the Pesaḥ sheep or goat, *men* would have smeared the blood of the slaughtered sheep or goat upon a domicile's doorposts and lintel, and *men* may also have taken responsibility for cooking this animal's meat. But during the associated Maṣṣot festival as depicted in Exod 12:15, 19; 13:7; and Deut 16:4, household space is transformed into sanctuary space through the acts—the purging of leaven from the home—and therefore through the agency of *women*.

In sum: despite what our sources initially seem to suggest, ancient Israel's Pesaḥ feast may not have been a ritual occasion that offered women significant opportunities for religious engagement. However, texts that describe the associated festival of Maṣṣot, especially Exod 12:15, 19; 13:7; and Deut 16:4, do assign women an important and even primary role in ensuring that Maṣṣot's rituals regarding leaven are properly observed and, thus, that the Israelite god is properly honored.

Women and the Summer Festival of Harvest/ Firstfruits/Shavu'ot

Concerning the second pilgrimage festival of the Israelite calendar, the so-called festival of the Harvest, or Firstfruits, or Shavu'ot ("Weeks"), we know by far the least. In large part, this is because among our most fulsome calendrical sources, those that stem from P, H, and related priestly traditions (Lev 23:4–38, Numbers 28–29, and Ezek 45:18–25), Harvest/Firstfruits/Shavu'ot is accorded little to no significance. For example, as I noted in this chapter's introductory remarks, the festival does not appear in Ezek 45:18–25 at all. Also, although Harvest/Firstfruits/Shavu'ot is included in the ritual calendars of Lev 23:4–38 and Numbers 28–29 (see Lev 23:15–21 and Num 28:26–31), and although it is called in Lev 23:21 and Num 28:26 a *miqrāʾ-qōdeš*, a "holy proclamation" (as are the pilgrimage festivals generally according to Leviticus 23 and Numbers 28–29), neither Lev 23:15–21 nor Num 28:26–31 labels Harvest/Firstfruits/Shavu'ot as a *ḥag.*[68]

Still, we do know that the particular harvest celebrated according to those texts that do enjoin the observance of Harvest/Firstfruits/Shavu'ot is that of the wheat, whose reaping follows the earlier barley harvest that takes place around the time of Pesaḥ-Maṣṣot.[69] More specifically, according to the Holiness Code of Leviticus 23, the celebration of the wheat harvest was held on the fiftieth day after the time of the barley harvest had passed, or just after an interval of seven weeks (Lev 23:16).[70] Thereby, H alludes to the name Shavu'ot ("Weeks") given to the wheat harvest festival in Exod 34:22, Num 28:26, and Deut 16:10, 16. The ritual calendars of Lev 23:15–21 and Num 28:26–31 further indicate that Harvest/Firstfruits/Shavu'ot lasts only one day, and Deut 16:9–12—by making no mention of a longer celebration—probably intimates this as well.[71]

These ritual calendars of Lev 23:15–21, Num 28:26–31, and Deut 16:9–12 in addition comment on the nature of the offerings to be dedicated at Harvest/Firstfruits/Shavu'ot. Perhaps most interesting for our purposes is the notice in Lev 23:17 that these offerings should include two special loaves of bread, in acknowledgment of the festival's association with the wheat harvest. These loaves were to be made from a type of flour called *sōlet.* Women of course, as we by now well know, would have ground the two- or four-tenths of an ephah of *sōlet* flour (4.4 to 8.8 liters) that the loaves require.[72] Traditionally, moreover, *sōlet* has been understood to be a fine flour, which means that women's grinding task, always time-consuming, would in this instance have been particularly so, as fine flour obviously takes longer to manufacture than the coarser flour (*qemaḥ*) that interpreters take to be the stuff of daily household use.[73] Indeed, Mesopotamian sources indicate that only 6.66 to 8 liters of fine flour could be ground per day.[74] This means that if four-tenths of an ephah of *sōlet* flour were needed for the Shavu'ot bread loaves, it could have taken an Israelite woman more than a day to grind the required amount. Not surprisingly, our sources therefore suggest that *sōlet* was a luxury product, appropriate to use in foods prepared for honored guests or in a king's household (Gen 18:6, 1 Kgs 5:2 [in most of the Bible's English versions, 4:22]) and appropriate also for God. For example, Lev 2:1–2, 4, 5, and 7 mandate that any grain offering made to Yahweh must be of *sōlet*. It is only in H texts such as Lev 23:17 and in related P writings such as Lev 2:1–2, 4, 5, and 7, however, that the requirement that Yahweh's grain offerings be of *sōlet* is articulated, and I thus wonder whether *sōlet* was considered such a luxury product that *sōlet* grain offerings were deemed to be an unrealistic expectation according to other biblical sources. For example, Hannah brings the more pedestrian *qemaḥ* flour to offer to Yahweh at Shiloh according to 1 Sam 1:24.

Yet even though women would have ground the *sōlet* flour that Lev 23:17 requires, we cannot be as sure, given texts such as Gen 19:3 and Judg 6:19, that they would have used this flour to bake two loaves of bread at their homesteads, as Lev 23:17 also mandates.[75] Nor can we know whether women would have been among those who brought these loaves to Yahweh's sanctuary as the firstfruits offering of the wheat harvest. Indeed, concerning the vexed question of whether women were thought to travel to the sanctuary—for Leviticus, the wilderness tent of meeting and then the succeeding Jerusalem temple—to participate in the presentation of the bread loaves, Lev 23:15–21 is silent. By definition, Lev 23:15–21 is thus also silent on the equally vexed question of what women's participation in the sanctuary rites at Harvest/Firstfruits/Shavu'ot might have entailed. Moreover, because Lev 23:15–21 comes from H, which many scholars consider to date from the exilic or postexilic period, the mandate of Lev 23:17 regarding the two loaves of bread made of *sōlet* flour, and the various ways in which women may have contributed to this project, may ultimately not be germane for the preexilic period that is the focus of this book.[76]

Numbers 28:26–31, the other and earlier text from a priestly source, P, that speaks of the celebration of Harvest/Firstfruits/Shavu'ot, is also silent on the issue of women's presence at the celebration. Generally, however, as we have seen in Chapter 6 in our discussion of purity laws, the P source is reluctant to embrace women's full engagement in the cult of the wilderness tent and the later Jerusalem temple. Jacob Milgrom also implies that during the busy wheat harvest season of Harvest/Firstfruits/Shavu'ot, a principle that he calls a "one-night and one-person stand" would have been in force.[77] By this Milgrom means that only a household's head could have taken the time to make a quick trip to Yahweh's sanctuary to observe the Harvest/Firstfruits/Shavu'ot festival before returning home to join all his household's other members in their agricultural labors.[78] Presumably this in addition means that only the household's head would have enjoyed the respite from the "work of your occupations" (*kol-mĕleʾket ʿăbōdâ*) that Num 28:26 mandates for the one day of the Harvest/Firstfruits/Shavu'ot festival. Indeed, even if women did join with men in the *miqrāʾ-qōdeš* indicated for Harvest/Firstfruits/Shavu'ot observance in Lev 23:21 and Num 28:26, it is not clear that they would have enjoyed respite from the "work of *their* occupations," given that in a different P-authored text, Exod 12:16, it is said of the *miqrāʾ-qōdeš* held on the first and seventh days of Maṣṣot that even though *kol-mĕlāʾkâ lōʾ-yēʿāśeh*, "no work is to be done," tasks of food preparation—that is, tasks that typically fall to women—are to continue unabated.[79]

The ritual calendar found in Exod 23:14–17—which arguably reflects (possibly along with Exod 34:18–23) the Bible's oldest festival register—is also mute concerning women's participating in any way in the celebration of Harvest/Firstfruits/Shavu'ot, as it specifically enjoins just males to undertake the three pilgrimages of the Israelite calendrical year. Similar language is found in Deut 16:16, although Deut 16:9–12 allows more latitude, by including among those who make the pilgrimage of Shavu'ot a household's daughters, female slaves, widows, and perhaps the paterfamilias's wife (depending, as I discussed in Chapter 6, on how one understands the problematic masculine singular "you"). Unfortunately, Deuteronomy says little more about the nature of this pilgrimage observance, not even designating the exact nature of the festival's sacrifice. Presumably, though, a *šĕlāmîm* offering is implied, since the pilgrimage's celebrants—including its women celebrants—are instructed to "rejoice" in Deut 16:11, and rejoicing, as Milgrom writes, is "the common denominator . . . in bringing a *šĕlāmîm*."[80] Thus, Deuteronomy's account of Shavu'ot allows us to envision a household's daughters, female slaves, widows, and perhaps its paterfamilias's wife enjoying the meat of a *šĕlāmîm* feast, as do the women of Elkanah's household in 1 Sam 1:4–5.

Numbers 29:39 may likewise indicate that *šĕlāmîm* offerings were made by worshippers at the festival of Harvest/Firstfruits/Shavu'ot (as at other "set occasions" or "appointed times" of the Israelite calendar).[81] However, as already noted, whether women would have been present to partake of this *šĕlāmîm* meal is unclear. Indeed, in the kindred Lev 23:19–20 as it stands, *šĕlāmîm* offerings associated with the festival of Harvest/Firstfruits/Shavu'ot are to be eaten only by the priests.[82] This means, according at least to later rabbinical tradition, that not even the women of the priests' families may share in this particular *šĕlāmîm* meal.[83]

And so, on that unpromising note, we come to an end of our ability to speak of women's roles and experiences in the Harvest/Firstfruits/Shavu'ot celebration. We can feel confident that women ground the *sōlet* flour required for the two special bread loaves mandated as a Firstfruits offering in Lev 23:17 and that at least some of a household's women would have joined in the Shavu'ot pilgrimage and the pilgrimage's *šĕlāmîm* feast enjoined in Deut 16:11. Otherwise, we can say nothing about women's engagement in the festival's rites. Our conclusions about the Harvest/Firstfruits/Shavu'ot festival, therefore, are probably best summed up not by using the "on one hand"/"on the other hand" dichotomization that has characterized some of my earlier analyses of Israelite women's ritual year. Rather, because of a lack of data, we are forced to realize that our hands are tied.

Women and the Autumn Festival of the Ingathering

While we know the least, generally, about Harvest/Firstfruits/Shavu'ot among Israel's three pilgrimage festivals, and thus the least about women's roles in its observance, we know the most about the third feast, Ingathering/Sukkot, both generally and more specifically concerning women's experiences during its observation. This is because, of the year's pilgrimage feasts, Ingathering/Sukkot was the most important (see Lev 23:39–43, Num 29:12–34, and Deut 31:10–13; also 1 Kgs 8:2, 65). Thus, while Maṣṣot, Harvest/Firstfruits/Shavu'ot, and Ingathering/Sukkot can all be described in the Bible using the term *ḥag*, "pilgrimage," only Sukkot is called simply *heḥāg*, "*the* pilgrimage feast" (as in 1 Kgs 8:2, 65), "with the definite article and without any qualification." This should identify it as "the most significant among the three *ḥaggîm*, the *ḥag par excellence*."[84]

Sukkot's preeminence stems from its position within the agricultural year, as it took place in the autumn, when the last crops of the year, primarily grapes and olives, were harvested and processed. The festival was thus a time of great celebration, with ritual observances far surpassing those of the celebrations associated with either Pesaḥ-Maṣṣot or Harvest/Firstfruits/Shavu'ot. According to the P calendar in Numbers 28–29, for example, a total of seventy bulls, fourteen rams, ninety-eight lambs, and seven male goats were to be sacrificed to Yahweh during the seven days of Ingathering/Sukkot (Num 29:12–34), as opposed to the fourteen bulls, seven rams, forty-nine lambs, and seven goats that this calendar mandates were to be offered during the seven days of Maṣṣot (28:17–25) and the two bulls, one ram, seven lambs, and one goat that Num 28:26–31 prescribes for the one-day festival of Harvest/Firstfruits/Shavu'ot. On all of these holidays, moreover, for each of the sacrificial animals except the goats, Numbers 28–29 mandates a corresponding grain offering: three-tenths of an ephah of flour per bull, two-tenths of a ephah of flour per ram, and one-tenth of an ephah of flour per lamb. This means that the increased number of animals sacrificed during the Ingathering/Sukkot festival is matched by a significantly enhanced grain offering.

Another way in which the festival calendar of Numbers 28–29, as well as the related H calendar of Lev 23:4–38, signals the exaggerated character of the Ingathering/Sukkot celebration is though its description of a "holiday season," so to speak, of which Sukkot is the centerpiece. For example, while the first day of every month—the new moon day—was, as we saw in the previous chapter, a festal day, Num 29:1–6 and Lev 23:23–25 indicate that the new moon day of the month of Ingathering/Sukkot was of particular significance. On it, according to Num 29:2–6, a special sacrificial offering is made that is almost the same as the regular new moon sacrifice but is presented in addition to that regular sacrifice (so that the new moon regular offering is nearly doubled).[85] According to Lev 23:24 and Num 29:1, the new moon day of the Sukkot month is also marked by horn blowing that seems to be of a different magnitude and of greater significance than the horn blowing that Num 10:10 prescribes for all new moons and for other festivals.[86] What's more, an important ritual is observed on the tenth day of the month of Ingathering/Sukkot, although this rite is of a sober quality as opposed to the joy that characterizes the preceding new moon day and the succeeding Ingathering/Sukkot celebration. It is the so-called Day of Purgation or Day of Expiation, on which the priests undertake exceptional rituals to purify the sanctuary of whatever defilements had contaminated it during the previous year (Lev 23:26–32, Num 29:7–11; see also Leviticus 16).[87] Additional sacrificial offerings are also prescribed for this day, as they are for the specially observed day that immediately follows the seven days of Ingathering/Sukkot (Lev 23:36, 39; Num 29:35–38). In both cases, these offerings are identical to the additional offerings dedicated on the month of Sukkot's first day.

Almost all of these ritual observances, however—in particular, the making of additional sacrificial offerings on Days 1, 10, 15–21, and 22 and the purging of the sanctuary on Day 10—pertain only to Israel's priestly caste. The sacrificial offerings catalogued above, for example, are all described as *ʿōlâ,* meaning they were whole burnt offerings consumed in their entirety by fire upon the altar and not used for a communal meal in which an assembled congregation partook. Moreover, the purging of the sanctuary on the Day of Expiation was an exclusively priestly obligation and especially an obligation of the high priest, who, according to biblical tradition, makes his once-a-year appearance before Yahweh on this day, originally, as Lev 16:11–19 would have it, by going behind the curtain or veil (the *pārōket*) that hung inside the wilderness tent of meeting in order to access the tent's inner sanctum where Yahweh resided, and later, by coming into Yahweh's presence in the Jerusalem's temple's inner chamber or "Holy of Holies." Yet this is not to say that the Israelite population at large was not deeply engaged in the seventh month's ritual occasions—and more engaged than during ritual observances that took place at other points in the course of the religious year. On the contrary, the P and H traditions reflected in Lev 23:33–36 and Num 29:12–34 and the Deuteronomic tradition reflected in Deut 16:13–15 and 31:10–13 all agree that all seven days of Ingathering/Sukkot were a time of pilgrimage and so were spent at Yahweh's sanctuary. This is as opposed both to Pesaḥ-Maṣṣot and to Harvest/Firstfruits/Shavuʿot. As noted above, Lev 23:7–8 and Num 28:18, 25 enjoin the people to join in a "holy proclamation" only for Maṣṣot's first and seventh days, whereas Deut 16:1–8 requires just an assembly for Pesaḥ on the first day of its combined Pesaḥ-Maṣṣot festivals.[88] Also, in Lev 23:15–21, Num 28:26–31, and, seemingly, Deut 16:9–12 Harvest/Firstfruits/Shavuʿot is treated as a one-day festival only.

Leviticus 23:25, 28, 35–36 and Num 29:1, 7, 12, and 35 in addition enjoin the people to desist from work on the first, tenth, fifteenth, and twenty-second days of the Sukkot festal month. Moreover, according to the conceit of Lev 23:25 and Num 29:1, the people are presumably to desist from work on only the new moon day of the month of Ingathering/Sukkot, as the injunction to refrain from work is not a requirement either Leviticus or Numbers imposes for other new moon celebrations (but cf. Amos 8:5).

Furthermore, according to the Leviticus and Numbers festal calendars, the people are to desist from their regular activities on the tenth day of the Ingathering/Sukkot month in a particularly substantial way, beyond just the abstaining from "the work of your occupations," or "laborious work," as Jacob Milgrom translates, that is required on the first, fifteenth, and twenty-second days.[89] The tenth day requires also of the people that they "afflict themselves," which commentators generally assume means that they fast.[90]

What did this all mean for women? As we have repeatedly seen in our discussion of the Israelite ritual calendar, I think we must posit for the time being (but see further below) an answer that is ambivalent in terms of its evaluation. While I see no reason, for example, to think that women did not join with men to fast on the Day of Expiation (just as Esther fasted along with her community in Esth 4:16), and while a fast day obviously relieves women of their obligations for food preparation, I wonder whether the tradition hints that it is women's pollution from which the sanctuary on this day needs especially to be purged. As Milgrom has noted, the chapter in Leviticus that describes the ritual acts whereby the high priest expurgated the sanctuary—Leviticus 16—originally followed directly upon Leviticus 10.[91] Chapters 11–15 were secondarily inserted because they enumerate the sorts of specific impurities that make necessary the sanctuary's expiation. Several different impurities are catalogued in these chapters, but notably prominent among them—especially in a book in which women are otherwise infrequently or obliquely present (in citations concerning the *nepeš* in Lev 2:1–2; 4:2, 27–31; 5:1–2, 4, 15, 17–18, 21–25 [in most of the Bible's English versions, 6:2–6]; 7:18, 20–21, 25, 27, for example)—are a woman's impurities that stem from childbirth (Lev 12:1–8) and the impurities a woman incurs during menstruation or during an abnormal genital flow (Lev 15:19–30).

Stanley K. Stowers points out, moreover, that these women's impurities—and especially the impurities associated with childbirth and menstruation—are really "incommensurable with the other pollutions" of Leviticus 11–15 in terms of the harm they potentially bring upon the Israelite community. This is because the other pollutions are, in comparison, mild (the one-day pollution suffered by a man who has had a seminal emission, for example) or only sporadic in their occurrence (for example, the abnormal genital discharges occasionally suffered by both men and women).[92] Even *ṣāraʿat,* or the skin ailment commonly (albeit incorrectly) translated as "leprosy," although it is classified as the tradition's most severe form of impurity in terms of the ramifications for the sufferer that it entails, "is random from the perspective of structuration in society."[93] Conversely, "menstruation and childbirth pollution are coextensive with women of childbearing age and potentially of all women." "One does not have to be an anthropologist or sociologist," Stowers concludes, "to see that these pollutions of women would have an enormous effect." Indeed he argues, as already indicated, that these women's pollutions would have an "incommensurate" effect compared with the other impurities Leviticus 11–15 catalogues.[94]

Does this indicate that, according to the book of Leviticus, women are considered a (or even the) primary cause of the Day of Expiation ritual? Moreover, while the thought world of Leviticus is in many ways distinctive, its ideology regarding women's impurities is not unique (see Chapter 6), and thus could Leviticus's juxtaposition of chapters 11–15 and chapter 16 be said to give us some more general indication about the way in which Israelite tradition regarded women in relation to the ritual expiation and purgation of Yahweh's sanctuary? If so, then perhaps women's fasting on the Day of Expiation, which I have presumed, carries with it more negative implications than their male counterparts' abstinence from food. Women fast because they have particularly threatened the sanctuary's holiness and thus particularly need to make supplication.

Further consideration of women's position during other of the seventh month's ritual occasions can yield similarly ambivalent conclusions. I have previously noted, for example, that Exod 12:16 indicates that even though *kol-mělāʾkâ lōʾ-yēʿāśeh,* "no work is to be done," on the first and seventh days of Maṣṣot, this does not include the task of food preparation that was primarily women's responsibility.[95] I have also suggested this same situation may well apply at Harvest/Firstfruits/Shavuʿot, in that the respite from the "work of your occupations" (*kol-mĕleʾket ʿăbōdâ*) that Num 28:26 mandates for that festival may not apply to women's work of food preparation. Does this mean as well that although *kol-mĕleʾket ʿăbōdâ lōʾ taʿăśû,* "you will not do the work of your occupations," is mandated by Lev 23:25, 35–36 and Num 29:1, 12, and 35 on the seventh month's first, fifteenth, and twenty-second days, women would still be obligated to undertake their food-preparation responsibilities? Likewise, in the same way that our discussions above of Pesaḥ-Maṣṣot and Harvest/Firstfruits/Shavuʿot have made clear that nowhere in the tradition is women's presence during these pilgrimages wholeheartedly embraced, so too is this the case in texts that concern the Sukkot pilgrimage to Yahweh's sanctuary. Indeed, four of our five ritual calendars—Exod 23:14–17, 34:18–23; Lev 23:4–38; and Numbers 28–29—

are completely silent about women's presence during all three pilgrimage feasts.

Still, we can imagine that women were more likely to participate in the annual Ingathering/Sukkot pilgrimage than they were in the pilgrimages of Pesaḥ-Maṣṣot and Harvest/Firstfruits/Shavu'ot. For example, because Sukkot entailed—at least according to Lev 23:33–36, Num 29:12–34, and Deut 16:13–15 and 31:10–13—a seven-day visit to a Yahwistic sanctuary (as opposed to the one- or two-day sanctuary visits that texts such as Exod 13:6; Lev 23:7–8; Num 28:17–25, 26; and Deut 16:1–7a specify for the festivals of Pesaḥ-Maṣṣot and Harvest/Firstfruits/Shavu'ot), it seems more likely that families would make this pilgrimage journey together, rather than just send a household's head as their representative. Because, moreover, Ingathering/Sukkot came at the end of the agricultural year, when the harvest was essentially complete, it is easier to imagine that all (or at least most of) a household's members—including women—could have taken the time to leave their home for a ritual celebration. Indeed, Deut 16:13–15 specifically includes a household's daughters, female slaves, and widows among Sukkot's participants, and Deut 31:10–13 mandates that all women join in the special celebrations of Ingathering/Sukkot every seven years during which the *tôrâ,* or "teaching," ascribed to Moses is read.

Deuteronomy also suggests—along with Lev 23:39–40 and perhaps Num 29:39, but unlike Exod 23:14–17 and 34:18–23, which are silent on the issue—that *šĕlāmîm* offerings can be made during the Ingathering/Sukkot celebration, either in lieu of or in addition to the *'ôlâ* sacrifices that Num 29:12–34 mandates.[96] I assume, moreover, that women who participated in the Sukkot pilgrimage partook of its *šĕlāmîm* meals, as Elkanah's wives Hannah and Peninnah, and possibly Peninnah's daughters, partook of the *šĕlāmîm* meals eaten during what I take to be their family's Sukkot pilgrimages to Shiloh in 1 Sam 1:1–2:26.[97] Still, Deut 16:14, in listing the participants in Sukkot's *šĕlāmîm* feast, deploys the ambiguous phrasing that includes a household's paterfamilias's wife only if she is subsumed in the masculine singular "you." I have argued in Chapter 6, though, that the wife is not necessarily a part of this "you," just as Hannah can, but does not necessarily, accompany Elkanah on their family's Sukkot journeys to Shiloh (1 Sam 1:21–23).

On one of the pilgrimage journeys to Shiloh in which Hannah does participate, however, she does something that is for our purposes rather extraordinary. In 1 Sam 2:1–10, she gives voice to a poetic composition that, it is usually presumed, was set to music; indeed, it is typically called the "Song of Hannah." Nor is Hannah, in my opinion, the only woman who should be identified with music-making traditions upon the occasion of the Ingathering/Sukkot festival. Rather, it is my presumption that while our discussion of women and Israel's ritual calendar has repeatedly revealed that women's presence at the communally celebrated events of the Israelite religious year was limited and their participation in these events constrained, the Sukkot pilgrimage—even though it also, as we have just seen, places limits on women's engagement—offered women one distinctive religious role during its celebration: to perform during the festival as ritual musicians. This distinguishes Ingathering/Sukkot from the Israelite calendar's other ritual events and moves it beyond the "on one hand"/"on the other hand" paradigm that has so dominated in this chapter and the last.

It is further the case that women's music-making in conjunction with the Ingathering/Sukkot celebration is part of a larger tradition of women's music-making in ancient Israelite religion. Thus I move to an examination of female musicianship, as well as other ritual specializations (for example, prophecy and magic) in which the women of ancient Israel engaged.

PART 3

Who? Women Religious Functionaries

9 "When the Young Women of Shiloh Come Out to Dance in the Dances": Women Ritual Musicians in Ancient Israel

Within preexilic tradition, we can identify three major arenas in which Israelite women assumed responsibilities as ritual musicians. The first, as I indicated at the end of the last chapter, is women's role as ritual musicians during the festival of Ingathering, or Sukkot—and arguably also, as we will see below, during the larger "holiday season" associated with Ingathering/Sukkot celebration. I have also already mentioned the second arena we can describe as a site of women's ritual musicianship. This is the role of women as music-makers in conjunction with various life-cycle rituals in ancient Israel: for example, as I noted briefly in Chapter 5, women's role in singing lamentations as part of Israelite mourning rites. The third and final context in which women assumed a role as ritual musicians is the singing of victory songs after an Israelite triumph in holy war—a war, that is, that Yahweh had sanctioned and whose success the deity had guaranteed. In this chapter, I describe each of these examples of women's musicianship in turn.

Women's Ritual Musicianship During the Sukkot Festival

In considering women's role as ritual musicians during the autumn festival of Ingathering, or Sukkot, I take as my starting point Judg 21:19–21 and its description of young women who come out "to dance in the dances" (*lāḥûl bamměḥōlôt*) during "the yearly pilgrimage festival of Yahweh held at Shiloh" (*ḥag-yhwh běšīlô miyyāmîm yāmîmâ*).[1] This latter phrase most logically refers to the annual pilgrimage of Ingathering/Sukkot. To be sure, Judg 21:19–21 does not explicitly mention Ingathering/Sukkot; however, as we saw in Chapter 8, it is only Sukkot, among the three yearly pilgrimages of the Israelite calendar, that can be designated as "the pilgrimage" (as in Lev 23:39 and 1 Kgs 8:2, 65) without being more specifically identified.[2] This suggests it is Ingathering/Sukkot that is meant by the otherwise imprecise phrase *ḥag-yhwh,* "the pilgrimage festival of Yahweh," in Judg 21:19. Indeed, this exact phrase—*ḥag-yhwh*—is used to refer to the Ingathering/Sukkot festival in Lev 23:39, and a very similar expression—*tāḥōg layhwh,* "you will keep the pilgrimage festival to Yahweh"—is used to refer to Ingathering/Sukkot in Deut 16:15.

Another reason for suggesting that the setting of Judg 21:19–21 is the festival of Ingathering/Sukkot is that, according to Judg 21:20–21, the young women's dancing took place in the vicinity of Shiloh's *vineyards* (*kĕrāmîm*). This is significant because Sukkot, as we again saw in Chapter 8, celebrated, among other things, the successful conclusion of the grape harvest and the concomitant pressing of the new wine. Indeed, Deut 16:13 specifically describes Ingathering/Sukkot as a celebration held in conjunction with the grape harvest.[3] What's more, some scholars have argued that the name Deuteronomy gives to the pilgrimage, *sukkōt,* or "Booths" (see also Lev 23:34, 42), may have its origins not in the historicized association of the festival with the Israelites' wilderness sojourn in "tents" or "booths" that is put forward in Lev 23:42–43 (see once more my comments in Chapter 8); rather, the name Sukkot may instead stem from the practice of agricultural laborers camping in their fields in temporary "booths" during the time of the grape harvest (Isa 1:8; see also, perhaps, Job 27:18).[4] Judges 9:27 in addition describes how jubilant celebrations—typically understood to be Sukkot festivities—ensue after the work of gathering grapes from the vineyards and treading them had ended. Analogously, many interpreters assume, as do I, that the vineyard dancing of Judg 21:19–21 is part of the jubilant celebrations of Ingathering/Sukkot.[5]

As I have now stated several times, another text whose "yearly festival" I take to be the festival of Ingathering, or Sukkot, is 1 Sam 1:1–2:26, the story of Hannah and of her family's annual pilgrimages to Shiloh.[6] At this point, however, let me not just repeat this claim but substantiate it. To do so, I first draw attention to the fact that, although this is obscured in Christian Bibles, where the non-Deuteronomistic book of Ruth is interposed between the books of Judges and 1 Samuel, the older Deuteronomistic History as found in the Hebrew Bible sets the 1 Samuel story of Hannah immediately subsequent to the Judges 21 story of the young women who dance in Shiloh's vineyards. Arguably, moreover, these two stories were not casually juxtaposed by the Deuteronomistic History's authors and/or redactors but were positioned intentionally to mirror one another. Certainly, they mirror one another in theme, as Judges 21 ends with the refrain that recurs repeatedly in the narrative complex that comprises the last five chapters of Judges, "In those days there was no king in Israel, and everyone did what was right in his or her own eyes" (Judg 17:6, 18:1, 19:1, 21:25). This is meant to signal how precarious the Israelite social order has become in the era these chapters describe because of a lack of stable and fixed leadership. First Samuel 1:1–2:26 then introduces the antidote to this problem, in the form of the agent who will resolve the Judges 17–21 crisis: Samuel, who, according to the biblical account, anoints Saul, Israel's first king, and subsequently his successor David and thereby establishes the institution of a permanent monarchy.

More significant than their thematic associations, though, are the ways in which Judg 21:19–21 and 1 Sam 1:1–2:26 are carefully linked in terms of time and place. Most obviously, both are set in Shiloh during celebrations that take place there annually. More strikingly, both use the exact same phrase, *miyyāmîm yāmîmâ,* "year by year" (Judg 21:19; 1 Sam 1:3, 2:19), to describe their celebrations' annual nature. This locution, moreover, is otherwise very rare, found at only two other points in the Hebrew Bible (Exod 13:10 and Judg 11:40). Judges 21:19–21 and 1 Sam 1:1–2:26 also both stress that their respective festivals are pilgrimage feasts. For example, in 1 Sam 1:3, 7, 21–22, 24, and 2:19, Hannah and her husband Elkanah are said to "go up" (*ʿālâ*) annually to Shiloh, which is typical language used of a pilgrimage.[7] Likewise, as indicated just above, Judg 21:19 explicitly describes its celebration as a "pilgrimage festival" or *ḥag.*[8] Because commentators almost unanimously agree, as we have also seen above, that the particular *ḥag* referred to in Judg 21:19–21 is the pilgrimage feast of Sukkot, then so too must the pilgrimage festival in the closely parallel text of 1 Sam 1:1–2:26 also be, I would insist, Sukkot. In fact, in Exod 34:22, the feast of Ingathering/Sukkot is specifically said to be celebrated *tĕqûpat haššānâ,* "at the turn of the year" (i.e., at the time of the year when the season turns from the last days of the harvest to the beginning of the next agricultural cycle), just as Hannah is said, in 1 Sam 1:20, to bear Samuel *tĕqūpôt hayyāmîm,* which might also be translated "at the turn of the year" and which, 1 Sam 1:21 implies, is the time when Elkanah's family journeys annually to make their pilgrimage to Shiloh.[9]

Understanding the Shiloh festival of 1 Sam 1:1–2:26 as the festival of Ingathering/Sukkot—which, as attested by the aforementioned Judg 9:27, included copious amounts of eating and drinking—also helps explain an otherwise enigmatic detail in 1 Sam 1:1–2:26: why the priest Eli, as he watches Hannah pray silently (and for the ancient Near East atypically), with only her lips moving, presumes she is drunk. Surely there are other, equally plausible explanations for Hannah's silent prayer: Why does Eli not assume, for example, that Hannah is mute? Only if we understand that the setting of the Hannah story is the Sukkot festival does it make sense for Eli to leap to the conclusion that Hannah, as a celebrant at the feast of the new wine, would be intoxicated.[10] Incidentally, the juice of newly harvested grapes ferments very quickly in the warm Levantine climate, meaning the wine consumed at the Sukkot celebration, although barely aged, would be plenty potent in terms of its alcohol content.[11]

Understanding the setting of the Hannah story to be the fall festival of Ingathering/Sukkot also explains a second enigmatic detail in 1 Sam 1:1–2:26: the presence of the so-called Song of Hannah in 1 Sam 2:1–10. Although this hymn of praise and thanksgiving is attributed to Hannah in v. 1, almost all interpreters agree it was only secondarily attached to the account of Hannah dedicating Samuel to a lifetime of divine service. This is in particular indicated by the significant variations found among the Bible's ancient Hebrew and Greek versions in the verses that immediately surround 1 Sam 2:1–10.[12] For example, while the verse that immediately precedes the song in 1 Sam 1:28 reads in the Masoretic Text, "And he [most likely Hannah's husband Elkanah; perhaps the priest Eli; much less probably Samuel] worshipped Yahweh there," the Samuel manuscript from the Dead Sea Scrolls reports, "And she [Hannah] left him [Samuel] there, and she worshipped Yahweh."[13] As for the Greek tradition, the Codex Vaticanus has no comparable remark at this point in the text but does read in 2:11, "And she [Hannah] left him [Samuel] there before Yahweh." The Greek Lucianic version follows the Masoretic tradition in 1:28 by reading, "So he [presumably Elkanah] worshipped Yahweh there," but then, in 2:11, it roughly parallels its Greek counterpart, Vaticanus, by reading, "And they [Hannah and Elkanah] left him there before Yahweh." It then adds, "And they worshipped Yahweh there."

Obviously, textual confusion runs rampant here, all of it stemming from the fact that the original narrative of Samuel's dedication was disturbed at a later point in the text's transmission when an editor added the

"Song of Hannah." The song's secondary status is also indicated by passages such as its v. 10, which presumes the existence of the monarchy, an institution otherwise not a part of the Samuel narrative until Samuel's secret anointing of Saul in 1 Sam 10:1 and the public proclamation of Saul's kingship that follows in 10:17–27.[14] So why the addition? According to many, although the "Song of Hannah" is itself anachronistic, the insertion of a hymn of jubilation for Hannah to sing is nevertheless appropriate, given that her prayer that her barrenness be reversed so that she might bear a son had been granted. The mention in v. 5 of the song of the barren woman who, through God's gift, bears seven children, as well as the entire poem's sense that Yahweh can bring about great reversals in the natural order, especially indicates to commentators that the ancient curators of the Samuel text acted in a reasonable—albeit inaccurate—fashion in putting this song into Hannah's mouth.[15]

But this explanation does not satisfy me completely, for there are, in addition to Hannah, five women in the Hebrew Bible who find their barrenness has been miraculously and unexpectedly reversed by God's giving to them the gift of a child: Sarah (Gen 18:9–15, 21:1–7), Rebekah (Gen 25:19–26), Rachel (Gen 30:1–8, 22–24), Manoah's wife (Judg 13:2–24), and the Shunammite woman (2 Kgs 4:8–17). Arguably, moreover, the reversal of at least some of these women's barrenness is just as miraculous as was the reversal of Hannah's—and plausibly even more so. Sarah, after all, is said to be ninety years of age (Gen 17:17) and to have ceased to menstruate (Gen 18:11) before she finally becomes pregnant; Rebekah also, according to Gen 25:20 and 26, is barren for a prolonged period—twenty years—before eventually giving birth; and Rachel, too, is depicted as infertile for many years before bearing, given that her sister Leah was able to deliver six sons and a daughter in the interim. But despite the fact that Sarah, Rebekah, and Rachel receive a gift of fertility from God that must be regarded—after such long delays—as wholly unexpected, and despite the command in Isa 54:1 to the barren one to "sing" (*ronnî ʿăqārâ*), the Bible's redactors place a song of thanksgiving *only* on the lips of Hannah.

Why just her? I suggest biblical tradition assigns Hannah alone a song of thanksgiving because Hannah's story of barrenness, alone among the Bible's barren women stories, is set during the celebration of the fall Sukkot festival. Hannah alone sings, that is, because as a woman participating in the Sukkot feast, the tradition expects her to play a special role in the making of ritual music. Hannah's song is thus *not,* according to this thesis, a response to her experience of barrenness reversed, but rather an example of the kind of ritual musicianship typically undertaken by women as they participate in Ingathering/Sukkot celebrations. This music-making, as we can see by considering the Hannah text in conjunction with its companion account in Judg 21:19–21, included both song (as in 1 Sam 2:1–10) and dance (in which Judges' "young women of Shiloh" engaged).

Another text that attests to this special role for women as singers and dancers in conjunction with the celebration of Ingathering/Sukkot is Jer 31:10–14. In this passage, which is set in the years just after the fall of the Southern Kingdom of Judah, Jeremiah expresses his hope that the Israelites will someday return from their exile in Babylon to experience once more God's goodness and munificence in Jerusalem. At that time, Jeremiah says (v. 12), the people will "sing out [*rinnĕnû*] on the height of Zion" over the flocks and the herds, and also over the grain (*dāgān*), the new wine (*tîrōš*), and the freshly pressed oil (*yiṣhār*). Generally, commentators see in this verse a fairly generic description of rejoicing over the bounty God will give to a restored Israel in a reconstituted Jerusalem with a rebuilt temple. But the references to the new wine (*tîrōš*) and the freshly pressed oil (*yiṣhār*) make clear that the context Jeremiah presumes is far more specific: it is the rejoicing that takes place during Sukkot to celebrate the ingathering of the recently ripened grapes and the concomitant harvest and pressing of the year's olive crop. Recognizing this temporal setting gives the next verse of Jeremiah's oracle (v. 13) a whole new significance:

> Then the young women[16] will rejoice in the dance (*bĕmāḥôl*),
> The young men and the old will be merry.[17]

The young women, that is, will rejoice by performing the same sort of Sukkot festal dance described in Judg 21:19–21.

The special place of women musicians during the grape harvest festival of Ingathering/Sukkot is also suggested by Isa 5:1–7, a composition that is in fact often called the "Song of the Vineyard." As it stands, this text is a parable, in which the "vineyard" represents the two nations of Israel and Judah, both of which have been lovingly tended by their "vintner," who is identified as God (v. 7).[18] Yet despite God's care, the "vineyard" has failed, yielding only what vv. 2 and 4 describe as "wild grapes," otherwise defined in v. 7 as "bloodshed" and "outcries." For the prophet Isaiah, the text thus comments on how Judah and Israel have failed to live up to God's expectations, even though God has treated the two nations with compassion and should deserve their fidelity. My interest, though, is in the tradition that stands behind this parable, for many scholars believe Isaiah, in shaping his polemic against God's people, quotes, especially in vv. 1–2, an actual song of the Sukkot festival.[19] What scholars have not noticed, however, is that the original singer of this song addresses a "beloved" (*yādîd*), who, given the reference to "*his* vineyard" in v. 1, must have been a male:[20]

> Let me sing a song for my beloved;
> A love song concerning his vineyard:
> My beloved had a vineyard on a very fertile hill.

The song's performer therefore must have been a woman. The basis of Isa 5:1, and by extension all of 5:1–7, is thus a woman's song of the vintage—and so a song again representative of women's special role in generating and executing the music of the Ingathering/Sukkot festival.

Three other texts from the book of Isaiah may also allude to music made by women during the Ingathering/Sukkot celebration. For example, Isa 24:4–13, an oracle of woe, depicts the chaos and catastrophe it envisions by describing how "the mirth of the frame drum," "the noise of the jubilant," "the mirth of the lyre," and "the singing" that accompany the celebration of the new wine will be stilled. Isaiah 30:29 likewise describes a "song" sung as a part of a celebratory *ḥag,* almost unanimously assumed by commentators to be the pilgrimage feast of Sukkot (given, again, that in the Bible, only Sukkot is referred to as simply *heḥāg,* "*the* pilgrimage"). Unfortunately for my purposes, neither Isa 24:4–13 nor 30:29 uses any gender-specific language that could identify the sex of its festival musicians. Isaiah 32:9–14, though, does associate women with the Sukkot festival, although here what is lacking is a description of celebratory music-making. Rather, the prophet condemns women for being complacent—for not, perhaps, engaging in the ritual music-making the festival requires of them?—and consequently, he says, the harvest at the time of the next vintage will fail. Then the women will mourn: that is, they will exchange, in my interpretation, the celebratory music they typically perform at Ingathering/Sukkot for the songs of lamentation more typical of women's performances during funerary and associated rituals (more on this below).

Women's music-making in conjunction with the Ingathering/Sukkot festival also might be associated with the larger "holiday season" of which the seven days of Ingathering/Sukkot were a part. For example, women might have assumed a responsibility for music-making during the period of the grape harvest and the pressing of the new wine that took place before the Ingathering celebration began. This is perhaps intimated in Isa 16:10, which, like Isa 24:4–13 and 32:9–14, is an oracle of woe, in this instance describing how the general joy and gladness that should be manifest during the process of treading the recently harvested grapes will be stilled in the face of imminent destruction. More specifically, the oracle mentions the "songs" and "vintage shout" that should be heard (but will not be) while those who labor in the wine presses tread the grapes (see similarly Jer 48:33). This suggests to Oded Borowski that "grape treading as an activity accompanied by music . . . may have been the custom of the Israelites," with the music seemingly employed to create a cadence for the treaders to follow as they marched in place to extract the grapes' juice.[21] If music was indeed used in this way, then women—because they are otherwise associated with music-making during Sukkot—might have been responsible for music-making during this antecedent period of grape treading as well.

More significant for this study, however (given my focus on women's *religious* lives), are the hints that might associate women's music-making with some of the rituals of the new moon day with which the month of the Sukkot celebration began. As we saw in Chapter 8, this new moon day, according at least to the Holiness (H) and Priestly (P) calendars (Lev 23:23–25, Num 29:1–6), was assigned a greater significance than the year's other new moon observances and thus was the occasion of extra sacrificial offerings and special horn blasts. More specifically, as Jacob Milgrom has pointed out, the new moon horn blasts of the Sukkot festival month are described in Num 29:1 using the noun *tĕrûʿâ,* whereas according to Num 10:10, the verb *tāqaʿ* is used with regard to the trumpet blasts with which other new moon days and festivals are marked. The instrument that Num 10:10 mandates is to be sounded on the other new moons and festivals is, moreover, the *ḥăṣōṣĕrâ*—"a trumpet made of beaten hammered silver, about a cubit long (40 centimeters), with a narrow body and a broad, bell-shaped end"—as opposed to the *šôpār,* or shofar—a goat's or ram's horn—that Milgrom suggests is used to make the blasts of the new moon day of the Sukkot festival month.[22] Milgrom supports this conclusion by citing Ps 47:6 (in most of the Bible's English versions, 47:5), where *tĕrûʿâ* (as in Num 29:1) and *šôpār*/shofar are used in parallel. Furthermore, Milgrom proposes, citing Josh 6:9, 13, and 20, that while to sound (*tāqaʿ*) the trumpets that Num 10:10 prescribes for the year's other new moon days and festivals is a responsibility of *priests* (see Num 10:8), the *tĕrûʿâ,* or horn blasts, made using the *šôpār*/shofar on the new moon day of the Sukkot festival month are sounded by the *people.*[23]

Could these "people" have included women? As we have seen, women are not necessarily included among the Israelite *ʿām,* "people," who gather for cultic assemblies.[24] But Ps 81:2–4 (in most of the Bible's English versions, 81:1–3) raises tantalizing possibilities about women's participation in the music-making associated with the Sukkot month's new moon. This text reads:

> Sing ringing songs to God, who is our strength;
> shout for joy to the God of Jacob.
> Lift up a song, sound a frame drum (*tĕnû tōp*),[25]
> [and] a sweet-voiced lyre (*kinnōr nāʿîm*), along with a deep-toned lyre (*nēbel*).[26]
> Blow a ram's horn at the new moon (*tiqʿû baḥōdeš šôpār*),
> at the full moon, for the day of our pilgrimage feast (*yôm ḥaggēnû*).

Several points here are of note. First, while the mention of the "new moon" in the penultimate line of this passage might suggest that Ps 81:2–4 (English 81:1–3) refers to any of the year's new moon celebrations, the parallel reference to the full moon day as the day of "our pilgrimage feast," or *ḥag,* indicates that the new moon and full moon days in question are those of the month of Ingathering/Sukkot.[27] Once more, that is, Ingathering/Sukkot appears in this text as a *ḥag* that can be identified without further elaboration because of its status as the *ḥag* par excellence. The designation of the horn to be blown on the new moon day (as well as the full moon day) as a *šôpār*/shofar in addition indicates the new moon and full moon days in question are those of the month of Sukkot (assuming, that is, that we follow Milgrom's analysis of Num 29:1 and Ps 47:6 [English 47:5] regarding the distinctive use of the *šôpār* on the Sukkot month's new moon day).

Equally significant is another of the musical instruments mentioned in this passage, the frame drum, or *tōp,* which Carol Meyers more specifically defines as a "hoop-shaped drum with a diameter much greater than the width of its frame."[28] Meyers, moreover, has drawn attention to the fact that in Ps 68:25–26 (in most of the Bible's English versions, 68:24–25), which I considered in Chapter 5 in conjunction with my discussion of women's participation in the rituals of the Jerusalem temple, the young women (*ʿălāmôt*) who participate in a procession into Yahweh's *qōdeš,* or sanctuary, are said to play frame drums.[29] Indeed, Meyers has at points argued that "the playing

Fig. 9.1. Clay figurine of a woman playing a frame drum. Courtesy of the Semitic Museum, Harvard University (photograph by Carl Andrews).

of these percussion instruments was a specifically female role in the ancient Mediterranean world."[30] She cites by way of evidence late second-millennium and first-millennium BCE iconographic evidence from Egypt, Cyprus, Phoenicia (Tyre, Achzib, Kharayeb), and sites like Shiqmona on the Israelite coast (Fig. 9.1).[31] Meyers also cites several other biblical passages that describe frame-drumming women (Exod 15:20 [twice], Judg 11:34, 1 Sam 18:6, and Jer 31:4) and at least one extrabiblical text.[32]

Several lines of evidence potentially converge here. I have now argued that women are particularly associated with music-making during the Ingathering/Sukkot festival and perhaps during the larger "holiday season" associated with that celebration; also, that the last line of Ps 81:4 (English 81:3) refers to Ingathering/Sukkot; and, in addition, that the larger stanza of which Ps 81:4 is a part, Ps 81:2–4 (English 81:1–3), refers to at least one event within the larger "holiday season" associated with Ingathering/Sukkot, the new moon day of the Sukkot festival month. What's more, Ps 81:3 (English 81:2) possibly refers to women music-makers who play the frame drum, or *tōp*, in conjunction with the Sukkot "holiday season," for while Meyers overstates, in my opinion, when she associates frame drum playing *exclusively* with women,[33] women are frequently associated with playing the frame drum. To be sure, the verb that exhorts the drummers of Ps 81:3 (English 81:2) to play is a masculine plural imperative form, but masculine plural verbs are characteristically used in Hebrew both when speaking of groups of men alone and when speaking of groups that include men and women. Likewise, the masculine plural imperative form used in Ps 81:4 (English 81:3) could possibly refer to women who are among the "people" (following here Milgrom) who are summoned to blow the *šôpār*/shofar on the new moon day of the month in which the Sukkot festival falls, as well as on the full moon day when the festival actually began.[34]

In short: it is conceivable that Ps 81:2–4 (English 81:1–3) attests that women's music-making extends beyond the seven days of the Ingathering/Sukkot festival to the special new moon observance that inaugurates the Sukkot "holiday season." On the basis of Psalm 81's evidence, it also is possible to suggest that just as women's music-making during the celebration of Ingathering/Sukkot proper can be multidimensional—involving dancing, according to texts such as Judg 21:19–21 and Jer 31:13, and singing, according to texts such as 1 Sam 2:1–10 and Isa 5:1–7—so too can the instrumental repertoire on which women musicians perform during the Sukkot "holiday season" be multidimensional and include not just the frame drums with which women are elsewhere associated, but also, as in Ps 81:2–4 (English 81:1–3), the "people's horn," the *šôpār*/shofar, and even perhaps the lyre. Frame drum and lyre are found together, after all (albeit not explicitly associated with women musicians), in the description of Sukkot musicianship found in Isa 24:4–13, and female lyre players are also relatively well attested in Late Bronze and Iron Age textual and iconographic sources from Israel's ancient Near Eastern neighbors.[35] Moreover, finds from the late ninth-century/early eighth-century BCE site of Kuntillet ʿAjrûd in the eastern Sinai, 50 kilometers south of Kadesh Barnea (see Fig. I.2), include an image of a female lyre player—although it must be admitted that this lyre player, who sits on the throne typical of royalty and deities, is hardly of the "people" as I have construed them here.[36] Still, the evidence from this Israelite site, in conjunction with the other data I have catalogued, indicates that it is possible that Israelite women performed ritual music upon the lyre, at least upon some occasions.[37]

Yet even if the lyre players, the drummers, and those who blow the *šôpār* according to Ps 81:2–4 (English 81:1–3) do not include women, Judg

21:19–21, 1 Sam 2:1–10, Isa 5:1–7, Jer 31:10–14, and possibly Isa 16:10, 24:4–13, and 32:9–14 still attest that the Ingathering/Sukkot festival and, perhaps, the longer Sukkot "holiday season" were remarkably productive forums for women's musicianship. Thus the Sukkot season of ritual celebration stands as an exception to the general pattern we observed in Chapters 7 and 8, whereby most of the events of the Israelite festival calendar—given their association with the formally constituted, temple-centered religious establishment—were occasions where women's ritual engagement was limited or constrained.

Women as Ritual Musicians During Life-Cycle Events

"Israel celebrated a fairly constant rota of festivals," Walter Brueggemann writes, "a long-standing sequence . . . that was geared to the varying agricultural seasons that ran from seed time to harvest, or alternatively, according to the human life cycle from birth to death."[38] We have just seen how at least one of the "festivals . . . geared to the varying agricultural seasons," Ingathering/Sukkot, was a site of women's ritual musicianship in preexilic Israel. Now I turn to explore instances of the latter: music-making undertaken by women in conjunction with various life-cycle rituals. To be sure, I indicated in the Introduction that I have come to understand the topic of life-cycle rituals as they pertain to women to be so significant that I have decided to make these rituals the subject of a separate study. Nevertheless, the observance of some life-cycle rituals involves women's musical performance, and I consider the data that concern this musicianship here.

A particularly well-attested instance of women's musicianship during ancient Israelite life-cycle rituals is women's role as singers of lamentation in conjunction with funerary rites and on other occasions where evocations of death and burial loom large. An oft-quoted passage in Jer 31:15, for example, speaks of how, at the time of the Babylonian invasions of the late seventh and early sixth centuries BCE, the voice of the long dead Rachel is heard weeping and performing a dirge over her devastated descendants (*nĕhî,* from the verb *nāhâ,* "to wail" or "to lament"). Second Samuel 1:24 similarly describes how David, as a part of the lament he sings after the deaths of Saul and Saul's son Jonathan, expects the "daughters of Israel" to weep over their dead king—or we can more specifically imagine, on the basis of Jer 31:15, that David expects them to sing mourning songs. Of course, the fact that David voices this expectation as part of his own song of lament, or *qînâ,* makes clear that men could assume roles as lament singers in ancient Israel as well as women.[39] Still, it is possible that while David sings his dirge on account of his personal association with and respect for the deceased Saul and Jonathan, the "daughters of Israel" in 2 Sam 1:24 were called upon to mourn in a *professional* capacity.[40]

Certainly it is clear from other texts that for some women, the task of singing ritual laments during funerary rites or at analogous times of mourning was a professional—as opposed to a personal—obligation. Women, for example, may be included among those "skilled" or "expert in dirges" (*yôdĕʿê nehî*) who are mentioned in Amos 5:16.[41] Moreover, a role for women as professional lament singers is indicated emphatically in Jer 9:16–20 (in most of the Bible's English versions, 9:17–21). There, in v. 16 (English v. 17), Yahweh, as part of an oracle concerning the forthcoming devastation of Jerusalem, commands that *the* lamenting women should be summoned (*qirʾû lamqônĕnôt*). The use of the definite article suggests a group of women specializing in lamentation, and this is also implied in the passage's next line, in which these women are identified as being "expert" or "learned" (*ḥăkāmôt*) in their craft (meaning, probably, specially trained). In v. 19 (English v. 20), moreover, these female lament singers are commanded to teach their daughters a dirge (*nĕhî*), possibly suggesting that the profession of the lament singer was handed down by women from one generation to the next.[42]

Phyllis Bird has in addition pointed out that in other cultures of the eastern Mediterranean and the ancient Near East, women played a prominent (although again, not an exclusive) role in the singing of lamentations and in related rituals of mourning.[43] In Greek tradition, for example, "women were the most active of the mourners," even when men joined in mourning rites.[44] In particular, Greek women assumed the role of singing funerary lamentations.[45] Also, like the lament singers of Jer 9:16–20 (English 9:17–21), some Greek women may have been "professional singers who sang dirges at the corpse, and presumably at the grave as well."[46] Women mourners—again, perhaps, professionals—are also found in the fourteenth-/thirteenth-century BCE epics of Aqhat and of Kirta, from the northern Levantine city-state of Ugarit (see Fig. I.2).[47] In the Aqhat Epic, women weepers (*bkyt,* from the verb *bky,* "to weep") arrive to mourn (*mšspdt,* from the verb *spd,* "to wail, lament") in the palace of King Dan'il after his son Aqhat is killed.[48] Similarly the Kirta Epic mentions women who sing laments as part of the larger mourning rites designated by the verb *spd* (and the related noun *mspd*): more specifically, "women's chanting" (*bd aṯt*) is listed as one of the mourning rites that would be performed if the ailing King Kirta were to die. Moreover, Kirta's daughter, Thitmanit, was expected to join in these lamentations, weeping (*bky*) and making moaning sounds (*dmm*, cognate with the Akkadian verb *damāmu*, which means "to mourn by moaning").

Evidence for women's role in mourning in the larger eastern Mediterranean and ancient Near Eastern worlds of which Israel was a part is also found within the Bible itself. We saw in Chapter 5, for example, that Ezek 8:14 speaks to the Mesopotamian ritual of women who, in imitation of the mythological figures of Ishtar (Inanna), Geshtinanna, and Ninsun, sing dirges to lament the untimely death of the young fertility god Tammuz. Meindert Dijkstra has proposed, moreover, that these women of Ezek 8:14, like the women of Jer 9:16–20 (English 9:17–21), should be identified as members of a professional class of lament singers: first, because like the women of Jer 9:16–20 (English 9:17–21), the women of Ezek 8:14 are described in the Masoretic tradition using the definite article—*hannāšîm*, "*the* women."[49] However, while this reading is possible, it is not wholly certain, as the ancient Greek translation of the Hebrew Bible does not place the direct article before "women." This means it may not have been present in the older Hebrew manuscripts of Ezekiel on which the Greek translation was dependent.[50] More secure, though, is Dijkstra's second argument: that the mourning women of Ezek 8:14 are depicted in the larger text of Ezekiel 8 as "a clearly defined group"—what Dijkstra calls a "college of women"—comparable to the clearly defined and identifiable groups of men who bracket the mourning women textually.[51] These are the seventy elders of Israel who are the subject of Ezek 8:7–13 and the twenty men who assemble at the temple's threshold in Ezek 8:16.[52] Dijkstra also proposes that Ezekiel's women lament singers, who are described as "sitting," *yōšěbôt*, at the northern gate of the Jerusalem temple compound, not only engage in the typical mourning activity of singing lamentations but also assume a traditional mourning pose, lowering themselves to the ground.[53] Following many other scholars, I take this to be a symbolic gesture of identification with the dead.[54]

Another typical mourning gesture is to raise one's hands to one's face or over one's head, sometimes in order to perform the traditional mourning behavior of pulling out one's hair or otherwise making oneself bald.[55] Mourners can also raise their hands over their heads to perform the

Fig. 9.2. Women mourners, from the tomb of Renini (EK 7), an Egyptian nomarch during the reign of Pharaoh Amenhotep I (r. 1514–1493 BCE). Located at el-Kab in Upper Egypt. Photograph by the author.

mourning rite of rubbing dirt or ashes into their scalps.[56] Or sometimes raised hands may draw attention to the mourning tradition of wearing one's hair unkempt, or the variant rite of covering one's head with a cloth or veil (Esth 6:12).[57] Whatever the particulars, though, this gesture is one frequently enacted by women mourners in the ancient Near East and eastern Mediterranean. It is well attested in Egyptian iconographical sources, for example (Fig. 9.2), in depictions of women mourners that are part of funeral scenes represented in New Kingdom tomb paintings (ca. 1539–1075 BCE). Perhaps some of these Egyptian mourners, moreover, are to be taken, as in Jer 9:16–20 (English 9:17–21) and Ezek 8:14, as professionals. As Gay Robins points out, a stele from the New Kingdom village of Deir el-Medina on the west bank of the Nile, opposite ancient Thebes, "was dedicated by a woman and her daughter who both use 'mourner' as a title, suggesting this was their occupation."[58]

Other representations of women performing the traditional mourning pose of raised hands—perhaps, again, representations of professional mourning women—are found in the art of Philistia, Israel's neighbor on the southwestern Levantine coast (roughly the region of today's Gaza strip; see Fig. I.2). The rim of a Philistine bowl from the Iron Age I period (ca. 1200–1000 BCE) that seemingly was used for burial rites is decorated, for instance, with images of four mourning women who, like their counterparts in Egyptian tomb paintings, have their arms raised above their heads.[59] The same image of women with arms upraised in a mourning gesture is found in the funerary art of Israel's Phoenician neighbors whose territory spanned roughly the region of modern-day Lebanon (see again Fig. I.2)—on the tenth-century BCE sarcophagus of King Ahiram of Byblos, for example.[60] Moreover, this gesture is enacted by women in the Bible (2 Sam 13:19, Lam 2:10), and at least once in conjunction with the singing of lamentations (Jer 7:29).[61]

That Israelite women assumed an important music-making role within funerary rituals thus appears to be part and parcel with the responsibility for mourning and lamentation assumed by women throughout the ancient Near East and eastern Mediterranean. However, one biblical text that speaks of women making music upon an occasion of mourning may reflect a more distinctively Israelite tradition. This is Judg 11:29–40, the story of Jephthah's daughter. This story begins by describing Jephthah's preparations as he goes forth to wage war against the nation of Ammon, which is oppressing Israel. These preparations include his vow that if he is successful, he will sacrifice to the deity as a burnt offering, or *'ôlâ*, whoever or whatever comes out of his house to meet him on his return from battle (the Hebrew *'ăšer* is ambiguous). Jephthah, one would want to imagine, has in mind that he will first encounter some animal from his flocks upon coming home, but as fate would have it, it is his daughter and only child who comes forth. He is greatly distressed, so much so that the first word out of his mouth is a cry of woe (*'ăhāh*, "Alas!"; Judg 11:35), and he engages in yet another act of mourning typical in the biblical world, tearing his clothes.[62] But he cannot, as he says, go back on his vow, as vows within biblical tradition are generally considered to be irrevocable (Deut 23:22 [in most of the Bible's English versions, 23:21]). Thus the daughter must be sacrificed as Jephthah has promised.

It is within the context of this tragic realization that the story introduces information relevant for our inquiry. The daughter, although she acknowledges the necessity of honoring her father's vow, asks for a short reprieve before the sacrifice takes place: two months to "wander" in the mountains with her companions, "so that I might bewail *'al-bĕtûlay,*" or, as it is usually translated, "so that I might bewail my virginity" (Judg 11:37).[63] This request Jephthah grants, the two-month period of bewailing is undertaken, and then, after the daughter is killed, we are told that a custom arose in Israel that every year, for four days, the daughters of Israel would go forth to *tannôt* Jephthah's daughter (Judg 11:40). In ancient translations of the Bible, and in many modern versions, this verbal infinitive form *tannôt* is rendered "to lament," which suggests the young women of 11:40 go forth annually to mourn the untimely demise of Jephthah's daughter. Under the terms of this interpretation, the young women of Judg 11:40 act just as the Israelite women whose mourning traditions I catalogued above, by performing lamentations in association with funerary rites and on occasions (as here) where evocations of death and burial loom large.

But *tannôt* really is better translated "to rehearse" or "recount."[64] Also, the daughter's stated intent to go into the mountains "so that I might bewail my virginity" is really better translated "so that I might bewail the onset of my womanhood," that is, her entry into puberty.[65] In the light of this, Peggy L. Day has persuasively argued that the "recounting" the young women of Israel are said annually to perform is not a lamentation over Jephthah's daughter's tragic death, but a reprise of the daughter's original bewailing that marked "her [Jephthah's daughter's] transition to physical maturity."[66] This annual reprise of the daughter's original mourning over her "transition to physical maturity" moreover functions, according to Day, as well as other scholars, as "a women's life-cycle ritual" for the daughters of Israel, who, like Jephthah's daughter, go forth at the time of their own entry into puberty (where to is not clear), so that they, again like the daughter, can "bewail" their own transition into physical maturity and the symbolic death of the childhood stage of life they leave behind.[67]

In other words, Day suggests that Jephthah's daughter's story serves as an etiological legend that "project[s] . . . contemporary practices backwards in time to their imagined point of origin,"[68] thereby to describe the putative foundation of and rationale for those practices. Under the terms of this etiological analysis, Jephthah's daughter's past actions serve as a model for a coming-of-age ritual of lamentation that all adolescent women are compelled to enact to mark the "death" of their prepubescent stage of life and, simultaneously, their entry into puberty and thus, according to the Israelite life-cycle calendar, the age of marriageability.[69] If Day is correct (and I believe she is), then we see here a somewhat different manifestation of women's role as lament singers upon occasions of mourning, for, while there is still in Judg 11:37–40, as within funerary rituals, a focus on lamentation in conjunction with death, the "death" in question—of the prepubescent stage of life—is located within a coming-of-age ritual. This in turn suggests that women's coming-of-age rituals should be listed along with funerary rites as Israelite life-cycle events that featured women's musical performances.

Weddings, too, may have been life-cycle events during which the women of ancient Israel were called upon to make music. To be sure, our evidence is sparse, and it is furthermore the case that most of the biblical passages we can cite regarding Israelite wedding music are not gender specific with regard to the music's performers. The notice in Ps 78:63, for example, that during a time of calamity for the Israelites, "Their young women of marriageable age were not praised/celebrated" (*bĕtûlōtâw lōʾ hûllālû*) or, as some commentators have interpreted, "Their maidens had no nuptial song," says nothing—even if the interpretation that refers to "nuptial songs" is correct—about the identity of these songs' performers.[70] Likewise, while Jer 7:34, 16:9, 25:10, and 33:11 are often taken to allude to wedding music when they associate sounds of mirth and gladness with the voices of the bride and bridegroom, there is no indication of who the music's performers might have been.

The Bible's fullest description of a wedding, the seven-day wedding celebration of Samson (Judg 14:10–18), is also ambiguous. Indeed, the text makes no explicit mention of music, although I think we can readily posit that music-making would have been a part of Samson's marriage festivities. The wedding feast, after all, is called a *mišteh,* or a drinking bout (Judg 14:10), and elsewhere in the ancient Near East, this sort of drinking feast typically included music-making. For example, in the fourteenth-/thirteenth-century BCE mythological texts about the storm god Baal that come from the northern Levantine city-state of Ugarit, music is a featured part of the lavish feast that celebrates the victory of Baal over the sea god Yamm; music also plays a prominent role in a feast in Baal's honor described in the Ugaritic Epic of Aqhat.[71] The music made at Samson's wedding feast, moreover, may have specifically included riddling songs, such as the riddle Samson poses to his guests in Judg 14:14. However, the fact that *Samson* performs this riddling song, if this is how we are to interpret, indicates that even if Israelite weddings were occasions on which music was made, it need not necessarily follow that *women* would have sung the nuptial songs.

Our comparative evidence can be equally unforthcoming. For example, several scholars have proposed that a poem from Late Bronze Age Ugarit in which a singer recounts the story of the marriage of the moon god Yariḫ and the goddess Nikkal-Ib (*KTU* 1.24) was commonly recited at weddings. The point, according to those who have put forward this theory, was "to ensure for the bride the same blessing and protection by the *katharat* [the divine patronesses of wedlock and conception] as was accorded the goddess Nikkal at her wedding."[72] Still, neither the poem nor the proponents of the theory regarding its customary performance at weddings offer any comment on the performer's sex.

There are, however, Greek marriage hymns sung by the bride or by a young women's chorus that speaks for her.[73] We might also note in this regard an account of the metaphorical wedding of Yahweh and Israel described in Hos 2:17 (in most of the Bible's English versions, 2:15), in which God promises Israel, pictured as Yahweh's bride-to-be, that she will be given vineyards as a wedding gift. Israel, the prophetic oracle goes on to say, "will respond," according to standard translations. But the verb used here, *ʿānâ,* might better be translated "to sing" or "to sing responsively."[74] If so, Hos 2:17 (English 2:15) might be seen as alluding to a tradition of women's music-making in association with weddings.

Yet whatever women's musical role at Israelite weddings, the persuasiveness (for me) of Day's reading of the story of Jephthah's daughter and the multiple pieces of evidence regarding women as singers of funerary laments confirm that Israelite women assumed responsibility for music-making during the observance of at least some life-cycle events. I therefore identify these life-cycle events as being, like the feast of Ingathering/Sukkot, religious occasions that called for women's performance as musical specialists.

Women and the Victory Song Tradition of Ancient Israel

The third and final arena we can describe as a site of women's ritual musicianship was originally studied by Eunice B. Poethig in her 1985 doctoral dissertation: this is women's responsibility for singing victory songs after an Israelite triumph in holy war.[75] The most famous examples are the two victory songs commonly called by the names of the women who performed them: the "Song of Miriam" in Exod 15:1–18, 20–21, which celebrates the defeat of the armies of Pharaoh at the time of the exodus from Egypt, and the similarly named "Song of Deborah" in Judg 5:1–31, which celebrates the defeat of the Canaanite army of Sisera during the early days of Israel's emergence in the "promised land."

Some analytical nuance is required, however, to appreciate fully women's role—and, more important, women's seemingly *exclusive* role—as singers of these and other victory songs. Judges 5:1, for example, ostensibly identifies both a man and a woman, Deborah and Barak, as singing the Judg 5:1–31 victory hymn. Yet close scrutiny suggests that in some older version of the text, the woman Deborah was identified as the sole performer, as her name comes first in v. 1 and the verb *šîr,* "to sing," is rendered in the third-person *feminine* singular (*wattāšar*). Somewhat similarly, Exod 15:1 identifies Moses, and not Miriam, as the singer of the Exod 15:1–18 victory song that praises Yahweh for drowning and thus defeating the Egyptians at the Reed (more traditionally, Red) Sea.[76] More than half a century ago, however, in a 1955 article, Frank Moore Cross and David Noel Freedman suggested that this attribution may not have been original.[77] Their argument is based on the fact that the second or "b" half of Exod 15:21 repeats almost verbatim the second half of 15:1. Thus, Exodus 15:1b reads, "I will sing to Yahweh, for he is highly exalted. Horse and chariotry, he has thrown into the sea," while 15:21b states, "Sing to Yahweh, for he is highly exalted. Horse and chariotry, he has thrown into the sea."[78] Yet in the first half of 15:21, the singer of these lines—and presumably, therefore, the singer of the larger hymn of which these lines are the incipit—is identified not as Moses, but as his sister, Miriam.[79] Cross and Freedman further argue that this identification of Miriam as the song's performer is the older ascription, as, over time, tradition would have more readily changed from assigning the song to Miriam in order to attribute it to her more famous brother. It is difficult to imagine, conversely, that a song originally ascribed to Moses later would have been accredited to a more minor character. As Cross and Freedman write, "It is easy to understand the ascription of the hymn to the great leader. It would be more difficult to explain the association of Miriam with the song as a secondary development."[80]

The victory song celebrating Yahweh's triumph over Pharaoh's Egyptian army thus was originally attributed to Miriam, not Moses; the attribution of the song to Miriam in Exod 15:21, moreover, is preceded in v. 20 by a description of how Miriam and all the women of Israel celebrated Yahweh's victory over the Egyptians by playing frame drums (*tuppîm*) and dancing (*mĕḥōlōt*). This is an indication that these acts of musical production were supplemental aspects of women's victory song performances. Frame drumming, dance, and victory song performance are also conjoined in 1 Sam 18:6–7, where the women of the towns of Israel serenade Saul as he marches back from doing battle against the Philistines by playing frame drums (*tuppîm*), dancing (*mĕḥōlōt*), and singing of his triumph.[81] Victory in holy war, frame-drum playing, and dancing again appear together in Judg 11:34, where the daughter of Jephthah goes forth to greet her father with drumming and dancing (*bĕtuppîm ûbimḥōlôt*) after he returns home victorious from battle against the Ammonites. No singing is mentioned, but surely song is implicit.[82] This episode in the story of Jephthah's daughter thus bears witness to another instance of women's victory song performance.

The tradition of women singing victory songs is found as well in Ps 68:12–13 (in most of the Bible's English versions, 68:11–12), where female heralds (*hamĕbaśśĕrôt*) are commissioned to sing out the news of Yahweh's victory in holy war, proclaiming, "The kings of the armies, they flee, they flee."[83] It may be, moreover, that we are to associate this victory song performance with the playing of frame drums (although not dancing), given that later on in Ps 68:25–26 (English 68:24–25), as I have now noted several times, the young women (*ʿălāmôt*) who participate in a procession into Yahweh's sanctuary play frame drums (*tôpēpôt*). Yet I have also noted (in Chapter 5) that the various stanzas of Psalm 68 originally may have come from disparate compositions, rather than forming a unified whole.[84] We thus might overstep in positing a relationship in Psalm 68 between the women who herald Yahweh's victory in vv. 12–13 (English vv. 11–12) and the drummers of vv. 25–26 (English vv. 24–25).

Whatever caveats we might raise, however, about Judg 11:34 and Ps 68:12–13, 25–26 (English 68:11–12, 24–25) as full manifestations of victory song performance, we have more than enough evidence to affirm that the performing of victory songs, in conjunction (often) with the playing of frame drums and dancing, stands as a third example of women's role as specialists in ritual musicianship.

10 "The Daughters of Your People Who Prophesy": Ancient Israel's Women Prophets

In 2 Kgs 3:9–20, King Jehoram of the Northern Kingdom of Israel, King Jehoshaphat of the Southern Kingdom of Judah, and the unnamed king of Edom, who are engaged in a joint military operation, find their armies' march stymied by a lack of water. They thus seek out the prophet Elisha so that he might solicit an oracle from Yahweh regarding their further prospects. Elisha, although initially reluctant, eventually agrees to inquire of God. However, in order that he might produce an oracle, Elisha tells the kings, "Get me a musician" (2 Kgs 3:15). A musician comes, starts to play (what instrument is unspecified), and as the performance proceeds, a state of rapture or ecstasy is induced. Elisha then begins to speak in Yahweh's name. Similarly, in 1 Sam 10:5, an ecstatic frenzy comes upon a band of prophets who are in the company of musicians who play the standard lyre (*kinnōr*), the deep-toned lyre (*nēbel*), the frame drum (*tōp*), and the pipe (*ḥālîl*).[1] So potent, in fact, is the power of these musicians to induce a rapturous trance that, according to 1 Sam 10:10, even the newly anointed King Saul is overtaken (and hence the origin of the saying, "Is Saul, too, among the prophets?").

Indeed, as Joachim Braun writes in his comprehensive study of Israelite music-making, "music as a means to induce prophecy, rapture, and ecstasy is deeply rooted in the cultural traditions of the ancient world."[2] Could the performers of such prophecy-inducing music have included women? The musician summoned to inspire Elisha's prophetic oracle was male (*mĕnaggēn*), but the mention in 1 Sam 10:5 of the frame drum (*tōp*) and the lyre (*kinnōr*) intimate that women might be included in prophecy-inducing musical ensembles.[3] After all, as we saw in Chapter 9, the frame drum is especially associated with women's musical performance, and evidence regarding women lyre players can be found throughout the biblical world.[4] An association of women musicians and prophetic utterance might also be indicated by the appearance of a prophet in Exod 15:20 in conjunction with the women of Israel who dance and play frame drums at the Reed (more traditionally, Red) Sea,[5] after Yahweh delivers the Israelites from the forces of Pharaoh who pursued them during their flight from Egypt. For my purposes in this chapter, however, more important than women's potential role in making prophecy-inducing music in Exod 15:20 is the fact that the prophet who appears in the company of the drumming and dancing women is herself a woman. This is Miriam, the sister of Moses and Aaron.[6]

Nor is Miriam the only woman labeled a prophet in the biblical record: the designation is in addition accorded to Deborah in Judg 4:4, Hulda in 2 Kgs 22:14–20 (paralleled in 2 Chr 34:22–28), and Noadiah in Neh 6:14. A group of women who seem to comprise a prophetic band or guild of some sort—the "daughters of your people who prophesy"—also appears in Ezek 13:17–23.[7] I would, however, resist including Isaiah's wife in this catalogue, even though she is called a *nĕbîʾâ,* "prophet," in Isa 8:3.[8] This is because, unlike Miriam, Deborah, Hulda, and Noadiah, Isaiah's wife does not engage in a prophet's typical work. She does not speak, for example, even though, as we will see just below, a core function of prophets is to deliver oracles on behalf of the deity. Instead, the sole action attributed to Isaiah's wife is an enterprise in which almost all ancient Israelite women engaged: conceiving by her husband and bearing their child. While it is true, moreover, that this child is of prophetic significance, this significance is on account of his symbolic name, which is determined by Yahweh and atypically bestowed on the infant boy not by his mother, but by his father (the name, Maher-Shalal-Hash-Baz, means something like "swift the spoil, prompt the plundering" and signifies the doom soon to come upon Judah's King Ahaz).[9] That is, by naming the child according to Yahweh's decree, the father Isaiah performs the real prophetic function of communicating Yahweh's oracle to Ahaz. It is also important to note that, unlike Miriam, Deborah, Hulda, and Noadiah (albeit like the anonymous "daughters . . . who prophesy" in Ezek 13:17–23), Isaiah's wife is not given a name. This is significant, for as we saw in Chapter 1, the giving of names in the Bible—especially the giving of names to women—is often an important marker of autonomy and authority.[10] The nameless status of Isaiah's wife, conversely, suggests relative powerlessness. In fact, I would argue that Isaiah's wife is assigned the title "prophet" only by virtue of her marriage to the male prophet Isaiah, in much the same way that, say, Esther is assigned the title "queen" by virtue of her marriage to the Persian king Ahasuerus, even though Esther herself is not of royal birth (Esth 2:22; 4:4; 5:2–3, 12; 7:1–3, 5–8; 8:1, 7; 9:12, 29, 31–32).

The Work of Women (and Men) Prophets in Ancient Israel

To discount the status of Isaiah's wife as "prophet" because, among other things, she did not engage in a prophet's typical work is, however, immediately to raise the question: What did a typical prophet do? As the story of Elisha's interactions with Kings Jehoram, Jehoshaphat, and the king of Edom may already have signaled, "the prophet was . . . one whose *primary function was to receive messages from the deity.*"[11] Yahweh's own account of the prophetic office as presented in Deut 18:18 similarly emphasizes this task: "I [Yahweh] will put my words in his [the prophet's] mouth." This Deuteronomy text then goes on to say that the prophet in turn "shall speak to them [the Israelite people] everything that I [Yahweh] command." That is, after receiving a message from the deity, the prophet's responsibility is to deliver that message in some form (an oracular declamation being the most common) to its intended recipient(s), whether they be the people as a whole, as Deut 18:18 envisions; some subset of the Israelites (the people of Judah and Jerusalem, say, as frequently in the book of Jeremiah—for example, Jer 4:3, 18:11, 35:13); or some individual or individuals who might represent their community or the Israelite people in some way (most often a king, as in 2 Kgs 3:9–20).[12]

This prophetic task of receiving and conveying divine messages describes particularly well the work of at least two of the Bible's women prophets, Deborah and Hulda.[13] As Hulda's story as recounted in 2 Kings 22 goes, she is living in Jerusalem when King Josiah, in the eighteenth year of his reign (ca. 622 BCE), sends his secretary, Shaphan, to the high priest of the temple in order to deliver Josiah's command that the institution's financial resources are to be allocated to fund needed repairs to the sanctuary complex (2 Kgs 22:3–7). In conjunction with these events (although the specific circumstances are not detailed), Hilkiah, the high priest, reports to Shaphan that the so-called book of the *tôrâ* or book of the law has been found amid the temple's holdings (2 Kgs 22:8). Scholars most typically identify this book, or more precisely scroll, as some version of what we now know as the book of Deuteronomy, whose teachings or law, as I have mentioned previously, stress (among other things) the need to worship Yahweh *only* at "the place that Yahweh your God will choose," or the temple in Jerusalem.[14] Yet when Shaphan brings the book to King Josiah and reads it to the monarch, Josiah is dismayed to realize that "our forefathers did not heed the words of this book" (2 Kgs 22:13). Josiah thus resolves to inaugurate a great religious reform, destroying all the shrines of the countryside to leave only the Jerusalem temple as a sanctuary for God's worship. Concurrently, he proposes to remove from the temple itself any cultic furnishings he perceives to be dedicated to gods other than Yahweh.

Before beginning this massive undertaking, however, Josiah seeks—as he reasonably might—to ensure that the commands of the "book of the *tôrâ*" truly reflect God's will. He thus sends Shaphan, along with Shaphan's son, Ahikam; the high priest Hilkiah; a royal servant, Asaiah; and a man named Achbor, son of Micaiah, to "inquire of Yahweh . . . concerning the words of this book that has been found" (2 Kgs 22:13). The verb used here for "inquire," *dāraš,* is, as we have seen in Chapter 4, a technical term that refers specifically to the soliciting of cultic oracles.[15] Shaphan and company thus appropriately go to an oracular specialist, or a prophet. This is Hulda, who is said to be the wife of Shallum, the keeper of the (king's) wardrobe, a datum that may be of significance. After all, there were presumably other prophets available in Jerusalem at this time: Jeremiah's prophetic work, for example, is said to have begun during the first half of Josiah's reign (Jer 1:2, 3:6, 25:3, 36:2), and Zeph 1:1 likewise identifies the prophet Zephaniah as active during "the days of King Josiah." Yet Shaphan chooses Hulda as opposed to these and other prophets, perhaps because she was known to him through her husband's position at the royal court.

When she is approached, Hulda does just as a prophet should: she speaks in the name of Yahweh concerning the book (or scroll) that Hilkiah has found, reporting that Josiah is right to be dismayed regarding the text, as Judah has indeed failed to live up to its statutes, which do reflect Yahweh's will. Thus the nation will be punished. Yet Hulda reports that Yahweh will look mercifully on Josiah himself because of the consternation he has expressed and the work of reformation he proposes. Whether, in the conceit of 2 Kings, we should actually consider this promise of Yahweh's mercy to have been fulfilled is not so clear, as Josiah dies a violent death in battle (2 Kgs 23:29–30) rather than going to his grave "in peace" as Hulda indicates will happen (2 Kgs 22:20).[16] Disaster for Judah, though, certainly does ensue, just as Hulda reports is inevitable, culminating in 586 BCE with the Babylonian conquest of Judah and the concomitant destruction of the Jerusalem temple and deposing of the Judahite monarchy. In 2 Kgs 23:1–25, Deuteronomistic tradition further signals its sense of the validity of Hulda's oracle by describing the massive crusade that Josiah undertook, some thirty-five years before the Babylonian destruction, to bring his kingdom into compliance with the description of Yahwistic tradition found in the scroll that Hulda had endorsed.

Deborah also performs the prophetic function of receiving messages from the deity and then communicating these messages to some individual(s) and/or the people as a whole on Yahweh's behalf. But describing the means by which she does this is somewhat more complicated than describing Hulda's work, in large part because Deborah appears in the biblical tradition in two distinct and, to a significant degree, different sources. Of course, Hulda appears in two sources as well, since her story, like many of the stories of the books of Samuel and Kings, is retold in 1–2 Chronicles, in 2 Chr 34:22–28. Moreover, many of the details of the larger 2 Kings 22 account of the finding of the "book of the *tôrâ*" differ significantly in the 2 Chronicles rendition. Still, in their presentation of the part of the story of greatest concern to us, Hulda's prophetic message, 2 Kgs 22:14–20 and 2 Chr 34:22–28 are practically identical. Conversely, our two sources regarding Deborah's prophetic work, Judg 4:4–24 and Judg 5:1–31, are not so readily harmonized. Nevertheless, as we will see, the pictures they present of Deborah's prophetic work are ultimately complementary.

It is in the first of these two sources as they appear in the biblical canon that Deborah is explicitly called a prophet (*nĕbîʾâ*): in Judg 4:4. She is also said in this same verse to be "judging Israel" (*šōpĕṭâ ʾet-yiśrāʾēl*). Judges 4:4 thereby suggests that the work of a prophet, in the opinion of this passage's authors and/or redactors, is synonymous, at least to some degree, with the role of "judge" (*šōpēṭ*), the title typically applied to the community's leaders in the premonarchic period of Israelite history during which both Judges 4 and Judges 5 are set. Yet how the two roles cohere is not necessarily clear, since nowhere else in the book of Judges does a "judge" in fact function as a prophet by delivering oracular decrees to individuals and/or the Israelite people as a whole, based on the declaimer's supernatural knowledge of the divine will.[17] However, this sort of divinatory role does seem to describe Samuel's work in "judging Israel" in 1 Sam 7:15–17, and we can therefore posit that this is the sense of a "judge-prophet" on which Judg 4:4 draws.[18]

Judges 4:5 in addition indicates that Deborah typically performed her prophetic role by waiting for petitioners to ask her for decrees (the text reports she used to sit under the so-called palm of Deborah, where the Israelites "came up to her for judgment"). This is similar to the way that many centuries later (according to biblical chronology), Hulda received the petitioners who were sent by King Josiah in her home and delivered to them an oracle when asked. Yet according to Judg 4:6, Deborah uses a somewhat different approach when she issues the decree that propels the action of the rest of Judges 4. In this verse, she summons, rather than receives, a man named Barak, to deliver to him a divine oracle that commands he raise an army from among the two Israelite tribes of Naphtali and Zebulun and take this militia into battle against Sisera, the general of the army of Jabin, king of the Canaanite city-state of Hazor (Judg 4:2, 17; see also Fig. I.1). Deborah further decrees the outcome of the battle: that "I [Deborah speaks here for Yahweh] will give him [Sisera] into your [Barak's] hand" (Judg 4:7).

Deborah can therefore be said to enact in Judges 4 the typical prophetic function of delivering a divinely decreed message on Yahweh's behalf (even though this oracle is, atypically for Deborah, unsolicited by a supplicant). The oracle Deborah delivers, moreover—a pronouncement that gives Yahweh's sanction for an Israelite military engagement and guarantees its success—is a type of decree that prophets elsewhere in the Bible often articulate. For example, after Elisha's musically induced prophetic oracle in 2 Kgs 3:16–20 reassures Kings Jehoram and Jehoshaphat and the king of Edom that pools of water will appear in normally dry riverbeds to slake their armies' thirst, the prophet goes on to promise the monarchs, in the name of Yahweh, that their enemy, the nation of Moab, will be handed over to them.[19] Similarly, in 1 Kgs 20:1–22, as King Ben-Hadad of Aram (modern Syria) lays siege to Samaria, the capital city of the Northern Kingdom, an unnamed prophet appears and delivers an oracle to the North's King Ahab. "Thus says Yahweh," the prophet begins, speaking, like Deborah, in the deity's name. Then, as God continues to speak through the prophet, an oracle sanctioning war in Yahweh's name is delivered: "Do you see all this great multitude? Behold, I [Yahweh] am giving it into your [Ahab's] hand today, and you shall know that I am Yahweh" (v. 13).

Still, while proclaiming these so-called holy war oracles is a common prophetic enterprise, the response of Barak in Judg 4:8—to refuse to respond to the oracle's command unless Deborah accompanies him to the battle site—is hardly the norm. In fact, it is more or less unparalleled: the closest analogies are Judg 6:36–40 and 11:29–31. In the former text, Gideon, having been commissioned to go forth in battle by an actual divine messenger, or angel, who also assures Gideon of his undertaking's success (Judg 6:11–24), nevertheless asks God for an additional sign that he will be victorious; in the latter, Jephthah, as we saw in Chapter 9, makes a vow to God in hope of securing divine succor, even though he has been previously imbued with the spirit of Yahweh, which should have been enough to guarantee a victory in battle.[20] So how to explain Barak's reluctance? One might be tempted to propose an answer based on gender: that because Deborah is a female prophet, Barak is less inclined to trust her oracular decree and act unquestioningly on it than are recipients of similar oracles delivered by male prophets. And, in fact, gender does influence certain dimensions of the Deborah account in Judges 4. For example, as noted above, the principal function of the "judge," or *šōpēṭ*, elsewhere in the book of Judges is not oracular; rather, it is to lead military engagements. Yet the authors and/or redactors of Judges 4 resist assigning this responsibility to Deborah the *šōpĕṭâ* (the feminine form of *šōpēṭ*), by depicting her instead as a divinatory judge who commissions a male war leader, Barak, to take charge of the fighting.

Gender issues cannot as readily be said to drive the Judges 4 account of Barak's reluctant response to Deborah's oracular pronouncement, however, given that Judges 4's authors and/or redactors, at least in the form of the text as it has come down to us, are the same Deuteronomistic Historians who are the authors and/or redactors of the Hulda account in 2 Kings 22. It thus seems unlikely these authors and/or redactors, who show no reservations about depicting Hulda as a legitimate and unquestioned source of prophetic authority in 2 Kings, would introduce concerns about gender by having Barak resist complying with a woman's prophetic oracle in Judges 4. Rather, as has been carefully documented by Baruch Halpern, what shapes the Judges 4 account in multiple respects—including the text's depiction of Barak's reluctance to accede to Deborah's commission—is that Judges 4 is literarily dependent on the second (and therefore obviously older) source in which Deborah (as well as Barak) appears, Judg 5:1–31.[21] In that text, Deborah is integrally involved in the actual prosecution of the war against Sisera; indeed, I have argued elsewhere that she is portrayed as the Israelite commander-in-chief in Judges 5, whereas Barak functions only as her second-in-command.[22] Judges 4, as noted above, resists going that far. But it reflects the lead of its Judges 5 source to the extent of having Deborah be present at the battle proper, through its conceit of having Barak refuse to fight unless she accompanies him to the scene of the conflict.

More of interest for my purposes, however, is the way in which Judg 4:4 derives its description of Deborah as a *nĕbîʾâ,* "prophet," from its source in Judg 5:1–31, given that Judges 5 never actually describes Deborah as a prophetic functionary. But Judges 5 does give several intimations of Deborah's prophetic status that the authors and/or redactors of Judges 4 then pick up on and make explicit. For example, Deborah is well described as having been "called" by God in Judg 5:1–31, as Yahweh summons her to "Awake!" (5:12) and muster an army for battle against Sisera. Likewise, the root meaning of the nouns *nābîʾ* ("prophet" in its masculine formulation) and *nĕbîʾâ* (the term's feminine rendering) can be determined by reference to the verb *nābāʾ*, "to call, proclaim, name," suggesting that a prophet is one who is "called" by Yahweh to proclaim the divine word (grammatically, *nābîʾ* and *nĕbîʾâ* are to be understood as passive participles of *nābāʾ*).[23] Moreover, as is implicit within the call to arms that Yahweh commands Deborah to issue in Judg 5:12 and explicit elsewhere in the text of Judges 5 (see especially vv. 4–5 and 19–21), the battle to which Deborah summons the Israelites is a holy war, in which God sanctions the combat and even goes forth to fight at Israel's side. We have seen above, of course, that to verify that a battle is an actual holy war of God is a major role assumed by prophets elsewhere in biblical tradition. In addition, in one of the Bible's holy war texts, 1 Kings 20, the prophetic adviser of Ahab not only declares that the war about to be fought is sanctioned by Yahweh, but also instructs the king regarding the mustering of an army and even goes so far as to dictate who should serve in this fighting force: "the young men who are in the service of the district governors" (v. 14). This parallels Deborah's role in Judges 5, which involves, first, summoning Barak for battle in Judg 5:12.[24] Then, in Judg 5:14–18, it is she (versus Barak, in Judges 4) who musters a coalition of Israel's northern tribes. Some scholars have further argued that the title "mother in Israel" assigned to Deborah in Judg 5:7 is a marker of her prophetic role, the counterpart of the title "father" assigned to male prophets such as Elijah and Elisha elsewhere in the Hebrew Bible (2 Kgs 2:12, 6:21, 13:14; see also 1 Sam 10:12).[25]

Together, these data suggest, as proposed above, that the Deuteronomistic authors and/or redactors of Judges 4 derived their explicit designation of Deborah as a prophet in 4:4 from indications found in the older text of Judges 5. More specifically, Judges 4 follows Judges 5 in presenting Deborah as a prophet who is called by God to announce the prosecution of a holy war and then to oversee it in some form.

In addition to mediating between the divine and human worlds by relaying messages from the former to an audience within the latter, prophets also mediated between these two worlds by ministering to those who were ill and effecting their healing.[26] This is because healing was understood in the ancient world as a divine prerogative.[27] As we saw in Chapter 7, for example, the Shunammite woman solicits the help of the prophet Elisha when her son is unexpectedly stricken and dies (2 Kgs 4:8–37), and the wife of King Jeroboam likewise solicits the prophet Ahijah in 1 Kgs 14:1–18 on behalf of her ailing son. Other prophetic healing stories can be found in 1 Kgs 17:17–24, 2 Kgs 5:1–14, and 2 Kgs 20:1–11 (= Isa 38:1–8). Nancy R. Bowen has suggested, moreover, that prophets' role in healing activities may underlie the fairly enigmatic passage concerning the cadre of "daughters . . . who prophesy" in Ezek 13:17–23.[28]

In making this argument, Bowen focuses on Ezek 13:18–21, where the passage's women prophets are said, first, to sew bands of cloth onto others' wrists.[29] They also put headbands (Bowen's preferred translation of the more usual "veils"; Hebrew *mispāḥôt*) on others' heads.[30] In addition, Ezekiel's women prophets are associated with "handfuls of barley" and "pieces of bread." All of these references remind Bowen of Mesopotamian (and we can add Hittite) rituals performed on behalf of childbearing women, both before and during the course of their pregnancy and at the time of delivery.[31] For example, special amulet stones could be tied to a Mesopotamian mother-to-be's body if she was experiencing difficulties, as in a text from the Neo-Assyrian period (ca. 934–609 BCE), which refers to nine stones tied around the waist of a pregnant women who was suffering from profuse vaginal bleeding.[32] Mesopotamian sources also describe a set of twelve amulet stones that can be tied to the hands, feet, and hips of a woman who struggles during labor and "does not give birth easily."[33] Other sources refer to a set of twenty-one stones strung on a linen thread and hung around the neck of a barren woman in order to help her conceive.[34]

More closely parallel to Ezek 13:18 are a Mesopotamian text from the Old Babylonian period (1894–1595 BCE) and a Middle Hittite period text from ca. 1450–1350 BCE. Both of these document how red wool threads can be bound to a mother during parturition to protect her.[35] Bowen also catalogues Mesopotamian rites of twining together and knotting threads of various colors, which are then tied to a pregnant woman's hand or other body parts to stop excessive vaginal bleeding, and she cites as well a ritual of tying a band on a Mesopotamian mother-to-be to prevent miscarriage.[36]

Note, moreover, as does Bowen, that the specific term for the "wrist bands" the daughters apply according to Ezek 13:18, *kĕsātôt,* is arguably related to the Akkadian verb *kasû,* "to bind."[37]

Mesopotamian ritual texts (as well as Egyptian tradition) in addition speak of the removal of bands or the untying of knots at the time of the actual birth.[38] This is because "knots [otherwise] . . . constrain birth" (so much so that, in Egypt, a parturient woman's hair was intentionally unbraided and left to hang unbound during delivery and in the period immediately after she gave birth [Fig. 10.1]).[39] Furthermore in Mesopotamia, a midwife might sprinkle a circle of flour on the floor during a pregnant

Fig. 10.1. An Egyptian woman shown with unbound hair after giving birth, while her maid offers a mirror and kohl. Ostracon from the Ramesside period, western Thebes. Musée du Louvre, Paris, France, inv. no. E25333. Photo: Christian Decamps. © RMN-Grand Palais/ Art Resource, NY.

woman's delivery, and offerings of bread could be made.[40] This latter ritual, Jo Ann Scurlock hypothesizes, was meant to sate the hunger of demons that might otherwise snatch newborn infants, and Bowen suggests that the association of the "daughters . . . who prophesy" in Ezek 13:17–23 with barley and bread indicates that they may have used these foodstuffs in a similar way.[41] All in all, Bowen concludes, "the activities that Ezekiel ascribes to the female prophets . . . share some of the same imagery as these various incantations associated with childbirth. In particular they share the imagery of the binding and removal of knots or bands of cloth (13:18, 20, 21) and the use of grain and bread for ritual use (13:19)."[42] It thereby can be proposed—although, needless to say, not all commentators agree—that Ezekiel's "daughters . . . who prophesy" "serv[ed] in a health-care capacity . . . as 'prophets' [who] could be consulted as 'medical professionals' during pregnancy and delivery."[43]

One might suggest, moreover, that to perform medical acts on behalf of childbearing women is a prophetic role especially assigned to *women* prophets. To be sure, in 2 Kgs 2:19–22, it is the *male* prophet Elisha who purifies a spring near Jericho so that the "miscarriage (*měšakkālet*) of the land," that is, its lack of fertility, is brought to an end, and perhaps by implication, we should understand that his act also brings to an end actual miscarriages as suffered by the city's pregnant women.[44] Also, in 2 Kgs 4:16–17, as we saw in Chapter 7, Elisha was able to bring about the pregnancy of the otherwise childless woman of Shunem, and somewhat similarly, in Gen 20:17–18, Abraham—who is called a prophet in Gen 20:7 (the only point in the Bible where Abraham is so identified)—intercedes with God to effect the healing of the women of the household of King Abimelek of Gerar, as they had been inflicted with barrenness.

Yet while these passages could suggest that a male prophet might respond to some of the difficulties faced by childbearing (or potentially childbearing) women, the specific rites a prophet might enact at the time of a woman's delivery—the binding on of red threads, the untying of other knotted bands, the making of bread offerings to baby-snatching demons—would more likely than not have been the responsibility of women functionaries, given what seems to be the Israelite tendency to separate men from a woman who is giving birth. Certainly, as we saw it Chapter 6, it seems clear that Israelite women were separated from their *husbands* during childbirth, as word must be brought after delivery to the father of Jeremiah that a son has been born to him (Jer 20:15).[45] We also saw in Chapter 6 that the Priestly (P) tradition as presented in Lev 12:1–8 considers pregnant women to be rendered impure at the time of their delivery and for one to two weeks afterwards and that this impurity is contagious. We can thereby surmise that in addition to their husbands, members of a recently delivered woman's community would have kept their distance from the polluted parturient—with the exception, of course, of a woman's midwife and possibly other women (1 Sam 4:20, Ruth 4:14) whose presence at childbirth was required. I would include Ezekiel's "daughters . . . who prophesy" in this cohort of childbirth attendants. From this it follows that while Hulda and Deborah perform their prophetic tasks in ways closely analogous to those employed by their male counterparts, the "daughters . . . who prophesy" in Ezek 13:17–23 may engage in a kind of reproductively focused prophetic work more associated with female practitioners than with men.

Perhaps this gendered nature of their work even helps explain why Ezekiel, in speaking of these women prophets, excoriates them. Granted, there are probably other reasons for Ezekiel's excoriation, which I discuss in Chapter 11; also, as Bowen points out, Ezekiel excoriates other groups of (male) prophets, in Ezek 12:21–25, 13:1–16, and 14:9–11. Bowen thus suggests that Ezekiel's denunciation of the women prophets of 13:17–23 is part of a larger program of condemnation that Ezekiel deploys to denigrate men and women among his prophetic contemporaries who cling to traditional preexilic theologies (for example, theologies of Jerusalem's inviolability and preexilic notions of covenant). These are ideological constructions, Bowen argues, that Ezekiel seeks to overturn in the light of the dramatically changed historical circumstance out of which he writes (the aftermath of the Babylonian conquest).[46] Still, as we have seen in discussing Jeremiah's denunciation of those who worship the Queen of Heaven in Chapter 2 (Jer 7:16–20; 44:15–19, 25), women can be the object of a prophet's special scorn even when both males and females together are being castigated. We might suppose, therefore, that—even if the denunciations of the "daughters . . . who prophesy" are a product of "Ezekiel's theology of radical discontinuity" (if we were to follow Bowen)[47]—a little professional jealousy underlies Ezekiel's harangue as well. However far-reaching and significant Ezekiel's work is as prophet, that is, he might resent women rivals who are able to fulfill prophetic responsibilities undertaken at the time of childbirth that he cannot.[48] Ezekiel, moreover, is not only a prophet but also a priest (Ezek 1:3), which might suggest that he is *especially* unable to fulfill whatever prophetic responsibilities would be undertaken at the time of childbirth, given that his priestly status means he must take special care to safeguard himself from the impurities that the process of delivery unleashes.[49]

Women's Prophetic Authority

The "daughters . . . who prophesy" of Ezek 13:17–23 are not the only women prophets who find their legitimacy as prophets challenged within biblical tradition. In fact, both Miriam and Noadiah, who is active in the postexilic period during the time of the Judaean governor Nehemiah (ca. 445 BCE), have their claims of prophetic authority questioned.[50] Indeed, virtually all we know about Noadiah is that she somehow stood in opposition to the project of rebuilding Jerusalem's walls that was championed by Nehemiah and is denigrated in Neh 6:14 for this stance.[51] The story that calls into question Miriam's prophetic authority, conversely, is fairly detailed (Num 12:1–15). The story, moreover, is particularly of interest for this study because of the role gender plays within it.

That said, Numbers 12, as it opens, seemingly has nothing to do with calling into question Miriam's prophetic authority: rather, it is Moses, Miriam's brother, who finds himself challenged, "on account of the Cushite wife whom he [Moses] had married" (Num 12:1). But Num 12:2 immediately introduces a different reason for the challenge to Moses and also, it seems, a slightly different view of Moses's challengers. In Num 12:1, while those who challenge Moses are identified as both Miriam and her other brother, Aaron, the verb that describes their speaking out against Moses is rendered in a feminine singular form. This suggests that in some older version of Num 12:1, Miriam was Moses's sole challenger concerning the issue of his marriage and what seems to be perceived as the inappropriate (non-Israelite) identity of his wife.[52] When the nature of the challenge changes, though, in Num 12:2, the verb form changes as well, to third-person plural, as both Miriam and Aaron speak out to question Moses's right to serve as Yahweh's sole spokesperson within the Israelite community.[53] "Has not he [Yahweh] also spoken through us?" they ask (Num 12:2). Aaron and Miriam continue to be presented in tandem as the text goes on (in, for example, vv. 5, 8, 9, and 11), and the initial concern expressed about Moses's marriage seems to be forgotten. Rather, the focus becomes exclusively the question of Yahweh's appropriate spokespeople, and, one might argue, reasonably so.[54] After all, this is the subject of the immediately preceding chapter in Numbers, in which the difficulties that Moses has faced in serving as the sole intermediary between Yahweh and the people are addressed. In addition, both Miriam and Aaron are designated as prophets in the larger exodus account of which Numbers 12 is a part: Aaron in Exod 7:1 and Miriam, as noted above, in Exod 15:20. Presumably, therefore, they are qualified to serve as Moses-like mediators between the divine and human worlds.

It must be admitted, however, that Exod 7:1 specifically designates Aaron as *Moses's* prophet, as Moses, according to Exod 4:10–16, suffers from a speech impairment, and so Aaron, in the conceit of the text, is cast as the mouthpiece who will convey Moses's words to the Egyptian pharaoh regarding the Israelites' enslavement and its hoped-for end. Also, neither Aaron nor Miriam is necessarily depicted anywhere within the exodus narrative as enacting the prophet's primary function of receiving messages from the deity and then passing them on to the appropriate recipient or recipients.[55] Still, the question these two raise with Moses in Num 12:2—"Has not he [Yahweh] also spoken through us?"—clearly indicates that they perceive themselves as able to fulfill the prophetic role of mediating between the divine and human realms. Furthermore, the deity seems to agree—at least at some level—that Aaron and Miriam are correct to claim that supernatural messages are delivered "to" (if not necessarily "through") them; thus, in Num 12:4, Yahweh speaks to Aaron and Miriam, along with Moses, and orders them to appear at the tent of meeting. Yahweh further directs—as I noted briefly in Chapter 5—that Aaron and Miriam are to approach the tent's entrance to hear the deity's words. Yet counter to Miriam's and Aaron's presumption, the speech Yahweh then delivers indicates that there is a difference between "prophets" such as the two of them and Moses, because it is to Moses alone that God speaks "mouth to mouth" (*peh 'el-peh*) or, more idiomatically, "face to face" (Num 12:8).

Then, according to Num 12:9, "the anger of Yahweh was kindled against *them* [Miriam and Aaron]" (emphasis mine) because of their affront. But as God's anger manifests itself, only Miriam is punished, afflicted with *ṣāraʿat,* which is traditionally translated as leprosy but is in fact better analyzed as some kind of eruptive skin disease (true leprosy, Hansen's disease, was unknown in the ancient Near East).[56] Aaron, conversely, remains unharmed. Moreover, even though it has been made clear through the words of Yahweh's pronouncement in Num 12:6–8 that Aaron's prophetic authority is less than Moses's, and even though Aaron's status as a prophet of Yahweh (versus Moses) is less than clear elsewhere in the exodus account, Aaron still seems able to intercede in a prophetlike way on Miriam's behalf, asking

Moses, the "lord" whom he serves as prophet according to Exod 7:1, to effect her healing (Num 12:11). What's more, the plea Aaron utters on Miriam's account—"do not let her be like one stillborn" (literally, "like one who dies when going forth from the womb of its mother"; Num 12:12)—could be said to recall, at least rhetorically, the role of Elisha in 2 Kgs 2:19–22 and the "daughters . . . who prophesy" in Ezek 13:17–23 in performing rituals that prevent miscarriages.

These inconsistencies—that Miriam is punished while Aaron is not and that some measure of prophetic identity and authority accrue to Aaron after the encounter with Yahweh at the tent of meeting, even as Miriam's prophetic claims seem wholly repudiated—have been major points of difficulty for interpreters of the passage.[57] They are particularly disturbing for those who see *Aaron* as the primary instigator of the Num 12:2–9 confrontation, a reading based on the fact that Aaron's name comes before Miriam's in Num 12:4 and 5.[58] To explain, I propose an analysis based on the tripartite pattern of rites of passage originally described by the French ethnographer and folklorist Arnold van Gennep.[59] More specifically, van Gennep argued that the three parts of any rite of passage were (1) separation, in which "a person or group becomes detached from an earlier fixed point in the social structure or from an earlier set of social conditions"; (2) margin or *limen* (from the Latin meaning "threshold), "when the state of the ritual subject is ambiguous; he is no longer in the old state and has not yet reached the new one"; and (3) reaggregation or reincorporation, "when the ritual subject enters a new stable state with its own rights and obligations."[60]

In describing this pattern's use, van Gennep focused his primary attention on life-cycle rituals, such as the rituals of coming-of-age, marriage, and death that I discussed in Chapter 9. I have suggested that the story of Jephthah's daughter, for example, describes a coming-of-age ritual whereby prepubescent girls are, with the onset of puberty, *separated* from their previous childhood identity. They then enter into a *liminal period,* during which they somehow go out (where to is not clear) and, like Jephthah's daughter, lament the loss of their old way of life as they transition into physical maturity. Finally, as this liminal phase concludes, they rejoin, or are *reintegrated* into their communities, but now with a new status—as young women who are soon thereafter, under the terms of the Israelite ritual calendar, to be married.

Yet while van Gennep's focus was this sort of life-cycle ritual that "passed" its human subjects from one stage of life to another, subsequent commentators have suggested that this tripartite model of separation-liminality-reaggregation might be applied to aspects of religious systems other than life-cycle rituals—and even to aspects of religious systems where a ritual practice or enactment is not the overt concern. For example, according to many scholars, van Gennep's rites-of-passage pattern structures the Bible's exodus account.[61] After all, during the course of the exodus narrative, the Israelites, as is typical in a rite of passage, are *separated* from "an earlier fixed point in the social structure or from an earlier set of social conditions":[62] their status as slaves in Egypt. Eventually, moreover, they are to assume a new identity: a people constituted as an independent polity resident within the land of Canaan. But in the interim come the Israelites' wilderness wanderings, which are well characterized as *liminal*—that is, to evoke a classic definition, "betwixt and between" in nature:[63] "betwixt and between" Egypt and Canaan, for example, and "betwixt and between" slave and free. As Ronald S. Hendel writes, "The entire account of the escape from Egypt, the covenant at Sinai, and the entry into the promised land can be viewed as an elaborate rite of passage, a transformation of the moral identity of the people from slaves to a free nation, from Egyptian bondage to the promised land."[64]

Still, the scholars who suggest that the Bible's exodus narrative can be read according to van Gennep's rites-of-passage pattern debate where within the story to locate the pattern's third element, *reaggregation*, "when the ritual subject enters a new stable state with its own rights and obligations."[65] The most obvious answer is that reaggregation occurs when the Israelites' forty years in the wilderness of the Sinai desert finally come to an end, at the moment in Joshua 3–5 when the people cross over the Jordan River to enter into the "promised land."[66] Indeed, much can be said on behalf of this interpretation. As noted just above, for example, the Israelites' wanderings before their entry into the land of Canaan are well characterized as belonging to reaggregation's preceding, or liminal stage, both because the act of wandering implies a quality of aimlessness reminiscent of the "betwixt and between" ambiguity that characterizes the liminal phase of a rite of passage and because the Israelites are homeless as they wander, which is another characteristic feature of liminality. That the wandering occurs in the wilderness is also significant, given that wilderness is *the* paradigmatic liminal space according to biblical tradition: "a 'betwixt and between' locality . . . which is neither fully in This World nor in The Other."[67] Moreover, the Israelites' lives during their wilderness wanderings are filled with the sorts of trials and ordeals that can be typical of liminality: the Israelites are pursued by the Egyptians, who change their minds after having been persuaded by Moses and Aaron to let the Israelites go free (Exod 14:1–18), and they thirst when encamped at Marah, where there is only bitter water to drink (Exod 15:22–26). They thirst again when they camp at Massah-Meribah, where there is no water at all (Exod 17:1–7), and they hunger in the wilderness of Sin, where there is nothing to eat (Exod 16:1–36).

Still, inspired by the stress placed by van Gennep's most notable interlocutor—the anthropologist and theorist of religion Victor Turner—on the "direct experience of the sacred, invisible, or supernatural order" as critically important to and, indeed, defining of the liminal phase of a rite of passage, Hendel has argued that "the liminal stage is represented by the encounter with Yahweh at the holy mountain, Sinai" and that the Israelites' post-mountain sojourn in the larger Sinai wilderness and their eventual entry into the "promised land" belong to the "third and final stage of reaggregation."[68] In support, Hendel points out that it is at Mount Sinai that Israel's new social and religious identity is forged and consecrated, given that it is during the Israelites' stay at Yahweh's holy mountain that the people and Yahweh enter into the covenant that binds them together in a complex web of mutual commitment and responsibility. Which is to say: under the terms of Hendel's analysis, the ceremony of covenant-making at Sinai (especially as it is depicted in Exod 24:3–8) and the concomitant articulation of the covenant's obligations mark the point of reaggregation, "when the ritual subject enters a new stable state with its own rights and obligations."[69]

I agree with Hendel on this point and, indeed, would adduce even more evidence to suggest that making the covenant at Sinai marks the culmination of Israel's liminal period and the beginning of reaggregation. Note, first, that while the Israelites do continue to experience liminal-like trials and ordeals after leaving Mount Sinai, these ordeals are not depicted in the same way as were the ordeals the Israelites experienced before arriving at God's holy mountain. These pre-Sinai trials, as is typical in liminality, were tests imposed upon the community by its spiritual authorities and especially by its spiritual overlord, Yahweh. It was *God,* for example, who hardened the heart of Pharaoh (Exod 14:4, 8), and the hearts of Egyptians as well (Exod 14:17).[70] Thus it was *God* who laid the foundations for the Egyptians' pursuit of the Israelites once they had escaped from slavery, which culminated with the life-threatening ordeal at the Reed Sea.[71] It was also *God* who put the Israelites to the test ("he [Yahweh] tested them [the people]"; *nissāhû*) when they thirsted immediately afterwards, according to the narrative's chronology, at Marah (Exod 15:25), where there was only bitter water to drink (Exod 15:22–26).[72] *God* again tested the people at Massah-Meribah (Exod 17:1–7), where there was no water at all (the very name Massah as given in Exod 17:7 comes from the root *nissâ*, "to test").[73] And it was once more *God* who is said to have tested the people when they hungered in the wilderness of Sin (Exod 16:4), where there was no food (Exod 16:1–36).

The Israelites' post-Sinai ordeals, conversely, are construed as examples of the people putting Yahweh on trial, demanding more and greater assurances of God's power and presence. For example, in Num 11:4–35, just after the Israelites leave Mount Sinai, we find a story about the people experiencing hunger that parallels in certain respects the Exod 16:1–36 account that describes how the Israelites hungered in the wilderness of Sin before their arrival at Yahweh's holy mountain. But while the Exodus 16 text is marked by liminal features—the characteristically liminal ordeal of fasting and the suggestion that Yahweh is testing the Israelites within the context of this ordeal ("I [Yahweh] will test them [the Israelites]," *'ănassennû*, God says in Exod 16:4)[74]—the Numbers 11 narrative has a very different sense. According to Num 11:4–6, the people hunger not because they lack food, as in Exodus 16, but because they are tired of eating the same food, the manna God causes to fall from the heavens day in and day out. That is, they are not suffering because of the characteristically liminal ordeals of fasting and of divinely imposed struggle; they are suffering because of their ungrateful and churlish nature. For Moses, moreover, this seems to suggest the community is testing Yahweh and has found the deity wanting (hence the people are said to have rejected Yahweh in Num 11:20). Yahweh is similarly described as regarding this incident and several other instances of the people's complaining after they leave Mount Sinai as tests the Israelites have imposed upon the deity ("they have tested me," *waynassû 'ōtî*, God says in Num 14:22). Furthermore, it is not clear how much liminal-like wandering the authors and/or redactors of the exodus tradition actually envision happening after the Israelites go forth from God's holy mountain. Instead, the people are depicted as spending the bulk of their time (up to thirty-eight of their forty years in the Sinai wilderness) at one location, Kadesh Barnea.[75] Kadesh Barnea, moreover, is not a particularly good exemplar of the typically liminal space of wilderness, given that it is an oasis location with three major springs.

Hence my agreement with Hendel that we should locate the Israelites' movement out of liminality at the time of their departure from Mount Sinai, which occurs in the exodus story at Num 10:12. According, therefore, to the narrative's structure, the Numbers 12 story of Aaron's and Miriam's challenge to Moses' sole authority as Yahweh's spokesperson occurs during the rite-of-passage's reaggregation phase. I propose—on the basis of an argument put forward by the noted historian of medieval Christianity Caroline Walker Bynum, in an article titled "Women's Stories, Women's Symbols: A Critique of Victor Turner's Theory of Liminality"—that this has important implications for the position of Miriam.

More specifically: Bynum suggests that throughout Turner's work, he follows van Gennep's lead in presenting the various features and characteristics of liminality (for example, the ordeals and onerous trials) as experiences endured *temporarily* by the individual or individuals going through a rite-of-passage event—during the interval, say, between some designated end of one's childhood and some socially recognized entry into puberty. Yet when it comes to women, Bynum notes that "at many points" in Turner's writings, "he suggests women are liminal or . . . marginals" not just temporarily, during key moments within certain ritual transitions, but as part of the *normal* course of their existence.[76] For example, Turner maintains that during the course of a ritual transition, "liminal entities" are often represented "as possessing nothing . . . to demonstrate that as liminal beings they have no status, property, insignia, secular clothing indicating rank or role, position in a kinship system."[77] Yet during many periods in history and in many cultures, women, as part of the *normal* course of their existence, have been unable to hold property, and they have also, as part of the *normal* course of their existence, been deemed peripheral or irrelevant in the delineation of kinship systems. In addition, they have often, in the *normal* course of their existence, been without rank or role, especially rank or role independent of some male in their lives. Instead, they have been required to submit passively and humbly to the demands of fathers, husbands, brothers, and/or other male authorities.

These observations correspond in many respects to the experiences of ancient Israelite women. For example, while it might seem that Micah's mother, whom I discussed in Chapter 1, was able to hold property, she probably was able to lay claim to her cache of eleven hundred silver pieces only after her husband, who typically would have controlled the couple's wealth, had died.[78] Similarly, we saw in Chapter 7 how peripheral women could be in the articulation of Israel's system of *patri*local and *patri*lineal kinship, and I suggested above that in Isa 8:3, Isaiah's wife is assigned the title "prophet"—and, more important, the social rank that goes with it—only by virtue of her marriage to the "real" prophet, Isaiah. Moreover, in a careful study of women's status in ancient Israel, T. M. Lemos suggests that "married women were in many ways subordinate to their husbands," as were daughters in many ways subordinate to their fathers, especially "in cases where sexuality is discussed," and "a father's or husband's . . . exclusive control" over the bodies of his household's women is presumed.[79] Overall, Gale A. Yee describes ancient Israelite women as "marginalized" and "disenfranchised," "particularly with respect to descent, inheritance, . . . and other social customs."[80] Or, we might say, following upon Bynum, that Israelite women were "liminal" as part of the *normal* course of their existence.

Ancient Israelite women can in addition be said to represent the ambiguity that Turner saw as liminality's most characteristic feature. For instance, in her 1993 book *Fragmented Women: Feminist (Sub)versions of Biblical Narrative,* J. Cheryl Exum includes a chapter whose title, "The (M)other's Place," and especially the parentheses within it, tries to capture the ambiguously "othered" position the matriarchs Sarah, Rebekah, Rachel, and Leah occupy in the book of Genesis. On one hand, as Exum sees it, these matriarchs are central to the forward movement of the Genesis narrative, since the generational progression on which Genesis relies cannot be accomplished without the patriarchs Abraham, Isaac, and Jacob begetting a son or sons with a "right" or proper wife. What makes a wife "right," moreover, is her *insider* status: she is not of the Canaanites, nor of some other people (like, say, Hagar, whose son by Abraham is unprivileged in his father's genealogy because his mother is an Egyptian). Instead, the "right" wife is of the patriarchs' ethnos and, indeed, of their own family: Sarah is Abraham's half-sister according to Gen 20:12; Rebekah and Isaac are patrilateral parallel cousins; Rachel and Leah are Jacob's matrilateral cross-cousins.

On the other hand, the matriarchs stand as outsiders: Rebekah, Leah, and Rachel, for example, are residents of far away lands they must leave to dwell with their husbands in Canaan, and once there, as Exum writes, "they are 'other.'"[81] More important, as Joseph Blenkinsopp points out, *all* ancient Israelite women are construed by the patrilocal conventions of Israelite marriage as, at least to some degree, "other." In his words: "the woman introduced into her husband's household always remained, in a certain sense, an outsider."[82] Phyllis Bird likewise notes that "to some extent . . .

married women are outsiders in the household of their husband and sons," and Bird has in addition, as we saw in Chapters 5 and 6, described Israelite women as holding a dual status as both insiders and outsiders with respect to cult.[83] Judith Romney Wegner, whose work I also quoted in Chapter 6, goes further still: as Wegner puts it, women were "so anomalous" within the arena of Israel's male-dominated cult "that [they] came to epitomize *otherness*."[84] This probably overstates; still, it seems clear that Israelite women were "to some degree always outsiders."[85] To define women as "outsiders" or as "other," moreover, is to associate them with that which is foreign (as we saw in discussing Exod 12:48 and Josh 5:5, 8 in Chapter 8).[86] And while the Bible often counsels compassion toward the *gēr,* the alien who sojourns among the Israelites but is not of them, foreigners are still, according to the tradition's generally xenophobic worldview, nonnormative, which is to say, paradoxical, disordered, anomalous, oppositional, or, in Turner's terms, liminal.[87]

So what happens, Bynum asks, when women, so associated with liminal features, characteristics, and symbols as part of their *normal* course of existence, participate in a rite of passage whose very structure, as van Gennep and Turner would have it, requires a movement *into* liminality as a central and constitutive part? In particular, as the shortened title of Bynum's article, "Women's *Stories*" (emphasis mine), makes clear, Bynum asks what happens to women in narrative accounts that are structured around a rites-of-passage pattern? Bynum's answer—based on narratives from the medieval period about the lives of that era's saints—considers authorship, for she argues that male authors tell rites-of-passage stories in a very distinctive way. More specifically: Bynum argues that when male biographers of the European Middle Ages tell stories of women who pursue a spiritual vocation, these biographers shape the women's stories according to men's typical experiences during rites of passage and rites-of-passage types of events, whereby men undergo profound reversals and inversions with regard to the positions of status and authority they normally hold. In his journey of spiritual transformation, for example, St. Francis of Assisi began by enthusiastically embracing every luxury and all sorts of frivolous pursuits, until he came, as a result of a religious calling, to renounce not only the riches but even the garb bestowed upon him by his wealthy cloth-merchant father. Thereby he enacted a dramatic separation from his previous existence, giving up every possible marker of his opulent past in order to live thereafter as a mendicant and an ascetic.

So too, according to Bynum, medieval men who are writing about women assume that women within their communities who are pursuing a religious vocation "flip-flop" by repudiating their previous identity and renouncing all markers of it. But while men are said to "flip-flop" by *giving up* markers of status, power, wealth, and authority as they enter into a rite of passage's liminal phase, Bynum argues that the male biographers of women saints describe these women as *taking on* the markers of status, power, wealth, and authority that they normally lack as they move into a period of liminality. The medieval women Bynum studies can be said by their biographers, for example, to "disguis[e] themselves as men" in order to "flee the world and join monasteries," thereby temporarily becoming—during this liminal phase of transition—higher-status males. "To men," Bynum writes, "women reverse images and 'become men' in renouncing the world."[88]

Needless to say, medieval Europe is not ancient Israel, nor are the Bible's prophets analogues of medieval Europe's saints. Nevertheless, Bynum's analysis regarding the rites-of-passage pattern as it is manifest in male-authored narratives about medieval women saints offers insight regarding the Bible's exodus account, a narrative that arguably follows van Gennep's rites-of-passage pattern and that also considers women but that I take to be authored by men (as, in my opinion, are all biblical texts; see my comments in the Introduction). According to these male authors, Miriam could be identified and even embraced as a prophet in Exod 15:20, at a point during the liminal phase of the exodus narrative (after the escape from Egypt but before reaggregation at Sinai), because in such liminal periods, women's empowerment and ability to accrue status is possible in the view of male narrators. Indeed, according to the paradigms of inversion and reversal that men see as crucial motifs during the liminal phase of a rite of passage, this enhancing of a woman's normally debased status is *required.* To paraphrase Bynum: in the exodus narrative's liminal phase, Miriam "reverses image" and "becomes" a high-status prophet, comparable to her male prophetic brothers. Not surprisingly, moreover, it is only at this point in the narrative that Miriam is identified by name, having been described before the Israelites' exodus (or "separation") from Egypt only as Moses's sister or "the young maid" (Exod 2:4, 7, 8).

Conversely, the perspective of the exodus account's male authors mandates that a return to women's normal state—and so disempowerment—characterize Miriam once the story's liminal phase is over and the reaggregated phase has begun. Thus, in Numbers 12, because liminality has come to an end, Miriam's claims about her prophetic stature are perceived as presumptuous, and far more presumptuous than are Aaron's, for while Aaron has only misconstrued the nature of his relationship to God as compared with that of Moses, Miriam has been guilty of this misconstrual *and* has overstepped the bounds of gender.[89] It is for this double transgression that Miriam is so harshly punished according to Num 12:10–15, and it is because Aaron is less reprobate within the logic of a rites-of-passage narrative that he emerges from this episode essentially unscathed. In fact, just as the logic of a rites-of-passage narrative would predict, Aaron, because he a man, can manifest power in Num 12:11–12, as well as the kinds of markers of status typical of men's existence outside of liminal time and space. For example, as noted above, Aaron seems able to assert a kind of prophetic authority even as Miriam is stricken and exiled from her community. Throughout the subsequent chapters of Numbers, moreover, Aaron appears again and again alongside Moses in a position of leadership among the people.[90] The now disenfranchised Miriam, conversely, appears only once more in the exodus story, in Num 20:1, to die. This confirms that, as opposed to Aaron, it was only during the exodus account's liminal period that Miriam could be pictured by the text's male authors as a true prophetic authority. In the reaggregated section of the narrative that begins in Num 10:12, the man Aaron can thrive, but any possibility of the woman Miriam's continued empowerment must be denied.

The Dearth of Israelite Women Prophets

These reflections on the constraints the tradition imposed on the prophetic authority of Miriam lead to a further consideration of the constraints that Israel's women prophets generally faced as they sought to assert their claims to legitimacy. To be sure, all Israelite prophets, whether male or female, faced certain challenges in manifesting their authority. This is because, as I already noted, the source of prophetic authority is a personal call or revelation the prophet receives from God to which only he or she is privy. Therefore, in order for the prophet to perform the prophetic function of passing on God's message to the people or some subset thereof and, more important, to get this audience to accept the message as valid, the prophet must persuade the recipients of the message of the veracity of his or her divine calling. But with no evidence supporting the prophet other than assertions of what the sociologist Max Weber famously described as "personal charisma,"[91] the task of acquiring the recognition of others is not easy—as the Bible's many stories of recognizing "true" versus "false" prophets indicate (1 Kgs 22:5–40; Jer 28:1–17; Ezek 13:1–16, 17–23; 14:9–11; Neh 6:14). Because two of these stories, moreover, assert the authority of a male (Ezekiel, Nehemiah) over that of women prophets (Ezek 13:17–23, Neh 6:14), we might suggest that within Israel's male-dominated society, the task women prophets faced in persuading an audience to accept their claims of prophetic legitimacy would have been especially challenging. "Personal charisma," Ronald S. Hendel writes, was "always . . . [a] tenuous and controverted basis for authority,"[92] and personal charismatics' claims to authority that were not supported by virtue of maleness may have been more "tenuous" and "controverted" still.

Yet if the odds of securing legitimization were not in women prophets' favor, what did facilitate the occasional recognition of women—Deborah, Hulda—as prophets? Useful here are some of the same insights of Carol Meyers and Jo Ann Hackett that I articulated in Chapter 6 about women's ability to accrue status and exercise power in certain social contexts as opposed to others: in domestic as opposed to nondomestic settings, for example, and similarly within rural as opposed to urban and urbanized environments. Conversely, "hierarchical and centrally structured institutions have been less open to participation by women than have local and nonhierarchical institutions," Hackett writes. Hackett adds, however, that during times of social dysfunction, whatever hierarchical structures and centralized institutions are in place within a community can break down to some degree, to give way to the sorts of localized control more conducive to an elevation in women's status and an increase in their ability to exercise power.[93] Meyers somewhat similarly proposes that during "pioneer" periods, when a community either seeks to establish itself in previously unsettled territories or reestablish itself in territories previously abandoned, it particularly needs and thus is particularly willing to assign value to the enterprises of all its members, including women.[94]

Consider Hulda in this regard. The major events of her prophetic work—that she is called upon by King Josiah to validate and in essence to enshrine a newly revealed version of Israel's covenant and, consequently, to set in motion Josiah's massive program of religious reforms—suggest that she was active in a period marked by at least some degree of religious upheaval. The biblical texts describing the reigns of Josiah's predecessors, Manasseh (r. 687–642 BCE) and Amon (r. 642–640 BCE), also suggest that certain religious instabilities existed within Judah and Jerusalem during Hulda's day. Granted, the accounts of Manasseh's and Amon's reigns have been quite heavily shaped by the authors and/or redactors of the Deuteronomistic History, so much so that they cannot indicate definitively the precise nature of any cultic disorder. Still, we can say with confidence that during the reigns of Manasseh and Amon, Jerusalem and the Southern Kingdom of Judah found themselves subject to the Assyrian Empire, and even though scholars have discounted the notion that the Assyrians imposed their own religious practices on their vassals,[95] it is nonetheless the case that Judah and Jerusalem would have experienced at least some degree of contact with the religious ideologies and practices of their suzerain. Mordechai Cogan, for example, speaks of "the *voluntary* adoption by Judah's ruling classes of the prevailing Assyro-Aramaean culture" (emphasis mine).[96] The result was surely some disruption of Judah's and Jerusalem's traditional religious routines. Can it be coincidence that Hulda is described as playing a major role in her community's cultic life during this period of religious disarray? The theoretical formulations put forward by especially Hackett would argue "no," suggesting instead that Hulda's prophetic role is directly linked to the period of religious destabilization during which she lived.

Hackett's work also suggests a second explanation for Hulda's preeminence: class. Class, of course, implies a hierarchical society and consequently, according to both Hackett and Meyers, one characterized by the relative disempowerment of women. Nevertheless, as Hackett points out, even within an otherwise male-dominated society, upper-class women, because of their families' associations with the leaders of their community, can find themselves able to exert power and achieve a relatively high degree of status.[97] Hulda is arguably this sort of upper-class woman, as she is, as we have seen, the wife of Shallum, the keeper of the (king's) wardrobe (2 Kgs 22:14, 2 Chr 34:22). Unfortunately, neither this position nor this particular Shallum is mentioned elsewhere in the Bible, and thus the specifics of Shallum's place in Judahite society and the responsibilities of his station are basically unknown to us. Surely, however, the keeper of the wardrobe was an official of at least some rank and status within the royal bureaucracy. Thus his wife Hulda, according to Hackett's thesis, may have been accorded greater opportunities to exert power.

Hackett's work, along with Meyers's, puts forward a third explanation for Hulda's preeminence: that Hulda's work as a prophet was conducted in an environment where certain aspects of the domestic and public spheres were not widely separated. Note in this regard that 2 Kgs 22:14 explicitly describes King Josiah's emissaries, Shaphan, Hilkiah, Ahikam, Asaiah, and Achbor, as going to Hulda's *house* in order to consult with her. It is precisely this sort of situation, where decision-making is done in or near the home, that according to Hackett and Meyers allows women greater potential for the exercise of power.

Finally, we can note that Hulda's home is—at least in terms of the biblical text's silence—atypical in Israelite tradition, in that no mention is made of Hulda having children. This is significant, for Esther Hamori has demonstrated that childlessness is another factor that facilitates women's ability to gain recognition as prophets. More specifically, Hamori has shown that in many different cultures, and at many different points in history (ancient, medieval, and modern), there is an "association" between "unusual access to the spirit world" and a "nonnormative social position," and that for women, this "nonnormative social position" is "often expressed through unconventional family structures," including "the lack of children."[98] Hamori suggests this is because of a cross-cultural preference for the male body and the authority that comes with male embodiment, meaning that female sexuality, including female sexuality as revealed through childbearing, needs to be effaced in order for women to assume positions as prophets (and also positions as other types of visionaries—for example, shamans—who mediate between the divine and human realms).[99] In particular, regarding biblical tradition, Hamori writes, "divine favor to a woman is commonly manifested through her becoming a mother," while for women such as Hulda, who are divinely favored with the gift of prophetic insight, motherhood seems precluded.[100]

Identifying the factors that support Deborah's claims to prophetic authority is somewhat more complex, given, as we have seen, that we have two fairly disparate sources that describe Deborah's prophetic work, and sources that are especially disparate concerning the issue that interests us the most—the explicit identification of Deborah as a prophet. Still, I have argued that Judg 4:4 derives its understanding of Deborah as a prophet from its source, Judg 5:1–31, and this is important, for unlike Judges 4 (which is a part of the Deuteronomistic History that, as indicated in the Introduction, I date to the late seventh and early sixth centuries BCE), Judges 5 dates, according to many scholars, to precisely the premonarchic period in which Deborah is said to have lived (ca. 1100 BCE).[101] This means that while Judg 4:4–24 allows us to ask only whether there were social and political conditions in the late seventh and early sixth centuries BCE that facilitated the Deuteronomistic History's "long after the fact" identification of Deborah as a prophet (presumably some of the same sorts of social and political conditions that I have argued effected Hulda's ability to be recognized as a prophetic authority), the evidence of Judg 5:1–31 pushes us to ask whether there were social and political conditions that marked Israel during Deborah's own day that led her contemporaries to accord her prophetic legitimacy.

Archaeological evidence from the premonarchic period suggests the answer must be "yes." More specifically, both archaeological excavations of individual twelfth- and eleventh-century BCE sites and large-scale surveys of twelfth- and eleventh-century BCE settlement patterns have demonstrated that a veritable population explosion occurred in the previously unoccupied hill country of the southern Levant during the period beginning in ca. 1200 BCE.[102] These new hill-country residents, according to the vast majority of scholars, are to be understood as the Israelites (or at least "proto-Israelites").[103] More important here, though, than these hill-country settlers' identity is the fact that they occupy territory that was not only previously uninhabited but also is an extremely challenging environment from which to eke out an existence. The southern Levantine highlands are, at best, marginally fertile. As Meyers writes, "the soils in the mountainous areas are rather poor . . . perennial sources of water are virtually nonexistent," and the topography—"an irregular configuration of hills and valleys"—makes the region "difficult" to settle and farm, even to the extent that the hill country can be, in the words of William G. Dever, "a *hostile* environment for human habitation" (emphasis mine).[104] Rainfall, too, is marginal and, David C. Hopkins adds, "is also highly variable," both with respect to "its distribution throughout the year" (as Hopkins explains, "rainfall in Palestine is concentrated in a few winter months and is highly intensive") and also with respect to "the achievement of average annual accumulation" ("one or two years out of ten might show more than a 25 percent deviation from the mean annual rainfall").[105] Moreover, "Israel's Mediterranean ecotype did not allow for an even spread of agricultural tasks throughout the year." Rather, "some seasons . . . required concentrated efforts."[106]

The early (or proto-)Israelites who struggled to establish themselves and then to subsist in this marginal environment are thus surely to be understood as the sort of pioneer community that, under the terms of Meyers's analysis, can accord women higher status and opportunities to exert power. Also, these Israelites' pioneer settlements were primarily rural or village-based, which is, of course, precisely the sort of setting that both Meyers and Hackett identify as being most conducive for generating positions of elevated status for women. Because these hill-country villages in addition contain no ruins of palaces or large residences, no public or administrative structures, and no monumental sanctuaries or temples, they seem to signal a relatively undifferentiated and unstratified social order, one without a political or religious elite and without a civil bureaucracy. Instead, the predominant architectural remains—the sorts of pillar-courtyard houses I discussed in Chapter 1—suggest communities made up of small-scale but nevertheless self-sufficient agriculturalists. This sort of nonhierarchical, noninstitutionalized, and domestically based society is again precisely the sort of environment in which, according to Meyers's and Hackett's analytical models, a woman such as Deborah could gain recognition as a prophetic authority.

What's more, Deborah is arguably depicted in both Judges 4 and Judges 5 as childless—and, indeed, as unmarried. To be sure, she is described in Judg 4:4 as *'ēšet lappîdôt,* usually translated as the "wife of Lappidoth," but also plausibly rendered "a fiery woman." And even if "the wife of Lappidoth" is the correct translation, it is striking that Judges 4 makes no mention of Deborah having children, given that—as I have now noted several times—Judges 4 is literarily dependent on Judges 5 and so was aware, presumably, of the description of Deborah in Judg 5:7 as "a mother in Israel." Yet despite the fact that the prose text of Judges 4 typically delivers an absolutely literal rendition of the poetic account found in Judges 5, Judges 4 does not interpret Judg 5:7 according to its plain meaning (which is to say, its biological sense). Perhaps, as noted above, this is because Judges 4 understands the phrase "a mother in Israel" to refer to Deborah's prophetic identity. But even if this specific interpretation is questioned, it seems clear that neither Judges 4 nor Judges 5 understands "a mother in Israel" to refer to Deborah as a childbearer. Rather, just as Hamori's work on women prophets suggests, Deborah seems to derive at least some measure of her prophetic authority from her nonnormative family status.

Yet this is not to say, I should be clear, that there actually was a prophet Deborah: elsewhere, I have followed the lead of Stephen C. Dempster and Peter C. Craigie to argue that Judg 5:1–31 is a composition powerfully influenced by older Canaanite mythology. This means that Judg 5:1–31, even though ostensibly presented as a historical account, reflects many supernatural elements in its overall recitation.[107] Because of this, the historical reliability of Judg 5:1–31 remains unknown. Still, we can claim that the early Israelites generated a piece of literature, Judg 5:1–31, in which a woman was portrayed as a significant actor in the religious (and also military) functioning of her society. I propose, following Hackett and Meyers, that among the factors that made such a portrayal possible is premonarchic Israel's character as a pioneering, rural, nonhierarchical, noninstitutionalized, and domestically based society in which women could hold positions of power. I further propose, following Hamori, that the tradition's understanding of Deborah as childless (and even unmarried) facilitated the Israelites' ability to accord her prophetic authority. Thereby, the authors of Judg 5:1–31, followed by the authors of Judg 4:4–24, were able to envision Deborah acting as a prophetic functionary.

Overall, I conclude that ancient Israel's women prophets could thrive *only* when some very particular social and historical circumstances were in place—and, indeed, often could thrive only when several of these particular social and historical circumstances were simultaneously manifest (for example, in the case of Deborah: a "pioneer" period within Israelite history, *and* a rural, village-based society, *and* a household-based economy, *and* a nonhierarchalized and nonbureaucratized social and political order, *and* an understanding within the tradition that Deborah was childless and perhaps even unmarried). It should not be surprising, then, that the same biblical tradition that recognizes just four women as prophets (Miriam, Deborah, Hulda, and Noadiah) assigns the title *nābîʾ* to at least seven times as many men (twenty-nine, by my count).[108] If, moreover, we assume, as I do, that most of the members of the various companies or bands of prophets mentioned in the Bible, such as the four hundred prophets of 1 Kgs 22:6, were exclusively (or at least almost exclusively) male (the "daughters . . . who prophesy" in Ezek 13:17–23 being the only obvious exception), then the number of men designated as "prophet" in the biblical account soars into the triple and even quadruple digits.[109] We can add to this soaring total, moreover, the names of the books attributed to six men from the preexilic period who, while not explicitly given the title *nābîʾ* in the biblical text, were certainly assumed by its redactors to be prophets: Amos, Hosea, Micah, Nahum, Obadiah, and Zephaniah.

Yet however one tallies up the specifics, any examination of the Bible's prophetic literature makes clear that the prophetic words and deeds that dominate are the prophetic words and deeds of men. What becomes noteworthy, then, about the women named as "prophet" in the Bible is how *few* of them there are compared with the number of men who were assigned the prophetic designation throughout Israel's history.[110] Miriam, Deborah, Hulda, and Noadiah, that is, ultimately appear to be not so much exemplars as anomalies, their role as prophets exceptional rather than acceptable within Israelite religion.

11 "Find Me a Woman Who Is a Medium": Ancient Israel's Women Magicians

An astute reader will have noticed that in the last two chapters certain lines of demarcation have begun to blur. For example, in Chapter 9 I described Miriam as a ritual musician who is depicted in Exod 15:20–21 as participating along with other women in singing a victory song after an Israelite triumph in holy war. Yet in Chapter 10, I focused on the label "prophet" that is assigned to Miriam in the same verses. Somewhat similarly, we might ask: If I have been correct in Chapter 10 to adopt the interpretation that sees the "daughters . . . who prophesy" in Ezek 13:17–23 as medical professionals who apply themselves particularly to matters concerning a woman's pregnancy and delivery, then how should we characterize these prophesying "daughters" in relation to other medical specialists who also apply themselves to matters concerning childbearing women—for example, midwives? After all, according to the interpretation of Ezek 13:17–23 that I have followed, the bands of cloth that the "daughters . . . who prophesy" tie on women's wrists to protect them during pregnancy and parturition are not so far removed from the red thread that a midwife ties around the hand of the baby Zeraḥ during the course of Tamar's delivery in Gen 38:28. This is especially the case if we accept Carol Meyers's proposal that despite the rather idiosyncratic use described for the red thread in the Tamar account (where it is used to mark which of Tamar's twin sons first breached the womb), the tying of a red thread around one of a newborn's limbs was an act performed routinely in ancient Israel, in order to protect an infant from the many sorts of evil he or she might face.[1]

More important for my current purposes, though, is the question of how to understand the health-care work undertaken by both the "daughters . . . who prophesy" and midwives in relation to the issue that is the subject of this chapter: the role that these and other Israelite women could play as magical specialists.[2] What is magic anyway, and what is its relationship to medicine? And what is the relationship of magic to religion—and, thus, what is the relationship of women magical specialists to this book's focus, which is women and religion? Again, lines of demarcation begin to blur. For example, concerning magic and medicine, consider the case of Hittite and Mesopotamian midwives, who, in addition to using their *medical* expertise in the service of delivering women, recite *magical* incantations to protect newborns.[3] Ancient Egyptian sources, as well as Hittite texts, similarly describe midwives as reciting magical incantations to protect delivering mothers during labor.[4] In one Hittite text, for example, the midwife is said repeatedly to conjure "The *Incantation* of Crying Out" (emphasis mine) as the woman is delivering, and she also recites an incantation over a ewe brought into the birth chamber, apparently as part of a magical rite meant to transfer onto the animal whatever evils might afflict the laboring woman.[5]

Indeed, Jo Ann Scurlock, who is responsible for cataloguing some of the Mesopotamian rituals related to childbearing that I cited in the last chapter—the tying of twined and knotted threads of various colors onto the hand of a pregnant woman who is suffering from excessive vaginal bleeding and the tying of a band on a mother-to-be to prevent miscarriage—does so in an essay whose subtitle is "*Medico-Magical* Means of Dealing with Some of the Perils of Motherhood in Ancient Mesopotamia" (emphasis mine).[6] Elsewhere, Scurlock has written of Mesopotamia that "separating the 'magic' from the 'medicine' has proved anything but easy," and so too has J. F. Borghouts written that in Egypt, "the exercise of a magical profession . . . could be combined with that of 'doctor' . . . so as to make it impossible to differentiate strictly between the two callings."[7] In Hittite tradition as well, there was no "clear distinction between the magical and the medical."[8] This conclusion surely pertained elsewhere in the ancient Near East and eastern Mediterranean, including Israel.

And what of the relation of the "medico-magical," and the just plain "magical," to religion? To answer is, in many respects, a book in itself.[9] Still, we can briefly say that although it has been a commonplace in the past to separate emphatically the categories of magic, on one hand, and religion, on the other, and to judge the former negatively in relation to the latter, scholars have increasingly argued—from the perspectives of the study of both religion as a whole and the religions of the ancient Near East in particular—that "there is . . . little point in attempting sharply to distinguish magic from religion."[10] After all, magic can be defined as "a form of communication involving the supernatural world in which an attempt is made to affect the course of present and/or future events by means of ritual actions . . . and/or . . . formulaic recitations,"[11] just as religion, at least in part, is "a form of communication involving the supernatural world" that employs "ritual actions . . . and/or . . . formulaic recitations," often in "an attempt . . . to affect the course of present and/or future events" (think, for example, of Hannah's prayer, vow, fasting, and weeping, all in the hope of reversing her barrenness and bearing a son).

Granted, many still maintain that even if there are not differences in kind between magic and religion, there are differences in degree.[12] Some argue, for example, that magic's ritual actions and formulaic recitations are more "problem" and/or "crisis" oriented, whereas religion's are more the regularized offerings of the daily cult and periodic festival observances.[13] According to others, "magic is practiced outside of considerations of moral boundaries," whereas religion involves "behaviors that attempt to cultivate a propitiatory relationship with [supernatural] powers" that "are imbued with moral overtones."[14] Nonetheless, in the ancient Near East, as elsewhere, both that which we tend to think of as magic and that which we tend to think of as religion "were part of the same belief system."[15] "Egyptian theology," for example, "does not contrast religion with magic."[16] Instead, in ancient Egypt, temple priests, traditionally taken to be representatives of "religion," could also serve as "freelance" magicians.[17] Indeed, "the priest was the author and compiler of magical spells and rites [and] also the performer and 'magician.'"[18] First Samuel 6:2, which groups together the Philistines' *kōhănîm,* or "priests," with their *qōsĕmîm,* "diviners" (who are typically understood as a group of magical specialists), may similarly signal that in Philistine culture, there was little distinction between "religious" and "magical" identities. Likewise in Mesopotamia, priests and exorcists (who, like diviners, are traditionally categorized as specialists in magic) "received the same education, served the same gods, and regarded each other as legitimate practitioners."[19]

Also in Israel, priests and prophets performed acts without censure that many would label "magic" or "divination"—for example, from among the prophetic accounts I described in Chapter 10, the prophet Elisha's purifying the "miscarrying" spring of Jericho by throwing a bowl of salt into it (2 Kgs 2:19–22), while at the same time reciting what is readily described as an incantation (v. 21); also, his determining the future prospects of the armies of Kings Jehoram and Jehoshaphat and the king of Edom by having a musician induce for him a prophetic trance (2 Kgs 3:9–20).[20] Indeed, texts such as 2 Kgs 3:9–20 have led Martti Nissinen, a specialist in the prophetic traditions of Israel and the ancient Near East, to comment that there is "a growing tendency in the study of biblical and ancient Near Eastern prophecy to consider prophecy, rather than being in contrast with divination . . . an integral part of it."[21] Brian B. Schmidt, in his contribution to the volume *Magic and Ritual in the Ancient World,* more sweepingly states that "magic and divination were . . . vital features of ancient Israel's *religious* ritual" (emphasis mine).[22]

Ancient Israel's magical specialists, it follows, should be counted among its religious functionaries, and thus Israel's women magicians are important subjects in this study of Israelite women's religious lives. I begin my examination by discussing two specific types of magical practice for which we have evidence of women's engagement: reproductive magic and necromancy. Then, provoked by my concern over Ezekiel's excoriation of the women specialists associated with the former of these two practices (according, at least, to the interpretation of Ezek 13:17–23 that I have followed), I turn to ask how biblical tradition overall regards its women magicians, especially in relation to male magical practitioners, both those male practitioners treated as legitimate such as Elisha (see above) and those male magicians who, like the "daughters . . . who prophesy," find themselves subject to censure.

Women's Reproductive Magic in Ancient Israel

Three texts in the Hebrew Bible arguably depict women engaged in acts of reproductive magic. Two of these we have encountered already: first, Ezek 13:17–23, where (to use Jo Ann Scurlock's terminology) "medico-magical" rites involving "knot magic" and the apotropaic use of special foodstuffs are, according to the interpretation I have adopted, enacted on behalf of expectant women during their pregnancies and at the time of parturition. The second text I have already cited is the kindred Gen 38:28, where the midwife who attends Judah's daughter-in-law Tamar as she gives birth ties a red thread around the hand of Tamar's son Zeraḥ as he breaches the womb. Most probably, as noted above, this is an apotropaic act meant to protect the baby from malevolent agents. In the words of Carol Meyers, the red thread's use "may reflect a set of practices involving the apotropaic character of strands of dyed yarn, with both their red color and the fact that they are bound on the infant's hand having magical protective powers."[23] As Meyers points out, this interpretation is consonant with the evidence cited in Chapter 10 regarding the protective red threads bound to parturient women according to both Old Babylonian (1894–1595 BCE) and Middle Hittite (ca. 1450–1350 BCE) tradition.[24] A better parallel still is found in the Hittite "Ritual of Papanikri," where a red thread is tied to a lamb that substitutes for the newborn, one among a series of acts this Hittite text details that were somehow meant to ensure the infant's well-being.[25]

The third biblical text that concerns women's reproductive magic is Gen 30:14–16. There, Rachel, who is barren (Gen 29:31), and her sister Leah, who has ceased to bear children (Gen 30:9), vie to use the "love plants" (*dûdāʾîm,* a term kindred to the noun *dôd,* meaning "love, beloved") that Leah's son Reuben has found in a field.[26] Their hope is to benefit from the love plants' powers as an aphrodisiac and their ability to facilitate reproduction. Meyers thus writes of Rachel and Leah engaging in a "magical act performed to promote fertility," and Marten Stol, who follows the standard interpretation that Leah's and Rachel's "love plants" were mandrake roots, describes the mandrake of Gen 30:14–16 as "a magical plant."[27]

Admittedly, this is not a large corpus of texts. It is also not a wholly uniform corpus. For example, as I discuss in my concluding remarks to this chapter, neither Leah's and Rachel's use of "plant magic" nor the apotropaic magic performed by Tamar's midwife is judged negatively by the biblical writers, even though Ezekiel, as we have seen, harshly condemns the "daughters . . . who prophesy" for (according to the interpretation I have followed) their acts of reproductive magic. Also, Ezekiel's "daughters . . . who prophesy" and Tamar's midwife, as my earlier discussion has indicated, are best classified as "medico-magical" specialists, even professionals, whose services are performed on behalf of others, as opposed to Rachel and Leah, who, along with their benefactor Reuben, seem better regarded (for lack of a better term) as amateurs—or what we might think of today as DIY-ers who aim to help themselves.[28] Regardless, I posit that whether enacted by amateurs or professionals, and however limited our textual witness, the practice of reproductive magic was quite common in ancient Israel. Indeed, I have argued already, in Chapter 2, that issues of human fertility and reproduction were integral among the (many) concerns addressed by practitioners of ancient Israelite household religion, and if we couple this observation with my arguments in this chapter regarding the close relationship between magic and religion, then it can only follow that, at least in the ancient Israelite household, acts of amateur reproductive magic, enacted by family members, would be common.[29] Similar arguments can be advanced about the professional practice of reproductive magic. Ann Fritschel has proposed regarding Ezekiel's "daughters . . . who prophesy," for example, that the "double *kl* (all) in verse eighteen [of Ezek 13:17–23] suggests that the women had many clients."[30]

The prevalence of ancient Israelite reproductive magic is also suggested by some of the realities of ancient Israelite demographics that I have mentioned elsewhere in this volume. We saw in Chapter 1, for example, that during the preexilic period, 80–90 percent of Israelites lived in rural villages,[31] where they were participants in an agrarian economy in which each household basically assumed responsibility for its own well-being. Yet as I documented in Chapter 10, fulfilling this responsibility was not so easy, as it required that the essentials of each family's subsistence be painstakingly procured from the marginally fertile Levantine highlands that were the heartland of Israel's territorial holdings. To survive and succeed in such an environment required, as Meyers writes, "the creation of an adequate labor supply," meaning, as Meyers notes elsewhere, that "successful reproduction was essential."[32] Tikva Frymer-Kensky similarly states: "The terrain and climactic conditions of Israel demanded a large labor force," and therefore "the encouragement of childbirth was vital to Israel's survival needs,"[33] and I have likewise noted in Chapter 2 how important the labor of sons and daughters was on the self-sufficient family farms that were the means of most Israelites' livelihood. Yet as many as one of two children may have died before reaching adulthood, or even before living a year.[34] Any and all acts that helped facilitate reproduction and allowed newborns to thrive must therefore have been commonplace, including, as I have posited, practices of reproductive magic.

That reproductive magic was abundantly practiced in Israel is further suggested by the many rituals in aid of reproduction that, as we saw earlier in this chapter and also in the last, were enacted within the larger ancient Near Eastern and eastern Mediterranean world of which Israel was a part. Also critical to note are the artifacts archaeologists have found in Israelite contexts that may be magical objects meant to enable reproductive success. For example, the many representations of the Egyptian demigod Bes found in the remains of Israelite domestic sites could well have been used to safeguard women during pregnancy and labor (Fig. 11.1).[35] After all, Bes was preeminently the divinity associated with safe pregnancies and deliveries in ancient Egypt, and the use of Bes amulets by pregnant and delivering Egyptian women is well attested.[36] Exemplars of the sorts of "pregnancy jars" used in Egypt, which are designed to resemble a childbearing figure (Fig. 11.2), have also been found in Syria-Palestine. Examples date from both the Late Bronze Age (ca. 1550–1200 BCE) and the Iron Age era that is the focus of this book (ca. 1200–586 BCE).[37] These vases held anointing oil, which was used by parturient women as part of the delivery process not only in Egypt and in Israel, but also in Mesopotamia and in the Hittite world.[38]

On the basis of Mesopotamian and Hittite rituals, moreover, we can reasonably presume that the anointing oil of parturition was used for magical purposes.[39] Consider, for example, the Hittite "Ritual of Papanikri" in which a lamb stands in for a newborn child.[40] As previously noted, this lamb has a red thread tied to it as a means of ensuring the newborn's well-being; here, we can add that the lamb is rubbed with oil. Like the tying of the red thread, this act of anointing the proxy lamb can only have had a magical, not a pragmatic purpose. An Assyrian text that describes a newborn's chest being massaged with oil during the course of an incantation likewise implies the oil's function is magical.[41] So too, then, should we take the ancient Israelites' use of anointing oil during parturition to be magical in nature. Other archaeological finds from Israelite sites associated with reproductive magic may include small model couches, such as those discussed in Chapter 2 that were found in the remains from Buildings (or Houses) 25 and 430 of eighth-century BCE Beersheba (see Fig. 2.6).[42] These model couches may be miniature representations of birth stools or birthing beds (a standard apparatus used during labor in the ancient Near East and eastern Mediterranean).[43] They thus may be meant magically to promote a woman's "ability to give birth."[44]

This archaeological evidence, when coupled with the other data I have surveyed, confirms that reproductive magic would have been abundantly practiced in ancient Israel, and it thereby follows that practitioners of reproductive magic were likewise abundant. I presume, moreover, that the practitioners of this reproductive magic would have included both women and men (for example, Elisha, if his efforts in 2 Kgs 2:19–22 include preventing actual miscarriages).[45] This is particularly the case when it comes to those I classified above as amateur practitioners. Here, we can again recall

Fig. 11.1. Bes amulets, from (*left to right*) Iron IA Azekah, Iron IIB Megiddo, and Iron IIB Lachish. After Christian Herrmann, *Ägyptische Amulette aus Palästina/Israel* IV: *Von der Spätbronzezeit IIB bis in römische Zeit* (OBO Series Archaeologica 38. Fribourg: Academic Press; Göttingen: Vandenhoeck & Ruprecht, 2016), 345 (Azekah: 0214.2006), 347 (Megiddo: 0409: 1994; Lachish: 0393: 1994). Drawing by Dorothea Ulrich.

Fig. 11.2. Calcite ointment jar, for holding anointing oil used by pregnant and parturient women. From Abydos, Egypt, ca. 1479–1352 BCE. Height, 19 centimeters. British Museum, London, BM no. EA65275. © Trustees of the British Museum.

my discussion in Chapter 2, where we saw that the men of Israelite households had as much reason as did their wives to want these women to bear and raise healthy children, especially sons, and thus they were as likely as were their wives to participate in whatever ritual and magical practices were at hand that could bring about reproductive success—such as the rituals of offering food and drink and of burning incense and/or aromatic plants on which I focused in Chapter 2.

Still, when it comes to performing many of the acts distinctive to the practice of reproductive magic (as opposed, say, to the ritual offerings discussed in Chapter 2, which I argued were directed to many different household imperatives), female professionals may have been more prevalently represented than males (just as the evidence of Gen 38:28 and Ezek 13:17–23 intimates, Elisha's efforts in 2 Kgs 2:19–22 notwithstanding). In particular, any specific rites a magician enacted at the time of a woman's delivery—the tying and untying of knotted threads and bands, the application of magical anointing oil, the making of bread offerings to baby-snatching demons—likely would have been the responsibility of women functionaries, given the tendency that I documented in Chapters 6 and 10 to separate men from a woman who is giving birth. To be sure, the evidence I have previously cited in support of this custom concerns predominantly the infant's father, but data from elsewhere in the ancient Near East suggest that the custom of excluding men from a birthing chamber often extended to male magicians and other ritual specialists.[46] For example, a Hittite text that describes ceremonies "carried out soon before . . . the actual birth" details how a male *patili*-priest performs purificatory rituals on behalf of the expectant mother, but as she seats herself on the birthing stool, "her husband [and] the *patili*-priests . . . go," and, furthermore, the priest "makes a sealing of" (meaning, presumably, that he seals shut) the birth chamber.[47] This situation pertains, moreover, elsewhere in Hittite tradition, for while "a significant proportion of the available textual occurrences of this [the *patili*] priest are in birth rituals . . . the *patili*-priest is *never* involved directly with parturition itself" (emphasis mine).[48] Rather, as noted above, it is Hittite *midwives* who recite incantations at the time of a woman's delivery and so provide whatever magical aid is needed.

In sum: reproductive magic must have been a widespread phenomenon in Israel, and while men and women performed certain acts of reproductive magical practice, many of the practitioners of reproductive magic, at least during the crucial periods of delivery and its aftermath, most logically would have been women. Therefore, women reproductive magicians—especially magically skilled midwives and other types of magical professionals specializing in reproduction, but homespun DIY-ers as well—must have been quite common within Israelite society.

Women Necromancers in Ancient Israel

The other magical practice for which we have evidence of Israelite women's engagement is necromancy, "the art or practice of magically conjuring up the souls of the dead . . . to obtain information from them, generally regarding the revelation of unknown causes or the future course of events."[49] As in our discussion of reproductive magic, three biblical texts command our attention: Lev 20:27, 1 Sam 28:3–25, and Isa 57:3–13. In addition, I consider Gen 31:19–35 and 1 Sam 19:11–17, where women—Rachel in the former, David's wife Michal in the latter—appear in conjunction with *tĕrāpîm*/teraphim, which (as we saw in Chapters 1 and 7) are best interpreted as ancestor figurines used in rituals of necromantic divination.[50]

Leviticus 20:27 appears at the end of a long body of ritual prescriptions that set out laws for the Israelites on matters as diverse as ritual slaughter (Lev 17:2–9), improper sexual relations (Lev 18:6–23, 20:10–21), agricultural dos and don'ts (Lev 19:9–10, 23–25), and grooming conventions (Lev 19:27–28). Scattered within this corpus are four passages that condemn various types of magical practice. Three of these, Lev 19:31, 20:6, and 20:27, explicitly condemn necromancy. In Lev 19:31 and 20:6, this means denouncing those who seek out "necromancers" (*ʾōbōt*) and "mediums" (*yiddĕʿōnîm*), but in Lev 20:27, the proscription is directed toward the necromancers and mediums themselves.[51] It is, moreover, directed to both male and female practitioners: "a man or a woman who has in them a spirit of the dead [*ʾôb ʾô yiddĕʿōnî*] will be put to death."[52] The means of execution is stoning.

It may be, moreover, that necromancy—with a possible allusion to female necromancers—is condemned in the fourth passage in the Leviticus ritual proscriptions that speaks to magical acts, Lev 19:26.[53] There, the practices of "augury" (*niḥēš*) and "conjuring" (*ʿōnēn*) are censured. This latter term occurs elsewhere in (among other places) Isa 57:3, where the city of Jerusalem, personified as a female, is called an *ʿōnĕnâ*, a "conjurer," as well as being condemned as an "adulteress" (*mĕnāʾepet*) and a "prostitute" or "harlot" (*zōnâ*).[54] All this invective is in service of the larger harangue that follows in 57:4–13, whose aim is to denounce Jerusalem's inhabitants as apostate. The language of this larger oracle can be difficult to interpret, however, meaning that the nature of the apostasies for which Jerusalem's people are condemned can be less than clear. Also, the precise meaning of the word used to describe Jerusalem as a magical practitioner, *ʿōnĕnâ*, is debated. Theodore J. Lewis has argued, though (following a suggestion that dates back to Julius Wellhausen),[55] that *ʿōnĕnâ* and the related forms *ʿōnēn* (as in Lev 19:26) and *mĕʿōnēn* (as in a list of magical practitioners in Deut 18:10–11) are etymologically kindred to the Arabic root *ʿanna*, meaning "to appear (to or before)," "to take shape," "to form," "to arise," or "to spring up." The Hebrew terms *ʿōnēn, ʿōnĕnâ,* and *mĕʿōnēn* thus would refer to one who causes apparitions or ghosts to "appear," "take shape," "arise," or "spring up": that is, a necromancer.[56]

Lewis goes on to point out that understanding woman Jerusalem to be condemned as a necromancer in Isa 57:3 makes good sense, given "the abundant death terminology" found in the rest of the Isa 57:3–13 pericope.[57] Some of this terminology is obvious (for example, the reference in v. 9 to sending envoys down to the underworld, or Sheol), but the majority is found in references Lewis has painstakingly uncovered within the otherwise oblique language of the passage. Regarding Isa 57:6, for example, Lewis follows William H. Irwin to show that the traditional (and basically nonsensical) translation of the first half of the verse, "with the smooth stones of the wadi is your portion," is far better understood to mean "among the departed [or 'dead'] of the wadi [a traditional Israelite place of burial] is your portion."[58] Likewise, Lewis points out that the term *qibbûṣayik* in v. 13, usually translated "your collection of idols," is far better understood as "your deceased ancestors,"[59] meaning that Yahweh—whose words of scathing denunciation this oracle pronounces—ends the jeremiad by condemning Jerusalem (which is to say, Jerusalem's inhabitants) to rely on the dead forebears the city has been accused of conjuring up in vv. 3 and 9. Yet according to the oracle, the people's intention is futile, as these dead spirits are powerless, as opposed to the might of the living God.

However, in 1 Sam 28:3–25, which is the biblical text that most emphatically associates women with the practice of necromancy, the dead are hardly powerless. Instead, just as necromantic practitioners desire, the ghost of the dead Samuel rises from the earth and delivers an oracle based on his supernatural knowledge. This story, moreover, which features the so-called "medium" (sometimes translated "witch"; Hebrew *ʾēšet baʿălat-ʾôb*) of the village of Endor (see Fig. I.1), allows us to learn something (whereas Lev

19:26, 31; 20:6, 27; and Isa 57:3–13 did not) about how necromantic rituals in ancient Israel were actually conducted.[60]

The narrative is set during the waning days of the reign of King Saul, at a time when the king, who had increasingly found himself under assault from incursions by the Philistine peoples who occupied the southwestern Levantine coast (today's Gaza Strip; see Fig. I.2), faces a Philistine threat once again. As is proper as he considers military action against this enemy, Saul seeks an oracle from Yahweh to determine whether such a war is in accord with the deity's will.[61] But when Saul "inquired" (*šāʾal*) of Yahweh for divine guidance, "Yahweh," according to 1 Sam 28:6, "did not answer him" through any of the standard divinatory techniques the king employs: the seeking of a divine visitation in a dream, as Solomon seeks in 1 Kgs 3:4–15 (2 Chr 1:1–13); the divinatory instrument of the Urim, upon which Saul's ritual specialists depend elsewhere (in 1 Sam 14:41); or the soliciting of a prophetic oracle, as Kings Jehoram and Jehoshaphat and the king of Edom solicit from Elisha in 2 Kgs 3:9–20.[62] Consequently Saul—although he is said previously to have banished all necromancers and mediums (*hēsîr hāʾōbôt wĕʾet-hayyiddĕʿōnîm*) from his land (1 Sam 28:3)—orders his servants to "find me a woman who is a necromancer" (*baqqĕšû-lî ʾēšet baʿălat-ʾôb*) so that he might "inquire" (*dāraš*) through her (1 Sam 28:7). More specifically, when he comes to the woman whom his servants have located, he asks her to raise and consult on his behalf the spirit of his deceased counselor Samuel. Instead, the woman raises an objection, pointing out the danger to her were she to act, given that Saul (whom she does not recognize at this point in the story) has ordered, as noted above, that all necromancers and mediums be banished from Israel. Yet Saul persists and indeed prevails, and in 1 Sam 28:11–13 the medium causes the spirit of Samuel to appear. Thus, even as the story's author(s) and/or redactor(s) express their qualms about the legitimacy of necromantic rites (in 1 Sam 28:3 and also 28:9), they register no doubts, according to 1 Sam 28:11–13, about the efficacy of this necromantic ritual.[63]

The spirit comes up from the ground according to 1 Sam 28:13—perhaps, certain Sumerian, Assyrian, Hittite, Ugaritic, and Greek data might indicate, from a pit dug specifically to facilitate communications with netherworld denizens.[64] Parallels from Hittite tradition also suggest that, as in 1 Sam 28:8, necromantic rites properly take place at night.[65] The fact that Saul is said in 1 Sam 28:20 to have eaten nothing preceding the ritual in addition suggests it was standard practice for those who sought a necromantic oracle to fast.[66] The spirit of Samuel that these ritual preparations and this ritual setting produce has bodily form: the woman describes its appearance as a man wrapped in a robe—although only she, and not Saul, can discern this (and thus she must indicate to Saul what the apparition looks like; 1 Sam 28:14).[67] The woman also describes the spirit as an *ʾĕlōhîm,* a term that here does not have its standard meaning of "god" (as in the "God of Israel," or some other high god of the Canaanite or Mesopotamian pantheon). Rather, Samuel is an *ʾĕlōhîm* in the sense of being one of the deified dead whom I discussed in Chapter 7 (see similarly, for this meaning of *ʾĕlōhîm,* 2 Sam 14:16; Isa 8:19; Num 25:2, as quoted in Ps 106:28; and probably Exod 21:6).[68] Samuel as an *ʾĕlōhîm* spirit, moreover, is able to do precisely what one would want of a deified apparition: deliver an oracle that conveys supernatural knowledge of divine matters.

Unfortunately for Saul, the divine will as reported by the *ʾĕlōhîm* Samuel is hardly to his benefit. Rather, Samuel tells Saul that Yahweh's favor has turned from him and that consequently the Israelite army will be given into the hands of the Philistines in the next day's battle. Moreover, Samuel decrees that in the course of the fighting, Saul and his sons will die (and thus will die any hopes Saul has of establishing a royal dynasty). Poignantly reflected here are the tragic circumstances that define, in the hands of the biblical narrators, almost every aspect of Saul's tenure as king.[69] In what follows, the woman necromancer, even though she, according to the narrative's conceit, has hardly been privy to all this tragedy's dimensions, is still depicted as grasping something of its enormity. Hence, when Saul falls to the ground upon hearing Samuel's words, "greatly afraid" (*wayyirāʾ mĕʾōd;* 1 Sam 28:20) and "terrified" (*nibhal mĕʾōd;* 1 Sam 28:21), she approaches the king with compassion and urges him to recover at least some of his physical strength by breaking the fast that was prelude to the necromantic rite. The meal she gives Saul, moreover, goes well beyond the mere morsel (*pat-leḥem*) she had originally pressed upon him. Instead, she prepares the sort of bounteous repast that a solicitous ancient Near Eastern host offers to an honored guest (see Gen 18:1–8), slaughtering a calf (the only point in the Bible where a woman is explicitly said to perform this task; see Chapter 3) and baking unleavened bread cakes.[70] After eating, Saul and his servants go on their way, and thus ends the story of Endor's medium, as well as this survey of the three biblical texts—Lev 20:27, 1 Sam 28:3–25, and Isa 57:3–13—that speak, either explicitly or obliquely, to women's engagement in necromantic rites.

Above, after surveying the corpus of biblical texts that associate women with the practice of reproductive magic, I noted, first, that the corpus was not a large one. Nevertheless, I argued that women practitioners of reproductive magic were in fact quite common in ancient Israel. Here, we must likewise note that the corpus of biblical texts that associates women with necromantic practice is not a large one. Nevertheless, many commentators have suggested that a conclusion similar to the one I posited regarding reproductive magic pertains: that women mediums were commonplace in ancient Israel, or at least more commonly represented than male necromancers. Carol Meyers, for example, cites ethnographic data regarding a Jerusalem-based community of elderly Jewish women, mostly Kurdish, others Yemeni, Iranian, Iraqi, and Moroccan in origin, who were studied by Susan Starr Sered in the 1980s, in order to suggest that these "women were especially skilled in invoking the dead" in "ways that may be analogous to some of the female necromancers of the biblical period."[71] Indeed, Meyers writes, "communing with the dead apparently was important for *many Israelite women*" (emphasis mine), especially, she suggests, "elderly women . . . mediating between the living and their dead ancestors . . . in the service of their daughters' fertility."[72] Kathryn Pfisterer Darr goes further, to suggest that the biblical evidence "may indicate that the raising of dead spirits was practiced *mainly* by women" (emphasis again mine), and Joseph Blenkinsopp, too, thinks that 1 Sam 28:7, in which Saul asks specifically for a woman necromancer, "suggests that mediums and controls were more often than not female."[73] Phyllis Bird and Karel van der Toorn also speak of "the predominance of women as mediums and clairvoyants [as] illustrated in the Hebrew Bible" (Bird) and "the custom particularly of [Israelite] women to get involved with necromancy" (van der Toorn), to the extent that, to continue to quote van der Toorn, "women *regularly* assumed the role of mediator in the interrogation of the shades" (once more, the emphasis is mine).[74] Ann Fritschel, following van der Toorn, further specifies that it was in "the domestic cult of the ancestors" that "many of the necromancers were women."[75]

I, however, am not so sanguine.[76] Note, for example, that in contrast to what we saw in our discussion of reproductive magic, there is no rich body of comparative evidence from the ancient Near East regarding women necromancers. In his voluminous study of women in ancient Mesopotamia, for example, Marten Stol cites only one text associating women and necromancy (an Old Assyrian letter in which two women claim to have consulted both divinatory specialists and "spirits of the dead" in order to support their claim that the letter's recipient, one Imdilum, owed them payment for cloth they had manufactured and that he then sold).[77] Moreover, the one other Mesopotamian text that mentions a woman necromancer, the *mušēlītu,* or "she who brings up (the spirits of the dead)" according to van der Toorn's translation,[78] is not very informative. It consists only of a list of professional titles and thus gives no indication of, say, female necromancers' prevalence in a Mesopotamian context.[79] Van der Toorn attempts to augment its evidence by arguing that the Mesopotamian *šā'iltu,* most commonly understood as a female dream interpreter, might also function at times as a necromancer. Yet Irving L. Finkel, in his article "Necromancy in Ancient Mesopotamia," cautions that "there is . . . no direct evidence to support this idea,"[80] and even van der Toorn must admit that only "one of the lexical texts [a text consisting, again, of a list of professional titles] places this 'female diviner' [the *šā'iltu*] directly before the 'one who summons [the spirits of the dead]'" in a way that might suggest that the two functionaries were somehow kindred. "Other lists," however, "suggest an affinity [of the *šā'iltu*] to the ecstatic prophets."[81] In addition, Brian B. Schmidt has called into question the rendering of the term *mušēlû* (the masculine form of *mušēlītu*) as "necromancer," suggesting this functionary may instead be an exorcist.[82]

All of this indicates it is a mistake to propose, as some have, that the *mšt'ltm* who appear in the fourteenth-/thirteenth-century BCE text from the northern Levantine city-state of Ugarit known as the "Feast of the Goodly Gods" (*KTU* 1.23.31, 35–36) are to be understood in relation to the Mesopotamian *mušēlītu* and so as female necromancers.[83] Rather, these *mšt'ltm* are best interpreted, more mundanely, as serving women.[84] What's more, female necromancers are mentioned nowhere else in the corpus of texts from Ugarit. Instead, "necromancy [at Ugarit] is a male profession."[85] As for Israel: I agree with Fritschel that the primary "social location" for the practice of necromancy was "the domestic cult of the ancestors,"[86] as it only makes sense that in a thought world where the dead do not rise happily from the grave (1 Sam 28:15), it is a family's forebears who will be most willing to suffer this disturbance, in order to offer aid to their descendants. But I cannot agree that women would have functioned as necromancers within this domestic context. Rather, my discussions in Chapter 7 of the male-dominated nature of the Israelite ancestor cult leads me to expect that it was *men* within a family who took charge of their kin group's necromantic rites. In fact, in a quotation I cited in Chapter 7, Alan M. Cooper and Bernard R. Goldstein make precisely this point regarding the solicitation of oracles from a clan's deities, including its deified dead. There, writing specifically of married women, Cooper and Goldstein state, "In a marital relationship, the wife has a right to ask her husband to intervene with the clan deities, but her contact is with her husband, not with those deities."[87] More generally, concerning both married women and other women within a clan, they aver, "a woman would have had the right to demand that her husband (or . . . the paterfamilias of her clan) petition the family's deities on her behalf," but this is not something she would do herself.[88] The conclusion that follows is that women would typically *not* have served as necromancers within an Israelite family's ancestor cult.

Consider also in this regard the story that I discussed in Chapter 1 of Micah's *bêt ʾĕlōhîm,* or shrine, which housed (I argued) Micah's mother's cast-metal figurine and Micah's *ʾēpôd*/ephod and *tĕrāpîm*/teraphim (or, depending on how one translates, his "ephoded teraphim"). In particular, recall the two points in this story where Micah appoints priestly functionaries to oversee his shrine, a responsibility that I have suggested included manipulating the *tĕrāpîm* figurines that represented Micah's ancestors in order to elicit oracular pronouncements from them. In both instances, the functionaries Micah appoints are *males:* first, in Judg 17:5, his son and then, in 17:11–12, the Levite sojourner from Bethlehem, who is said to have become to Micah like one of his sons upon his appointment. This might be meant to indicate that Micah assigned the Levite a status of "fictive kin" within his family precisely so that the Levite, as an ostensible member of Micah's patriline, would be able to solicit oracles from Micah's ancestral *tĕrāpîm* and could expect them to deliver a response. More important for my purposes, though: the language of "son" in Judg 17:5 and 11–12 indicates that it was *men* who took charge of soliciting *tĕrāpîm* for necromantic oracles within a family's ancestor cult.

Yet what of the two biblical texts in which women are associated with *tĕrāpîm*/teraphim? These are the stories of Rachel's theft of her father's *tĕrāpîm* in Gen 31:19–35 and of Michal's putting a *tĕrāpîm* in David's bed as a doppelgänger for her fugitive husband in 1 Sam 19:11–17. It must be admitted that both these narratives are domestic in terms of their setting, and I also, as just above, have admitted my agreement with those who assign a necromantic function to the *tĕrāpîm.* So do not Gen 31:19–35 and 1 Sam 19:11–17, by associating women and *tĕrāpîm,* intimate a role for women in household-based necromantic ritual? In fact, no, as neither Gen 31:19–35 nor 1 Sam 19:11–17 indicates that their women protagonists use the *tĕrāpîm* figurines with which they are associated to solicit oracles from their families' deceased ancestors. Indeed, in the eight biblical texts where the *tĕrāpîm* appear,[89] it is *only* in the two accounts that involve women that no allusion is made to the *tĕrāpîm*'s divinatory powers. The conclusion that follows is that women did not use *tĕrāpîm* for necromantic purposes, just as, more generally, women did not serve as necromancers within their families' ancestor cult.

In short: despite Fritschel's claims that it was in "the domestic cult of the ancestors" that "many of the necromancers were women,"[90] we really have no evidence of women playing a role as necromantic functionaries within their family homes. Indeed, a significant body of data suggests otherwise. Within the public realm that Fritschel identifies as the other "social location" of Israelite necromantic activity,[91] evidence for women necromancers (as Fritschel seems to agree) is also hard to find.

Biblical Condemnations of Women Magicians

The results of my discussion thus far could be summarized as follows: that while female practitioners of reproductive magic were arguably commonplace in ancient Israel, female practitioners of necromancy were rare. Nevertheless, I have identified some similarities between women reproductive magicians and women necromancers. It just so happens, for example, that three key biblical texts speak to the topics of, respectively, women's reproductive magic (Gen 30:14–16, 38:28; Ezek 13:17–23) and women's necromancy (Lev 20:27, 1 Sam 28:3–25, Isa 57:3–13). More significantly, in each case, these three key texts can vary strikingly in terms of tone. For instance, as we saw in discussing women's reproductive magic, Ezek 13:17–23 harshly condemns its "daughters . . . who prophesy" for their works (as I have interpreted) of reproductive magic, while neither Gen 30:14–16 nor Gen 38:28 comments negatively on Leah's and Rachel's magical use of plants or Tamar's midwife's magical use of a red thread. Likewise, in Lev 20:27 and Isa 57:3–13, female necromancers, whether real (Lev 20:27) or metaphorical (Isa 57:3–13), are castigated, even to the point, in Lev 20:27, of being subject to execution, and necromancy itself is in addition denounced in at least two and arguably three other verses in the Leviticus text of which Lev 20:27 is a part (Lev 19:26, 31; 20:6). However, in 1 Sam 28:3–25, the text's attitude is not so wholly condemnatory, for even as the author(s) and/or redactor(s) responsible for 1 Sam 28:3–25 seem to suggest King Saul did right in banishing mediums and necromancers from his land, both Saul, in seeking out a necromancer, and the medium of Endor, who performs the necromantic rite on Saul's behalf, are represented sympathetically.[92]

To explain these differing sensibilities, let us begin with necromancy and a consideration of the historical context of our three key passages. Leviticus 20:27 and the kindred Lev 19:26, 31, and 20:6 all come from H, or the Holiness Code, and while scholars differ regarding H's date, we saw in the Introduction that many consider it to come from the exilic or postexilic period of Israel's history. Elsewhere, I have argued that Isa 57:3–13 likewise comes from the early postexilic period, more specifically, from somewhere between 535 and 520 BCE.[93] Leviticus 19:26, 31; 20:6, 27; and Isa 57:3–13 thus arguably reflect a significant religious development that occurred in Israel at the end of the seventh century BCE, in conjunction with the program of reformation enacted by King Josiah (r. 640–609 BCE) that I described briefly in Chapter 10. Without going into too much detail, given my intention to treat the Josianic reform and its effects upon women in a separate study (see the Introduction), we still can note here that a major target of that reformation was the ancestor cult.[94] This is because the ancestor cult, which is so constitutive of *clan*-based identities and loyalties, stands fundamentally in opposition to Josiah's goal of centralizing worship at the *state*-sponsored temple in Jerusalem—and thereby constituting among the temple's worshippers an identity defined by the state, to which their loyalty would in turn be directed. It is no wonder, then, that "after renewing the covenant with the people, getting rid of the now-unsanctioned vessels and priests, smashing altars, breaking pillars, and burning bones,"[95] the culminating act of Josiah's reform efforts is the elimination of mediums and necromancers from the kingdom of Judah and the eradication of the *tĕrāpîm*/teraphim (2 Kgs 23:24). This extirpation of various components of the ancestor cult is fundamental if Josiah is to shift the base of power from kin to king so that his centralized state can thrive.

And, in fact, even though Josiah, as we saw in the last chapter, suffered a violent and untimely death that stymied his reform's progress, his agenda of centralization and all the policies that undergirded it did come to dominate Israel's self-understanding by the late exilic and early postexilic period.[96] The result is (among other things) the persistent and harsh condemnations of necromancers—both real and metaphorical—in (arguably) late exilic and early postexilic texts such as Lev 19:26, 31; 20:6, 27; and Isa 57:3–13 and in late preexilic texts closely tied to Josiah's program of reform. These include the book of Deuteronomy and the closely related Deuteronomistic History: see, for example, the condemnations of necromancy found in Deut 18:10–11 and 2 Kgs 21:6. Still, what of the story of the medium of Endor? After all, it appears within the Deuteronomistic History, which, as just noted, supported King Josiah in his eradication of necromantic practice.[97] But in the Endor story, as also noted above, both Saul and the medium are treated sympathetically.

To be sure, parts of 1 Sam 28:3–25 do in fact denigrate necromantic ritual—most obviously, the indication in vv. 3 and 9 that Saul had expelled mediums and necromancers from his land. Nevertheless, the potentially odious necromancer of Endor need not be disparaged in the same way as are her counterparts in Lev 20:27 and Isa 57:3–13 because, in the conceit of 1 Sam 28:3–25, the medium manifests an attitude that is in line with what supporters of the Josianic reform hoped to encourage. That is: she does *not* act, as a typical necromancer would, in the service of a family's ancestor cult and thus in support of clan interests. Rather, she acts in the service of (and so can be said to give her loyalty to) the king—Saul, yet simultaneously, in the minds of the story's author(s) and/or redactor(s), Josiah. Under the terms of this interpretation, 1 Sam 28:3–25 is a sort of "have your cake and eat it too" composition. As Deuteronomic and Deuteronomistic ideology recommend, necromancy is denigrated, yet one of necromancy's potentially abominable practitioners is said to act independently of the familial/clan context where, in Israel, necromancy most naturally thrived. Instead, the necromancer of Endor directs her allegiances to the crown, just as the story's author(s) and/or redactor(s) want their audience to do. Paradoxically, therefore, Josiah's antinecromancy agenda and the ideology that motivates it are maintained even within a text in which the necromancer is treated sympathetically.

Still, what about gender? If, from the point of view of the Josianic reform, necromancy as a *practice* is the problem, and if, as my previous analysis has shown, necromancers were typically *male,* why are *women* necromancers specifically singled out in two of our reform-influenced texts (1 Sam 28:3–25 and Isa 57:3–13) and indicted, along with men, in the third (Lev 20:27)? To answer, we need to consider further another antinecromancy text from the Josianic era that I mentioned briefly above, Deut 18:10–11. This text, its late preexilic date notwithstanding, envisions its setting to be some six hundred years earlier, during the final days of the Israelites' exodus sojourn and immediately before the people's entry into the "promised land." In preparation for this event, Moses warns the Israelite assembly, "When you come to the land that Yahweh your God is giving you, you shall not learn to act according to the abominable practices" of the nations already within it (Deut 18:9). In Deut 18:10–11, Moses then enumerates what some of these "abominable practices" are by citing necromancy, along with at least four additional magical specialties (divination, augury, sorcery, and the casting of spells).[98] He concludes by reiterating the notion that such practices are "abominable" (v. 12) and also stresses that it is on account of the nations' engaging in these magical acts that Yahweh is driving them out of the land Israel will inhabit.

Several points are of note here. First, whatever the consensus of modern-day scholars as sketched out in this chapter's introductory comments—that "there is . . . little point in attempting sharply to distinguish magic from religion"[99]—the author(s) and/or redactor(s) of Deut 18:10–11 (as well as the authors and/or redactors of many other biblical texts) pointedly differentiate between what to them are illegitimate magical practices (necromancy, divination, augury, sorcery, and casting spells) and other practices that they consider legitimate within the exercise of Israelite religion. They do this, moreover, through what Brian B. Schmidt describes as a "Canaanizing" rhetorical strategy—that is, a strategy of proscribing the practices they deem to be illicit by associating them with the Canaanite foreigners whose land, according to the conceit of Deut 18:10–11, the Israelites are preparing to possess.[100] This, it turns out, is a well-established trope throughout the ancient Near East and eastern Mediterranean. Thus, Sarah Iles Johnston writes, "in antiquity, *magic* . . . almost always referred to someone else's religious practices; it was a term that distanced those practices from the norm—that is, from one's own practices, which constituted religion."[101] Likewise, according to Jacob Neusner, "one group's holy man is another's magician," and Robert K. Ritner is almost as pithy: "magic," he writes, "is simply the religious practices of one group viewed with disdain by another."[102] The Bible's excoriated magicians are, in short, its "others," so that, in the words of Stephen D. Ricks, "magic . . . is quintessentially the activity of the 'outsider' in the Bible."[103]

Yet while Deut 18:10–11 focuses on foreigners—those who are treated by the biblical writers as ethnically "other" than the Israelites and who, in terms of their political and religious affiliations, stand outside the Israelite commonwealth—we know from Chapter 10 that there is another group in Israelite society that is readily classified as "foreign," as "alien," and even, in the words of Carol A. Newsom, as the "quintessential other":[104] this is ancient Israel's women. To be a woman magician in ancient Israel, that is, is to be doubly othered, both as a magical practitioner and because of gender. The effect of this double othering is, colloquially speaking, a double whammy, as magic, the art of the "other," and women, the "other sex," are brought together into an ideological synthesis that is then used by the Bible's authors and/or redactors to produce texts that are particularly vitriolic in their efforts to censure and even condemn their subjects. Consider, for example, texts whose goal is to condemn magic in general or some magical act in particular. In these texts, the ideological synthesis that brings together magic, the art of the "other," and women, the "other sex," can be used to enhance the critique by identifying the magical practitioners as women. By associating magic with women as representatives of the "quintessential other," that is, magic can be vilified to a greater degree.

This is the rhetorical strategy deployed, at least to some degree, in 1 Sam 28:3–25. As I have already noted above, this text, even though it treats its woman necromancer sympathetically, nevertheless denigrates necromancy as a ritual practice—most obviously in vv. 3 and 9, where it is twice reported that Saul had expelled the mediums and necromancers from Israel. What is important to add here is that these critiques of necromancy in vv. 3 and 9 neatly bracket the notice in 1 Sam 28:7 that Saul explicitly asked his servitors to find him "a *woman* who is a necromancer" (emphasis mine). Yet, as I have argued, what underlies this request is *not* any historical reality whereby women commonly served as necromancers in ancient Israel. Rather, what we see here is an example of a phenomenon we might describe as "polemic run amok," whereby the author(s) and/or redactor(s) of 1 Sam 28:3–25 seek to exacerbate their condemnations of necromancy in vv. 3 and 9 by affiliating the rite with a particularly suspect group of magical practitioners—namely, women. Which is to say: while I have previously argued (for example, in Chapters 1, 2, and 3 and also in my Chapter 10 discussion of the women prophets of Ezek 13:17–23) that biblical polemics can typically be stripped of their derisive intent in order to reveal reliable historical information about the society of their day, some of the polemics that associate women with magic tend to be so overstated and even overwrought that they completely lose touch with the realities of women's magical practice and the roles played by women magicians within Israelite tradition. This is the case in 1 Sam 28:3–25, where the rhetoric used in vv. 3 and 9 to condemn necromancy as the art of the Canaanite "other" (so much so that its practitioners are to be banished from Israel) is enhanced in v. 7 by deviating from the normative understanding of Israelite necromancers as male in order to depict the 1 Samuel 28 necromancer as a woman. Interestingly enough, this rhetorical strategy continues to succeed even today, as some modern commentators have been so seduced by its power that they follow the lead of Josh 17:11–12 and take the necromancer's village, Endor, to be a Canaanite city.[105] Thereby the medium is identified as Canaanite and rendered as triply suspect: a magician, a foreign "other," and a member of the "other sex."

Another text that deliberately although unrealistically identifies a woman as its magical practitioner in order to promote more forcefully its critique of necromancy is Isa 57:3–13. There, as we have seen, the city of Jerusalem, personified as a woman, is called a necromancer (*ʿōnĕnâ*) in v. 3, and the city's role as a necromancer is also alluded to in v. 9, where she is said to send envoys down to the underworld, or Sheol. Presumably, this is done in order to solicit necromantic oracles from the underworld's denizens and in particular to solicit oracles from the *qibbûṣayik*, or "your [Jerusalem's] deceased ancestors,"[106] on whom the city is accused of relying in v. 13, instead of relying on God.

But a city, obviously, does not have ancestors, at least not in a literal sense. Nor can a city actually perform rituals of necromancy. Rather, as noted above, the aim of the oracle found in Isa 57:3–13 is to denounce Jerusalem's *inhabitants* for ritual activities the oracle's author(s) and/or redactor(s) deem to be apostate, including necromancy. The inhabitants of Jerusalem also seem to be condemned for devoting themselves to gods other than Yahweh, which I take to be the force of the language of sexual impropriety that is found, for example, in v. 5. There the Jerusalemites are said to "burn with lust" under "every green tree," a phrase often used in biblical literature to describe the site of other gods' worship (Jer 2:20; 3:6, 13; Ezek 6:13; also, concerning specifically the worship of the goddess Asherah, Deut 12:2–3, 1 Kgs 14:23, 2 Kgs 17:10, Jer 17:2).

Verse 5 is further of interest because it, along with vv. 3–4, is explicitly addressed to Jerusalem's inhabitants (the nominal and verb forms used in these verses are all rendered in the masculine plural), demonstrating conclusively that the oracle's critique is really about Jerusalem's people, not the city itself. Still, it is Jerusalem who is called a necromancer in 57:3, as well as being called an "adulteress" and a "prostitute" or "harlot."[107] This language of sexual impropriety suggests the city is being accused of devoting herself to other gods, just as the language of sexual impropriety in v. 5 suggests of Jerusalem's inhabitants. Formally, what we see here is a relatively simple metonymy, where the image of a personified Jerusalem can readily alternate with references to the people who live there. (We do the same thing: when we say, for instance, "Washington is in an uproar," what we are really referring to is discord and strife among the government officials and political operatives who work in the U.S. capital city.) Rhetorically, however, the metonymy in Isa 57:3–13 does far more than represent a ready interchange of people and place. Rather, it greatly exacerbates the critique of Jerusalem's inhabitants, and especially the critique of those inhabitants as necromancers, by associating necromancy with Jerusalem as a (metaphorical) woman. Thereby the magical practice of necromancy, already suspect from the point of view of the author(s) and/or redactors(s) of Isa 57:3–13, is made even more suspect by its being linked to women as a class of particularly problematic magical practitioners.

As in 1 Sam 28:3–25, that is, identifying a woman—even a metaphorical woman—as a necromancer in Isa 57:3, 9, and 13 promotes more forcefully the text's critique of necromancy, even though again, as in 1 Sam 28:3–25, this really is "polemic run amok." Which is to say: while I do not doubt that necromantic rituals were in fact being enacted in Jerusalem during the period in which Isa 57:3–13 is set (to this extent, the Isa 57:3–13 polemic is accurate),[108] the specific understanding on which the metaphor of Isa 57:3, 9, and 13 depends—a predominant role for women as necromantic practitioners—is not supported, as we have seen, by ancient Israelite or Near Eastern historical data.

A related rhetorical strategy that brings together magic, the art of the "other," and women, the "other sex," for censorious purposes relies on, yet reverses the strategy of 1 Sam 28:3–25 and Isa 57:3–13. More specifically: while 1 Sam 28:3–25 and Isa 57:3–13 deliberately although unrealistically identify women—whether real or metaphorical—as magical practitioners in order to promote more forcefully a critique of necromancy, other texts deploy a reverse rhetorical strategy that uses negative views about magic in order to vilify women. That is, in texts that seek to censure women, the authors' and/or redactors' misogynistic critique can more aggressively be advanced by suggesting women's association with magic. Consider, for example, 2 Kgs 9:22, in which Jezebel, the text's villain (in the eyes of its author[s] and/or redactor[s]), is denounced for "her sorceries" (*kĕšāpêhâ*) by

Jehu, the usurper king, who subsequently orders, in 2 Kgs 9:33, that she be thrown out of a window and killed.

To be sure, one could argue that Jehu in 2 Kgs 9:33 is simply acting in accord with a legal prescription found in Exod 22:17 (in most of the Bible's English versions, 22:18), which reads, "You shall not let live (*lōʾ tĕḥayyeh*) a woman sorcerer (*mĕkaššēpâ*)." But in fact, the charge of sorcery found in 2 Kgs 9:22 is better interpreted as a metaphorical attack used to exacerbate the text's censure of Jezebel. Note in this regard that in the same breath that Jehu speaks of Jezebel's sorceries, he denounces her "harlotries," and this even though sexual improprieties are not among the otherwise manifold wrongdoings of which Jezebel, in the opinion of the biblical writers, is guilty. Instead, in the same way that the term "harlot" is used metaphorically in Isa 57:3 to attack Jerusalem, and thereby the city's inhabitants, for worshipping gods other than the Israelite god Yahweh, so too does Jehu use the allegation of harlotry in 2 Kgs 9:22 to condemn Jezebel because of her unacceptable devotion (as the author[s] and/or redactor[s] of 2 Kings see it) to the Canaanite storm god Baal (1 Kgs 16:31–32, 18:19, 21:25). The accusation of "sorcery" likewise describes evils that Jehu takes Jezebel to represent metaphorically, not who she is literally.[109]

Yet although the accusation of sorcery in 2 Kgs 9:22 is not to be taken literally, one nevertheless gets a clear sense from this verse how magic, construed as the art of the "other," and women, "the other sex," can cohere together in an ideological synthesis that is used forcefully to denigrate women—or, in this case, an individual woman. Indeed, 2 Kgs 9:22 represents yet again the sort of overwrought polemic I discussed above, whereby the resolution of a text's author(s) and/or redactor(s) to vilify a woman becomes so intense that the text loses touch with any historical reality regarding women and magical practice. The result, in the words of Ann Fritschel, in one of the few scholarly studies to focus specifically on woman's magicianship in ancient Israel, is an irrational and inaccurate "gendering of magic users."[110]

Fritschel points out, moreover, that this situation pertains in other regions of the ancient Near East and eastern Mediterranean. Fritz Graf has shown, for example, that in the Greek and Roman world, most incantations concerning erotic magic were scripted for use by male performers. Yet in these same cultures' literary sources, which were primarily authored by men, women are commonly portrayed as the primary practitioners of erotic magic and are judged negatively on that account.[111] In late antique

Jewish tradition, too, male authors (the rabbinic authorities responsible for the Talmud) depict women as particularly and problematically engaged in magical practice, even when actual magical materials (for example, Hebrew and Aramaic amulets and incantation bowls) might suggest otherwise.[112] Indeed, the rabbis are so inclined to blame women for magical wrongdoing that in addition to assuming that most magicians are women, they lay claim to the far more sweeping corollary: that "most women are witches" (b. Sanhedrin 67a).[113] Thereby, these male writers disproportionately assign the evils they associate with magical practice to women, whatever (and arguably despite) the historical reality, and thus gender the notion of magical malfeasance.[114]

A final example of the way magical malfeasance can be gendered is found in Ezek 13:17–23. Here, as opposed to the Greek, Roman, and rabbinic-era texts just cited, the text is arguably to be taken as accurate when it speaks of women who act as magical practitioners. Still, if we consider Ezekiel's denunciation of the "daughters . . . who prophesy" in Ezek 13:17–23 in relation to Ezekiel's denunciations of the (presumably) male prophets of Ezek 13:1–16 and 14:9–11, we see that women magicians are excoriated to a degree significantly beyond that experienced by their male counterparts. For example, in 13:17–23, the women prophets are censured for prophesying falsely "out of their own imagination" (literally, "from their heart"), whereas in 14:9–11, the condemnatory tone is at least in part mitigated because *God* takes responsibility for deceiving the (presumably) male prophets who speak falsely. Somewhat similarly: while the same language of prophesying out of one's own imagination used of the female prophets in Ezek 13:17–23 is also used to describe the (presumably) male prophets denounced in 13:1–16, the punishments that God threatens to bring upon the accused are very different. In Ezek 13:1–16, the punishment is primarily directed against a seemingly flimsy "wall" that is imagined to have been built by the people and then "whitewashed" by the (presumably) male prophets with whom this oracle is concerned. That is, in 13:1–16, God threatens violence against the mistaken ideas of the people (this is the flimsy wall) and the (presumably) male prophets' "whitewashing" rhetoric, which has supported the people's misguided notions. In 13:17–23, however, God's threats focus directly on those whom the women prophets have served and, by implication, the women prophets themselves. What's more, the specific language that 13:17–23 uses—that God will tear off the bands of cloth and the headbands that (under the terms of the interpretation I have followed) the women prophets have affixed to childbearing women's wrists and heads—is frighteningly reminiscent of the imagery of sexual abuse and violence that is used in such horrifying ways to attack women elsewhere in Ezekiel (in Ezek 16:1–52 and 23:1–49; especially 16:39, 23:10, and 23:26–30). In these texts, women are described as being stripped bare and then physically assaulted.

The Ezekiel 13 "daughters . . . who prophesy" also seem to be denounced to a degree beyond that experienced by their male counterparts elsewhere in the Bible. For example, Ezekiel, in addition to critiquing the daughters' use of "knot magic" and the apotropaic use of barley and bread, censures them for practicing divination (*tiqsamnâ;* Ezek 13:23), whereas the occasional biblical text can extend to male diviners, as well as to other men engaged in divinatory practice, at least a modicum and sometimes a significant amount of respect. Thus, in 1 Kgs 20:33, it passes unremarked that the unnamed king of Israel (presumably King Ahab)[115] is perceived by the defeated soldiers of the Syrian king Ben-Hadad as engaging in an act of cledonomancy. This is the giving of an omen that the soldiers are able to augur, or divine (*yĕnaḥăšû*), through the interpreting of the king's "chance utterances," which are "overheard and considered endowed with ominous meanings."[116] Somewhat similarly in Isa 3:2–3, the "diviner" (*qōsēm*), as well as the "skilled magician" (*ḥăkam ḥărāšîm*) and the one who "understands enchantment" (*nĕbôn lāḥaš*), is included in a seemingly matter-of-fact way (certainly, without opprobrium) in a list of respected community authorities:[117] the *gibbôr,* or "warrior"; the *šōpēṭ*, or "judge"; the *nābîʾ*, or "prophet"; the *zāqēn,* or "elder"; and the *yôʿēṣ*, or "counselor." All these terms, including "diviner" (*qōsēm*), are rendered in the Hebrew text in the masculine singular and thus most obviously refer to *men* who filled these various leadership roles in Israelite society during Isaiah's day. It is also a *man*—indeed, a king—who is affirmed as just and virtuous for giving voice to divinatory oracles in Prov 16:10. Moreover, this Proverbs text uses the same terminology (*qāsam*/*qōsēm*/*qesem*) that is used positively of the "diviner" in Isa 3:2–3 but negatively of Ezekiel's "daughters . . . who prophesy" in Ezek 13:23.

Another example of this same phenomenon—the excoriating of women magical practitioners while their male counterparts are accorded a modicum and sometimes a significant amount of respect—is found in Exod 22:17 (English 22:18), where, as noted above, it is commanded that a woman sorcerer be put to death. Yet nowhere in Exodus or elsewhere in the Bible's legal corpora is there a similar decree concerning the woman sorcerer's male counterpart, the *mĕkaššēp*.[118] Indeed, according to prophetic tradition, the judgment to which sorcerers (*mĕkaššĕpîm*) are subject is left ambiguous, determined by the will of God (Mal 3:5; see similarly Mic 5:11 [in most of the Bible's English versions, 5:12], regarding the abstract noun "sorceries"). Granted, it could be that these sorcerers include women, given that Hebrew uses grammatically masculine forms, such as Malachi's masculine plural participle *mĕkaššĕpîm*, when referring to collectives that include both men and women. It could also be that women are included in the male collective form *mĕkaššēp*, "sorcerer," who is condemned (although not to death) in Deut 18:10. Still, in 2 Chronicles 33, God—although angered enough by King Manasseh's practice of sorcery (*kiššēp*) to have him made prisoner of the king of Assyria (2 Chr 33:11–12)—ultimately forgives him and restores him to his throne (2 Chr 33:13). To be sure, there are ideological reasons that drive this account of restoration, as the authors and redactors of 2 Chronicles, in contradistinction to their source in 2 Kings, seek to absolve Manasseh from charges of egregious wrongdoing.[119] Nevertheless, it seems that the negative judgments the biblical writers can render concerning sorcery accrue disproportionately to women, as women accused of sorcery (as in Exod 22:17 [English 22:18]) remain subject to execution, even as their male counterparts (as in 2 Chr 33:13) can be exonerated. Once more, that is, women magicians seem to be impugned in ways that far exceed the censure directed toward their male colleagues.

Yet what of Gen 30:14–16 and 38:28? In these texts, neither Leah's and Rachel's engagement in an act of "plant magic" nor the apotropaic magic performed by Tamar's midwife is judged negatively. Why are these women practitioners of magic not condemned, as are their counterparts in Ezek 13:17–23 and as are women magicians more generally, in texts like Exod 22:17 (English 22:18), Lev 20:27, and Isa 57:3–13?

To answer, we can begin by reminding ourselves that the magical acts depicted in Gen 30:14–16 and 38:28 are deployed in the interests of facilitating reproduction, either by enhancing women's reproductive abilities (Gen 30:14–16) or by safeguarding the well-being of a newly delivered child (Gen 38:28). This has led Fritschel, who, as I noted above, is one of the few scholars who has commented specifically on women's magicianship in ancient Israel, to suggest that women's magical practice—otherwise so suspect in biblical tradition—can be sanctioned or at least tolerated by the biblical authors as long as it is performed in the service of the constitutive unit of Israelite society, the "house of the father," or the patrilineal family.[120]

Conversely, Fritschel argues that women who perform magic outside the sphere of the patrilineal family, or in ways that act against family interests, are condemned.[121] Fritschel, I should make clear, does not unequivocally follow the interpretation that sees the women prophets of Ezek 13:17–23 as performing magical acts associated with pregnancy and childbirth, and thus she need not see Ezekiel's denunciation of these women as contradicting her thesis regarding sanctioned magical practices.[122] I, however, do find this interpretation of Ezek 13:17–23 to be of merit. Nevertheless, Fritschel's overarching understanding of women's reproductive magic is compelling. Indeed, it reminds me of J. Cheryl Exum's very compelling studies of the women of Moses's birth story as recounted in Exod 1:8–2:10.[123] In that text, no fewer than six women are portrayed as laudatory characters (the two midwives Shiphrah and Puah, Moses's mother, Moses's sister, Pharaoh's daughter, and the daughter's maidservant). However, these women are portrayed as laudatory, Exum argues, because all act in service of a patrilineal agenda: saving the lives of Hebrew male babies in general and the life of the baby boy Moses in particular. Likewise, Fritschel suggests, women who deploy magical practices in the service of the reproductive health of a family's patriline are treated as acting acceptably by the biblical writers.

Still, the women reproductive magicians of Gen 30:14–16 and 38:28, even as they are treated as acting acceptably, are not exactly lavished with praise on account of their efforts. Moreover, there is arguably some obfuscation regarding the magical significance of the red thread in Gen 38:28, where it is suggested that its use was only pragmatic (to make clear which of Tamar's twin sons first breached the womb) and not an apotropaic rite generally performed by a midwife on behalf of a newly delivered child. Thereby, the respect that should be accorded Rachel and Leah for their homespun endeavors to increase fertility and to Tamar's midwife as a specialist in reproductive magic is undermined. The importance of reproductive magic and of its women practitioners is also undermined by women's reproductive magic being largely ignored (as we have seen) within the biblical text, despite the fact the women's reproductive magic, I have argued, must have been quite common in ancient Israel. And, of course, another means by which the significance of women reproductive magicians is undermined is through condemnation: both condemnation of specialists in reproductive magic, as in Ezek 13:17–23, and condemnation of the larger community of women magicians elsewhere in the Bible, a condemnation that can be expressed, as we have seen, in the harshest possible terms.

Karel van der Toorn has argued that women in Israel and the ancient Near East turned to magic because positions of power were otherwise so unavailable to them.[124] My argument, with respect to reproductive magic, is in many respects the converse: that women as practitioners of reproductive magic would have been able to lay claim to so much power in Israelite tradition that however much the society needed them, the biblical writers acted to suppress their significance. They did this through failing to acknowledge these women and their work's importance and/or its true nature (Gen 30:14–16 and 38:28), through ignoring them, through denouncing them (Ezek 13:17–23), and through stigmatizing the larger class of women magicians of which they were a part. Despite the power that women reproductive magicians should be able to claim and despite the service to their communities these magicians provided, the biblical writers ultimately enforce their position as "others" and so place them at the margins of Israelite tradition and culture.

12 "The *Ṣōbĕ'ôt* Who Served at the Entrance to the Tent of Meeting": Determining Their Religious Role

Twice in the Bible, we find references to women functionaries called *ṣōbĕ'ôt* who served at the entrance to the tent of meeting. Exodus 38:8 reads, "He [Bezalel, one of the chief craftsmen responsible for the tent of meeting's construction] made the bronze [or copper] basin with its bronze [or copper] stand from the mirrors of the *ṣōbĕ'ôt* who served at the entrance to the tent of meeting."[1] First Samuel 2:22 reports, "Now Eli [the priest] . . . heard . . . how they [his two sons, Hophni and Phinehas] lay with the *ṣōbĕ'ôt* women who served at the entrance to the tent of meeting." The "tent of meeting" we know well from Chapters 5 and 6: this is the tent shrine that, according to the predominant strain in biblical tradition, was Israel's central place of worship during the nation's premonarchic era. In the biblical conceit, this tent of meeting was especially central to the Israelites' religious life during their exodus sojourn in the Sinai wilderness. Indeed, the setting of Exod 38:8 is the Sinai wilderness, at a point in the exodus story that follows immediately upon the people's covenant-making encounter with Yahweh at Mount Sinai, when the Israelites, as Yahweh had instructed, engage in the tent of meeting's fabrication. According to the Bible's chronology, 1 Sam 2:22 is set some 150 to 200 years later, after the people's entry into Canaan and at a time, moreover, when they seem to have become reasonably well constituted in what was the heartland of Israelite settlement, the central hill country of the southern Levant. So settled are these Israelites, in fact, that as the larger pericope of 1 Sam 1:1–2:26 presents it, they have been able to establish for themselves a regional sanctuary at Shiloh that includes an actual shrine building (1 Sam 1:7, 9, 24; 3:3, 15; see also Judg 18:31). How, though, to understand this shrine *building* in relation to the reference in

1 Sam 2:22 (also Josh 18:1, 19:51; Ps 78:60) that locates the "*tent* of meeting" in Shiloh is, as we saw in Chapter 3, something of an enigma.

This enigma is further complicated by the fact that the reference in 1 Sam 2:22 to Eli's sons lying with the women who served at the tent of meeting's entrance is missing in two of the most important witnesses to the books of Samuel's ancient text: the "a," or first, Samuel scroll found among the Dead Sea Scrolls (4QSam[a]) and the ancient Greek translation of the Hebrew Bible preserved in the Codex Vaticanus. For some commentators—most notably, perhaps, P. Kyle McCarter in his Anchor Yale Bible commentary on 1 Samuel—this indicates that this 1 Sam 2:22 text was not a part of the original (and preexilic) Samuel account but was added by a postexilic redactor in order to denigrate the priesthood of Shiloh.[2] Other commentators, however, note that the 1 Sam 2:22 text is present in the Greek rendering of the Bible represented in the so-called Lucianic group of minuscules and that the text was also known to the first-century CE Jewish historian Josephus (*Antiquities* 5.339). Thus, these scholars argue that the reference in 1 Sam 2:22 was original to the Samuel story and was deliberately deleted in the line of manuscript transmission represented by Codex Vaticanus and 4QSam[a] because it was just too scurrilous (sexual perversity among priests!).[3]

Ambiguities, albeit smaller, that plague the analysis of Exod 38:8 include the fact that women are anachronistically described as serving at the entrance to the tent of meeting even though the tent was at that point in the narrative still under construction.[4] In addition, concerning the women, neither Exod 38:8 nor 1 Sam 2:22 tells us very much. We learn in Exod 38:8 that these women possess mirrors that, like mirrors typically in the ancient world, were made of bronze (or copper), and perhaps the biblical writers mean for us to imagine—assuming we envision mirrors of the same size as those found in archaeological excavations and in ancient artistic representations (see Fig. 10.1)—that many such mirrors were in the women's possession. After all, Bezalel, one of the artisans in charge of the tent of meeting's construction, melts the women's mirrors down and uses their bronze/copper to fashion what biblical tradition elsewhere understands to be two fairly substantial items (see 1 Kgs 7:27–38): a basin to be used in the precinct of the tent of meeting for washing and that basin's stand. Perhaps moreover, if we are meant to imagine the presence of *many* mirrors, we are to imagine the presence of *many* women: one woman per mirror, say. Contrary to the biblical text's reckoning, however, bronze stands for holding basins known from ancient Near Eastern archaeological excavations are rather small. For example, a well-preserved wheeled stand often compared with the biblical account found in 1 Kgs 7:27–38 stands only 29.2 centimeters tall (without the wheels), and a similar stand is only slightly taller (34 centimeters).[5] If we take these stands as a guide, we should perhaps imagine that the metal of only a few mirrors would be needed to produce the tent of meeting's bronze stand and associated laver.[6] If only a few mirrors, should we analogously imagine only a few women? Indeed, maybe we should envision only two women at the tent of meeting's entrance, assuming that the 1 Sam 2:22 account of Hophni's and Phinehas's sexual encounters posits there to be one woman for each priest.

Of greater ambiguity than the women's number, however, is the question of their function. In addressing this issue, scholars often throw up their hands in despair. "The best we can do," John I. Durham writes, is "to confess ignorance," and Martin Noth gives voice to the same sentiment, albeit in less dramatic terms: "The reason for this note [about the women servitors] remains obscure."[7] Others, though, are somewhat more optimistic. Already in 1898, for example, in a rather revolutionary article titled "Women in the Ancient Hebrew Cult," Ismar J. Peritz suggested that the various forms of the root *ṣ-b-ʾ* used repeatedly to describe the women at the tent's entrance—in Exod 38:8, they are called *haṣṣōbĕʾōt ʾăšer ṣābĕʾû* (the "*ṣōbĕʾōt-women who ṣābā(ʾ)-ed,*" in William H. C. Propp's rendering),[8] and in 1 Sam 2:22, they are *hannāšîm haṣṣōbĕʾōt* (the "*ṣōbĕʾōt-women,*" to paraphrase Propp)—could be of significance in understanding the women's role. Most commonly in the Bible, *ṣ-b-ʾ* refers to some kind of military service; the noun *ṣābāʾ*, for example, usually means "army." But because this same noun refers to the work of the Levitical priesthood at the tent of meeting in Num 4:3, 23, 35, 39, 43, and 8:24–25, Peritz suggested that the women who served at the tent's entrance likewise "render[ed] service in connection with the tabernacle in a Levitical capacity."[9] As to what that service might more specifically be, Propp imagines that the women might somehow assist with sacrifice, or they might be charged with examining women worshippers who come to the tent of meeting to ensure these women's ritual purity (similar to the role Levitical priests assume in 2 Chr 23:19).[10] Other commentators have argued that the *ṣōbĕʾōt* women's role might have been to perform more menial cultic tasks: weaving fabric, tanning hides, cleaning, baking.[11]

Still others have proposed that the women may have been responsible for some kind of ritual music-making at the tent's entrance.[12] Or, Irmtraud

Fischer suggests, the women may have been prophets who recorded their prophetic revelations on "vision tablets" (which is Fischer's preferred rendering of *mar'ōt* in Exod 38:8).[13] Conversely, among scholars who follow the more traditional translation of *mar'ōt* as "mirrors," some focus on the mirrors as items of self-beautification and/or the descriptions of Hophni's and Phinehas's sexual improprieties in 1 Sam 2:22, in order to propose that the *ṣōbĕ'ōt* women were agents of some sort of inappropriate sexual activity.[14] This sexual activity is, moreover, often taken to be religiously inflected in character and most commonly described as "cultic" or "sacred prostitution."[15] A kindred, yet less polemically charged interpretation takes the women to be the sexual partners (which is to say wives) of the tent of meeting's priests.[16]

In the face of such ambiguity, it is perhaps futile to speculate still more. Nevertheless, in what follows I pursue a line of interpretation intimated already in Jerome's late fourth-century CE Latin translation of the Bible (the Vulgate), in which the *ṣōbĕ'ōt* women at the tent's entrance are understood, particularly in Exod 38:8, as guards (Jerome renders *haṣṣōbĕ'ōt* as *mulierum quae excubabant,* "the women who keep watch or guard," in Exod 38:8; in 1 Sam 2:22, he renders *hannāšîm haṣṣōbĕ'ōt* as *mulieribus quae observabant,* literally, "the women who observe," but also "the women who watch, keep their eyes on").[17] As his translation of Exod 38:8 in particular makes clear, Jerome's inspiration was surely the military connotations of the root *ṣ-b-'* that I have previously mentioned.[18] My interpretation, though, draws on archaeological evidence: a corpus of small ceramic models of shrine buildings and related objects that has increasingly attracted scholars' attention in the past several years.[19]

To be sure, working with this corpus presents significant challenges. Most problematic is the fact that several of the model shrines were not found during the course of scientifically controlled archaeological excavations but were pillaged by looters from ancient sites. These shrines thus lack the sorts of contextualizing evidence scholars crave. For example, were they found in Israel? in Transjordan? elsewhere? in a domestic setting? at a cult site? in a grave? And what is their date: the Middle Bronze Age? the Late Bronze Age? the Iron Age? or some other period altogether? Yet even shrines that are archaeologically provenanced can present difficulties.[20] The model shrines, for example, while typically rich in decoration, are uninscribed, meaning they offer no written clues about how their imagery is to be understood.

Still, some things seem straightforward. First, enough of the model shrines do come from scientifically controlled archaeological excavations to allow us to suggest that such shrines were a feature of the religious culture of both Israel and Transjordan during the Iron Age—both the Iron Age I period (ca. 1200–1000 BCE) and the Iron Age II period (ca. 1000–586 BCE) that was the heyday of biblical Israel. The oldest known Transjordanian exemplars come from eleventh- or tenth-century BCE Tall al-'Umayri, a site that sits about 15 kilometers south of Amman in the highlands that overlook the northeastern shores of the Dead Sea (see Fig. I.1). There, archaeologists found a fairly well-preserved shrine and fragments from at least two other shrine models lying on the floor of a large courtyard that they have described as a *temenos* (a precinct that is enclosed or otherwise demarcated in order to signify it as sacred).[21] The nearly complete shrine measures approximately 25–30 centimeters wide, 38 centimeters high, and 24 centimeters deep (Fig. 12.1).[22] Also from Transjordan come two shrinelike objects from eleventh- or tenth-century BCE Pella, in the northern Jordan River Valley (see again Fig. I.1).[23] While not model shrines per se, these are best understood as closely related representations of multistory temples.[24] Unfortunately, however, the piece in which I am most interested, which measures 23 centimeters wide by 59.5 centimeters high, is so fragmentary that it is hard to define its identity even this precisely (Figs. 12.2 and 12.3).[25]

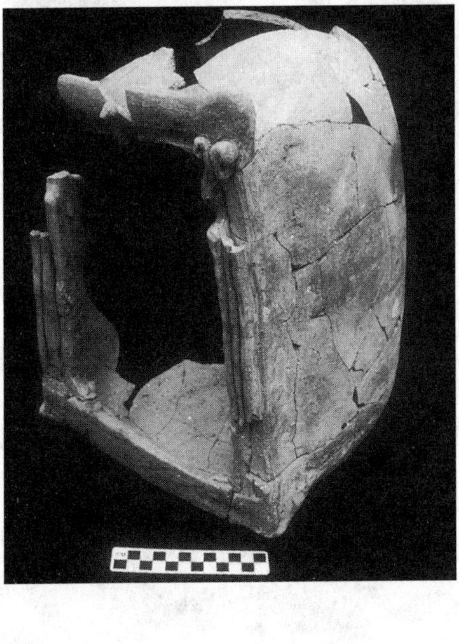

Fig. 12.1. Eleventh- or tenth-century BCE model shrine from Tall al-'Umayri. From Larry G. Herr and Douglas R. Clark, "From the Stone Age to the Middle Ages in Jordan: Digging up Tall al-Umayri," *NEA* 72 (2009): 90; the complete article is available on the online journal platform of University of Chicago Press. Photograph courtesy of Larry G. Herr and Douglas R. Clark.

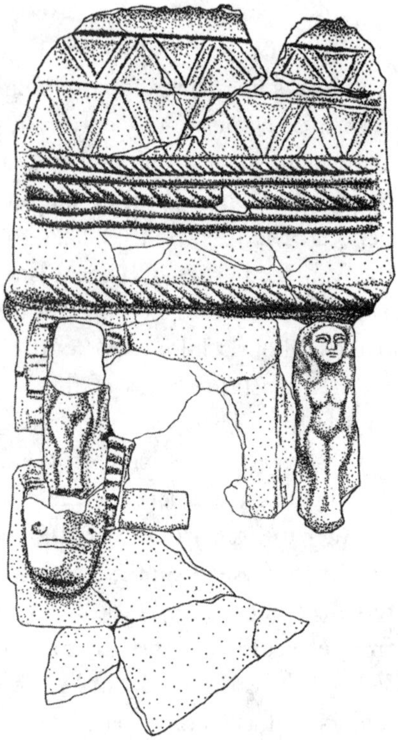

Fig. 12.2. Remains of a model temple from eleventh- or tenth-century BCE Pella, based on recovered pieces of Pella Cult Stand, RN 72066, IVE 21.2. Courtesy of the Pella Excavation Project, University of Sydney. Drawing by Dorothea Ulrich.

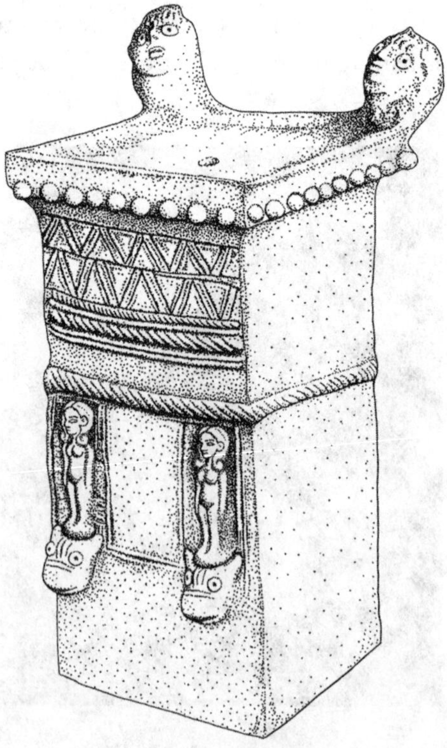

Fig 12.3. Reconstruction of the Pella model temple/Pella Cult Stand, RN 72066, IVE 21.2, based on a photograph from the Ashmolean Museum, Oxford. Courtesy of the Pella Excavation Project, University of Sydney. Drawing by Dorothea Ulrich.

Fig. 12.4. Late seventh-/early sixth-century BCE model shrine from the Edomite site of Ḥorvat Qitmit, as reconstructed by Pirhiya Beck. From Pirhiya Beck, "Catalogue of Cult Objects and Study of the Iconography," in *Ḥorvat Qitmit: An Edomite Shrine in the Biblical Negev,* ed. Itzhaq Beit-Arieh (Monograph Series of the Institute of Archaeology, Tel Aviv University 11. Tel Aviv: Institute of Archaeology of Tel Aviv University, 1995), 103. Courtesy of the Institute of Archaeology of Tel Aviv University.

Across the Jordan in the south, at the late seventh-/early sixth-century BCE Edomite site of Ḥorvat Qitmit (see yet again Fig. I.1), fragments from the remains found there were used by Pirhiya Beck to reconstruct at least four model shrines, including one with tree-shaped pilasters with volutes, very like the Israelite model shrine from Tell el-Farʿah North that I discuss below, and one decorated with two nude female figures, who are described by Beck as "pregnant" and who clutch their breasts as they flank the shrine's entry (Fig. 12.4).[26] Until recently, only one model shrine had been found in the territory of the Southern Kingdom of Judah, a very plain and very small exemplar (5.5 centimeters wide, 8.5 centimeters high, and 7 centimeters deep) that comes from Jerusalem and that dates to ca. 700 BCE.[27] In May 2012, however, Yosef Garfinkel announced that during excavations at the site of Khirbet el-Qeiyafa (biblical Shaaraim?) in the valley of Elah, about 30 kilometers west-southwest of Jerusalem (see once more Fig. I.1), two larger and more elaborate model shrines had been discovered. Garfinkel and his excavation team have dated these two shrines, as well as one other model shrine from Qeiyafa, to the tenth century BCE.[28]

Several model shrines have been found in the territory of the Northern Kingdom of Israel. Most significant for my purposes are the following:

1. a complete tenth- or ninth-century BCE model shrine, 12.6–13.9 centimeters wide, 20.8 centimeters high, and 10.5 centimeters deep

Fig. 12.5. Tenth- or ninth-century BCE model shrine from Tell el-Far'ah North. Musée du Louvre, Paris, France, inv. no. AO21689. Photo: Christophe Chavan. © Musée du Louvre, Dist. RMN-Grand Palais/ (Christophe Chavan) Art Resource, NY.

(Fig. 12.5), from the Iron Age II remains at Tell el-Far'ah North (probably biblical Tirzah; see Fig. I.1);[29]

2. a fairly crude model shrine, 15.5–18 centimeters wide, 26.5 centimeters high, and 25.3 centimeters deep, that was found by schoolchildren on or just below the ground's surface at Tel Rekhesh, in the Lower Galilee, about 8 kilometers southeast of Mount Tabor (see Fig. I.1), which can be "loosely attributed to the Iron I period," according to Ziony Zevit's survey of Israelite and Transjordanian model shrines but which dates from the Iron Age II period (ca. 900 BCE) according to Joachim Bretschneider's and Béatrice Muller's more extensive catalogues and Garfinkel's and Madeleine Mumcuoglu's recent study (Fig. 12.6);[30] and

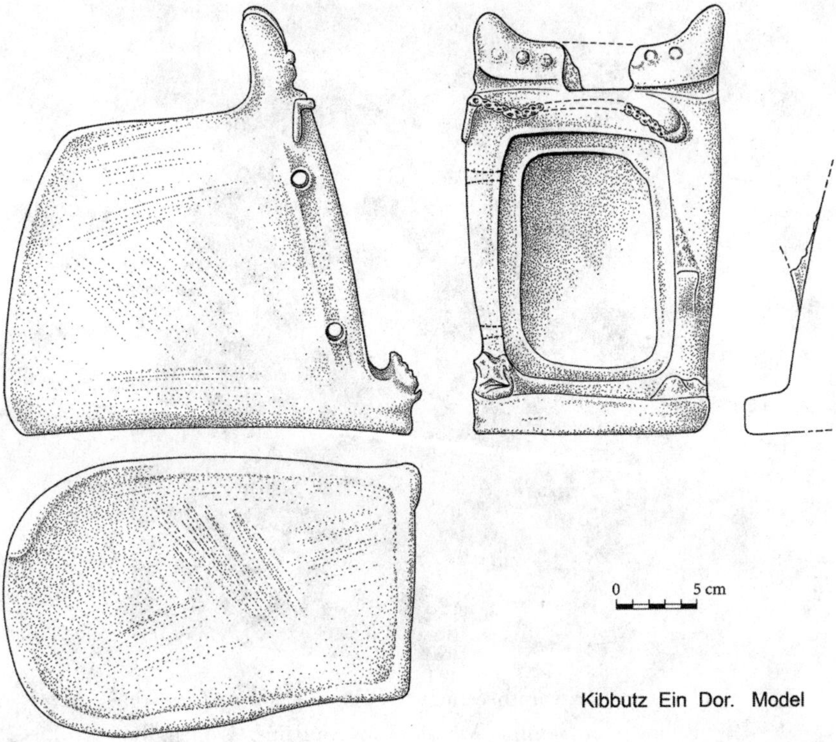

Fig. 12.6. Model shrine from ca. 900 BCE from Tel Rekhesh. From Yosef Garfinkel and Madeleine Mumcuoglu, "A Shrine Model from Tel Rekhesh," *STRATA: Bulletin of the Anglo-Israel Archaeological Society* 33 (2015): 74, Fig. 9. Courtesy of Yosef Garfinkel, The Hebrew University of Jerusalem.

3. a model shrine from early ninth-century BCE Tel Reḥov (see Fig. I.1) and five closely related clay altars from Reḥov, one, unfortunately, quite fragmentary (Fig. 12.7).[31]

Although there is some variation in size and shape, the model shrines of this corpus all are roughly box- or beehive-shaped, with a fairly large opening on one side that is clearly meant to represent the shrine's entrance. This entrance is often, although by no means always, flanked by two columns, sometimes free-standing, sometimes engaged: examples from among the shrines catalogued above include shrines from Tall al-ʿUmayri, Ḥorvat Qitmit, Khirbet el-Qeiyafa, and Tell el-Farʿah North. Biblical scholars can readily compare the columns Jachin and Boaz that flanked the entrance to the Jerusalem temple (1 Kgs 7:21). Indeed, somewhat like Jachin and

Fig. 12.7. Early ninth-century BCE model shrine from Tel Reḥov. From Amihai Mazar and Nava Panitz-Cohen, "It Is the Land of Honey: Beekeeping at Tel Reḥov," *NEA* 70 (2007): 211; the complete article is available on the online journal platform of University of Chicago Press. Published courtesy of the Tel Reḥov Excavations, Institute of Archaeology, The Hebrew University of Jerusalem.

Boaz, whose capitals were decorated with pomegranates suspended from a decorative net (see 1 Kgs 7:20, 42; 2 Kgs 25:17; Jer 52:22–23; 2 Chr 3:16, 4:13),[32] seemingly to suggest fruits hanging on a tree, the model shrines' columns can be treelike in appearance. These columns can be depicted with fronds, for example (as in the example from Idalion, Cyprus, discussed below; Fig. 12.8), or with palmette volutes (as in one of the Ḥorvat Qitmit shrines and in the Tell el-Far'ah North shrine; see Fig. 12.5).[33] Over the model shrines' entryways, there is often, although again not always, a large entablature that again often, but not always, features some form of decoration (Zevit describes these entablatures as "billboard frontons," "on which symbols of the deity whose shrine it was could be placed").[34] The model shrine from Tel Reḥov, however, lacks an entablature. Instead, it features a

Fig. 12.8. Sixth-century BCE model shrine from Idalion, Cyprus. Musée du Louvre, Paris, France, inv. no. N3294. Photo: The Chuzeville brothers. © RMN-Grand Palais/ Art Resource, NY.

lion that lies sprawled on its belly across the shrine's rounded roof, with the beast's front paws extending downward to press atop two human heads that are affixed to the shrine's façade, above and just to the right and left of the entryway (see Fig. 12.7).

Yet although the heads that appear on the Reḥov shrine's façade represent humans (whether males or females is unclear),[35] it seems certain that just as the ancients understood an actual shrine or temple to be the place where the deity or deities worshipped there resided, so too do the interiors of model shrines represent a divine dwelling place. Indeed, on the floor of one of the Khirbet el-Qeiyafa shrines, "opposite its entrance and near its rear wall, is a small rectangular depression," which the excavators suggest might have held a base atop which "a statue or a symbol of a divinity" could be placed.[36] By way of parallel, Qeiyafa's excavators cite a Middle Bronze Age shrine from the site of Ashkelon, on the southern coast of modern-day Israel (see Fig. I.1), that contained "a bronze figurine of a calf covered with silver," undoubtedly a representation of the god that shrine was meant to house.[37] We can also note a chronologically closer (Iron Age II) analogue from the Transjordanian site of Wadi ath-Thamad 13, about 8 kilometers northeast of ancient Dibon (see again Fig I.1). There, remains included a model shrine that had "residual clay on the interior wall that suggests an attached figure," presumably, again, a representation of the deity whom the shrine was understood to house.[38] The site's excavator, P. M. Michèle Daviau, compares a model shrine from sixth-century BCE Idalion, Cyprus, 21 centimeters wide, 27 centimeters high, and 21 centimeters deep (see Fig. 12.8).[39] This shrine, in the collection of the Louvre, has standing inside of it a female figurine that peers out of the model's doorway and is certainly to be interpreted as a goddess who is resident within (according to the Louvre's website, for example, she is winged).[40] Female figurines peer from windows on either side of the Idalion shrine as well.[41] These are perhaps, again, representations of the shrine's resident goddess, or perhaps more than one goddess was thought to be resident in the Idalion shrine.[42] Consider in this regard female figures, nude, that peer from what appear to be shrine windows carved into the side of one of Tel Reḥov's clay (and unfortunately fragmentary) altars.[43] Their nudity indicates that each of these figures depicts a goddess, but we cannot say whether they represent the same goddess or multiple goddesses worshipped together in the same shrine.[44]

Far more interesting for my purposes, however, than the female figures that peer out from the interior of Idalion's model shrine and the shrine windows of Reḥov's clay altar are the female figures that appear on the exteriors of at least six model shrines and related objects, often flanking the sanctuaries' entrances, either in addition to or in lieu of the columns often found in this position. For example, a Late Bronze Age or early Iron Age model shrine, 16–18.3 centimeters wide, 22.5 centimeters high, and 10–14 centimeters deep, unfortunately unprovenanced and now in the collection of the American University of Beirut, shows two standing female figures, nude, flanking the shrine's entrance instead of columns (Fig. 12.9).[45] Another unprovenanced shrine model, in the collection of the Jordan Archaeological Museum, 14.9 centimeters wide by 15.9 centimeters high by 10 centimeters deep and said to come from near Kerak, in Transjordan (see Fig. I.1), and to date from the eleventh, tenth, or ninth century BCE, likewise features two female figures, nude (or nearly so—each may wear a girdle around her waist), flanking its entrance (Fig. 12.10).[46] The eleventh- or tenth-century BCE fragmentary cult object from Pella (Figs. 12.2 and 12.3)—although not a model shrine per se but perhaps, as noted above, a rendering of the façade of a multistory temple—similarly shows two mold-made female figures, nude, standing on either side of "what looks to be an

Fig. 12.9. Late Bronze Age or early Iron Age model shrine, from the collection of the American University of Beirut. From Helga Seeden, "A Small Clay Shrine in the AUB Museum," *Berytus* 27 (1979): 17 (Plate VI). Used by permission.

Fig. 12.10. Eleventh-, tenth-, or ninth-century BCE model shrine from near Kerak, in Transjordan, from the collection of the Jordan Archaeological Museum. After Fawzi Zayadine, "Sculpture in Ancient Jordan," in *Treasures from an Ancient Land: The Art of Jordan,* ed. Piotr Bienkowski (Stroud, Gloucestershire: Alan Sutton; Liverpool: National Museums and Galleries of Merseyside, 1991), 39, Fig. 37. Drawing by Dorothea Ulrich.

open window."[47] According to Beck, all three of these exemplars—the Beirut and Kerak model shrines and the Pella temple façade, plus a similarly decorated cylindrical stand from Megiddo—inspired her reconstruction of the model shrine flanked by two nude, pregnant female figures at Ḥorvat Qitmit (Fig. 12.4).[48]

We can note as well that one of the ninth-century BCE Reḥov clay altars that is, like the Pella stand, kindred to a model shrine if not such an object exactly, shows a two-story tower (the excavators interpret it as a model of a city-gate tower) to which two mold-made female figures, nude, were affixed to the left and right of the double window of the tower's lower story (Fig. 12.11).[49] Somewhat similarly, the busts of two females are positioned atop the entrance of a tenth- to eighth-century BCE model shrine, 16–27 centimeters wide, 29.7 centimeters high, and 10.8 centimeters deep, said to have been found in the vicinity of Mount Nebo, in Transjordan (see Fig. I.1), and now in the collection of the University of Missouri, Columbia, Museum of Art and Archaeology.[50] More specifically, the figures sit on either side of a metope and within niches formed, on the left and right, by the capitals of columns flanking the shrine's entry and by the large entablature above (Fig. 12.12).[51]

Fig. 12.11. Early ninth-century BCE model altar from Tel Reḥov, representing a city-gate tower. From Amihai Mazar and Nava Panitz-Cohen, "It Is the Land of Honey: Beekeeping at Tel Reḥov," *NEA* 70 (2007): 209; the complete article is available on the online journal platform of University of Chicago Press. Published courtesy of the Tel Reḥov Excavations, Institute of Archaeology, The Hebrew University of Jerusalem.

Fig. 12.12. Drawing of a tenth-, ninth-, or eighth-century BCE model shrine, said to have been found in the vicinity of Mount Nebo, in Transjordan, in the collection of the University of Missouri, Columbia, Museum of Art and Archaeology. From Saul S. Weinberg, "A Moabite Shrine Group," *MUSE* 12 (1978): 33.

Almost everyone who has commented on the female figures that flank the entries or otherwise appear on the façades of these six model shrines and their analogues describes them as goddesses,[52] and it is by no means my intent to disagree. Rather, as I have intimated already, I take the figures' nudity—a feature characteristically used in southern Levantine representations of female divinities but not of human women—to be determinative.[53] Each of the Pella figures also stands, as would goddesses but obviously not human women, atop a lion's head (see Figs. 12.2 and 12.3).[54] The female figures on the Pella stand furthermore wear the "Hathor headdress"—that is, a hairstyle typical of the Egyptian goddess Hathor—that is generally taken to indicate divine status.[55] The female figures of the American University of Beirut model shrine may somewhat similarly wear bird headdresses that would seemingly mark these women as divine rather than human (see Fig. 12.9).[56] In addition, elaborate jewelry, which is one of the iconic elements that marks representations of female deities,[57] adorns the figures that flank the entries of the American University of Beirut, Kerak, and Qitmit model shrines and the Reḥov city-gate altar.

Still, I am not as convinced as are most about these goddesses' specific identity. For example, while Othmar Keel and Christoph Uehlinger admit that there could be a difference between the identity of a goddess or goddesses placed *within* a model shrine or its analogue and the identity of goddesses who can *flank* the shrine's or its analogue's entryway, they conclude that the deities of the interior and exterior are one and the same. They further argue that to put images of a goddess to whom a shrine is dedicated flanking that shrine's entry is a way of marking the shrine as belonging to said goddess and of emphasizing her accessibility.[58] William G. Dever interprets much the same; indeed, he proposes that the goddess can be specifically identified as Asherah, the great mother goddess of the Canaanite world. He writes, therefore, of the nude female figures that flank the entryway of one model shrine, "most likely, these females are symbolic of Asherah, 'at home in her house,' and beckoning to her devotees."[59]

A considerable amount of evidence, moreover, lends credence to Dever's suggestion. The tree-shaped columns with which the flanking females can be associated, for example (either because the female figures somehow stand in proximity to tree columns or because the females replace the trees), readily bring to mind Asherah, who, as noted in Chapter 5, can symbolically be presented as a stylized tree in both iconographic and textual sources.[60] The lion pedestals atop which the tree-shaped columns can stand (Khirbet el-Qeiyafa) or with which the flanking females are sometimes conjoined (Pella) recall as well various mythological and artistic traditions that associate Asherah with lions.[61] In fact, Asherah can seemingly be depicted as standing atop a lion (more on this in Chapter 13), in much the same way that the female figures that flank the entry of the Pella temple façade stand atop lions' heads (see Figs. 12.2 and 12.3). Crouching lions that flank or seemingly flanked the façades of other model shrines, as at Tel Rekhesh (see Fig 12.6),[62] even though they can appear independent of tree columns or female figures, might also be said to represent Asherah, as might the lion sprawled on its belly across the roof of the model shrine from Tel Reḥov (see Fig 12.7).

Nevertheless, we must raise cautions. For example, as P. R. S. Moorey points out regarding model shrines from both the mid-second millennium BCE and the Iron Age, "the use of identical pairs [of flanking female figures] is not documented when the subjects are indisputably ranking goddesses [such as Asherah]." Instead, regarding the "duplicated" female figures that stand on lions' heads flanking the "doorway or aperture in a tower wall" of the Pella shrinelike object (see Figs. 12.2 and 12.3), Moorey writes, "it may be doubted whether a major goddess, such as Astarte or Asherah, would be duplicated in such a subordinate role."[63] Indeed, despite the compelling arguments that Dever puts forward, his assumption, like the assumption of Keel and Uehlinger, that the goddess of a shrine—say, Asherah—stands beside her sanctuary's doorway to beckon to her devotees and to signal her easy accessibility, seems to me to run counter to much of what we know from the ancient world about how doorways and related entries were perceived. Rather, as Alan M. Cooper and Bernard R. Goldstein especially make clear, while doorways, doorposts, city gates, and other entryways were places associated with the divine presence—consonant with Keel's, Uehlinger's, and Dever's understanding—this renders them as anything but warm and welcoming spaces. Instead, they are locations fraught with all the risks and uncertainties that an unmediated encounter with the divine—even a friendly divine agent—can bring. Cooper and Goldstein thus describe entry spaces in Near Eastern tradition as "liminal," evoking with this term, perhaps, liminal in its most literal sense of a "threshold" (Latin *limen*) that lies, in the cases I am considering here, between our mundane world and the supernatural domain.[64] More significantly, though, Cooper and Goldstein evoke the sense of the liminal as dangerous, as is captured in Mary Douglas's succinct statement, "to have been in the margins [or at the *limen*] is to have been in contact with danger."[65]

What properly stands at the ancient world's liminal junctures, therefore, are not its religious traditions' great and powerful gods, but less potent mediating agents that can negotiate the safety of the human-divine encounter on behalf of either or both parties. For instance, in Exod 12:22–23 (to use the example Cooper and Goldstein cite as the locus classicus of liminal entryways' imperiled nature), the party that requires protection is human—the firstborn of the Israelites—and the mediating agent that negotiates their safety is the blood smeared on the doorposts of Israelite houses.[66] This prompts Yahweh to prohibit the "Destroyer" that otherwise is killing off each Egyptian family's oldest child from entering the Israelites' homes.[67] In sanctified spaces, conversely, it is the deity resident there who needs protection, from, for example, the impurities that humans can carry into the god's holy presence, but also, I would argue, from the same sorts of demonic threats represented by a being such as the "Destroyer" of Exod 12:22–23 or the demon "Sin" that lurks at the door in Gen 4:7.[68] It follows that, no less than the Israelites' homes in Exod 12:22–23, a sanctuary space needs a mediating agent or agents that can safeguard its entryway. These mediating agents can include, I submit, columns that somehow provide security through their "stability" and "strength" (paradigmatically, the Jerusalem temple's Jachin and Boaz, whose very names are derived from the roots *k-w-n*, "to be established, set up, fixed," and *ʿ-z-z*, "to be strong").

They can also include lions, as do model shrines from Tel Rekhesh, Tel Reḥov, and Khirbet el-Qeiyafa, as well as model shrine fragments from Tall al-ʿUmayri, Khirbet ʿAtaruz (probably biblical Ataroth; see Fig. I.1), and the University of Missouri collection.[69] Indeed, even Dever describes these lions as functioning as "*guardians* at the entrance to the *naos* temples [*naos* being the technical name for a model shrine]" (emphasis mine).[70]

Most important for my purposes, though: a model shrine's guardians can include anthropomorphized representations of supernatural beings. These supernatural beings are perhaps, as Zevit writes of the nude goddesses of the Late Bronze or early Iron Age model shrine now in Beirut (see Fig. 12.9), "mythological associates of the particular deity whose shrine was represented."[71] More crucially, I take them to be—as intimated above and as Joel S. Burnett, in a superb study of the entryway's flanking figures, has suggested—"mediating divine figures" whose role is to "mark the boundary between the sacred and profane realms, between the divine and human," and thereby to "oversee and mediate access to the divine."[72]

Burnett, moreover, has stressed that to understand a shrine's divine guardians as "mediating," or as "intermediaries," is to understand them to be, like the entryways they flank, "betwixt and between," or, more simply put, liminal. This can result in rendering these figures as composites that are "betwixt and between" animals and humans in form, like the cherubs—composite animal-bird-human beings—assigned to guard the Garden of Eden in Gen 3:24.[73] Indeed, two of the cherubs' near relative, the sphinx, flank the windowed façade of a model shrine from Iron Age (Stratum IV) Megiddo, thereby serving as the shrine's "betwixt and between" guardians.[74] Similarly, "betwixt and between" guardians can combine male and female characteristics, as on the Tall al-ʿUmayri model shrine, where each figure flanking that shrine's doorway has a small female breast, while the preserved head of the right-hand figure wears a helmet that appears to represent a male soldier's military headgear (see Fig. 12.1).[75] This connotes these figures, as Burnett puts it, "as represent[ing] a crossing of boundaries," or as intermediaries who stand between the two sexes as normatively defined.[76]

But as we learned in Chapter 10, women are liminal not only when they are made part of "betwixt and between" androgynes; rather, women in many societies are liminal as part of the *normal* course of their existence. Moreover, I argued in that discussion that this characterization aptly described ancient Israelite women, including the women of Israelite sites such as ninth-century BCE Reḥov, from which comes the gate-tower clay altar (see Fig. 12.11) that has window openings flanked by what I now maintain are *liminal* female figures that are stationed at an entryway as (to quote again Burnett) "divine intermediaries."[77] As such, they, like the tower to which they are affixed, signify protection. Indeed, just as twinned gate towers at a city gate served actually to guard the entry into an ancient city, the twinned female figures of the Reḥov city-gate altar symbolically guard the boundary between the city's interior and the dangerous world without. They thus protect the city and its god(s) from whatever dangers of the outside world, either human or supernatural, that might otherwise seek to penetrate the city's fortifications.

A characterization of women as liminal is in addition, as I see it, consistent with the way women were conceptualized throughout the ancient Near East and eastern Mediterranean, and this includes the women of sites such as Transjordanian Pella, with its shrinelike object whose doorway is flanked by female figures that again, I argue, play a role as "divine intermediaries" who safeguard the deity (or deities) housed within that shrine's interior from whatever dangers might be introduced from the mundane world that lies without (see Figs. 12.2 and 12.3). Likewise, the female figures that flank the entry of the Late Bronze Age or early Iron Age model shrine housed at the American University of Beirut (see Fig. 12.9); the female figures that flank the entries of the model shrines said to come from Transjordanian Kerak and Mount Nebo (see Figs. 12.10 and 12.12); and the female figures that flank the entryway of one of the model shrines at Ḥorvat Qiṭmit as reconstructed by Beck (see Fig. 12.4) are to be interpreted, I believe, as liminal divine agents who safeguard the deity (or deities) housed within those shrines. Indeed, Sarit Paz proposes that the Kerak figures wear masks, which can be a characteristically liminal form of costume,[78] and pregnancy too—as manifest by the two figures that, according to Beck's reconstruction, flank the entryway of one of the model shrines at Ḥorvat Qiṭmit—is a characteristically liminal state, as it positions a woman (especially a woman pregnant for the first time) "betwixt and between" the states of "not mother" and "mother."

Moreover, Beck, in her reconstruction of this Ḥorvat Qiṭmit shrine, follows Rudolph Henry Dornemann in specifically describing the female figures represented upon the analogues on which she draws—those that flank the entryways of the Beirut and Kerak model shrines, as well as the female figures that flank the entry of the Pella temple model and those that stand on either side of an opening on a cylindrical cult stand from

Megiddo—as "protecting" the object in question.[79] Leila Badre also speaks of the entry of the Kerak model shrine as "guarded" by its flanking female figures.[80] I therefore conclude that as previous commentators have argued, the female figures that flank the entryways of model shrines and their analogues are supernatural beings. But they are not, contrary to most previous interpreters' evaluation, the same supernatural beings envisioned as resident within the shrine. Rather, they are guardian figures that are particularly able—because of their liminal nature—to protect the shrine's divine occupant(s) from the dangers that lurk at its liminally fraught door.[81]

This brings us very close to Exod 38:8 and 1 Sam 2:22, where the "*ṣōbĕʾōt-women . . . ṣābā(ʾ)-ed*" (to use again Propp's rendering) at the entrance to the tent of meeting. Certainly, we have in these texts the same sort of liminally fraught entryway that characterizes the model shrines and these shrines' analogues; indeed, the very subject of the article in which Cooper and Goldstein write of "doorposts, city gates, and entryways of all sorts" as "liminal spaces" is the entrance to the tent of meeting.[82] Certainly, moreover, the repeated use of the root *ṣ-b-ʾ* of the women stationed at the entry, given its military resonances, can easily suggest guardianship. Furthermore, as we saw in Chapter 6, the Priestly, or P tradition of which Exod 38:8 is a part (and from which the 1 Sam 2:22 text seems clearly derived)[83] unambiguously understands the tent of meeting to be the place where Yahweh dwells among the Israelites. Therefore I suggest that in Exod 38:8 and 1 Sam 2:22, women, as paradigmatically liminal beings, are identified as the appropriate *ṣōbĕʾōt,* or guardians, of the liminal threshold of Yahweh's tent shrine, and that 1 Sam 2:22, by associating the *ṣōbĕʾōt* women with the *two* sons of Eli, may especially suggest that a pair of *ṣōbĕʾōt* women were to flank the entrance to the tent of meeting to safeguard it, just as a pair of *ṣōbĕʾōt* guard the entries of certain model shrines and certain of these shrines' analogues.

Yet even though my understanding of the female figures that flank the entryways of model shrines and these shrines' analogues—that they are guardian figures that protect the shrines' divine occupants—brings us very close to the "*ṣōbĕʾōt-women who ṣābā(ʾ)-ed*" of Exod 38:8 and 1 Sam 2:22, a discrepancy remains, for while I have agreed with previous commentators that the model shrines' flanking female figures are supernatural beings, the P authors of Exod 38:8, and likewise those responsible for the derivative tradition found in 1 Sam 2:22, could never admit such a trespass against Yahweh's sole sovereignty. Their *ṣōbĕʾōt* are instead represented as human, as especially can be seen in 1 Sam 2:22, where the *ṣōbĕʾōt* are depicted as the sexual partners of the all-too-human priests of Shiloh, Hophni and Phinehas.

How to explain? One possibility is that in the P account in Exod 38:8, as well as in the derivative reference in 1 Sam 2:22, the *ṣōbĕʾôt* women are deliberately "brought down to earth," so to speak. That is: even as the P authors of Exod 38:8, followed by the author(s) and/or redactors(s) of 1 Sam 2:22, drew on a "guardian goddess" tradition from the southern Levantine world, they moved to demythologize this aspect of their cultural heritage by refashioning the originally divine guardian figures as human.[84] I am more inclined, however, to think that the P authors of Exod 38:8 inserted their reference to the "*ṣōbĕʾôt-women who ṣābā(ʾ)-ed*" without having any awareness that it was to *supernatural* guardian figures that this phrase originally referred. Under the terms of such an account, the "*ṣōbĕʾôt-women who ṣābā(ʾ)-ed*" should be taken as a frozen idiom whose referent was no longer understood by its P users, just as today, we continue to use the idiom "to dial a telephone," although practically no one younger than the age of forty has ever dialed a telephone—and may, in fact, never have seen a telephone with a dial. Similarly (and to take an analogy from the realm of architecture, which might be more appropriate, given that my argument hinges on architectural models of shrine buildings): consider how many contemporary Euro-American houses have a "powder room" near their living room, dining room, or other rooms used for entertaining, even though, unlike gentlemen in the eighteenth century, no guest today needs to excuse himself from a party to repowder his wig. In the twenty-first century, that is, we have totally forgotten the original meaning of the phrase "powder room," even as we continue to use the idiom. What's more, just as we rely on an idiom from two centuries past in speaking of a "powder room," so too does P, in drawing (as I have proposed) on the motif of guardian *ṣōbĕʾôt* that is illustrated by model shrines with flanking females, rely on a tradition that generally predates P by a century or two (the shrines and their analogues predominantly date from the tenth and ninth centuries BCE, and I assume, as discussed in the Introduction, that P's roots lie in the late preexilic period [the late eighth and seventh centuries BCE]). In addition, the P tradition, based in Jerusalem, was geographically removed from the Transjordanian plateau and the Jordan River's northern valley where the model shrines with flanking females are most prevalently represented. As a result P, I suggest, was ignorant of the greater Levantine sensibility that understood that it was *supernatural* female beings who stood guard at shrine entrances. Rather, P used this motif from Israel's cultural orbit to refer to *human* women.

Indeed, note that despite my repeated evocations of Propp's rendering, the "*ṣōbĕʾōt-women who ṣābā(ʾ)-ed*," the noun *nāšîm*, "women," is absent in Exod 38:8. This may well suggest that the idiom regarding the *ṣōbĕʾōt* did not originally refer to human cult servitors, but to supernatural guardian figures. The P tradition then naively applied this older phraseology to its description of *ṣōbĕʾōt* at the entrance to the tent of meeting. Thus does the original supernatural identity of the *ṣōbĕʾōt* disappear, and P's guardian figures become human. Moreover, as we think, in the context of this study, about women cultic agents in ancient Israelite religion, it is important to remember that the Bible's *ṣōbĕʾōt* women are *imaginary* humans, given that the tent of meeting whose entrance the *ṣōbĕʾōt* women safeguard according to my reconstruction is only a product of the literary imagination of the P tradition. That is: the P tradition used the model of the Jerusalem temple, with which it was closely allied, to imagine an antecedent tent of meeting that served as the sanctuary space of the Israelites during their wilderness wanderings (and, according to certain strains of biblical tradition, within the land of Israel before the temple was built). The tent of meeting's form, its furnishings, and its functionaries are in this respect nothing but a fiction.

Still, could not the *ṣōbĕʾōt* of the imaginary antecedent tent be retrojections of actual *ṣōbĕʾōt* who served at the temple in Jerusalem, analogous, say, to the way the tent of meeting's priests are retrojections of the temple's priesthood, or the way in which the bronze stand and basin that the tent of meeting's craftsman, Bezalel, fashioned out of the *ṣōbĕʾōt*'s mirrors in Exod 38:8 are retrojections of the ten bronze stands and basins that flanked the north and south sides of the Jerusalem temple according to 1 Kgs 7:27–38? Possibly, but the fact of the matter is that just as the tent of meeting essentially disappears from the biblical text after the Jerusalem temple is built (see 1 Kgs 8:4), so too do its *ṣōbĕʾōt* disappear, by becoming transformed, like Lot's wife, into pillars—although, in their case, not pillars of salt (Gen 19:26). Rather, the *ṣōbĕʾōt* are transformed into (at best) genderless or the (quite plausibly) male-connoted pillars of Jachin and Boaz that embody "stability" (Jachin) and "strength" (Boaz) and that take over the function of guarding the entryway of Yahweh's earthly home. The conclusion that follows is that while the guardianship function of the *ṣōbĕʾōt* women remains important, the idea that female cult specialists could have responsibility for this role is repudiated.[85] The public face of the temple cult, as represented both "in the sanctuary and in the priesthood," Gale A. Yee argues, was "male."[86] Thus the "*ṣōbĕʾôt-women who ṣābā(ʾ)-ed*" at the tent of meeting's entrance must be replaced in 1 Sam 1:9 by the male priest, Eli, who sat beside the doorpost(s) of Yahweh's temple at Shiloh (see further Chapter 4), and, in Jerusalem, by (again, quite plausibly) masculinized pillars. No actual *ṣōbĕʾôt* women were part of the ancient Israelite cult.

13 "The *Qĕdēšâ* Among the Daughters of Israel": Defining Her Identity Within the Israelite Cult

In Chapter 12, in discussing the *ṣōbĕʾōt* women, I noted that some scholars—because they understand the mirrors in Exod 38:8 as items of self-beautification, and/or because they assign special significance to the 1 Sam 2:22 account of Eli's sons' sexual intercourse with the *ṣōbĕʾōt*—conclude that the *ṣōbĕʾōt* women's function is sexual yet also religious in nature: that they are agents of what is commonly described as "cultic" or "sacred prostitution."[1] As these scholars define it, this institution required of both men and women who had been specially consecrated that they engage in sexual intercourse with worshippers who came to them in a sanctified setting, as an act of imitative or sympathetic magic meant to "emulate," and thereby "stimulate," in the words of Marvin H. Pope, the gods who brought fertility.[2] According also to these commentators, this practice of "cultic" or "sacred prostitution" was widespread throughout the ancient Near East—indeed, so widespread that even scholars who do not interpret Exod 38:8 or 1 Sam 2:22 as referring to "cultic" or "sacred prostitutes" can nevertheless maintain that the tradition was found in Israel, especially among worshippers unduly influenced by allegedly foreign religious practices.

The biblical passage preeminently cited in support of this claim is Hos 4:13–14. Like 1 Sam 2:22, this passage contains both religious and seemingly scurrilous sexual imagery (for example, references in v. 13 to sacrifice and to women who are accused of harlotry and adultery). More important, in v. 14 it refers to Israelite men interacting with "prostitutes" or "harlots" (*zōnôt,* a feminine plural form). Then immediately following in this poetic colon is a description of these men sacrificing with individuals described as *qĕdēšôt,* a feminine plural noun derived from the root *q-d-š,* "consecrated," "sanctified," or "holy," that can most literally be translated as "consecrated women" or "sanctified women." According to the norms that define Hebrew poetry, the two lines of this couplet should be taken as parallel, both in structure and in content, meaning that the second line's *qĕdēšôt* can be taken as somehow related to the first line's *zōnôt.* Thus *qĕdēšôt* can be interpreted as referring to women who are "consecrated" or "sanctified" as prostitutes: that is, as above, women who served as "cultic" or "sacred prostitutes." James Luther Mays summarizes: "Sacred prostitutes (*qĕdēšôt*) are professionals who served as cultic personnel at the shrines where fertility rites were practiced . . . for the sake of the land's fertility."[3]

The terms "prostitute"/"harlot" (*zônâ;* the feminine singular form of *zōnôt*) and *qĕdēšâ* (the feminine singular form of *qĕdēšôt*) also occur in conjunction in Gen 38:15, 21–22—the story of Tamar's disguising herself as a prostitute in order to seduce her father-in-law Judah and become impregnated by him—and in Deut 23:18–19 (in most of the Bible's English versions, 23:17–18). Under the precepts of the "sacred prostitution" interpretation, these concurrences further suggest that the term *qĕdēšâ* refers to a kind of "prostitute" (*zônâ*) who is *qādôš,* or culticly sanctified. Furthermore, the term *qĕdēšâ* appears in conjunction with its masculine counterpart, *qādēš,* in Deut 23:18 (English 23:17), where both the *qĕdēšâ* and the *qādēš* are condemned and, presumably, so the "sacred prostitution" interpretation goes, for the same reason: because both the female *qĕdēšâ* and the male *qādēš* engage in what Deuteronomy's authors deem to be religiously illicit sexual intercourse. From this, it follows that condemnations of the *qādēš* and *qĕdēšîm* (the masculine plural form of *qādēš*) that are found in the kindred Deuteronomistic History, in 1 Kgs 14:24, 15:12, 22:47 (English 22:46), and 2 Kgs 23:7, although these condemnations occur independent of any sexual imagery, are likewise to be taken as references to "cultic" or "sacred prostitutes"—perhaps just male "cultic" or "sacred prostitutes," if we follow slavishly the grammatical gender of *qādēš* and *qĕdēšîm,* or perhaps both male and female, given that Hebrew masculine forms can be used to refer to both male and female subjects. Regardless of how the grammatical intricacies of *qādēš* and *qĕdēšîm* are addressed, however, the terms *qādēš/qĕdēšîm* (masculine) and *qĕdēšâ/qĕdēšôt* (feminine) as found in Gen 38:21–22; Deut 23:18 (English 23:17); 1 Kgs 14:24, 15:12, 22:47 (English 22:46); 2 Kgs 23:7; and Hos 4:13–14 are commonly taken to refer to some sort of sexual-religious functionaries.

This understanding is reflected, for example, in many translations of the Bible, including some of its most recent: the 1985 and 1999 NJPS versions, the 1985 NJB, the 1989 REB, the 1989 NRSV, and the 2011 NABRE.

Already in 1973, however, scholars had begun to question whether "cultic" or "sacred prostitution" really existed in Israel, or at least whether it existed among Israel's ancient Near Eastern neighbors, especially in Mesopotamia.[4] Doubts arose, at least in part, because the major source that indicates the institution's Mesopotamian presence—an account offered by the Greek historian Herodotus (*Histories* 1, 199) regarding the Ishtar temple in Babylon—is so compromised in nature.[5] For example, although Herodotus wrote during the fifth century BCE, the Babylonian tradition he purports to describe dates, according to the *Histories,* from the century before and thus from a period very different from Herodotus's day, during which the Persians dominated Babylon. Moreover, the custom of "cultic" or "sacred prostitution" that Herodotus reports is not "cultic" or "sacred prostitution" as it is generally understood—an institution to which some men and women are specially and permanently, or at least semipermanently, consecrated—but instead a once-in-a-lifetime event of ritual intercourse in which every Babylonian woman must engage to "[make] herself holy in the goddess's sight."[6]

More damning still is the fact that Herodotus's report in the *Histories* is unabashedly tendentious in nature: he begins, for example, by speaking of "the *foulest* Babylonian custom . . ." (emphasis mine).[7] He thereby signals that his purpose is not necessarily accurate reportage but culturally driven denigration, as he seeks to confirm to his Greek audience that the Babylonians are, in fact, the heinous "barbarians" that the Greeks think them to be.[8] Thus he can, in the words of Robert A. Oden, "contrast . . . civilized Greece and the bizarre East," and so, according to Tikva Frymer-Kensky, "prov[e] the superiority of the Greeks."[9] Or, at a minimum, in the passage we are considering, Herodotus aims to prove the superiority of the Persians vis-à-vis the Babylonians. Thus he can "excogitate a distinctive niche for Babylon in his cabinet of ways to be un-Greek," in order to explain "how Cyrus' Persia conquered and supplanted it."[10] "Father of History" or no, what Herodotus offers in *Histories* 1, 199 cannot be taken as good historical data.

Indeed, "no cuneiform [that is, indigenously Mesopotamian] text supports the idea that the women of Assyria or Babylon" performed the act of "sacred prostitution" that Herodotus claims.[11] Nor does the indigenous evidence evinced by those who would repudiate the extremes of Herodotus's position, while still laying claim to a more authentically Mesopotamian form of "cultic" or "sacred prostitution," stand up to close scrutiny.[12] Most important, the fairly rich corpus of Mesopotamian texts that pertain to the *qadištu* women (*qadištu* being the term cognate to Hebrew *qĕdēšâ*) gives no indication that these women were agents of "cultic" or "sacred prostitution." Rather, the *qadištu* woman is one whose sexual activities are carefully circumscribed, either because she was married or because she was celibate.[13]

If married, moreover, the *qadištu* was more associated with "the task of procreation and nurture" than she was with her sexual relationship with her husband.[14] More specifically, according to both Babylonian and Assyrian texts that span the second and first millennium BCE, as well as older third-millennium BCE Sumerian texts, the *qadištu* (or, in Sumerian, the *nu-gig*) is commonly associated with childbirth and wet-nursing.[15] For example, in the Old Babylonian "Epic of Atrahasis" (Tablet I, lines 290–91), the *qadištu* woman appears, together with the midwife, in a line just before a description of "the pregnant woman giving birth." The *qadištu* also can be closely (although not exclusively) associated with the god Adad, whose sister Bēlet-ilī was the goddess of childbirth. According to ritual texts from the Middle Assyrian period of Mesopotamian history (1366–1077 BCE), for instance, "the *qadištu*-woman officiated in the Adad cult in Assur," through, among other acts, making meal and purification offerings and "inton[ing] the *inhu*-chant."[16] Likewise, the *qadištu* can appear in Old Babylonian texts as a votary of Adad in his temples in the cities of Kish and Sippar.[17]

Concerning Mesopotamia, therefore, Joan Goodnick Westenholz concludes that while *qadištu* women were known to have special relationships with certain deities and took responsibility for certain religious obligations (sometimes on behalf of these deities), the notion that these obligations ever included "sacred prostitution" stems from "an amalgam of misconceptions, presuppositions, and inaccuracies."[18] So too, Westenholz concludes, are any claims made about "sacred prostitution" at the northern Levantine city-state of Ugarit during the Late Bronze Age (ca. 1550–1200 BCE) misconceived and inaccurate. There, the term *qdšm* (cognate to the Hebrew masculine plural form *qĕdēšîm*) occasionally occurs (there are, incidentally, no male analogues to the *qadištu* women found in Mesopotamian sources). There are also two references in the Ugaritic corpus to *qdšt* (cognate to the Hebrew feminine singular form *qĕdēšâ* or perhaps the Hebrew feminine plural form *qĕdēšôt*). These Ugaritic *qdšt* references, however, are found in clan names, and so little can be deduced from them.[19] Conversely, the Ugaritic *qdšm*—as the root meaning of *q-d-š*, "holy," "sanctified," or "consecrated," suggests—can be described as some sort of religious functionaries, and perhaps fairly important functionaries within the religious hierarchy. This is indicated by the five instances where they show up in administrative texts, listed immediately following the *khnm* (the tradition's major priests). It is also indicated by passages within these same texts in which the *qdšm* are accorded the same privileges and assume some of the same civic (although not necessarily religious) obligations as the *khnm*.[20] On the basis of our sources, it is difficult to say, however, just what religious obligations might fall to the *qdšm*, although in one ritual text (*KTU* 1.112.21), a *qdš* functions as a singer during a sacrificial rite over which *khnm* presumably preside.[21] None of these sources, however, associates the *qdšm* with any sort of sexual role within the Ugaritic cult.[22]

What, then, of the Israelite *qĕdēšîm* and *qĕdēšôt* to whom these Ugaritic *qdšm* and Mesopotamian *qadištu* women are at least etymologically kindred? Arguably, the Israelite *qĕdēšîm* and *qĕdēšôt* and the Ugaritic *qdšm* and Mesopotamian *qadištu* women are religiously kindred as well. As already noted, the root form of the Hebrew terms *qĕdēšîm* and *qĕdēšôt*, *q-d-š*, means "consecrated," "sanctified," or "holy," suggesting that the work of the Israelite *qĕdēšîm* and *qĕdēšôt* is sanctified in nature. It is also the case that of the eight biblical texts in which the terms *qādēš*/*qĕdēšîm* (masculine) and *qĕdēšâ*/*qĕdēšôt* (feminine) occur, four are blatantly religious in terms of their larger setting (1 Kgs 14:24, 15:12; 2 Kgs 23:7; Hos 4:13–14), and two others (Deut 23:18 [English 23:17] and 1 Kgs 22:47 [English 22:46]) are reasonably interpreted as having a religious referent as well: Deut 23:18 (English 23:17) is "linked editorially with the following verse," which concerns matters of temple administration,[23] and 1 Kgs 22:47 (English 22:46) refers back to the religiously inflected 1 Kgs 15:12. In addition, even though Gen 38:21–22 apparently stands independent of a religious context or setting, I argue below that religious allusions may be in play in the text. Unfortunately, the eighth and final passage in which the *qĕdēšîm* appear, Job 36:14, is so hopelessly enigmatic (as, indeed, are huge chunks of the book of Job) that it is impossible to incorporate it in any sort of analysis.[24]

More important: just as the cultic responsibilities of the Mesopotamian *qadištu* women and the Ugaritic *qdšm* cannot be described in sexual terms, so too the role of the Israelite *qādēš*/*qĕdēšîm* and *qĕdēšâ*/*qĕdēšôt*—although seemingly to be regarded as religious—cannot be said to be sexual. Indeed, as my previous comments have again indicated, only three of the seven biblical texts in which the terms *qādēš/qĕdēšîm* and *qĕdēšâ/qĕdēšôt* occur (I exclude here the basically unintelligible text of Job 36:14) have any sexually related imagery: Gen 38:21–22, Deut 23:18–19 (English 23:17–18), and Hos 4:13–14. Moreover, the Hosea passage is so sexually charged that it must, like Herodotus's description of sixth-century BCE Babylon and like several of the texts associating women with magic that I discussed in Chapter 11, be read as "polemic run amok"—an overwrought attempt to use the language of sexual licentiousness to denigrate, deride, and humiliate Israelites who engage in religious practices of which Hosea disapproves.[25] Which is to say: the term *zōnôt,* "prostitutes," is used metaphorically in Hos 4:13–14 in order for the prophet to accuse those who commit apostasy in his eyes of "whoring" after other gods. It follows that all that is revealed in the Hos 4:13–14 juxtaposition of *zōnôt* and *qĕdēšôt* is that the cultic activities of the *qĕdēšôt* are viewed by Hosea as religiously inappropriate. To characterize the nature of the inappropriateness as "cultic" or "sacred prostitution" goes beyond what our evidence allows.

Phyllis Bird has in addition noted that the idea of *male* cult prostitutes (*qādēš/qĕdēšîm*), as some see in Deut 23:18 (English 23:17); 1 Kgs 14:24, 15:12, 22:47 (English 22:46); and 2 Kgs 23:7, makes no sense in Israel, given Israelite sexual mores and the rationale of a presumed fertility cult. For example, Israelite sexual mores, while they could conceivably allow for rituals in which female "cultic prostitutes" engaged in intercourse with men who came to sacred precincts to lie with them, could not possibly countenance the opposite: that women, whose sexuality, unlike men's, was rigidly controlled to protect the integrity of a man's patriline, could come to a sanctuary to lie with male "cultic prostitutes" who were not their husbands. The occasionally proposed alternative, that the male *qādēš/qĕdēšîm* engaged in male-male sexual encounters, likewise "has no place," in Bird's words, "in a fertility cult," as "it fails to support, and in fact threatens, the primary symbolism of the cult (as commonly reconstructed), which centers in the union of male and female."[26] The idea of cult prostitutes in sanctuary settings, whether male or female, also makes no sense if we presume that the purity dictates regarding seminal emissions and menstrual discharge articulated in Leviticus and related biblical texts were actually operative at some point in Israelite history and within some circles of Israelite society, including (as I have argued in Chapter 6) the preexilic period on which this book is focused.

But if not agents of sexual intercourse, then what do the *qĕdēšîm* and *qĕdēšôt* do? The most honest answer is that we do not know, and this may be because the Israelite *qĕdēšîm* and *qĕdēšôt* did not have an explicitly defined religious function (as may also be the case, on the basis of the information available to us, concerning the *qdšm* at Ugarit). Still, I am intrigued by the fact that of the seven biblical texts in which the terms *qādēš*/*qĕdēšîm* and *qĕdēšâ*/*qĕdēšôt* appear (excluding, again, the enigmatic Job 36:14), four have either explicit or implicit references to the worship of the mother goddess Asherah.[27] The verse that immediately precedes the 1 Kgs 14:24 reference to the *qĕdēšîm*, for example, describes how the peoples of the Southern Kingdom of Judah had erected *'ăšērîm* or "asherah images" in their land. These asherah images, as noted in Chapter 5, are wooden, pole-shaped icons that represented the trees commonly associated with Asherah in both Canaanite and Israelite tradition.[28] I further noted in Chapter 5 that like her countrymen according to 1 Kgs 14:23, Ma'acah, the queen mother (*gĕbîrâ*) of King Asa of Judah, is said to have made an Asherah icon in 1 Kgs 15:13—an action reported to be so offensive to Asa that he removed her from the position of *gĕbîrâ*. What we can add here is that "in the same breath," so to speak, in 1 Kgs 15:12, Asa removed all the *qĕdēšîm* from his land. That is: in both 1 Kgs 14:23–24 and 1 Kgs 15:12–13, *qĕdēšîm* and asherah images—which is to say, *qĕdēšîm* and the goddess Asherah—are closely linked.

The link is even closer in 2 Kgs 23:7, a passage I also mentioned in Chapter 5. There, women said to be weaving for Asherah (probably manufacturing garments that are somehow to be draped over the goddess's tree-shaped asherah image)[29] are described as doing this work in the houses of the *qĕdēšîm* that stood within the Jerusalem temple compound. Less explicit is the connection between Asherah worship and the *qĕdēšôt* in Hos 4:13–14. Still, the site of the religious activities that Hosea condemns in this passage, including the religious activities involving the *qĕdēšôt*, is "on mountain tops," "on hills," and "under oak, styrax tree, and terebinth," which is much the same as the site "on every high hill and under every green tree" that 1 Kgs 14:23, among other passages (Deut 12:2–3, 2 Kgs 17:10, Jer 17:2), associates with *'ăšērîm* or "asherah images." Moreover, the "oak" and "terebinth" trees that Hosea mentions seem closely tied to Asherah worship, given that their names—*'allôn*, "oak," and *'ēlâ*, "terebinth"—are linked etymologically to one of Asherah's well-known epithets at the northern Levantine city-state of Ugarit, Elat (*'lt*), a name that simply means "goddess." In fact, the Hebrew term *'ēlâ* and Ugaritic *'lt*/Elat are etymologically identical.

Asherah is also referred to at Ugarit, as well as elsewhere within the ancient Near Eastern world, by the epithet Qudšu (Qudshu). At Ugarit, for example, the pantheon of gods can be called the *bn qdš*, the "children of Qudšu,"[30] just as they can be called the *bn il,* the "children of El." This is because all of the deities of the pantheon (even those who are described in the tradition as being born of different parents) belong metaphorically to the divine entourage headed by El as the father of the gods and his consort Asherah, the divine mother. Certain humans, too—for example, the epic hero King Kirta—can be metaphorically denoted as the son of the god El (Kirta is described, for example, using the epithet *bn il,* "son of El"), and Kirta is also called *šph ltpn wqdš,* "the offspring of *ltpn* and *qdš*" (*KTU* 1.16.1.10–11, 21–22). The term *ltpn* is typically taken as an El epithet meaning "the Compassionate One," and many scholars also take *qdš* to be an El epithet that means "the Holy One" (as have I in the past).[31] But I am now more inclined to take *qdš* as referring to El's consort, Asherah/Qudšu, who serves as metaphorical divine mother to Kirta in the same way El serves as metaphorical divine father.[32] These Ugaritic materials in turn suggest that a Nineteenth Dynasty (1292–1190 BCE) plaque from Egypt showing a goddess who is identified as "Qudšu, the beloved of Ptah" represents Asherah.[33] So too should a similar Egyptian stele that reads "Qudšu, lady of the sky and mistress of all the gods" be taken as representing Asherah.[34] Indeed, both these representations show the goddess Qudšu standing astride a lion, which I noted in Chapter 12 is the animal with which Asherah is characteristically associated.[35] Thereby, we can suggest that the goddess depicted standing atop a lion on an Egyptian plaque from the collection of Winchester College, dated to the Nineteenth (1292–1190 BCE) or Twentieth (1190–1075 BCE) Dynasty, although identified as a composite deity Qudšu-Astarte-Anat, is in fact Asherah/Qudšu.[36]

In the light of all of these data, I suggest—as already indicated—that there may be a connection between Asherah/Qudšu and the Israelite *qĕdēšîm* and *qĕdēšôt.* Does Hosea imagine, for example, that *qĕdēšôt* are present to participate in sacrifices "on mountain tops," "on hills," and "under oak, styrax tree, and terebinth" because these spaces—and especially the spaces "under oak, styrax tree, and terebinth"—are locales where the patron goddess of the *qĕdēšôt,* Asherah/Qudšu, is being worshipped? Do the women who weave for Asherah in 2 Kgs 23:7 work within the houses of the *qĕdēšîm* because these *qĕdēšim* are religious functionaries responsible for the upkeep and well-being of the Asherah/Qudšu cult that was present in the Jerusalem temple compound during the time chronicled in the 2 Kings 23 passage? Does Asa simultaneously depose the *'ăšērâ*-making Ma'acah and the *qĕdēšîm* in 1 Kgs 15:12–13 because the acts of Asherah worship engaged in by the former are at one with the religious practices of the latter? Are *'ăšērîm*, or "asherah images," and *qĕdēšîm* said to be in the land of Judah at the same time in 1 Kgs 14:23–24 because they are closely associated with one another?

Moreover, does associating the *qĕdēšîm* and *qĕdēšôt* with the cult of Asherah help explain the vehemence and vigor with which both *qĕdēšîm* and *qĕdēšôt* can be denounced in biblical sources? In a 1987 study of the cult of Asherah in ancient Israel, Saul M. Olyan argued that the worship of Asherah enjoyed wide-scale acceptance during the preexilic period, in both the Northern Kingdom and the South and among both political and religious aristocrats (kings and priests) and the populace at large, because these devotees considered Asherah to be the consort of the Israelite god Yahweh.[37] The evidence (both textual and archaeological) that Olyan cites in support of this conclusion has also been catalogued by many other scholars (myself included),[38] and I will not rehearse it here. Rather, what is important for my purposes is Olyan's argument that the notable exceptions to this wide-scale acceptance of the Asherah cult in preexilic Israel were those who were adherents of Deuteronomic and Deuteronomistic tradition or those who were heavily influenced by Deuteronomic/Deuteronomistic theology. As he writes, "anti-asherah polemic in the Hebrew Bible . . . is restricted to the Deuteronomistic History or to materials which betray the influence of deuteronomistic language and theology."[39]

For example, from the book of Deuteronomy, we can cite Deut 16:21 and its ringing denunciation of those who would erect an *'ăšērâ* or "asherah image": "You shall not plant for yourself as an *'ăšērâ* any tree beside the altar of Yahweh, your God." From the related Deuteronomistic History, we can note 1 Kgs 16:33, where the statement that King Ahab of the Northern Kingdom of Israel erected an *'ăšērâ* (seemingly in his capital city of Samaria) is followed immediately by the claim that "Ahab did more to anger Yahweh, the God of Israel, than had all the kings of Israel before him." Among texts influenced by Deuteronomic and/or Deuteronomistic theology, Olyan cites the prose sections of the book of Jeremiah, whose affinities with Deuteronomic and/or Deuteronomistic theology are well known.[40] It thus comes as no surprise to find Asherah worship condemned in Jer 17:2. Olyan also argues that the condemnations of Asherah worship found in Exod 34:13–14; Isa 17:8, 27:9; and Mic 5:13 (in most of the Bible's English versions, 5:14) betray Deuteronomic and/or Deuteronomistic influence.[41]

In terms of the thesis I am pursuing here—the possible understanding of the *qĕdēšîm* and *qĕdēšôt* as Asherah cult functionaries—Olyan's hypothesis neatly explains why we find these individuals so harshly condemned in Deut 23:18 (English 23:17) and their existence likewise excoriated (although not in such vehement terms) in the Deuteronomistic History, in 1 Kgs 14:24, 15:12, 22:47 (English 22:46), and 2 Kgs 23:7.[42] I also think the denigration of the *qĕdēšôt* in Hos 4:13–14 is well explained by Olyan's work, although Olyan himself would seemingly not agree, as he counts Hosea as among the biblical sources accepting of Asherah worship.[43] Like Jeremiah, however, Hosea is well known for his theological affinities with Deuteronomic thought: Hosea's ideology regarding kingly authority, for example, is often described as closely kindred to the mandates that constrain royal power in Deut 17:14–20. Hosea, moreover, shares with Deuteronomic thought the sense that Israelite worship at hilltop sanctuaries and "under every green tree" (to use the language of the Deuteronomistic cliché) is anathema; in fact, in an essay titled "Hosea and Deuteronomy," Moshe Weinfeld specifically cites affinities between Deut 12:2 ("You must destroy completely all the [worship] sites . . . on the mountain tops, on the hills, and under every green tree") and the first verse of the Hosea passage that has been a focus of my attention in this discussion, Hos 4:13, and its condemnations of hilltop worship and worship under terebinths, styrax trees, and oaks.[44]

What's more, immediately following the Deut 12:2 condemnation of the worship sites on hilltops and under green trees is a condemnation of an *'ăšērâ* image. Likewise, I have suggested there are allusions to Asherah worship—and allusions that judge this worship unfavorably—in Hos 4:13–14 in conjunction with condemnations of hilltop worship sites and worship under certain luxuriantly leafy trees. I suggest, then, that although there are no explicit mentions of Asherah worship in Hosea (on this point, Olyan is quite correct),[45] Hosea nevertheless shares the Deuteronomic school's antipathy toward the goddess's cult. It should further follow that as Hosea shares the Deuteronomic aversion toward Asherah worship, he shares (under the terms of my analysis) the Deuteronomic aversion toward the *qĕdēšîm* and *qĕdēšôt* as Asherah cult functionaries. Ergo, the *qĕdēšôt* are treated as objects of scorn in Hos 4:14, and, as a result, the interpretation that I have proposed—that the *qĕdēšîm* and *qĕdēšôt* in Deut 23:18 (English 23:17); 1 Kgs 14:24, 15:12, 22:47 (English 22:46); 2 Kgs 23:7; and Hos 4:14 are Asherah cult functionaries—stands as a coherent whole.

What, though, about the Bible's remaining reference to *qĕdēšîm* and *qĕdēšôt,* the labeling of Tamar as a *qĕdēšâ* in Gen 38:21–22? If a *qĕdēšâ* is not a cult (or some other kind of) prostitute, then how is the conjunction of the terms *qĕdēšâ* and *zônâ* in this text to be explained? I have to admit, I do not have a clear sense, and other scholars also struggle to provide a convincing exegesis. Frymer-Kensky, for example, suggests that although the terms *zônâ,* "prostitute"/"harlot," and *qĕdēšâ* seem positioned as synonyms in Gen 38:15 and 21–22, what makes them synonymous is not a mode of sexual practice that the *zônâ* and *qĕdēšâ* have in common, but the fact that both stand outside normal family or household structure and as such are vulnerable to men's sexual approaches.[46] Westenholz somewhat similarly argues that because the Mesopotamian *qadištu,* and, by analogy, the Israelite *qĕdēšâ,* did not belong to an organized household, her social location was defined to be the street, which is also the location associated with the *zônâ;* hence, while "Tamar pretended to be a prostitute standing in the street," she "could also be mistaken for a *qadištu*-woman in that location."[47] Bird likewise proposes that while a *qĕdēšâ* is not a prostitute, the term can be used as a euphemism for *zônâ* because the two "may share some important characteristics," which, in Bird's account, might "includ[e] sexual intercourse with strangers."[48] In his Anchor Yale Bible commentary on Genesis, E. A. Speiser evokes an explanation based on euphemism as well. More specifically, Speiser suggests that while Judah slept with Tamar in Gen 38:18 believing her to be (as in 38:15) a *zônâ,* "prostitute," Judah's comrade Hirah, when he returned to the site of the sexual encounter in 38:20–21 to make payment to Tamar on Judah's behalf, covered up for his friend's peccadilloes by pretending to those to whom he spoke, asking for Tamar, that the kid that Judah had sent to her as compensation was to be given not to a *zônâ,* but to a *qĕdēšâ* as a sacrifice.[49]

Clearly, Gen 38:15, 21–22 defies easy explanation. Still, despite having indicated above that I, too, have no ironclad interpretation to offer, I nevertheless propose to add a suggestion to the mix, and one that tries to move beyond the confines of the three verses in Genesis 38 in which the terms *zônâ* and *qĕdēšâ* appear to consider these terms' resonance within the larger story. I begin by noting the circumstances that, in the story's conceit, led to Tamar's act of prostitution: she, having been twice widowed, first by the eldest son of Judah, Er, and then by Er's younger brother, Onan, without in either case having borne a son, remains obligated, under the terms of Israel's law of the levir, to marry her deceased husbands' surviving brother, Judah's third and youngest son, Shelah, and bear by him a son who would be counted as Er's. Thus this son would promulgate Er's otherwise extinguished patriline. Judah, however, has resisted marrying Tamar to Shelah, as he has already lost two sons to such nuptials. Thus Tamar—trapped in a commitment to marry Shelah that will never lead to resolution—decides to take matters into her own hands, by disguising herself as a *zônâ* and presenting herself at a time when and in a place where she knows Judah will be sure to encounter her. Her goal is that he will lie with her and father the son that she, according to levirate law, is obligated to bear. And Judah does indeed encounter Tamar as she intends and contracts for her services, by promising he will later send to her a kid from his flock. They then have intercourse, and she conceives (we subsequently learn) twin sons, who are delivered in Gen 38:27–30. In the interim, Judah's emissary, Hirah, returns to the site of the sexual union to attempt to deliver payment on Judah's behalf to the woman he calls a *qĕdēšâ.*

As I just noted, Tamar's motivation in lying with Judah was, in a sense, retrospective—a look back to the death of her husband Er and an attempt to bear for him, after the fact, the son that Israelite social convention ideally would have had her bear during Er's lifetime. The biblical authors' motivation for telling us Tamar's story, however, is prospective: they look forward from the birth of Tamar's son Perez (the twin who forces his way past his brother Zeraḥ to emerge from the womb first) to Perez's son, then grandson, then great-grandson, and so on, to the seventh generation of great-grandsons, the youngest of whom is the great king of biblical tradition, David (1 Sam 16:6–13, Ruth 4:18–22). From the biblical writers' point of view, Tamar thus acts not to promulgate the line of Er, but to establish the line of David. Tamar in this respect could be described as a foreshadowing of, and even as the founding queen mother within the Davidic royal line, to the extent that she might be said to represent, metaphorically and proleptically, David's queen mother (and we might recall in this regard, as we saw concerning Ma'acah in Chapter 5, that the queen mother or *gĕbîrâ* need not be the actual biological mother of a king).

I also argued in Chapter 5 that the queen mothers of Judah (and one notes here David's Judahite ancestry) played a special religious role within their sons' courts, serving as the human representative or even the earthly counterpart of the goddess Asherah. To this end, I suggested, the queen mother Ma'acah made an Asherah icon for her divine patron (1 Kgs 15:13), and likewise it might have been some queen mother in the seventh century BCE who stationed a group of women weavers in the Jerusalem temple compound to make "garments" to drape over the *'ăšērâ* or "asherah image" that stood in the temple's grounds (2 Kgs 23:7). These two incidents I have also cited earlier in this chapter, as each associates Asherah worship with the *qĕdēšîm:* in 1 Kgs 15:12–13, King Asa deposes both the *qĕdēšîm* and Ma'acah, on account of her Asherah icon, and in 2 Kgs 23:7, it is in the houses of the *qĕdēšîm* in which the women who weave on Asherah's behalf do their work.

As in 1 Kgs 15:12–13 and 2 Kgs 23:7, so too in Genesis 38? That is, if I am correct to view Tamar in Genesis 38 as a metaphorical *gĕbîrâ* from the biblical writers' point of view, could this explain the shift in language from *zônâ* in Gen 38:15 to *qĕdēšâ* in Gen 38:21–22? In Gen 38:18, after Judah lies with Tamar, the story's audience is told what even Tamar herself cannot yet know: that she has conceived. An Israelite audience, moreover (or at least an audience generally familiar with its own historical traditions), would surely appreciate what Tamar's pregnancy meant for the future of the Davidic monarchy. Do the biblical authors thus give a nod to their audience's "insider knowledge" by having Judah's friend Hirah—when he comes to Tamar to deliver payment of the agreed-upon kid—refer to her as a *qĕdēšâ,* that is, as a functionary of Asherah, kindred to the sort of functionary that the Davidic *gĕbîrâ* will be in the monarchy-to-come?

According to this reading, Gen 38:18 is transformative for Tamar, in that she conceives her twin sons and thus begins to embody her metaphorical role as the Davidic line's proleptic, or even founding *gĕbîrâ.* Yet to become a *gĕbîrâ* is simultaneously to become a special devotee of Asherah. So too the *qĕdēšâ,* I have argued, is dedicated to the Asherah cult. Hence Hirah in Gen 38:21–22 is made to call Tamar a *qĕdēšâ* by the story's authors, not to gloss the term *zônâ* by which she has earlier, in 38:15, been described, but to gloss the identity of proleptic *gĕbîrâ* that through her pregnancy (38:18), she has assumed.

Epilogue

In Chapters 10–11 of the apocryphal/deuterocanonical book of Judith, Judith, the book's title character, enacts a ruse to gain the favor of the Assyrian general Holofernes, who is besieging her town of Bethulia. Her strategy is twofold: first, she puts on fine clothes, anoints herself with precious oils, and bedecks her body with abundant jewelry, so that Holofernes's soldiers will be seduced by her looks and take her into Holofernes's camp (Jdt 10:3–10). Then, once she is brought into Holofernes's presence, she claims to be Holofernes's ally by declaring herself dismayed by her countrymen's response to Assyria's siege, as the Israelites propose (according to Judith's account) to augment their food supply, which is running out, by "kill[ing] their livestock" and using these animals for food, even though this is something "God by his laws has forbidden them to eat." The besieged Bethulians, Judith goes on to say, also propose "to consume the first fruits of the grain, and the tithes of the wine and oil," which otherwise had been "consecrated and set aside for the priests" (Jdt 11:12–13, NRSV).

These sins will cause God, still according to Judith's report, to withdraw the deity's blessings from Bethulia so that Holofernes will be able to capture the town. Judith indicates, moreover, that she will be able to determine for Holofernes precisely when the people's sinful use of consecrated foodstuffs and the consequent withdrawing of God's protective oversight will occur, by going out from the Assyrian camp every night to pray and receive God's revelation. "He will tell me," she says, "when they have committed their sins" (Jdt 11:17, NRSV). In the conceit of the ruse, this "going forth" is of strategic significance, for it sets the stage for Judith to achieve her true objective: to assassinate Holofernes and then successfully escape by leaving the Assyrian camp in the evening in the usual way, only this time with the deliverance of her people assured.

Yet whatever the strategic considerations that motivate Judith's ruse, the book of Judith makes clear that, in many respects, the ways in which she presents herself to Holofernes are in fact intrinsic to her character. According to Jdt 8:7, for example, Judith was indeed "beautiful in appearance," and the succeeding verse reports that just as she told Holofernes, she did in truth "fear God with great devotion" (NRSV). Many other verses in the book also speak to Judith's piety. For example, Jdt 8:4 tells us that Judith had, at the time of Holofernes's attack on Bethulia, been widowed for some time—three years and four months—and during all that time, according to Jdt 8:5, she had scrupulously observed at least one of the standards that earlier Israelite tradition had defined for mourners: the wearing of sackcloth.[1] During the day, she also fasted as part of her mourning ritual, except—according to Jdt 8:6—on "the day before the sabbath and the sabbath itself, the day before the new moon and the day of the new moon, and the festivals and days of rejoicing of the house of Israel" (NRSV). On these days, presumably, Judith participated in the celebratory festivities as Israelite tradition required.

Further evidence of Judith's piety is found in Jdt 8:9–27, where, after Judith protests the plan of Bethulia's elders to surrender to Holofernes, Uzziah, who is seemingly the head of the elders' council, affirms she is "God-fearing" (Jdt 8:31). Uzziah then exhorts her to pray for rain, so that at least Bethulia's cisterns will be filled and the people will have water. And, in Jdt 9:2–14, Judith does pray, although not for rain, but for God's help in her more ambitious plan to deceive Holofernes and kill him. This is one of the several instances of women's prayer in apocryphal/deuterocanonical and New Testament texts that I catalogued in Chapter 4.

Judith also, in Jdt 16:19, is said to dedicate the canopy from Holofernes's bedchamber, which she had taken after she had assassinated him, as a "votive offering" to God (NRSV). The use here of the term "votive" implies that Judith had earlier made a vow to give the deity such a donation, in exchange, presumably, for God's aid in carrying out her plan to deliver her people. Just so are women, as we again saw in Chapter 4, frequently said to make vows where they promise to give to God some gift or service in exchange for God's providing the boon or favor for which the petitioner has asked. Moreover, in Jdt 12:1–2, 7–9, Judith observes various purity rites somewhat similar to those I discussed in Chapter 6. In her case, these rites involve careful adherence to Jewish dietary laws and a commitment to eating only foods classified as "clean"—and hence she brings her own food with her to Holofernes's camp when she allows herself to be captured, rather than eating of the "delicacies" that Holofernes serves her (Jdt 12:1, NRSV). She also bathes daily as a purification ritual.

In addition, in Jdt 15:13–14 and 16:1–17, Judith is said to join with other women in dancing, playing frame drums, and singing a victory song to celebrate the Bethulians' (and God's) victory in their struggle against Holofernes, just as in Chapter 9, we saw Miriam, Deborah, the daughter of Jephthah, and other women of Israel singing, dancing, and/or playing frame drums to celebrate Israelite victories in holy war. Indeed, like Miriam in Exod 15:20–21 and Deborah in Judg 5:1–31, Judith is said (in Jdt 16:1) to give voice to the hymn that celebrates God's and the Israelites' triumph over the Assyrians.

Thus, although the book of Judith is a late text within the biblical corpus (second–first century BCE),[2] and so well beyond the preexilic purview of my analysis, Judith can nevertheless be said to exemplify in many respects the means by which preexilic women asserted themselves as ritual agents: by offering prayers and making vows (Chapter 4); by maintaining standards of ritual purity (Chapter 6); by observing key events in the Israelite ritual calendar—the Sabbath, the day of the new moon, and the other festival days of the religious year (Chapters 7–8); by participating in mourning rituals and in a victory song celebration (Chapter 9); and even—if we were to take Judith's words to Holofernes in Jdt 11:17 seriously—by claiming a position as a prophet (Chapter 10). After all, Judith anticipates in that discourse that she will hear the word of God revealed to her during prayer and will in turn reveal it to a male leader (in Judith's case, Holofernes, the head of the Assyrian army), just as Deborah and Hulda, say, revealed God's word to, respectively, Barak and Josiah.

Yet it is equally important to note that Judith exemplifies in many respects the constraints I have argued were placed on preexilic women in their exercise of religious agency. For example, she is presented, like the women of preexilic times, as someone whose access to public sanctuary space is limited. Note in this regard that although Judith is said in Jdt 8:6 to keep the Sabbath, the day of the new moon, and the other festival days of the Israelite ritual calendar regularly and seemingly with meticulous attention to these days' proper observance, Jdt 10:2 implies that she does this at home (this verse refers to Judith's "house where she lived on sabbaths and on her festal days" [NRSV], as opposed to the tent on this house's roof where Judith—as part of her mourning rituals of self-deprivation—normally dwelt). Also telling is Judith 9, the passage in which Judith prays to God, asking the deity to abet her in her attempts to deliver her people. The setting is her home in Bethulia, but Jdt 9:1 describes her prayer as taking place "at the very time" when the evening incense that was part of the daily offering "was being offered in the house of God in Jerusalem" (NRSV). During this ritual moment in the Israelite calendar (on which see also Exod 30:8 and Num 28:1–8), Judith's opportunity for religious self-expression is thus affirmed. Still, she is far from the primary locus of the ritual's observance, and she is alone.

To be sure, Judith, in 9:1, could hardly be in Jerusalem for the offering of the evening incense, given that her village is under siege. However, elsewhere in the book of Judith, in Jdt 16:18–20, she is said to accompany all of the people of Bethulia on a visit to Jerusalem—and more specifically, given v. 18's stress on worship, burnt offerings, and freewill offerings, to the Jerusalem temple. Verse 20 confirms that in Jerusalem, Bethulia's inhabitants were "feasting . . . before the sanctuary," or the temple, and that they stayed there (rather astonishingly) "for three months" (NRSV).

Let us consider the chronology of this visit a little more carefully, and to begin, let us return to Jdt 8:2–3 and the notice that Judith's husband Manasseh had died when he was overcome by heatstroke during the course of the barley harvest. The barley harvest, we know from our discussion in Chapter 8, was associated with the festival of Maṣṣot, and we further know, from that same chapter, that Maṣṣot is said to begin—at least according to priestly authored sources (Lev 23:6, Num 28:17)—on the fifteenth day of the first month in the spring, or on the first full moon day following the vernal equinox. The vernal equinox, we have further noted, occurs on about March 20 according to our calendar, so let us say that by our reckoning, Manasseh died somewhere, roughly, between April 4 and 11 (that is, at some point during the seven-day period of the Maṣṣot celebration, were the full moon day to come as early as possible after the equinox). In Jdt 8:4, Judith is then said to have mourned for the next three years and four months; if we assume that the three years were counted by the circuit of the sun and the four months were counted by the cycles of the moon,[3] this gets us to a date somewhere between July 31 and August 7 on our calendar. This, incidentally, coordinates well with the indications in Jdt 7:20–21 and 8:31 that Bethulia's cisterns were going dry, as well they would be in the summer dry season typical of the southern Levant.

As our story continues, in Jdt 12:10 Judith is said to be in the Assyrians' camp for four days (until somewhere between August 4 and 11, according to the calendrical reckoning we are considering). Then, after she assassinates Holofernes and returns to Bethulia, the Israelites are said to plunder the camp of the Assyrians, according to Jdt 15:11, for thirty days, that is, until somewhere between September 3 and 10. Then the Bethulians go to Jerusalem, making their way there, depending on whether one uses the September 3 or September 10 date, two to three weeks before the autumn equinox, which we will once more recall from Chapter 8 occurs on about September 23 according to our system of date reckoning. We should in addition recall from Chapter 8 that this equinox coincided, at least roughly, with the beginning of the fall festival of Ingathering, or Sukkot (Lev 23:34, Num 29:12, Ezek 45:25). What all this means is that once the people of Bethulia arrive in Jerusalem according to Jdt 16:18, they arrive to celebrate Ingathering/Sukkot and, more generally, to participate in the observances of the longer holiday season of which Ingathering/Sukkot, as we again saw in Chapter 8, is a part.

It is no wonder, then, that the Bethulians can stay in Jerusalem for a prolonged period of time (although three months is surely an exaggeration), for even though Israel during the time in which Judith was written was less overwhelmingly agricultural than it was during the preexilic period that has been the focus of my study, agriculture still dominated the economy. Consequently, it was the agricultural calendar—which allowed for a period of nonagricultural activities after the harvest had been completed—that made a protracted stay in Jerusalem possible. Understanding the date of Judith's assassination of Holofernes to fall in the period leading up to Sukkot, moreover, explains why—in her deceitful words to Holofernes in Jdt 11:13—Judith proclaims herself to be so concerned, among other things, about the Israelites' illicit eating of the "first fruits . . . of the wine and oil, which they had consecrated and set aside for the priests." Judith's alleged concern, that is, is the new wine and the freshly pressed oil that was being produced in the weeks leading up to the Sukkot festival.

Most important for my purposes: understanding the setting of Jdt 16:18–20 as Ingathering/Sukkot explains why Judith and, presumably, all (or almost all) of the other women of Bethulia are in Jerusalem for the festival's celebration, whereas Jdt 10:2 implies that Judith, even before she had been trapped in Bethulia by Holofernes's siege, spent Sabbaths and other festival days in her home. After all, Ingathering/Sukkot, as we have seen, is the ritual occasion when women seem most likely to have participated in sanctuary-based celebrations, whether these be at regional sanctuaries such as Shiloh or at the Jerusalem temple. Thus, it is to the former that Hannah, I have argued in Chapters 3–4, journeyed annually to celebrate Sukkot with her husband, Elkanah, and the rest of Elkanah's family, and it is at the latter, as we saw in Chapter 5 and again in Chapter 8, where many among a household's women are commanded to be present annually to celebrate Sukkot according to Deut 16:14 and where all women, according to Deut 31:10–13, are commanded to assemble every seven years for a special Sukkot celebration.

In addition, note that if the calendrical calculations put forward above are of merit, then Judith journeys together with the people of Bethulia two to three weeks before the start of Sukkot proper, which means they travel—especially if we were to use the "two weeks before" chronology—just around the time of the special new moon day that inaugurates the month of Sukkot and the larger Sukkot holiday season. In Chapter 9, I suggested that the special music-making associated with this new moon day may be, along with the music-making of Sukkot, the particular responsibility of women performers. Thus, the victory song performance in which Judith and other women engage according to Jdt 15:13–14 and 16:1–17 might simultaneously be understood as an example of women's music-making in conjunction with the special new moon day of the month of Sukkot. Note, moreover, that according to Jdt 15:13–14, it is all the women of *Israel* who are said to have danced with Judith; it is all the men of *Israel* who are said to follow; and it is before all of *Israel* that Judith is said to sing her thanksgiving hymn. Judith's victory song performance, it is thereby implied, did not take place in Bethulia, and, indeed, Jdt 16:18, which immediately follows the hymn's conclusion and which begins "when they arrived at Jerusalem" (NRSV), more readily suggests that the singing and dancing that celebrates the Bethulians' victory over Holofernes took place on the way from Bethulia to Jerusalem at about the time of the Sukkot month's new moon celebration. Again, then, we might imagine that Judith's victory song celebration simultaneously marks the Sukkot month's new moon, just as we might also imagine that, when Judith arrived in Jerusalem, she and the women of Israel kept making music, in celebration of Sukkot proper.

Yet even if this supposition overreaches, we still can claim that, as a character, Judith embodies much of what we have learned in the preceding chapters about women and the practice of ancient Israelite religion. In the positions she assumes as a mourner, a musician, and a prophet (at least in her hypothetical description of herself as one who will receive and then transmit revelations from God), she represents in many ways the "who" of women religious functionaries. As a celebrant of Sabbaths, of new moon days, and of other festival occasions, preeminently Sukkot, she represents in many ways the "when" of women's ritual observances. And as a religious practitioner whose primary domain of ritual observance is the home and who only now and then visits larger sanctuary settings (seemingly only annually, for the festival of Sukkot), she represents in many ways the "where" typical of women's religious culture. As such, she represents both the possibilities for religious performance available to women in ancient Israel and also the limitations. Thereby she represents a fitting conclusion to this book.

Notes

Unless otherwise noted, all translations of biblical and other ancient texts are my own.

Introduction

1. Meyers, "From Household to House of Yahweh," 281; Meyers, *Households and Holiness,* 13–14.
2. The latest text in the Hebrew Bible is generally taken to be the book of Daniel, which dates in the form that we have it to ca. 165 BCE. See J. J. Collins, *Daniel,* 24–38.
3. The first mention of Israel in ancient sources is found in the so-called Merenptah Stele, a monumental slab erected in ca. 1209/1208 BCE to commemorate the military exploits of the Egyptian pharaoh Merenptah (r. 1213–1204 BCE). This stele mentions "Israel" among the peoples that Merenptah encounters in his campaigns in southern Canaan, yet designates "Israel" as a tribal community without a fixed city-state home. This has suggested to many that late thirteenth-century BCE "Israel" was a nascent polity, just beginning to establish itself in the southern Levantine hills. Scholarly discussions are numerous: for a representative sample, see Dever, *Who Were the Early Israelites?,* 201–8; Grabbe, *Ancient Israel,* 77–80; and Stager, "Forging an Identity," 91–93.
4. Fleming, *Legacy of Israel,* 23, citing Faust, "Rural Community," 17–39.
5. The precise chronology of Josiah's reformation program is reported differently in 2 Kgs 22–23, where the reform occurs in "one fell swoop," so to speak, in 622 BCE, versus 2 Chr 34–35, where Josiah has begun his efforts at reform already in ca. 628 BCE, and they culminate in 622 BCE.
6. To this extent, I agree with Albertz, "Introduction," in Albertz and Schmitt, *Family and Household Religion,* 18, that "the Josianic reform of the late 7th century" had "a strong impact on Israelite family and household religion" (similarly ibid., 4), with the result that within the family and household, as well as elsewhere, "the traditional religious practices of women"—in the words of J. J. Collins, *Bible After Babel,* 129—"were

especially disrupted" (see similarly Dijkstra, "Women and Religion," 180–88, esp. 187–88). While Albertz, however, seems to view this late seventh-century BCE disruption as so transformative that he and his co-author Schmitt limit their study's chronological scope to the period before Josiah's reformation efforts, Collins and Dijkstra are more sensitive to the eventual (versus immediate) impact of the reform program (see, e.g., J. J. Collins, *Bible After Babel,* 128, and Dijkstra, "Women and Religion," 188). Elsewhere I have argued much the same regarding the reform's eventual versus immediate impact, in Ackerman, *Under Every Green Tree,* esp. 213–17. Hence my sense that I can separate Josiah's reform program and its effects upon women's religious lives from the analysis I undertake in this volume, while still describing aspects of women's religious experience that come from the four decades or so of the preexilic period that postdate the reform yet were not (in my view) affected by it.

7. Bird, "Notes on Gender," 223.
8. For discussion of the Bible's chronology as it pertains to the book of Genesis, see, e.g., McCarter, "Patriarchal Age," 2–3, with further comments in Hendel, "Revisions," 2–3.
9. Morris, "Use and Abuse of Homer," 88.
10. On the date of 1 Sam 1:1–2:26, and Samuel's tribal affiliation, see Chapter 3 and nn. 8 and 22 there.
11. Olyan, *Asherah,* 7–8, 14–17.
12. My thinking with regard to what follows has been particularly influenced by Dever, *Recent Archaeological Discoveries,* 6–8, 122–24; Dever, *Did God Have a Wife?,* 68–72; Meyers, *Discovering Eve,* 4–5, 11–14; Meyers, "Archaeology—A Window," 63–67; Meyers, *Rediscovering Eve,* 2–4, 18–25; and Stavrakopoulou and Barton, "Introduction," 2, 4–5.
13. That Solomon and his father David actually ruled over a "united monarchy" of North and South in the tenth century BCE is increasingly a matter open to question: see the references collected in Ackerman, *When Heroes Love,* 284–85, nn. 40–42, and, more recently, Garfinkel, Kreimerman, and Zilberg, *Debating Khirbet Qeiyafa,* 226, and the references there. See also my discussion in Chapter 5.
14. Dever, *Did God Have a Wife?,* 18. See also Meyers, *Rediscovering Eve,* 42, who notes that 94 percent of the population of fourteenth-century England were agriculturalists, as were 97 percent of the population of eighteenth-century Russia.
15. Chapter 1 and n. 43 there.
16. I engage in more detail below with the literary complexity of Exodus, Leviticus, and Numbers, but here I follow the lead of Fleming, in "Israelite Festival Calendar," 20, n. 37, and in "Break in the Line," 162, n. 2, by simplifying the terminology scholars use for the various literary strands within this corpus (preeminently P, or the Priestly source, and H, or the Holiness Code) by calling it

all "priestly," as these source divisions (which are, at any rate, debated) are not essential for my current point.

17. Mic 1:1 identifies the prophet as coming from Moresheth, usually taken to be a small village about 8 kilometers northeast of Lachish and about the same distance southwest of Azekah.
18. See, e.g., Jer 7:1–15, 20:1–6, 26:4–11, 36:10–26, 37:11–16, 38:1–6.
19. Dever, *Did God Have a Wife?,* 70, speaks of the prophets' "lofty literary style," their "elegant Hebrew," their "complex syntax," their "sophisticated literary allusions," and their "subtle play on words."
20. I have documented several attempts to identify female authors within the Hebrew Bible in Ackerman, *Warrior, Dancer,* 23, n. 34. But this scholarship is so speculative that it has persuaded few. In addition, as Bird observes in "Women's Religion in Ancient Israel," 285–86, n. 8, the smattering of compositions that the Hebrew Bible does put in the mouths of women (e.g., Judg 5:1–31, 1 Sam 2:1–10) "have all been transmitted to us in the compositions of scribal guilds, which I would view as male associations." Hence, Bird writes, "I believe that we have no *direct* or *unmediated* access to the words or lives of women in the Hebrew scriptures." See similarly Bird, "Women in the Ancient Mediterranean World," 32.
21. The identity of Deuteronomy's authors has been debated, with commentators suggesting the book was produced by scribes or wise men of the Jerusalem royal court (e.g., Levinson, *Deuteronomy,* 18, 64; Weinfeld, *Deuteronomy and the Deuteronomic School,* 158–78), by some prophetic community or prophetic school (e.g., E. W. Nicholson, *Deuteronomy,* 58–82), or by tribal elders (e.g., Hoppe, "Elders and Deuteronomy," 259–72; Hoppe, "Levitical Origins of Deuteronomy," 27–36). Given, though, that the Israelites who figure most prominently within the book are Levitical priests, von Rad's theory that assigns the book's authorship to the Levites seems to me to remain valid (von Rad, *Studies in Deuteronomy,* 60–69, esp. 66–68; von Rad, *Deuteronomy,* 23–26). For further discussion, see O'Brien, "Book of Deuteronomy," 102–3.
22. Bird, "Women in the Ancient Mediterranean World," 32.
23. Gould, "Law, Custom, and Myth," 38.
24. Exum, "Feminist Criticism," 66–67. See similarly Ebeling, *Women's Lives,* 8; Nakhai, "Gender and Archaeology," 515; and both Dever and Meyers as cited in n. 12 above.
25. Bynum, "Women's Stories," 33.
26. Stavrakopoulou and Barton, "Introduction," 1.
27. Stavrakopoulou, "'Popular' Religion and 'Official' Religion," 41.
28. My thinking with regard to what follows has been particularly influenced by Carol Meyers's scholarship over the years: most recently, Meyers, "Archaeology—A Window," 68–72; Meyers, *Rediscovering Eve,* 27–32; and Meyers, "Double Vision," 117–22.

29. Meyers, *Discovering Eve,* 17; Meyers, *Rediscovering Eve,* 28.
30. Hackett, "In the Days of Jael," 17–18; Hackett, "Women's Studies," 147–48; Meyers, *Discovering Eve,* 139–64; and Meyers, *Rediscovering Eve,* 125–46.
31. Meyers, *Rediscovering Eve,* 30.
32. Meyers has made this point in several publication: perhaps first in Meyers, "Material Remains and Social Relations," 429–30; more recently in Meyers, *Rediscovering Eve,* 29–30, and Meyers, "Double Vision," 120–22. See similarly (drawing on Meyers) Ebeling, *Women's Lives,* 7.
33. See also Meyers, *Rediscovering Eve,* 26; Meyers, "Double Vision," 116.
34. On women priests in the ancient Near East and eastern Mediterranean, see Ackerman, "Women and the Religious Culture," 259–89; Ackerman, "Mother of Eshmunazor," 158–78.
35. King and Stager, *Life in Biblical Israel,* 7.
36. Morris, *Burial and Ancient Society,* 45.
37. Morris, "Use and Abuse of Homer," 88.
38. Ibid., 90; Morris, *Burial and Ancient Society,* 44–45.
39. Morris, *Burial and Ancient Society,* 44.
40. King and Stager, *Life in Biblical Israel,* 7, quoting Burckhardt, *The Greeks,* 5.
41. King and Stager, *Life in Biblical Israel,* 7, citing Murray, "Introduction," xxxi. See similarly Meyers, *Rediscovering Eve,* 24–25.
42. Morris, "Use and Abuse of Homer," 89.
43. King and Stager, *Life in Biblical Israel,* 7.
44. Brettler, "Woman's Voice," 163.
45. As well described in E. W. Nicholson, *The Pentateuch,* 13–14, 21, 70–72, the case for a tenth-century BCE date for J was forcefully made by von Rad, *Das formgeschichtliche Problem,* as opposed to the ninth- and eighth-century BCE dates that had been proposed some half a century earlier by, respectively, Wellhausen, in his *Prolegomena,* and by Dillmann, *Die Genesis.* Van Seters's arguments dating J to the exilic era were first articulated in book form in Van Seters, *Abraham in History and Tradition,* and then developed and reiterated in multiple publications, including Van Seters's recent summary and synthetic statement of his views: Van Seters, *The Yahwist.*
46. H. H. Schmid, *Der sogenannte Jahwist;* M. Rose, *Deuteronomist und Jahwist.*
47. See, e.g., Römer, "Elusive Yahwist," 9–27; Römer, "Zwischen Urkunden," 2–24; and the summary comments (with additional bibliography) of Albertz, "Recent Discussion," 67–68.
48. A theory positing two editions of the Deuteronomistic corpus, one preexilic and one exilic, was advanced already in the nineteenth century by both Abraham Kuenen and Julius Wellhausen (as pointed out by Cross, in *Canaanite Myth,* 275, n. 6, and Lohfink, "Cult Reform of Josiah," 462). For modern proponents, see the bibliographies assembled in Knoppers, "Aaron's Calf," 93–94, n. 5, and Miano, *Shadow on the Steps,* 5, n. 10, to which add, more recently, Leuchter,

Samuel and the Shaping of Tradition, 13–21. I have identified what I take to be the most crucial works of the recent European reassessment in Ackerman, *When Heroes Love,* 282, n. 6. For a position that combines the American and European views, see Römer, *So-Called Deuteronomistic History.*

49. A mid-eighth-century BCE date for P has been proposed by Milgrom, *Leviticus 1–16,* 28. Proponents of a late eighth-century BCE date include Cooper and Goldstein in numerous publications, most recently in "Development of the Priestly Calendars," 2–3, 5; Friedman, *Who Wrote the Bible?*, 161–216, esp. 210–14 (but cf. Friedman, *Exile and Biblical Narrative,* 44–119, as cited just below); Haran, *Temples,* 132–48, esp. 146–47; and Haran, "Behind the Scenes of History," 321–33. A seventh-century BCE date is suggested in Friedman, *Exile and Biblical Narrative,* 44–119; Halpern, "Jerusalem and the Lineages," 58; and Weinfeld, *Deuteronomy and the Deuteronomic School,* 179–89. Arguments for a sixth-century BCE date are advanced by many: e.g., Blenkinsopp, *The Pentateuch,* 26, 238; Cross, *Canaanite Myth,* 294–95, quoting the conclusions he had previously stated in "The Tabernacle," 57–58; D. P. Wright, "Ritual Theory, Ritual Texts," 215; and Zevit, *Religions,* 47, n. 62 (but cf. Zevit, "Converging Lines of Evidence," 510, where he writes that "the exile of 586 B.C.E. is the *terminus ad quem* for the composition of P"). A postexilic date for P was originally put forward by Wellhausen in his *Prolegomena* and has many advocates still today, especially among German scholars: e.g., Gertz, Berlejung, Schmid, and Witte, *Handbook of the Old Testament,* 301, and Zenger, "Das priester(schrift)liche Werk," in Zenger et al., *Einleitung,* 156–75.
50. Haran, "Behind the Scenes of History," 330 and n. 13 on that page, cites Yehezkel Kaufmann's view (with which Haran does not agree) regarding a twelfth-century BCE date for P; those who propose a tenth-century BCE date include Knohl, *Sanctuary of Silence,* 220–22, and Rendsburg, "Once More the Dual," 37–38. See also Rendsburg, "Late Biblical Hebrew," 65–80, regarding an "early" (albeit unspecified) date for P.
51. E. W. Nicholson, *The Pentateuch,* 220.
52. Ibid., 220–21.
53. Hurowitz, "P," 46.
54. Propp, *Exodus 19–40,* 732; Levine, *Numbers 1–20,* 104; and Gertz, Berlejung, Schmid, and Witte, *Handbook of the Old Testament,* 301.
55. Knohl, first in Knohl, "Priestly Torah," 65–177, and then in Knohl, *Sanctuary of Silence,* turned the earlier scholarly understanding upside down, by arguing and—in the opinion of many, myself included—proving that H postdates rather than predates P. This position has been further articulated, refined, and (in some cases) modified by Milgrom, *Leviticus 1–16,* 13–35; Milgrom, *Leviticus 17–22,* 1349–52; Nihan, *From Priestly Torah to Pentateuch;* Nihan, "Israel's Festival Calendars," 177–231; B. J. Schwartz, *Holiness Legislation;* and Stackert, *Rewriting the Torah.*

56. E. W. Nicholson, *The Pentateuch,* vi.
57. See Friedman, *Who Wrote the Bible?,* 87; R. M. Wright, *Linguistic Evidence.*
58. Friedman, *Who Wrote the Bible?,* 87, and Jenks, *The Elohist;* also on E, see Stackert, *Prophet like Moses,* 70–125, and (albeit without a discussion of the date) Baden, *J, E, and the Redaction of the Pentateuch;* Baden, *Composition of the Pentateuch,* 103–28, esp. 116–28.
59. This is not necessarily to imply, however, the existence of a redacted JE document (R^{JE}): on this, see, preeminently, Baden, *J, E, and the Redaction of the Pentateuch.*
60. This thesis was first articulated by the German scholar W. M. L. de Wette in his 1805 doctoral dissertation; for a more recent affirmation, see (among others) Rofé, *Deuteronomy,* 4–9. O'Brien, "Book of Deuteronomy," 103–5, surveys other scholarly positions.
61. Matthews and Benjamin, *Social World of Ancient Israel,* xiii.
62. Meyers, "Household Religion," 121.
63. By the late twentieth century, however, important exceptions began to appear: P. D. Miller, *Religion;* Niditch, *Ancient Israelite Religion;* Soggin, *Israel in the Biblical Period;* and Zevit, *Religions.* Note also Albertz, *History of Israelite Religion* 1–2. Here, even as Albertz maintains a chronologically based system of organization (moving from the "period before the state," to the monarchy, to the exile, and then to the postexilic period), he modifies and nuances this diachronic trajectory significantly by focusing concurrently on the "internal religious pluralism" (see Albertz, *History of Israelite Religion* 1, 95–99)—the religion of the family, of the village community, and of the "people" as a whole, or the state—that was manifest simultaneously within the Israelite polity during each of the historical periods that he examines.
64. King and Stager, *Life in Biblical Israel,* 6.
65. My thinking with regard to what follows has been particularly influenced by Dever, *Recent Archaeological Discoveries,* 121–28, esp. 125–26; Dever, *Did God Have a Wife?,* 1–4, 35–39, 59–62; Meyers, "From Household to House of Yahweh," 278, 280–81; Meyers, *Households and Holiness,* 4–5, 6–9, 13–14; Meyers, *Rediscovering Eve,* 148; and Meyers, "Women's Religious Life," 511–12.
66. Olyan, "Search for the Elusive Self," 40–41.
67. Stavrakopoulou and Barton, "Introduction," 1.
68. Meyers, "Household Religion," 121; van der Toorn, "Nine Months," 396; note also Meyers, "Women's Religious Life," 511–12, and van der Toorn, "Introduction," 423.
69. Meyers, *Households and Holiness,* 14.
70. This definition of "cult" as used in common parlance comes from *OED Online,* s.v. "Cult, n.2b,"http:// www .oed .com .dartmouth .idm .oclc .org/ view/ Entry/ 45709?rskey=rsd2nY&result=1.
71. De Vaux, *Ancient Israel,* 271.

72. Zevit, *Religions*, 11.
73. See similarly Bird, who in her programmatic essay, "Place of Women," 401, writes of the need of assessing the sphere of women's religious activities "spatially [my 'where'], temporally [my 'when'], and functionally [my 'who' and 'how']."

Chapter 1. "Micah's Mother Had Made a Cast-Metal Figurine"

1. See Chapter 3 and n. 9 there.
2. See similarly, with respect to a tripartite typology of Israelite sacred spaces, Albertz, *History of Israelite Religion* 1, implicitly on 19 and 21 (regarding a tripartite division of religious practitioners) and more explicitly throughout; Nakhai, *Archaeology*, 191; and Weippert, *Jahwe und die anderen Götte*, 9–19. But cf. just below, n. 3.
3. Several other types of cult places are known, especially from the archaeological record (e.g., gate shrines and work-related cult sites). Indeed, Schmitt, in "Typology of Iron Age Cult Places," in Albertz and Schmitt, *Family and Household Religion*, 220–41, has proposed an *eight-part* taxonomy of Israelite cult places, and Schmitt further divides four of his taxa into subgroups. Nevertheless, I restrict my discussion to the types of sacred space I have listed here, both because I take these to be among the most important of Israelite cult sites and because the Bible's textual evidence allows me to comment on women's experiences at these three types of sites in ways that are not possible regarding others of Israel's religious venues due to a lack of data.
4. Others who hold this view include Albertz, "Introduction," in Albertz and Schmitt, *Family and Household Religion*, 10–11, who notes the "significance of women . . . for Israelite family and household religion, in stark contrast to their restricted roles in the official cult of Yhwh"; Bird, "Place of Women," 401, 411; Bird, "Israelite Religion," 101–2; Bird, "Gender and Religious Definition," 13; Bird, "Notes on Gender," 221–22; and P. D. Miller, *Religion*, 39, 201. In addition, see Meyers, "From Household to House of Yahweh," 283 and also n. 30 on that page, who cites Bird's conclusions with approval, as well as the similar conclusions reached by van der Toorn in *From Her Cradle to Her Grave* and *Family Religion*. Likewise, see Meyers, *Households and Holiness*, 17 and 77, n. 10, and, more significantly, Meyers's attempts throughout Meyers, "From Household to House of Yahweh" and *Households and Holiness*, and in Meyers, *Rediscovering Eve*, 147–70, esp. 168–70, to identify the household as the typical site of women's religious practice.
5. Grammatically, the phrase *pesel ûmassēkâ*, which is referred to in Judg 17:4 using a singular verb, is best understood as a hendiadys, whereby two nouns (*pesel*, "image," and *massēkâ*, "molten image") are connected by *û*, "and," to indicate a single concept: a "cast-metal figurine": so, e.g., Boling, *Judges*, 256; Martin, *Book*

of Judges, 185; and Soggin, *Judges,* 265. But cf. (among the standard commentaries) Gunn, *Judges,* 231; Niditch, *Judges,* 172, 177, n. g, and 181; and Schneider, *Judges,* 233. These scholars, on the basis of the wording of Judg 18:17, 18, and perhaps of 18:20, 30, 31, understand the phrase *pesel ûmassēkâ* to refer to two separate objects, "an image," *pesel,* and "a molten image," *massēkâ.*

6. Several scholars (esp. Boling, *Judges,* 258–59, and van der Toorn, *Family Religion,* 247) have proposed that Judg 17:1–4 was originally a separate tale from the episode that follows in Judg 17:7–13; this is particularly indicated by the fact that Micah's name is rendered differently in the two passages (*mîkāyĕhû* in Judg 17:1, 4 versus *mîkâ* in Judg 17:8, 9, 10, 12, 13). Judg 17:5–6, according to this reconstruction, was added by a redactor to bring 17:1–4 and 7–13 together. Leuchter, "'Now There Was a [Certain] Man,'" 436–38, argues similarly but takes 17:5 to be part of the account found in 17:1–4. A thorough discussion can be found in Mueller, *Micah Story,* 7–15.
7. Women name their children in about 63 percent of the naming episodes recounted in the Hebrew Bible, although the exact percentage that commentators cite can differ, depending on how, exactly, one counts: see, among many others, Albertz, "Personal Names and Family Religion," in Albertz and Schmitt, *Family and Household Religion,* 247, n. 9; Bohmbach, "Names and Naming in the Biblical World," 37; Meyers, "From Household to House of Yahweh," 291; Meyers, *Households and Holiness,* 42; and Meyers, *Rediscovering Eve,* 158. According to Albertz, "Introduction," in Albertz and Schmitt, *Family and Household Religion,* 8, women's role in "naming ceremonies" was first suggested by Bird, "Place of Women," 409–10.
8. As is suggested, e.g., by Dohmen, "*massēkâ,*" 432, 434–35; King and Stager, *Life in Biblical Israel,* 9; and van der Toorn, "Nature of the Biblical Teraphim," 211. The most recent discussion is Kletter, "To Cast an Image," 197–99.
9. Note, however, regarding the date of Isaiah, that many have suggested that the prophet's oracles were heavily redacted in the sixth century BCE, to the extent that, for some, the eighth-century BCE oracles cannot be considered a corpus independent of a sixth-century BCE context. See Williamson, *Book Called Isaiah,* and, with regard specifically to Isa 30:22, Kaiser, *Isaiah 13–39,* 302. Regarding the date of Judg 17:1–18:31, see my discussion below.
10. Kletter, "To Cast an Image," 201, with references.
11. Examples from the Middle and Late Bronze Ages (ca. 2000–1550 BCE and 1550–1200 BCE) have been well documented by Negbi, *Canaanite Gods in Metal.* Early Iron Age examples (ca. 1200–1000 BCE) are somewhat harder to come by: see, though, Keel and Uehlinger, *Gods, Goddesses, and Images of God,* 117, Fig. 139 (= *ANEP,* no. 494).
12. For this interpretation, see, e.g., Ahlström, *Aspects of Syncretism,* 26, and van der Toorn, *Family Religion,* 250. See also Faraone, Garnand, and López-Ruiz, "Micah's Mother," 164, n. 13, who argue not only that the phrase *'ēpôd ûtĕrāpîm*

is a hendiadys (above, n. 5), but that it should furthermore be taken as referring to the *pesel ûmassēkâ* of 17:4 (which they also interpret as a hendiadys), with *tĕrāpîm* referring specifically to the *pesel* or image proper and *'ēpôd* to its molten plating or *massēkâ.* Other commentators (e.g., Burney, *Book of Judges,* 409; LaRocca-Pitts, *"Of Wood and Stone,"* 60; and G. F. Moore, *Critical and Exegetical Commentary,* 378) similarly take *pesel ûmassēkâ* and *'ēpôd ûtĕrāpîm* to be equivalent, with *pesel ûmassēkâ* stemming from one stratum in the history of the textual development of Judg 17–18 and the variant *'ēpôd ûtĕrāpîm* from another. However, while Judg 17:1–18:31 no doubt has a multilayered redactional history (n. 6 above), the plainest meaning of the text—and the one embraced by the redactor of Judg 17:1–18:31 in 18:17, 18, 20—is to see the *pesel ûmassēkâ* and the *'ēpôd ûtĕrāpîm* as distinct objects. See further Albertz, *History of Israelite Religion* 1, 37: "the teraphim . . . are here [in Judg 17:1–18:31] distinguished clearly from a cultic image of the god proper [i.e., the *pesel ûmassēkâ*]," and Bray, *Sacred Dan,* 63: "it is clear that this object [the *pesel*] is to be distinguished from . . . the ephod and teraphim."

13. The most up-to-date and persuasive works on the *tĕrāpîm*/teraphim and their function are van der Toorn, "Nature of the Biblical Teraphim," 203–22; van der Toorn and Lewis, *"tĕrāpîm,"* 777–89; and Lewis, "Teraphim," 844–50. For additional bibliography, see Cox and Ackerman, "Micah's Teraphim," 2, n. 5, and 4, n. 12.
14. P. D. Miller, *Religion,* 67.
15. For other alternatives still regarding the *'ēpôd*/ephod, see van der Toorn, "Nature of the Biblical Teraphim," 211–13; van der Toorn and Houtman, "David and the Ark," 212–19, 230; and van der Toorn and Lewis, "*tĕrāpîm,*" 784–87. For further bibliography, see Cox and Ackerman, "Micah's Teraphim," 9, n. 20, to which add de Vaux, *Ancient Israel,* 349–52; Dolansky, *Now You See It,* 49–50; Haran, "Priestly Image of the Tabernacle," 208–11; and Jeffers, *Magic and Divination,* 202–9.
16. Schroer, "Ancient Near Eastern Pictures," 43, and van der Toorn, "Nine Months," 396, similarly suggest that *tĕrāpîm* were made of wood; see also van der Toorn, "Israelite Figurines," 54, where van der Toorn suggests *tĕrāpîm* were made of wood or clay.
17. Cox and Ackerman, "Micah's Teraphim," 23–24.
18. So Bray, *Sacred Dan,* 89, 95, 126, 138; Cody, *History of Old Testament Priesthood,* 53 (with references in n. 55); and M. S. Moore, "Role Pre-Emption," 326. Particularly significant here is Micah's bestowing upon his Levite priest the title "father," which is assigned to prophetic figures who speak on behalf of God in 1 Sam 10:12; 2 Kgs 2:12, 6:21, 13:14 (Boling, *Judges,* 257).
19. On the dialectal variants of Israel's North and South, see Garr, *Dialect Geography;* Rendsburg, *Linguistic Evidence;* and Rendsburg, *Israelian Hebrew.* But cf. Pat-El, "Israelian Hebrew," 1–37.

20. According to Danish archaeological excavations of Shiloh in 1926, 1929, 1932, and 1963, and according especially to the 1963 excavators' reevaluation of the older results (Buhl and Holm-Nielsen, *Shiloh*), Shiloh was destroyed during the Assyrian invasions of the second half of the eighth century BCE. According to I. Finkelstein, however, who excavated at Shiloh from 1981 to 1984, Shiloh was destroyed much earlier (in ca. 1050 BCE, perhaps by the Philistines, according to I. Finkelstein, "History and Archaeology of Shiloh," 388–89; a century or so later, according to I. Finkelstein, "Iron I Shiloh," 146, on the basis of the "low chronology" Finkelstein put forward in 1996 in I. Finkelstein, "Archaeology of the United Monarchy," 177–87). In I. Finkelstein, "History and Archaeology of Shiloh," 388–89, Finkelstein also argues, contra the Danish excavators' conclusions, that no significant resettlement happened after this destruction, describing the evidence for renewed activity at Shiloh in the seventh and possibly eighth centuries BCE as "meagre."
21. Above, n. 6.
22. My characterization of the polemic in Judg 17–18 is taken primarily from van der Toorn, *Family Religion,* 247–48; see similarly Ahlström, *Aspects of Syncretism,* 26–27, and Yee, "Ideological Criticism," 151. See also, regarding the story as a polemic against the Levitical priesthood, Brettler, "Book of Judges," 409 (following Noth, "Background of Judges 17–18," 68–85), and, regarding the story as a polemic against the sanctuary at Dan, Bray, *Sacred Dan,* 42; Martin, *Book of Judges,* 182–83, 187; and Soggin, *Judges,* 268–69, 277–78. Brettler ("Book of Judges," 409) further argues, still following Noth, that the story implies a negative attitude about the Danites, "who conquer the unsuspecting peaceful residents of Laish." But cf. Boling, *Judges,* 258–59, who, while he also sees the story as polemical, takes the thrust of the polemic to be directed against Micah. Others have described the story's polemical character in different terms still: e.g., Amit, *Hidden Polemics,* 100–109; Bartusch, *Understanding Dan,* 171; and McMillion, "Worship in Judges 17–18," 234 (citing D. R. Davis, "Comic Literature," 156–63). Mueller, *Micah Story,* 26–35, surveys various interpretations and at pp. 51–128 offers her own.
23. M. K. Wilson, "'As You Like It,'" 81.
24. L. R. Klein, *Triumph of Irony,* 149.
25. Ibid. See likewise, among older commentaries, Burney, *Book of Judges,* 420. More recently, this position has been put forward by Amit, *Hidden Polemics,* 105; Brettler, "Book of Judges," 409; Exum, "Centre Cannot Hold," 426; Mueller, *Micah Story,* 54, 78; Soggin, *Judges,* 268; and Yee, "Ideological Criticism," 149. This possibility is also raised, although not necessarily embraced, by Martin, *Book of Judges,* 185.
26. For a similar conclusion, with more extensive commentary, see Bray, *Sacred Dan,* 16–28, 138, as well as the arguments for a pre-Deuteronomistic date recently advanced by Hutton, "Levitical Aspirations," 98–108, esp. 104–5.

27. See only 2 Kgs 10:29, to which compare the multiple references in the Deuteronomistic History to Dan's sister sanctuary at Bethel, which seems to have remained a functioning cult site after the Assyrian conquest and, according to 2 Kgs 23:15–20, even up until the time of the Josianic reform in the late seventh century BCE (although on the purported Josianic provenance and thus the date of 2 Kgs 23:15, 16b–17, 19–20, see Barrick, *The King and the Cemeteries,* 107–8).
28. On these possibilities, see Brettler, "Book of Judges," 416, and van der Toorn, *Family Religion,* 248–49.
29. Van der Toorn, *Family Religion,* 247, 250.
30. Faraone, Garnand, and López-Ruiz, "Micah's Mother," 161–86.
31. Scharbert, "*'ālâ,*" 262; see also Meyers, "Mother of Micah," 248.
32. According to Albertz, "Methodological Reflections," in Albertz and Schmitt, *Family and Household Religion,* 37, this interpretation of Judg 18:22 was first put forward by Gottwald in his magisterial *Tribes of Yahweh,* 291. As Albertz indicates in ibid., 37–38, n. 29, he disagrees, but many others have followed Gottwald's lead, including Halpern, "Jerusalem and the Lineages," 51; Meyers, "Family in Early Israel," 17; P. D. Miller, *Religion,* 68; Stager, "Archaeology of the Family," 22; van der Toorn, *Family Religion,* 197–98; and Zevit, *Religions,* 626.
33. The premier presentation of this reconstruction of ancient Israelite household and family structure is Stager, "Archaeology of the Family." Other helpful discussions include Borowski, *Daily Life,* 13–21; Dever, *Who Were the Early Israelites?,* 102–7; Dever, *Did God Have a Wife?,* 18–29; Dever, *Lives of Ordinary People,* 186–87; King and Stager, *Life in Biblical Israel,* 9–19, 28–43; and van der Toorn, *Family Religion,* 194–99.
34. The premier presentation of this reconstruction of ancient Israelite household and family structure is Schloen, *House of the Father,* 150–55, who has sought to modify Stager's reconstruction (above, n. 33) by proposing that multiple generations of a family like Micah's would have lived together within the same domicile, while the occupants of the other buildings of a household compound comprise other multigenerational family units (one per domicile). All of these multigenerational family units then belonged, as Schloen would have it, to the same clan or patronymic association.
35. See similarly Blenkinsopp, "Family in First Temple Israel," 52, and, provocatively, on the significance of the "gate," Schloen, *House of the Father,* 160, n. 34.
36. Above, nn. 5 and 12.
37. This definition of a shrine corner or a shrine niche is from Zevit, *Religions,* 123.
38. Mettinger, *No Graven Image?,* 141, citing de Pury, *Promesse divine,* 427–28.
39. E.g., the editors of the *BHS,* note on Judg 18:15; Martin, *Book of Judges,* 193; and G. F. Moore, *Critical and Exegetical Commentary,* 397.
40. Niditch, *Judges,* 175, seems to embrace such an interpretation.

41. Boling, *Judges,* 264.
42. See similarly Blenkinsopp, "Family in First Temple Israel," 52; Bray, *Sacred Dan,* 63; Halpern, "Jerusalem and the Lineages," 51; P. D. Miller, *Religion,* 68; Soggin, *Judges,* 272, 274; and van der Toorn, *From Her Cradle to Her Grave,* 44.
43. For this population estimate, see Dever, *Did God Have a Wife?,* 18; King and Stager, *Life in Biblical Israel,* 21; and Meyers, "Household Religion," 120. But cf. Borowski, *Daily Life,* 9, 13, who estimates that only 66 percent of the Israelite population, at least during the Iron Age II period (ca. 1000–586 BCE), lived in rural locations.
44. Succinct but nevertheless comprehensive summaries of views on these issues, with references, can be found in Albertz, "Methodological Reflections," in Albertz and Schmitt, *Family and Household Religion,* 34–41; Baadsgaard, "Taste of Women's Sociality," 17–18; Ebeling, *Women's Lives,* 26; and Halpern, "Jerusalem and the Lineages," 50.
45. Halpern, "Jerusalem and the Lineages," 50.
46. On whether a "single-family house" housed a nuclear family or a family composed of multiple generations, see nn. 33–34 above. See also Faust and Bunimovitz, "Four Room House," 26, who write, "the urban four-room house . . . housed nuclear families, comprising two parents and a couple of unmarried children," whereas "the rural houses . . . housed extended families of at least three generations"; similarly Faust, "Differences in Family Structure," 243–47, and Faust, "Rural Community," 19.
47. On household ovens, see Baadsgaard, "Taste of Women's Sociality," 25–41, esp. 28–29, and, most recently, Shafer-Elliott, "'He Shall Eat Curds and Honey,'" 286–87.
48. Dever, *Lives of Ordinary People,* 131; King and Stager, *Life in Biblical Israel,* 35; and Meyers, "Archaeology—A Window," 79.
49. As noted by many: e.g., Dever, *Lives of Ordinary People,* 131, and Meyers, "Archaeology—A Window," 79.
50. This has been noted by many. The best discussion remains that of Stager, "Archaeology of the Family," 12, 16–17.
51. Dever, *Who Were the Early Israelites?,* 104–5; similarly Hardin, "Household Archaeology," 545; Holladay, "Kingdoms of Israel and Judah," 392; and Meyers, "In the Household and Beyond," 22.
52. But note Ruth 2:3, 8–9, 15–16, 22–23, where women, including Ruth, glean grain left behind by male reapers.
53. This account of the various agricultural roles assumed by men in ancient Israel has been put forward by many: e.g., Borowski, *Daily Life,* 14, 22, 114–16; Dever, *Did God Have a Wife?,* 26–27; Dever, *Lives of Ordinary People,* 173; King and Stager, *Life in Biblical Israel,* 16; and Meyers, "From Field Crops to Food," 77.
54. Meyers, "Material Remains and Social Relations," 431, citing Murdock and Provost, "Factors in the Division of Labor by Sex," Tables 1, 5; see also Mey-

ers's comments in several subsequent publications: most recently, Meyers, *Rediscovering Eve,* 128–32, and Meyers, "Women's Daily Life," 489–90. Also see Baadsgaard, "Taste of Women's Sociality," 14, 19, 41–44, and the references assembled at 14, n. 5, and 19, n. 27; Bird, "Women (OT)," 954; Borowski, *Daily Life,* 113–14, 123–25; Dever, *Lives of Ordinary People,* 173, 188; and Faust, "Burnished Pottery," 59.

55. Meyers, "Material Remains and Social Relations," 433, citing Murdock and Provost, "Factors in the Division of Labor by Sex," Table 1, and also Costin, "Exploring the Relationship Between Gender and Craft," Table 4.1. See also Bird, "Women (OT)," 954; Borowski, *Daily Life,* 32, 123; Dever, *Lives of Ordinary People,* 173, 187–89; Meyers, *Rediscovering Eve,* 133; Meyers, "Women's Daily Life," 490–91; and H. M.-L. Miller, *Archaeological Approaches to Technology,* 68.
56. Prov 31:10–31 may not, however, date from the preexilic period that is the focus of this book. Yoder, *Wisdom as a Woman of Substance,* 15–39, has argued for a Persian-era date, but Fox, *Proverbs 10–31,* 899–902, has raised significant doubts (without offering an alternative).
57. Traditions of Cypriot women's pottery production have been preeminently documented by London, "Cypriot Potters," 320–21; London, "Fe(male) Potters," 159–62; London, Egoumenidou, and Karageorghis, *Traditional Pottery in Cyprus,* 22–25; and London, *Ancient Cookware,* 27. On women potters elsewhere in the Near East, see Bourriau, Nicholson, and Rose, "Pottery," 141; London, *Ancient Cookware,* 32, 34, 35–36; and Meyers, "Women's Daily Life," 491 (all with additional references). On women as particularly responsible for the manufacture of hand-made pots, versus vessels thrown on kick-wheels, see Ebeling, *Women's Lives,* 55; R. H. Johnston, "Cypriot Potter," 138; London, *Ancient Cookware,* 34; H. M.-L. Miller, *Archaeological Approaches to Technology,* 190–91; and Wood, *Sociology of Pottery,* 23–24, along with the references there.
58. Borowski, *Daily Life,* 113–14, 116–18, 121–22, 124–26; King and Stager, *Life in Biblical Israel,* 15; and Meyers, "Family in Early Israel," 27.
59. While the pillar-courtyard house is well known in Israelite cities as well as in rural villages (Dever, *Lives of Ordinary People,* 132), the constraints of urban space, and the differences in the urban economy and in urban demographics, militate against multiple houses being configured together or compounded in the same way as they are in rural spaces. See Holladay, "House, Israelite," 310. But cf., regarding Tell en-Naṣbeh, my comments just below and also, regarding Tell en-Naṣbeh, Tell Beit Mirsim, and Tell el-Far'ah North, Stratum VIIb, King and Stager, *Life in Biblical Israel,* 13; Schloen, *House of the Father,* 167; and Stager, "Archaeology of the Family," 22.
60. King and Stager, *Life in Biblical Israel,* 12, 19; Meyers, "Family in Early Israel," 16; and Stager, "Archaeology of the Family," 18.
61. On courtyard ovens: Baadsgaard and Shafer-Elliott as cited in n. 47 above, and also (among others) Ebeling, *Women's Lives,* 51; Ebeling and Homan, "Baking

and Brewing Beer," 61. On gardens: Borowski, *Daily Life,* 29, 118; King and Stager, *Life in Biblical Israel,* 17–19, 33.

62. Mazar, "Religious Practices," 29.
63. Brody, "Archaeology of the Extended Family," 237–54, esp. 252–54.
64. Marquet-Krause, *Les fouilles de 'Ay,* 23 (this quotation brought to my attention by Nakhai, *Archaeology,* 173).
65. Zevit, *Religions,* 153–56. See also the briefer discussions of Dever, *Did God Have a Wife?,* 113; Nakhai, *Archaeology,* 173; and Schmitt, "Elements of Domestic Cult," in Albertz and Schmitt, *Family and Household Religion,* 74–76.
66. But cf. Schmitt, "Elements of Domestic Cult," in Albertz and Schmitt, *Family and Household Religion,* 75–76, who describes the conclusion that Room 65 is "a cultic place" as "uncertain" while nevertheless suggesting that "the objects and installations [found in Room 65] were quite likely associated with . . . ritual actions" and that Room 65 "could well have comprised a neighborhood shrine integrated within the domestic area."
67. Nakhai, *Archaeology,* 173; Zevit, *Religions,* 153.
68. Willett, "Women and Household Shrines," 203; Zevit, *Religions,* 153.
69. Z. Herzog, "Fortress Mound at Arad," 56, 62.
70. On the height, see Willett, "Women and Household Shrines," 203. The feet were originally called leonine by Marquet-Krause, *Les fouilles de 'Ay,* 23. Dever, *Did God Have a Wife?,* 113, interprets them as human.
71. Reported by Zevit, *Religions,* 153.
72. Schmitt, "Elements of Domestic Cult," in Albertz and Schmitt, *Family and Household Religion,* 75; Zevit, *Religions,* 153, 155.
73. Nakhai, *Archaeology,* 173; Schmitt, "Elements of Domestic Cult," in Albertz and Schmitt, *Family and Household Religion,* 75; and Zevit, *Religions,* 153.
74. Callaway, "Ai," 130. Hopkins, "Life on the Land," 182, suggests that "if Ai with its densely packed houses is taken as typical, then early Iron Age villages boasted no more than 200 to 300 individuals." That said, there is no consensus among scholars regarding the number of occupants who lived in individual houses and in extended household compounds. In *Who Were the Early Israelites?,* 78, Dever reckons there were as many as ten to fifteen inhabitants per individual house at twelfth-century BCE Tel Masos, and he similarly argues in *Lives of Ordinary People,* 154, that a larger village/rural house could have held a family of nine to thirteen people. This is basically consistent with the view of Schloen, *House of the Father,* 150–55, and Ebeling, *Women's Lives,* 23, 26, who, following Schloen, envisions twelve members of a multigenerational family living in an individual house in the hypothetical village of Iron Age I Israel (ca. 1200–1000 BCE) that she reconstructs. However, in *Life in Biblical Israel,* 12, King and Stager assume a much smaller household size, as they propose there were approximately 12.5 people living within the several houses of a family compound. Meyers, "Family in Early Israel," 19, and van der Toorn, *Family Religion,* 197, view the matter similarly. See also Meyers, *Rediscovering Eve,* 111.

75. Albertz, *History of Israelite Religion* 1, 100; Albertz, "Family Religion in Ancient Israel," 97, citing Daviau, "Family Religion," 223; and Albertz, "Introduction," in Albertz and Schmitt, *Family and Household Religion,* 6, 8, citing Bodel and Olyan, "Comparative Perspectives," 279. See also my discussion in Chapters 3–6.
76. Although whether most households would have had "access to such a rare commodity as frankincense" is doubtful: Daviau, "Family Religion," 207–8.
77. Zevit, *Religions,* 154, 156.
78. Dever, *Did God Have a Wife?,* 121–22, and Dever, "Folk Religion," 429. See also Schmitt, "Elements of Domestic Cult," in Albertz and Schmitt, *Family and Household Religion,* 69, on the many ways stands such as the one found at Ai could be used for making offerings.
79. On the archaeological data, see Wood, *Sociology of Pottery,* 15–50; on the biblical data, see Meyers, *Discovering Eve,* 148. On comparative data that point to men as staffing pottery workshops, see R. H. Johnston, "Cypriot Potter," 138; note likewise Bourriau, Nicholson, and Rose, "Pottery," 136; H. M.-L. Miller, *Archaeological Approaches to Technology,* 190–91; and Sanders, "Fingerprints," 223–38.
80. Faust, "Burnished Pottery," 54; Meyers, *Rediscovering Eve,* 20.
81. Esse, "Collared Pithos," 98; note also Bird, "Women (OT)," 954, who remarks that industrialized pottery production by males may have been a "male professionalization" of a craft "originally practiced exclusively by women."
82. Willett, "Women and Household Shrines," 203.
83. Dever, *Did God Have a Wife?,* 121; similarly Dever, "Folk Religion," 429.
84. Willett, "Women and Household Shrines," 212.
85. Meyers, "Hannah and Her Sacrifice," 96–99; Meyers, "Hannah Narrative," 120–22. But cf. Reinhartz, *"Why Ask My Name?"*
86. For this characterization of Samson's mother, see Exum, *Fragmented Women,* 61–93, esp. 63–68, and Reinhartz, "Samson's Mother," 25–37.
87. Above, n. 20.
88. English Bibles traditionally render Hebrew *yām-sûp* as "Red Sea" on the basis of its translation in the Latin Vulgate as *Mare Rubrum.* Yet while Hebrew *yam* is correctly translated as "sea," the word *sûp* means not "red" but "reed." It is generally taken to be a loanword from Egyptian *ṯwf,* "papyrus plant."

Chapter 2. "The Women Knead Dough"

1. On the date and the attribution of Jer 7:1–8:3 to Jeremiah, see Ackerman, *Under Every Green Tree,* 6.
2. The consonantal Hebrew text in Jer 7:18, 44:17, 18, 19, and 25 reads *lmlkt,* "for the Queen of [Heaven]." But the Masoretic tradition vocalizes *limleket,* as if the word were *lml'kt,* "for the work of [heaven]," meaning, presumably, "the heavenly host" that is referred to in 8:2. Many Hebrew manuscripts in fact read *lml'kt* in 7:18 and 44:17, 18, 19, 25. But as commonly recognized (Gordon, "Aleph Apologeticum," 112), the Masoretic pointing is an attempt to remove any hint

that the people of Judah worshipped the Queen of Heaven. The correct reading, *lĕmalkat,* "for the Queen of," is supported by the Greek translations of Aquila, Symmachus, and Theodotion; by the rendering of 44:17, 18, 19, 25 in the LXX; and by the Latin Vulgate.

3. Ackerman, *Under Every Green Tree,* 8–34; Ackerman, "Women and the Worship of Yahweh," 195.
4. The dates of Cult Corner 2081 and, especially, Room 340 in Building 338 are debated. The most recent discussions of Building 338's date, with references to previous publications, are Kleiman and Finkelstein, "Date of Building 338," 50–55, and Ussishkin, "Date of Building 338," 232–36. For discussion of the Megiddo remains, see Holladay, "Religion in Israel and Judah," 252–53; Kempinski, *Megiddo,* 187–88; Nakhai, *Archaeology,* 177–78; and Zevit, *Religions,* 220–25, 227–31. Also see, on Room 340, Stern, "Schumacher's Shrine," 102–7; Ussishkin, "Schumacher's Shrine," 149–72; and Ussishkin, "Fresh Examination of Old Excavations," 67–85.
5. Mazar, "Religious Practices," 41–42.
6. So Ussishkin, "Schumacher's Shrine," 162; see similarly Ussishkin, "Fresh Examination of Old Excavations," 78–79. Ussishkin (among others) also suggests that the building in which Cult Corner 2081 was located may have been a palace ("Schumacher's Shrine," 172), but this is debated: see Albertz, *History of Israelite Religion* 1, 99; Schmitt, "Kultinventare," 449–51; and Schmitt, "Elements of Domestic Cult," in Albertz and Schmitt, *Family and Household Religion,* 134–37 (with multiple references).
7. Jer 7:18 is usually translated "the children gather wood," rendering the Hebrew *bānîm* (the plural of *bēn,* "son") as a generic rather than as gender specific. But a comparison with Lam 5:13, a composition closely related to the book of Jeremiah that describes young *boys* (*nĕʿārîm*) carrying loads of wood, suggests that wood-gathering was a task more typically assigned to males. See further my discussion of gathering wood on the Sabbath in Chapter 7.
8. The various modes of baking are discussed in Meyers, "From Field Crops to Food," 71, and Meyers, "Having Their Space," 23. See also Ebeling, *Women's Lives,* 50, and Lev 2:4–5, 7, 7:9; 1 Kgs 19:6.
9. Zorn, "Naṣbeh, Tell en-," 101.
10. Brody, "Archaeology of the Extended Family," 252–53.
11. Hardin, "Understanding Domestic Space," 76–77, 79; Hardin, *Lahav* II, 133–43; and Hardin, "Household Archaeology," 533–36.
12. Hardin, *Lahav* II, 139.
13. Zevit, *Religions,* 123.
14. In addition to my discussion that follows, see, on the remains from Khirbet Qeiyafa, Garfinkel and Hasel, "Sanctuary Buildings," 16–24. On the Megiddo materials, see Nakhai, *Archaeology,* 177, citing Shiloh, "Iron Age Sanctuaries," 149, and Shiloh, "Megiddo," 1017; see also Schmitt, "Elements of Domestic Cult," in Albertz and Schmitt, *Family and Household Religion,* 141–57. On

the Tell Beit Mirsim and Hazor materials, see Holladay, "Religion in Israel and Judah," 276, 278–29, as well as (on Hazor) Dever, *Lives of Ordinary People,* 267, 269, and Schmitt, "Elements of Domestic Cult," in Albertz and Schmitt, *Family and Household Religion,* 105–6. On Lahav/Tell Halif, see, in addition to the references cited above in n. 11, Schmitt, "Elements of Domestic Cult," in Albertz and Schmitt, *Family and Household Religion,* 99–102, and Willett, "Women and Household Shrines," 154–56.

15. Dever, *Did God Have a Wife?,* 115; Nakhai, *Archaeology,* 173–74; and Schmitt, "Elements of Domestic Cult," in Albertz and Schmitt, *Family and Household Religion,* 164–65.
16. The remains of domestic cult from Tell el-Far'ah North are dated to the tenth century BCE by Dever, *Did God Have a Wife?,* 115, 117, and by Willett, "Women and Household Shrines," 118, but to the ninth century BCE by Zevit, *Religions,* 241.
17. Zevit, *Religions,* 328.
18. The shrine was originally published by Chambon, *Tell el-Far'ah,* 77–78 and Pl. 66:1. For discussion and analysis, see Bretschneider, *Architekturmodelle,* 129, 233; Dever, *Did God Have a Wife?,* 114–15, 117; Katz, *Portable Shrine Models,* 43–44; Keel and Uehlinger, *Gods, Goddesses, and Images of God,* 162; Muller, *Les "maquettes architecturales"* 1, 53–54 and 339–42; Willett, "Women and Household Shrines," 123, 127; and Zevit, *Religions,* 241, 337–38.
19. See further my discussion in Chapter 12, regarding, especially, a tenth-century BCE model shrine from Khirbet Qeiyafa, a ninth-century BCE clay altar from Tel Reḥov, an Iron Age II model shrine from the Transjordanian site of Wadi ath-Thamad 13, and a sixth-century BCE model shrine from Idalion, Cyprus. But cf. Schmitt, "Elements of Domestic Cult," in Albertz and Schmitt, *Family and Household Religion,* 68.
20. Willett, "Women and Household Shrines," 125–27; Zevit, *Religions,* 241.
21. Willett, "Women and Household Shrines," 127.
22. Dever, *Lives of Ordinary People,* 269; Holladay, "Religion in Israel and Judah," 275–76.
23. Beit-Arieh, "Western Quarter," 422; Z. Herzog, "Southern Quarter," 264, 267.
24. Dever, *Lives of Ordinary People,* 280.
25. Kletter, *Judean Pillar-Figurines,* 49, but cf. Vriezen, "Cakes and Figurines," 253, and Vriezen, "Archaeological Traces of Cult," 70.
26. Van der Toorn similarly imagines that Israelite worshippers would take divine images made of terra-cotta back to their homes after acquiring them on a visit to a temple: see van der Toorn, "Israelite Figurines," 59–61, and van der Toorn, "Nine Months," 395–96. Note also the brief comments of Schroer, "Ancient Near Eastern Pictures," 31.
27. This is, in fact, unclear in the Masoretic Text, but the ancient Greek translation of the Bible represented in the Lucianic minuscules (thought to date back to the third century CE and based on older traditions still) reads *kai hai gynaikes*

eipon, "and the women said," in identifying those who speak of making libation and incense offerings and bread cakes for the Queen of Heaven in Jer 44:19. As is clear, moreover, from the reference later in the verse to the speakers' "husbands," this reference to women is necessary for the sense.

28. Gerstenberger, *Theologies,* 42, somewhat similarly ventures the conclusion that "the household cult was women's business" (likewise ibid., 49).
29. Willett, "Women and Household Shrines," 10, 12, 16, 407, 457.
30. Ibid., 127.
31. Ibid., 142–43, 145–46.
32. Ibid., 150, 153.
33. Zevit, *Religions,* 175–76.
34. Dever, *Did God Have a Wife?,* 117.
35. Albertz and Schmitt, "Summary," 479, and Schmitt, "Typology of Iron Age Cult Places," 227, both in Albertz and Schmitt, *Family and Household Religion.*
36. Willett, "Women and Household Shrines," 16.
37. The remains of the domestic cult from Tel Masos are dated to the twelfth and eleventh centuries BCE by Willett, "Women and Household Shrines," 107, but Willett also notes that "some scholars" (she does not specify who) date the "four-room pillared 'Israelite' houses" whose religious remains are the focus of her discussion to "the eleventh and tenth centuries."
38. Willett, "Women and Household Shrines," 109, 117.
39. Ibid., 139.
40. Zevit, *Religions,* 175; on Beersheba as a site of an Israelite altar (and temple?), and so a town where priests would have been resident, see Chapter 6.
41. Beit-Arieh, "Western Quarter," 420.
42. Willett, "Women and Household Shrines," 127.
43. Zevit, *Religions,* 241.
44. Meyers, "From Household to House of Yahweh," 283; also Meyers, *Households and Holiness,* 17; Meyers, *Rediscovering Eve,* 154; and Meyers, "Women's Religious Life," 519.
45. Meyers, "Family in Early Israel," 27; similarly Meyers, *Rediscovering Eve,* 153.
46. These rituals are detailed in the fourteenth-/thirteenth-century BCE Epic of Aqhat, from the northern Levantine city-state of Ugarit: see *KTU* 1.17.1.26–33. Within Israelite tradition, "the erection of a commemorative stele by Absalom because he had no son to do so (2 Sam 18:18) may . . . be a reflection of the practice of a son honoring his father by setting up a funerary stele to the ancestral spirit of his father" (P. D. Miller, *Religion,* 55). Indeed, as van der Toorn writes, "to die without a son was feared as a major misfortune" (*Family Religion,* 208).
47. Meyers has argued this in several places: most recently in Meyers, *Rediscovering Eve,* 97–98. See also Meyers as cited in Chapter 11, n. 32, and Ebeling, *Women's Lives,* 97.
48. Hopkins, "Life on the Land," 189.

49. In addition to the cautions raised here, see Olyan, "What Do We Really Know?," 60–61, and, specifically in response to Meyers, White, "Review of Carol Meyers, *Households and Holiness.*"
50. Willett, "Women and Household Shrines," 146.
51. Van der Toorn, *From Her Cradle to Her Grave,* 41.
52. This is especially the case if instead of the Masoretic Text's *ʾtm wnšykm,* "you [masculine plural] and your wives," we read Jeremiah as addressing "you women" in 44:25, as in the LXX and in accordance with the feminine plural verbs that follow. But the matter is confused, since, as noted above, the objects of these verbs are rendered with masculine plural suffixes.
53. Note, however, apropos of the preexilic focus of this study, that Ecclesiastes (Qoheleth) is a late text within biblical tradition: Persian-era (Seow, "Linguistic Evidence and the Dating of Qoheleth," 643–66) or Hellenistic (Krüger, *Qoheleth,* 19–22).
54. Curtis, *Ancient Food Technology,* 115; Markoe, "28a Servant Statue" and "28b Servant Statue," 91; and Samuel, "Brewing and Baking in Ancient Egyptian Art," 180.
55. Meyers has argued this in numerous places: perhaps first in Meyers, "Family in Early Israel," 25 and 45, n. 67; most recently, in Meyers, *Rediscovering Eve,* 130, and Meyers, "Women's Daily Life," 490. See too Baadsgaard, "Taste of Women's Sociality," 19, 25, and Ebeling and Homan, "Baking and Brewing Beer," 53.
56. Dever, *Lives of Ordinary People,* 170; Ebeling, *Women's Lives,* 48.
57. On an individual's daily flour needs, see Borowski, *Daily Life,* 72, who cites Smelik, *Writings from Ancient Israel,* 106; see also Meyers, "Having Their Space," 22, who cites "Common Roots," 4. In Meyers, *Rediscovering Eve,* 130, and Meyers, "Women's Daily Life," 490, Meyers cites Broshi, *Bread, Wine, Walls, and Scrolls,* 123–25.
58. Meyers, *Discovering Eve,* 146–47; Meyers, *Rediscovering Eve,* 185.
59. Meyers, "Women as Bread Bakers," 213–14; Meyers, "Having Their Space," 26; and Meyers, "From Field Crops to Food," 74. Note, however, that Lev 26:26 is a text from the H or Holiness source, whose date may put it beyond the purview of this study. See the Introduction.
60. Meyers, *Discovering Eve,* 163.
61. Borowski, *Daily Life,* 134, n. 31, gives the measure of an ephah as 5.8 gallons (22 liters, or 0.6 of a bushel); Meyers, "Ethnoarchaeological Analysis of Hannah's Sacrifice," 84, reports that an ephah is somewhere between three-eighths and two-thirds of a bushel.
62. Oppenheim, *Ancient Mesopotamia,* 183.

Chapter 3. "She Went Up with Her Husband to Offer the Annual Sacrifice"

1. Chapter 1, n. 20.
2. Chapter 1, n. 7.
3. Peninnah's daughters are a part of the family party according to 1 Sam 1:4 of the Masoretic Text, but they are not mentioned in the LXX. McCarter, *I Samuel,* 51, suggests the Greek text preserves the better reading, but R. W. Klein, *1 Samuel,* 2, raises the possibility that the "daughters" were deliberately omitted in the Greek "by someone who felt daughters would/should not participate in the sacrifices." Cf., however, Tov as cited in n. 85 below, concerning the Masoretic Text's greater misogyny in 1 Sam 1:1–2:26 as compared with the Greek.
4. McCarter, *I Samuel,* 51, citing Driver, *Notes on the Hebrew Text,* 1; see similarly H. P. Smith, *Critical and Exegetical Commentary,* 6.
5. E.g., Ackroyd, *First Book of Samuel,* 18; Driver, *Notes on the Hebrew Text,* 1; Hertzberg, *I and II Samuel,* 21; R. W. Klein, *1 Samuel,* 1–2; McCarter, *I Samuel,* 51; and H. P. Smith, *Critical and Exegetical Commentary,* 6. As Driver, Klein, McCarter, and Smith point out, the mistaken reading of *ṣôpîm* arose when the *m* of the following phrase *mēhar 'eprāyim* was mistakenly copied twice and thus appended to the original *ṣûpî.*
6. E.g., P. M. Arnold, "Ramah," 613; Tsumura, *First Book of Samuel,* 107, 124–25.
7. So Edelman, "Saul's Journey," 54–57; see also van der Toorn, "Saul and the Rise of Israelite State Religion," 522, and van der Toorn, *Family Religion,* 270.
8. So, e.g., Hertzberg, *I and II Samuel,* 23; R. W. Klein, *1 Samuel,* 5; McCarter, *I Samuel,* 58, 61–62; and Meyers, "Ethnoarchaeological Analysis of Hannah's Sacrifice," 85–86. But cf. Haran, "Zeḇaḥ Hayyamîm," 15–16, and Haran, *Temples,* 307–8, who argues (on the basis of the fact that Ephrath and Ephraim can be used in the Bible to refer to Bethlehem) that Samuel should be understood as a Judahite.
9. Ramah/er-Ram lies about 22.5 kilometers south and slightly west of Shiloh as the crow flies, or, as near as I can figure, about 25 kilometers if one were to travel by ancient roads. Arimathea/Rentis lies about 26.2 kilometers to the west and a little south of Shiloh as the crow flies, or again, about 30 kilometers via ancient roads. Khirbet Raddana lies about 18.1 kilometers southwest of Shiloh as the crow flies, or, once more, about 25.2 kilometers via ancient roads.
10. According to King and Stager, *Life in Biblical Israel,* 186, "a day's journey in biblical times averaged between twenty-seven and thirty-seven kilometers"; Garfinkel, Kreimerman, and Zilberg, *Debating Khirbet Qeiyafa,* 226–27, similarly write that "the distance that can be covered in a day on foot or using pack animals is no more than 30 km." Josephus in addition reports that in the Roman era, it took three days to journey the 105 kilometers from the Galilee to Jerusalem, meaning travelers covered a little more than 32 kilometers in a day.

See M. S. Smith, with contributions by Bloch-Smith, *Pilgrimage Pattern,* 58, citing Dorsey, *Roads and Highways,* 12.

11. Milgrom, *Leviticus 1–16,* 32.
12. This is the highway that modern scholars often designate as the "Hill Road," the "Ridge Route," the "Watershed Route," or the "Watershed Highway," so called because it "followed the crest or watershed of the highlands for much of its length" (Dorsey, *Roads and Highways,* 117).
13. Certain biblical scholars also promote this understanding: e.g., P. D. Miller, *Religion,* 79; Wenham, "Deuteronomy," 98–99; and Willis, "Cultic Elements," 44, 46; also, although he expresses some caveats, McKane, *I and II Samuel,* 35.
14. On a seventh-century BCE date for Ps 78, see Clifford, "In Zion and David a New Beginning," 139–41, as well as the many references collected by van der Toorn and Houtman, "David and the Ark," 226, n. 60. There is, however, debate: various views are summarized by Leuchter, "Reference to Shiloh in Psalm 78," 1–19; on pp. 19–31, Leuchter stakes out his own position. On the date of Jer 7:12 and the related 26:4–9, see Ackerman, *Under Every Green Tree,* 6 and n. 3 on that page.
15. On Jerusalem as Deuteronomy's "chosen place," see Chapter 5, n. 50. See also on Deuteronomy's ideology, and for a refutation of those who would interpret the Deuteronomy materials differently, E. W. Nicholson, *Deuteronomy,* 53–55.
16. Weinfeld, *Deuteronomy and the Deuteronomic School,* 218.
17. Ibid., 170, 219.
18. A similar understanding of Shiloh as a regional sanctuary is well articulated by van der Toorn, *Family Religion,* 244 and n. 39 on that page; see also Berlin, "Hannah and Her Prayers," 227; Bird, "Notes on Gender," 226, n. 21; Driver, *Notes on the Hebrew Text,* 12; Milgrom, *Leviticus 1–16,* 31–32; Milgrom, *Leviticus 17–22,* 1504; Olyan, "What Do We Really Know?," 63; Shiloh, "Iron Age Sanctuaries," 153; M. S. Smith, with contributions by Bloch-Smith, *Pilgrimage Pattern,* 73; and van der Toorn and Houtman, "David and the Ark," 226. Shiloh is in addition described as a local or regional sanctuary by Albertz, "Personal Names and Family Religion," in Albertz and Schmitt, *Family and Household Religion,* 271, and by Schmitt, "Rites of Family and Household Religion," in ibid., 389, 404, and 415, but cf. Schmitt, "Elements of Domestic Cult," in ibid., 169, who writes of the archaeological remains from Shiloh: "the decorated cult stand and other figurative material seem to be ritual essentials from an early Iron Age *domestic* cult assemblage" (emphasis mine). Note also ibid., 498, 533.
19. See similarly Olyan, "Family Religion in Israel," 123, n. 15, and Schmitt, "Typology of Iron Age Cult Places," in Albertz and Schmitt, *Family and Household Religion,* 234–35, 237, 244.
20. On Gilgal as a regional sanctuary, see Hos 4:15, 12:12 (English 12:11); Amos 5:5. On Lachish and Nebo, see Stern, "From Many Gods to One God," 396–97; also, on Lachish, see Ganor and Kreimerman, "Eighth-Century B.C.E. Gate

Shrine," 227; Köckert, "YHWH in the Northern and Southern Kingdom," 378; and Na'aman, "No Anthropomorphic Graven Image," 404–5; and, on Nebo, see M. S. Smith, *Where the Gods Are,* 96 and 176, n. 219, and Stern, "Phoenician Source of Palestinian Cults," 316. On Carmel, see A. R. Davis, *Tel Dan,* 116–18, and Edelman, "Cultic Sites," 84. On Dor, see Avigad, "Priest of Dor," 103–4, and Stern, "Phoenician Source of Palestinian Cults," 317. On Tel Motza, see Kisilevitz, "Iron IIA Judahite Temple," 147–64, and on Tel Reḥov, see Edelman, "Cultic Sites," 91–92. Van der Toorn, *Family Religion,* 311, includes Jericho on this list.

21. McCarter, *1 Samuel,* 93. See similarly R. W. Klein, *1 Samuel,* 5, who writes, "no clear evidence of the [Deuteronomistic] historian's hand is present" in 1 Sam 1.
22. McCarter, *1 Samuel,* 22, citing Birch, *Rise of the Israelite Monarchy,* 152–54.
23. E.g., P. D. Miller, *Religion,* 91.
24. The Masoretic Text reads a singular form, *mĕzûzâ;* other ancient sources reflect the plural *mĕzûzôt.*
25. McCarter, *1 Samuel,* 100.
26. E.g., Barrick, "High Place," 199; McCarter, *I Samuel,* 55, following several older authorities (see BDB, 545b); and Parry, "Hannah in the Presence of the Lord," 63. See as well Fincke, *Samuel Scroll,* 8, and Ulrich, ed., *Biblical Qumran Scrolls,* 259, both of whom restore a reference to a *liškâ* in the 4QSam[a] scroll from Qumran.
27. Zevit, *Religions,* 218.
28. See I. Finkelstein, "History and Archaeology of Shiloh," 384–85; I. Finkelstein, "Iron I Shiloh," 143–44.
29. On Finkelstein's evolving views regarding the date of the Iron Age I period, and so the date of this destruction, see Chapter 1, n. 20.
30. I. Finkelstein, "Seilun, Khirbet," 1072. Finkelstein describes himself as "non-commital," however, on the identification of Shiloh as a regional or "pan-Israelite" sacred center: see I. Finkelstein, "History and Archaeology of Shiloh," 385–86.
31. I. Finkelstein, "History and Archaeology of Shiloh," 377; I. Finkelstein, "Iron I Shiloh," 143.
32. I. Finkelstein, "Seilun, Khirbet," 1071.
33. I. Finkelstein, "History and Archaeology of Shiloh," 381–82; I. Finkelstein, "Iron I Shiloh," 144.
34. I. Finkelstein, "Seilun, Khirbet," 1072; also I. Finkelstein, "History and Archaeology of Shiloh," 386–87. See similarly Milgrom, "Priestly ('P') Source," 460, who reports the number of sites surrounding Shiloh as twenty-two.
35. Similarly I. Finkelstein, "Iron I Shiloh," 149.
36. Indeed, during the Iron Age II period (ca. 1000–586 BCE), there may have been an Israelite preference for open-air sanctuaries as opposed to sanctuary sites with buildings: see Farber, "Religion in Eighth-Century Judah," 440–41, and Faust, "Israelite Temples," 1–26.

37. Mazar, "Bull Site," 383.
38. Mazar, "The 'Bull Site,'" 32; Nakhai, *Archaeology,* 170; and Zevit, *Religions,* 176.
39. Mazar, "The 'Bull Site,'" 33; Zevit, *Religions,* 178.
40. Mazar, "The 'Bull Site,'" 33–34.
41. Ibid., 34–35, 36.
42. Ibid., 27.
43. For references to El as "Bull," see M. S. Smith, *Origins of Biblical Monotheism,* 32; for Baal bull images, see the catalogue in Mazar, "The 'Bull Site,'" 29–32.
44. Reading **'abbîr* ["the Bull of"] *ya'ăqōb* and **'abbîr* ["the Bull of"] *yiśrā'ēl,* for the Masoretic Text's *'ăbîr* ["the Mighty One of"] *ya'ăqōb* and *'ăbîr* ["the Mighty One of"] *yiśrā'ēl.* Alternatively, see Cross, *Canaanite Myth,* 4, n. 6, who argues that *'ābîr* originally meant "bull" or "stallion," or (similarly) Kapelrud, "*'ābîr, 'abbîr,*" 42, who describes the doubling of the *b* in *'abbîr* as "an artificial distinction which the Masoretes invented to avoid any suspicion that Yahweh was to be identified with [a] bull."
45. King and Stager, *Life in Biblical Israel,* 343–44; Stager, "Canaanite Silver Calf," 580. However, unlike King and Stager, who take the bull image on the Taanach cult stand to be "the beast of Yahweh, not Yahweh himself" (*Life in Biblical Israel,* 343), I see the bull as a Yahweh image.
46. Van der Toorn, *Family Religion,* 245, 254.
47. Mazar, "The 'Bull Site,'" 35–36; Nakhai, *Archaeology,* 170.
48. Milgrom, *Leviticus 1–16,* 205–8.
49. On the archaeological evidence that indicates *šĕlāmîm* offerings were boiled, see Greer, *Dinner at Dan,* 82.
50. Zevit, *Religions,* 180. On the evidence, textual and archaeological, that indicates that *šĕlāmîm* meals were both cooked and eaten within a sanctuary's courtyard, see Greer, *Dinner at Dan,* 80–82, 92–93, 120–22; Milgrom, *Leviticus 1–16,* 223, 619–21; and Segal, *Hebrew Passover,* 133; also Daviau, "Family Religion," 223, who cites Mazar, *Excavations at Tell Qasile,* Fig. 14.9–20 (Locus 110), in order to argue that "communal meals were definitely part of the ceremonies at public shrines and temples, such as at Tell Qasile where cooking was practiced."
51. Anderson, "Sacrifice," 873, 878; similarly Bergman, Lang, and Ringgren, "*zābaḥ, zebaḥ,*" 10; Eberhart, "Sacrifice? Holy Smokes!," 26–27; Levine, *Leviticus,* 15; and Milgrom, *Leviticus 1–16,* 218.
52. See similarly Bird, "Notes on Gender," 226 (on 1 Sam 1:4–5); Bray, *Sacred Dan,* 95, 139 (on 1 Sam 1:4–5 and 1 Sam 1:1–2:26 generally); and Greer, *Dinner at Dan,* 121 (on 1 Sam 1:4–5 and 2:13). But cf. Olyan, *Rites and Rank,* 11, who imagines (Olyan's word) that in 1 Sam 1:3–5, after Elkanah, as the head of his household, slaughters the sacrifice and "strips the skin off the slaughtered animal and divides it into portions," "the components of the sacrifice are then passed to the priests for further processing," before Elkanah "receives back portions of cooked meat to distribute to his dependents."

53. On the site of a sacrificial animal's slaughter in relation to the site of the altar, see de Vaux, *Ancient Israel,* 416; Eberhart, "Sacrifice? Holy Smokes!," 27; Greer, *Dinner at Dan,* 116–19; Milgrom, *Leviticus 1–16,* 164; Propp, *Exodus 19–40,* 698; and Zevit, *Religions,* 168, 278.
54. De Vaux, *Ancient Israel,* 356.
55. On the relation of Ezekiel to P and other priestly sources, see Haran, "Ezekiel, P, and the Priestly School," 211–18; Hurvitz, *Linguistic Study;* Milgrom, *Leviticus 1–16,* 451–53; and Zimmerli, *Ezekiel 1,* 46–52.
56. Milgrom, *Leviticus 1–16,* 55.
57. Olyan, *Rites and Rank,* 19.
58. See McCarter, *1 Samuel,* 92, who writes of 1 Sam 2:27–36 as "replete with the devices and clichés of the . . . [Deuteronomistic] historian"; see similarly Brettler, "Composition of 1 Samuel 1–2," 665: "2:27–36 is . . . a secondary, Deuteronomistic addition . . . full of Deuteronomistic language and ideology"; also Willis, "Anti-Elide Narrative Tradition," 288, n. 3, who lists 1 Sam 2:27–36 as among "relatively the latest passages" in 1 and 2 Samuel, most of which he further characterizes as having "*some* affinities in thought and expression with Dt [Deuteronomy]." But cf., specifically in response to Brettler, Rendsburg, "Some False Leads," 35–45. For further discussion, see Leuchter, "Something Old, Something Older."
59. Although cf. Milgrom, *Leviticus 1–16,* 222: "the blood rite is . . . the quintessential element in the well-being [*šĕlāmîm*] offering."
60. McCarter, *1 Samuel,* 77. Other translators who render in the passive include the LXX (both in 2:15 and 2:16); the JB (in 2:15); the NEB (in 2:15); the REB (in 2:15); the NJPS (in 2:15); the RSV (in 2:15); the NJB (in both 2:15 and 16); the NAB (in both 2:15 and 16); the NABRE (in both 2:15 and 16); Hertzberg, *I and II Samuel,* 32 (in both 2:15 and 16); and Tsumura, *First Book of Samuel,* 153–54 and 153, n. 91 (in both 2:15 and 16). See further, on Tsumura's understanding of "impersonal passives" as used in 2:15–16, n. 83 below.
61. McCarter, *1 Samuel,* 79.
62. Braulik, "Were Women, Too, Allowed to Offer Sacrifices?," 921.
63. Nelson, *Raising Up a Faithful Priest,* 46–47; Cody, *History of Old Testament Priesthood,* 72.
64. Blenkinsopp, *Sage, Priest, Prophet,* 74, suggests that "sacrifice at local sanctuaries" may have been officiated over by "the cultic specialist of the kinship unit."
65. See similarly van der Toorn, "Theology, Priests, and Worship," 2050; also, in a discussion that considers the Bull Site along with other similar venues, Albertz, *History of Israelite Religion 1,* 85: "this . . . type of sanctuary" was a place where "the whole of the local community could assemble . . . under the guidance of a man of God, if one happened to be present, or a priest engaged for a season."
66. 1 Sam 7:17 describes Samuel as erecting an altar in Ramah; 1 Sam 9:11–14, 19, 22–25 then describe Samuel as coming to preside over a sacrifice that commen-

tators most typically interpret as taking place at that same shrine (although this is, in fact, not specified). But cf. McCarter, *1 Samuel,* 163, 175, who, while he unequivocally locates the shrine mentioned in 1 Sam 7:17 in Benjaminite Ramah (ibid., 148), understands the shrine in 1 Sam 9 to be located in Ephraimite Ramathaim, the town that McCarter takes one strand of the Samuel tradition to identify as Samuel's hometown (above, n. 8). Hertzberg, *I and II Samuel,* 79, somewhat similarly sees two strands of tradition in 1 Sam 9, one of which concerns (and originally stemmed from) Benjaminite Ramah and the other of which concerns (and originally stemmed from) the tradition that located Samuel's hometown in Ramathaim.

67. McKane, *I and II Samuel,* 73; P. D. Miller, *Religion,* 162; see similarly ibid., 176. Willis, "Cultic Elements," 45, also understands Samuel to play a priestly role in 1 Sam 9:11–14, 19, 22–25, and Willis speaks of Samuel's priestly role more generally in ibid., 44–48, with other references listed at 47, n. 50. But cf. Cody, *History of Old Testament Priesthood,* 72–80, who rejects the view that Samuel in 1 Sam 9 or, indeed, anywhere is understood as a priest.

68. The translation of *bāmâ* (singular)/*bāmôt* (plural) as "high place(s)" comes into English via the Latin Vulgate, which rendered *bāmâ* as *excelsus* (Barrick, "High Place," 196; Barrick, BMH *as Body Language,* 1). But this translation is misleading: for example, while biblical texts can speak of hills and mountains as the sites of *bāmôt,* the *bāmâ* at the Tophet in Jerusalem was in the *valley* of Hinnom (Jer 7:31, 19:5–6, 32:35), and Ezek 6:3 refers to the *bāmôt* of both the hills and *valleys.* Nor is it necessarily clear, whatever some have argued (e.g., de Vaux, *Ancient Israel,* 284–88; Haran, *Temples,* 18–25; and Vaughan, *Meaning of "bāmâ,"* 31, 55), that *bāmôt* are always associated with manmade elevations (Barrick, "High Place," 197). Overall, as P. D. Miller points out (*Religion,* 236, n. 21), "there is much that is still unclear" regarding the *bāmôt.* In addition to a 1980 article by Barrick, "What Do We Really Know About the 'High Places'?," 50–57, Miller directs readers, as would I, to Emerton, "Biblical High Place," 116–32, and Gleis, *Die Bamah.*

69. Some *bāmôt,* in my opinion, are better understood as more centralized and even national sanctuaries. See, e.g., my discussion in Chapter 7 of the *bāmâ* associated with King Saul's fief in Gibeah according to 1 Sam 10:5, 13, and some Greek versions of 1 Sam 22:6.

70. For this translation of *ʿîr* (singular)/*ʿārîm* (plural), see Meyers, *Rediscovering Eve,* 41–42.

71. Barrick, in addition to objecting to the translation of *bāmâ* as "high place" (above, n. 68), also objects to the characterization of *bāmôt* as local sanctuaries: in his monograph BMH *as Body Language,* he criticizes Emerton, "Biblical High Place," 129–30; Gleis, *Die Bamah,* 32–234; and Whitney, "'Bamoth' in the Old Testament," 138, for holding this view, and in "Why Do We Associate Biblical Bamoth with Israelite 'Popular' Religion?," he similarly faults King

and Stager, *Life in Biblical Israel,* 319; P. D. Miller, *Religion,* 76 and 236, n. 22; Nakhai, *Archaeology,* 163–64; and Zevit, *Religions,* 262–63. But if I read Barrick correctly, what really concerns him is the association he believes all these scholars presume between local sanctuaries and "popular" religious practices, by which Barrick means, at a minimum, practices that were engaged independent of state sanction and that could, more maximally, be described as nonnormative in the sense of being (in his words) "neo-Canaanite" and "non-Yahwistic." Yet I see no reason to assume this equation (although I do not doubt that many have made it), which is to say: I maintain the *bāmôt* can be "local" in the sense I have described (shrines used by worshippers who live within a 25–30-kilometer radius or so), yet used for ritual practices that, for their congregations, are a part of normative Yahwistic cult. That said, I am grateful to Professor Barrick for having provided me with a copy of the unpublished manuscript cited above before his untimely death.

72. P. D. Miller, *Religion,* 76–77. See similarly Blenkinsopp, "Family in First Temple Israel," 79, who characterizes *bāmôt* as "regional sanctuaries," and LaRocca-Pitts, *"Of Wood and Stone,"* 147, who describes the Israelite and Moabite *bāmôt* of Isa 15:2, 16:12; Hos 10:8; Amos 7:9; Mic 1:5, 3:12 (= Jer 26:18) as "small-scale sites of worship . . . when compared with the greater state-level cult centers."
73. Halpern, "Sybil, or the Two Nations?," 303.
74. Gerstenberger, *Theologies,* 105.
75. Meyers, *Discovering Eve,* 147; likewise Meyers, *Rediscovering Eve,* 184.
76. In the fourteenth-/thirteenth-century BCE Kirta Epic from the northern Levantine city-state of Ugarit, King Kirta's wife, Lady Hurriya, also serves as cook (*ṭbḫ)* when Kirta's nobles visit the palace for a feast (*KTU* 1.15.4.4, 15, 1.15.5.1). Gen 41:10, however, identifies the "chief baker" in the palace of the Egyptian pharaoh as male.
77. Above, n. 3.
78. For this terminology, see Anderson, "Sacrifice," 878; Bergman, Lang, and Ringgren, "*zābaḥ, zebaḥ,*" 10; Milgrom, *Leviticus 1–16,* 218; and P. D. Miller, *Religion,* 112.
79. McCarter, *I Samuel,* 57, and Tov, "Different Editions of the Song of Hannah," 154; also Fincke, *Samuel Scroll,* 9 and 30, note on Col. II, lines 9–10, and Ulrich, ed., *Biblical Qumran Scrolls,* 260.
80. For some, however, the journey of 1 Sam 1:24–25 was a trip to Shiloh that Elkanah and Hannah made to dedicate the newly weaned Samuel to Yahweh's service, as, according to 1 Sam 1:11, Hannah had vowed to do (more on this in Chapter 4). This suggestion, which goes back to Wellhausen, *Der Text der Bücher Samuelis,* 41, is based on the reference to Hannah going to Shiloh with Samuel "when she had weaned him" in v. 24, which, Wellhausen argued, indicated a journey made to Shiloh *not* at the time of Elkanah's usual yearly visit (see further Walters, "Hannah and Anna," 400–401 and 401, n. 25). Some commentators (e.g., P. D. Miller, *Religion,* 71; Zevit, *Religions,* 665) even see in

1 Sam 1:24–25 a description of a sacrifice (with a feast to follow) that was explicitly made in celebration of Samuel's weaning. I, however, take weaning feasts to be home-based, as opposed to sanctuary-based rituals (Gen 21:8), and for this reason, among the others I have detailed here, I see 1 Sam 1:24–25 as an account of one of Elkanah's family's regular journeys to Shiloh.

81. On the translation "skin"/"vessel," see Meyers, "Ethnoarchaeological Analysis of Hannah's Sacrifice," 84.

82. As Driver (*Notes on the Hebrew Text,* 20) and McCarter (*I Samuel,* 56–57), among others, point out, the Masoretic Text has suffered a simple corruption here, as the *m* of the original reading *bpr mšlš,* a "three-year-old bull," has been mistakenly repositioned to yield *bprym šlšh,* "three bulls." But cf. Braulik, "Were Women, Too, Allowed to Offer Sacrifices?," 920, n. 38, who argues (drawing on the work of Walters, "Hannah and Anna," 402) that "three bulls" is the correct reading, as one bull was to be sacrificed for each of the three people involved (Elkanah, Hannah, and Samuel).

83. That Hannah and Elkanah (as opposed to Hannah and Samuel) are the subjects of the third-person plural verbs of v. 25 in the Masoretic Text is well argued by Walters, "Hannah and Anna," 401, who notes both that it is unlikely that Hannah and Samuel would have traveled alone to Shiloh without the company of their male head of household, i.e., Elkanah, and that 1 Sam 2:11, which speaks of Elkanah as returning to Ramah "while the boy [Samuel] remained to serve Yahweh," confirms Elkanah was present at Shiloh along with Hannah to dedicate their son to Yahweh's service in 1 Sam 1:25–28. For further discussion, including an analysis of how Elkanah was originally present but then dropped out of the Masoretic Text of v. 24, see Tov, "Different Editions of the Song of Hannah," 153–54. But cf. Driver, *Notes on the Hebrew Text,* 21; McKane, *I and II Samuel,* 35; and Willis, "Cultic Elements," 60, who propose that some otherwise unmentioned *šōḥăṭîm* (Driver), "temple attendants" (McKane), or "temple servants or attendants" (Willis) were the ones who, in Willis's words, "slew the bull and brought Samuel to Eli." Tsumura, *First Book of Samuel,* 132, renders the verbs of v. 25 as what he calls "impersonal passives," thus translating "the bull was slaughtered" and "the boy was brought to Eli."

84. L. R. Klein, "Hannah," 91; similarly Meyers, "Hannah and Her Sacrifice," 100–101, and Meyers, "Hannah Narrative," 123; somewhat similarly (although without accusing the Greek of deliberately "patriarchalizing"), Walters, "Hannah and Anna," 400–409.

85. Tov, *Textual Criticism,* 254; see similarly Tov, "Different Editions of the Song of Hannah," 155–57, where he argues with regard to 1 Sam 1:28 and 2:11 that the Masoretic Text, in the words of Fidler ("Wife's Vow," 375, n. 10), "'reflects a revision' that marginalizes the role of Hannah in favour of Elkanah." Fidler's own conclusions, especially as summarized in ibid., 387, are similar: "Ultimately, his [Elkanah's] active involvement seems superimposed on an essentially woman-centered story."

86. Paraphrasing here W. Dietrich's remarks about the Dead Sea Scroll text of 1 Sam 1:28 ("Doch ein Text hinter den Texten?," 150: "In diesem Fall hat also einzig Q den ursprünglichen, Hanna-freundlichen Text bewahrt").
87. See further Tov, "Different Editions of the Song of Hannah," 154–55, n. 26, who argues that after the textual mishap that deleted Elkanah from v. 24 (above, n. 83), the masculine singular verb of v. 25, "and he slaughtered," became incomprehensible to the text's copyists and transmitters and so it was mistakenly changed to a plural form.
88. See similarly Bird, "Place of Women," 405, 408, and 415–16, n. 34; Bird, "Women's Religion," 293; P. D. Miller, *Religion,* 69 (but cf. ibid., 205); Vos, *Woman in Old Testament Worship,* 80; Winter, *Frau und Göttin,* 38–40; and, specifically of the sacrifice under consideration here, Wegner, "'Coming Before the LORD': *lpny yhwh,*" 82; Wegner, "*'Coming Before the Lord':* The Exclusion of Women," 455.
89. Ackerman, "Mother of Eshmunazor," 174–77; Henshaw, *Female and Male,* 3; and Stowers, "Greeks Who Sacrifice," 296–98, 327, 332.
90. Jay, *Throughout Your Generations Forever.*
91. Jay, "Sacrifice as Remedy," 284.
92. This text and its significance were brought to my attention by Vos, *Woman in Old Testament Worship,* 80, 148.
93. Children in ancient Israel, as elsewhere in the ancient world, were typically not weaned until three years of age. See 2 Macc 7:27, and, among many modern commentators, Gruber, "Breast-Feeding Practices," 72 (citing Granqvist, *Child Problems,* 79); Stol, *Birth,* 181; and Stol, *Women,* 376. See also the references assembled by Berlinerblau, *The Vow,* 109, n. 37, and note as well that Blenkinsopp, "Family in First Temple Israel," 97, n. 42, has proposed that Hannah is said in 1 Sam 1:24 to bring a *three-year-old* bull to Shiloh when she comes to dedicate Samuel to God's service because this animal is the same age as the newly weaned boy (following here the Greek, versus the Masoretic Text's reading of "three bulls"; see my discussion above). This interpretation is also put forward by Fokkelman, *Narrative Art and Poetry,* 67, and Pfeifer, "Entwöhnung," 342.
94. On the size of an ephah, see Chapter 2, n. 61.
95. See Borowski, *Agriculture in Iron Age Israel,* 102–12, and Hopkins, "'All Sorts of Field Work,'" 162–67, for many of the biblical references cited here and for the technical details concerning wine production. For Egyptian images of the grape-harvesting process, see James, "Earliest History of Wine," 205, 208–11, and Lesko, "Egyptian Wine Production," 217–18, 220.
96. Similarly Bird, "Notes on Gender," 227.
97. Oppenheim, *Ancient Mesopotamia,* 183.

Chapter 4. "She Prayed to Yahweh, She Wept . . . and She Made a Vow"

1. Chapter 3, n. 82.
2. Cf. Meyers, "Hannah and Her Sacrifice," 94 (likewise, Meyers, "Hannah Narrative," 117), who proposes that "Elkanah's differential allotment of the sacrificial portions—only one portion to Hannah, for she was only one individual—caused her to weep."
3. 1 Sam 1:9 is not preserved in the texts from the Dead Sea Scrolls.
4. See, among older sources, Driver, *Notes on the Hebrew Text,* 11–12, and the discussion in GKC, §91e; for more recent comments, see Tsumura, *First Book of Samuel,* 115–16, n. 67, and Walters, "After Drinking," 528, n. 4.
5. For scholars who hold this view, see the excellent catalogue assembled by Walters, "After Drinking," 531–33.
6. Similarly (among others) Ackroyd, *First Book of Samuel,* 23, 25; Amit, "'Am I Not More Devoted to You Than Ten Sons?,'" 71 and 71–72, n. 3; Berlin, "Hannah and Her Prayers," 228, n. 4; Driver, *Notes on the Hebrew Text,* 12; Fokkelman, *Narrative Art and Poetry,* 32; and H. P. Smith, *Critical and Exegetical Commentary,* 8–9.
7. Chapter 3, n. 24.
8. Cartledge, *Vows in the Hebrew Bible,* 25; also Berlinerblau, *The Vow,* 175.
9. Hebrew *šēkār,* the term that presumably underlies the Vaticanus text's *methysma,* "an intoxicating drink," is often translated "beer." But this translation is by no means certain: see Ebeling and Homan, "Baking and Brewing Beer," 48, and Homan, "Beer, Barley, and *šēkār,*" 28–38.
10. McCarter, *I Samuel,* 54; see likewise Fincke, *Samuel Scroll,* 8, and Ulrich, ed., *Biblical Qumran Scrolls,* 259.
11. Although as Brettler has pointed out (in "Women and Psalms," 31, n. 27), some midrashic traditions interpret the odd phrase *nōkaḥ 'ištô* in Gen 25:21 to mean that Rebekah joined together with Isaac during his entreaty (*'ātar*) to God regarding Rebekah's barrenness.
12. P. D. Miller, in "Things Too Wonderful," 237, identifies what he describes as ten or eleven instances of women praying in the Hebrew Bible (although he then lists thirteen—Gen 21:16–17, 25:22, 29:35, 30:24; Exod 15:21; Judg 5:1–31; 1 Sam 1:10, 12–15, 2:1–10; 1 Kgs 10:9; Ps 131; Ruth 1:8–9, 4:14); see also P. D. Miller, *They Cried to the Lord*), 413, n. 2. Miller is followed in his analysis of Ps 131 by J. G. Janzen, "Prayer and/as Self-Address," 115–17; Knowles, "Woman at Prayer," 385–89; and Strawn, "Woman at Prayer," 421–26. But see n. 16 below.
13. Brettler, "Woman's Voice," 155–70, esp. 162–63.
14. On Gen 25:22, see P. D. Miller, as cited in n. 12 above; for Judg 17:2, see Blank, "The Curse," 95, and Scharbert, "*'ālâ,*" 265.
15. My reservations with regard to the other examples catalogued by Miller in n. 12 above concern Miller's sense of what should be classified as prayer, which

I define more narrowly than he, limiting the category of prayer to moments in which an individual or a community speaks directly to God. I thus would not, contrary to Miller, see Gen 21:16–17 as prayer, since there is no indication that Hagar's words in this verse are directed to God; similarly, I would argue that Leah's words in Gen 29:35 and Rachel's words in Gen 30:24, which are spoken as part of wordplays that gloss the names of their sons Judah and Joseph, are addressed not to God but to the family members and others (e.g., midwives) who might attend these women at birth. Naomi's words in Ruth 1:8–9 likewise seem to me words that are addressed to her daughters-in-law, and Exod 15:21 and Judg 5:1–31, although addressed to Yahweh, are *hymns* of thanksgiving, a genre I differentiate from prayer. Somewhat similarly, I categorize the Bethlehemite women's words in Ruth 4:14 and the Queen of Sheba's words in 1 Kgs 10:9 as benedictions, not prayers, whose intended audience, moreover, is not really the deity.

16. Brettler, "Women and Psalms," 39; Craven, "'From Where Will My Help Come?,'" 95–96.
17. Brettler, "Woman's Voice," 160–62.
18. On both these points—the object of Eli's rebuke and the oddity of silent prayer—see Brettler, "Women and Psalms," 45.
19. Brettler, "Woman's Voice," 163–64.
20. See the references cited in Frevel, "Gifts to the Gods?," 31–32; Marsman, *Women*, 574–75 (although discount Marsman's reference in n. 10, which is to the text of an incantation, not a prayer); and P. D. Miller, *They Cried to the Lord*, 367–68, n. 28. See also Singer, *Hittite Prayers*, 43–44 (Prayer of Taduhepa) and 101–5 (Puduhepa's Prayer), and *KAI* 88 and 164.
21. For the dates of the Esther and Susannah texts discussed here, see McDowell, *Prayers of Jewish Women*, 35, 68.
22. On women's prayers in these various apocryphal/deuterocanonical texts, see further ibid., 34–57, 67–84, and Craven, "'From Where Will My Help Come?,'" 99–100, 102–8.
23. Men's vows: Jacob in Gen 28:20; Jephthah in Judg 11:30; Elkanah, according to 1 Sam 1:21; Absalom in 2 Sam 15:7–8; David, according to Ps 132:2; the sailors of Jonah 1:16; Jonah, according to the psalm that is put in his mouth in Jonah 2:10 (English 2:9); Judas Maccabeaus in 1 Macc 5:5; Heliodorus in 2 Macc 3:35; Antiochus in 2 Macc 9:13; unnamed "heads of families" in 1 Esd 5:44; Artaxerxes in 1 Esd 8:13; Paul in Acts 18:18; four men in Jerusalem at the time of Paul's visit there, according to Acts 21:23.
24. The Nazirite vow discussed in Num 6:2 (and more generally in Num 6:1–21) is somewhat different from the definition of a vow I offered above, in that it is unclear that one takes on the obligations of Nazirite service in *response* to some favor that the deity has granted. Nevertheless, the Nazirite's imposing on himself or herself special obligations on behalf of Yahweh is close enough to the

conceptual world of the vow that the Nazirite vow can be included in this discussion. See Berlinerblau, *The Vow,* 175–76, in response to Cartledge, *Vows in the Hebrew Bible,* 18–26, and to Cartledge, "Were Nazirite Vows Unconditional?," 409–22.

25. Van der Toorn ("Female Prostitution," 193–205) has suggested that Deut 23:19 (English 23:18), which forbids using the wages earned by a female prostitute to pay a vow, speaks more generally to ordinary women, who made frequent vows according to van der Toorn's understanding but did not necessarily have adequate resources to fulfill their commitments. Hence they resorted to prostitution to raise the necessary funds. Cf. Berlinerblau, *The Vow,* 103–7.
26. Commentators who hold this position are well catalogued by Berlinerblau, *The Vow,* 133 and 148, n. 25; add only, among those whose work appeared after Berlinerblau's study had been completed, Albertz, "Personal Names and Family Religion," in Albertz and Schmitt, *Family and Household Religion,* 271; Dever, *Did God Have a Wife?,* 190–92, 195, 241; Tita, *Gelübde;* van der Toorn, *From Her Cradle to Her Grave,* 97–102; and van der Toorn, "Nine Months," 408.
27. Cartledge, *Vows in the Hebrew Bible,* 75, quoting Falkenstein, *Sumerische und akkadische Hymnen und Gebete,* 218–19, no. 41.
28. Cartledge, *Vows in the Hebrew Bible,* 102–3, 105–7.
29. Marsman, *Women,* 574; Singer, *Hittite Prayers,* 101–5 (Puduhepa's Prayer).
30. For vows with prayer, see *KAI* 88 and 164. Other examples of women's vows, as catalogued by Berlinerblau, *The Vow,* 139, and n. 13 on that page, and Gursky, "Reproductive Rituals," 48, include *KAI* 40, 87, 109, and 155, as well as *CIS* 378 and 515. Note, however, that *KAI* 40 does not actually concern a woman's vow: rather, this text, from a third-century BCE stele from Idalion, Cyprus, describes how a grandmother, on behalf of her three grandsons, fulfilled a vow to the god RŠP-MKL that had been made by her (presumably deceased) son MRYḤY. A brief discussion can be found in Cartledge, *Vows in the Hebrew Bible,* 130.
31. *KAI* 109, as discussed in Berlinerblau, *The Vow,* 139.
32. McCarter, *I Samuel,* 55.
33. Because the verb that refers to "a man or a woman" (*'îš 'ô-'iššâ*) in Num 6:2 is in the third-masculine singular, it might be argued that the original text referred only to a man (*'îš*) who vowed himself as a Nazirite and that the phrase "or a woman" is a secondary gloss. But while Num 5:6, where *'îš 'ô-'iššâ* takes a third-masculine plural verb, might support this interpretation, the typical Hebrew idiom is, in fact, to use a singular verb with the compound subject *'îš 'ô-'iššâ:* see Exod 21:28; Lev 13:29, 38; 20:27; Deut 17:2, 29:17 (English 29:18).
34. Chapman, *House of the Mother,* 136–37.
35. See similarly Blenkinsopp, "Structure and Style," 66; Exum, "Promise and Fulfillment," 49; and Gunn, "Samson of Sorrows," 229.
36. Berlin, "Hannah and Her Prayers," 228.

37. Gruber, *Aspects of Nonverbal Communication,* 385.
38. Werline, "Prayer, Politics, and Power," 9.
39. See likewise Hamori, *Women's Divination,* 97, who, while understanding Hannah to be emotionally upset, argues "Hannah is not sad, she is angry" because Peninnah has enraged her; similarly J. G. Janzen, "Prayer and/as Self-Address," 124.
40. I have discussed some of the materials that support this conclusion more fully in Ackerman, "Deception of Isaac," 92–120; see also Olyan, *Biblical Mourning,* 62–96. Observations somewhat similar to my analysis of the Hannah story are in addition offered by Gursky, "Reproductive Rituals," 34–42; Kim, *Incubation,* 263–342; and Neufeld, "Barrenness," 139–40.
41. Text and translation in Güterbock, "Die historische Tradition," 49–65 (with commentary), and in Mouton, *Rêves hittites,* 109–10. For further discussion, see Oppenheim, *Interpretation of Dreams,* 188, 200.
42. In addition to my catalogue here, see Ackerman, "Deception of Isaac," 110, and a fragmentary Mesopotamian text from the Late Babylonian period that details, on the obverse, an account of a lady, perhaps named Qatantu, weeping at a gate (of a city? of a temple?) and, on the reverse, a dream appearance to King Kurigalzu by the god Bel in the Esagila temple. In his editio princeps of this text ("Dream of Kurigalzu," 75–80), Finkel speculates that Qatantu may be both King Kurigalzu's wife and barren. If so, the text can be said to represent a fascinating cooperation in terms of ritual solicitation (the barren wife engages in the weeping that, I propose, induces a dream vision that the husband lies on a couch in the Esagila to receive). Obviously, this text's focus on barrenness also offers an intriguing parallel to the Hannah account (as Finkel duly notes).
43. Winckler, *Sammlung von Keilinschrifttexten,* K. 3040; discussed in Oppenheim, *Interpretation of Dreams,* 188, 190, 200–201, and translated on p. 249, no. 10.
44. The importance of weeping in this text was first suggested by Greenfield, "Some Glosses," 62. Greenfield also proposes that in addition to weeping, the verb *qmṣ* in line 35 "refers to lying down in a recumbent position to induce a dream."
45. Kim, *Incubation,* 185–86.
46. The discussion that follows concentrates on weeping as a means of producing a divine *oracle,* but it is important to note that weeping in the Bible can be more generally practiced in conjunction with cultic petitions: see, e.g., Num 25:6, where the Israelites are said to be weeping at the entrance to the tent of meeting in an effort to petition the deity (as vv. 8–9 imply) to stop the plague that was ravaging their camp; Deut 1:45, where the Israelites weep before Yahweh, presumably seeking forgiveness after they had disobeyed the divine command by attempting to enter the "promised land" from the south and had been rebuffed; and 2 Kgs 22:19 (2 Chr 34:27), where King Josiah is similarly said to have wept before Yahweh, seeking forgiveness for his failure to uphold God's com-

mands as articulated in the scroll that had recently been found in the Jerusalem temple.

47. Bosworth, "Weeping in the Psalms," 39.
48. Other Psalms texts that mention nighttime weeping, presumably in the hope of receiving a divine response that resolves one's woes and even brings rejoicing come morning, include Ps 30:6 (English 30:5) and, more obliquely, Pss 5:4 (English 5:3), 46:6 (English 46:5), 88:14 (English 88:13), and 90:14, references all brought to my attention by Bosworth, "Weeping in the Psalms," 40.
49. Fuhs, "*šā'al,*" 258–61; see also Kuemmerlin-McLean, "Divination and Magic," 94–98, and Sasson, *Judges 1–12,* 121–22.
50. Wagner, "*biqqēš,*" 236–39.
51. As in n. 46 above, the discussion that follows concentrates on fasting as a means of producing a divine *oracle,* but like weeping, fasting in the Bible can more generally be practiced in conjunction with cultic petitions. For discussion, see Olyan, *Biblical Mourning,* 65–69, 71, 75–76, and the excellent catalogue of late biblical and postbiblical examples found in Anderson, *Time to Mourn,* 72, n. 44. Note also Ps 69:11 (English 69:10), where weeping along with fasting is undertaken in order to petition God, and the additional examples of weeping in conjunction with fasting in the context of petition found in postexilic texts that are otherwise not the topic of this study: e.g., Joel 2:12–17; Ezra 10:1, 6; Neh 1:4.
52. Wagner, "*dāraš,*" 302–4; see also Kuemmerlin-McLean, "Divination and Magic," 98–103.
53. David's fasting and weeping in 2 Sam 12:15–23 are, like Hannah's acts in 1 Sam 1:9–18, often taken to be expressions of grief or, more specifically in David's case, rites of "anticipatory mourning" over the imminent death of his infant son: for references, see Bosworth, "Faith and Resilience," 693–94 and 694, n. 8, and Jacobs, "Death of David's Son," 568 and n. 4 on that page. But as Bosworth, "Faith and Resilience," 693–94, emphatically states, David's fasting and weeping are acts of *supplication,* not to be "confused with mourning," just as I have proposed that Hannah's fast and her tears are not expressions of grief but rites of petition.
54. Stager, "Archaeology of the Family," 16.
55. Note, however, that only after the child has died, in v. 20, is David said to go to the "house of Yahweh." Thus, if David did go to a sacred precinct in conjunction with his ritual acts of fasting and weeping, it was not Yahweh's temple in Jerusalem. Indeed, according to the logic of the larger biblical tradition, David could not have gone to the temple even after his ritual of fasting and weeping, since the temple is not said to have been built until the time of his son, Solomon!
56. Ackerman, "Deception of Isaac," 115 (with references).
57. But cf. Kim, *Incubation,* 300–302.

58. Reading *hš'ylh* with 4QSam[a] in 1 Sam 2:20 for the nonsensical *šā'al* of the Masoretic Text.
59. This issue is one that has generated much discussion in the scholarly literature, with most commentators suggesting that the birth story of Samuel—or at least significant parts of it—must have originally been told about Saul, for only by substituting Saul's name for Samuel's do the wordplays of v. 20 and v. 28 make sense ("She [Hannah] called his name Samuel [*šěmû'ēl*], for [she said], 'It was from Yahweh that I asked him [*šě'iltîw*]"; "I have dedicated him [*hiš'iltīhû*] to Yahweh . . . he is dedicated [*šā'ûl*] to Yahweh" [literally, "he is Yahweh's Saul"]). For an extensive review of the literature, see Na'aman, "Samuel's Birth Legend," 51–57.
60. As Cooper and Goldstein, "At the Entrance to the Tent," 209, write: "Once Eli has ascertained Hannah's sincerity and sobriety, he does his job, uttering what we would take to be the intermediary's formal response to a bona fide petition." Indeed, we might take Eli's "job" here, uttering an oracle in "response to a bona fide petition," to be the predominant task of priestly functionaries according to 1 Sam 1:1–2:26 (and related texts; note, e.g., the oracular functions performed by Micah's Levite priest in Judg 17:1–18:31), this as opposed to the task of presiding at sacrificial rites, especially the sacrificial rites of altar service, from which—as we saw in Chapter 3—the Shiloh priesthood (as well as, I argued, the priesthoods of the Bull Site and the sanctuary of 1 Sam 9) is seemingly detached. See similarly Cody, *History of Old Testament Priesthood,* 72, 74, and Nelson, *Raising Up a Faithful Priest,* 42, 123.
61. See similarly Albertz, "Personal Names and Family Religion," in Albertz and Schmitt, *Family and Household Religion,* 273, and Schmitt, "Rites of Family and Household Religion," in ibid., 389, 411; also, Bray, *Sacred Dan,* 96; Brueggemann, *Worship,* 32; Kim, *Incubation,* 305, 309; Willis, "Anti-Elide Narrative Tradition," 291, n. 10; and Willis, "Cultic Elements," 59, n. 96 (in both cases with additional references). Cartledge, *Vows in the Hebrew Bible,* 187, and R. W. Klein, *1 Samuel,* 9, also admit the possibility that Eli's words convey a promise and not just a wish, although neither commits to a particular translation.
62. Amit, "'Am I Not More Devoted to You Than Ten Sons?,'" 68–76.
63. See somewhat similarly, Ackroyd, *First Book of Samuel,* 25, and Fokkelman, *Narrative Art and Poetry,* 28; also Kim, *Incubation,* 309, 313.
64. These many instances of Hannah being "before the Lord" or "before Yahweh" are well catalogued in Parry, "Hannah in the Presence of the Lord," 70–71.
65. Haran, *Temples,* 26, n. 24, identifies 230 instances of the phrase *lipnê yhwh* in the Bible; Fowler, "Meaning of *lîpnê* YHWH," 384 and 387, counts 236 citations, with 62 in Leviticus.
66. Wegner, "'Coming Before the LORD': *lpny yhwh,*" 86–87; Wegner, "'*Coming Before the Lord':* The Exclusion of Women," 459–60.
67. Chapter 3, n. 85.

68. On the subjects of the third-person plural verbs of v. 25 in the Masoretic Text, see Chapter 3, n. 83.
69. Translation McCarter, *I Samuel,* 57.
70. Ibid.; see also Ulrich, ed., *Biblical Qumran Scrolls,* 260.
71. McCarter, *I Samuel,* 57–58.
72. For discussion, see Walters, "Hannah and Anna," 401, who notes that most commentators follow Wellhausen, *Der Text der Bücher Samuelis,* 12, in taking Elkanah as the subject of the Masoretic Text's v. 28; Walters, however, suggests it is Samuel, as does Parry, "Hannah in the Presence of the Lord," 68–69. Fokkelman, *Narrative Art and Poetry,* 73, takes the subject of the "bowing down" to be Eli.
73. On Exod 19:15, see Chapter 5 and n. 51 there.

Chapter 5. "This Is the King's Sanctuary and a Temple of the Kingdom"

1. On these dates, see Meyers, "Temple," 365; similarly, Grossman, "Women and the Jerusalem Temple," 20 and 32, n. 37.
2. Quoted in Meyers, "Temple," 365.
3. While the archaeological remains from Herod's temple are in many respects "meager" (Netzer, *Architecture of Herod,* 137), those that are extant make clear the complex's monumental scale, on which see (for the dimensions given here) Lalor, "Temple Mount," 97, and Meyers, "Temple," 365. Slightly different figures are given in Netzer, *Architecture of Herod,* 160.
4. Meyers, "Temple," 365, citing Ben-Dov, *In the Shadow of the Temple,* 77.
5. Lalor, "Temple Mount," 98, 113.
6. Ibid., 111.
7. On this courtyard, see Netzer, *Architecture of Herod,* 140, 160, and, for its date, Jacobson, "Plan of Herod's Temple," 48.
8. Jacobson, "Plan of Herod's Temple," 48; Netzer, *Architecture of Herod,* 157.
9. Bird, "Place of Women," 403.
10. For an excellent assessment of Jerusalem's status as a capital city in the tenth and ninth centuries BCE, see Uziel and Shai, "Iron Age Jerusalem," 161–70.
11. Dan's status as a Northern Kingdom sanctuary site has been challenged by Noll, who argues that the archaeological remains from Dan that most scholars associate with a Northern Kingdom state sanctuary represent instead a religious complex dedicated to the god Hadad, whose worship was promoted by the Aramaeans who ruled in pre-Assyrian Dan (as Noll sees it) for all but "a brief [Israelite] period in the latter tenth and/or early ninth century . . . and . . . a few decades at most in the middle of the 8th century" (Noll, "God Who Is Among the Danites," 14; similarly Noll, "City of Dan in the Pre-Assyrian Iron Age," 150). Noll's views, however, have not found a following, and, indeed,

I have outlined multiple grounds for rejecting them in Ackerman, "E-Dan," 160–67. There, too, I have briefly registered my disagreement with those who hold that the large ashlar masonry platform that dominates the allegedly religious precinct at Dan is not to be interpreted as having a cultic function, but instead is to be understood as the remains of a palace or administrative center. In addition, I have pointed to the far more substantial refutation offered by A. R. Davis, "Tel Dan," 53–60, and the briefer comments in A. R. Davis, *Tel Dan,* 28–29.

12. This is not to say that the tent shrine that David purportedly used to house the ark in Jerusalem is to be equated with the "tent of meeting" (*ʾōhel môʿēd*) that biblical accounts in Exodus, Leviticus, and Numbers describe as housing the ark earlier in Israelite history; see, preeminently, Haran, "Shiloh and Jerusalem," 14–24, and Haran, *Temples,* 189–204. But cf. Cross, "The Tabernacle," 45–68, where Cross first articulated arguments for the two tents' equivalence that he reiterated throughout his career. For a recent and thorough discussion (with additional bibliography), see Homan, *To Your Tents,* 4, 129–37, esp. 133–37.
13. A thorough discussion can be found in Halpern, *David's Secret Demons,* 107–226. For a good summary, see Meyers, "Kinship and Kingship," 183–85.
14. Major studies putting forth this argument are catalogued in Ackerman, *When Heroes Love,* 282, n. 6.
15. Ibid., 153–64.
16. Meyers, "Kinship and Kingship," 183; also Halpern, *David's Secret Demons,* 107–226.
17. Halpern, *David's Secret Demons,* 341.
18. McKenzie, *King David,* 146.
19. Halpern, *David's Secret Demons,* 333–41.
20. Dever, "What Did the Biblical Writers Know?," 350–52.
21. P. D. Miller, *Religion,* 91. See similarly Uziel and Shai, "Iron Age Jerusalem," 167.
22. According to the Austro-German excavations from 1913–1914 and the 1920s and 1930s, and the Drew-McCormick excavations of the 1950s and 1960s, pre-Israelite Shechem had two temples dating from the Middle Bronze and Late Bronze Ages (ca. 2000–1550 BCE and 1550–1200 BCE). Lawrence E. Stager has argued, moreover, that the so-called Tower Temple or Fortress Temple from the Middle Bronze Age continued to stand during Israel's premonarchic era, until ca. 1100 BCE: see Stager, "Fortress-Temple at Shechem," 228–49. Nonetheless, arguments which posit that an Israelite royal sanctuary stood in Shechem two hundred years later, during the time of Jeroboam, are speculative: see P. D. Miller, *Religion,* 191 and 283, n. 91.
23. The name of the priest's grandfather is actually rendered in the Hebrew text as *mnšh,* or "Manasseh," versus *mšh,* "Moses," but the *n* is "suspended," meaning it probably represents a secondary addition to the text, as is attested in some

ancient Greek manuscripts of the Bible and in the Latin Vulgate, which read "Moses." See, e.g., Boling, *Judges,* 265–66; Cross, *Canaanite Myth,* 197, n. 18; Gunn, *Judges,* 232; Martin, *Book of Judges,* 195–96; and Soggin, *Judges,* 268–69.

24. Cogan and Tadmor, *II Kings,* 296.
25. 1 Kgs 14:21; 15:1–2, 9–10; 22:41–42; 2 Kgs 8:25–26; 12:2 (English 12:1); 14:1–2; 15:1–2, 32–33; 18:1–2; 21:1, 19; 22:1; 23:31, 36; 24:8, 18.
26. Ackerman, *Warrior, Dancer,* 133–38.
27. Ibid., 142–54.
28. Cross, *Canaanite Myth,* 241–65.
29. Although cf. M. S. Smith, *Early History of God* (1st ed.), 80–94, and also the more nuanced position Smith puts forward in this volume's 2nd ed., xxx–xxxvi, and in *Where the Gods Are,* 40–41.
30. Ackerman, *Under Every Green Tree,* 189–91.
31. Ackerman, "Women and the Worship of Yahweh," 189–90; Ackerman, "Asherah," 18–19.
32. Hebrew *tōp* is more commonly translated as "timbrel" or "tambourine," but as Meyers has documented in multiple publications, this translation is anachronistic, as the "timbrel" or "tambourine," an instrument that adds jingles to a frame drum, was not invented until after the biblical period. For Meyers's original presentations of this argument, see Meyers, "Terracotta at the Harvard Semitic Museum," 120, and Meyers, "Of Drums and Damsels," 18. For an image of a woman playing a frame drum, see Fig. 9.1.
33. See, e.g., Dahood, *Psalms II,* 147, who interprets *qōdeš* as a holy habitation *from which* God marches and a reference to "either Sinai . . . or heaven." See also Knohl, "Psalm 68," 1–21, who, unlike Dahood, takes Ps 68:25 (English 68:24) to refer to a procession *into* the deity's temple (p. 9), yet understands the temple to be "the cultic center at Mount Bashan" (p. 19).
34. The classic presentation of this "disassociated" reading of the stanzas of Ps 68 is Albright, "Catalogue," 1–39.
35. See further Japhet, *I and II Chronicles,* 444, who notes that the daughters are unnecessary for the context in 1 Chr 25:5 but are probably mentioned in order to demonstrate the "unusual proliferation of Heman," to whom fourteen of the twenty-four divisions listed in 1 Chr 25 are ascribed. She goes on to say, moreover, that "the numbers . . . are certainly typological, and are identical with those of Job's children after his restoration." A similar point is made by Williamson, *1 and 2 Chronicles,* 168; see also, somewhat similarly, Grossman, "Women and the Jerusalem Temple," 19, and Meyers, "Daughters (and Sons) of Heman," 281. Cf., however, Meyers's less cautious assessments of this passage in Meyers, "Mother to Muse," 62, and in Meyers, *Rediscovering Eve,* 176, and the similarly less cautious assessment of Gruber, "Women in the Cult," 66.
36. Albright, *Archaeology,* 127; Braun, *Music in Ancient Israel/Palestine,* 86.
37. De Vaux, *Ancient Israel,* 382.

38. Blenkinsopp, "Family in First Temple Israel," 102–3, n. 89, calls this hypothesis "precarious."
39. I have discussed my understanding of the geographical layout of Ezek 8 in Ackerman, *Under Every Green Tree,* 53–55.
40. Note, e.g., the laments of Inanna/Ishtar, Geshtinanna, and Ninsun collected by Jacobsen, *Treasures of Darkness,* 49–55; see also Jacobsen's comments in "Toward the Image of Tammuz," 77–78, and Kramer, "Weeping Goddess," esp. 76–79.
41. Alster, "Tammuz," 831.
42. On the relationship between this tent shrine and the wilderness "tent of meeting," see above, n. 12.
43. Num 27:1–11 has been assigned to H by Knohl, *Sanctuary of Silence,* 100.
44. Cross, *Canaanite Myth,* 202, n. 34.
45. Meyers, "Person (Female or Male) Presenting an Offering," 203; also Meyers, "From Household to House of Yahweh," 279–80; Meyers, *Households and Holiness,* 10; and, most recently, Meyers, "Contributing to Continuity," 6–7. For Gruber's discussion, see "Women in the Cult," 62–64; for Milgrom's, see *Leviticus 1–16,* 178–79. See as well Braulik, "Were Women, Too, Allowed to Offer Sacrifices?," 941–42; Henshaw, *Female and Male,* 27 (albeit with some caveats); P. D. Miller, *Religion,* 205; and Vos, *Woman in Old Testament Worship,* 79.
46. Gruber, "Women in the Cult," 62, 64; Milgrom, *Leviticus 1–16,* 145. See also Braulik, "Were Women, Too, Allowed to Offer Sacrifices?," 941–42, and P. D. Miller, *Religion,* 205, but cf. ibid., 69.
47. Gruber, "Women in the Cult," 64.
48. Braulik, "Were Women, Too, Allowed to Offer Sacrifices?," 925–26; Braulik, "Rejection of the Goddess Asherah," 178–79.
49. Greer, *Dinner at Dan,* 121; on the archaeological remains that drive Greer's interpretation, see also ibid., 80–82, 91–93, and my comments in Chapter 3, n. 50.
50. Although Deuteronomy never explicitly identifies this "place that Yahweh will choose" as Jerusalem, a vast majority of scholars agrees that this formula refers—and always referred, even in the text of Deuteronomy's underlying strata—to Jerusalem. For discussion, with references, see Levinson, *Deuteronomy,* 4, n. 4, and 23, n. 1.
51. Note also my discussions of Josh 5:5, 8 in Chapter 8 and of Num 25:1–2 in Ackerman, "Who Is the Baal of Peor?," 184. Note as well Exod 20:17 and Deut 5:21, where the tenth commandment, although seemingly part of a corpus addressed to all the Israelites, actually applies only to men, at least in its requirement not to covet the wife of one's neighbor, and note too Gen 14:16, 26:10, and Ps 128:1–4. This Psalms text, in which "everyone who fears Yahweh" (v. 1) turns out to include only those (men) who have "wives" (v. 3), was brought to my attention by Bird, "Place of Women," 402, where Exod 20:17 and Deut 5:21 are also discussed. On Exod 19:15, see also Bird, "Images of Women," 50, and, on

both Exod 19:15 and Jer 44:24, see Bird, "Women's Religion," 286, n. 9. On Exod 20:17 and Deut 5:21, see too Brenner, "An Afterword," 255–58.

52. But cf. Lev 10:14, which presumes priestly dwellings outside the precinct of the wilderness tent of meeting and so, presumably, outside the precincts of the Jerusalem temple that succeeded it: Milgrom, *Leviticus 1–16,* 619; also Wegner, "*'Coming Before the Lord':* The Exclusion of Women," 453.
53. Cogan and Tadmor, *II Kings,* 296.

Chapter 6. "At the Time of Her Menstruation, She Shall Be Unclean"

1. Meyers, *Discovering Eve,* 139, 145.
2. Hackett, "In the Days of Jael," 17–18.
3. Ibid., 17; also Hackett, "Women's Studies," 147.
4. Meyers, *Discovering Eve,* 190.
5. Ibid., 191–92.
6. For Meyers's own comments on this reformulation, see Meyers, *Rediscovering Eve,* ix.
7. Chapter 1, n. 43.
8. Meyers, "Material Remains and Social Relations," 434; see similarly Meyers, "From Field Crops to Food," 77, and Meyers, *Rediscovering Eve,* 139–46, 184–85.
9. Meyers, "Material Remains and Social Relations," 435–36. Meyers has also put forward this argument in several other publications: e.g., Meyers, "From Field Crops to Food," 77–78, and Meyers, *Rediscovering Eve,* 130, 140–41.
10. Meyers, "From Household to House of Yahweh," 303; Meyers, *Households and Holiness,* 73.
11. Meyers, "From Household to House of Yahweh," 280; Meyers, *Households and Holiness,* 10.
12. E.g., Meyers, "Women with Hand-Drums, Dancing," 189–91; Meyers, "Person (Female or Male) Presenting an Offering," 203; Meyers, "Daughters (and Sons) of Heman," 281; Meyers, "Women (and Men and Children) in Assembly," 286; and Meyers, "Women, Part of the Assembly of People," 288.
13. Greer, *Dinner at Dan,* 66–67, 74–76, 85.
14. Ibid., 94.
15. Ibid., 101–5, with references.
16. A. R. Davis, *Tel Dan,* 73, 90, 97–98.
17. A. R. Davis, "Tel Dan," 129.
18. Levine, "Priests," 688; Tuell, *Law of the Temple,* 131.
19. See Chapter 5 and n. 45 there.
20. See Chapter 5 and the references to Braulik's work cited in n. 48 there.
21. Braulik, "Were Women, Too, Allowed to Offer Sacrifices?," 936.
22. See similarly regarding the masculine singular "you," Bird, "Women (OT)," 955 (on the related Deut 16:11, 14); Meyers in several publications, most recently,

Meyers, "Contributing to Continuity," 7; Vos, *Woman in Old Testament Worship,* 119; and Weinfeld, *Deuteronomy and the Deuteronomic School,* 291. See also Berman, *Created Equal,* 13 and 60, but as pointed out by Olyan, "Equality and Inequality," 40, n. 91, cf. Berman, *Created Equal,* 80, where Berman does seem [implicitly] to take the masculine singular "you" to refer to the individual Israelite male.

23. In addition to what follows, see Ackerman, "Only Men Are Created Equal," 19–22; note also Altmann, "Material Culture and the Symbolic Meaning of Meat," 22, who takes the *'attâ,* "you," of Deut 12:18 as referring to "the (male) heads of household," and Olyan, "Equality and Inequality," 40.
24. Carmichael, "Death and Sexuality," 226.
25. Ibid., citing Péter-Contesse and Ellington, *Translator's Handbook,* 316.
26. Both Carmichael, "Death and Sexuality," 226, and Milgrom, *Leviticus 17–22,* 1798, cite Hartley, *Leviticus,* 347, by way of example.
27. Levine, *Leviticus,* 142; Milgrom, *Leviticus 17–22,* 1798.
28. See further Chapter 5, n. 51; also, Brettler, "Women in the Decalogue," 189–90.
29. Chapter 3, n. 93.
30. Bird, "Place of Women," 404.
31. P. D. Miller, *Religion,* 202.
32. Eitan, "Antiquities Director Confronts Problems," 30.
33. Eitan, "Vered Yeriho," 106; Stern, "Eastern Border," 404; Stern, *Archaeology,* 134.
34. Stern, "Eastern Border," 399, 406–7; Stern, *Archaeology,* 137–38.
35. Riklin, "Fortress of Michmash," 69–79; see also Stern, *Archaeology,* 138, 202.
36. Chapter 3, n. 12.
37. See Chapter 3 and n. 66 there.
38. On the date of 2 Kgs 23, see Cross, *Canaanite Myth,* 274–89, especially 284–85; Friedman, *Exile and Biblical Narrative,* 1–26; and Nelson, *Double Redaction of the Deuteronomistic History,* 13–28, 119–28. On 2 Kgs 23:8 specifically, see Barrick, *The King and the Cemeteries,* 107–8.
39. 2 Kgs 23:8 refers to all the shrines "from Geba to Beersheba," a phrase that is best interpreted to mean any shrine found within Judah's boundaries as they stretched from Geba, on the kingdom's northern border, to Beersheba, on its southern frontier.
40. See originally Y. Aharoni, "Arad," 30, and, among Aharoni's followers, P. M. Arnold, "Geba," 921–22; P. D. Miller, *Religion,* 88 and 234–35, n. 230; and Schunck, "Zentralheiligtum, Grenzheiligtum und 'Hohenheiligtum,'" 136–37.
41. Dorsey, *Roads and Highways,* 136–38; Schniedewind, "Search for Gibeah," 719–21.
42. P. M. Arnold, *Gibeah,* 67; P. M. Arnold, "Mizpah," 879–80.
43. Zorn, "Naṣbeh, Tell en-," 101–2.
44. At Ḥorvat 'Uza, excavations revealed a fieldstone platform that has been interpreted as an altar near the gateway of a small fort (42 by 51 meters). Likewise

at Ḥorvat Radum, a platform seemingly used for cultic purposes was found. See Beit-Arieh, *Ḥorvat 'Uza and Ḥorvat Radum,* 29, 31, 316–17; also Edelman, "Cultic Sites," 95–96, and Stern, *Archaeology,* 151–54, 202. In addition, on Ḥorvat 'Uza, see Beit-Arieh and Cresson, "Ḥorvat 'Uza," 126–35.

45. Z. Herzog, "Social, Historical, and Cultural Ramifications," 1459–75; Z. Herzog, "Beersheba," 289.
46. Z. Herzog, "Beersheba," 290–91.
47. 2 Kgs 23:8, which refers to all the shrines "from Geba to Beersheba," has also been taken to suggest the presence of a temple in Beersheba in the late seventh or early sixth century BCE. This interpretation is, however, problematic: see above, n. 39. Correlating 2 Kgs 23:8 with the archaeological evidence from Beersheba is also problematic because Beersheba's temple (if there was one; this is debated) was arguably dismantled at the end of the eighth century BCE (see further below). Moreover, the entire city was destroyed by the Assyrians in 701 BCE.
48. For these measurements, see Z. Herzog, "Social, Historical, and Cultural Ramifications," 1476–77, as opposed to the measurements earlier proposed by the excavation team, reported in Z. Herzog, "Beersheba," 290. The altar's discovery was originally reported by Y. Aharoni, "Horned Altar," 2–6, and Y. Aharoni, "Excavations at Tel Beer-sheba," 154, 156.
49. The quoted material here is taken from Zevit, *Religions,* 174; for Aharoni's and his followers' reconstruction regarding Beersheba's temple, and its possible location, see Y. Aharoni, "Horned Altar," 5; Y. Aharoni, "Excavations at Tel Beer-sheba," 158, 160, 162–63; Z. Herzog, "Israelite Sanctuaries," 120–21; and Z. Herzog, Rainey, and Moshkovitz, "Stratigraphy at Beer-sheba," 56–58. But cf. Z. Herzog, "Perspectives on Southern Israel's Cult Centralization," 176: "there is no convincing answer to the question of the original location of the Tel Beer-sheba altar [and, so, the temple presumably associated with it]." Indeed, there was perhaps only an altar and no temple at Beersheba: see Chapter 3, n. 36.
50. Y. Aharoni, "Horned Altar," 6, and Z. Herzog in many publications: most recently, Z. Herzog, "Perspectives on Southern Israel's Cult Centralization," 177–83, 193–97, and Z. Herzog, "Social, Historical, and Cultural Ramifications," 1477–78.
51. In Josh 15:21, if the Hebrew *'ēder* results from a mistaken transposition of *r* and *d,* then, when corrected, an original reading of *'rd,* "Arad," would result. See Z. Herzog, M. Aharoni, Rainey, and Moshkovitz, "Israelite Fortress at Arad," 1, and Z. Herzog, "Arad," 174.
52. Z. Herzog, M. Aharoni, Rainey, and Moshkovitz, "Israelite Fortress at Arad," 1–2; Z. Herzog, "Arad," 174; and Z. Herzog, "Fortress Mound at Arad," 3–4, 6.
53. Y. Aharoni, "Arad," 5; Z. Herzog, M. Aharoni, Rainey, and Moshkovitz, "Israelite Fortress at Arad," 6; Z. Herzog, "Arad," 174; and Mazar, *Archaeology,* 438–41.

54. A tenth-century BCE date for the inauguration of Arad's fortress compound was suggested by Y. Aharoni in "Excavations at Tel Arad," 135, and was subsequently maintained by Aharoni and by his followers in Y. Aharoni, "Arad," 5, 9, and Z. Herzog, M. Aharoni, Rainey, and Moshkovitz, "Israelite Fortress at Arad," 6–8. A ninth-century BCE date is proposed by Mazar, "Chronology of the Pottery Assemblages," 89–90; see also Mazar, *Archaeology*, 439.
55. The major scholarly discussions of this temple, and it associated courtyard and altar, include the references cited in nn. 52–53 above and Dever, "Were There Temples in Ancient Israel?," 310–15; Z. Herzog, "Date of the Temple at Arad," 156–78; Z. Herzog, "Perspectives on Southern Israel's Cult Centralization," 169–75; Mazar, *Archaeology*, 496–98; Ussishkin, "Date of the Judean Shrine at Arad," 142–57; and Zevit, *Religions*, 156–71.
56. Z. Herzog, "Date of the Temple at Arad," 164–70; Z. Herzog, "Fortress Mound at Arad," 12, 21, 27, 32–40, 49–72; and Z. Herzog, "Perspectives on Southern Israel's Cult Centralization," 169.
57. See already Z. Herzog, "Arad," 175; similarly Z. Herzog, "Date of the Temple at Arad," 170; Z. Herzog, "Fortress Mound at Arad," 66–67; and Z. Herzog, "Perspectives on Southern Israel's Cult Centralization," 175, 177–97.
58. On the date of Isa 10:27b–32, see Ackerman, "Isaiah," 973.
59. Eitan, "Vered Yeriho," 106–7; Eitan, "Antiquities Director Confronts Problems," 30.
60. Beit-Arieh, *Ḥorvat 'Uza*, 55; Beit-Arieh and Cresson, "Ḥorvat 'Uza," 132.
61. Beit-Arieh, *Ḥorvat 'Uza*, 29, 31, 33, 43; Beit-Arieh and Cresson, "Ḥorvat 'Uza," 130.
62. Z. Herzog, "Social, Historical, and Cultural Ramifications," 1472.
63. Dever, *Lives of Ordinary People*, 70.
64. Singer-Avitz, "Household Activities," 1441.
65. Bird, "Place of Women," 401.
66. On postpartum uterine discharges as the source of a recently delivered woman's impurity, see Burnette-Bletsch, "Women After Childbirth," 204; D. P. Wright and Jones, "Discharge," 205; and Whitekettle, "Leviticus 12," 397, 405–8.
67. The differences between the biblical concept of purity and more modern, especially Christian notions of purity are well discussed by Poorthuis and J. Schwartz, "Purity and Holiness," 4 and n. 10 on that page; a related discussion, on the differences between the biblical concept of the "holy" and more modern notions of holiness, is that of B. J. Schwartz, "Israel's Holiness," 49.
68. The bibliography on what Jonathan Klawans defines as "moral impurities" as opposed to "ritual impurities" is extensive. In addition to Klawans, "Concepts of Purity," 2041–47, and Klawans, *Impurity and Sin*, vii, 22–23, 26–27, the following discussions are helpful: Attridge, "Pollution, Sin, Atonement, Salvation," 72–73; Frymer-Kensky, "Pollution, Purification, and Purgation," 399–414; Milgrom, "Israel's Sanctuary,'" 390–99; Nihan, "Forms and Functions of Purity," 339–50;

D. P. Wright, "Two Types of Impurity," 180–93; D. P. Wright, "Spectrum of Priestly Impurity," 150–81; and D. P. Wright, "Unclean and Clean," 729–41.

69. Attridge, "Pollution, Sin, Atonement, Salvation," 72.
70. P. D. Miller, *Religion,* 150.
71. D. P. Wright, "Spectrum of Priestly Impurity," 158.
72. Olyan, *Rites and Rank,* 39.
73. Maccoby, "Holiness and Purity," 152.
74. Milgrom, *Leviticus 1–16,* 751–52; P. D. Miller, *Religion,* 137–38.
75. Milgrom, *Leviticus 1–16,* 279–80 (regarding Nazirites); P. D. Miller, *Religion,* 138–39, and Olyan, "Gender-Specific Pollution," 161, n. 5 (regarding priests).
76. D. Janzen, "Priestly Sacrifice in the Hebrew Bible," 41.
77. P. D. Miller, *Religion,* 131.
78. Poorthuis and J. Schwartz, "Purity and Holiness," 12.
79. On the terms *ʾōhel môʿēd* and *miškān* as synonyms in P and related sources, see Haran, "Nature of the 'Ohel Moʿedh,'" 61; Haran, *Temples,* 272; and Levine, *Numbers 1–20,* 129–30.
80. Olyan, "Sin, Pollution, and Purity," 502.
81. B. J. Schwartz, "Israel's Holiness," 59.
82. Milgrom, *Leviticus 1–16,* 616.
83. Milgrom, *Leviticus 1–16,* 953; also Exum, *Fragmented Women,* 138 and n. 78 on that page; Gruber, "Women in the Cult," 67, n. 40; Marsman, *Women,* 543; and Olyan, *Rites and Rank,* 57 and 150, n. 79.
84. Chapter 3, n. 93.
85. Van der Toorn, *From Her Cradle to Her Grave,* 86, 92.
86. Ibid., 85. Note also, from Ugaritic tradition, *KTU* 1.23.52–53, 59–60, where word is brought to the patriarch of the gods, El, regarding the birth of his children, named Dawn and Dusk in 1.23.52–53 and the "goodly gods" in 1.23.59–60; likewise in *KTU* 1.10.3.33–36, word must be brought to the god Baal that a theriomorphic son (a bull) has been born to him. See also Chapter 11 and nn. 46 and 48 there, about the seeming exclusion of male ritual specialists from a woman's birth chamber.
87. Olyan, *Disability,* 59.
88. Olyan, *Rites and Rank,* 57–58.
89. Pitkänen, *Central Sanctuary,* 46.
90. For more sustained discussion, see, e.g., Haran, "Priestly Image of the Tabernacle," 200–207; Haran, *Temples,* 158–65; Jensen, *Graded Holiness,* 36–55, 89–114; and D. P. Wright, *Disposal of Impurity,* 231–47. Note also, regarding Dan, my discussion above concerning restrictions on the laity's access to the sanctuary's western chambers and, as time went on, to the courtyard's central altar.
91. On this translation, see Olyan, *Rites and Rank,* 20, with references on 133, n. 30.
92. Block, "Marriage and Family," 57, n. 113, and Meyers, "Women's Daily Life," 492; see also Ezek 16:8, where, just before the rites that enact Yahweh's betrothal

to Jerusalem, personified in Ezek 16 as female, the city is said to have reached her *ʿēt dōdîm.* Literally, this means "the age of love"; more accurately, though, as Greenberg, *Ezekiel 1–20,* 277, points out (on the basis of parallels in Ezek 23:17; Prov 7:18; Cant 4:10, 7:13 [English 7:12]), *ʿēt dōdîm* refers to a young woman's coming into puberty.

93. Although it significantly postdates the scope of our study, Luke 2:36–37, which describes the prophet Anna, who "never left the temple," as "a woman of great age" and "a widow to the age of eighty-four," may similarly indicate that postmenopausal women could access the Jerusalem temple's precinct in ways that women of childbearing age could not.

94. Chapter 5, n. 39.

95. P. D. Miller, *Religion,* 39 and 234, n. 179, citing Zimmerli, *Ezekiel 1,* 242.

96. Milgrom, *Leviticus 1–16,* 907.

97. Wegner, "'Coming Before the LORD': *lpny yhwh,*" 84–85; Wegner, "*'Coming Before the Lord':* The Exclusion of Women," 457.

98. Van der Toorn, "Theology, Priests, and Worship," 2052; Olyan, *Disability,* 59.

99. Wegner, "'Coming Before the LORD': *lpny yhwh,*" 81; Wegner, "*'Coming Before the Lord':* The Exclusion of Women," 453–54.

100. Wegner, "'Coming Before the LORD': *lpny yhwh,*" 84; Wegner, "*'Coming Before the Lord':* The Exclusion of Women," 457. Note also that the man is required in Lev 15:13 to wash his clothes and bathe, whereas no similar requirement is imposed upon the woman. This is because, according to Wegner, the woman does not come *lipnê yhwh* and so is not required to enter into the state of cultic purity that the cleansing of one's clothes and bathing bring about (Wegner, "'Coming Before the LORD': *lpny yhwh,*" 85). But in her article "Bathing, Status and Gender," 66–81, Nicole Ruane has shown that there is something far more systemic (and sinister) at work, as the P texts of which Leviticus 15 is a part consistently portray bathing as "almost exclusively a male cultic activity" (ibid., 67) and moreover use this portrayal to characterize "women as having inferior cultic status and as being more closely related to the low status of impurity" (ibid., 78).

101. Wegner, "'Coming Before the LORD': *lpny yhwh,*" 84, and Wegner, "*'Coming Before the Lord':* The Exclusion of Women," 456, in both cases citing Milgrom, *Leviticus 1–16,* 944.

102. Cohen, "Menstruants and the Sacred," 292, n. 9.

103. As Sarah Shectman has shown in a careful study of gendered and gender-neutral terminology in the P corpus, the terms *ʾîš* and *ʾiššâ,* "man" and "woman," "are used almost exclusively in places where it becomes necessary to clarify the gender of the offerant": see Shectman, "Women in the Priestly Laws," 6.

104. Above and Chapter 5, with references in n. 45 there.

105. Wegner, "'Coming Before the LORD': *lpny yhwh,*" 84; Wegner, "*'Coming Before the Lord':* The Exclusion of Women," 457.

106. Ackerman, "Women and the Religious Culture," 275–76.
107. Chapter 1, n. 13.
108. See, e.g., McCarter, *II Samuel,* 286, and D. P. Wright, "David Autem Remansit in Hierusalem," 218 and n. 10 on that page.
109. On this translation, see Olyan, *Rites and Rank,* 137, n. 71, and 146, n. 29, and D. P. Wright, "David Autem Remansit in Hierusalem," 218, n. 9.
110. But see Milgrom, *Leviticus 1–16,* 934–35, who argues that purification by immersion at the end of a woman's menstrual period is an underlying assumption in Lev 15:19–24.
111. Van der Toorn, *From Her Cradle to Her Grave,* 53.
112. Frymer-Kensky, "Pollution, Purification, and Purgation," 399. See similarly Lemos, "Where There Is Dirt," 289.
113. Olyan, *Disability,* 32.
114. Olyan, *Rites and Rank,* 62; see similarly ibid., 55.
115. See, e.g., W. R. Smith, *Lectures,* 238, as cited by MacDonald, *What Did the Ancient Israelites Eat?,* 74.
116. Olyan, *Rites and Rank,* 55; see similarly Milgrom, *Leviticus 1–16,* 221–22, and P. D. Miller, *Religion,* 125.
117. This estimate is based on a calculation that sacrifices, with a meal following at which the sacrificial meat was served, took place at the monthly celebrations of the new moon (on which see Chapter 7 and also, with regard to meat consumption, van der Toorn, "Nine Months," 401), at a clan's annual sacrifice (on which see Chapter 7), at the year's three pilgrimage feasts (on which see Chapter 8), and perhaps at a few other occasions as well. But cf. Gruber, "Private Life in Canaan and Ancient Israel," 638, who, writing of typical rural families of Late Bronze Age Ugarit, estimates that flock sizes and ewes' rates of reproduction were such that these families could have slaughtered a sheep only every six weeks (or about eight or nine times per year) without reducing the size of their herd. See similarly, regarding ancient Israel, Welton, "Ritual and the Agency of Food," 614–15.
118. Meyers, "Function of Feasts," 144, quoting W. R. Smith, *Lectures,* 269.
119. Meyers, "Function of Feasts," 141, citing Dietler, "Feasts and Commensal Politics," 89, and Meyers, "Function of Feasts," 152.
120. Meyers, "Function of Feasts," 157, citing Connerton, *How Societies Remember,* 66, and Meyers, "Function of Feasts," 162. See similarly Meyers, *Rediscovering Eve,* 163.
121. Van der Toorn, "Nine Months," 401; Meyers, "Function of Feasts," 159, citing Twiss, "Home Is Where the Hearth Is," 52.
122. Olyan, *Rites and Rank,* 55–56, 62.
123. Ibid., 57.
124. See similarly, regarding women's lack of access to feasts formally celebrated in cultic settings, Bird, "Women's Religion in Ancient Israel," 294; Bird, "Gender

and Religious Definition," 19; Bird, "Israelite Religion," 106; and Faust, "Burnished Pottery," 59–60, 66. But cf. Meyers, "Function of Feasts," 150–51.

125. Lehman, "Gendered Rhetoric of Sukkah Observance," 310.
126. P. D. Miller, *Religion,* 123.
127. Olyan, *Rites and Rank,* 62; Olyan, *Disability,* 32.
128. Chapter 1, n. 75.
129. Bird, "Place of Women," 403.

Chapter 7. "There Is a Yearly Sacrifice . . . for All the Family"

1. The third commandment assigned exclusively to women concerns immersion in a ritual bath after the end of each menstrual period.
2. The "taking of challah" does not in fact concern just the special challah bread customarily baked for the Sabbath but all bread-making; however, the correspondence in terminology between the commandment's name and the Sabbath's characteristic bread, in addition to the fact that Sabbath is often the only time when modern Jewish families bake bread, means that Sabbath has become a preeminent occasion at which women observe the "taking of challah" commandment.
3. Plaskow, *Standing Again at Sinai,* 49, citing Ozick, "Notes Toward Finding the Right Question," 129–30.
4. Zborowski and Herzog, *Life Is with People,* 45, 131.
5. As Cooper and Goldstein observe in "Development of the Priestly Calendars," 10, n. 19, "The . . . scholarship on this topic [Sabbath] is voluminous." They, as would I, refer readers to the surveys found in standard biblical dictionaries and encyclopedias and, for more comprehensive treatments, Andreasen, *Old Testament Sabbath;* G. F. Hasel, "Sabbath in the Pentateuch," 21–43; G. F. Hasel, "'New Moon and Sabbath,'" 37–64; G. F. Hasel and Murdoch, "Sabbath in the Prophetic and Historical Literature," 44–56; H. A. McKay, *Sabbath and Synagogue,* esp. 11–42; Robinson, *Origin and Development;* and B. J. Schwartz, "Sabbath."
6. Although see below, nn. 16 and 18, regarding *šabbāt* materials in P and in D.
7. This theory was first articulated by Lotz, *Quaestiones de Historia Sabbati,* and then developed by Meinhold, *Sabbat und Woche im Alten Testament.* See further on this position (without, necessarily, endorsement) Albertz, *History of Israelite Religion* 2, 408–9; Andreasen, *Old Testament Sabbath,* 1–5, 11; de Vaux, *Ancient Israel,* 476–78; G. F. Hasel, "'New Moon and Sabbath,'" 37–38; P. D. Miller, *Religion,* 247, n. 132; and Robinson, *Origin and Development,* 34–36. In addition, Andreasen, *Old Testament Sabbath,* 95–96, n. 1; G. F. Hasel, "'New Moon and Sabbath,'" 37–38, 58, n. 62; and G. F. Hasel, "Sabbath in the Pentateuch," 37, n. 6, although both disagree with the "*šabbāt* = full moon" hypothesis, have catalogued a long list of adherents. Albertz lists other adherents still, in *History of*

Israelite Religion 2, 607, n. 35, to which add Cooper and Goldstein, "Festivals of Israel and Judah," 20–21; Cooper and Goldstein, "Development of the Priestly Calendars," 12; and, more recently, Farber, "Israelite Festivals," 2–5; J. L. Wright, "Shabbat of the Full Moon"; and J. L. Wright, "How and When the Seventh Day Became Shabbat."

8. This translation is forcefully argued by Haag, "*šābat,*" 382–85, and by Robinson, "Idea of Rest," 37–40; see also the brief comments of Andreasen, *Old Testament Sabbath,* 105–6; Andreasen, "Recent Studies in the Old Testament Sabbath," 459; and de Vaux, *Ancient Israel,* 475.
9. Robinson, *Origin and Development,* 306; J. L. Wright, "How and When the Seventh Day Became Shabbat."
10. Haag, "*šabbāt,*" 388; see similarly (with multiple references), Andreasen, "Recent Studies in the Old Testament Sabbath," 455–56, and nn. 10–11 on those pages.
11. Haag, "*šabbāt,*" 391–92.
12. Fleming, "Break in the Line," 174, n. 31; for the critiques of Propp and Soggin, see Propp, *Exodus 19–40,* 175–76, and Soggin, *Israel in the Biblical Period,* 139–40.
13. This is particularly well detailed by Lemaire, "Le Sabbat," 162–64; see also G. F. Hasel, "'New Moon and Sabbath,'" 39.
14. But cf. H. A. McKay, *Sabbath and Synagogue,* 31, who follows Kaiser, *Isaiah 1–12,* 25, 31, in dating "this oracle as coming from the beginning of the Second Temple."
15. See Propp, *Exodus 19–40,* 660. While Propp, however, understands virtually all of Exod 25–31, 35–40 to be the work of P (ibid., 365–66), and while Propp further understands the P materials to have preexilic roots (see the Introduction and n. 54 there), several scholars assign Exod 35:3 to H: so Knohl, "Priestly Torah," 73–74; Knohl, *Sanctuary of Silence,* 16; Milgrom, *Leviticus 17–22,* 1338–39; Nihan, *From Priestly Torah to Pentateuch,* 568; and Stackert, "Compositional Strata," 19. Thus, depending on how one dates H (see the Introduction), Exod 35:3 may stand outside the preexilic scope that I have defined for this book.
16. Is it found, say, in the P source? Knohl ("Priestly Torah," 72–77, esp. 76–77; Knohl, *Sanctuary of Silence,* 14–19, esp. 18), followed by Cooper and Goldstein ("Development of the Priestly Calendars," 5, 13), has forcefully argued that it is not, but Olyan ("Exodus 31:12–17," 201–9, esp. 203, 208–9) has urged the opposite conclusion. See also B. J. Schwartz, "Sabbath," 10–13, and Stackert, "Compositional Strata," 14–20.
17. Cooper and Goldstein, "Development of the Priestly Calendars," 12–13, following Cazelles, "Ex 34, 21," 223–26.
18. See Cooper and Goldstein, "Festivals of Israel and Judah," 28; Cooper and Goldstein, "Development of the Priestly Calendars," 13; Haran, *Temples,* 291–92, n. 7; and B. J. Schwartz, "Sabbath," 9–10, although note that Haran and Schwartz, unlike Cooper and Goldstein, do not take Deut 5:14 to refer to something other than a weekly *šabbāt* tradition.

19. For discussion, see Andreasen, *Old Testament Sabbath,* 260; also G. F. Hasel, "'New Moon and Sabbath,'" 43–45.
20. On the date of Jer 17:19–27, see McKane, *Critical and Exegetical Commentary,* 416–19 (as pointed out by Cooper and Goldstein, "Development of the Priestly Calendars," 11–12, n. 20).
21. On the language of this passage, and what that might mean about its authorship, see Knohl, "Priestly Torah," 74–76; Knohl, *Sanctuary of Silence,* 17–18; Propp, *Exodus 1–18,* 588–90; and B. J. Schwartz, "Sabbath," 3–5.
22. On Exod 35:3, see above, n. 15. Regarding the source attribution and date of Num 15:32–36, see Chavel, "Numbers 15, 32–36," 45–55; Novick, "Law and Loss," 1–14; and Stackert, "Compositional Strata," 19, all of whom ascribe Num 15:32–36 to H, which means—depending on how one chooses to date H (see the Introduction)—that this text might postdate the preexilic focus of this book.
23. Modern translations often render the term for "reaping" (*qāṣîr*) in this Exodus passage using the more generic word "harvest" (with the crop unspecified). But overwhelmingly in the Bible, *qāṣîr* specifically denotes the harvesting of grain and even more specifically the harvesting of wheat.
24. See Chapter 6, and the references to Braulik and other adherents of this position who are cited in nn. 21 and 22 there. Brettler, "Women in the Decalogue," 190, also allows for (although does not necessarily embrace) Braulik's interpretation of masculine singular forms as they pertain to *šabbāt* observance. But cf. Andreasen, "Festival and Freedom," 285, and H. A. McKay, *Sabbath and Synagogue,* 13, n. 8.
25. Although, regarding "the people" (*hā'ām*), note the caveats I raised in Chapter 5 regarding Exod 19:15 and Jer 44:24 and the caveats regarding Gen 14:16, 26:10; Exod 20:17; Num 25:1–2; Deut 5:21; Josh 5:5, 8; and Ps 128:1–4 cited in n. 51 there. Also see, regarding "the congregation" (*hā'ēdâ*), as well as "the people" (*hā'ām*), Bird, "Women's Religion in Ancient Israel," 286: "We cannot assume without further evidence that such designations as 'the people' (*hā'ām*), 'the congregation' (*haqqāhāl* or *hā'ēdâ*), or 'Israel' include, or exclude, women."
26. Some have suggested, on the basis of Exod 16:5 and 23, that tasks of food preparation were to be suspended on *šabbāt,* both during the time of the exodus and in the later postexodus community. But as W. A. M. Beuken persuasively argues ("Exodus 16.5, 23," 3–14), all that is forbidden is gathering of manna on the seventh day and not the preparation of it. Rather, while the preparation *can* be done before the seventh day, this is not required.
27. See Chapter 1 and n. 53 there.
28. On the date of Prov 31:10–31, see Chapter 1, n. 56.
29. I find this a rather surprising datum; given the responsibilities that Israelite women assumed within their homes for food preparation, one might think that the responsibility for making fire, so essential to the food preparation

task, would be assigned to them as well. Do we see here a homologizing between the cult and the home?—that as the male priesthood takes responsibility for the fires on Yahweh's altars, so too do men throughout Israelite culture assume the responsibility (or perhaps we should say right) of fire-making.

30. But cf. Levine, *Numbers 21–36,* 383, who takes the terminology of Exod 12:16 regarding work to be both anomalous and imprecise and so (presumably) not useful for determining ancient Israelites' assumptions regarding women's work in food preparation on days when other work is suspended. Elsewhere (in *Leviticus,* 262), Levine argues that cooking and baking *were* supposed to be suspended on the Sabbath. See further n. 26 above.
31. But see above, n. 14, on the date of Isa 1:13.
32. Albertz, *History of Israelite Religion* 2, 408.
33. On the source attribution (P or H) and so the date of Exod 31:15 and Exod 35:2, and the larger pericopes (Exod 31:12–17 and Exod 35:1–3) of which they are a part, see above, nn. 15 and 16. More specifically, among the scholarly references cited there, see Stackert, "Compositional Strata," 14–20, on Exod 31:15 and 35:2, which Stackert understands to be part of an underlying P stratum subsequently augmented by H. That said, Stackert, in ibid., 80, excises the term *šabbātôn* on which I presently comment as an H addition to Exod 31:15 and 35:2, even though he admits (at ibid., 80, n. 60), that "it is possible that *šbtwn* [*šabbātôn*] belongs to P."
34. Milgrom, *Leviticus 1–16,* 1055, 1057; see also Milgrom, *Leviticus 23–27,* 1959, 1977–78.
35. Cooper and Goldstein, "Development of the Priestly Calendars," 12.
36. H. A. McKay, *Sabbath and Synagogue,* 15; see also ibid., 30, and H. A. McKay, "New Moon or Sabbath?," 15.
37. See somewhat similarly van der Toorn, *From Her Cradle to Her Grave,* 96, who writes: "In ancient times, the new moon and sabbath were important sacred days . . . if one visited the 'man of God' on those days, it was probably not for consultation but to perform some ceremony in the sanctuary where he stayed."
38. See, e.g., the references cited in Robinson, *Origin and Development,* 93, n. 15, to which add de Vaux, *Ancient Israel,* 470; G. F. Hasel, "'New Moon and Sabbath,'" 58, n. 67; and G. F. Hasel and Murdoch, "Sabbath in the Prophetic and Historical Literature," 51.
39. On the presumption that Rebekah sought the counsel of an oracular specialist, see Ackerman, "Blind, the Lame, and the Barren," 30–32.
40. Although he does not link Gen 25:19–26, 1 Kgs 14:1–18, and 2 Kgs 4:22–25 as explicitly with *šabbāt* observance as I have hypothesized here, P. D. Miller, *Religion,* 72–73, also discusses the three texts in question in tandem with one another and in tandem with *šabbāt* tradition.
41. Note, however, that Cooper and Goldstein, "Festivals of Israel and Judah," 21, see the new moon celebration as a feature of the Northern Kingdom of Israel only.

42. Keel, *Goddesses and Trees,* 104. But cf. van der Toorn, *Family Religion,* 211–18, who associates the new moon with the so-called interlunium days, i.e., the several days when the moon is dark before the lunar crescent reappears.
43. But see above, n. 14, on the date of Isa 1:13.
44. So, e.g., Hertzberg, *I and II Samuel,* 175, who speaks of "the scene in the king's *house*" (emphasis mine) when describing the new moon feast of 1 Sam 20; H. A. McKay, *Sabbath and Synagogue,* 26, who describes the "new moon . . . as a holy day to be celebrated in *Saul's family home*" (emphasis again mine); and Tsumura, *First Book of Samuel,* 525, who writes, "it is possible that the New Moon was celebrated . . . at the *royal palace*" (emphasis once more mine). Driver's rather idiosyncratic interpretation of 1 Sam 20:5 (*Notes on the Hebrew Text,* 161) also assumes that the setting of Saul's new moon feast is the king's home, and this assumption seems to underlie Farber's description of the event as a "family feast day" ("Israelite Festivals," 3).
45. Chapter 3, n. 50.
46. On 1 Sam 1:18, see Chapter 3, n. 26.
47. On the translation of *bāmâ,* and its problematic nature, see Chapter 3, n. 68.
48. The bibliography on the identification of Gibeah is extensive. See P. M. Arnold, *Gibeah;* Brooks, "From Gibeon to Gibeah," 40–59; Demsky, "Geba, Gibeah, and Gibeon," 26–31; J. M. Miller, "Geba/Gibeah of Benjamin," 145–66; Schniedewind, "Search for Gibeah," 711–22; Sinclair, "Archaeological Study of Gibeah," 52–64; and Sinclair and Cleveland, *Archaeological Study of Gibeah.*
49. Among those who hold these two assumptions (that Gibeath-elohim in 1 Sam 10:5 is identical to Gibeah in 1 Sam 10:10–12, and that both are names for the "Gibeah of Saul"), see, preeminently, van der Toorn, "Saul and the Rise of Israelite State Religion," 520–21, and van der Toorn, *Family Religion,* 268–69; also Tsumura, *First Book of Samuel,* 285. J. M. Miller, "Geba/Gibeah of Benjamin," 165, somewhat similarly equates "Geba, Geba of Benjamin, Gibeah, Gibeah of Benjamin, Gibeah of Saul, and probably Gibeath-elohim," and he has been followed in this interpretation by his student, P. M. Arnold, preeminently in Arnold's book *Gibeah.*
50. E.g., Hertzberg, *I and II Samuel,* 78, takes *gbʿh* in 1 Sam 10:10 to be the common noun "hill" (it does, after all, have the definite article prefixed), and he then follows the LXX in understanding that the Masoretic Text's reading of *habbāmâ* in 1 Sam 10:13 (on which see further below) refers to a different "high place," as in a "hill," i.e., the Gibeah of Saul. Thus, he interprets that in 1 Sam 10:13, Saul went to Gibeah, his hometown, after his encounter in 10:10–12 with the prophetic band on some "Hill of God" that lay elsewhere. R. W. Klein, *1 Samuel,* 91, 93, equates the Gibeath-elohim of 1 Sam 10:5, which he says must be identical with the Gibeah, or "the hill" of 1 Sam 10:10–12, with Geba, which he locates about 3 miles (4.8 kilometers) northeast of the "Gibeah of Saul." Demsky, "Geba, Gibeah, and Gibeon," 26–27, on the basis of 1 Chr 8:29–40 and

9:35–44, takes Saul's hometown to be Gibeon (Tell el-Jîb), not Tel el-Fûl, the site many commentators identify as the "Gibeah of Saul" (see most recently Schniedewind, "Search for Gibeah," passim, but esp. 722, arguing against J. M. Miller, "Geba/Gibeah of Benjamin," passim, but esp. 165, and P. M. Arnold, *Gibeah*). Demsky furthermore takes the Gibeath-elohim of 1 Sam 10:5 to be the same as the Gibeah of 10:10–12 and sees both as references to Gibeon, whose well-known *bāmâ* he also believes is referred to in 1 Sam 10:13 (pp. 27–28). Yet while Demsky and I would agree that 1 Sam 10:5 and 10:10–12 (and also 10:13) all refer to the same site, Demsky would not, as opposed to my interpretation, see this as the site of Saul's royal fief as described in 1 Sam 20. Rather, Demsky sees Saul as having moved from his ancestral home of Gibeon to a fief at the "Gibeah of Saul" at some point following his coronation (Demsky, "Geba, Gibeah, and Gibeon," 28). See similarly Brooks, "From Gibeon to Gibeah," 57.

51. On the place name Gibeah, see, e.g., Josh 24:33, regarding the town Gibeah in Ephraim, and also the place names Gibeath-Haaraloth (Josh 5:3), Gibeath-Kiriath (Josh 18:28), Gibeath-Moreh (Judg 7:1), Gibeath-Hachilah (1 Sam 23:19; 26:1, 3), and Gibeath-Ammah (2 Sam 2:24).
52. McCarter, *I Samuel,* 361, 363.
53. Chapter 3, n. 66.
54. Mastin, "Jonathan at the Feast," 120–24; also Tsumura, *First Book of Samuel,* 515.
55. Knauf, "Saul, David, and the Philistines," 15–16.
56. As pointed out by van der Toorn, "Saul and the Rise of Israelite State Religion," 528, and van der Toorn, *Family Religion,* 274.
57. Whether David's presence was expected because he was a kinsman to Saul or a courtier is not necessarily clear: see Hertzberg, *I and II Samuel,* 173, and R. W. Klein, *1 Samuel,* 206.
58. Olyan, *Rites and Rank,* 57–58.
59. As Miano, *Shadow on the Steps,* 26–27, notes, the new moon festival envisioned in 1 Sam 20 probably lasts two days because the period between new moons actually "fluctuates slightly" from month to month (29.5 days, plus or minus thirteen hours), yet "with no apparent pattern." Thus, the "most useful phenomena" for determining the new moon is "to observe the moon's phases," although, as pointed out by Tsumura, *First Book of Samuel,* 505, "the new moon cannot be actually observed in the evening of the festival in certain months." This means the festival must carry over into a second day if celebrants err on the early side regarding the lunar crescent's appearance in the sky. For further discussion, Tsumura cites his article published in Japanese (with an English summary), "'New Moon' and 'Sabbath' in Samuel," 77–99.
60. On corpse impurity, see P (Num 5:2–3, 9:6–12, 19:11–22, 31:19–20), H (Lev 21:1–6), the Deuteronomistic History (2 Kgs 23:14, 16), the prophet Ezekiel (Ezek 9:7, 39:12–14, 43:7–9), and D. P. Wright, "Unclean and Clean," 730.
61. H. A. McKay, *Sabbath and Synagogue,* 15; see also ibid., 30, and H. A. McKay, "New Moon or Sabbath?," 15.

62. Levine, *Numbers 21–36,* 403; van der Toorn, *From Her Cradle to Her Grave,* 96.
63. On Carmel as the site of a monarchic-era regional sanctuary, see Chapter 3, n. 20, and, as there, A. R. Davis, *Tel Dan,* 116–18, and Edelman, "Cultic Sites," 84.
64. Paraphrasing here P. D. Miller's comments, in *Religion,* 123, on the Hannah story; see further my discussion in Chapter 6.
65. On the meaning "*yearly* sacrifice" for the phrase *zebaḥ hayyāmîm* (which literally means "the sacrifice of days"), see McCarter, *1 Samuel,* 53 and 62.
66. De Vaux, *Ancient Israel,* 470.
67. This is what Haran seems to imply, in "Zeḇaḥ Hayyamîm," 14–15, and in *Temples,* 306–7.
68. Alternatively, one could follow the Dead Sea Scrolls (4QSam[b]) and the Greek tradition (Codex Vaticanus) to read that David's "brothers" commanded him to attend their clan's yearly sacrifice.
69. P. D. Miller, *Religion,* 69.
70. Haran, *Temples,* 34, 307–8.
71. Haran, in "Zeḇaḥ Hayyamîm," 13, and in *Temples,* 306, argues that it is clear women and children were included in clans' sacrificial banquets, on the basis of his assumption that 1 Sam 1:1–2:26 is a narrative concerning the annual clan feast of Elkanah's family. As we will see, however, the matter is not so clear-cut if this text is excluded (as I propose in Chapter 9) from a catalogue of "annual clan sacrifice" accounts.
72. On brother(s), see above, n. 68.
73. Bergant, "Anthropological Approach," 50.
74. Blenkinsopp, "Family in First Temple Israel," 79 (see similarly Blenkinsopp, "Deuteronomy," 7); Malamat, "King Lists," 173, n. 29.
75. Halpern, "Jerusalem and the Lineages," 58.
76. See, e.g., Blenkinsopp, "Deuteronomy," 6–8; Blenkinsopp, "Family in First Temple Israel," 81; Lewis, *Cults of the Dead,* 178; van der Toorn, "Ancestors and Anthroponyms," 9–10; and van der Toorn, *Family Religion,* 211–14.
77. Cox and Ackerman, "Rachel's Tomb," 135–48.
78. Olyan, "Some Neglected Aspects," 602–3.
79. Somewhat similarly, the bodies of kings who die outside their capital cities can be transported to their royal seats for burial. For example, in 2 Kgs 9:28 and 2 Kgs 23:30, the bodies of Kings Ahaziah and Josiah, respectively, are brought to Jerusalem after they are killed during battles at Megiddo. Also in 2 Kgs 14:20, King Amaziah's body is said to have been brought from Lachish, where he was killed, to be buried in Jerusalem, and in 1 Kgs 22:37, the body of an unnamed Israelite king killed in battle (usually thought to be Ahab) is brought to Samaria.
80. See also Exod 13:19, Josh 24:32.
81. Cox and Ackerman, "Micah's Teraphim," 11, 15–16, 23–24. See similarly Schmitt, "Elements of Domestic Cult," in Albertz and Schmitt, *Family and Household Religion,* 61: "*tĕrāpîm* are perhaps best understood as (male) figurines used in

the context of domestic and familial religion, especially for interrogating ancestor spirits."

82. Malamat, "King Lists," 173, n. 29.
83. Noegel, "Maleness, Memory, and the Matter of Dream Divination," 72–74 and 74, n. 44; see also Ackerman, *Under Every Green Tree,* 106–7, n. 14, and Lewis, *Cults of the Dead,* 150.
84. Van der Toorn, *Family Religion,* 229.
85. Van der Toorn, "Family Religion in Second Millennium West Asia," 27.
86. Ibid., 28; Stol, *Women,* 631.
87. Further on the *nadītu,* with references, see Ackerman, "Women and the Religious Culture," 271–72, and Stol, *Women,* 587–607.
88. Van der Toorn, "Family Religion in Second Millennium West Asia," 28.
89. Ibid., 29.
90. J. J. Finkelstein, "Genealogy of the Hammurapi Dynasty," 95–118; Stol, *Women,* 630.
91. Van der Toorn, "Family Religion in Second Millennium West Asia," 28.
92. On *ʾĕlōhîm* with the meaning "deceased spirit(s)," see 1 Sam 28:13; 2 Sam 14:16; Isa 8:19; Num 25:2, as cited in Ps 106:28; and probably Exod 21:6. Also, on Exod 21:6, see van der Toorn and Lewis, "*tĕrāpîm,*" 783, and the references cited there. On Num 25:2 as cited in Ps 106:28, see Lewis, *Cults of the Dead,* 167, and Lewis, "Ancestral Estate," 602. On 2 Sam 14:16, see Lewis, "Ancestral Estate," passim. On 1 Sam 28:13, see Hutter, "Religionsgeschichtliche Erwägungen," 32–36, and Lewis, *Cults of the Dead,* 115–16, but cf. Schmidt, *Israel's Beneficent Dead,* 210–20, and Schmidt, "'Witch' of En-Dor," 120–26.
93. Van der Toorn, "Ancestors and Anthroponyms," 6.
94. Ibid., 7.
95. Meyers, "Contributing to Continuity," 4, and Stol, *Women,* 628, but cf. Bayliss, "Cult of Dead Kin," 118–19, who suggests that while women may have taken responsibility for seeing that the proper offerings were made to the dead, they may not have made the offerings themselves.
96. Bayliss, "Cult of Dead Kin," 123–24.
97. Stol, *Women,* 628; see also, regarding the specific cases of Emar and Nuzi, van der Toorn, "Gods and Ancestors," 44, 49–50, 53, 55–56.
98. Lewis, *Cults of the Dead,* 28, 79.
99. Marsman, *Women,* 591; cf. the more optimistic assessment of Meyers, "Contributing to Continuity," 5.
100. Blenkinsopp, "Family in First Temple Israel," 79; see also Block, "Marriage and Family," 99.
101. Van der Toorn, "Nine Months," 401–2.
102. Cooper and Goldstein, "At the Entrance to the Tent," 214.

Chapter 8. "You Will Make Three Pilgrimage Journeys to Me"

1. There are also once-a-year celebrations that are without religious significance, e.g., the festival that seems to have taken place annually in conjunction with sheepshearing (Gen 31:19, 38:12; 1 Sam 25:2–38; 2 Sam 13:23–29).
2. If a month does begin, as suggested in Chapter 7, with the appearance of the new moon (see n. 42 there), then the full moon would generally appear thirteen days thereafter and not fifteen. Nevertheless, as Propp, *Exodus 1–18,* 383, writes, "it is quite possible that . . . the Israelites considered the fifteenth day the full moon, irrespective of astronomical reality."
3. Scholars debate what season marked the beginning of the Israelite year: the spring or the autumn. Thorough discussions can be found in Clines, "Evidence for an Autumnal New Year," 22–40, and Propp, *Exodus 1–18,* 384–87.
4. Wagenaar, *Origin and Transformation,* 80–83; Weyde, *Appointed Festivals,* 3.
5. See Levinson, "Goethe's Analysis of Exodus 34," 213, n. 6, for references, including, recently and thoroughly, Gesundheit (Bar-On), "Festival Calendars," 161–93, and Gesundheit, *Three Times a Year,* 12–42. Gesundheit seeks to demonstrate that Exod 34:18–23 is dependent on, and thus later than, Exod 23:14–17 (making the traditional ascription of Exod 34:18–23 to J impossible, given that J is generally taken as a source independent of E). Instead, Gesundheit argues that Exod 34:18–23 is post-Deuteronomic. Cooper and Goldstein, however, while accepting Gesundheit's claim that Exod 34:18–23 is dependent on Exod 23:14–17, still take Exod 34:18–23 to be from a relatively early source, namely, R^{JE} (see Cooper and Goldstein, "Development of the Priestly Calendars," 3–4, esp. 4, n. 10), that is, the redactor who brought together J and E in (in their view) the mid-eighth century BCE (see ibid., 2; Cooper and Goldstein, "Festivals of Israel and Judah," 27–28; and Cooper and Goldstein, "Exodus and *Maṣṣôt,*" 17, 25). But cf. Baden, *J, E, and the Redaction of the Pentateuch.*
6. P. D. Miller, *Religion,* 84.
7. As Haran notes (*Temples,* 291 and 300–303), there are also references to *ḥaggîm* in Exod 5:1, 10:9, and 32:5–6 that do not seem to concern the pilgrimage festivals of Maṣṣot, Harvest/Firstfruits/Shavu'ot, and Ingathering/Sukkot. Haran takes these verses as anachronistic retrojections inserted into the exodus account by later writers. See my discussion ahead on the exceptional descriptions of Pesaḥ (Passover) as a *ḥag* in Exod 34:25 and in (apparently) Ezek 45:21. On the possibility that Pesaḥ is described as a *ḥag* in Exod 12:14, see n. 13 below.
8. Assuming here, with almost all commentators, that the form *šěbū'ōt* that appears in Ezek 45:21 should be vocalized *šib'at* so that the reference, which immediately follows this calendar's injunctions regarding Pesaḥ, is to the "seven days" of Maṣṣot. See Wagenaar, "Passover," 240–41, and Zimmerli, *Ezekiel 2,* 481.
9. On the names Pesaḥ/Passover, see Glasson, "'Passover,' a Misnomer," 79–84, esp. 80; Milgrom, *Leviticus 23–27,* 1970; and Milgrom, *Leviticus,* 276.

10. On the date of these texts, see above, n. 5.
11. See Alexander, "Passover Sacrifice," 9; de Vaux, *Ancient Israel,* 471; Haran, "Passover Sacrifice," 96–101; Haran, *Temples,* 327–32; and Weyde, *Appointed Festivals,* 43–52. But cf. May, "Relation of the Passover to the Festival of Unleavened Cakes," 66, who insists "the reference to the passover in verse 25 of Exodus 34 is palpably a later interpolation." See similarly Levinson, *Deuteronomy,* 69 and n. 52 on that page (with references, along with direction to more references still).
12. As in n. 11 just above, see Alexander, "Passover Sacrifice," 9; Haran, "Passover Sacrifice," 96–101; and Haran, *Temples,* 327–32; also the comments of Propp, *Exodus 19–40,* 284 and 616. But cf. Milgrom, *Leviticus 23–27,* 2068–70, and again as in n. 11 above, May, "Relation of the Passover to the Festival of Unleavened Cakes," 66, as well as Wagenaar, "Passover," 250, 253 and n. 13 on that page, and Wagenaar, *Origin and Transformation,* 40.
13. Pesaḥ may be referred to as a *ḥag* in Exod 12:14, depending on whether the reference to *ḥag* in that verse is understood as looking back to the Pesaḥ ritual described in Exod 12:1–13 or forward to the ritual of Maṣṣot described in Exod 12:15–20. See further Wagenaar, "Passover," 250, 253, and n. 13 on that page, and Wagenaar, *Origin and Transformation,* 94.
14. The grammar of Ezek 45:21 is strange, as the noun *ḥag* appears after Pesaḥ, not before, and in the absolute as opposed to the construct form. For discussion, see Wagenaar, "Passover," 240, and Zimmerli, *Ezekiel 2,* 480–81, nn. a and b on Ezek 45:21.
15. Propp, *Exodus 1–18,* 447.
16. There is a long and complex literature on the specific type of sanctuary or temple that pilgrimage celebrants were required to visit. Deuteronomy, in keeping with its imperative that all sacrificial rituals be centrally observed, insists pilgrimage must be made to the temple in Jerusalem. As I have intimated in my discussions of the P and H tent of meeting and the succeeding Jerusalem temple in Chapters 5–6, I take the Bible's P, H, and related calendars also to assume centralized worship, a position originally articulated by Wellhausen; see his *Prolegomena,* 34–39. See similarly Haran, "Zeḇaḥ Hayyamiîm," 13, n. 1; Haran, "Complex of Ritual Acts," 290, n. 18; Levine, *Numbers 21–36,* 50, 365; and Propp, *Exodus 1–18,* 448, citing Friedman, *Who Wrote the Bible?,* 171–72. But cf. Kaufmann, *Religion of Israel,* 175–84; Milgrom, *Leviticus 1–16,* 29–34; Milgrom, "Does H Advocate the Centralization of Worship?," 59–76; and Milgrom, *Leviticus 17–22,* 1504–14. Cf. also Knohl, *Sanctuary of Silence,* 112–13, 204–12, who argues for a compromise position: that while P does not insist on centralization, H does.
17. On the translation "holy proclamation," see Haran, *Temples,* 291, and, similarly, Propp, *Exodus 1–18,* 365, 404, who renders *miqrāʾ-qōdeš* as a "calling of holiness." For the translation "a holy convocation," see Brueggemann, *Worship,* 15; P. D.

Miller, *Religion,* 141–42; and some (but not all) renditions of the term *miqrāʾ-qōdeš* in the NRSV. On the translation "sacred assembly," see Levine, *Leviticus,* 154, 157, and similarly MacRae, "Meaning and Evolution," 257, who translates "solemn assemblies." But cf. Levine, *Numbers 21–36,* 381–82, where *miqrāʾ-qōdeš* is translated as "sanctuary convocation." The translation "sacred occasion" comes from the NJPS, and it is adopted by Cooper and Goldstein, "Development of the Priestly Calendars," 16, and Milgrom, *Leviticus 23–27,* 1957–58. Nihan, "Israel's Festival Calendars," 179, n. 9; Wagenaar, "Passover," 260; and Wagenaar, *Origin and Transformation,* 192, argue for "holy day" or "holiday," following Kutsch, "*miqrāʾ*," 247–53.

18. This interpretation of Deuteronomy's festal calendar in 16:1–8 (one day in Jerusalem, with the next six days in one's family homestead) has perhaps been argued most forcefully by Levinson, *Deuteronomy,* 53–56, 69, 72, 79–80, 89. Cf., however, the equally forceful critique of Gesundheit, "Der deuteronomische Festkalendar," 57–68, and Gesundheit, *Three Times a Year,* 96–149.
19. Milgrom, *Leviticus 23–27,* 1976; Milgrom, *Leviticus,* 277.
20. On the translation of *śeh,* see Alexander, "Passover Sacrifice," 21, n. 27; Meyers, *Exodus,* 96; and Propp, *Exodus 1–18,* 388.
21. This position is well presented (although not necessarily endorsed) by P. D. Miller, *Religion,* 82–83, and also by Soggin, *Israel in the Biblical Period,* 92–94. It was in essence proposed more than a century ago by Wellhausen in his great *Prolegomena:* see, e.g., the summary of Wellhausen's position as presented by Alexander, "Passover Sacrifice," 1–2, and by Van Seters, "Place of the Yahwist," 160. Its most forceful contemporary spokesperson is Levinson, *Deuteronomy,* 55–97, esp. 56–62 and 65–97, and see as well pp. 21 and 53. But cf. Cooper and Goldstein, "Festivals of Israel and Judah," 22, 25–26, 27–29; Cooper and Goldstein, "Exodus and *Maṣṣôt,*" 17, 25, 27; and Cooper and Goldstein, "Development of the Priestly Calendars," 2, 5, who likewise take Pesaḥ and Maṣṣot to have been originally separate observances, but to have been separated not by *type,* but by *place,* Pesaḥ being, in their view, a festival that was originally a part of the calendar only of the South, whereas Maṣṣot was a festival that was originally only of the North.
22. But cf. above, nn. 5 and 11.
23. P. D. Miller, *Religion,* 82.
24. This position is presented by P. D. Miller, *Religion,* 81–82, citing Mayes, *Deuteronomy,* and by Segal, *Hebrew Passover,* 175. In Miller's subsequent discussion, on p. 83, he does not take a stand on this proposition's validity, but elsewhere (on pp. 69, 92, and 256, n. 251), he does seem to signal his endorsement.
25. Although note that Maṣṣot goes unmentioned in the 2 Kings account.
26. Propp, *Exodus 1–18,* 428.
27. Although cf. Wagenaar, "Passover," 259, who takes the reference to unleavened bread in Exod 12:8 as secondary.

28. Cooper and Goldstein, "Exodus and *Maṣṣôt,*" 32, n. 59, indeed wonder whether Sarah's *'ūgôt* are to be compared to the *'ūgōt maṣṣôt,* the "unleavened bread cakes," of Exod 12:39.
29. On the translation "bitter lettuces," see Propp, *Exodus 1–18,* 394, and Segal, *Hebrew Passover,* 169.
30. See Chapter 1 and n. 58 there.
31. Alexander, "Passover Sacrifice," 6–8; Haran, "Passover Sacrifice," 109–16; Haran, *Temples,* 341–48; Meyers, *Exodus,* 96–98; and Propp, *Exodus 1–18,* 448–51. But cf. Levinson, *Deuteronomy,* 60–62.
32. Alexander, "Passover Sacrifice," 6–7; Meyers, *Exodus,* 96; Niditch, *Folklore,* 55; and Propp, *Exodus 1–18,* 389.
33. Indeed, it is because there needs to be an adequate number of people to consume the meat in one night that smaller households, according to Exod 12:4, must procure and prepare the sheep or goat jointly with their neighbors. See Alexander, "Passover Sacrifice," 8, and Propp, *Exodus 1–18,* 388–89.
34. Propp, *Exodus 1–18,* 396–97.
35. Hendel, "Sacrifice as a Cultural System," 384–85; also Niditch, *Folklore,* 58–60.
36. See also Exod 23:18; 29:2, 23; 34:25; Lev 2:4–5; 6:9–10 (English 6:16–17); 7:12; 8:2, 26; 10:12; Num 6:15; Judg 6:19–21; and 2 Kgs 23:9, references all pointed out by Propp, *Exodus 1–18,* 393, and Segal, *Hebrew Passover,* 168, n. 5; see also Milgrom, *Leviticus 23–27,* 2003. See too Levine, *Leviticus,* 42–43, 159, and Propp, *Exodus 1–18,* 433, on Lev 7:13 and 23:17, which describe leavened offerings that were brought to Yahweh's sanctuary but that were allowable because they were only "presented before God" but did not "ascend to the altar" (Levine, *Leviticus,* 159).
37. Meyers, *Exodus,* 97–98. See similarly Alexander, "Passover Sacrifice," 7, who states that "there can be little doubt that this [the Pesaḥ ritual as described in Exod 12:1–13] constituted a sacrifice"; Bergant, "Anthropological Approach," 52, who writes of "the sacrificial feature of the meal"; and Jenks, "Eating and Drinking," 254, who notes "the Passover supper takes on nearly sacramental significance."
38. See similarly Bergant, "Anthropological Approach," 51.
39. This was brought to my attention by Meyers, *Exodus,* 95.
40. Although see Knohl, who in "Priestly Torah," 77–79, 113, and *Sanctuary of Silence,* 19–21, 52, attributes Exod 12:1–20 to H.
41. Segal, *Hebrew Passover,* 135; Vos, *Woman in Old Testament Worship,* 124. Segal, *Hebrew Passover,* 35, also points out, by way of a chronologically much later example, that Jesus's Last Supper, envisioned as a Pesaḥ meal in the New Testament's Synoptic Gospels, had male participants only.
42. See similarly my discussion in Chapter 5 of Exod 19:15 and Jer 44:24; see also, as cited in Chapter 5, n. 51, Gen 14:16, 26:10; Exod 20:17; Num 25:1–2; Deut 5:21; and Ps 128:1–4.
43. But cf. Exod 12:22, as interpreted by Levinson, *Deuteronomy,* 58–60, who reads for the usual translation "the blood which is in the basin," "the blood which is

upon the threshold." That is, Levinson understands that the Pesaḥ slaughter as described in Exod 12:21–22 takes place on the doorway threshold of each Israelite's house.

44. Meyers, *Exodus,* 95.
45. Bird, "Women's Religion in Ancient Israel," 286. I have also cited this quotation in Chapter 7, n. 25, in relation to my discussion of Exod 16:4–5, 22–30.
46. Segal, *Hebrew Passover,* 134.
47. Bergant, "Anthropological Approach," 50.
48. Some commentators take this text as coming from a different source than Exod 12:1–13: see Friedman, *Who Wrote the Bible?,* 250, who identifies the author(s) of Exod 12:21–23 as J; Propp, *Exodus 1–18,* 356, who identifies the author(s) of this passage as E; and Segal, *Hebrew Passover,* 49, who identifies the author(s) of Exod 12:21 as the combined JE. Propp lists, however (on p. 376), numerous scholars who attribute all of Exod 12:1–27 to P.
49. Bergant, "Anthropological Approach," 50.
50. Ibid., 52.
51. Meyers, *Discovering Eve,* 147; likewise Meyers, *Rediscovering Eve,* 184.
52. Haran, "Passover Sacrifice," passim, but esp. 109–16; Haran, *Temples,* 317–48, esp. 341–48; and Propp, *Exodus 1–18,* 445–51, esp. 448–51.
53. Haran, "Passover Sacrifice," 110, 114–16; Haran, *Temples,* 342, 347–48; and Propp, *Exodus 1–18,* 448, 450. On centralized worship in P, see also above, n. 16.
54. On the Mishnah's language, see Propp, *Exodus 1–18,* 445.
55. Haran, *Temples,* 348; see similarly Haran, "Passover Sacrifice," 115.
56. Haran, *Temples,* 348; see similarly Haran, "Passover Sacrifice," 116.
57. Propp, *Exodus 1–18,* 450.
58. Haran, *Temples,* 342–43; see similarly Haran, "Passover Sacrifice," 110–11.
59. Haran, *Temples,* 347–348; see similarly Haran, "Passover Sacrifice," 115.
60. Fretheim, *Exodus,* 133.
61. Propp, *Exodus 1–18,* 448–49.
62. Ibid., 437; see also ibid., 457.
63. Although see Cooper and Goldstein, "Festivals of Israel and Judah," 21–22.
64. Propp, *Exodus 1–18,* 393, 433; Wagenaar, *Origin and Transformation,* 52–53, 56.
65. Propp, *Exodus 1–18,* 433; see similarly Segal, *Hebrew Passover,* 169, 178, 180, and, somewhat similarly, Milgrom, *Leviticus 1–16,* 188; Milgrom, *Leviticus,* 26.
66. Propp, *Exodus 1–18,* 433; Segal, *Hebrew Passover,* 169.
67. Propp, *Exodus 1–18,* 433.
68. On the translation of *miqrāʾ-qōdeš,* see above, n. 17.
69. Milgrom, *Leviticus,* 277; see also Milgrom, *Leviticus 23–27,* 1966, 1982.
70. Exactly how this fifty days is to be counted according to Lev 23:16, however, has been a matter of some controversy in Jewish tradition. A succinct summary of the various positions, along with an equally succinct but well-chosen bibliography of scholarly discussion, can be found in Wagenaar, "Priestly Festival Calendar," 218, n. 1.

71. Soggin, *Israel in the Biblical Period,* 107.
72. The Hebrew here is ambiguous: it is clear that two loaves of bread are to be baked, but it is unclear whether each loaf is to be made from two-tenths of a ephah of flour or whether two-tenths of an ephah of flour is to be used to make both loaves. See Milgrom, *Leviticus 23–27,* 2004, and, on the size of an ephah, see Chapter 2, n. 61.
73. However, as Milgrom points out (*Leviticus 1–16,* 179; *Leviticus 23–27,* 2095), rabbinical tradition takes *sōlet* to be a coarser product than was *qemaḥ*.
74. Stol, *Women,* 351.
75. For an imaginative reconstruction that does have women baking the loaves, see Ebeling, *Women's Lives,* 43.
76. On the date of H, see the Introduction.
77. Milgrom, *Leviticus,* 279.
78. Milgrom, *Numbers,* 245; Milgrom, *Leviticus 23–27,* 1980, 2000–2001; and Milgrom, *Leviticus,* 278–79.
79. Although cf. Chapter 7, n. 30, regarding Levine's interpretation of this verse.
80. Milgrom, *Leviticus 1–16,* 419; see similarly ibid., 218.
81. Milgrom, *Numbers,* 249–50; cf. Levine, *Numbers 21–36,* 392–93.
82. On possible redactional layers within this text, see Milgrom, *Leviticus 23–27,* 2006–7.
83. Ibid., 2008.
84. Haran, *Temples,* 298. See similarly ibid., 296; also, de Vaux, *Ancient Israel,* 495; Fleming, "Israelite Festival Calendar," 30, 32; Levine, *Numbers 21–36,* 50; MacRae, "Meaning and Evolution," 258, 261; P. D. Miller, *Religion,* 84, 196; Nihan, "Israel's Festival Calendars," 185; Rubenstein, *History of Sukkot,* 2, 15, 17–19; Soggin, *Israel in the Biblical Period,* 115; and Weinfeld, *Deuteronomy and the Deuteronomic School,* 219.
85. Milgrom, *Numbers,* 245; Nihan, "Israel's Festival Calendars," 184–85.
86. Milgrom, *Numbers,* 75, 246, 372–73; see also my discussion in Chapter 9.
87. On the translation of this day's name, see Olyan, *Rites and Rank,* 20, with references on 133, n. 30.
88. Above, n. 18.
89. Milgrom, *Leviticus 1–16,* 1055.
90. Milgrom, *Numbers,* 246–47.
91. Milgrom, *Leviticus 1–16,* 1011; Milgrom, *Leviticus,* 167.
92. Stowers, "On the Comparison of Blood," 190.
93. On the translation of *ṣāraʿat,* see Chapter 10 and n. 56 there.
94. Stowers, "On the Comparison of Blood," 190.
95. Although as noted in n. 79 above, cf. Chapter 7, n. 30.
96. Presuming here, as in my discussion of Harvest/Firstfruits/Shavuʿot above, that the command in Lev 23:40 and Deut 16:14 to "rejoice" during Sukkot's celebration implies a *šĕlāmîm* feast: see above, n. 80.
97. See my discussion just ahead, at the beginning of Chapter 9.

Chapter 9. "When the Young Women of Shiloh Come Out to Dance in the Dances"

1. On women's Sukkot musicianship, see also Ackerman, *Warrior, Dancer,* 253–87, and the brief discussion, couched in veiled terms, of van der Toorn, "Nine Months," 405.
2. Chapter 8, n. 84.
3. On the relationship between the grape harvest and Ingathering/Sukkot, see further Rubenstein, "Sukkot Wine Libation," 575–91, esp. 577–81, and Rubenstein, *History of Sukkot,* 14.
4. Vintners did this in order to protect their crop from marauding bands of animals (and humans!) as it ripened, and/or to have easy access to the rapidly maturing grapes. See Hopkins, "'All Sorts of Field Work,'" 166; Matthews, "Treading the Winepress," 20, 26–27; Rubenstein, *History of Sukkot,* 15, 17, 25–27 (with further references in nn. 33–38); and Walsh, *Fruit of the Vine,* 128–42.
5. Spokespeople for this position include Albertz, *History of Israelite Religion* 1, 91; de Vaux, *Ancient Israel,* 495–96; Haran, *Temples,* 299; Martin, *Book of Judges,* 224–25; Rubenstein, "Sukkot Wine Libation," 577; Rubenstein, *History of Sukkot,* 14; M. S. Smith, with contributions by Bloch-Smith, *Pilgrimage Pattern,* 60, 65; and Soggin, *Israel in the Biblical Period,* 112.
6. This interpretation is hardly unique to me; it was suggested already by Wellhausen, *Prolegomena,* 92–94. More modern proponents include Ackroyd, *First Book of Samuel,* 20, 26, 27; Braulik, "Were Women, Too, Allowed to Offer Sacrifices?," 918; M. S. Smith, with contributions by Bloch-Smith, *Pilgrimage Pattern,* 65; Wagenaar, *Origin and Transformation,* 12; and Walters, "After Drinking," 539, 541–42. Others, though, take the 1 Sam 1:1–2:26 feasts to be private family or clan observances: Albertz, *History of Israelite Religion* 1, 101–2; Cooper and Goldstein, "Festivals of Israel and Judah," 21; A. R. Davis, "Tel Dan," 126–27, 250–52; Haran, "Zeḇaḥ Hayyamîm," 11–14; Haran, *Temples,* 304–7; Kim, *Incubation,* 286, n. 82; R. W. Klein, *1 Samuel,* 6; McCarter, *1 Samuel,* 58; Meyers, "Hannah and Her Sacrifice," 101–2; Meyers, "Hannah Narrative," 123–24; H. P. Smith, *Critical and Exegetical Commentary,* 185; and Tsumura, *First Book of Samuel,* 109.
7. Fuhs, *ʿālâ,* 89; Hertzberg, *I and II Samuel,* 24.
8. Unfortunately, in translations of Judg 21:19, *ḥag* often is rendered as just "festival" or the like: see, e.g., the NRSV, the JB, the NJB, the NAB, the NABRE, and the NJPS, all of which translate "feast." But cf. the REB, "pilgrimage."
9. So Ackroyd, *First Book of Samuel,* 26.
10. See similarly ibid., 25; de Vaux, *Ancient Israel,* 496; Rubenstein, "Sukkot Wine Libation," 577, n. 8; and Rubenstein, *History of Sukkot,* 14, n. 4. But cf. Hamori, *Women's Divination,* 97, who—on the basis of her reading of Hannah in 1 Sam 1:4–18 as embittered and enraged (Chapter 4, n. 39)—understands Hannah's

silent prayer to be enacted with such gesticulations of fury that Eli, Sukkot festival or no, would have assumed that she was drunk.

11. See Hopkins, "'All Sorts of Field Work,'" 166–67; Matthews, "Treading the Winepress," 20; Rubenstein, "Sukkot Wine Libation," 589; and Walsh, *Fruit of the Vine,* 189.
12. In addition to my comments that follow, see my Chapter 4 discussion of 1 Sam 1:25–28 and also Brettler, "Composition of 1 Samuel 1–2," 602–3; McCarter, *1 Samuel,* 57–58; Tov, "Different Editions of the Song of Hannah," 151–56, 169; and Willis, "Song of Hannah," 139–40, nn. 8–9.
13. On the translation of the Masoretic Text of 1 Sam 1:28, see Chapter 4, n. 72.
14. Scholars also suggest (1) that the military metaphor found in v. 4a is difficult to imagine as coming from Hannah's mouth; (2) that the reference in v. 5 to the *seven* children of the barren woman cannot refer to Hannah, who, according to 1 Sam 2:21, had only six offspring; and (3) that the overall tone of the poem is nationalistic rather than the sort of personal hymn of thanksgiving that Hannah might be expected to sing. See further R. W. Klein, "Song of Hannah," 676–77, n. 4.
15. R. W. Klein (ibid., 677, n. 4) adds that vv. 1 and 3 express well the difficulties Hannah had suffered at the hands of Peninnah; see similarly Hamori, *Women's Divination,* 100–101.
16. The Masoretic Text reads a singular form, *bĕtûlâ,* but almost all commentators translate in the plural for the sake of the parallelism with the second half of the verse. That *bĕtûlâ* designates a stage in life, "a young woman" (more specifically, a young woman who has entered into puberty), rather than the more usual "virgin," has been preeminently demonstrated by Wenham, "*Betûlāh,*" 326–48. See also Pressler, *View of Women,* 25–28, with multiple references.
17. Reading here *yiḥdû,* "they will be merry," with the LXX, for the Masoretic Text *yaḥdāw,* "together."
18. The genres "love song," "lawsuit," "fable," "parable," and "allegory" have all been proposed for this text: see Graffy, "Literary Genre," 401–4; Korpel, "Literary Genre," 119–23; and Niehr, "Zur Gattung von Jes 5, 1–7," 99–100, nn. 1–6. Most, however, follow Willis, "Genre of Isa 5:1–7," 337–62, in regarding the passage as a parable, although many accept the modification of "juridical parable" proposed by Yee, "Form Critical Study," 30–40. See also Sheppard, "More on Isaiah 5:1–7," 45–47.
19. References are collected by Willis, "Genre of Isa 5:1–7," 362, n. 116; see also Matthews and Benjamin, *Social World of Ancient Israel,* 47, and Matthews, "Treading the Winepress," 24.
20. Among those scholars who do comment on the identity of the male "beloved," most assume that he is a close friend of the prophet on whose behalf the prophet sings; then, in v. 3, as the parabolic language of the poem begins to reveal itself, it is made clear that this "beloved friend" is Yahweh (so, e.g., Scott,

"Introduction and Exegesis," 197). But this interpretation ignores the sexual connotations elsewhere associated with the term "beloved" (*yādîd*). It also ignores the description of the song as a "love song" (*šîrat dôdî*) and the juxtaposition of the terms *yādîd* and *dôd,* both meaning "beloved," with the term *kerem,* "vineyard," in v. 1. Frequently in ancient Near Eastern poetry, these words appear in conjunction to designate lovers. See Williams, "Frustrated Expectations," 460–61.

21. Borowski, *Agriculture,* 112; see similarly Ebeling, *Women's Lives,* 89, and van der Toorn, "Nine Months," 405.
22. On these two instruments, see Braun, *Music,* 15, 26.
23. Milgrom, *Numbers,* 75, 246, 372–73.
24. See Chapter 5, n. 51, and Chapter 7, n. 25.
25. For the translation of *tōp,* see Chapter 5, n. 32, and my discussion below.
26. Typically, Hebrew *nēbel* is rendered as "harp." But as Braun, *Music,* 23, points out, "no harps dating to the pre-Hellenistic period have yet been found in the territory of Canaan and ancient Israel." He thus follows Bayer, "Negina v'zimra," 755–82, in understanding the *nēbel* as a thicker-stringed lyre than was a *kinnōr* and also one deeper in tone.
27. See similarly de Vaux, *Ancient Israel,* 477; Levine, *Leviticus,* 268; and Levine, *Numbers 21–36,* 387.
28. Meyers, "Mother to Muse," 57.
29. Meyers, "Women with Hand-Drums," 190.
30. Ibid.; likewise Meyers, "Guilds and Gatherings," 166 (but cf. the less emphatic language Meyers uses in n. 23 on that page). See also Paz, *Drums,* 89 (regarding iconographic evidence from across the ancient Near East), and Werner, "Jewish Music, Liturgical," 619.
31. Meyers has cited this iconographic evidence in numerous publications: originally in Meyers, "Terracotta at the Harvard Semitic Museum," 120–21; most recently in Meyers, "Miriam, Music, and Miracles," 34–35.
32. The extrabiblical text Meyers mentions is "a reference to the Canaanite goddess Anath with a frame-drum" (Meyers, "Women with Hand-Drums," 190). Unfortunately, Meyers does not give an exact citation, and I do not know the text to which she alludes; n. 6 on p. 51 of Meyers's article "Mother to Muse" suggests Meyers has taken her information from Eaton-Krauss, "Figure of a Female Drummer," 303, who similarly claims, without a specific citation, that Anat is "described in a text found at Ugarit as a tambourine player." But, again, I know of no Ugaritic text that describes Anat as a drummer, although she does perhaps play a lyre in *KTU* 1.3.3.4–5 (below, n. 35), and she is present at a banquet at which the frame drum (*tp*) is played, along with other instruments, according to *KTU* 1.108.1–9. It is the case, however, that according to some scholars, the daughter of King Kirta, Thitmanit, is instructed by her father to take up a *tp* in *KTU* 1.16.1.41–42. See, e.g., Greenstein, "Kirta," 32 and 46, n. 122.

33. Indeed, Meyers in certain publications is less emphatic about associating women exclusively with frame-drum playing than in the sources cited in n. 30 above: see, e.g., Meyers, "Mother to Muse," 66, 68–70; Meyers, "In the Household and Beyond," 29; and Meyers, *Rediscovering Eve,* 176. Less emphatic still is Meyers, in "Of Drums and Damsels," 19, 21, where she writes (contra Werner) that while there is "a preponderance of females as hand drummers," "the contention . . . that the hand-drum was exclusively a women's instrument cannot be substantiated."
34. To be sure, Ps 81:4 (English 81:3) uses the verb *tāqa*ʿ, which Milgrom associates with priestly performance, in its command that the *šôpār*/shofar be sounded. But Milgrom explains that nonpriestly sources, such as Ps 81, did not necessarily observe the careful terminological distinctions between *ḥăṣōṣĕrâ* and *šôpār* and *tāqa*ʿ and *tĕrûʿâ* that priestly sources such as Num 10 and 29 deployed. Thus, while "the masses may not have been aware of the technical name for the wind instrument blown by the priests" and of other technical terminology, this does not mean that the distinction between the priestly *ḥăṣōṣĕrâ* and the people's *šôpār* did not hold in texts such as Ps 81:2–4 (English 81:1–3). See Milgrom, *Numbers,* 373.
35. From the Late Bronze Age, see the textual reference to the goddess Anat playing a lyre that is frequently restored in an otherwise broken context in *KTU* 1.3.3.4–5, based on *KTU* 1.101.16 (so, e.g., M. S. Smith, "Baal Cycle," 109 and 167, n. 54). For Late Bronze Age artistic representations of women lyre players, see *ANEP,* no. 208; Burgh, *Listening to the Artifacts,* 54; and Keel, *Symbolism,* 337 (Fig. 450); also Braun, *Music,* 96 (but cf. Burgh, *Listening to the Artifacts,* 89). For the Iron Age, see the representations of female lyre players found on several of the so-called Phoenician bowls, as pictured in Markoe, *Phoenician Bronze and Silver Bowls,* 252, 328–29, and 347.
36. The most thorough discussions of the ʿAjrûd lyre player and her throne are those of Beck, "Drawings from Ḥorvat Teiman," 31–36; Beck, "Drawings and Decorative Designs," 169–73; and Dever, "Asherah, Consort of Yahweh?," 22–25. See also Braun, *Music,* 151–54, and Dever, *Did God Have a Wife?,* 164–67.
37. But cf. Braun, *Music,* 157, who suggests that when lyres and frame drums are played in conjunction, as in Ps 81:2–4 (English 81:1–3), it is more typical to find a "male-female duo of chordophone [lyre] and membranophone [drum]."
38. Brueggemann, *Worship,* 12.
39. On men as lament singers, see also 2 Sam 3:33; Ezek 19:1, 14; 26:17; 27:2; 28:12; 32:2, 18; Amos 5:1; 2 Chr 35:25; and, possibly, Isa 19:8 and Ezek 27:32 (assuming the fishermen and sailors who are gendered grammatically as male in these texts are, in fact, men).
40. See, e.g., Meyers, "Mother to Muse," 64; Meyers, "Guilds and Gatherings," 168; and Meyers, *Rediscovering Eve,* 175.
41. The form *yôdĕʿê* is in the masculine plural, which, as noted above, can be used in Hebrew both when speaking of groups of men alone and also when speaking

of groups that include both men and women. Further on lamentation in Amos 5:16, see Henshaw, *Female and Male,* 121.

42. The significance of this Jeremiah passage was originally pointed out by Bird, "Women's Religion in Ancient Israel," 295–96; see similarly Bird, "Israelite Religion," 106, and Brenner, *Israelite Woman,* 37.
43. Bird, "Israelite Religion," 106, and Bird, "Notes on Gender and Religious Ritual," 227. See also Henshaw, *Female and Male,* 27 and 72, n. 57, for further references.
44. Dillon, *Girls and Women,* 279; see similarly ibid., 271–72, 277, and 285.
45. See, e.g., Alexiou, *Ritual Lament,* 6–7, 10–13, 21–22, and 212, n. 107; Blundell, *Women in Ancient Greece,* 50, 72–73, 85, 162–63; Dillon, *Girls and Women,* 268–70, 282–83, 285, 288–89; and Klinck, *Women's Songs,* 15–16, 18–19.
46. Dillon, *Girls and Women,* 269.
47. See *KTU* 1.16.1.5, 19, 30 (Kirta) and *KTU* 1.19.4.9–10, 20–22 (Aqhat). On the mourners as professionals, see Dahood, *Psalms II,* 247.
48. On *mšspdt,* see Scharbert, "*sāpad, mispēd,*" 299–303.
49. Dijkstra, "Goddess, Gods, Men, and Women," 203–14, and Dijkstra, "Women and Religion," 173–76. See also Jost and Seifert, "Ezekiel," 348.
50. Discussed in Ackerman, *Under Every Green Tree,* 44 and n. 33 on that page.
51. Dijkstra, "Women and Religion," 174–75.
52. The Masoretic Text locates twenty-five worshippers in the temple courtyard in Ezek 8:16, whereas the LXX reads twenty. Twenty seems the more likely reading; twenty-five is a secondary assimilation to Ezek 11:1.
53. See Ackerman, *Under Every Green Tree,* 53–55, for my understanding of the geographical layout presumed in Ezek 8. For "sitting" as a mourning pose, see *KTU* 1.5.6.12–14, where the god El retires from his throne to sit on a low stool and, in the parallel colon, the ground itself when he hears of the death of the storm god Baal. See similarly, Isa 3:26, 47:1; Ezek 26:16; Lam 2:10; and note the Jewish custom of sitting *shiva* after a death, which continues until this day.
54. See, e.g., Olyan, *Biblical Mourning,* 39–45, who both surveys scholarly opinion and discusses his own.
55. Among biblical sources, see Lev 21:5; Isa 15:2, 22:12; Jer 7:29, 16:6, 47:5, 48:37; Ezek 27:31; Amos 8:10; Mic 1:16; for Greek tradition, see Dillon, *Girls and Women,* 269–70, 275, 277, 279, and 281; for Egyptian tradition, see Ritner, "Household Religion in Ancient Egypt," 173. Further discussion in Ackerman, *Under Every Green Tree,* 85–86 and 86, n. 143.
56. See *KTU* 1.5.6.14–16, where the god El, upon hearing of the death of the storm god Baal (above, n. 53), rubs dirt (paralleled by dust) on his head, and, in the Bible, Ezek 27:30. Jer 6:26, 25:34, and Esth 4:3 speak more generally of covering one's body with dust as a mourning gesture—as does Mic 1:10, regarding an otherwise unspecified female subject (reading here a feminine singular im-

perative *hitpallāšî* with the *qĕrê,* rather than the first-person perfect form reflected by the *kĕtîb*). For further discussion of this custom in Egypt, see Ritner, "Household Religion in Ancient Egypt," 173; for other ancient Near Eastern and eastern Mediterranean evidence, see Ackerman, *Under Every Green Tree,* 85 and n. 141 on that page.

57. Olyan, *Biblical Mourning,* 32.
58. Robins, *Women in Ancient Egypt,* 164.
59. Dothan, *Philistines,* 237–46; Keel and Uehlinger, *Gods, Goddesses, and Images of God,* 124, Fig. 150.
60. Conveniently reproduced in *ANEP,* no. 459.
61. See also Mic 1:16, where an unidentified female subject is commanded to make herself bald.
62. Gen 37:34; 2 Sam 1:2, 11; 3:31; 13:31; Job 1:20, 2:12; Esth 4:1; see also the Epic of Gilgamesh, Tablet VIII, line 64, where King Gilgamesh of Uruk "rip[s] off his finery" upon the death of his bosom companion Enkidu.
63. Reading here the verb *rād,* "to wander," for the Masoretic Text *yārad,* "to go down."
64. The Hebrew verb *tinnâ* is found elsewhere in the Bible only in Judg 5:11, where it means "to recount," with the more specific sense of recounting to commemorate. See P. L. Day, "From the Child Is Born the Woman," 67, n. 4, and the references there; also, van Dijk-Hemmes, "Traces of Women's Texts," 90.
65. See above, n. 16, on translating *bĕtûlâ* as "young woman," and more specifically as a "young woman who has entered into puberty." By extension, in Judg 11:37, the abstract form *bĕtûlîm* should be translated as "young womanhood" (i.e., the point when a girl enters into puberty). The most thorough discussion within the context of Judg 11:29–40 is P. L. Day, "From the Child Is Born the Woman," 59–60.
66. Ibid., 58.
67. Ibid.; see similarly Bal, *Death and Dissymmetry,* 46–49, 110–13; Niditch, *Ancient Israelite Religion,* 115–16; and van Dijk-Hemmes, "Traces of Women's Texts," 88–90.
68. Halperin, *One Hundred Years of Homosexuality,* 21.
69. Chapter 6 and n. 92 there.
70. For the translation "nuptial songs," see, e.g., the NRSV, the NJPS (note on the translation), the JB, the NJB, and the NABRE; also Dahood, *Psalms II,* 247. Cf. the NEB, the NAB, the REB, and the RSV.
71. *KTU* 1.3.1.4–22; *KTU* 1.17.6.30–32; see also *KTU* 1.108.1–9.
72. Marcus, "Betrothal of Yarikh and Nikkal-Ib," 215; see also M. Dietrich and Loretz, *Studien zu den ugaritischen Texten,* 145; Lewis, "Family, Household, and Local Religion," 65; Wyatt, *Religious Texts from Ugarit,* 336; and, somewhat similarly, M. S. Smith, "Is Genesis 1 a Creation Myth?," 81.

73. While the remains of women's wedding songs from ancient Greece are "meagre" (Seaford, "Tragic Wedding," 111), enough are extant to be clear regarding their existence and basic character. See (among others) Blundell, *Women in Ancient Greece,* 80; Hague, "Marriage Athenian Style," 34–36; Oakley and Sims, *Wedding in Ancient Athens;* and Thomsen, *Ritual and Desire,* 244, n. 11.
74. Sasson, "Worship of the Golden Calf," 157, in fact suggests that the distinction standard lexica draw between *ʿānâ,* "to respond," and *ʿānâ,* "to sing," is unnecessary, arguing that the type of antiphonal singing that *ʿānâ,* "to sing," describes is fully a part of the larger context of *ʿānâ,* "to respond." See similarly, on *ʿānâ* in Exod 15:21, Henshaw, *Female and Male,* 119.
75. Poethig, "Victory Song Tradition," passim.
76. Chapter 1, n. 88.
77. Cross and Freedman, "Song of Miriam," 237–50.
78. For *rekeb,* "chariotry," for the Masoretic Text's *rōkĕbô,* "his rider," in 15:1b, see Cross, *Canaanite Myth,* 127, n. 48.
79. It has been argued that Miriam's song does not *begin* with the couplet found in 15:21, but that 15:21 is Miriam's song in its entirety. This view has been well refuted by Cross and Freedman, "Song of Miriam," 237; see also Cross, *Canaanite Myth,* 123–24. But cf. R. J. Burns, *Has the Lord Indeed Spoken Only Through Moses?,* 13–16.
80. Cross and Freedman, "Song of Miriam," 237. See also Brenner, *Israelite Woman,* 52–56; Meyers, "Miriam, Music, and Miracles," 29–31; and Trible, "Bringing Miriam out of the Shadows," 19–20 and 34, n. 5.
81. Reading *lāšîr,* "to sing," in v. 6 with the *qĕrê,* rather than the *kĕtîb lāšûr.*
82. As noted by Meyers in several publications: originally in Meyers, "Of Drums and Damsels," 22; most recently in Meyers, "Miriam, Music, and Miracles," 33, 39.
83. Meyers, "Mother to Muse," 72, n. 61; see also Meyers, "Those Who Bear Tidings," 299. But cf. Dahood, *Psalms II,* 140–41.
84. Albright, "Catalogue," 1–39.

Chapter 10. "The Daughters of Your People Who Prophesy"

1. Typically, *ḥālîl* is translated "flute." But as Braun points out in *Music,* 13–14, the *ḥālîl* is more like an oboe. For the translations of *kinnōr, nēbel,* and *tōp,* see Chapter 5, n. 32, and Chapter 9, n. 26.
2. Braun, *Music,* 219.
3. Meyers, "Guilds and Gatherings," 166, n. 23; Meyers, "In the Household and Beyond," 29 and 39, n. 50; and Meyers, *Rediscovering Eve,* 176.
4. See Chapter 9, and nn. 30–31 and 35 there. See also Ebeling, *Women's Lives,* 87–88, regarding women's association with multiple types of musical instruments.
5. Chapter 1, n. 88.

6. On Miriam as she is presented in the Bible's genealogical accounts, as well as Miriam's relationship to Moses and Aaron according to other biblical texts, see Fischer, *Gotteskünderinnen,* 82–85; Gafney, *Daughters of Miriam,* 79–80; Leuchter and Farber, "Pre-Biblical Aaron, Miriam, and Moses"; and Meyers, "Miriam, Music, and Miracles," 42, n. 4.
7. On these women as constituting a guild, see Meyers, "Engendering Ezekiel," 291.
8. See similarly Brenner, *Israelite Woman,* 57; Dijkstra, "Women and Religion," 182; Huffmon, "Company of Prophets," 66; and Jepsen, "Die Nebiah," 267–68. Others, though, interpret differently: see most recently, Hamori, *Women's Divination,* 100–101, and Williamson, "Prophetesses in the Hebrew Bible," 65, 75, both of whom draw particular attention to the arguments of Wildberger, *Isaiah 1–12,* 337.
9. On naming as a more typically maternal role, see Chapter 1 and n. 7 there.
10. But cf. Fischer, *Gotteskünderinnen,* 216, who argues that the presence of the definite article *ha-*, "the," before the designation *nĕbîʾâ* in Isa 8:3 indicates that this woman is so well known in her community that she need not be identified by name.
11. P. D. Miller, *Religion,* 177.
12. Huffmon, "Company of Prophets," 67; Nissinen, "Biblical Prophecy," 445–50.
13. More generally, scholars have suggested that there is no particular difference in the work of female and male prophets, either in the Bible or elsewhere in the Near East. See Hamori, *Women's Divination,* 39–40, with references, but cf. my discussion below of Ezek 13:17–23.
14. The thesis regarding the identification of the "book of the *tôrâ*" as some form of Deuteronomy is one of the oldest and most venerable in modern biblical scholarship, promulgated already by W. M. L. De Wette in his 1805 doctoral dissertation (and in even earlier sources still, according to Lohfink, "Cult Reform of Josiah," 459). For more recent discussions, sometimes with modifications, see O'Brien, "Book of Deuteronomy," 98–100; Römer, "Book of Deuteronomy," 191–94; and Weinfeld, *Deuteronomy 1–11,* 81–84.
15. Wagner, "*dāraš,*" 302–4.
16. 2 Chr 35:20–25 shifts the story to explain away this discrepancy: for discussion, see Halpern, "Why Manasseh Is Blamed," 501–5; Hamori, "Prophet and the Necromancer," 841–43; and also the interchange between Williamson, "Death of Josiah," 242–48; Begg, "Death of Josiah," 1–8; and Williamson, "Reliving the Death of Josiah," 9–15.
17. Spronk, "Deborah, a Prophetess," 235.
18. Ibid.
19. Although this victory does not, in fact, ensue: for discussion, see B. O. Long, "2 Kings III," 337–48; Sprinkle, "Deuteronomic 'Just War,'" 285–301; and Westbrook, "Elisha's True Prophecy," 530–32; with a response by J. C. Long, "Elisha's Deceptive Prophecy," 168–71.

20. Somewhat further afield (because there is no military connotation), note Moses's reluctance to serve as the deliverer of the Israelite people, despite having been commissioned by God at the burning bush (Exod 3:13; 4:1, 10, and 13), and Jonah's reluctance to go to Nineveh to prophesy after having received God's commission ordering him to do so: Jonah 1:1–3.
21. Halpern, "Resourceful Israelite Historian," 379–401; Halpern, *First Historians,* 76–103.
22. Ackerman, *Warrior, Dancer,* 31–32.
23. But cf. Fleming, "Etymological Origins of the Hebrew *nābî',*" 217–24; Fleming, "Prophets and Temple Personnel," 61–64.
24. On this reading, see Ackerman, *Warrior, Dancer,* 34, drawing upon Halpern, "Resourceful Israelite Historian," 384, 396, 401, and Halpern, *First Historians,* 87.
25. See Boling, *Judges,* 257; Hackett, "In the Days of Jael," 28; and Meyers, *Discovering Eve,* 159–60. Note also Chapter 1, n. 18, concerning the title "father."
26. See especially Avalos, *Illness and Health Care,* 260–77, and Schmitt, *Magie,* 219–54.
27. Ackerman, "Illnesses and Other Crises: Syria-Canaan," 459–60, and Avalos, "Illnesses and Other Crises: Israel," 460–61; see also Avalos, *Illness and Health Care,* 238–46.
28. Bowen, "Daughters of Your People," 417–33.
29. Reading *yādayim,* "hands, wrists," for the Masoretic Text *yāday,* "my hands."
30. Bowen, "Daughters of Your People," 424, n. 31.
31. To be sure, Ezek 13:20–21, where the bands are said to be tied to "your [masculine plural] arms" and where the headbands are likewise described using a second-person masculine plural suffix, might seem to disallow any suggestion that the wrist and headbands are bound onto *women,* whether childbearing or not. But as Zimmerli points out (*Ezekiel 1,* 289), these and other masculine forms used in 13:20 and 21 are extremely problematic (note preeminently the wholly illogical use of a *masculine* plural pronoun, *'attem,* to denounce the "*daughters* who prophesy" at the end of v. 20). The masculine forms of 13:20–21, Zimmerli therefore concludes, may be the result of textual corruption or come from material that was secondarily added to Ezekiel's original oracle. Or "the changes in grammatical gender" may be, as in Ezek 1, "the result of the redactional processes that shaped the entire prophetic book": so Stökl, "The *mtnb'wt,*" 63. Whatever the case, these grammatical oddities need not contradict Bowen's analysis.
32. Scurlock, "Baby-Snatching Demons," 136; Stol, *Birth,* 203.
33. Stol, *Birth,* 132–33; see also ibid., 49–52, 116, and 203.
34. Nemet-Nejat, "Women in Ancient Mesopotamia," 91, citing Biggs, "Medicine, Surgery, and Public Health," 1917.
35. For the Old Babylonian text, see Gursky, "Reproductive Rituals," 66, n. 6 (also ibid., 75), who cites as her source Finkel, "Crescent Fertile," 37–52, esp. 47. For

the Hittite ritual, see Beckman, *Hittite Birth Rituals,* Text H (pp. 86–115): II, lines 26–27 (pp. 90–91); also Gursky, "Reproductive Rituals," 69, and Pringle, "Hittite Birth Rituals," 140. For this Hittite text's date, see Beckman, *Hittite Birth Rituals,* 98.

36. Bowen, "Daughters of Your People," 424, citing Scurlock, "Baby-Snatching Demons," 136–39. Note similarly the Egyptian spell quoted by Robins, "Women and Children in Peril," 27, whereby a piece of knotted material was placed in a hemorrhaging woman's vagina to keep her from miscarrying.
37. Bowen, "Daughters of Your People," 424. See also Davies, "Archaeological Commentary on Ezekiel 13," 121; Fritschel, "Women and Magic," 127, n. 4, and 130; and Stökl, "The *mtnb'wt,*" 64.
38. Bowen, "Daughters of Your People," 424, citing Scurlock, "Baby-Snatching Demons," 139 and 141, and Foster, *Before the Muses* 1, 136 (II.30.b).
39. Ritner, "Household Religion in Ancient Egypt," 174.
40. Bowen, "Daughters of Your People," 424, citing Scurlock, "Baby-Snatching Demons," 140, 151, 157, and 182.
41. Bowen, "Daughters of Your People," 424, citing Scurlock, "Baby-Snatching Demons," 157, and also Foster, *Before the Muses* 2, 550 (III.35).
42. Bowen, "Daughters of Your People," 424.
43. Ibid., 426. Yet those who disagree include, curiously enough, Bowen herself, who after carefully documenting how "the language of tying and binding is found in incantations concerning pregnancy and childbearing," notes that this language is "also found generally in . . . incantations to cure various illnesses or maladies that are attributed to witches, sorcerers, sorceresses, and demons." "This means," Bowen goes on to say, "that it is nearly impossible to . . . decide with any certainty whether these female prophets were conducting childbirth rituals": see Bowen, "Daughters of Your People," 428–29. Others who associate the acts of Ezekiel's "daughters . . . who prophesy" with rituals other than those that pertain to childbirth include Darr, "Daughters Who Prophesy," 336, and Stökl, "The *mtnb'wt,*" 69–74, who propose that the "daughters . . . who prophesy" are engaged in rituals of necromancy. This has also been suggested by several other scholars (catalogued in Ackerman, "'I Have Hired You,'" 25, n. 8). In ibid., 16, I have described this interpretation more thoroughly, as well as the somewhat kindred interpretation of Jeffers, *Magic and Divination,* 94, and put forward my objections. For still other interpretations of Ezek 13:17–23, see Jost, "Die Töchter deines Volkes prophezeien," 59–65; Jost and Seifert, "Ezekiel," 351; Schmitt, *Magie,* 283–87, 360–62; Schmitt, "Problem of Magic and Monotheism," 5–6; Schmitt, "Theories Regarding Witchcraft Accusations," 190–92; and Zevit, *Religions,* 561–62.
44. Meyers, "From Household to House of Yahweh," 290; Meyers, *Households and Holiness,* 40.
45. Chapter 6 and n. 86 there.

46. Bowen, "Daughters of Your People," 430–32.
47. Ibid., 432.
48. A similar conclusion, although one derived by a different line of argumentation, is put forward by Stökl, "The *mtnb'wt*," 75.
49. See somewhat similarly Schmitt, *Magie*, 283–87, 360–62, and Schmitt, "Theories Regarding Witchcraft Accusations," 191–92.
50. While the date of Ezra's mission to Jerusalem and its chronological relationship to the missions of Nehemiah are debated among scholars (see the various positions summarized in Clines, *Ezra, Nehemiah, Esther*, 16–24, and in Kellermann, "Erwägungen zum Problem der Esradatierung," 55–87), there is almost unanimous agreement that the first year of Nehemiah's initial mission, during which the story of Noadiah is set, should be dated to ca. 445 BCE. Cf. only Saley, "Date of Nehemiah Reconsidered," 151–65.
51. Along with most commentators, I take Noadiah in Neh 6:14 as a woman prophet (*nĕbî'â*) who was associated with a larger community of prophets (*hannĕbî'îm*) who wanted to make Nehemiah afraid (*mĕyārĕ'îm*). The LXX, however, reads a masculine form for the Hebrew *nĕbî'â*, and the Greek Codices Vaticanus and Sinaiticus read *hiereōn*, "priests," for *hannĕbî'îm*. The Lucianic tradition, moreover, reads *enouthetoun*, "warned," reflecting Hebrew *mbynym*, for *mĕyārĕ'îm*, thereby suggesting that Noadiah was an ally rather than an opponent of Nehemiah.
52. This is by far the most common interpretation of Num 12:1: see, e.g., Milgrom, *Numbers*, 93. But cf. Levine, *Numbers 1–20*, 328.
53. This discrepancy is but one of the many difficulties encountered in Num 12:1–15, and as a consequence, the bibliography is extensive. In addition to the standard commentaries, see R. J. Burns, *Has the Lord Indeed Spoken Only Through Moses?*, 41–79; Coats, "Humility and Honor," 97–107; Culley, "Five Tales of Punishment," 25–34; Jobling, "Structural Analysis of Numbers 11–12," 31–65; Stackert, *Prophet like Moses*, 108–17; Trible, "Bringing Miriam out of the Shadows," 14–25, 34; and Trible, "Eve and Miriam," 15–24.
54. Cooper and Goldstein, "At the Entrance to the Tent," 205.
55. Indeed, just as she discounts Miriam's primacy as the singer of the song celebrating Yahweh's victory over the forces of Pharaoh (Chapter 9, n. 79), R. J. Burns, *Has the Lord Indeed Spoken Only Through Moses?*, 46–48, argues that the title prophet was only secondarily ascribed to Miriam in Exod 15:20. Likewise, P. D. Miller, *Religion*, 280, n. 55, writes that "the plausibility of the designation of Miriam as a prophet is questionable."
56. Hulse, "Nature of Biblical 'Leprosy,'" 87–105; Zias, "Lust and Leprosy," 27–31.
57. Most commonly, interpreters posit that only Miriam is punished because, according to the verb form in Num 12:1, only Miriam spoke out against Moses's wife: see, e.g., Coats, "Humility and Honor," 97 (citing Noth, *Exodus*, 93); Cross, *Canaanite Myth*, 204; and Milgrom, *Numbers*, 93. Yet, as I have argued, the real issue in the Num 12 pericope is the challenge to Moses's sole leadership.

Since this challenge is mounted by Miriam and Aaron *together* in v. 2, then the question of why both were not punished remains.

58. The Greek Codices Vaticanus and Alexandrinus, however, place Miriam's name first in 12:4.
59. Van Gennep, *Les rites de passage.*
60. Deflem, "Ritual, Anti-Structure, and Religion," 7–8, paraphrasing V. Turner, *Forest of Symbols,* 94.
61. Cohn, *Shape of Sacred Space,* 7–23; Haldar, *Notion of the Desert,* 5; Hendel, "Sacrifice as a Cultural System," 375; Hendel, "Exodus in Biblical Memory," 617; Propp, *Exodus 1–18,* 35–36; Talmon, "'Desert Motif,'" 50, 54.
62. Above, n. 60.
63. V. Turner, *Ritual Process,* 95.
64. Hendel, "Sacrifice as a Cultural System," 375.
65. Above, n. 60.
66. Cohn, *Shape of Sacred Space,* 13; Propp, *Exodus 1–18,* 35; and Talmon, "'Desert Motif,'" 54.
67. Leach, "Anthropological Approaches to the Study of the Bible," 16.
68. Hendel, "Sacrifice as a Cultural System," 374–75, citing V. Turner, "Pilgrimages as Social Processes," 197.
69. Above, n. 60.
70. This "hardening of the heart" motif has been much discussed in the literature: see, e.g., Chisholm, "Divine Hardening," 410–34; Gunn, "'Hardening of Pharaoh's Heart,'" 72–96; and R. R. Wilson, "Hardening of Pharaoh's Heart," 18–36.
71. Chapter 1, n. 88.
72. The Hebrew *nissāhû,* "he tested him," is in fact ambiguous regarding the identity of the tester and the one tested. I follow most in assuming God as the subject and Israel as the object. For further discussion, see Propp, *Exodus 1–18,* 577–79.
73. On God's role as "tester" at Massah-Meribah, see Deut 33:8 and Ps 81:8 (English 81:7). However, in Exod 17:2, 7, and also in Deut 6:16 and Ps 95:8–9, it is the Israelites who are said to test Yahweh at Massah-Meribah. As my argument makes obvious, it is my inclination to take God's identity as "tester" as the primary tradition. The identification of God as "tester" in Exod 15:22–26 (above, n. 72) and 16:1–36, the two pericopes that immediately precede and generally stand parallel to Exod 17:1–7, suggests this.
74. On fasting as a liminal ordeal, see Droogers, "Symbols of Marginality," 106.
75. For a brief but nevertheless helpful discussion of the confusing chronology of the Israelites' Kadesh Barnea sojourn, see Milgrom, *Numbers,* 164.
76. Bynum, "Women's Stories," 33, footnoting as examples V. Turner, *Ritual Process,* 99–105, and V. Turner, *Process, Performance, and Pilgrimage,* 104–5.
77. V. Turner, *Ritual Process,* 95.
78. Cox and Ackerman, "Micah's Teraphim," 12–13.
79. Lemos, "Were Israelite Women Chattel?," 238.

80. Yee, "Recovering Marginalized Groups," 12.
81. Exum, *Fragmented Women,* 110.
82. Blenkinsopp, "Family in First Temple Israel," 59.
83. Bird, "Women (OT)," 952; Bird, "Place of Women," 403.
84. Wegner, "'*Coming Before the Lord*': The Exclusion of Women," 452.
85. Bird, "Women (OT)," 953.
86. Exum, *Fragmented Women,* 72–73; see also L. A. Hoffman, *Covenant of Blood,* 47, who goes so far as to draw the structural equation, men:women :: Israelite: foreigner.
87. Myerhoff, Camino, and E. Turner, "Rites of Passage," 382.
88. Bynum, "Women's Stories," 38.
89. Although her overall analysis differs from mine, Exum, "Second Thoughts About Secondary Characters," 86, also speaks of Miriam's overstepping of gender boundaries in Num 12 in order to explain why only she, and not Aaron, is punished.
90. E.g., Num 13:26; 14:2, 5, 26; 15:33; 16:3, 11, 16–22; 17:1–5, 6–15, 16–26 (English 16:36–40, 41–50; 17:1–11); 18:1–7; 19:1; 20:2, 6, 8, 10.
91. See, e.g., Weber, *Ancient Judaism,* 96, 284.
92. Hendel, "Prophets, Priests, and the Efficacy of Ritual," 186.
93. Hackett, "In the Days of Jael," 17, 19; Hackett, "Women's Studies," 149–51.
94. Meyers, *Discovering Eve,* 50–71, 196.
95. Cogan, *Imperialism and Religion;* Cogan, "Judah Under Assyrian Hegemony," 403–14; and J. W. McKay, *Religion in Judah Under the Assyrians.*
96. Cogan, *Imperialism and Religion,* 113.
97. Hackett, "In the Days of Jael," 18–19; Hackett, "Women's Studies," 149.
98. Hamori, "Childless Female Diviners," 178; see also Hamori, "Prophet and the Necromancer," 829, n. 9.
99. Hamori, "Childless Female Diviners," 182, 190–91.
100. Ibid., 170.
101. See, most recently, Hendel and Joosten, *How Old?*, 101–4.
102. For a comprehensive presentation of the archaeological data, see I. Finkelstein, *Archaeology of the Israelite Settlement.* Particularly useful summaries include Dever, *Who Were the Early Israelites?*, 91–100, and Stager, "Forging an Identity," 97–100.
103. The term "proto-Israelites" is predominantly associated with Dever, first used by him in Dever, *Recent Archaeological Discoveries,* 78 (although see Dever's acknowledgment of others' prior use of the term, in Dever, *Who Were the Early Israelites?*, 194).
104. Meyers, *Discovering Eve,* 51; Dever, *Did God Have a Wife?*, 14.
105. Hopkins, "Life on the Land," 184.
106. Meyers, *Discovering Eve,* 61.
107. Ackerman, *Warrior, Dancer,* 56–59, following Craigie, "Deborah and Anat," 374–81, and Dempster, "Mythology and History," 33–53.

108. These are (in alphabetical order) Aaron, Abraham, Ahijah, Elijah, Elisha, Ezekiel, Gad, Habakkuk, Haggai, Hananiah, Iddo, Isaiah, Jehu, Jeremiah, Jonah, Micaiah, Moses, Nathan, Oded, Samuel, Shemiah, Zechariah, and the anonymous, but clearly male prophets of Judg 6:8; 1 Kgs 13:11, 18; 20:13, 38; 2 Kgs 9:4; and 2 Chr 25:15. Moreover, this list counts only men whom the biblical record labels *nābîʾ*; if we were to include those men who bear the kindred titles of "seer," "man of God," and the like, and those, like Uriah in Jer 26:20, who are said to prophesy but are not explicitly called "prophet," our total would be still higher.

109. An extensive, if not comprehensive list of these prophetic bands can be found in Huffmon, "Company of Prophets," 64. In ibid., 66, Huffmon indicates he is inclined, as am I, to see these companies as exclusively, or at least almost exclusively, male; see similarly Brenner, *Israelite Woman,* 57. But cf. Gafney, *Daughters of Miriam,* 15, 39–40, 100, 116, 175, n. 12, and 194, n. 136, where Gafney argues that multiple passages which refer to *nĕbîʾîm,* a masculine plural form meaning "prophets," designate prophetic bands that include both men and women. Others who suggest this include Fischer, *Gotteskünderinnen,* 18–20; Meyers, "In the Household and Beyond," 31; Meyers, *Rediscovering Eve,* 174; and Stökl, *Prophecy in the Ancient Near East,* 191.

110. A very similar conclusion has been reached by Brenner, *Israelite Woman,* 66, and also by Bird, "Place of Women," 407–8, and by Stökl, "Ištar's Women, YHWH's Men?," 87–100, both of whom have explored, as have I, the dearth of women prophets in the Bible while proposing different explanations. But cf. Stökl, *Prophecy in the Ancient Near East,* 190 and 216, where he states that "women prophets were nothing unusual" in ancient Israel, meaning that "it seems unlikely that female prophets were quite as rare as the text of the Hebrew Bible seems to suggest." See likewise Butting, *Prophetinnen gefragt,* 201–3; P. D. Miller, *Religion,* 177; and Williamson, "Prophetesses in the Hebrew Bible," 74, 76, in addition to the arguments of Fischer, Gafney, and Meyers as cited in n. 109 above.

Chapter 11. "Find Me a Woman Who Is a Medium"

1. Meyers, "From Household to House of Yahweh," 290, 296; Meyers, *Households and Holiness,* 38–39. See similarly Bowen, "Daughters of Your People," 426.
2. See, e.g., Bowen, "Daughters of Your People," 418–23; Davies, "Archaeological Commentary on Ezekiel 13," 121–22; Fritschel, "Women and Magic," 126–56; Jeffers, *Magic and Divination,* 93–95; Schmitt, *Magie,* 283–87, 360–62; Schmitt, "Problem of Magic and Monotheism," 5–6; and Schmitt, "Theories Regarding Witchcraft Accusations," 190–92. All of these scholars invoke the term "magic" in discussing Ezek 13:17–23.
3. Beckman, *Hittite Birth Rituals,* 234; Nemet-Nejat, "Women in Ancient Mesopotamia," 92; Pringle, "Hittite Birth Rituals," 132, 135; and Stol, *Birth,* 69.

4. Beckman, "Birth and Motherhood," 323; Capel, "8a. Statuette of Woman" and "8b. Relief of Woman and Child," 59, citing Pinch, *Magic,* 128–30.
5. Beckman, *Hittite Birth Rituals,* Text B (pp. 32–41) §3, line 10′, and §6, lines 25′–27′ (pp. 32–33).
6. Scurlock, "Baby-Snatching Demons," 137–85.
7. Scurlock, "Physician, Exorcist, Conjurer, Magician," 69; Borghouts, "Witchcraft, Magic, and Divination," 1784.
8. Beckman, "From Cradle to Grave," 27.
9. Studies pertaining to magic and its relationship to religion that are particularly useful for students of the Bible include Braman, "Problem of Magic in Ancient Israel," 4–127; Cryer, *Divination in Ancient Israel,* 42–95; Dolansky, *Now You See It,* 27–36; C. A. Hoffman, "Fiat Magica," 179–94, esp. 179–85; Jeffers, *Magic and Divination,* 4–7; Kuemmerlin-McLean, "Divination and Magic," 41–43; and Schmitt, *Magie,* 1–66.
10. Cryer, *Divination,* 91.
11. Scurlock, "Magic," 464.
12. The phrasing here is Fritschel's, from "Women and Magic," 180.
13. Borghouts, "Witchcraft, Magic, and Divination," 1775; Schmidt, "Canaanite Magic vs. Israelite Religion," 256; and Scurlock, "Magic," 464–65.
14. Dolansky, *Now You See It,* 6.
15. Scurlock, "Magic," 465.
16. Ritner, "Household Religion in Ancient Egypt," 172.
17. S. I. Johnston, "Magic," 142.
18. Ritner, *Mechanics of Ancient Egyptian Magical Practice,* 220.
19. Scurlock, "Magic," 465.
20. On this act as "magic," see Jeffers, "Magic from Before the Dawn of Time," 130.
21. Nissinen, *References to Prophecy,* 6. A catalogue of biblical passages that associate prophecy and divination has been helpfully assembled by Gafney, *Daughters of Miriam,* 27.
22. Schmidt, "Canaanite Magic vs. Israelite Religion," 256.
23. Meyers, "From Household to House of Yahweh," 290; Meyers, *Households and Holiness,* 38–39.
24. Chapter 10, n. 35.
25. Beckman, *Hittite Birth Rituals,* "Ritual of Papanikri" (pp. 116–23): IV, lines 6–7 (pp. 118–19).
26. I take the translation "love plants" from Avalos, *Illness and Health Care,* 255.
27. Meyers, *Households and Holiness,* 38 (see similarly Meyers, "From Household to House of Yahweh," 289, and Meyers, *Rediscovering Eve,* 154); Stol, *Birth,* 56.
28. Gerstenberger, "Healing Rituals," 166–67, offers a more general discussion of medico-magical professionals and amateurs in the Bible.
29. In addition to my discussion below, see Meyers, "From Household to House of Yahweh," 282–84, 286–94, 300–301, and Meyers, *Households and Holiness,* 15–17, 31–47, 62–69, whose arguments and conclusions about the ubiquity of

household-based reproductive magic have helped inspire mine. That said, as noted in Chapter 2, I am not as convinced as is Meyers that reproductive magic was the predominant focus of women's religious culture in the household cult. See similarly Olyan and White, as cited in Chapter 2, n. 49.

30. Fritschel, "Women and Magic," 152; see similarly ibid., 148–49.
31. Chapter 1, n. 43.
32. Meyers, *Discovering Eve,* 62; Meyers, "From Household to House of Yahweh," 298, and Meyers, *Households and Holiness,* 59. See also Chapter 2, n. 47.
33. Frymer-Kensky, *In the Wake of the Goddesses,* 97.
34. Angel, "Ecology and Population," 94–95, 97, estimates, on the basis of Greek data, that in the early Iron Age there were an average of 4.1 births per female, with 1.9 survivors. Somewhat similarly, in *Discovering Eve,* 112, Meyers discusses a tomb group from ancient Israel where 35 percent of the individuals died before the age of five, and in *Rediscovering Eve,* 98–99, she cites comparative data that put infant mortality rates at somewhere between 50 and 70 percent. Robins, "Women and Children in Peril," 28, notes that in Egypt, at three New Kingdom (ca. 1539–1075 BCE) and Third Intermediate Period (ca. 1075–715 BCE) cemeteries, infant graves comprised 50 percent, 48 percent, and 42 percent of total burials. Garnand, Stager, and Greene, "Infants as Offerings," 207, similarly estimate that "before the demographic transition of the 18th–19th century in the industrialized West, one would expect the mortality rate during infancy (< 12 months) to exceed 50% and the rate before reproductive age (< 15 years) to exceeded [*sic*] 60%."
35. Herrmann, *Ägyptische Amulette aus Palästina/Israel* IV, 123 and 342–55, catalogues up to 263 Bes amulets that come from Iron Age sites that today are located in Israel and the Palestinian territories, including Beth Shean, Beth Shemesh, Gezer, Jerusalem, Jezreel, Tel Reḥov, Achzib, Dor, Samaria, Tell eṣ-Ṣafi, Tell en-Naṣbeh, Lachish, Megiddo, Tell Jemme, Ashkelon, Tell el-Hesi, Tell el-Far'ah South, Tell el-Ajjul, Deir el-Balah, and Khirbet el-Qôm. Moreover, Keel and Uehlinger, *Gods, Goddesses, and Images of God,* 220 and 221, Illus. 225e, draw attention to a mold for making Bes figurines from Gezer, showing that in ancient Israel, Bes amulets were produced indigenously.
36. Robins, "Women and Children in Peril," 29; see also Willett, "Women and Household Shrines," 309–10.
37. See Keel and Uehlinger, *Gods, Goddesses, and Images of God,* 106; also Janssen and Janssen, *Growing Up in Ancient Egypt,* 4, although the Janssens unfortunately do not indicate the specific find spots or dates for the Syro-Palestinian "pregnancy vases" that they mention.
38. Janssen and Janssen, *Growing Up in Ancient Egypt,* 3–4; Pringle, "Hittite Birth Rituals," 131; and Stol, *Birth,* 124.
39. But cf., regarding the Egyptian evidence, Ritner, "Household Religion in Ancient Egypt," 182, and Romano, "11. Jar in the Form of a Woman," 63.
40. Above, n. 25.

41. Stol, *Birth,* 177.
42. For references, see Chapter 2, n. 23.
43. See Exod 1:16; birthing stools are also mentioned in a Late Bronze Age Ugaritic text (*KTU* 1.12.1.17–18) and are well attested among Ugarit's Hittite neighbors: see Beckman, *Hittite Birth Rituals,* 250. The birth stool seems to be the norm in Greek and Roman culture as well (Stol, *Birth,* 121–22).
44. Zevit, *Religions,* 175–76.
45. Meyers, "From Household to House of Yahweh," 290; Meyers, *Households and Holiness,* 40.
46. Olyan, "What Do We Really Know?," 64, citing Stol, *Birth,* 133–134, draws attention to one bilingual Sumerian/Akkadian prayer where a male conjurer, an *āšipu,* prays to the sun god Utu/Shamash that the "knot" that seems to be impeding a woman's delivery be loosened, but whether this prayer is uttered within the birth chamber is not specified. Ritner, "Household Religion in Ancient Egypt," 177, documents the presence of male magicians in Egyptian nurseries postparturition but not during the birth process itself.
47. Beckman, *Hittite Birth Rituals,* 98, and Text H (pp. 86–115), §18, lines 34–36, 38, and §19, line 39 (pp. 92–93).
48. Ibid., 236, 238. But cf. Beckman, "Birth and Motherhood," 324.
49. Bourguignon, "Necromancy," 6451, as quoted in Schmidt, *Israel's Beneficent Dead,* 11; see also Nihan, "1 Samuel 28," 24.
50. Chapter 1, n. 13.
51. Determining the proper translation of *ʾōbōt* and *yiddĕʿōnîm* is difficult, as *ʾôb* (plural *ʾōbōt* [or *ʾôbôt*]) seems sometimes to mean a dead spirit and sometimes the person who summons that spirit, and refers as well, according to Harry A. Hoffner (among others), to a pit in the earth in which the spirit appears (see Hoffner, "Second Millennium Antecedents," 385–401, and Hoffner, "*ʾôb,*" 130–34, esp. 133–34). Similarly, *yiddĕʿōnîm* may refer at times to a dead spirit and at other times to the magician who has summoned that spirit: see Kuemmerlin-McLean, "Divination and Magic," 89–94, and Kuemmerlin-McLean, "Magic," 469. Lewis (*Cults of the Dead,* 113, 163, and "Dead," 229–30) thus suggests that *ʾôb* and *yiddĕʿōnîm* refer primarily to spirits of the dead and, elliptically, to the magicians who conjured them.
52. Here, the terms *ʾôb* and *yiddĕʿōnî* must refer to dead spirits as opposed to the people who summon them (see above, n. 51). Moreover, Lewis (*Cults of the Dead,* 163) proposes that when the terms *ʾôb* and *yiddĕʿōnî* occur in conjunction, as they do in Lev 20:27, they "functioned as a hendiadys denoting 'spirits of the dead'" (see likewise ibid., 114, and Lewis, "Dead," 230). See also Nihan, "1 Samuel 28," 30, and, on *ʾôb* and *yiddĕʿōnî* in Deut 18:11, Zevit, *Religions,* 517, n. 19.
53. Some would see allusions to female necromancers also in Lev 19:31 and 20:6, based on a suggestion that of the two terms used for necromancers and mediums in those texts, the *ʾōbōt* (a feminine plural form) are to be taken as female and the *yiddĕʿōnîm* (a masculine plural form) are to be taken as male. See, e.g.,

Blenkinsopp, "Saul and the Mistress of the Spirits," 53, n. 8; Jobling, *1 Samuel,* 185–86; and (tentatively) Lewis, *Cults of the Dead,* 114. But cf. Hamori, *Women's Divination,* 109.

54. The Masoretic Text condemns Jerusalem's inhabitants as the "seed" of a *mn'p wtznh,* which means, literally, the "seed" of "an adulterer and she played the harlot." Since this is obviously nonsensical, most commentators emend to *mn'p wznh,* based on the Greek *moichon kai pornēs,* thereby understanding the verse to refer to Jerusalem's inhabitants as the "seed" of a city characterized as "an adulterer and a harlot." But given the well-known biblical convention that genders cities as female, I prefer to read *mn'pt wznh,* "an adulter*ess* and a harlot." The corruption of this original text began when a misplaced word divider yielded *mn'p twznh.* This corrupt text begat the further error of a metathesis of *wāw* and *tāw,* yielding *mn'p wtznh.*
55. Wellhausen, *Reste arabischen Heidentums,* 204.
56. Lewis, *Cults of the Dead,* 146–47. Lewis also catalogues alternative etymologies, as do Dolansky, *Now You See It,* 41; Fritschel, "Women and Magic," 44–45, 226; Jeffers, *Magic and Divination,* 78–79; and Kuemmerlin-McLean, "Divination and Magic," 71–72.
57. Lewis, *Cults of the Dead,* 147.
58. Ibid., 147–49, following Irwin, "'Smooth Stones of the Wady'?," 31–40.
59. Lewis, *Cults of the Dead,* 151–52.
60. There has been some debate over the location of Endor, although a location in the Jezreel Valley, near Mount Tabor, seems clear. See Cogan, "Road to En-Dor," 319, n. 1, who cites Kallai, "En-Dor," 168–70.
61. Blenkinsopp, "Saul and the Mistress of the Spirits," 60–61, and Cogan, "Road to En-Dor," 320, cite 1 Sam 23:2–4, 9–12; 30:7–8; and 2 Sam 5:19, 22–25 as examples of oracle solicitation before battle found within the books of Samuel; Jeffers, *Magic and Divination,* 237, adds (from the larger biblical corpus) Judg 20:26–28; 1 Kgs 22:15; Jer 21:1–2; 37:7, 17; 2 Chr 20:3–4.
62. See the very similar Plague Prayer of the Hittite King Mursilis (*ANET,* 394–96), §11, cited by (among others) Cogan, "Road to En-Dor," 321. This text quotes King Mursilis as saying, "Either let me see it [some god's oracle] in a dream, or let it be discovered by divination, or let a 'divinely inspired man' declare it."
63. As is noted by many: e.g., Cogan, "Road to En-Dor," 326; Dolansky, *Now You See It,* 48–49; Fritschel, "Women and Magic," 191, 194, 199; Hertzberg, *I and II Samuel,* 221; Kuemmerlin-McLean, "Divination and Magic," 169–70; Lewis, "Dead," 230; and Schmidt, *Israel's Beneficent Dead,* 163–64.
64. See, preeminently, Hoffner, "Second Millennium Antecedents," 385–401, and Hoffner, "*'ôb,*" 131–33; also B. J. Collins, "Necromancy, Fertility and the Dark Earth," 226.
65. B. T. Arnold, "Necromancy and Cleromancy," 201; Hoffner, "Second Millennium Antecedents," 393, 401; Hoffner, "*'ôb,*" 132–33; Lewis, *Cults of the Dead,* 12 and 114; and Spronk, *Beatific Afterlife,* 256.

66. As proposed, e.g., by Blenkinsopp, "Saul and the Mistress of the Spirits," 55, and Jeffers, *Magic and Divination,* 179, and argued more forcefully by Lewis, *Cults of the Dead,* 114, and by McCarter, *I Samuel,* 421.

67. On the precise understanding of the woman's vision, and whether she sees Samuel in the form of an "old man" (*'îš zāqēn*), as most translations would have it, or in the form of a "startling being" (*'îš zāqēp*), a reading reflected in the LXX, see Fritschel, "Women and Magic," 189, n. 40, and Lewis, *Cults of the Dead,* 116. McCarter, *1 Samuel,* 419, reads *'îš zāqēp,* as does Lewis, but translates "an erect man."

68. The scholarly discussion concerning the term *'ĕlōhîm* in 1 Sam 28:13 is extensive and concerns, in the main, the precise nature of its meaning. Lewis, *Cults of the Dead,* 115–16, argues *'ĕlōhîm* is meant to signify that Samuel is some sort of preternatural spirit, as opposed to Schmidt, "'Witch' of En-Dor," 125, who sees the *'ĕlōhîm* as "deities of the netherworld [who] are called upon [by the necromancer] in order to insure the appearance of the ghost of the dead." For Schmidt's full discussion of this issue, see *Israel's Beneficent Dead,* 210–20; for other scholarly discussions on *'ĕlōhîm* in 1 Sam 28:13 and related passages, see Chapter 7, n. 92.

69. See, preeminently, Exum, *Tragedy and Biblical Narrative,* 16–44, and Gunn, *Fate of King Saul.*

70. The verb used to describe the woman's slaughter is *zābaḥ*, a term that typically refers to sacrificial slaughter (Chapter 3, nn. 51 and 78), and unleavened cakes are likewise appropriate for sacrificial occasions, as we have seen in discussing the Maṣṣot festival in Chapter 8. Still, there is no sense that an altar and the other ritual apparatus requisite for sacrifice are present, and thus the suggestion that "the food the woman prepares for Saul and his men . . . is some kind of sacrificial ritual meal connected to necromancy . . . lacks support" (Hamori, *Women's Divination,* 122).

71. Meyers, *Households and Holiness,* 53–54, citing Sered, *Women as Ritual Experts,* 18–29; see similarly Meyers, "From Household to House of Yahweh," 296.

72. Meyers, *Households and Holiness,* 64.

73. Darr, "Daughters Who Prophesy," 336; Blenkinsopp, "Saul and the Mistress of the Spirits," 53.

74. Bird, "Gender and Religious Definition," 13; van der Toorn, *From Her Cradle to Her Grave,* 46, 126.

75. Fritschel, "Women and Magic," 97, citing van der Toorn, *From Her Cradle to Her Grave,* 46. But cf. van der Toorn, *Family Religion,* 233, where van der Toorn rejects the idea that "consultation of the dead was an essential part of early Israelite family religion." I confess that do not know how to take this statement, given that elsewhere in his writings (see Chapter 1, n. 13) and, indeed, elsewhere in *Family Religion,* van der Toorn has powerfully affirmed that "the early Israelites were well acquainted with the phenomenon of ancestor figurines [*tĕrāpîm*] . . . [that] were found . . . in the houses of the Israelites" (pp. 224–25),

that the "function" of the "teraphim as ancestor figurines . . . [was] divination" (p. 223), and that "the 'consultation of the teraphim' was a type of necromancy" (p. 224).

76. See also in this regard Hamori, "Prophet and the Necromancer," 831: "we do not have enough information, in historical or literary terms, to judge whether a medium was more likely to be female"; likewise Hamori, *Women's Divination,* 117–18.
77. Stol, *Women,* 618.
78. Van der Toorn, *From Her Cradle to Her Grave,* 124.
79. Finkel, "Necromancy," 1; Tropper, *Nekromantie,* 59.
80. Finkel, "Necromancy," 1, n. 1.
81. Van der Toorn, *From Her Cradle to Her Grave,* 125.
82. Schmidt, *Israel's Beneficent Dead,* 215; Schmidt, "'Witch' of En-dor," 118, n. 25.
83. For discussion, with references, see Tropper, *Nekromantie,* 156–59.
84. M. S. Smith, *Rituals and Myths of the Feast of the Goodly Gods,* 74–77.
85. Marsman, *Women,* 527, citing *KTU* 1.124, as discussed by M. Dietrich and Loretz, *Mantik in Ugarit,* 205–40, esp. 215–16, and Tropper, *Nekromantie,* 151–156. But cf. Cryer, *Divination,* 182; Schmidt, *Israel's Beneficent Dead,* 79–80; Schmidt, "'Witch' of En-Dor," 114–15, n. 14; and Spronk, *Beatific Afterlife,* 193–95.
86. Fritschel, "Women and Magic," 97.
87. Cooper and Goldstein, "At the Entrance to the Tent," 214.
88. Ibid., 217.
89. In addition to Gen 31:19–35, Judg 17–18, and 1 Sam 19:11–17, these are 1 Sam 15:23, 2 Kgs 23:24, Ezek 21:26 (English 21:21), Hos 3:4, and Zech 10:2.
90. Fritschel, "Women and Magic," 97.
91. Ibid.
92. On the necromancer being represented sympathetically, see Fritschel, "Women and Magic," 53, 194, and 197–98, with additional references at 194, n. 61.
93. Ackerman, *Under Every Green Tree,* 111–14, with additional references at 114, n. 36.
94. See, provisionally, Ackerman, "Cult Centralization," 19–30.
95. Hamori, "Prophet and the Necromancer," 832.
96. Many of the Bible's authors and/or redactors would like to think that Josiah's reform efforts took effect immediately, and, as noted in the Introduction, n. 6, some modern scholars follow suit. Yet as also noted in the Introduction, n. 6, my own sense is that Josiah's reform efforts came to fruition only later: in the late exilic and early postexilic period.
97. See further B. T. Arnold, "Necromancy and Cleromancy," 206–7; Blenkinsopp, "Saul and the Mistress of the Spirits," 49, who describes 1 Sam 28:3–25 as having "many points of contact . . . with the ethos and style of the [Deuteronomistic] History"; and Cogan, "Road to En-Dor," 325–26, who notes a "terminological affinity" between 1 Sam 28:3–25 and "Deuteronomistic tradition," including the language the Deuteronomists use in their descriptions of Josiah's reform.

But cf. Friedman and Overton, "Death and Afterlife," 51 ("the story of the medium at En-Dor . . . does not contain any of the characteristic language of the Deuteronomistic historian"), and note also that Cogan ultimately opts to follow Hertzberg, *I and II Samuel,* 217, in viewing 1 Sam 28:3–25 as a "very ancient [i.e., pre-Deuteronomistic] narrative." Van der Toorn, *Family Religion,* 318, also rejects understanding Saul's prohibition of necromancy as "a Deuteronomistic anachronism," even as he puts forward—as I have here—an interpretation whereby the king's banning of necromancy is an attempt to curb the "potentially dangerous influences of family religion" and, more specifically, necromancy's "potential threat to the stability of the royal rule."

98. The translation of these terms is debated. For discussion, and discussion of other terms that comprise the Bible's magical vocabulary, see, e.g., Blenkinsopp, *Sage, Priest, Prophet,* 123–29; Dolansky, *Now You See It,* 38–55, esp. 40–53; Fritschel, "Women and Magic," 40–80; Jeffers, *Magic and Divination,* 25–124; Kuemmerlin-McLean, "Divination and Magic," 60–106; Kuemmerlin-McLean, "Magic," 468–69; and Schmitt, *Magie,* 107–22.
99. Cryer, *Divination,* 91.
100. Schmidt, *Israel's Beneficent Dead,* 138–39; Schmidt, "Canaanite Magic vs. Israelite Religion," 256.
101. S. I. Johnston, "Magic," 140.
102. Neusner, "Introduction," 4; Ritner, "Religious, Social, and Legal Parameters," 44.
103. Ricks, "Magician as Outsider," 132.
104. Newsom, "Women and the Discourse of Patriarchal Wisdom," 148.
105. See, e.g., Schmidt, "'Witch' of En-Dor," 111, n. 3. Cf. n. 60 above regarding Endor's location.
106. Lewis, *Cults of the Dead,* 151–52.
107. Above, n. 54.
108. Ackerman, *Under Every Green Tree,* 115–17.
109. See the very similar analysis of Fritschel, "Women and Magic," 234–45; also, less fully, Schmitt, *Magie,* 108, 374–76, and Schmitt, "Theories Regarding Witchcraft Accusations," 187.
110. Fritschel, "Women and Magic," 113. Indeed, this phenomenon of the "gendering of magic" and the negative consequences that women suffer as a result is the overall focus of Fritschel's study, and my discussion here is indebted to her in many respects. See also the discussion of Schmitt, "Theories Regarding Witchcraft Accusations," 186–89, 193, and the brief comments, specific to 1 Sam 28:3–25, of Jeffers, "'Nor by Dreams, nor by Urim,'" 137–38.
111. Graf, "How to Cope with a Difficult Life," 95–96; see similarly S. I. Johnston, "Magic," 150.
112. Aubin, "Gendering Magic in Late Antique Judaism," as cited in Fritschel, "Women and Magic," 19–21, nn. 67–73, and 115–16, nn. 76–77. See similarly S. I. Johnston, "Magic," 150.

113. Cited in Schmitt, *Magie,* 339, and in Schmitt, "Theories Regarding Witchcraft Accusations," 189. Schmitt also quotes like statements from elsewhere in the rabbinic corpus.
114. Male translators do this too, as Kuemmerlin-McLean, "Divination and Magic," 80, perceptively points out, regarding the KJV rendering of Deut 18:10, where the grammatically masculine singular form *mĕkaššēp* is translated using the English feminine term "witch."
115. Cogan, *I Kings,* 471–74.
116. Ibid., 468, citing Oppenheim, "Sumerian: inim.gar," 55.
117. On the translation of these terms for magical practitioners, see n. 98 above.
118. Although cf. Dolansky, *Now You See It,* 43, who suggests, on the basis of the LXX of Exod 22:17 (English 22:18), that "perhaps the original text implicated both sexes . . . with haplography in the Hebrew responsible for the singling out of female sorcerers." The Greek rendering, though, which implies that Exod 22:17 (English 22:18) refers to both male and female sorcerers, is better read as a secondary expansion: see Fritschel, "Women and Magic," 57, n. 110.
119. Halpern, "Why Manasseh Is Blamed," 474.
120. Fritschel hints at this in her Ph.D. dissertation ("Women and Magic," 39); the idea was much more fully developed in Fritschel, "Gender and Magic in the Hebrew Bible."
121. Note also in this regard Meyers, "From Household to House of Yahweh," 300, n. 110, and Meyers, *Households and Holiness,* 65, who suggests (following Brenner, *Intercourse of Knowledge,* 84–86) that the reason the female sorcerer is condemned in Exod 22:17 (English 22:18) is that she may have been "expert at preventing conception or inducing abortion, both procedures abhorrent to clan ideology encouraging procreation."
122. Fritschel, "Women and Magic," 126–42.
123. Exum, "'You Shall Let Every Daughter Live,'" 63–82; Exum, "Second Thoughts About Secondary Characters," 75–87.
124. Van der Toorn, *From Her Cradle to Her Grave,* 113, 116.

Chapter 12. "The *Ṣōbĕʾôt* Who Served at the Entrance to the Tent of Meeting"

1. On the translation "copper" for the more usual "bronze," see Greenstein, "Recovering 'The Women Who Served,'" 166, and Propp, *Exodus 19–40,* 665.
2. McCarter, *I Samuel,* 81, 92–93. See likewise Ackroyd, *First Book of Samuel,* 36, and Driver, *Notes on the Hebrew Text,* 33. Note also Brettler, "Composition of 1 Samuel 1–2," 609, who, like Ackroyd, Driver, and McCarter, takes 1 Sam 2:22 to be a late addition to 1 Sam 1:1–2:26, but perhaps not as late as Ackroyd, Driver, and McCarter would have it. R. W. Klein, *1 Samuel,* 26, seems to imply something similar.
3. So Greenstein, "Recovering 'The Women Who Served,'" 170–71. Haran, *Temples,* 199, n. 17; Harvey, "*Tendenz* and Textual Criticism," 72–73; and McKane,

I and II Samuel, 38, also suggest the reference to "the women who served at the entrance to the tent of meeting" in 1 Sam 2:22 may be original.

4. Noted by Everhart, "Serving Women," 50–51; Greenstein, "Recovering 'The Women Who Served,'" 167 (with additional references); Meyers, *Exodus,* 278; and Propp, *Exodus 19–40,* 667.
5. The former of these stands is in the collection of the British Museum (museum no. 1946, 1017.1), and information on its dimensions can be found at the British Museum, "vessel-stand; stand," https:// research .britishmuseum .org/ research/ collection_online/ collection_object_details .aspx?objectId = 464314& partId=1&searchText=Bronze+AND+wheeled+&page=1. For the latter stand, see Catling, *Cypriot Bronzework,* 207–8 and Pl. 36a (catalogue no. 36a), and Matthäus, *Metallgefäße und Gefäßuntersätze der Bronzezeit,* 318–19 and Pl. 108 (catalogue no. 708).
6. Note in this regard that the British Museum stand cited in n. 5 above weighs 3.2 kilograms, to which compare an Egyptian mirror held in the collection of my home institution, Dartmouth College Hood Museum of Art, object no. 157.25.13960. This mirror weighs 354.6 grams, meaning it would take about nine exemplars of the Dartmouth mirror—which I take to be generally representative of ancient Near Eastern mirrors—to yield the metal needed to make the British Museum wheeled stand.
7. Durham, *Exodus,* 488; Noth, *Exodus,* 278.
8. Propp, *Exodus 19–40,* 666.
9. Peritz, "Women in the Ancient Hebrew Cult," 145. This interpretation has subsequently been noted by many: see, e.g., Dijkstra, "Women and Religion," 182; Driver, *Notes on the Hebrew Text,* 33; Everhart, "Serving Women," 45–47; Gruber, "Women in the Cult," 54–55; Marsman, *Women,* 565–66; and Propp, *Exodus 19–40,* 666.
10. Propp, *Exodus 19–40,* 666.
11. Propp (ibid.) cites among exponents of this view Dillmann, *Exodus und Leviticus,* 363. Greenstein, "Recovering 'The Women Who Served,'" 165, n. 4, adds other references. This position is also put forward by Dijkstra, "Women and Religion," 182; R. W. Klein, *1 Samuel,* 26; Meyers, *Exodus,* 278; and Meyers, "Women at the Entrance," 202. But cf. Meyers, *Rediscovering Eve,* 173 (n. 13 below).
12. As noted by Durham, *Exodus,* 487, and Cornelis Houtman, *Exodus* 3, 570, both of whom cite additional references; see also Propp, *Exodus 19–40,* 666.
13. Fischer, *Gotteskünderinnen,* 104–7, followed by Meyers, *Rediscovering Eve,* 173. But cf. n. 11 above.
14. Greenstein, "Recovering 'The Women Who Served,'" 171–73.
15. Cornelis Houtman, *Exodus* 3, 570, and Propp, *Exodus 19–40,* 666, cite various proponents of this view, to which add Durham, *Exodus,* 487; Willis, "Cultic Elements," 56; and Yamauchi, "Cultic Prostitution," 218 (although

note that Yamauchi does not embrace the sacred prostitution interpretation unreservedly).

16. A speculation (his term) advanced by Propp, *Exodus 19–40,* 666.
17. Ibid.
18. This point has also inspired Spencer, "Tasks of the Levites," 267–71, who argues that in *all* the cases where *ṣ-b-'* is used to describe the work of cultic functionaries at the tent of meeting, the term has military connotations. On *ṣ-b-'* as having military connotations in Exod 38:8, see also Gafney, *Daughters of Miriam,* 153–56, and Vos, *Woman in Old Testament Worship,* 164, although note that Gafney's overall understanding differs considerably from mine.
19. On this corpus, see, preeminently, Bretschneider, *Architekturmodelle;* Katz, *Portable Shrine Models;* Muller, *Les "maquettes architecturales"*; Muller, *Maquettes antiques;* and Zevit, *Religions,* 328–43.
20. On these model shrines' geographical and chronological range, and the different find spots with which they are associated, see the helpful charts assembled by Muller, *Maquettes antiques,* 250–51 and 262.
21. Herr, "Late Iron Age I Ceramic Assemblage," 136.
22. Elkins, "Model Shrine," 436.
23. In the original publication, Potts suggested a "broad eleventh-nineth [*sic*] century B.C. range" for the Pella objects, "with the tenth century perhaps the most likely": see Potts, "Late Bronze–Early Iron Age," 204. Bretschneider, *Architekturmodelle,* 214, and Muller, *Les "maquettes architecturales"* 1, 57 and 353–54, date the shrinelike object in which I am interested to the eleventh or tenth century BCE.
24. Dever, "Temple Built for Two," 85, n. 13.
25. For this stand's measurements, see Potts, "Cultic Stands," 98. For discussion, see ibid., 97–100, as well as Potts, "Late Bronze–Early Iron Age," 204, and also Bretschneider, *Architekturmodelle,* 80–81, 214; Hadley, *Cult of Asherah,* 165–69; Katz, *Portable Shrine Models,* 87; Keel and Uehlinger, *Gods, Goddesses, and Images of God,* 101, 103; and Muller, *Les "maquettes architecturales"* 1, 57 and 354.
26. Beck, "Catalogue of Cult Objects," 99–103 (re Figs. 3.66–3.69), 143–44 (re Fig. 3.95), and 171 (re Fig. 3.119a and b).
27. Moorey, *Idols of the People,* 53 and Pl. 16; Zevit, *Religions,* 338 and Fig. 4.21.
28. Garfinkel and Mumcuoglu, "Elaborate Clay Portable Shrine," 83–100; Garfinkel and Mumcuoglu. "Limestone Portable Shrine," 101–26; and Zilberg, "Simple Clay Portable Shrine," 73–81.
29. For this shrine's measurements, see Muller, *Les "maquettes architecturales"* 1, 53 and 341; for further references, see Chapter 2, n. 18. Because the shrine was retrieved from an unsecure stratigraphic context (a pit), the date is debated. Dever, *Did God Have a Wife?,* 115, gives a tenth-century BCE date, as does Willett, "Women and Household Shrines," 118. Keel and Uehlinger, *Gods, Goddesses, and Images of Gods,* 162, date the shrine to the late tenth century BCE.

Katz, *Portable Shrine Models,* 43, and Muller, *Les "maquettes architecturales"* 1, 53, propose a tenth- to ninth-century BCE date; Bretschneider, *Architekturmodelle,* 233, suggests a date of ca. 900 BCE; Zevit, *Religions,* 337, dates the shrine to the ninth or eighth century BCE.

30. Bretschneider, *Architekturmodelle,* 237; Garfinkel and Mumcuoglu, "Shrine Model from Tel Rekhesh," 85; Muller, *Les "maquettes architecturales"* 1, 57 and 355; Muller, *Maquettes antiques,* 251; and Zevit, *Religions,* 337 (see similarly Katz, *Portable Shrine Models,* 41).
31. Mazar and Panitz-Cohen, "It Is the Land of Honey," 209–13; Mazar, "Religious Practices and Cult Objects," 32–38.
32. For these references, see Greer, "Israelite *Mizrāq?,*" 35.
33. This motif is discussed in detail by Dever, "Temple Built for Two," 59, 61, and by Elkins, "Model Shrine," 441–42. In ibid., 438, Elkins also describes the capitals of the columns on the Tall al-'Umayri shrine as precursors to later volute capitals.
34. Zevit, *Religions,* 329.
35. Mazar and Panitz-Cohen, "It Is the Land of Honey," 210–11; Mazar, "Religious Practices and Cult Objects," 36.
36. Garfinkel, Ganor, and Hasel, *In the Footsteps of King David,* 154. See also Schroer, "Iconography of the Shrine Models," 141, who notes not only the depression in the shrine's floor, near the rear wall, but the presence of "two holes in the back wall," positioned, Schroer proposes, so that a divine figurine housed in the shrine "could be secured with a copper wire or a string."
37. Garfinkel, Ganor, and Hasel, *In the Footsteps of King David,* 155; see also Stager, "Canaanite Silver Calf," 577–80.
38. Daviau, "Ceramic and Architectural Models," 301.
39. For these measurements, see Bretschneider, *Architekturmodelle,* 218.
40. Louvre, "Model of a Shrine," http://www.louvre.fr/en/oeuvre-notices/model-shrine.
41. This actually cannot be determined from the readily available drawings or photographs, but see Dever, *Did God Have a Wife?,* 222; Dever, "Temple Built for Two," 58; and Louvre, "Model of a Shrine," http://www.louvre.fr/en/oeuvre-notices/model-shrine.
42. For other model shrines from Cyprus that have a divine figure housed within, see Katz, *Portable Shrine Models,* 13 (Fig. 2.16) and 53–54 (Figs. 3.53–3.58, 3.60–3.62). For similar shrines from the Phoenician coast, see ibid., 52 (Figs. 3.47, 3.49–3.50). See also Muller, *Maquettes antiques,* 203–4 and 252–53.
43. Mazar and Panitz-Cohen, "It Is the Land of Honey," 210; Mazar, "Religious Practices and Cult Objects," 34–35.
44. On a female figure's nudity as a mark of divinity in the art of the southern Levant, see Bloch-Smith, "Acculturating Gender Roles," 1–2.
45. Seeden, "Small Clay Shrine," 7–19, 23–25; see also Bretschneider, *Architekturmodelle,* 127–28, 229; Katz, *Portable Shrine Models,* 50–51; Muller, *Les "maquettes*

architecturales" 1, 59–60 and 370–72; and Zevit, *Religions,* 339. Zevit, *Religions,* 339, dates this shrine to the Late Bronze Age, but Muller, *Les "maquettes architecturales"* 1, 59, n. 164, prefers an early Iron Age date. Yet Muller, in *Maquettes antiques,* 251, proposes a fifth-century BCE date. Bretschneider, *Architekturmodelle,* 128 and 229, and Katz, *Portable Shrine Models,* 50, suggest a date of the eleventh or tenth century BCE.

46. For discussion, see Badre, "Terra Cotta Anthropomorphic Figurines," 465; Bretschneider, *Architekturmodelle,* 127, 228–29; Katz, *Portable Shrine Models,* 50; Muller, *Les "maquettes architecturales"* 1, 62–63 and 386–87; and Paz, *Drums,* 34.
47. Keel and Uehlinger, *Gods, Goddesses, and Images of God,* 103; see similarly Moorey, *Idols of the People,* 42. But cf. Daviau, "Ceramic and Architectural Models," 295, who describes the female figures as standing *in* two windows.
48. Beck, "Catalogue of Cult Objects," 122–23. For the Megiddo stand, see *ANEP,* no. 582.
49. Mazar and Panitz-Cohen, "It Is the Land of Honey," 209, 212–13; Mazar, "Religious Practices and Cult Objects," 33.
50. For the measurements of this shrine, see Muller, *Les "maquettes architecturales"* 1, 64 and 394. Bretschneider, *Architekturmodelle,* 236, dates the shrine to ca. 900 BCE; Katz, *Portable Shrine Models,* 51, and Muller, *Maquettes antiques,* 251, give a date of the tenth to the eighth century BCE, but Muller, *Les "maquettes architecturales"* 1, 64, suggests the tenth or ninth century BCE.
51. Weinberg, "Moabite Shrine Group," 31–33; further discussion can be found in Bretschneider, *Architekturmodelle,* 130, 236; Katz, *Portable Shrine Models,* 51; Muller, *Les "maquettes architecturales"* 1, 64 and 393–95; and Zevit, *Religions,* 332–33.
52. See, e.g., Bretschneider, *Architekturmodelle,* 127 (regarding the figures on the Kerak shrine); Burnett, "What Kind of Goddess?" (regarding the model shrines' figures generally); Mazar, "Religious Practices and Cult Objects," 33 (regarding the Reḥov city-gate altar); Muller, *Les "maquettes architecturales"* 1, 57 and 354 (regarding the figures on the Pella façade); 1, 372 (regarding the figures on the shrine in the collection of American University of Beirut); and 1, 163–68 and 171–73 (regarding the model shrines' figures generally). But cf. Daviau, "Ceramic and Architectural Models," 301, regarding what she describes as "human figures" who flank the doorways of model shrines from Jordan, and Culican, "Terracotta Shrine from Achzib," 53, and Zayadine, "Sculpture in Ancient Jordan," 39, who describe the females flanking the entry of the American University of Beirut and Kerak model shrines and those who appear in the niches above the entry of the University of Missouri model shrine as "hierodules." Paz, *Drums,* 78 and 118, also interprets the Kerak shrine's female figures as cultic functionaries, and Böhm, *Die "Nackte Göttin,"* 138, takes the female figures who flank the model shrines' entries to be cultic or sacred prostitutes.
53. Above, n. 44.

54. Technically speaking, it is only the left-hand female figure at Pella that stands atop a lion's head, as the pedestal atop which the right-hand figure stood has not been preserved. Further on the Pella lion pedestals, see Bretschneider, *Architekturmodelle,* 214; Burnett, "What Kind of Goddess?"; Hadley, *Cult of Asherah,* 168–69; Keel and Uehlinger, *Gods, Goddesses, and Images of God,* 103; Muller, *Les "maquettes architecturales"* 1, 57 and 354; Potts, "Late Bronze–Early Iron Age," 204; and Potts, "Cultic Stands," 99.
55. Technically, as in n. 54 above, only the right-hand figure at Pella can be said to wear a Hathor headdress, since the head of the left-hand figure has not been preserved. Further on the Pella headdresses, see Hadley, *Cult of Asherah,* 168; Muller, *Les "maquettes architecturales"* 1, 57 and 354; Potts, "Late Bronze–Early Iron Age," 204; and Potts, "Cultic Stands," 98–99. On Hathor headdresses generally, see Burnett, "What Kind of Goddess?," citing Schroer, "Die Göttin auf den Stempelsiegeln," 174–85.
56. Seeden, "Small Clay Shrine," 15, but cf. Bretschneider, *Architekturmodelle,* 127 and 229, who suggests the headdresses are perhaps crowns. Muller, *Les "maquettes architecturales"* 1, 354, agrees that the headdresses are not birds but does not propose what they otherwise might represent.
57. Meyers, "Terracottas Without Texts," 120.
58. Keel and Uehlinger, *Gods, Goddesses, and Images of God,* 103, 105.
59. Dever, "Temple Built for Two," 61. See similarly, although not quite so emphatically, regarding the interpretation of the Pella figures, Hadley, *Cult of Asherah,* 169. Potts, "Late Bronze–Early Iron Age," 204, identifies the Pella figures as the goddess Astarte; in Potts, "Cultic Stands," 98, he modifies his position to identify them as Astarte-Asherah.
60. Chapter 5, n. 30.
61. On the Khirbet Qeiyafa lions, see Garfinkel and Mumcuoglu, "Elaborate Clay Portable Shrine," 86–91. On the textual and iconographic evidence that associates Asherah with lions, see Ackerman, "Queen Mother and the Cult in Ancient Israel," 396–97, with references.
62. On the lions of the Tel Rekhesh shrine, see Garfinkel and Mumcuoglu, "Shrine Model from Tel Rekhesh," 82, 86, and Zevit, *Religions,* 337, although, as Zevit notes, the Tel Rekhesh model shrine is in poor enough shape that it is possible to interpret the crouching animals as dogs. Muller, *Maquettes antiques,* 235, refers to them as "beasts."
63. Moorey, *Idols of the People,* 41–42; see also Burnett, "What Kind of Goddess?" Muller, *Maquettes antiques,* 193, similarly indicates that the female figures found on the exteriors of model shrines are not to be confused with high goddesses of Semitic pantheons, such as Ishtar or Astarte. See also Mazar and Panitz-Cohen, "The Apiary," caption to Fig. 21 (Hebrew text, p. 40), regarding the gate-tower clay altar from Tel Reḥov (Fig. 12.11): "a tree," which Mazar and Panitz-Cohen take to represent Asherah, "is incised on the façade and flanked

by two nude female figurines," whom Mazar and Panitz-Cohen take to be fertility goddesses who stand at Asherah's side.

64. Cooper and Goldstein, "At the Entrance to the Tent," 204. Note similarly Matthews, "Entrance Ways and Threshing Floors," 26, who, quoting van den Boorn, "*Wḏʿ-ryt* and Justice at the Gate," 10, writes of how gates in ancient Near Eastern cultures "operate 'in certain contexts . . . as a "channel" between two regions'—the world of men and the 'enclosed world' of the god." Garfinkel and Mumcuoglu, *Crossing the Threshold,* 36, likewise state that "as a transition point between the earthly world and heaven, the gate of a temple is a *classic liminal zone*" (emphasis mine). Even more significant for my discussion here is Nissinen and Münger, "'Down the River,'" 1376, who describe a model shrine's opening as "marking the *liminal* space between the world of those looking through it and those residing inside the modeled space" (emphasis again mine).
65. Douglas, *Purity and Danger,* 97. Note similarly Grimes, "Portals," 7333, who writes of a portal as "any gateway or doorway . . . [that] often separates a sacred precinct from a profane one . . . [and that] as a structure that is both inside and outside the same zone . . . attracts dangerous as well as beneficent forces."
66. Cooper and Goldstein, "At the Entrance to the Tent," 204.
67. As Levinson, *Deuteronomy,* 58–59, writes, "By framing the doorway with blood, the head of each Israelite family established a liminal barrier between 'within the house'—as a refuge—and *mptḥ bytw* 'outside the door of the house' (Exod 12:22)—as the realm of otherwise uncontrolled demonic energies."
68. Speiser, *Genesis,* 32–33. Propp, *Exodus 1–18,* 441, who brought this reference to my attention, in addition points out that in the ancients' minds, doorways were such dangerous spaces that both Philistines (in 1 Sam 5:5) and Israelites (Zeph 1:9) leaped over the threshold.
69. Three crouching lion fragments found at Tall al-ʿUmayri are hypothesized to come from two different model shrines: see Dabrowski, "Preliminary Report," 226–27, 229; Elkins, "Ceramic Architectural Models," 99–102, 117–24; and also Katz, *Portable Shrine Models,* 47 and Fig. 3.33. For crouching lions positioned at the column bases of a model shrine from Khirbet ʿAtaruz, see again Elkins, "Ceramic Architectural Models," 201–9. Twin crouching lions in the collection of the Museum of Art and Archaeology of the University of Missouri, Columbia, appear to be from the façade of a shrine model: see Burnett, "What Kind of Goddess?"; Daviau, "Ceramic and Architectural Models," 297; Muller, *Les "maquettes architecturales"* 1, 64 and 395–96, and 2, Fig. 183a–c; Weinberg, "Moabite Shrine Group," 34, 43; and Zevit, *Religions,* 332–33 and Fig. 4.14. Note also the full-size lion figures that served as guardians of temples, palaces, and gateways at locations throughout the ancient Near East, catalogued in Strawn, *What Is Stronger than a Lion?,* 86–88, 217–24, to which add a magnificently carved stone lion figure associated with the citadel gate complex at Tel Tayinat

that was discovered in 2011: see, e.g., Harrison, "Recent Discoveries at Tayinat," 408 and 424, Fig. 4.

70. Dever, "Temple Built for Two," 61; see also Katz, *Portable Shrine Models,* 28, who describes the lion draped over the roof of the Reḥov model shrine as a "*guardian* figure," and Zevit, *Religions,* 337, who describes the lions/dogs/beasts (above n. 62) that appear at the entry of the Tel Rekhesh shrine as "crouching *guardian* animals" (emphasis in both cases mine).
71. Zevit, *Religions,* 329, n. 143.
72. Burnett, "What Kind of Goddess?" I am very grateful to Professor Burnett for making a copy of this unpublished paper from 2008 available to me. Almost simultaneously, in 2007, a similar argument, interpreting the female figures that flank model shrines as supernatural guardians, was put forward by Schroer, "Frauenkörper als architektonische Elemente," 425–50. Darby, *Interpreting Judean Pillar Figurines,* 331–32, n. 99, and 346, n. 159, also suggests that females who flank the entrances to model shrines and related cult stands are divine guardian figures. Schroer, "Iconography of the Shrine Models," 153, in addition captures Burnett's sense of the figures' mediating role, which is also briefly articulated by Bloch-Smith in "Acculturating Gender Roles," 4: "naked females flanking a [model] shrine entrance are . . . divine associates that protect and mediate access to the deity that presides from inside."
73. Burnett, "What Kind of Goddess?"
74. May, *Material Remains of the Megiddo Cult,* Pl. XIII; May, "The Ark," Fig. 1 (p. 216). See also Bretschneider, *Architekturmodelle,* 217 and Pl. 60–61 (Fig. 52a–b), and Katz, *Portable Shrine Models,* 88 and Fig. 4.39.
75. Burnett, "What Kind of Goddess?"; Elkins, "Model Shrine," 437–38, 440–41.
76. Burnett, "What Kind of Goddess?"
77. Ibid.
78. Paz, *Drums,* 34. On masks as a liminal form of costume, see Rubenstein, "Purim, Liminality, and Communitas," 259–63. Others, though, are less sure of how to interpret the Kerak figures' faces: Bretschneider, *Architekturmodelle,* 127, speaks only of a possible forehead ornament on each figure.
79. Beck, "Catalogue of Cult Objects," 122–23, citing Dornemann, *Archaeology of the Transjordan,* 143–45.
80. Badre, "Terra Cotta Anthropomorphic Figurines," 465.
81. Ornan, "In the Likeness of Man," 130–32, offers a very similar analysis of anthropomorphized images of "lower status" deities in Mesopotamian tradition, most commonly the goddess Lama, that were placed "at the entrance to a building," where they "functioned as . . . apotropaic figure[s] warding off evil"; see similarly Schroer, "Iconography of the Shrine Models," 153.
82. Cooper and Goldstein, "At the Entrance to the Tent," 204.
83. Cross, *Canaanite Myth,* 202, n. 34.

84. Such a move seems paralleled elsewhere in the Hebrew Bible: see Craigie, "Deborah and Anat," 374–81; Dempster, "Mythology and History," 33–53; also Ackerman, *Warrior, Dancer,* 56–59, 66–68.
85. See somewhat similarly the analyses of Everhart, "Serving Women," 48–54, and Winter, *Frau und Göttin,* 58–65, both of whom associate the mirrors said to be in the possession of the *ṣōbĕʾōt* women with the iconography of female deities, and both of whom thus see the melting down of the *ṣōbĕʾōt*'s mirrors as a means of repudiating any goddess's worship in Israel. As a result, the *ṣōbĕʾōt* were repudiated as well: "As the mirrors became a 'washbasin' for priests," Everhart writes on p. 50 of her article, "the women's service seems also to have been washed away." Interpretations of Exod 38:8 that likewise give primacy to the role of the mirrors include Görg, "Der Spiegeldienst der Frauern," 9–13, and Wacker, "Die Spiegel der Frauen," 142–55.
86. Yee, *Poor Banished Children,* 96.

Chapter 13. "The *Qĕdēšâ* Among the Daughters of Israel"

1. Chapter 12, n. 15.
2. Pope, "Fertility Cults," 265.
3. Mays, *Hosea,* 75.
4. The pioneering 1973 study is by Arnaud, "La prostitution sacrée en Mésopotamie," 111–15. See also the foundational studies that followed: Barstad, *Religious Polemics of Amos,* 21–34; Bird, "'To Play the Harlot,'" 85–89; Bird, "End of the Male Cult Prostitute," 37–80; Fisher, "Cultic Prostitution?," 225–36; Frevel, *Aschera und der Ausschliesslichkeitsanspruch YHWHs,* 629–737; Frymer-Kensky, *In the Wake of the Goddesses,* 199–202; Oden, *Bible Without Theology,* 131–53; Westenholz, "Tamar, *Qĕdēšā, Qadištu,*" 245–65; and Winter, *Frau und Göttin,* 334–42.
5. In Herodotus, the temple is actually said to be dedicated to Mylitta, but Herodotus takes this to be the Assyrian name of the Greek goddess Aphrodite (= Ishtar).
6. Herodotus, as quoted in Oden, *Bible Without Theology,* 141.
7. Ibid.
8. Frymer-Kensky, *In the Wake of the Goddesses,* 200.
9. Oden, *Bible Without Theology,* 145; Frymer-Kensky, *In the Wake of the Goddesses,* 200.
10. Beard and Henderson, "With This Body I Thee Worship," 64.
11. Frymer-Kensky, *In the Wake of the Goddesses,* 200.
12. But cf. J. B. Burns, "*qādēš* and *qĕdēšâ,*" 159–60; van der Toorn, "Female Prostitution," 201–5; van der Toorn, "Cultic Prostitution," 510–13; and Wilhelm, "Marginalien zu Herodot, Klio 199," 514–15, all of whom, while rejecting the notion of "cultic" or "sacred prostitution" as it has conventionally been understood, suggest, in one way or another, that "in Mesopotamia, prostitution was carried

out by women attached to temples" who "were actually organized and . . . 'dedicated' to the temple to that precise intent" (quoting here from J. B. Burns, "*qādēš* and *qĕdēšâ*," 159). Short critiques can be found in Bird, "End of the Male Cult Prostitute," 38–39, nn. 5 and 8; Bird, "Prostitution," 57, n. 16; J. Day, "Does the Old Testament Refer to Sacred Prostitution?," 8–9; and Olyan, "'And with a Male,'" 181–82, n. 6.

13. On married *qadištu* women, see Budin, "Sacred Prostitution in the First Person," 81; Budin, *Myth of Sacred Prostitution,* 24–25; Henshaw, *Female and Male,* 207–8, 210; Marsman, *Women,* 499; Oden, *Bible Without Theology,* 149; Westenholz, "Tamar, *Qĕdēšā, Qadištu,*" 252, 254; and Yamauchi, "Cultic Prostitution," 214. On *qadištu* who are celibate, see Westenholz, "Religious Personnel," 294; also Marsman, *Women,* 499.
14. Westenholz, "Tamar, *Qĕdēšā, Qadištu,*" 254.
15. Budin, "Sacred Prostitution in the First Person," 81; Budin, *Myth of Sacred Prostitution,* 24–25; Henshaw, *Female and Male,* 208, 211–12; Marsman, *Women,* 500, 570; and Westenholz, "Tamar, *Qĕdēšā, Qadištu,*" 252–54, 258–60.
16. Westenholz, "Tamar, *Qĕdēšā, Qadištu,*" 253–54; see also Budin, "Sacred Prostitution in the First Person," 81; Budin, *Myth of Sacred Prostitution,* 24; Gruber, "Hebrew *qĕdēšāh,*" 28–31; Henshaw, *Female and Male,* 209; and Marsman, *Women,* 500.
17. Gruber, "Hebrew *qĕdēšāh,*" 33–34; Westenholz, "Tamar, *Qĕdēšā, Qadištu,*" 253.
18. Westenholz, "Tamar, *Qĕdēšā, Qadištu,*" 263.
19. Bird, "End of the Male Cult Prostitute," 44, and n. 26 on that page; Gruber, "Hebrew *qĕdēšāh,*" 43–44; Henshaw, *Female and Male,* 213, 222–23, 225; and Westenholz, "Tamar, *Qĕdēšā, Qadištu,*" 249–50.
20. Westenholz, "Tamar, *Qĕdēšā, Qadištu,*" 249; see similarly, although less fully, Budin, *Myth of Sacred Prostitution,* 46; Frymer-Kensky, *In the Wake of the Goddesses,* 201; and Henshaw, *Female and Male,* 225.
21. See Pardee, *Ritual and Cult at Ugarit,* 36–38, with further discussion in Bird, "End of the Male Cult Prostitute," 44, n. 26; Budin, *Myth of Sacred Prostitution,* 46; Gruber, "Hebrew *qĕdēšāh,*" 18, n. 2; and Westenholz, "Tamar, *Qĕdēšā, Qadištu,*" 249.
22. This Ugaritic material has led Gruber, in a series of publications, beginning in 1983 ("The *qadesh* in the Book of Kings," 167–76; see also Gruber, "Hebrew *qĕdēšāh,*" 17–47, an article based on a 1978 conference paper) and most recently in 2005 ("Prostitute and Prostitution," 20–29) to argue that the biblical *qādēš* is to be understood as a temple singer. However, the term *qĕdēšâ,* according to Gruber, does have sexual connotations, but the reference is just to a common prostitute. Yet as several commentators have pointed out (Budin, *Myth of Sacred Prostitution,* 34; J. Day, "Does the Old Testament Refer to Sacred Prostitution?," 3–6; Frymer-Kensky, *In the Wake of the Goddesses,* 201; and Westenholz, "Tamar, *Qĕdēšā, Qadištu,*" 248), Gruber's rather arbitrary separating of the *qādēš* from the *qĕdēšâ* seems "a most curious viewpoint" (J. Day, "Does the Old Testament

Refer to Sacred Prostitution?," 3), to the extent of being "contrary to reason" (Westenholz, "Tamar, *Qĕdēšā, Qadištu,*" 248). For Gruber's rebuttal, see Gruber, "Review of Stephanie Lynn Budin, *Myth of Sacred Prostitution,*" n. 6.

23. Bird, "End of the Male Cult Prostitute," 47.
24. Ibid., 46, n. 32, and 75–77.
25. See the comments of Bird, "'To Play the Harlot,'" 87–89; Bird, "Prostitution," 52; Keefe, *Women's Body and the Social Body,* 53–57; and Yee, *Poor Banished Children,* 89, as well as the much more detailed analysis of Adams, "Metaphor and Dissonance," 291–305.
26. Bird, "End of the Male Cult Prostitute," 41–42.
27. A somewhat similar point about Asherah worship and the *qĕdēšîm* and *qĕdēšôt* is made by J. B. Burns, "*qādēš* and *qĕdēšâ,*" 162–64, and also, in passing—and with less specificity than I posit—by Bird, "End of the Male Cult Prostitute," 70; Budin, *Myth of Sacred Prostitution,* 35; J. Day, "Does the Old Testament Refer to Sacred Prostitution?," 17–18; Dijkstra, "Women and Religion," 177; Frymer-Kensky, *In the Wake of the Goddesses,* 201; Keefe, *Women's Body and the Social Body,* 55; Tigay, *Deuteronomy,* 216 (on the *qĕdēšîm* of 1 and 2 Kings only); Wacker, "'Kultprostitution' im Alten Israel?," 70–72; and Wacker, "Hosea," 376–77. But Bird ultimately rejects this hypothesis (see "End of the Male Cult Prostitute," 75), and Day ("Does the Old Testament Refer to Sacred Prostitution?"), unlike I, would see the *qĕdēšîm* and *qĕdēšôt* as cult prostitutes, although more in the vein of actors who "engage in sexual intercourse as a form of devotion to a deity" (p. 18) and not as "a form of imitative magic, encouraging the deity to bring fertility to the land" (p. 16).
28. Chapter 5, n. 30.
29. Chapter 5, n. 31.
30. Some commentators take the epithet *bn qdš* to mean "the holy ones," a general designation for the Ugaritic pantheon's gods (see, e.g., M. S. Smith, *Ugaritic Baal Cycle,* 294–95). But the translation "children of Qudšu/Asherah" is supported by comparing *KTU* 1.2.3.19–20, on one hand, and *KTU* 1.3.5.38–39 and *KTU* 1.4.4.51, on the other. In all these passages, the formulaic couplet of *'ilm* // *bn*+DN occurs, yet with the epithet *qdš* in the former and appellation *aṯrt,* Asherah, in the latter two. This suggests that *bn qdš* and *bn aṯrt*—and so *qdš* and *aṯrt*—are synonymous. For this same point, see Hadley, *Cult of Asherah,* 48–49, and, as Hadley notes, Meier, "Baal's Fight with Yam," 247. But cf. Wyatt, *Religious Texts from Ugarit,* 54–55, n. 78.
31. Ackerman, *Under Every Green Tree,* 137; see also Pope, *El in the Ugaritic Texts,* 44; Wiggins, "Myth of Asherah," 387–89; and Wyatt, *Religious Texts from Ugarit,* 221.
32. See similarly Hadley, *Cult of Asherah,* 47–48.
33. *ANEP,* no. 470.
34. *ANEP,* no. 474; see also no. 473.
35. Chapter 12, n. 61.

36. Edwards, "Relief of Qudshu-Astarte-Anath," 49–51; pictured in *ANEP,* no. 830.
37. Olyan, *Asherah,* 1–37.
38. See, most recently, Ackerman, "At Home with the Goddess," 455–59; Ackerman, "Women and the Worship of Yahweh," 189–90.
39. Olyan, *Asherah,* 3.
40. See Hyatt, "Deuteronomic Edition of Jeremiah," 247–67; Thiel, *Die deuteronomische Redaktion von Jeremia 1–25;* Thiel, *Die deuteronomische Redaktion von Jeremia 26–45;* and Weinfeld, *Deuteronomy and the Deuteronomic School,* 320–61.
41. Olyan, *Asherah,* 13–18.
42. Bird, "End of the Male Cult Prostitute," 46, notes briefly the Deuteronomic/Deuteronomistic context of many of the *qĕdēšîm/qĕdēšôt* passages, as does, more substantially, Oden, *Bible Without Theology,* 131–32.
43. Olyan, *Asherah,* 7, 9, 17, 19–22.
44. Weinfeld, "Hosea and Deuteronomy," in Weinfeld, *Deuteronomy and the Deuteronomic School,* 366.
45. Olyan, *Asherah,* 7.
46. Frymer-Kensky, *In the Wake of the Goddesses,* 201.
47. Westenholz, "Tamar, *Qĕdēšā, Qadištu,*" 251.
48. Bird, "Harlot as Heroine," 126.
49. Speiser, *Genesis,* 299–300.

Epilogue

1. See Gen 37:34; 2 Sam 3:31; Isa 22:12, 32:11; Jer 6:26, 48:37, 49:3; Ezek 27:31; Amos 8:10; and Ps 30:12 (English 30:11); see also, from the corpus of texts from Late Bronze Age Ugarit, *KTU* 1.5.6.16–17, 31. For further discussion, see Ackerman, *Under Every Green Tree,* 85 and n. 141 on that page, and Ackerman, *When Heroes Love,* 270, n. 112.
2. Wills, *Judith,* 14–16.
3. See Miano, *Shadow on the Steps,* 48, 205, and Soggin, *Israel in the Biblical Period,* 157, on the ancient Israelites' use of a lunisolar calendar that depended on both the 29.5-day lunar cycle, to define the month, and the 365.25-day solar cycle, to define the year.

Bibliography

Ackerman, Susan. "Asherah, the West Semitic Goddess of Spinning and Weaving?" *JNES* 67 (2008): 1–30.

———. "At Home with the Goddess." Pages 455–68 in *Symbiosis, Symbolism, and the Power of the Past: Canaan, Ancient Israel, and Their Neighbors from the Late Bronze Age Through Roman Palaestina.* Edited by William G. Dever and Seymour Gitin. Winona Lake, Ind.: Eisenbrauns, 2003.

———. "The Blind, the Lame, and the Barren Shall Not Come into the House." Pages 29–45 in *Disability Studies and Biblical Literature.* Edited by Candida R. Moss and Jeremy Schipper. New York: Palgrave Macmillan, 2011.

———. "Cult Centralization, the Erosion of Kin-Based Communities, and the Implications for Women's Religious Practices." Pages 19–30 in *Social Theory and the Study of Israelite Religion: Essays in Retrospect and Prospect.* Edited by Saul M. Olyan. RBS 71. Atlanta: Society of Biblical Literature, 2012.

———. "The Deception of Isaac, Jacob's Dream at Bethel, and Incubation on an Animal Skin." Pages 92–120 in *Priesthood and Cult in Ancient Israel.* Edited by Gary A. Anderson and Saul M. Olyan. JSOTSup 125. Sheffield: JSOT Press, 1991.

———. "E-Dan." *JANER* 13 (2013): 153–87.

———. "'I Have Hired You with My Son's Mandrakes': Women's Reproductive Magic in Ancient Israel." Pages 15–29 in *Sex in Antiquity: Exploring Gender and Sexuality in the Ancient World.* Edited by Mark Masterson, Nancy Rabinowitz, and James Robson. Rewriting Antiquity 1. New York: Routledge, 2015.

———. "Illnesses and Other Crises: Syria-Canaan." Pages 459–60 in *Religions of the Ancient World: A Guide.* Edited by Sarah Iles Johnston. Cambridge, Mass.: Harvard University Press, 2004.

———. "Isaiah." Pages 955–1049 in *The New Interpreter's Study Bible.* Edited by Walter J. Harrelson et al. Nashville, Tenn.: Abingdon, 2003.

———. "The Mother of Eshmunazor, Priest of Astarte: A Study of Her Cultic Role." *Die Welt des Orients* 43 (2013): 158–78.

———. "Only Men Are Created Equal." In Saul M. Olyan, ed., "In Conversation with Joshua A. Berman, *Created Equal: How the Bible Broke with Ancient Political Thought* (Oxford University Press, 2008)." *JHS* 10 (2010): 14–27.

———. "The Queen Mother and the Cult in Ancient Israel." *JBL* 112 (1993): 385–401.

———. *Under Every Green Tree: Popular Religion in Sixth-Century Judah.* HSM 46. Atlanta: Scholars Press, 1992.

———. *Warrior, Dancer, Seductress, Queen: Women in Judges and Biblical Israel.* AYBRL. New York: Doubleday, 1998.

———. *When Heroes Love: The Ambiguity of Eros in the Stories of Gilgamesh and David.* Gender, Theory, and Religion 2. New York: Columbia University Press, 2005.

———. "Who Is the Baal of Peor?" Pages 175–91 in *Mighty Baal: Essays in Honor of Mark S. Smith.* Edited by Stephen C. Russell and Esther J. Hamori. Harvard Semitic Studies 66. Leiden: Brill, 2020.

———. "Women and the Religious Culture of the Ancient Levant's State Temples, Or: Priestesses, Purity, and Parturition." Pages 259–89 in *Temple Building and Temple Cult: Architecture and Cultic Paraphernalia of Temples in the Levant (2.-1. Mill. B.C.E.).* Edited by Jens Kamlah. ADPV 41. Wiesbaden: Harrassowitz, 2012.

———. "Women and the Worship of Yahweh in Ancient Israel." Pages 189–97 in *Confronting the Past: Archaeological and Historical Essays on Ancient Israel in Honor of William G. Dever.* Edited by Seymour Gitin, J. Edward Wright, and J. P. Dessel. Winona Lake, Ind.: Eisenbrauns, 2006.

———. See also Cox, Benjamin D.

Ackroyd, Peter R. *The First Book of Samuel.* CBC. Cambridge: Cambridge University Press, 1971.

Adams, Karin. "Metaphor and Dissonance: A Reinterpretation of Hosea 4:13–14." *JBL* 127 (2008): 291–305.

Aharoni, Miriam. See Herzog, Ze'ev.

Aharoni, Yohanan. "Arad: Its Inscriptions and Temple." *BA* 31 (1968): 2–32.

———. "Excavations at Tel Arad: Preliminary Report on the First Season, 1962." *IEJ* 14 (1964): 131–47.

———. "Excavations at Tel Beer-sheba: Preliminary Report of the Fifth and Sixth Seasons, 1973–1974." *TA* 2 (1975): 146–68.

———. "The Horned Altar of Beer-sheba." *BA* 37 (1974): 2–6.

Ahlström, Gösta W. *Aspects of Syncretism in Israelite Religion.* Horae Soederblomianae 5. Lund: C. W. K. Gleerup, 1963.

Albertz, Rainer. "Family Religion in Ancient Israel and Its Surroundings." Pages 89–112 in *Household and Family Religion in Antiquity.* Edited by John Bodel and Saul M. Olyan. Oxford: Blackwell, 2008.

———. *A History of Israelite Religion in the Old Testament Period.* 1: *From the Beginnings to the End of the Monarchy,* and 2: *From the Exile to the Maccabees.* OTL. Louisville: Westminster/John Knox, 1994.

———. "The Recent Discussion on the Formation of the Pentateuch/Hexateach." *Hebrew Studies* 59 (2018): 65–92.

Albertz, Rainer, and Rüdiger Schmitt. *Family and Household Religion in Ancient Israel and the Levant.* Winona Lake, Ind.: Eisenbrauns, 2012.

Albright, William Foxwell. *Archaeology and the Religion of Israel.* OTL. Louisville: Westminster/John Knox, 2006.

———. "A Catalogue of Early Hebrew Lyric Poems (Psalm LVIII)." *HUCA* 23 (1950–1951): 1–39.

Alexander, T. Desmond. "The Passover Sacrifice." Pages 1–24 in *Sacrifice in the Bible.* Edited by Roger T. Beckwith and Martin J. Selman. Carlisle, U.K.: Paternoster; Grand Rapids: Baker, 1995.

Alexiou, Margaret. *The Ritual Lament in Greek Tradition.* 2nd ed. Revised by Dimitrios Yatromanolakis and Panagiotis Roilos. Lanham, Md.: Rowman & Littlefield, 2002.

Alster, Bendt. "Tammuz." Pages 828–34 in *DDD.*

Altmann, Peter. "Material Culture and the Symbolic Meaning of Meat in Deuteronomy 12." Paper presented in the Biblical Law Section of the Annual Meeting of the Society of Biblical Literature, Boston, Mass., November 25, 2008. Posted online at https://biblicallaw.files.wordpress.com/2013/07/altmann.pdf.

Amit, Yairah. "'Am I Not More Devoted to You Than Ten Sons?' (1 Samuel 1:8): Male and Female Interpretations." Pages 68–76 in *A Feminist Companion to Samuel and Kings.* Edited by Athalya Brenner. FCB 5. Sheffield: Sheffield Academic, 1994.

———. *Hidden Polemics in Biblical Narrative.* Biblical Interpretation Series 25. Leiden: Brill, 2000.

Anderson, Gary A. "Sacrifice and Sacrificial Offerings (OT)." Pages 870–86 in *ABD* 5.

———. *A Time to Mourn, a Time to Dance: The Expression of Grief and Joy in Israelite Religion.* University Park: Pennsylvania State University Press, 1991.

Andreasen, Niels-Erik A. "Festival and Freedom: A Study of an Old Testament Theme." *Interpretation* 28 (1974): 281–97.

———. *The Old Testament Sabbath.* SBLDS 7. Missoula, Mont.: Scholars Press, 1972.

———. "Recent Studies in the Old Testament Sabbath: Some Observations." *ZAW* 86 (1974): 453–69.

Angel, J. Lawrence. "Ecology and Population in the Eastern Mediterranean." *World Archaeology* 4 (1972): 88–105.

Arnaud, Daniel. "La prostitution sacrée en Mésopotamie, un mythe historiographique." *Revue de l'histoire des religions* 123 (1973): 111–15.

Arnold, Bill T. "Necromancy and Cleromancy in 1 and 2 Samuel." *CBQ* 66 (2004): 199–213.

Arnold, Patrick M. "Geba." Pages 921–22 in *ABD* 2.

———. *Gibeah: The Search for a Biblical City.* JSOTSup 79. Sheffield: JSOT Press, 1990.

———. "Mizpah." Pages 879–81 in *ABD* 4.

———. "Ramah." Pages 613–14 in *ABD* 5.

Attridge, Harold W. "Pollution, Sin, Atonement, Salvation." Pages 71–83 in *Religions of the Ancient World: A Guide.* Edited by Sarah Iles Johnston. Cambridge, Mass.: Harvard University Press, 2004.

Aubin, Melissa. "Gendering Magic in Late Antique Judaism." PhD diss., Duke University, 1998.

Avalos, Hector. *Illness and Health Care in the Ancient Near East: The Role of the Temple in Greece, Mesopotamia, and Israel.* HSM 54. Atlanta: Scholars Press, 1995.

———. "Illnesses and Other Crises: Israel." Pages 460–61 in *Religions of the Ancient World: A Guide.* Edited by Sarah Iles Johnston. Cambridge, Mass.: Harvard University Press, 2004.

Avigad, Nahman. "The Priest of Dor." *IEJ* 25 (1975): 101–5.

Baadsgaard, Aubrey. "A Taste of Women's Sociality: Cooking as Cooperative Labor in Iron Age Syro-Palestine." Pages 13–44 in *The World of Women in the Ancient and Classical Near East.* Edited by Beth Alpert Nakhai. Newcastle upon Tyne: Cambridge Scholars, 2008.

Baden, Joel S. *The Composition of the Pentateuch: Renewing the Documentary Hypothesis.* AYBRL. New Haven: Yale University Press, 2012.

———. *J, E, and the Redaction of the Pentateuch.* FAT 68. Tübingen: Mohr Siebeck, 2009.

Badre, Leila. "The Terra Cotta Anthropomorphic Figurines." *Studies in the History and Archaeology of Jordan* 5 (1995): 457–68.

Bal, Mieke. *Death and Dissymmetry: The Politics of Coherence in the Book of Judges.* Chicago: University of Chicago Press, 1988.

Bar-On, Shimon. See Gesundheit, Shimon.

Barrick, W. Boyd. BMH *as Body Language: A Lexical and Iconographical Study of the Word* BMH *When Not a Reference to Cultic Phenomena in Biblical and Post-Biblical Hebrew.* New York: T&T Clark, 2008.

———. "High Place." Pages 196–200 in *ABD* 3.

———. *The King and the Cemeteries: Toward a New Understanding of Josiah's Reform.* VTSup 88. Leiden: Brill, 2002.

———. "What Do We Really Know About the 'High Places'?" *Svensk exegetisk årsbok* 45 (1980): 50–57.

———. "Why Do We Associate Biblical Bamoth with Israelite 'Popular' Religion?" Unpublished paper presented at the joint meeting of the Midwest Region of the Society of Biblical Literature, the Middle West Branch of the American

Oriental Society, and the American Schools of Oriental Research, at Bourbonnais, Ill., February 20–22, 2004.

Barstad, Hans M. *The Religious Polemics of Amos: Studies in the Preaching of Am 2:7b–8, 4:1–13, 5:1–27, 6:4–7, 8:14.* VTSup 34. Leiden: Brill, 1984.

Barton, John. See Stavrakopoulou, Francesca.

Bartusch, Mark W. *Understanding Dan: An Exegetical Study of a Biblical City, Tribe and Ancestor.* JSOTSup 379. London: Sheffield Academic, 2003.

Bayer, Bathja. "Negina v'zimra [Instrumental Performance and Singing]." Pages 755–82 in *Encyclopaedia Miqra'it* 5. Jerusalem: Bialek Institute, 1968 (Hebrew).

Bayliss, Miranda. "The Cult of Dead Kin in Assyria and Babylonia." *Iraq* 35 (1973): 115–25.

Beard, Mary, and John Henderson. "With This Body I Thee Worship: Sacred Prostitution in Antiquity." Pages 56–79 in *Gender and the Body in the Ancient Mediterranean.* Edited by Maria Wyke. Oxford: Blackwell, 1998.

Beck, Pirhiya. "Catalogue of Cult Objects and Study of the Iconography." Pages 27–197 in *Ḥorvat Qitmit: An Edomite Shrine in the Biblical Negev.* Edited by Itzhaq Beit-Arieh. Monograph Series of the Institute of Archaeology, Tel Aviv University 11. Tel Aviv: Institute of Archaeology of Tel Aviv University, 1995.

———. "The Drawings and Decorative Designs." Pages 143–204 in Ze'ev Meshel, *Kuntillet 'Ajrud (Ḥorvat Teman): An Iron Age II Religious Site on the Judah-Sinai Border.* Jerusalem: Israel Exploration Society, 2012.

———. "The Drawings from Ḥorvat Teiman (Kuntillet 'Ajrûd)." *TA* 9 (1982): 3–68.

Beckman, Gary M. "Birth and Motherhood Among the Hittites." Pages 319–28 in *Women in Antiquity: Real Women Across the Ancient World.* Edited by Stephanie Lynn Budin and Jean MacIntosh Turfa. London: Routledge, 2016.

———. "From Cradle to Grave: Women's Role in Hittite Medicine and Magic." *Journal of Ancient Civilizations* 8 (1993): 25–39.

———. *Hittite Birth Rituals.* 2nd rev. ed. Studien zu den Boğazköy-Texten 29. Wiesbaden: Harrassowitz, 1983.

Begg, Christopher T. "The Death of Josiah in Chronicles: Another View." *VT* 37 (1987): 1–8.

Beit-Arieh, Itzhaq. *Ḥorvat 'Uza and Ḥorvat Radum: Two Fortresses in the Biblical Negev.* Tel Aviv: Emery and Claire Yass Publications in Archaeology, 2007.

———. "The Western Quarter." Pages 412–24 in Ze'ev Herzog and Lily Singer-Avitz, *Beer-Sheba* III: *The Early Iron IIA Enclosed Settlement and the Late Iron IIA–Iron IIB Cities.* Monograph Series of the Sonia and Marco Nadler Institute of Archaeology, Tel Aviv University 34. Tel Aviv: Emery and Claire Yass Publications in Archaeology; Winona Lake, Ind.: Eisenbrauns, 2016.

Beit-Arieh, Itzhaq, and Bruce C. Cresson. "Ḥorvat 'Uza: A Fortified Outpost on the Eastern Negev Border." *BA* 54 (1991): 126–35.

Ben-Dov, Meir. *In the Shadow of the Temple: The Discovery of Ancient Jerusalem.* New York: Harper & Row, 1985.

Benjamin, Don C. See Matthews, Victor H.

Bergant, Dianne. "An Anthropological Approach to Biblical Interpretation: The Passover Supper in Exodus 12:1–20 as a Case Study." Pages 43–62 in *Transformation, Passages, and Processes* (= *Semeia* 67). Edited by Mark McVann and Bruce Malina, 1994.

Bergman, J., B. Lang, and H. Ringgren. "*zābaḥ, zebaḥ*." Pages 8–29 in *TDOT* 4.

Berlejung, Angelika. See Gertz, Jan Christian.

Berlin, Adele. "Hannah and Her Prayers." *Scriptura* 87 (2004): 227–32.

Berlinerblau, Jacques. *The Vow and the "Popular Religious Groups" of Ancient Israel: A Philological and Sociological Inquiry*. JSOTSup 210. Sheffield: Sheffield Academic, 1996.

Berman, Joshua A. *Created Equal: How the Bible Broke with Ancient Political Thought*. Oxford: Oxford University Press, 2008.

Beuken, W. A. M. "Exodus 16.5, 23: A Rule Regarding the Keeping of the Sabbath." *JSOT* 32 (1985): 3–14.

Biggs, Robert D. "Medicine, Surgery, and Public Health in Ancient Mesopotamia." Pages 1911–24 in *CANE* 3–4.

Birch, Bruce C. *The Rise of the Israelite Monarchy: The Growth and Development of I Samuel 7–15*. SBLDS. Missoula, Mont.: Scholars Press, 1976.

Bird, Phyllis. "The End of the Male Cult Prostitute: A Literary-Historical and Sociological Analysis of Hebrew *qādēš-qĕdēšîm*." Pages 37–43 in *Congress Volume: Cambridge 1995*. Edited by J. A. Emerton. VTSup 66. Leiden: Brill, 1997.

———. "Gender and Religious Definition: The Case of Ancient Israel." *Harvard Divinity Bulletin* 20/2 (1990): 12–13, 19–20.

———. "The Harlot as Heroine: Narrative Art and Social Presumption in Three Old Testament Texts." Pages 119–39 in *Narrative Research on the Hebrew Bible* (= *Semeia* 46). Edited by Miri Amihai, George W. Coats, and Anne M. Solomon, 1989.

———. "Images of Women in the Old Testament." Pages 44–88 in *Religion and Sexism: Images of Women in the Jewish and Christian Traditions*. Edited by Rosemary Radford Ruether. New York: Simon & Schuster, 1974.

———. "Israelite Religion and the Faith of Israel's Daughters: Reflections on Gender and Religious Definition." Pages 97–108 in *The Bible and the Politics of Exegesis: Essays in Honor of Norman K. Gottwald on His Sixty-Fifth Birthday*. Edited by David Jobling, Peggy L. Day, and Gerald T. Sheppard. Cleveland: Pilgrim, 1991.

———. "Notes on Gender and Religious Ritual in Ancient Israel." Pages 221–33 in *To Break Every Yoke: Essays in Honor of Marvin L. Chaney*. Edited by Robert B. Coote and Norman K. Gottwald. SWBA 2/3. Sheffield: Sheffield Phoenix, 2007.

———. "The Place of Women in the Israelite Cultus." Pages 397–419 in *Ancient Israelite Religion: Essays in Honor of Frank Moore Cross*. Edited by Patrick D. Miller, Paul D. Hanson, and S. Dean McBride. Philadelphia: Fortress, 1987.

———. "'To Play the Harlot': An Inquiry into an Old Testament Metaphor." Pages 75–94 in *Gender and Difference in Ancient Israel.* Edited by Peggy L. Day. Minneapolis: Fortress, 1989.

———. "Prostitution in the Social World and Religious Rhetoric of Ancient Israel." Pages 40–58 in *Prostitutes and Courtesans in the Ancient World.* Edited by Christopher A. Faraone and Laura K. McClure. Wisconsin Studies in Classics. Madison: University of Wisconsin Press, 2006.

———. "Women in the Ancient Mediterranean World: Ancient Israel." *BR* 39 (1994): 31–45.

———. "Women (OT)." Pages 951–57 in *ABD* 6.

———. "Women's Religion in Ancient Israel." Pages 283–98 in *Women's Earliest Records from Ancient Egypt and Western Asia.* Edited by Barbara S. Lesko. BJS 166. Atlanta: Scholars Press, 1989.

Blank, Sheldon H. "The Curse, Blasphemy, the Spell, and the Oath." *HUCA* 23 (1950/1951): 73–95.

Blenkinsopp, Joseph. "Deuteronomy and the Politics of Post-Mortem Existence." *VT* 45 (1995): 1–16.

———. "The Family in First Temple Israel." Pages 48–103 in Leo G. Perdue, Joseph Blenkinsopp, John J. Collins, and Carol Meyers, *Families in Ancient Israel.* The Family, Religion, and Culture. Louisville: Westminster/John Knox, 1997.

———. *The Pentateuch: An Introduction to the First Five Books of the Bible.* AYBRL. New York: Doubleday, 1992.

———. *Sage, Priest, Prophet: Religious and Intellectual Leadership in Ancient Israel.* Library of Ancient Israel. Louisville: Westminster/John Knox, 1995.

———. "Saul and the Mistress of the Spirits (1 Samuel 28.3–25)." Pages 49–62 in *Sense and Sensitivity: Essays on Reading the Bible in Memory of Robert Carroll.* Edited by Alastair G. Hunter and Phillip R. Davies. JSOTSup 348. Sheffield: Sheffield Academic, 2002.

———. "Structure and Style in Judges 13–16." *JBL* 82 (1963): 65–76.

Bloch-Smith, Elizabeth M. "Acculturating Gender Roles: Goddess Images as Conveyors of Culture in Ancient Israel." Pages 1–18 in *Image, Text, Exegesis: Iconographic Interpretation and the Hebrew Bible.* Edited by Izaak J. de Hulster and Joel M. LeMon. London: Bloomsbury, 2014.

———. See also Smith, Mark S.

Block, Daniel I. "Marriage and Family in Ancient Israel." Pages 33–102 in *Marriage and Family in the Biblical World.* Edited by Ken M. Campbell. Downers Grove, Ill.: InterVarsity, 2003.

Blundell, Sue. *Women in Ancient Greece.* Cambridge, Mass.: Harvard University Press, 1995.

Bodel, John, and Saul M. Olyan. "Comparative Perspectives." Pages 276–82 in *Household and Family Religion in Antiquity.* Edited by John Bodel and Saul M. Olyan. Oxford: Blackwell, 2008.

Böhm, Stephanie. *Die "Nackte Göttin": Zur Ikonographie und Deutung unbekleideter weiblicher Figuren in der frühgriechischen Kunst.* Mainz am Rhein: von Zabern, 1990.

Bohmbach, Karla G. "Names and Naming in the Biblical World." Pages 33–39 in *WIS.*

Boling, Robert G. *Judges: A New Translation with Introduction and Commentary.* AYB 6A. Garden City, N.Y.: Doubleday, 1975.

Boorn, G. P. F. van den. "*Wḏ'-ryt* and Justice at the Gate." *JNES* 44 (1985): 1–25.

Borghouts, J. F. "Witchcraft, Magic, and Divination in Ancient Egypt." Pages 1775–85 in *CANE* 3–4.

Borowski, Oded. *Agriculture in Iron Age Israel.* Reprint ed. Boston: American Schools of Oriental Research, 2002.

———. *Daily Life in Biblical Times.* Atlanta: Society of Biblical Literature, 2003.

Bosworth, David A. "Faith and Resilience: King David's Reaction to the Death of Bathsheba's Firstborn." *CBQ* 73 (2011): 691–707.

———. "Weeping in the Psalms." *VT* 62 (2013): 36–46.

Bourguignon, Erika. "Necromancy." Pages 6451–54 in *ER* 10.

Bourriau, Janine, Paul Nicholson, and Pamela Rose. "Pottery." Pages 121–47 in *Ancient Egyptian Materials and Technology.* Edited by Paul T. Nicholson and Ian Shaw. Cambridge: Cambridge University Press, 2000.

Bowen, Nancy R. "The Daughters of Your People: Female Prophets in Ezekiel 13:17–23." *JBL* 118 (1999): 417–33.

Braman, Robert Michael. "The Problem of Magic in Ancient Israel: A Century of Studies." PhD diss., Drew University, 1989.

Braulik, Georg. "The Rejection of the Goddess Asherah in Israel: Was the Rejection as Late as Deuteronomistic and Did It Further the Oppression of Women in Israel?" Pages 165–82 in *The Theology of Deuteronomy: Collected Essays by Georg Braulik, O.S.B.* North Richland Hills, Tex.: BIBAL, 1994.

———. "Were Women, Too, Allowed to Offer Sacrifices in Israel? Observations on the Meaning and Festive Form of Sacrifice in Deuteronomy." *Hervormde teologiese studies* 55 (1999): 909–42.

Braun, Joachim. *Music in Ancient Israel/Palestine: Archaeological, Written, and Comparative Sources.* The Bible in Its World. Grand Rapids: Eerdmans, 2002.

Bray, Jason S. *Sacred Dan: Religious Tradition and Cultic Practice in Judges 17–18.* LHBOTS 449. New York: T&T Clark, 2006.

Brenner, Athalya. "An Afterword: The Decalogue—Am I an Addressee?" Pages 255–58 in *A Feminist Companion to Exodus to Deuteronomy.* Edited by Athalya Brenner. FCB 6. Sheffield: Sheffield Academic, 1994.

———. *The Intercourse of Knowledge: On Gendering Desire and "Sexuality" in the Bible.* Biblical Interpretation Series 26. Leiden: Brill, 1997.

———. *The Israelite Woman: Social Role and Literary Type in Biblical Narrative.* The Biblical Seminar 2. Sheffield: JSOT Press, 1985.

Bretschneider, Joachim. *Architekturmodelle in Vorderasien und der östlichen Ägäis vom Neolithikum bis in das 1. Jahrtausend: Phänomene in der Kleinkunst an Beispielen aus Mesopotamien, dem Iran, Anatolien, Syrien, der Levante und dem ägäischen Raum unter besonderer Berücksichtigung der bau- und der religionsgeschichtlichen Aspekte.* AOAT 229. Neukirchen-Vluyn: Neukirchener; Kevelaer: Butzon & Bercker, 1991.

Brettler, Marc Zvi. "The Book of Judges: Literature as Politics." *JBL* 108 (1989): 395–418.

———. "The Composition of 1 Samuel 1–2." *JBL* 116 (1997): 601–12.

———. "A Woman's Voice in the Psalter: A New Understanding of Psalm 113." Pages 155–70 in *Built by Wisdom, Established by Understanding: Essays on Biblical and Near Eastern Literature in Honor of Adele Berlin.* Edited by Maxine L. Grossman. Bethesda, Md.: CDL, 2013.

———. "Women and Psalms: Toward an Understanding of the Role of Women's Prayer in the Israelite Cult." Pages 25–56 in *Gender and Law in the Hebrew Bible and the Ancient Near East.* Edited by Victor H. Matthews, Bernard M. Levinson, and Tikva Frymer-Kensky. JSOTSup 262. Sheffield: Sheffield Academic, 1998.

———. "Women in the Decalogue." Pages 191–92 in *WIS.*

Brody, Aaron J. "The Archaeology of the Extended Family: A Household Compound from Iron II Tell en-Naṣbeh." Pages 237–54 in *Household Archaeology in Ancient Israel and Beyond.* Edited by Assaf Yasur-Landau, Jennie R. Ebeling, and Laura B. Mazow. CHANE 50. Leiden: Brill, 2011.

Brooks, Simcha Shalom. "From Gibeon to Gibeah: High Place of the Kingdom." Pages 40–59 in *Temple and Worship in Biblical Israel.* Edited by John Day. LHBOTS 422. London: T&T Clark, 2005.

Broshi, Magen. *Bread, Wine, Walls, and Scrolls.* Journal for the Study of the Pseudepigrapha: Supplement Series 36. Sheffield: Sheffield Academic, 2001.

Brueggemann, Walter. *Worship in Ancient Israel: An Essential Guide.* Nashville: Abingdon, 2005.

Budin, Stephanie Lynn. *The Myth of Sacred Prostitution in Antiquity.* Cambridge: Cambridge University Press, 2008.

———. "Sacred Prostitution in the First Person." Pages 77–92 in *Prostitutes and Courtesans in the Ancient World.* Edited by Christopher A. Faraone and Laura K. McClure. Wisconsin Studies in Classics. Madison: University of Wisconsin Press, 2006.

Buhl, Marie-Louise, and Svend Holm-Nielsen. *Shiloh, the Danish Excavations at Tell Sailun, Palestine, in 1926, 1929, 1932 and 1963.* 1: *The Pre-Hellenistic Remains.* Publications of the National Museum, Archaeological Historical Series 12. Copenhagen: National Museum of Denmark, 1969.

Bunimovitz, Shlomo. See Faust, Avraham.

Burckhardt, Jacob. *The Greeks and Greek Civilization.* Edited, with an introduction by Oswyn Murray. New York: St. Martin's, 1998.

Burgh, Theodore W. *Listening to the Artifacts: Music Culture in Ancient Palestine.* New York: T&T Clark, 2006.

Burnett, Joel S. "What Kind of Goddess? Terra-Cotta Shrine Figurines from Iron Age Jordan." Unpublished paper, 2008.

Burnette-Bletsch, Rhonda. "Women After Childbirth." Page 204 in *WIS.*

Burney, C. F. *The Book of Judges, with Introduction and Notes.* 2nd ed. London: Rivington's, 1920.

Burns, John Barclay. "*qādēš* and *qĕdēšâ:* Did They Live Off Immoral Earnings?" *Proceedings: Eastern Great Lakes and Midwest Biblical Societies* 15 (1995): 157–68.

Burns, Rita J. *Has the Lord Indeed Spoken Only Through Moses? A Study of the Biblical Portrait of Miriam.* SBLDS 84. Atlanta: Scholars Press, 1987.

Butting, Klara. *Prophetinnen gefragt: die Bedeutung der Prophetinnen im Kanon aus Tora und Prophetie.* Biblisch-feministische Texte 3. Knesebeck: Erev-Rav, 2001.

Bynum, Caroline Walker. "Women's Stories, Women's Symbols: A Critique of Victor Turner's Theory of Liminality." Pages 27–51 in *Fragmentation and Redemption: Essays on Gender and the Human Body in Medieval Religion.* New York: Zone Books, 1991.

Callaway, Joseph A. "Ai." Pages 125–30 in *ABD* 1.

Camino, Linda A. See Myerhoff, Barbara G.

Capel, Anne K. "8a. Statuette of Woman Dressing Hair of Nursing Mother" and "8b. Relief of Woman and Child Between Trees (Tomb of Mentuemhat)." Pages 59–60 in *Mistress of the House, Mistress of Heaven: Women in Ancient Egypt.* Edited by Anne K. Capel and Glenn E. Markoe. New York: Hudson Hills, in conjunction with the Cincinnati Art Museum, 1996.

Carmichael, Calum. "Death and Sexuality Among Priests (Leviticus 21)." Pages 225–44 in *The Book of Leviticus: Composition and Reception.* Edited by Rolf Rendtorff and Robert A. Kugler. VTSup 93. Leiden: Brill, 2003.

Cartledge, Tony W. *Vows in the Hebrew Bible and the Ancient Near East.* JSOTSup 147. Sheffield: JSOT Press, 1992.

———. "Were Nazirite Vows Unconditional?" *CBQ* 51 (1989): 409–22.

Catling, Hector William. *Cypriot Bronzework in the Mycenaean World.* Oxford: Clarendon, 1964.

Cazelles, Henri. "Ex 34, 21: Traite-t-il du sabbat?" *CBQ* 23 (1961): 223–26.

Chambon, Alain. *Tell el-Far'ah.* I: *L'âge du fer.* Paris: Éditions Recherche sur les Civilisations, 1984.

Chapman, Cynthia R. *The House of the Mother: The Social Roles of Maternal Kin in Biblical Hebrew Narrative and Poetry.* AYBRL. New Haven: Yale University Press, 2016.

Chavel, Simeon. "Numbers 15, 32–36—A Microcosm of the Living Priesthood and Its Literary Production." Pages 45–55 in *The Strata of the Priestly Writings: Contemporary Debate and Future Directions.* Edited by Sarah Shectman and Joel S. Baden. ATANT 95. Zürich: Theologischer Verlag, 2009.

Chisholm, Robert B. "Divine Hardening in the Old Testament." *Bibliotheca sacra* 153 (1996): 410–34.

Cleveland, Ray L. See Sinclair, Lawrence A.

Clifford, Richard J. "In Zion and David a New Beginning: An Interpretation of Psalm 78." Pages 121–41 in *Traditions in Transformation: Turning-Points in Biblical Faith.* Edited by Baruch Halpern and Jon D. Levenson. Winona Lake, Ind.: Eisenbrauns, 1981.

Clines, David J. A. "The Evidence for an Autumnal New Year in Pre-Exilic Israel Reconsidered." *JBL* 93 (1974): 22–40.

———. *Ezra, Nehemiah, Esther.* New Century Bible Commentary. Grand Rapids: Eerdmans; London: Marshall Morgan & Scott, 1984.

Coats, George W. "Humility and Honor: A Moses Legend in Numbers 12." Pages 97–107 in *Art and Meaning: Rhetoric in Biblical Literature.* Edited by David J. A. Clines, David M. Gunn, and Alan J. Hauser. JSOTSup 19. Sheffield: JSOT Press, 1982.

Cody, Aelred. *A History of Old Testament Priesthood.* Analecta biblica 39. Rome: Pontifical Biblical Institute, 1969.

Cogan, Mordechai. *I Kings: A New Translation with Introduction and Commentary.* AYB 10. New York: Doubleday, 2001.

———. *Imperialism and Religion: Assyria, Judah and Israel in the Eighth and Seventh Centuries B.C.E.* SBLMS 19. Missoula, Mont.: Scholars Press, 1974.

———. "Judah Under Assyrian Hegemony: A Reexamination of *Imperialism and Religion.*" *JBL* 112 (1993): 403–14.

———. "The Road to En-Dor." Pages 319–26 in *Pomegranates and Golden Bells: Studies in Biblical, Jewish, and Near Eastern Ritual, Law, and Literature in Honor of Jacob Milgrom.* Edited by David P. Wright, David Noel Freedman, and Avi Hurvitz. Winona Lake, Ind.: Eisenbrauns, 1995.

Cogan, Mordechai, and Hayim Tadmor. *II Kings: A New Translation with Introduction and Commentary.* AYB 11. Garden City, N.Y.: Doubleday, 1988.

Cohen, Shaye J. D. "Menstruants and the Sacred in Judaism and Christianity." Pages 273–99 in *Women's History and Ancient History.* Edited by Sarah B. Pomeroy. Chapel Hill: University of North Carolina Press, 1991.

Cohn, Robert L. *The Shape of Sacred Space: Four Biblical Studies.* AAR Studies in Religion 23. Chico, Calif.: Scholars Press, 1981.

Collins, Billie Jean. "Necromancy, Fertility and the Dark Earth: The Use of Ritual Pits in Hittite Cult." Pages 224–41 in *Magic and Ritual in the Ancient World.* Edited by Paul Mirecki and Marvin Miller. Religions in the Graeco-Roman World 141. Leiden: Brill, 2002.

Collins, John J. *The Bible After Babel: Historical Criticism in a Postmodern Age.* Grand Rapids: Eerdmans, 2005.

———. *Daniel: A Commentary on the Book of Daniel.* Hermeneia. Minneapolis: Fortress, 1993.

"Common Roots." *Neot Kedumim News,* April–May 1999, 4.

Connerton, Paul. *How Societies Remember.* Cambridge: Cambridge University Press, 1989.

Cooper, Alan M., and Bernard R. Goldstein. "At the Entrance to the Tent: More Cultic Resonances in Biblical Narrative." *JBL* 116 (1997): 201–15.

———. "The Development of the Priestly Calendars (I): The Daily Sacrifice and the Sabbath." *HUCA* 74 (2003): 1–20.

———. "Exodus and *Maṣṣôt* in History and Tradition." *Maarav* 8 (1992): 15–37.

———. "The Festivals of Israel and Judah and the Literary History of the Pentateuch." *JAOS* 110 (1990): 19–31.

Costin, Cathy L. "Exploring the Relationship Between Gender and Craft in Complex Societies: Methodological and Theoretical Issues of Gender Attribution." Pages 111–40 in *Gender and Archaeology.* Edited by Rita P. Wright. Philadelphia: University of Pennsylvania Press, 1996.

Cox, Benjamin D., and Susan Ackerman. "Micah's Teraphim." *JHS* 12 (2012): 1–37.

———. "Rachel's Tomb." *JBL* 128 (2009): 135–48.

Craigie, Peter C. "Deborah and Anat: A Study of Poetic Imagery." *ZAW* 90 (1978): 374–81.

Craven, Toni. "'From Where Will My Help Come?' Women and Prayer in the Apocryphal/Deuterocanonical Books." Pages 95–109 in *Worship and the Hebrew Bible: Essays in Honour of John T. Willis.* Edited by M. Patrick Graham, Rick R. Marrs, and Steven L. McKenzie. JSOTSup 284. Sheffield: Sheffield Academic, 1999.

Cresson, Bruce C. See Beit-Arieh, Itzhaq.

Cross, Frank Moore. *Canaanite Myth and Hebrew Epic: Essays in the History of the Religion of Israel.* Cambridge, Mass.: Harvard University Press, 1973.

———. "The Tabernacle: A Study from an Archaeological Approach." *BA* 10 (1947): 45–68.

Cross, Frank Moore, and David Noel Freedman. "The Song of Miriam." *JNES* 14 (1955): 237–50.

Cryer, Frederick H. *Divination in Ancient Israel and Its Near Eastern Environment: A Socio-Historical Investigation.* JSOTSup 142. Sheffield: Sheffield Academic, 1994.

Culican, William. "A Terracotta Shrine from Achzib." *ZDPV* 92 (1976): 47–53.

Culley, Robert C. "Five Tales of Punishment in the Book of Numbers." Pages 25–34 in *Text and Tradition: The Hebrew Bible and Folklore.* Edited by Susan Niditch. Atlanta: Scholars Press, 1990.

Curtis, Robert I. *Ancient Food Technology.* Technology and Change in History 5. Leiden: Brill, 2001.

Dabrowski, Boguslav. "A Preliminary Report on Figurines and Clay Objects." Pages 215–37 in *Madaba Plains Project: The 1992 Season at Tall al-'Umayri and Subsequent Studies.* Edited by Larry G. Herr, Douglas R. Clark, Lawrence T. Geraty, Randall

W. Younker, and Oystein Sakara LaBlanca. Berrien Springs, Mich.: Andrews University, 2000.

Dahood, Mitchell. *Psalms II, 51–100: Introduction, Translation, and Notes.* AYB 17. Garden City, N.Y.: Doubleday, 1968.

Darby, Erin. *Interpreting Judean Pillar Figurines: Gender and Empire in Judean Apotropaic Ritual.* Tübingen: Mohr Siebeck, 2014.

Darr, Katheryn Pfisterer. "Daughters Who Prophesy." Page 336 in *WIS.*

Daviau, P. M. Michèle. "Ceramic and Architectural Models from Transjordan and the Syrian Tradition." Pages 293–308 in *Proceedings of the 4th International Congress of the Archaeology of the Ancient Near East, 29 March–3 April 2004, Freie Universität Berlin. 1: The Reconstruction of Environment: Natural Resources and Human Interrelations Through Time. Art History: Visual Communication.* Edited by Hartmut Kühne, Rainer Maria Czichon, and Florian Janoscha Kreppner. Wiesbaden: Harrassowitz, 2008.

———. "Family Religion: Evidence for the Paraphernalia of the Domestic Cult." Pages 199–229 in *The World of the Aramaeans II: Studies in History and Archaeology in Honour of Paul-Eugène Dion.* Edited by P. M. Michèle Daviau, John W. Wevers, and Michael Weigl. JSOTSup 325. Sheffield: Sheffield Academic, 2001.

Davies, Graham I. "An Archaeological Commentary on Ezekiel 13." Pages 108–25 in *Scripture and Other Artifacts: Essays on the Bible and Archaeology in Honor of Philip J. King.* Edited by Michael D. Coogan, J. Cheryl Exum, and Lawrence E. Stager. Louisville: Westminster/John Knox, 1994.

Davis, Andrew R. "Tel Dan in Its Northern Cultic Context." PhD diss., The Johns Hopkins University, 2010.

———. *Tel Dan in Its Northern Cultic Context.* Society of Biblical Literature Archaeological and Biblical Studies 20. Atlanta: Society of Biblical Literature, 2013.

Davis, Dale Ralph. "Comic Literature—Tragic Theology: A Study of Judges 17–18." *WTJ* 46 (1984): 156–63.

Day, John. "Does the Old Testament Refer to Sacred Prostitution and Did It Actually Exist in Ancient Israel?" Pages 2–21 in *Biblical and Near Eastern Essays: Studies in Honour of Kevin J. Cathcart.* Edited by Carmel McCarthy and John F. Healey. London: T&T Clark, 2004.

Day, Peggy L. "From the Child Is Born the Woman: The Story of Jephthah's Daughter." Pages 109–24 in *Gender and Difference in Ancient Israel.* Edited by Peggy L. Day. Minneapolis: Fortress, 1989.

Deflem, Mathieu. "Ritual, Anti-Structure, and Religion: A Discussion of Victor Turner's Processual Symbolic Analysis." *Journal for the Scientific Study of Religion* 30 (1991): 1–25.

Dempster, Stephen G. "Mythology and History in the Song of Deborah." *WTJ* 41 (1978): 33–53.

Demsky, Aaron. "Geba, Gibeah, and Gibeon: An Historico-Geographic Riddle." *BASOR* 212 (1973): 26–31.

de Pury, Albert. See Pury, Albert de.

de Vaux, Roland. See Vaux, Roland de.

Dever, William G. "Asherah, Consort of Yahweh? New Evidence from Kuntillet 'Ajrûd." *BASOR* 255 (1984): 21–37.

———. *Did God Have a Wife? Archaeology and Folk Religion in Ancient Israel.* Grand Rapids: Eerdmans, 2005.

———. "Folk Religion in Ancient Israel: The Disconnect Between Text and Artifact." Pages 425–39 in *Berührungspunkte Studien zur Sozial- und Religionsgeschichte Israels und seiner Umwelt. Festschrift für Rainer Albertz zu seinem 65. Geburtstag.* Edited by Ruth Ebach, with Ingo Kottsieper, Rüdiger Schmitt, and Jakob Wöhrle. AOAT 350. Münster: Ugarit-Verlag, 2008.

———. *The Lives of Ordinary People in Ancient Israel: Where Archaeology and the Bible Intersect.* Grand Rapids: Eerdmans, 2012.

———. *Recent Archaeological Discoveries and Biblical Research.* Seattle: University of Washington Press, 1990.

———. "A Temple Built for Two: Did Yahweh Share a Throne with His Consort Asherah?" *BAR* 34/2 (March/April 2008): 54–62, 85.

———. "Were There Temples in Ancient Israel? The Archaeological Evidence." Pages 300–16 in *Text, Artifact, and Image: Revealing Ancient Israelite Religion.* Edited by Gary M. Beckman and Theodore J. Lewis. BJS 346. Providence: Brown Judaic Studies, 2006.

———. "What Did the Biblical Writers Know, and When Did They Know It?" Pages 241–57 in *Hesed ve-Emet: Studies in Honor of Ernest S. Frerichs.* Edited by Jodi Magness and Seymour Gitin. BJS 320. Atlanta: Scholars Press, 1998.

———. *Who Were the Early Israelites and Where Did They Come From?* Grand Rapids: Eerdmans, 2003.

Dietler, Michael. "Feasts and Commensal Politics in the Political Economy: Food, Power, and Status in Prehistoric Europe." Pages 87–125 in *Food and the Status Quest: An Interdisciplinary Perspective.* Edited by Polly Wiessner and Wulf Schiefenhövel. Providence: Berghahn, 1996.

Dietrich, Manfried, and Oswald Loretz. *Mantik in Ugarit: Keilalphabetische Texte der Opferschau, Omensammlungen, Nekromantie.* Anhandlungen zur Literatur Alt-Syren-Palästinas und Mesopotamiens 3. Münster: Ugarit-Verlag, 1990.

———. *Studien zu den ugaritischen Texten* 1. Münster: Ugarit-Verlag, 2000.

Dietrich, Walter. "Doch ein Text hinter den Texten? Vorläufige textkritische Einsichten eines Samuel-Kommentators." Pages 133–60 in *Archaeology of the Books of Samuel: The Entangling of the Textual and Literary History.* Leiden: Brill, 2010.

Dijk-Hemmes, Fokkelien van. "Traces of Women's Texts in the Hebrew Bible." Pages 43–48 in Athalya Brenner and Fokkelien van Dijk-Hemmes, *On Gendering Texts: Female and Male Voices in the Hebrew Bible.* Leiden: Brill, 1993.

Dijkstra, Meindert. "Goddess, Gods, Men, and Women." Pages 83–114 in *On Reading Prophetic Texts: Gender-Specific and Related Studies in Memory of Fokkelien van*

Dijk-Hemmes. Edited by Bob Becking and Meindert Dijkstra. Leiden: Brill, 1996.

———. "Women and Religion in the Old Testament." Pages 164–88 in Bob Becking, Meindert Dijkstra, Marjo Korpel, and Karel Vriezen, *Only One God? Monotheism in Ancient Israel and the Veneration of the Goddess Asherah*. The Biblical Seminar 77. London: Sheffield Academic, 2001.

Dillmann, August. *Exodus und Leviticus*. Kurzgefasstes exegetische Handbuch. Leipzig: S. Hirzel, 1880.

———. *Die Genesis*. 6th ed. Leipzig: S. Hirzel, 1892.

Dillon, Matthew. *Girls and Women in Classical Greek Religion*. London: Routledge, 2002.

Dohmen, C. "*massēkâ*." Pages 431–37 in *TDOT* 8.

Dolansky, Shawna. *Now You See It, Now You Don't: Biblical Perspectives on the Relationship Between Religion and Magic*. Winona Lake, Ind.: Eisenbrauns, 2008.

———. See also Friedman, Richard Elliott.

Dornemann, Rudolph Henry. *The Archaeology of the Transjordan in the Bronze and Iron Ages*. Milwaukee: Milwaukee Public Museum, 1983.

Dorsey, David A. *The Roads and Highways of Ancient Israel*. ASOR Library of Bible and Near Eastern Archaeology. Baltimore: Johns Hopkins University Press, 1991.

Dothan, Trude. *The Philistines and Their Material Culture*. New Haven: Yale University Press, 1982.

Douglas, Mary. *Purity and Danger: An Analysis of the Concepts of Pollution and Taboo*. London: Ark Paperbacks, 1966.

Driver, Samuel R. *Notes on the Hebrew Text and the Topography of the Books of Samuel, with an Introduction on Hebrew Paleography and the Ancient Versions and Facsimiles of Inscriptions and Maps*. 2nd ed. Oxford: Clarendon, 1913.

Droogers, André. "Symbols of Marginality in the Biographies of Religious and Secular Innovators." *Numen* 27 (1980): 105–21.

Durham, John I. *Exodus*. WBC 3. Waco, Tex.: Word, 1987.

Eaton-Krauss, Marianne. "Figure of a Female Drummer." Page 303 in *Ebla to Damascus: Art and Archaeology of Ancient Syria*. Edited by Harvey Weiss. Washington, D.C.: Smithsonian Institution Traveling Exhibition Service, 1985.

Ebeling, Jennie R. *Women's Lives in Biblical Times*. London: T&T Clark, 2010.

Ebeling, Jennie R., and Michael M. Homan. "Baking and Brewing Beer in the Israelite Household: A Study of Women's Cooking Technology." Pages 45–62 in *The World of Women in the Ancient and Classical Near East*. Edited by Beth Alpert Nakhai. Newcastle upon Tyne: Cambridge Scholars, 2008.

Eberhart, Christian A. "Sacrifice? Holy Smokes! Reflections on Cult Terminology for Understanding Sacrifice in the Hebrew Bible." Pages 17–32 in *Ritual and Metaphor: Sacrifice in the Bible*. RBS 68. Atlanta: Society of Biblical Literature, 2011.

Edelman, Diana. "Cultic Sites and Complexes Beyond the Jerusalem Temple." Pages 82–103 in *Religious Diversity in Ancient Israel and Judah*. Edited by Francesca Stavrakopoulou and John Barton. London: T&T Clark, 2010.

———. "Saul's Journey Through Mt. Ephraim and Samuel's Ramah (1 Sam 9:4–5; 10:2–5)." *ZDPV* 104 (1988): 44–58.

Edwards, I. E. S. "A Relief of Qudshu-Astarte-Anath in the Winchester College Collection." *JNES* 14 (1955): 49–51.

Egoumenidou, Frosso. See London, Gloria A.

Eitan, Avraham. "Antiquities Director Confronts Problems and Controversies (*BAR* Interviews Avraham Eitan)." *BAR* 12/4 (July/August 1986): 30–38.

———. "Vered Yeriho." *Excavations and Surveys in Israel* 2 (1983): 106–7.

Elkins, Stefanie. "Ceramic Architectural Models from the Madaba Plains Region: A Selected Art Historical Analysis." PhD diss., Andrews University, 2019.

———. "A Model Shrine from Tall al-ʿUmayri." Pages 433–46 in *Madaba Plains Project 7: The 2000 Season at Tall al-ʿUmayri and Subsequent Studies.* Edited by Larry G. Herr, Douglas L. Clark, and Lawrence T. Geraty. Winona Lake, Ind.: Eisenbrauns, 2017.

Ellington, John. See Péter-Contesse, René.

Emerton, J. A. "The Biblical High Place in the Light of Recent Study." *PEQ* 129 (1997): 116–32.

Esse, Douglas L. "The Collared Pithos at Megiddo: Ceramic Distribution and Ethnicity." *JNES* 51 (1992): 81–103.

Everhart, Janet S. "Serving Women and Their Mirrors: A Feminist Reading of Exodus 38:8b." *CBQ* 66 (2004): 44–54.

Exum, J. Cheryl. "The Centre Cannot Hold: Thematic and Textual Instabilities in Judges." *CBQ* 52 (1990): 410–31.

———. "Feminist Criticism: Whose Interests Are Being Served?" Pages 65–89 in *Judges and Method: New Approaches in Biblical Studies.* 2nd ed. Edited by Gale A. Yee. Minneapolis: Fortress, 2007.

———. *Fragmented Women: Feminist (Sub)versions of Biblical Narratives.* Valley Forge, Pa.: Trinity Press International, 1993.

———. "Promise and Fulfillment: Narrative Art in Judges 13." *JBL* 99 (1980): 43–59.

———. "Second Thoughts About Secondary Characters: Women in Exodus 1.8–2.10." Pages 75–87 in *A Feminist Companion to Exodus to Deuteronomy.* Edited by Athalya Brenner. FCB 6. Sheffield: Sheffield Academic, 1994.

———. *Tragedy and Biblical Narrative: Arrows of the Almighty.* Cambridge: Cambridge University Press, 1992.

———. "'You Shall Let Every Daughter Live': A Study of Exodus 1:8–2:10." Pages 63–82 in *The Bible and Feminist Hermeneutics* (= *Semeia* 28). Edited by Mary Ann Tolbert, 1983.

Falkenstein, Adam. *Sumerische und akkadische Hymnen und Gebete.* Die Bibliothek der alten Welt: Der alte Orient. Zurich: Artemis, 1953.

Faraone, C. A., B. Garnand, and C. López-Ruiz. "Micah's Mother (Judg. 17:1 4) and a Curse from Carthage (*KAI* 89): Canaanite Precedents for Greek and Latin Curses Against Thieves?" *JNES* 64 (2005): 161–86.

Farber, Zev I. "Israelite Festivals: From Cyclical Time Celebrations to Linear Time Commemorations." *Religions* 10 (2019): 1–19.

———. "Religion in Eighth-Century Judah: An Overview." Pages 431–53 in *Archaeology and History of Eighth-Century Judah.* Edited by Zev I. Farber and Jacob L. Wright. ANEM 23. Atlanta: SBL Press, 2018.

———. See also Leuchter, Mark.

Faust, Avraham. "Burnished Pottery and Gender Hierarchy in Iron Age Israelite Society." *Journal of Mediterranean Archaeology* 15 (2002): 53–73.

———. "Differences in Family Structure Between Cities and Villages in Iron Age II." *TA* 26 (1999): 233–52.

———. "Israelite Temples: Where Was Israelite Cult Not Practiced, and Why." *Religions* 10 (2019): 1–26.

———. "The Rural Community in Ancient Israel During the Iron Age II." *BASOR* 317 (2000): 17–39.

Faust, Avraham, and Shlomo Bunimovitz. "The Four Room House: Embodying Iron Age Israelite Society." *NEA* 66 (2003): 22–31.

Fidler, Ruth. "A Wife's Vow—The Husband's Woe? The Case of Hannah and Elkanah (1 Samuel 1, 21–23)." *ZAW* 118 (2006): 374–88.

Fincke, Andrew. *The Samuel Scroll from Qumran: 4QSam[a] Restored and Compared to the Septuagint and 4QSam[c].* Studies on the Texts of the Desert of Judah 43. Leiden: Brill, 2001.

Finkel, Irving L. "The Crescent Fertile." *AfO* 27 (1980): 37–52.

———. "The Dream of Kurigalzu and the Tablet of Sins." *Anatolian Studies* 33 (1983): 75–80.

———. "Necromancy in Ancient Mesopotamia." *AfO* 29–30 (1983–1984): 1–17.

Finkelstein, Israel. *The Archaeology of the Israelite Settlement.* Jerusalem: Israel Exploration Society, 1988.

———. "The Archaeology of the United Monarchy: An Alternative View." *Levant* 28 (1996): 177–87.

———. "The History and Archaeology of Shiloh from the Middle Bronze Age II to Iron Age II." Pages 371–89 in Israel Finkelstein, Shlomo Bunimovitz, and Zvi Lederman, *Shiloh: The Archaeology of a Biblical Site.* Edited by Israel Finkelstein. Tel Aviv: Monograph Series of Tel Aviv University, 1993.

———. "Iron I Shiloh: Twenty Years Later." Pages 142–52 in *Historie og konstruktion: Festskrift til Niels Peter Lemche i anledning af 60 års fødselsdagen den 6. september 2005.* Edited by Mogens Müller and Thomas L. Thompson. Forum for Bibelsk Eksegese 14. Copenhagen: Københavns Universitet, Museum Tusculanums Forlag, 2005.

———. "Seilun, Khirbet." Pages 1069–72 in *ABD* 5.

———. See also Kleiman, Assaf.

Finkelstein, J. J. "The Genealogy of the Hammurapi Dynasty." *Journal of Cuneiform Studies* 20 (1966): 95–118.

Fischer, Irmtraud. *Gotteskünderinnen: zu einer geschlechterfairen Deutung des Phänomens der Prophetie und der Prophetinnen in der Hebräischen Bibel.* Stuttgart: Kohlhammer, 2002.

Fisher, Eugene J. "Cultic Prostitution in the Ancient Near East? A Reassessment." *Biblical Theology Bulletin* 5 (1976): 225–36.

Fleming, Daniel E. "A Break in the Line: Reconsidering the Bible's Diverse Festival Calendars." *RB* 106 (1999): 161–74.

———. "The Etymological Origins of the Hebrew *nābî'*: The One Who Invokes God." *CBQ* 55 (1993): 217–24.

———. "The Israelite Festival Calendar and Emar's Ritual Archive." *RB* 106 (1999): 8–34.

———. *The Legacy of Israel in Judah's Bible: History, Politics, and the Reinscribing of Tradition.* Cambridge: Cambridge University Press, 2012.

———. "Prophets and Temple Personnel in the Mari Archives." Pages 44–64 in *The Priests in the Prophets: The Portrayal of Priests, Prophets, and Other Religious Specialists in the Latter Prophets.* Edited by Lester L. Grabbe and Alice Ogden Bellis. LHBOTS 408. London: T&T Clark, 2004.

Fohrer, Georg. *Geschichte der israelitischen Religion.* Berlin: de Gruyter, 1969.

Fokkelman, J. P. *Narrative Art and Poetry in the Books of Samuel: A Full Interpretation Based on Stylistic and Structural Analyses.* 4: *Vow and Desire (I Sam. 1–12).* Studia semitica neerlandica. Assen: Van Gorcum, 1993.

Foster, Benjamin R. *Before the Muses: An Anthology of Akkadian Literature* 1–2. Bethesda, Md.: CDL, 1996.

Fowler, Mervyn D. "The Meaning of *lipnê* YHWH in the Old Testament." *ZAW* 99 (1987): 384–90.

Fox, Michael V. *Proverbs 10–31: A New Translation with Introduction and Commentary.* AYB 18B. New Haven: Yale University Press, 2009.

Freedman, David Noel. See Cross, Frank Moore.

Fretheim, Terence E. *Exodus.* Interpretation. Louisville: John Knox, 1991.

Frevel, Christian. *Aschera und der Ausschliesslichkeitsanspruch YHWHs: Beiträge zu literarischen, religionsgeschichtlichen und ikonographischen Aspekten der Ascheradiskussion* 2. Bonner biblische Beiträge 94/2. Weinheim: Beltz Athenäum, 1995.

———. "Gifts to the Gods? Votives as Communication Markers in Sanctuaries and Other Places in the Bronze and Iron Ages in Palestine/Israel." Pages 25–48 in *"From Ebla to Stellenbosch": Syro-Palestinian Religions and the Hebrew Bible.* Edited by Izak Cornelius and Louis Jonker. ADPV 37. Wiesbaden: Harrassowitz, 2008.

Friedman, Richard Elliott. *The Exile and Biblical Narrative: The Formation of the Deuteronomistic and Priestly Works.* HSM 22. Chico, Calif.: Scholars Press, 1981.

———. *Who Wrote the Bible?* New York: Summit, 1987.

Friedman, Richard Elliott, and Shawna Dolansky Overton. "Death and Afterlife: The Biblical Silence." Pages 35–60 in *Judaism in Late Antiquity. 4: Death, Life-*

After-Death, Resurrection and the World-to-Come in the Judaisms of Antiquity. Edited by Alan J. Avery-Peck and Jacob Neusner. Handbuch des Orientalistik 1, Erste Abteilung: Nahe und Mittlere Osten 55. Leiden: Brill, 2000.

Fritschel, Ann. "Gender and Magic in the Hebrew Bible: Sex, Lies, and Amorphous Shapes." Paper presented at the annual meeting of the European Association of Biblical Studies, Pázmány Péter Catholic University, Piliscaba, and Károly Gáspar Reformed University, Budapest, August 2006.

———. "Women and Magic in the Hebrew Bible." PhD diss., Emory University, 2003.

Frymer-Kensky, Tikva. *In the Wake of the Goddesses: Women, Culture, and the Biblical Transformation of Pagan Myth*. New York: Free Press, 1992.

———. "Pollution, Purification, and Purgation in Biblical Israel." Pages 399–414 in *The Word of the Lord Shall Go Forth. Essays in Honor of David Noel Freedman in Celebration of His Sixtieth Birthday*. Edited by Carol L. Meyers and Michael O'Connor. Winona Lake, Ind.: Eisenbrauns, 1983.

Fuhs, H. F. *'ālâ*. Pages 76–95 in *TDOT* 11.

———. "*šā'al*." Pages 249–64 in *TDOT* 14.

Gafney, Wilda C. *Daughters of Miriam: Women Prophets in Ancient Israel*. Minneapolis: Fortress, 2008.

Ganor, Saar, and Igor Kreimerman. "An Eighth-Century B.C.E. Gate Shrine at Tel Lachish." *BASOR* 381 (2019): 211–36.

Garfinkel, Yosef, Saar Ganor, and Michael G. Hasel. *In the Footsteps of King David*. London: Thames & Hudson, 2018.

Garfinkel, Yosef, and Michael G. Hasel. "The Sanctuary Buildings." Pages 15–53 in Yosef Garfinkel, Saar Ganor, and Michael G. Hasel, *Khirbet Qeiyafa Vol. 4. Excavation Report 2007–2013: Art, Cult, and Epigraphy*. Edited by Martin G. Klingbeil. Jerusalem: Israel Exploration Society, 2018.

Garfinkel, Yosef, Igor Kreimerman, and Peter Zilberg. *Debating Khirbet Qeiyafa: A Fortified City in Judah from the Time of King David*. Jerusalem: Israel Exploration Society; Hebrew University of Jerusalem, 2015.

Garfinkel, Yosef, and Madeleine Mumcuoglu. *Crossing the Threshold: Architecture, Iconography, and the Sacred Entrance*. Oxford: Oxbow, 2018.

———. "An Elaborate Clay Portable Shrine." Pages 83–100 in Yosef Garfinkel, Saar Ganor, and Michael G. Hasel, *Khirbet Qeiyafa Vol. 4. Excavation Report 2007–2013: Art, Cult, and Epigraphy*. Edited by Martin G. Klingbeil. Jerusalem: Israel Exploration Society, 2018.

———. "A Limestone Portable Shrine." Pages 101–26 in Yosef Garfinkel, Saar Ganor, and Michael G. Hasel, *Khirbet Qeiyafa Vol. 4. Excavation Report 2007–2013: Art, Cult, and Epigraphy*. Edited by Martin G. Klingbeil. Jerusalem: Israel Exploration Society, 2018.

———. "A Shrine Model from Tel Rekhesh." *STRATA: Bulletin of the Anglo-Israel Archaeological Society* 33 (2015): 77–87.

Garnand, Brien K., Lawrence E. Stager, and Joseph A. Greene. "Infants as Offerings: Palaeodemographic Patterns and Tophet Burials." *Studi Epigrafici e Linguistici* 29–30 (2012–2013): 193–222.

———. See also Faraone, C. A.

Garr, W. Randall. *The Dialect Geography of Syria-Palestine, 1000–586 B.C.E.* Philadelphia: University of Pennsylvania Press, 1985.

Gennep, Arnold van. *Les rites de passage.* Paris: E. Nourry, 1909. Translated by Monika B. Vizedom and Gabrielle L. Caffee as *The Rites of Passage.* Chicago: University of Chicago Press, 1960; 2nd ed. 2019.

Gerstenberger, Erhard S. "Healing Rituals at the Intersection of Family and Society." Pages 165–81 in *Family and Household Religion—Toward a Synthesis of Old Testament Studies, Archaeology, Epigraphy, and Cultural Studies.* Edited by Rainer Albertz, Beth Alpert Nakhai, Saul M. Olyan, and Rüdiger Schmitt. Winona Lake, Ind.: Eisenbrauns, 2014.

———. *Theologies in the Old Testament.* London: T&T Clark, 2002.

Gertz, Jan Christian, Angelika Berlejung, Konrad Schmid, and Markus Witte. *T&T Clark Handbook of the Old Testament.* London: T&T Clark, 2012.

Gesundheit (Bar-On), Shimon. "Der deuteronomische Festkalendar." Pages 57–68 in *Das Deuteronomium.* Edited by Georg Braulik. Österreichische biblische Studien 23. Frankfurt am Main: Peter Lang, 2003.

———. "The Festival Calendars in Exodus XXIII 14–19 and XXXIV 18–26." *VT* 48 (1998): 161–93.

———. *Three Times a Year: Studies on Festival Legislation in the Pentateuch.* FAT 82. Tübingen: Mohr Siebeck, 2012.

Glasson, T. Francis. "The 'Passover,' a Misnomer: The Meaning of the Verb *pasach.*" *Journal of Theological Studies* 10 (1959): 79–84.

Gleis, Matthias. *Die Bamah.* BZAW 251. Berlin: de Gruyter, 1997.

Goldstein, Bernard R. See Cooper, Alan M.

Gordon, R. P. "Aleph Apologeticum." *JQR* 69 (1978–1979): 112–16.

Görg, Manfred. "Der Spiegeldienst der Frauern." *BN* 23 (1984): 9–13.

Gottwald, Norman K. *The Tribes of Yahweh: A Sociology of the Religion of Liberated Israel, 1250–1050 B.C.E.* 2nd ed. Maryknoll, N.Y.: Orbis Books, 1981.

Gould, John. "Law, Custom, and Myth: Aspects of the Social Position of Women in Classical Athens." *Journal of Hellenic Studies* 100 (1980): 38–59.

Grabbe, Lester L. *Ancient Israel: What Do We Know and How Do We Know It?* London: T&T Clark, 2007.

Graf, Fritz. "How to Cope with a Difficult Life: A View of Ancient Magic." Pages 93–114 in *Envisioning Magic: A Princeton Seminar and Symposium.* Edited by Peter Schäfer and Hans G. Kippenberg. Studies in the History of Religions 85. Leiden: Brill, 1997.

Graffy, Adrian. "The Literary Genre of Isaiah 5, 1–7." *Biblica* 60 (1979): 400–409.

Granqvist, Hilma. *Child Problems Among the Arabs.* Helsinki: Söderström, 1950.

Greenberg, Moshe. *Ezekiel 1–20: A New Translation with Introduction and Commentary.* AYB 22. Garden City, N.Y.: Doubleday, 1983.
Greene, Joseph A. See Garnand, Brien K.
Greenfield, Jonas C. "Some Glosses on the Keret Epic." *ErIsr* 9 (1969): 60–65.
Greenstein, Edward L. "Kirta." Pages 9–48 in *Ugaritic Narrative Poetry.* Edited by Simon B. Parker. SBLWAW 9. Atlanta: Scholars Press, 1997.
———. "Recovering 'The Women Who Served at the Entrance.'" Pages 165–73 in *Studies in Historical Geography and Biblical Historiography: Presented to Zechariah Kallai.* Edited by Gershon Galil and Moshe Weinfeld. VTSup 81. Leiden: Brill, 2000.
Greer, Jonathan S. *Dinner at Dan: Biblical and Archaeological Evidence for Sacred Feasts at Iron Age II Tel Dan and Their Significance.* CHANE 66. Leiden: Brill, 2013.
———. "An Israelite *Mizrāq* at Tel Dan?" *BASOR* 358 (2010): 27–45.
Grimes, Ronald L. "Portals." Pages 7333–35 in *ER* 11.
Grossman, Susan. "Women and the Jerusalem Temple." Pages 15–37 in *Daughters of the King. Women and the Synagogue: A Survey of History, Halakhah, and Contemporary Realities.* Edited by Susan Grossman and Rivka Haut. Philadelphia: Jewish Publication Society, 1992.
Gruber, Mayer I. *Aspects of Nonverbal Communication in the Ancient Near East.* Studia Pohl: Dissertationes Scientificae de Rebus Orientis Antiqui 12/1. Rome: Biblical Institute Press, 1980.
———. "Breast-Feeding Practices in Biblical Israel and in Old Babylonian Mesopotamia." Pages 69–107 in *The Motherhood of God and Other Studies.* South Florida Studies in the History of Judaism 57. Atlanta: Scholars Press, 1992.
———. "Hebrew *qĕdēšāh* and Her Canaanite and Akkadian Cognates." Pages 17–47 in *The Motherhood of God and Other Studies.* South Florida Studies in the History of Judaism 57. Atlanta: Scholars Press, 1992.
———. "Private Life in Canaan and Ancient Israel." Pages 633–48 in *CANE* 1–2.
———. "Prostitute and Prostitution in the Biblical World." *Zemanim* 90 (2005): 20–29 (Hebrew).
———. "The *qadesh* in the Book of Kings and in Other Sources." *Tarbiz* 52 (1983): 167–76 (Hebrew).
———. "Review of Stephanie Lynn Budin, *The Myth of Sacred Prostitution in Antiquity.*" *Review of Biblical Literature* [http://www.bookreviews.org] (2009).
———. "Women in the Cult According to the Priestly Code." Pages 49–68 in *The Motherhood of God and Other Studies.* South Florida Studies in the History of Judaism 57. Atlanta: Scholars Press, 1992.
Gunn, David M. *The Fate of King Saul: An Interpretation of a Biblical Story.* JSOTSup 14. Sheffield: JSOT Press, 1980.
———. "The 'Hardening of Pharaoh's Heart': Plot, Character and Theology in Exodus 1–14." Pages 72–96 in *Art and Meaning: Rhetoric in Biblical Literature.*

Edited by David J. A. Clines, David M. Gunn, and Alan J. Hauser. JSOTSup 19. Sheffield: JSOT Press, 1982.

———. *Judges.* Blackwell Bible Commentaries. Oxford: Blackwell, 2005.

———. "Samson of Sorrows: An Isaianic Gloss on Judges 13–16." Pages 225–53 in *Reading Between Texts: Intertextuality and the Hebrew Bible.* Edited by Danna Nolan Fewell. Louisville: Westminster/John Knox, 1992.

Gursky, Marjorie D. "Reproductive Rituals in Biblical Israel." PhD diss., New York University, 2001.

Güterbock, Hans Gustav. "Die historische Tradition und ihre literarische Gestaltung bei Babyloniern und Hethitern bis 1200." *ZA* 44 (N.F. 10; 1938): 49–65.

Haag, E. "*šābat.*" Pages 381–86 in *TDOT* 14.

———. "*šabbāt.*" Pages 387–97 in *TDOT* 14.

Hackett, Jo Ann. "In the Days of Jael: Reclaiming the History of Women in Ancient Israel." Pages 15–38 in *Immaculate and Powerful: The Female in Sacred Image and Social Reality.* Edited by Clarissa W. Atkinson, Constance H. Buchanan, and Margaret R. Miles. Boston: Beacon, 1985.

———. "Women's Studies and the Hebrew Bible." Pages 141–64 in *The Future of Biblical Studies: The Hebrew Scriptures.* Edited by Richard Elliott Friedman and H. G. M. Williamson. Atlanta: Scholars Press, 1987.

Hadley, Judith M. *The Cult of Asherah in Ancient Israel and Judah: Evidence for a Hebrew Goddess.* Cambridge: Cambridge University Press, 2000.

Hague, Rebecca. "Marriage Athenian Style." *Archaeology* 41/3 (June 1988): 32–36.

Haldar, Alfred. *The Notion of the Desert in Sumero-Accadian and West-Semitic Religions.* Uppsala universitets årsskrift 1950: 3. Uppsala: Almqvist & Wiksell, 1950.

Halperin, David M. *One Hundred Years of Homosexuality.* New York: Routledge, 1990.

Halpern, Baruch. *David's Secret Demons: Messiah, Murderer, Traitor, King.* Grand Rapids: Eerdmans, 2001.

———. *The First Historians: The Hebrew Bible and History.* San Francisco: Harper & Row, 1988.

———. "Jerusalem and the Lineages in the Seventh Century BCE: Kinship and the Rise of Individual Moral Liability." Pages 11–107 in *Law and Ideology in Monarchic Israel.* Edited by Baruch Halpern and Deborah W. Hobson. JSOTSup 124. Sheffield: Sheffield Academic, 1991.

———. "The Resourceful Israelite Historian: The Song of Deborah and Israelite Historiography." *HTR* 76 (1983): 379–401.

———. "Sybil, or the Two Nations? Archaism, Alienation, and the Elite Redefinition of Traditional Culture in Judah in the 8th–7th Centuries B.C.E." Pages 291–338 in *The Study of the Ancient Near East in the Twenty-First Century: The William Foxwell Albright Centennial Conference.* Edited by Jerrold S. Cooper and Glenn M. Schwartz. Winona Lake, Ind.: Eisenbrauns, 1996.

———. "Why Manasseh Is Blamed for the Babylonian Exile: The Evolution of a Biblical Tradition." *VT* 48 (1998): 473–514.

Hamori, Esther J. "Childless Female Diviners in the Bible and Beyond." Pages 169–91 in *Prophets Male and Female: Gender and Prophecy in the Hebrew Bible, the Eastern Mediterranean, and the Ancient Near East.* Edited by Jonathan Stökl and Corrine L. Carvalho. Ancient Israel and Its Literature 15. Atlanta: Society of Biblical Literature, 2013.

———. "The Prophet and the Necromancer: Women's Divination for Kings." *JBL* 132 (2013): 827–43.

———. *Women's Divination in Biblical Literature: Prophecy, Necromancy, and Other Arts of Knowledge.* AYBRL. New Haven: Yale University Press, 2015.

Haran, Menahem. "Behind the Scenes of History: Determining the Date of the Priestly Source." *JBL* 100 (1981): 321–33.

———. "The Complex of Ritual Acts Performed Inside the Tabernacle." Pages 272–302 in *Studies in the Bible.* Edited by Chaim Rabin. Scripta hierosolymitana 8. Jerusalem: Magnes, 1961.

———. "Ezekiel, P, and the Priestly School." *VT* 58 (2008): 211–18.

———. "The Nature of the 'Ohel Mo'edh' in Pentateuchal Sources." *Journal of Semitic Studies* 5 (1960): 50–65.

———. "The Passover Sacrifice." Pages 86–116 in *Studies in the Religion of Ancient Israel.* VTSup 23. Leiden: Brill, 1972.

———. "The Priestly Image of the Tabernacle." *HUCA* 36 (1965): 191–226.

———. "Shiloh and Jerusalem: The Origin of the Priestly Tradition in the Pentateuch." *JBL* 81 (1962): 14–24.

———. *Temples and Temple-Service in Ancient Israel: An Inquiry into the Character of Cult Phenomena and the Historical Setting of the Priestly School.* Oxford: Clarendon, 1978.

———. "Zeḇaḥ Hayyamîm." *VT* 19 (1969): 11–22.

Hardin, James W. "Household Archaeology from the Southern Levant: An Example from Iron Age Tell Halif." Pages 519–56 in *New Perspectives on Household Archaeology.* Edited by Bradley J. Parker and Catherine P. Foster. Winona Lake, Ind.: Eisenbrauns, 2012.

———. *Lahav II: Households and the Use of Domestic Space at Iron II Tell Halif: An Archaeology of Destruction.* Winona Lake, Ind.: Eisenbrauns, 2010.

———. "Understanding Domestic Space: An Example from Iron Age Tel Halif." *NEA* 67 (2004): 71–83.

Harrison, Timothy P. "Recent Discoveries at Tayinat (Ancient Kunulua/Calno) and Their Biblical Implications." Pages 396–425 in *Congress Volume: Munich 2013.* Edited by Christl M. Maier. Leiden: Brill, 2014.

Hartley, John E. *Leviticus.* WBC 4. Dallas: Word, 1992.

Harvey, John E. "*Tendenz* and Textual Criticism in 1 Samuel 2–10." *JSOT* 96 (2001): 71–81.

Hasel, Gerhard F. "'New Moon and Sabbath' in Eighth Century Israelite Prophetic Writings (Isa 1:13; Hos 2:13; Amos 8:5)." Pages 37–64 in *"Wünschet Jerusalem Frieden": Collected Communications to the XIIth Congress of the International Organization for the Study of the Old Testament, Jerusalem, 1986.* Edited by Matthias Augustin and Klaus-Dietrich Schunk. Beiträge zur Erforschung des Alten Testaments und des antiken Judentum 13. Frankfort am Main: Peter Lang, 1988.

———. "The Sabbath in the Pentateuch." Pages 21–43 in *The Sabbath in Scripture and History.* Edited by Kenneth A. Strand. Washington, D.C.: Review and Herald Publishing Association, 1982.

Hasel, Gerhard F., and W. G. C. Murdoch. "The Sabbath in the Prophetic and Historical Literature of the Old Testament." Pages 44–56 in *The Sabbath in Scripture and History.* Edited by Kenneth A. Strand. Washington, D.C.: Review and Herald Publishing Association, 1982.

Hasel, Michael G. See Garfinkel, Yosef.

Hendel, Ronald S. "The Exodus in Biblical Memory." *JBL* 120 (2001): 601–22.

———. "Prophets, Priests, and the Efficacy of Ritual." Pages 185–98 in *Pomegranates and Golden Bells: Studies in Biblical, Jewish, and Near Eastern Ritual, Law, and Literature in Honor of Jacob Milgrom.* Edited by David P. Wright, David Noel Freedman, and Avi Hurvitz. Winona Lake, Ind.: Eisenbrauns, 1995.

———. "Revisions to 'The Patriarchal Age: Abraham, Isaac, and Jacob.'" Pages 1–31 in *Ancient Israel: From Abraham to the Roman Destruction of the Temple.* Rev. and expanded ed. Edited by Hershel Shanks. Englewood Cliffs, N.J.: Prentice-Hall; Washington, D.C.: Biblical Archaeology Society, 1999.

———. "Sacrifice as a Cultural System: The Ritual Symbolism of Exodus 24, 3–8." *ZAW* 101 (1989): 366–90.

Hendel, Ronald S., and Jan Joosten. *How Old Is the Hebrew Bible? A Linguistic, Textual, and Historical Study.* AYBRL. New Haven: Yale University Press, 2018.

Henderson, John. See Beard, Mary.

Henshaw, Richard A. *Female and Male: The Cultic Personnel: The Bible and the Rest of the Ancient Near East.* Allison Park, Pa.: Pickwick Publications, 1994.

Herr, Larry G. "The Late Iron Age I Ceramic Assemblage from Tall al-'Umayri." Pages 135–45 in *"Up to the Gates of Ekron": Essays on the Archaeology and History of the Eastern Mediterranean in Honor of Seymour Gitin.* Edited by Sidnie White Crawford, with Amnon Ben-Tor et al. Jerusalem: W. F. Albright Institute of Archaeological Research and the Israel Exploration Society, 2007.

Herrmann, Christian. *Ägyptische Amulette aus Palästina/Israel* IV: *Von der Spätbronzezeit IIB bis in römische Zeit.* OBO Series Archaeologica 38. Fribourg: Academic Press; Göttingen: Vandenhoeck & Ruprecht, 2016.

Hertzberg, Hans Wilhelm. *I and II Samuel: A Commentary.* OTL. Philadelphia: Westminster, 1964.

Herzog, Elizabeth. See Zborowski, Mark.

Herzog, Ze'ev. "Arad: Iron Age Period." Pages 174–76 in *OEANE* 1.

———. "Beersheba." Pages 287–91 in *OEANE* 1.

———. "The Date of the Temple at Arad: Reassessment of the Stratigraphy and the Implications for the History of Religion in Judah." Pages 156–78 in *Studies in the Archaeology of the Iron Age in Israel and Jordan.* Edited by Amihai Mazar. JSOTSup 331. Sheffield: Sheffield Academic, 2001.

———. "The Fortress Mound at Arad: An Interim Report." *TA* 29 (2002): 3–109.

———. "Israelite Sanctuaries at Arad and Beer-Sheba." Pages 120–22 in *Temples and High Places in Biblical Times: Proceedings of the Colloquium in Honor of the Centennial of Hebrew Union College-Jewish Institute of Religion, Jerusalem, 14–16 March, 1977.* Edited by Avraham Biran. Jerusalem: Nelson Glueck School of Biblical Archaeology of Hebrew Union College-Jewish Institute of Religion, 1981.

———. "Perspectives on Southern Israel's Cult Centralization: Arad and Beer-sheba." Pages 169–99 in *One God—One Cult—One Nation: Archaeological and Biblical Perspectives.* Edited by Reinhard G. Kratz and Hermann Spieckermann. BZAW 405. Berlin: de Gruyter, 2010.

———. "Social, Historical, and Cultural Ramifications." Pages 1452–85 in Ze'ev Herzog and Lily Singer-Avitz, *Beer-Sheba* III: *The Early Iron IIA Enclosed Settlement and the Late Iron IIA–Iron IIB Cities.* Monograph Series of the Sonia and Marco Nadler Institute of Archaeology, Tel Aviv University 34. Tel Aviv: Emery and Claire Yass Publications in Archaeology; Winona Lake, Ind.: Eisenbrauns, 2016.

———. "The Southern Quarter." Pages 242–309 in Ze'ev Herzog and Lily Singer-Avitz, *Beer-Sheba* III: *The Early Iron IIA Enclosed Settlement and the Late Iron IIA–Iron IIB Cities.* Monograph Series of the Sonia and Marco Nadler Institute of Archaeology, Tel Aviv University 34. Tel Aviv: Emery and Claire Yass Publications in Archaeology; Winona Lake, Ind.: Eisenbrauns, 2016.

Herzog, Ze'ev, Miriam Aharoni, Anson F. Rainey, and Shmuel Moshkovitz, "The Israelite Fortress at Arad." *BASOR* 254 (1984): 1–34.

Herzog, Ze'ev, A. F. Rainey, and Sh. Moshkovitz. "The Stratigraphy at Beer-sheba and the Location of the Sanctuary." *BASOR* 225 (1977): 49–58.

Hoffman, C. A. "Fiat Magica." Pages 179–94 in *Magic and Ritual in the Ancient World.* Edited by Paul Mirecki and Marvin Miller. Religions in the Graeco-Roman World 141. Leiden: Brill, 2002.

Hoffman, Lawrence A. *Covenant of Blood: Circumcision and Gender in Rabbinic Judaism.* Chicago Studies in the History of Judaism. Chicago: University of Chicago Press, 1996.

Hoffner, Harry A. "*'ôb.*" Pages 130–34 in *TDOT* 1.

———. "Second Millennium Antecedents to Hebrew *'ôb.*" *JBL* 86 (1967): 385–401.

Holladay, Jr., John S. "House, Israelite." Pages 308–18 in *ABD* 3.

———. "The Kingdoms of Israel and Judah: Political and Economic Centralization in the Iron IIA–B (ca. 1000–750 BCE)." Pages 368–98 in *The Archaeology of*

Society in the Holy Land. Edited by Thomas E. Levy. New York: Facts on File, 1995.

———. "Religion in Israel and Judah Under the Monarchy: An Explicitly Archaeological Approach." Pages 249–99 in *Ancient Israelite Religion: Essays in Honor of Frank Moore Cross.* Edited by Patrick D. Miller, Paul D. Hanson, and S. Dean McBride. Philadelphia: Fortress, 1987.

Holm-Nielsen, Svend. See Buhl, Marie-Louise.

Homan, Michael M. "Beer, Barley, and *šēkār* in the Hebrew Bible." Pages 25–38 in *Le-David Maskil: A Birthday Tribute for David Noel Freedman.* Edited by Richard Elliott Friedman and William H. C. Propp. Winona Lake, Ind.: Eisenbrauns, 2004.

———. *To Your Tents, O Israel! The Terminology, Function, Form, and Symbolism of Tents in the Hebrew Bible and the Ancient Near East.* CHANE 12. Leiden: Brill, 2002.

———. See also Ebeling, Jennie R.

Hopkins, David C. "'All Sorts of Field Work': Agricultural Labor in Ancient Palestine." Pages 149–72 in *To Break Every Yoke: Essays in Honor of Marvin L. Chaney.* Edited by Robert B. Coote and Norman K. Gottwald. SWBA 2/3. Sheffield: Sheffield Phoenix, 2007.

———. "Life on the Land: The Subsistence Struggles of Early Israel." *BA* 50 (1987): 178–91.

Hoppe, Leslie J. "Elders and Deuteronomy: A Proposal." *Église et théologie* 14 (1983): 259–72.

———. "The Levitical Origins of Deuteronomy Reconsidered." *BR* 28 (1983): 27–36.

Houtman, Cees. See Toorn, Karel van der.

Houtman, Cornelis. *Exodus* 3. Historical Commentary on the Old Testament. Leuven: Peeters, 2000.

Huffmon, Herbert B. "A Company of Prophets: Mari, Assyria, and Israel." Pages 47–70 in *Prophecy in Its Ancient Near Eastern Context: Mesopotamian, Biblical, and Arabian Perspectives.* Edited by Martti Nissinen. SBLSymS 13. Atlanta: Society of Biblical Literature, 2000.

Hulse, E. V. "The Nature of Biblical 'Leprosy' and the Use of Alternative Medical Terms in Modern Translations of the Bible." *PEQ* 107 (1975): 87–105.

Hurowitz, Victor. "P—Understanding the Priestly Source." *BRev* 12/3 (June 1996): 30–37, 44–47.

Hurvitz, Avi. *A Linguistic Study of the Relationship Between the Priestly Source and the Book of Ezekiel: A New Approach to an Old Problem.* Cahiers de la Revue biblique 20. Paris: J. Gabalda, 1982.

Hutter, Manfred. "Religionsgeschichtliche Erwägungen zu 'elohîm in 1 Sam 28:13." *BN* 21 (1983): 32–36.

Hutton, Jeremy M. "Levitical Aspirations and Saintly Foundation Stories in Judges 17–18." *ErIsr* 33 (2018): 98–108.

Hyatt, J. Philip. "The Deuteronomic Edition of Jeremiah." Pages 247–67 in *A Prophet to the Nations: Essays in Jeremiah Studies.* Edited by Leo G. Perdue and Brian W. Kovacs. Winona Lake, Ind.: Eisenbrauns, 1984.

Irwin, William H. "'The Smooth Stones of the Wady'? Isaiah 57, 6." *CBQ* 29 (1967): 31–40.

Jacobs, Jonathan. "The Death of David's Son by Bathsheba (II Sam 12:13–25): A Narrative in Context." *VT* 63 (2013): 566–76.

Jacobsen, Thorkild. "Toward the Image of Tammuz." Pages 73–101 in *Toward the Image of Tammuz and Other Essays on Mesopotamian History and Culture.* Edited by William L. Moran. Cambridge, Mass.: Harvard University Press, 1970.

———. *The Treasures of Darkness: A History of Mesopotamian Religion.* New Haven: Yale University Press, 1976.

Jacobson, David M. "The Plan of Herod's Temple." *Bulletin of the Anglo-Israel Archaeological Society* 10 (1990–1991): 36–66.

James, T. G. H. "The Earliest History of Wine and Its Importance in Ancient Egypt." Pages 227–44 in *The Origins and Ancient History of Wine.* Edited by Patrick E. McGovern, Stuart J. Fleming, and Solomon H. Katz. Food and Nutrition in History and Anthropology 11. Luxembourg: Gordon and Breach, 1995.

Janssen, Rosalind M., and Jac. J. Janssen. *Growing Up in Ancient Egypt.* London: Rubicon, 1990.

Janzen, David. "Priestly Sacrifice in the Hebrew Bible: A Summary of Recent Scholarship and a Narrative Reading." *Religion Compass* 2 (2008): 38–52.

Janzen, J. Gerald. "Prayer and/as Self-Address: The Case of Hannah." Pages 113–27 in *A God So Near: Essays on Old Testament Theology in Honor of Patrick D. Miller.* Edited by Brent A. Strawn and Nancy R. Bowen. Winona Lake, Ind.: Eisenbrauns, 2003.

Japhet, Sara. *I and II Chronicles: A Commentary.* OTL. Louisville: Westminster/John Knox, 1993.

Jay, Nancy. "Sacrifice as Remedy for Having Been Born of Woman." Pages 283–309 in *Immaculate and Powerful: The Female in Sacred Image and Social Reality.* Edited by Clarissa W. Atkinson, Constance H. Buchanan, and Margaret R. Miles. Boston: Beacon, 1985.

———. *Throughout Your Generations Forever: Sacrifice, Religion, and Paternity.* Chicago: University of Chicago Press, 1992.

Jeffers, Ann. *Magic and Divination in Ancient Palestine and Syria.* Studies in the History and Culture of the Ancient Near East 8. Leiden: Brill, 1996.

———. "Magic from Before the Dawn of Time: Understanding Magic in the Old Testament: A Shift in Paradigm (Deuteronomy 18:9–14 and Beyond)." Pages 123–32 in *A Kind of Magic: Understanding Magic in the New Testament and Its Religious Environment.* Edited by Michael Labahn and Bert Jan Lietaert Peerbolte. London: T&T Clark, 2007.

———. "'Nor by Dreams, nor by Urim, nor by Prophets': The Story of the Woman at the Pit in 1 Samuel 28." Pages 129–40 in *Seeing with Different Eyes: Essays in*

Astrology and Divination. Edited by Patrick Curry and Angela Voss. Newcastle upon Tyne: Cambridge Scholars, 2007.

Jenks, Alan W. "Eating and Drinking in the Old Testament." Pages 250–54 in *ABD* 2.

———. *The Elohist and North Israelite Traditions.* Missoula, Mont.: Society of Biblical Literature, 1977.

Jensen, Philip Peter. *Graded Holiness: A Key to the Priestly Conception of the World.* JSOTSup 106. Sheffield: Sheffield Academic, 1992.

Jepsen, Alfred. "Die Nebiah in Jes 8:3." *ZAW* 72 (1960): 267–68.

Jobling, David. *1 Samuel.* Berit Olam. Collegeville, Minn.: Liturgical Press, 1998.

———. "A Structural Analysis of Numbers 11–12." Pages 31–65 in *The Sense of Biblical Narrative: Structural Analyses in the Hebrew Bible* 1. 2nd ed. JSOTSup 7. Sheffield: JSOT Press, 1986.

Johnston, Robert H. "The Cypriot Potter." Pages 130–39 in Lawrence E. Stager, Anita Walker, and G. Ernest Wright, *American Expedition to Idalion, Cyprus: First Preliminary Report, Seasons of 1971 and 1972.* Bulletin of the American Schools of Oriental Research: Supplement Series 18. Cambridge, Mass.: American Schools of Oriental Research, 1974.

Johnston, Sarah Iles. "Magic." Pages 139–52 in *Religions of the Ancient World: A Guide.* Edited by Sarah Iles Johnston. Cambridge, Mass.: Harvard University Press, 2004.

Jones, Richard N. See Wright, David P.

Joosten, Jan. See Hendel, Ronald S.

Jost, Renate. "Die Töchter deines Volkes prophezeien." Pages 59–65 in *Für Gerechtigkeit streiten: Theologie im Alltag einer bedrohten Welt.* Edited by Dorothee Sölle. Gütersloh: Chr. Kaiser/Gütersloher, 1994.

Jost, Renate, and Elke Seifert. "Ezekiel: Male Prophecy with Female Imagery." Pages 345–60 in *Feminist Biblical Interpretation: A Compendium of Critical Commentary on the Books of the Bible and Related Literature.* Edited by Luise Schottroff and Marie-Theres Wacker. Grand Rapids: Eerdmans, 2012.

Kaiser, Otto. *Isaiah 1–12: A Commentary.* OTL. London: SCM, 1983.

———. *Isaiah 13–39: A Commentary.* OTL. Philadelphia: Westminster, 1974.

Kallai, Zekharyah. "En-Dor." *ErIsr* 16 (1982): 168–70 (Hebrew).

Kapelrud, A. S. "*'ābîr, 'abbîr.*" Pages 42–44 in *TDOT* 1.

Karageorghis, Vassos. See London, Gloria A.

Katz, Hava. *Portable Shrine Models: Ancient Architectural City Models from the Levant.* BAR International Series 2791. Oxford: British Archaeological Reports, 2016.

Kaufmann, Yehezkel. *The Religion of Israel: From Its Beginnings to the Babylonian Exile.* Translated and abridged by Moshe Greenberg. Chicago: University of Chicago Press, 1960, 1977.

Keefe, Alice A. *Woman's Body and the Social Body in Hosea.* Gender, Culture, and Theory 10. JSOTSup 338. London: Sheffield Academic, 2001.

Keel, Othmar. *Goddesses and Trees, New Moons and Yahweh: Ancient Near Eastern Art and the Hebrew Bible.* JSOTSup 261. Sheffield: Sheffield Academic, 1998.

———. *Symbolism of the Biblical World: Ancient Near Eastern Iconography and the Book of Psalms.* Winona Lake, Ind.: Eisenbrauns, 1997.

Keel, Othmar, and Christoph Uehlinger. *Gods, Goddesses, and Images of God in Ancient Israel.* Minneapolis: Fortress, 1998.

Kellermann, Ulrich. "Erwägungen zum Problem der Esradatierung." *ZAW* 80 (1968): 55–87.

Kempinski, Aharon. *Megiddo: A City-State and Royal Centre in North Israel.* Materialien zur Allgemeinen und Vergleichenden Archäeologie 40. Munich: C. H. Beck, 1989.

Kim, Koowon. *Incubation as a Type-Scene in the 'Aqhatu, Kirta, and Hannah Stories: A Form-Critical and Narratological Study of KTU 1.14 I–1.15 III, 1.17 I–II, and 1 Samuel 1:1–2:11.* VTSup 145. Leiden: Brill, 2011.

King, Philip J., and Lawrence E. Stager. *Life in Biblical Israel.* Library of Ancient Israel. Louisville: Westminster/John Knox, 2001.

Kisilevitz, Shua. "The Iron IIA Judahite Temple at Tel Moza." *TA* 42 (2015): 147–64.

Klawans, Jonathan. "Concepts of Purity in the Bible." Pages 2041–47 in *The Jewish Study Bible.* Edited by Adele Berlin and Marc Zvi Brettler. Oxford: Oxford University Press, 2004.

———. *Impurity and Sin in Ancient Judaism.* Oxford: Oxford University Press, 2000.

Kleiman, Assaf, and Israel Finkelstein. "The Date of Building 338 at Megiddo: *Eppur Si Muove!*" *IEJ* 68 (2018): 50–55.

Klein, Lillian R. "Hannah." Pages 90–91 in *WIS.*

———. *The Triumph of Irony in the Book of Judges.* JSOTSup 68. Bible and Literature Series 14. Sheffield: Almond, 1988.

Klein, Ralph W. *1 Samuel.* WBC 10. Waco, Tex.: Word, 1983.

———. "The Song of Hannah." *Concordia Theological Monthly* 41 (1970): 674–87.

Kletter, Raz. *The Judean Pillar-Figurines and the Archaeology of Asherah.* BAR International Series 636. Oxford: Tempus Reparatum, 1996.

———. "To Cast an Image: Masks from Iron Age Judah and the Biblical *Masekah.*" Pages 189–208 in *"Up to the Gates of Ekron": Essays on the Archaeology and History of the Eastern Mediterranean in Honor of Seymour Gitin.* Edited by Sidnie White Crawford, with Amnon Ben-Tor et al. Jerusalem: W. F. Albright Institute of Archaeological Research and the Israel Exploration Society, 2007.

Klinck, Anne L. *Women's Songs in Ancient Greece.* Montreal: McGill-Queen's University Press, 2008.

Knauf, Ernst Axel. "Saul, David, and the Philistines: From Geography to History." *BN* 109 (2001): 15–18.

Knohl, Israel. "The Priestly Torah Versus the Holiness School: Sabbath and the Festivals." *HUCA* 58 (1987): 65–177.

———. "Psalm 68: Structure, Composition and Geography." *JHS* 12 (2012): 1–21.

———. *The Sanctuary of Silence: The Priestly Torah and the Holiness School.* Minneapolis: Fortress, 1995.

Knoppers, Gary N. "Aaron's Calf and Jeroboam's Calves." Pages 92–104 in *Fortunate the Eyes That See: Essays in Honor of David Noel Freedman in Celebration of His Seventieth Birthday.* Edited by Astrid B. Beck, Andrew H. Bartelt, Paul R. Raabe, and Chris A. Franke. Grand Rapids: Eerdmans, 1995.

Knowles, Melody D. "A Woman at Prayer: A Critical Note on Psalm 131:2b." *JBL* 125 (2006): 385–89.

Köckert, Matthias. "YHWH in the Northern and Southern Kingdom." Pages 357–94 in *One God—One Cult—One Nation: Archaeological and Biblical Perspectives.* Edited by Reinhard G. Kratz and Hermann Spieckermann. BZAW 405. Berlin: de Gruyter, 2010.

Korpel, Marjo C. A. "The Literary Genre of the Song of the Vineyard (Isa. 5:1–7)." Pages 119–55 in *The Structural Analysis of Biblical and Canaanite Poetry.* Edited by Willem van der Meer and Johannes C. de Moor. JSOTSup 74. Sheffield: JSOT Press, 1988.

Kramer, Samuel N. "The Weeping Goddess: Sumerian Prototypes of the *Mater Dolorosa.*" *BA* 46 (1983): 69–80.

Kreimerman, Igor. See Ganor, Saar, and Garfinkel, Yosef.

Krüger, Thomas. *Qoheleth: A Commentary.* Hermeneia. Minneapolis: Fortress, 2004.

Kuemmerlin-McLean, Joanne K. "Divination and Magic in the Religion of Israel: A Study in Perspectives and Methodology." PhD diss., Vanderbilt University, 1986.

———. "Magic (OT)." Pages 468–71 in *ABD* 4.

Kutsch, Ernst. "*miqrāʾ*." *ZAW* 65 (1953): 247–53.

Lalor, Brian. "The Temple Mount of Herod the Great at Jerusalem: Recent Excavations and Literary Sources." Pages 95–116 in *Archaeology and Biblical Interpretation.* Edited by J. R. Bartlett. London: Routledge, 1997.

Lang, B. See Bergman, J.

LaRocca-Pitts, Elizabeth C. *"Of Wood and Stone": The Significance of Israelite Cultic Items in the Bible and Its Early Interpreters.* HSM 61. Winona Lake, Ind.: Eisenbrauns, 2001.

Leach, Edmund. "Anthropological Approaches to the Study of the Bible During the Twentieth Century." Pages 7–32 in Edmund Leach and D. Alan Aycock, *Structuralist Interpretations of Biblical Myth.* Cambridge: Cambridge University Press and Royal Anthropological Institutes of Great Britain and Ireland, 1983.

Lehman, Marjorie. "The Gendered Rhetoric of Sukkah Observance." *JQR* 96 (2006): 309–35.

Lemaire, André. "Le Sabbat à l'époque royale Israélite." *RB* 80 (1973): 162–64.

Lemos, T. M. "Were Israelite Women Chattel?" Pages 227–41 in *Worship, Women, and War: Essays in Honor of Susan Niditch.* Edited by John J. Collins, T. M. Lemos, and Saul M. Olyan. BJS 357. Providence: Brown Judaic Studies, 2015.

———. "Where There Is Dirt, Is There System? Revisiting Biblical Purity Constructions." *JSOT* 37 (2013): 265–94.

Lesko, Leonard H. "Egyptian Wine Production During the New Kingdom." Pages 245–61 in *The Origins and Ancient History of Wine.* Edited by Patrick E. McGovern, Stuart J. Fleming, and Solomon H. Katz. Food and Nutrition in History and Anthropology 11. Luxembourg: Gordon and Breach, 1995.

Leuchter, Mark. "'Now There Was a [Certain] Man': Compositional Chronology in Judges-1 Samuel." *CBQ* 69 (2007): 429–39.

———. "The Reference to Shiloh in Psalm 78." *HUCA* 77 (2006): 1–31.

———. *Samuel and the Shaping of Tradition.* Biblical Refigurations. Oxford: Oxford University Press, 2013.

———. "Something Old, Something Older: Reconsidering 1 Sam. 2:27–36." *JHS* 4 (2002). DOI: 10.5508/jhs.2002.v4.a6.

Leuchter, Mark, and Zev Farber. "Pre-Biblical Aaron, Miriam, and Moses." TheTorah.com (2020). https://thetorah.com/article/pre-biblical-aaron-miriam-and-moses.

Levine, Baruch A. *Leviticus: The Traditional Hebrew Text with the New JPS Translation.* JPS Torah Commentary. Philadelphia: Jewish Publication Society, 1989.

———. *Numbers 1–20: A New Translation with Introduction and Commentary.* AYB 4. New York: Doubleday, 1993.

———. *Numbers 21–36: A New Translation with Introduction and Commentary.* AYB 4A. New York: Doubleday, 2000.

———. "Priests." Pages 687–90 in *The Interpreter's Dictionary of the Bible, Supplementary Volume.* Edited by Keith Crim. Nashville: Abingdon, 1976.

Levinson, Bernard M. *Deuteronomy and the Hermeneutics of Legal Innovation.* Oxford: Oxford University Press, 1997.

———. "Goethe's Analysis of Exodus 34 and Its Influence on Wellhausen: The *Pfropfung* of the Documentary Hypothesis." *ZAW* 114 (2002): 212–23.

Lewis, Theodore J. "The Ancestral Estate (*naḥălat 'ĕlōhîm*) in 2 Samuel 14:16." *JBL* 110 (1991): 597–612.

———. *Cults of the Dead in Ancient Israel and Ugarit.* HSM 39. Atlanta: Scholars Press, 1989.

———. "Dead." Pages 223–31 in *DDD.*

———. "Family, Household, and Local Religion at Late Bronze Age Ugarit." Pages 60–88 in *Household and Family Religion in Antiquity.* Edited by John Bodel and Saul M. Olyan. Oxford: Blackwell, 2008.

———. "Teraphim." Pages 844–50 in *DDD.*

———. See also Toorn, Karel van der.

Lohfink, Norbert. "The Cult Reform of Josiah of Judah: 2 Kings 22–23 as a Source for the History of Israelite Religion." Pages 459–75 in *Ancient Israelite Religion: Essays in Honor of Frank Moore Cross.* Edited by Patrick D. Miller, Paul D. Hanson, and S. Dean McBride. Philadelphia: Fortress, 1987.

London, Gloria A. *Ancient Cookware from the Levant: An Ethnoarchaeological Perspective.* Worlds of the Ancient Near East and Mediterranean. Sheffield: Equinox, 2016.

———. "Cypriot Potters: Past and Present." Pages 319–22 in *Report of the Department of Antiquities, Cyprus, 1987.* Nicosia: Department of Antiquities, Cyprus, 1987.

———. "Fe(male) Potters as the Personification of Individuals, Places, and Things as Known from Ethnoarchaeological Studies." Pages 155–80 in *The World of Women in the Ancient and Classical Near East.* Edited by Beth Alpert Nakhai. Newcastle upon Tyne: Cambridge Scholars, 2008.

London, Gloria A., Frosso Egoumenidou, and Vassos Karageorghis, *Traditional Pottery in Cyprus/Töpferei auf Zypern, damals-heute.* Mainz am Rhein: von Zabern, 1990.

Long, Burke O. "2 Kings III and Genres of Prophetic Narrative." *VT* 23 (1973): 337–48.

Long, Jesse C. "Elisha's Deceptive Prophecy in 2 Kings 3: A Response to Raymond Westbrook." *JBL* 126 (2007): 168–71.

López-Ruiz, C. See Faraone, C. A.

Loretz, Oswald. See Dietrich, Manfried.

Lotz, Wilhelm. *Quaestiones de Historia Sabbati.* Leipzig: J. C. Hinrichs, 1883.

Maccoby, Hyam. "Holiness and Purity: The Holy People in Leviticus and Ezra-Nehemiah." Pages 153–70 in *Reading Leviticus: A Conversation with Mary Douglas.* Edited by John F. A. Sawyer. JSOTSup 227. Sheffield: Sheffield Academic, 1996.

MacDonald, Nathan. *What Did the Ancient Israelites Eat? Diet in Biblical Times.* Grand Rapids: Eerdmans, 2008.

MacRae, George W. "The Meaning and Evolution of the Feast of Tabernacles." *CBQ* 22 (1960): 251–76.

Malamat, Abraham. "King Lists of the Old Babylonian Period and Biblical Genealogies." Pages 163–73 in *Essays in Memory of E. A. Speiser.* Edited by William W. Hallo. American Oriental Series 53. New Haven: American Oriental Society, 1968.

Marcus, David. "The Betrothal of Yarikh and Nikkal-Ib." Pages 215–18 in *Ugaritic Narrative Poetry.* Edited by Simon B. Parker. SBLWAW 9. Atlanta: Scholars Press, 1997.

Markoe, Glenn E. *Phoenician Bronze and Silver Bowls from Cyprus and the Mediterranean.* Classical Studies 26. Berkeley: University of California Press, 1985.

———. "28a Servant Statue: Woman Grinding Grain" and "28b Servant Statue: Woman Straining Mash for Beer." Pages 91–92 in *Mistress of the House, Mistress of Heaven: Women in Ancient Egypt.* Edited by Anne K. Capel and Glenn E. Markoe. New York: Hudson Hills, in conjunction with the Cincinnati Art Museum, 1996.

Marquet-Krause, Judith. *Les fouilles de 'Ay (et-Tell), 1933–35*. Bibliothèque Archéologique et Historique 45. Paris: Geuthner, 1949.

Marsman, Hennie J. *Women in Ugarit and Israel: Their Social and Religious Position in the Context of the Ancient Near East*. OtSt/OTS 49. Leiden: Brill, 2003.

Martin, James D. *The Book of Judges*. CBC. Cambridge: Cambridge University Press, 1975.

Mastin, B. A. "Jonathan at the Feast: A Note on the Text of 1 Samuel xx 25." Pages 113–24 in *Studies in the Historical Books of the Old Testament*. Edited by J. A. Emerton. VTSup 30. Leiden: Brill, 1979.

Matthäus, Hartmut. *Metallgefäße und Gefäßuntersätze der Bronzezeit, der geometrischen und archaischen Periode auf Cypern*. Munich: C. H. Beck'sche, 1985.

Matthews, Victor H. "Entrance Ways and Threshing Floors: Legally Significant Sites in the Ancient Near East." *Fides et historia* 19 (1987): 25–40.

———. "Treading the Winepress: Actual and Metaphorical Viticulture in the Ancient Near East." Pages 19–32 in *Food and Drink in the Biblical World* (= *Semeia* 86). Edited by Athalya Brenner and Jan Willem van Henten, 1999.

Matthews, Victor H., and Don C. Benjamin. *Social World of Ancient Israel: 1250–587 BCE*. Peabody, Mass.: Hendrickson, 1993.

May, Herbert G. "The Ark: A Miniature Temple." *American Journal of Semitic Languages and Literature* 52 (1936): 215–34.

———. *Material Remains of the Megiddo Cult*. Oriental Institute Publications 26. Chicago: University of Chicago Press, 1935.

———. "The Relation of the Passover to the Festival of Unleavened Cakes." *JBL* 55 (1936): 65–82.

Mayes, A. D. H. *Deuteronomy: Based on the Revised Standard Version*. New Century Bible Commentary. Grand Rapids: Eerdmans, 1981.

Mays, James Luther. *Hosea: A Commentary*. OTL. Philadelphia: Westminster, 1969.

Mazar, Amihai. *Archaeology of the Land of the Bible, 10,000–586 B.C.E.* AYBRL. New York: Doubleday, 1990.

———. "Bull Site." Pages 183–84 in *OEANE* 1.

———. "The 'Bull Site'—An Iron Age I Open Cult Place." *BASOR* 247 (1982): 27–42.

———. "Chronology of the Pottery Assemblages from Arad." Pages 89–90 in Amihai Mazar and Ehud Netzer, "On the Israelite Fortress at Arad." *BASOR* 263 (1986): 87–91.

———. *Excavations at Tell Qasile, Part 2. The Philistine Sanctuary: Various Finds, the Pottery, Conclusions, Appendices*. Qedem 20. Jerusalem: Hebrew University, 1985.

———. "Religious Practices and Cult Objects During the Iron Age IIA at Tel Reḥov and Their Implications Regarding Religion in Northern Israel." *HeBAI* 4 (2015): 25–55.

Mazar, Amihai, and Nava Panitz-Cohen. "The Apiary (*hmkwwrt*)." Pages 25e–31e (English) and 32–45 (Hebrew) in *It Is the Land of Honey: Discoveries from Tel*

Reḥov, the Early Days of the Israelite Monarchy. Tel Aviv: Eretz Israel Museum, 2016.

———. "It Is the Land of Honey: Beekeeping at Tel Reḥov." *NEA* 70 (2007): 202–19.

McCarter, Jr., P. Kyle. *I Samuel: A New Translation with Introduction and Commentary.* AYB 8. Garden City, N.Y.: Doubleday, 1980.

———. "The Patriarchal Age: Abraham, Isaac, and Jacob." Pages 1–29 in *Ancient Israel: A Short History from Abraham to the Roman Destruction of the Temple.* Edited by Hershel Shanks. Englewood Cliffs, N.J.: Prentice-Hall; Washington, D.C.: Biblical Archaeology Society, 1988.

———. *II Samuel: A New Translation with Introduction and Commentary.* AYB 9. Garden City, N.Y.: Doubleday, 1984.

McDowell, Markus. *Prayers of Jewish Women: Studies of Patterns of Prayer in the Second Temple Period.* Tübingen: Mohr Siebeck, 2006.

McKane, William. *A Critical and Exegetical Commentary on Jeremiah* 1. ICC 20. Edinburgh: T&T Clark, 1986.

———. *I and II Samuel: A Commentary.* Torch Bible Commentaries. London: SCM, 1963.

McKay, Heather A. "New Moon or Sabbath?" Pages 12–27 in *The Sabbath in Jewish and Christian Traditions.* Edited by Tamara C. Eskenazi, Daniel J. Harrington, and William H. Shea. New York: Crossroad, 1991.

———. *Sabbath and Synagogue: The Question of Sabbath Worship in Ancient Judaism.* Religions in the Graeco-Roman World 122. Leiden: Brill, 1994.

McKay, John W. *Religion in Judah Under the Assyrians.* Studies in Biblical Theology 2/26. Naperville, Ill.: Alan R. Allenson, 1973.

McKenzie, Steven L. *King David: A Biography.* New York: Oxford University Press, 2000.

McMillion, Phillip E. "Worship in Judges 17–18." Pages 225–43 in *Worship and the Hebrew Bible: Essays in Honour of John T. Willis.* Edited by M. Patrick Graham, Rick R. Marrs, and Steven L. McKenzie. JSOTSup 284. Sheffield: Sheffield Academic, 1999.

Meier, Sam. "Baal's Fight with Yam (KTU 1.2.I, IV): A Part of the Baal Myth as Known in KTU 1.1, 3–6?" *UF* 18 (1986): 241–54.

Meinhold, Johannes. *Sabbat und Woche im Alten Testament.* Forschungen zur Religion und Literatur des Alten und Neuen Testaments 5. Göttingen: Vandenhoeck & Ruprecht, 1905.

Mendenhall, George. *Ancient Israel's Faith and History: An Introduction to the Bible in Context.* Louisville: Westminster/John Knox, 2001.

Mettinger, Tryggve N. D. *No Graven Image? Israelite Aniconism in Its Ancient Near Eastern Context.* Coniectanea biblica: Old Testament Series 42. Stockholm: Almqvist & Wiksell, 1995.

Meyers, Carol. "Archaeology—A Window to the Lives of Israelite Women." Pages 61–108 in *The Bible and Women: An Encyclopaedia of Exegesis and Cultural History.*

Edited by Irmtraud Fischer and Mercedes Navarro Puerto, with Andrea Taschl-Erber. Leiden: Brill, 2011.

———. "Contributing to Continuity: Woman and Sacrifice in Ancient Israel." Pages 1–19 in *Women, Religion, and the Gift: An Abundance of Riches.* Edited by Morny Joy. Sophia Studies in Cross-cultural Philosophy of Traditions and Cultures 17. Basel: Springer, 2017.

———. "Daughters (and Sons) of Heman." Page 281 in *WIS.*

———. *Discovering Eve: Ancient Israelite Women in Context.* Oxford: Oxford University Press, 1988.

———. "Double Vision: Textual and Archaeological Images of Women." *HeBAI* 5 (2016): 112–31.

———. "Engendering Ezekiel: Female Figures Reconsidered." Pages 281–97 in *Birkat Shalom: Studies in the Bible, Ancient Near Eastern Literature, and Postbiblical Judaism Presented to Shalom M. Paul on the Occasion of His Seventieth Birthday* 1. Edited by Chiam Cohen, Victor Avigdor Hurowitz, Avi Hurvitz, Yochanan Muffs, Baruch J. Schwartz, and Jeffrey Tigay. Winona Lake, Ind.: Eisenbrauns, 2008.

———. "An Ethnoarchaeological Analysis of Hannah's Sacrifice." Pages 77–91 in *Pomegranates and Golden Bells: Studies in Biblical, Jewish, and Near Eastern Ritual, Law, and Literature in Honor of Jacob Milgrom.* Edited by David P. Wright, David Noel Freedman, and Avi Hurvitz. Winona Lake, Ind.: Eisenbrauns, 1995.

———. *Exodus.* NCBC. Cambridge: Cambridge University Press, 2005.

———. "The Family in Early Israel." Pages 1–47 in Leo G. Perdue, Joseph Blenkinsopp, John J. Collins, and Carol Meyers, *Families in Ancient Israel.* The Family, Religion, and Culture. Louisville: Westminster/John Knox, 1997.

———. "From Field Crops to Food: Attributing Gender and Meaning to Bread Production in Iron Age Israel." Pages 67–84 in *The Archaeology of Difference: Gender, Ethnicity, Class and the "Other" in Antiquity. Studies in Honor of Eric M. Meyers.* Edited by Douglas R. Edwards and C. Thomas McCullough. Annual of the American Schools of Oriental Research 60/61. Boston: American Schools of Oriental Research, 2007.

———. "From Household to House of Yahweh: Women's Religious Culture in Ancient Israel." Pages 277–303 in *Congress Volume: Basel 2001.* Edited by André Lemaire. VTSup 92. Leiden: Brill, 2002.

———. "The Function of Feasts: An Anthropological Perspective on Israelite Religious Festivals." Pages 141–68 in *Social Theory and the Study of Israelite Religion: Essays in Retrospect and Prospect.* Edited by Saul M. Olyan. RBS 71. Atlanta: Society of Biblical Literature, 2012.

———. "Guilds and Gatherings: Women's Groups in Ancient Israel." Pages 154–84 in *Realia Dei: Essays in Archaeology and Biblical Interpretation in Honor of Edward F. Campbell, Jr., at His Retirement.* Edited by Prescott H. Williams, Jr., and Theodore Hiebert. Atlanta: Scholars Press, 1999.

———. "Hannah and Her Sacrifice: Reclaiming Female Agency." Pages 93–104 in *A Feminist Companion to Samuel and Kings.* Edited by Athalya Brenner. FCB 5. Sheffield: Sheffield Academic, 1994.

———. "The Hannah Narrative in Feminist Perspective." Pages 117–26 in *Go to the Land I Will Show You: Studies in Honor of Dwight W. Young.* Edited by Joseph E. Coleson and Victor H. Matthews. Winona Lake, Ind.: Eisenbrauns, 1996.

———. "Having Their Space and Eating There Too: Bread Production and Female Power in Ancient Israelite Households." *Nashim: A Journal of Jewish Women's Studies and Gender Issues* 5 (2002): 14–44.

———. "Household Religion." Pages 118–34 in *Religious Diversity in Ancient Israel and Judah.* Edited by Francesca Stavrakopoulou and John Barton. London: T&T Clark, 2010.

———. *Households and Holiness: The Religious Culture of Israelite Women.* Minneapolis: Fortress, 2005.

———. "In the Household and Beyond: The Social World of Israelite Women." *ST* 63 (2009): 19–41.

———. "Kinship and Kingship: The Early Monarchy." Pages 165–205 in *The Oxford History of the Biblical World.* Edited by Michael D. Coogan. Oxford: Oxford University Press, 1998.

———. "Material Remains and Social Relations: Women's Culture in Agrarian Households of the Iron Age." Pages 425–44 in *Symbiosis, Symbolism, and the Power of the Past: Canaan, Ancient Israel, and Their Neighbors from the Late Bronze Age Through Roman Palaestina.* Edited by William G. Dever and Seymour Gitin. Winona Lake, Ind.: Eisenbrauns, 2003.

———. "Miriam, Music, and Miracles." Pages 27–48 in *Mariam, the Magdalen, and the Mother.* Edited by Deirdre Good. Bloomington: Indiana University Press, 2005.

———. "Mother of Micah." Page 248 in *WIS.*

———. "Mother to Muse: An Archaeomusicological Study of Women's Performance in Israel." Pages 50–77 in *Recycling Biblical Figures: Papers Read at a Noster Colloquium in Amsterdam, 12–13 May 1997.* Edited by Athalya Brenner and Jan Willem van Henten. Studies in Theology and Religion 1. Leiden: Deo, 1999.

———. "Of Drums and Damsels: Women's Performance in Ancient Israel." *BA* 54 (1991): 16–27.

———. "Person (Female or Male) Presenting an Offering." Page 203 in *WIS.*

———. *Rediscovering Eve: Ancient Israelite Women in Context.* Oxford: Oxford University Press, 2013.

———. "Temple, Jerusalem." Pages 350–69 in *ABD* 6.

———. "A Terracotta at the Harvard Semitic Museum and Disc-holding Female Figurines Reconsidered." *IEJ* (1987): 116–22.

———. "Terracottas Without Texts: Judean Pillar Figurines in Anthropological Perspective." Pages 115–30 in *To Break Every Yoke: Essays in Honor of Marvin L.*

Chaney. Edited by Robert B. Coote and Norman K. Gottwald. SWBA 2/3. Sheffield: Sheffield Phoenix, 2007.

———. "Those Who Bear Tidings: Heralds." Page 299 in *WIS*.

———. "Women (and Men and Children) in Assembly." Page 286 in *WIS*.

———. "Women as Bread Bakers." Pages 213–14 in *WIS*.

———. "Women at the Entrance to the Tent of Meeting." Page 202 in *WIS*.

———. "Women, Part of the Assembly of People." Page 288 in *WIS*.

———. "Women with Hand-Drums, Dancing." Pages 189–91 in *WIS*.

———. "Women's Daily Life (Iron Age Israel)." Pages 488–500 in *Women in Antiquity: Real Women Across the Ancient World*. Edited by Stephanie Lynn Budin and Jean MacIntosh Turfa. London: Routledge, 2016.

———. "Women's Religious Life (Iron Age Israel)." Pages 511–20 in *Women in Antiquity: Real Women Across the Ancient World*. Edited by Stephanie Lynn Budin and Jean MacIntosh Turfa. London: Routledge, 2016.

Miano, David. *Shadow on the Steps: Time Measurement in Ancient Israel*. RBS 64. Atlanta: Society of Biblical Literature, 2010.

Milgrom, Jacob. "Does H Advocate the Centralization of Worship?" *JSOT* 88 (2000): 59–76.

———. "Israel's Sanctuary: The Priestly 'Picture of Dorian Gray.'" *RB* 33 (1976): 390–99.

———. *Leviticus: A Book of Ritual and Ethics*. Continental Commentaries. Minneapolis: Fortress, 2004.

———. *Leviticus 1–16: A New Translation with Introduction and Commentary*. AYB 3. New York: Doubleday, 1991.

———. *Leviticus 17–22: A New Translation with Introduction and Commentary*. AYB 3A. New York: Doubleday, 2000.

———. *Leviticus 23–27: A New Translation with Introduction and Commentary*. AYB 3B. New York: Doubleday, 2000.

———. *Numbers: The Traditional Hebrew Text with the New JPS Translation*. JPS Torah Commentary. Philadelphia: Jewish Publication Society, 1990.

———. "Priestly ('P') Source." Pages 454–61 in *ABD* 5.

Miller, Heather M.-L. *Archaeological Approaches to Technology*. Amsterdam: Elsevier/Academic Press, 2007.

Miller, J. Maxwell. "Geba/Gibeah of Benjamin." *VT* 25 (1975): 145–66.

Miller, Patrick D. *The Religion of Ancient Israel*. Library of Ancient Israel. London: SPCK; Louisville: Westminster/John Knox, 2000.

———. *They Cried to the Lord: The Form and Theology of Biblical Prayer*. Minneapolis: Fortress, 1994.

———. "Things Too Wonderful: Prayers of Women in the Old Testament." Pages 237–51 in *Biblische Theologie und gesellschaftlicher Wandel: Für Norbert Lohfink SJ*. Edited by Georg Braulik, Walter Gross, and Sean E. McEvenue. Freiburg: Herder, 1983.

Moore, George F. *A Critical and Exegetical Commentary on Judges.* 2nd ed. ICC 7. Edinburgh: T&T Clark, 1903.

Moore, Michael S. "Role Pre-Emption in the Israelite Priesthood." *VT* 46 (1996): 316–29.

Moorey, P. R. S. *Idols of the People: Miniature Images of Clay in the Ancient Near East.* Schweich Lectures of the British Academy 2001. Oxford: Oxford University Press, for the British Academy, 2003.

Morris, Ian. *Burial and Ancient Society: The Rise of the Greek City-State.* Cambridge: Cambridge University Press, 1987.

———. "The Use and Abuse of Homer." *Classical Antiquity* 5 (1986): 81–138.

Moshkovitz, Shmuel. See Herzog, Ze'ev.

Mouton, Alice. *Rêves hittites: Contribution à une histoire et une anthropologie du rêve en Anatolie ancienne.* CHANE 28. Leiden: Brill, 2007.

Mueller, E. Aydeet. *The Micah Story: A Morality Tale in the Book of Judges.* Studies in Biblical Literature 34. New York: Peter Lang, 2001.

Muller, Béatrice. *Maquettes antiques d'Orient: de l'image d'architecture au symbole.* Paris: Éditions Picard, 2016.

———. *Les "maquettes architecturales" du Proche-Orient Ancien: Mésopotamie, Syrie, Palestine du IIIe au Ier millénaire av. J.-C.* 1–2. Bibliothèque archéologique et historique 160. Beirut: Institut Français d'Archéologie du Proche-Orient, 2002.

Mumcuoglu, Madeleine. See Garfinkel, Yosef.

Münger, Stefan. See Nissinen, Martti.

Murdoch, W. G. C. See Hasel, Gerhard F.

Murdock, George P., and Caterina Provost. "Factors in the Division of Labor by Sex: A Cross-Cultural Analysis." *Ethnology* 12 (1973): 203–25.

Murray, Oswyn. "Introduction." Pages xi–xliv in Jacob Burckhardt, *The Greeks and Greek Civilization.* Edited, with an introduction by Oswyn Murray. New York: St. Martin's, 1998.

Myerhoff, Barbara G., Linda A. Camino, and Edith Turner. "Rites of Passage: An Overview." Pages 380–86 in *The Encyclopedia of Religion* 12. 1st ed. Edited by Mircea Eliade. New York: Macmillan; London: Collier Macmillan, 1987.

Na'aman, Nadav. "No Anthropomorphic Graven Image: Notes on the Assumed Anthropomorphic Cult Statues in the Temples of YHWH in the Pre-Exilic Period." *UF* 31 (1999): 391–415.

———. "Samuel's Birth Legend and the Sanctuary of Shiloh. *Journal of Northwest Semitic Languages* 43 (2017): 51–61.

Nakhai, Beth Alpert. *Archaeology and the Religions of Canaan and Israel.* ASOR Books 7. Boston: American Schools of Oriental Research, 2001.

———. "Gender and Archaeology in Israelite Religion." *Religion Compass* 1 (2007): 512–28.

Negbi, Ora. *Canaanite Gods in Metal: An Archaeological Study of Ancient Syro-Palestinian Figurines.* Tel Aviv: Tel Aviv University Institute of Archaeology, 1976.

Nelson, Richard D. *The Double Redaction of the Deuteronomistic History.* JSOTSup 18. Sheffield: JSOT Press, 1981.

———. *Raising Up a Faithful Priest: Community and Priesthood in Biblical Theology.* Louisville: Westminster/John Knox, 1993.

Nemet-Nejat, Karen Rhea. "Women in Ancient Mesopotamia." Pages 85–114 in *Women's Roles in Ancient Civilizations: A Reference Guide.* Edited by Bella Vivante. Westport, Conn.: Greenwood, 1999.

Netzer, Ehud. *The Architecture of Herod, the Great Builder.* Tübingen: Mohr Siebeck, 2006.

Neufeld, Dietmar. "Barrenness: Trance as Protest Strategy." Pages 128–41 in *Ancient Israel: The Old Testament in Its Social Context.* Edited by Philip F. Esler. Minneapolis: Fortress, 2006.

Neusner, Jacob. "Introduction." Pages 3–7 in *Religion, Science, and Magic: In Concert and in Conflict.* Edited by Jacob Neusner, Ernest S. Frerichs, and Paul V. McCracken Flesher. New York: Oxford University Press, 1989.

Newsom, Carol A. "Women and the Discourse of Patriarchal Wisdom: A Study of Proverbs 1–9." Pages 142–60 in *Gender and Difference in Ancient Israel.* Edited by Peggy L. Day. Minneapolis: Fortress, 1989.

Nicholson, Ernest W. *Deuteronomy and Tradition.* Philadelphia: Fortress, 1967.

———. *The Pentateuch in the Twentieth Century: The Legacy of Julius Wellhausen.* Oxford: Clarendon, 1998.

Nicholson, Paul. See Bourriau, Janine.

Niditch, Susan. *Ancient Israelite Religion.* New York: Oxford University Press, 1997.

———. *Folklore and the Hebrew Bible.* Minneapolis: Fortress, 1993.

———. *Judges: A Commentary.* OTL. Louisville: Westminster/John Knox, 2008.

Niehr, Herbert. "Zur Gattung von Jes 5, 1–7." *Biblische Zeitschrift* 30 (1986): 99–104.

Nihan, Christophe L. "1 Samuel 28 and the Condemnation of Necromancy in Persian Yehud." Pages 23–54 in *Magic in the Biblical World.* Edited by Todd Klutz. Journal for the Study of the New Testament: Supplement Series 242. New York: T&T Clark, 2003.

———. "Forms and Functions of Purity in Leviticus." Pages 311–68 in *Purity and the Forming of Religious Traditions in the Ancient Mediterranean World and Ancient Judaism.* Edited by Christian Frevel and Christophe Nihan. Dynamics in the History of Religion 3. Leiden: Brill, 2013.

———. *From Priestly Torah to Pentateuch: A Study in the Composition of the Book of Leviticus.* FAT 2/25. Tübingen: Mohr Siebeck, 2007.

———. "Israel's Festival Calendars in Leviticus 23, Numbers 28–29 and the Formation of 'Priestly' Literature." Pages 177–231 in *The Books of Leviticus and Numbers.* Edited by Thomas Römer. Bibliotheca ephemeridum theologicarum lovaniensium 215. Leuven: Peeters, 2008.

Nissinen, Martti. "Biblical Prophecy from a Near Eastern Perspective: The Cases of Kingship and Divine Possession." Pages 441–68 in *Congress Volume: Ljubljana 2007.* Edited by André Lemaire. VTSup 133. Leiden: Brill 2010.

———. *References to Prophecy in Neo-Assyrian Sources*. State Archives of Assyria Studies 7. Helsinki: Neo-Assyrian Text Corpus Project, 1998.

Nissinen, Martti, and Stefan Münger. "'Down the River . . .': A Shrine Model from Tel Kinrot in Its Context." Pages 129–44 in *A Timeless Vale: Archaeological and Related Essays on the Jordan Valley in Honour of Gerrit van der Kooij on the Occasion of His Sixty-Fifth Birthday*. Edited by Eva Kaptijn and Lucas P. Petit. Archaeological Studies Leiden University 19. Leiden: Leiden University Press, 2009.

Noegel, Scott B. "Maleness, Memory, and the Matter of Dream Divination in the Hebrew Bible." Pages 61–90 in *Perchance to Dream: Dream Divination in the Bible and the Ancient Near East*. Edited by Esther J. Hamori and Jonathan Stökl. ANEM 21. Atlanta: SBL Press, 2018.

Noll, K. L. "The City of Dan in the Pre-Assyrian Iron Age." *Proceedings: Eastern Great Lakes and Midwest Biblical Societies* 15 (1995): 145–56.

———. "The God Who Is Among the Danites." *JSOT* 80 (1998): 3–23.

Noth, Martin. "The Background of Judges 17–18." Pages 68–85 in *Israel's Prophetic Heritage: Essays in Honor of James Muilenburg*. Edited by Bernhard W. Anderson and Walter Harrelson. New York: Harper & Row, 1962.

———. *Exodus: A Commentary*. OTL. Philadelphia: Westminster, 1962.

Novick, Tzvi. "Law and Loss: Response to Catastrophe in Numbers 15." *HTR* 101 (2008): 1–14.

Oakley, John H., and Rebecca H. Sims. *The Wedding in Ancient Athens*. Wisconsin Studies in Classics. Madison: University of Wisconsin Press, 1993.

O'Brien, Mark A. "The Book of Deuteronomy." *Currents in Research: Biblical Studies* 3 (1995): 95–128.

Oden, Jr., Robert A. *The Bible Without Theology: The Theological Tradition and Alternatives to It*. San Francisco: Harper & Row, 1987.

Olyan, Saul M. "'And with a Male You Shall Not Lie the Lying Down of a Woman': On the Meaning and Significance of Leviticus 18:22 and 20:13." *Journal of the History of Sexuality* 5 (1994): 179–206.

———. *Asherah and the Cult of Yahweh in Israel*. SBLMS 34. Atlanta: Scholars Press, 1988.

———. *Biblical Mourning: Ritual and Social Dimensions*. Oxford: Oxford University Press, 2004.

———. *Disability in the Hebrew Bible: Interpreting Physical and Mental Differences*. Cambridge: Cambridge University Press, 2008.

———. "Equality and Inequality in the Socio-Political Visions of the Pentateuch's Sources." In Saul M. Olyan, ed., "In Conversation with Joshua A. Berman, *Created Equal: How the Bible Broke with Ancient Political Thought* (Oxford University Press, 2008)." *JHS* 10 (2010): 35–41.

———. "Exodus 31:12–17: The Sabbath According to H, or the Sabbath According to P and H?" *JBL* 124 (2005): 201–9.

———. "Family Religion in Israel and the Wider Levant of the First Millennium BCE." Pages 113–26 in *Household and Family Religion in Antiquity*. Edited by John Bodel and Saul M. Olyan. Oxford: Blackwell, 2008.

———. "Gender-Specific Pollution in the Hebrew Bible." Pages 159–67 in *Gender and Social Norms in Ancient Israel, Early Judaism and Early Christianity: Texts and Material Culture.* Journal of Ancient Judaism Supplements 28. Edited by Michaela Banks, Katharina Galor, and Judith Hartenstein. Göttingen: Vandenhoeck & Ruprecht, 2019.

———. *Rites and Rank: Hierarchy in Biblical Representations of Cult.* Princeton: Princeton University Press, 2000.

———. "The Search for the Elusive Self in Texts of the Hebrew Bible." Pages 40–50 in *Religion and the Self in Antiquity.* Edited by David Brakke, Michael E. Satlow, and Steven Weitzman. Bloomington: Indiana University Press, 2005.

———. "Sin, Pollution, and Purity: Syria-Canaan." Pages 501–2 in *Religions of the Ancient World: A Guide.* Edited by Sarah Iles Johnston. Cambridge, Mass.: Harvard University Press, 2004.

———. "Some Neglected Aspects of Israelite Interment Ideology." *JBL* 124 (2005): 601–16.

———. "What Do We Really Know About Women's Rites in the Israelite Family Context?" *JANER* 10 (2010): 55–67.

———. See also Bodel, John.

Oppenheim, A. Leo. *Ancient Mesopotamia: Portrait of a Dead Civilization.* Rev. ed. Chicago: University of Chicago Press, 1977.

———. *The Interpretation of Dreams in the Ancient Near East, with a Translation of an Assyrian Dream-Book.* Transactions of the American Philosophical Society 46/3. Philadelphia: American Philosophical Society, 1956.

———. "Sumerian: inim.gar, Akkadian: *egirrû* = Greek: *kledon.*" *AfO* 17 (1954–1956): 49–55.

Ornan, Tallay. "In the Likeness of Man: Reflections on the Anthropocentric Perception of the Divine in Mesopotamian Art." Pages 93–151 in *What Is a God? Anthropomorphic and Non-Anthropomorphic Aspects of Deity in Ancient Mesopotamia.* Edited by Barbara Nevling Porter. Transactions of the Casco Bay Assyriological Institute 2. Winona Lake, Ind.: Eisenbrauns, 2009.

Overton, Shawna Dolansky. See Friedman, Richard Elliott.

Ozick, Cynthia. "Notes Toward Finding the Right Question." Pages 120–51 in *On Being a Jewish Feminist: A Reader.* Edited by Susannah Heschel. New York: Schocken, 1983.

Panitz-Cohen, Nava. See Mazar, Amihai.

Pardee, Dennis. *Ritual and Cult at Ugarit.* SBLWAW 10. Atlanta: Society of Biblical Literature, 2002.

Parry, Donald W. "Hannah in the Presence of the Lord." Pages 53–74 in *Archaeology of the Books of Samuel: The Entangling of the Textual and Literary History.* Leiden: Brill, 2010.

Pat-El, Na'ama. "Israelian Hebrew: A Re-Evaluation." *VT* 67 (2017): 1–37.

Paz, Sarit. *Drums, Women, and Goddesses: Drumming and Gender in Iron Age II Israel.* OBO 232. Fribourg: Academic Press; Göttingen: Vandenhoeck & Ruprecht, 2007.

Peritz, Ismar J. "Women in the Ancient Hebrew Cult." *JBL* 17 (1898): 111–48.

Péter-Contesse, René, and John Ellington. *A Translator's Handbook on Leviticus.* New York: United Bible Societies, 1990.

Pfeifer, Gerhard. "Entwöhnung und Entwöhnungsfest im Alten Testament: der Schlüssel zu Jesaja 28, 7–13?" *ZAW* 84 (1972): 341–47.

Pinch, Geraldine. *Magic in Ancient Egypt.* Austin: University of Texas Press, 1995.

Pitkänen, Pekka. *Central Sanctuary and Centralization of Worship in Ancient Israel: From the Settlement to the Building of Solomon's Temple.* Gorgias Dissertations, Near Eastern Studies 5. Piscataway, N.J.: Gorgias, 2003.

Plaskow, Judith. *Standing Again at Sinai: Judaism from a Feminist Perspective.* San Francisco: Harper & Row, 1990.

Poethig, Eunice B. "The Victory Song Tradition of the Women of Israel." PhD diss., Union Theological Seminary, 1985.

Poorthuis, Marcel, and Joshua Schwartz. "Purity and Holiness: An Introductory Survey." Pages 3–26 in *Purity and Holiness: The Heritage of Leviticus.* Edited by M. J. H. M. Poorthuis and J. Schwartz. Jewish and Christian Perspectives Series 2. Leiden: Brill, 2000.

Pope, Marvin H. *El in the Ugaritic Texts.* VTSup 2. Leiden: Brill, 1955.

———. "Fertility Cults." Page 265 in *The Interpreter's Dictionary of the Bible* 2. Edited by G. A. Butterick. Nashville: Abingdon, 1962.

Potts, T. F. "The Cultic Stands." Pages 97–101 in *Pella in Jordan 2: The Second Interim Report of the Joint University of Sydney and College of Wooster Excavations at Pella, 1982–1985.* Edited by Anthony W. McNicoll et al. Sydney: Meditarch, 1992.

———. "The Late Bronze–Early Iron Age (Areas III and IV)." Pages 202–4 in T. F. Potts, S. M. Colledge, and P. C. Edwards, "Preliminary Report on a Sixth Season of Excavation by the University of Sydney at Pella in Jordan (1983/84)." *Annual of the Department of Antiquities of Jordan* 29 (1985): 181–210.

Pressler, Carolyn. *The View of Women Found in Deuteronomic Family Laws.* Berlin: de Gruyter, 1993.

Pringle, Jackie. "Hittite Birth Rituals." Pages 128–41 in *Images of Women in Antiquity.* Edited by Averil Cameron and Amélie Kuhrt. London: Routledge, 1983, 1993.

Propp, William H. C. *Exodus 1–18: A New Translation with Introduction and Commentary.* AYB 2. New York: Doubleday, 1998.

———. *Exodus 19–40: A New Translation with Introduction and Commentary.* AYB 2A. New York: Doubleday, 2006.

Provost, Caterina. See Murdock, George P.

Pury, Albert de. *Promesse divine et légende cultuelle dans le cycle de Jacob. Genèse 28 et les traditions patriarcales.* Paris: J. Gabalda, 1975.

Rad, Gerhard von. *Deuteronomy: A Commentary.* OTL. Philadelphia: Westminster, 1966.

———. *Das formgeschichtliche Problem des Hexateuchs.* Beiträge zur Wissenschaft vom Alten und Neuen Testament 26. Stuttgart: Kohlhammer, 1938.

———. *Studies in Deuteronomy.* Chicago: H. Regnery, 1953.

Rainey, Anson F. See Herzog, Ze'ev.

Reinhartz, Adele. "Samson's Mother: An Unnamed Protagonist." *JSOT* 55 (1992): 25–37.

———. *"Why Ask My Name?" Anonymity and Identity in Biblical Narrative.* Oxford: Oxford University Press, 1998.

Rendsburg, Gary A. *Israelian Hebrew in the Book of Kings.* Bethesda, Md.: CDL, 2002.

———. "Late Biblical Hebrew and the Date of 'P.'" *Journal of the Ancient Near Eastern Society of Columbia University* 12 (1980): 65–80.

———. *Linguistic Evidence for the Northern Origin of Selected Psalms.* Atlanta: Scholars Press, 1990.

———. "Once More the Dual: With Replies to J. Blau and J. Blenkinsopp." *Ancient Near Eastern Studies* 38 (2001): 28–41.

———. "Some False Leads in the Identification of Late Biblical Hebrew Texts: The Case of Genesis 24 and 1 Samuel 2:27–36." *JBL* 121 (2002): 23–46.

Ricks, Stephen D. "The Magician as Outsider in the Hebrew Bible and the New Testament." Pages 131–43 in *Ancient Magic and Ritual Power.* Edited by Marvin Meyer and Paul Mirecki. Leiden: Brill, 2001.

Riklin, Shimon. "The Fortress of Michmash on the Northeastern Boundary of the Judaean Desert." *Judea and Samaria Research Studies* 4 (1994): 69–79 (Hebrew).

Ringgren, Helmer. *Israelitische Religion.* Stuttgart: Kohlhammer, 1963.

———. See also Bergman, J.

Ritner, Robert K. "Household Religion in Ancient Egypt." Pages 127–58 in *Household and Family Religion in Antiquity.* Edited by John Bodel and Saul M. Olyan. Oxford: Blackwell, 2008.

———. *The Mechanics of Ancient Egyptian Magical Practice.* Studies in Ancient Oriental Civilizations 54. Chicago: Oriental Institute of the University of Chicago, 1993.

———. "The Religious, Social, and Legal Parameters of Traditional Egyptian Magic." Pages 43–60 in *Ancient Magic and Ritual Power.* Edited by Marvin Meyer and Paul Mirecki. Leiden: Brill, 2001.

Robins, Gay. "Women and Children in Peril: Pregnancy, Birth and Infant Mortality in Ancient Egypt." *Kmt* 5/4 (1994–1995): 24–35.

———. *Women in Ancient Egypt.* Cambridge, Mass.: Harvard University Press, 1993.

Robinson, Gnana. "The Idea of Rest in the Old Testament and the Search for the Basic Character of the Sabbath." *ZAW* 92 (1980): 32–42.

———. *The Origin and Development of the Old Testament Sabbath: A Comprehensive Exegetical Approach.* Beiträge zur biblischen Exegese und Theologie 21. Frankfurt am Main: Peter Lang, 1988.

Rofé, Alexander. *Deuteronomy: Issues and Interpretation.* London: T&T Clark, 2002.

Romano, James F. "11. Jar in the Form of a Woman." Page 63 in *Mistress of the House, Mistress of Heaven: Women in Ancient Egypt.* Edited by Anne K. Capel and Glenn E. Markoe. New York: Hudson Hills, in conjunction with the Cincinnati Art Museum, 1996.

Römer, Thomas C. "The Book of Deuteronomy." Pages 178–212 in *The History of Israel's Traditions: The Heritage of Martin Noth.* Edited by Steven L. McKenzie and M. Patrick Graham. JSOTSup 182. Sheffield: Sheffield Academic, 1994.

———. "The Elusive Yahwist: A Short History of Research." Pages 9–27 in *A Farewell to the Yahwist? The Composition of the Pentateuch in Recent European Interpretation.* Edited by Thomas B. Dozeman and Konrad Schmid. SBLSymS 34. Atlanta: Society of Biblical Literature, 2006.

———. *The So-Called Deuteronomistic History: A Sociological, Historical, and Literary Introduction.* London: T&T Clark, 2007.

———. "Zwischen Urkunden, Fragmenten und Ergänzungen: zum Stand der Pentateuchforschung." *ZAW* 125 (2013): 2–24.

Rose, Martin. *Deuteronomist und Jahwist: Untersuchungen zu den Berührungspunkten beider Literaturwerke.* ATANT 67. Zürich: Theologischer Verlag, 1981.

Rose, Pamela. See Bourriau, Janine.

Ruane, Nicole. "Bathing, Status and Gender in Priestly Ritual." Pages 66–81 in *A Question of Sex? Gender and Difference in the Hebrew Bible and Beyond.* Edited by Deborah W. Rooke. Hebrew Bible Monographs 14. Sheffield: Sheffield Phoenix, 2007.

Rubenstein, Jeffrey L. *The History of Sukkot in the Second Temple and Rabbinic Periods.* BJS 302. Atlanta: Scholars Press, 1995.

———. "Purim, Liminality, and Communitas." *Association for Jewish Studies Review* 17 (1992): 247–77.

———. "The Sukkot Wine Libation." Pages 575–91 in *Ki Baruch Hu: Ancient Near Eastern, Biblical, and Judaic Studies in Honor of Baruch A. Levine.* Edited by Robert Chazan, William W. Hallo, and Lawrence H. Schiffman. Winona Lake, Ind.: Eisenbrauns, 1999.

Saley, Richard J. "The Date of Nehemiah Reconsidered." Pages 151–65 in *Biblical and Near Eastern Studies: Essays in Honor of William Sanford LaSor.* Edited by Gary A. Tuttle. Grand Rapids: Eerdmans, 1978.

Samuel, Delwen. "Brewing and Baking in Ancient Egyptian Art." Pages 173–81 in *Food in the Arts: Proceedings of the Oxford Symposium on Food and Cookery 1998.* Edited by Harlan Walker. Devon, U.K.: Prospect Books, 1999.

Sanders, Akiva. "Fingerprints, Sex, State, and the Organization of the Tell Leilan Ceramic Industry." *Journal of Archaeological Science* 57 (2015): 223–38.

Sasson, Jack M. *Judges 1–12: A New Translation with Introduction and Commentary.* AYB 6D. New Haven: Yale University Press, 2014.

———. "The Worship of the Golden Calf." Pages 151–59 in *Orient and Occident: Essays Presented to Cyrus H. Gordon on the Occasion of His Sixty-Fifth Birthday.*

Edited by Harry A. Hoffner. AOAT 22. Neukirchen-Vluyn: Neukirchener; Kevelaer: Butzon & Bercker, 1973.

Scharbert, J. "*'ālâ*." Pages 261–66 in *TDOT* 1.

———. "*sāpad, mispēd.*" Pages 299–303 in *TDOT* 10.

Schloen, J. David. *The House of the Father as Fact and Symbol: Patrimonialism in Ugarit and the Ancient Near East.* Winona Lake, Ind.: Eisenbrauns, 2001.

Schmid, Hans Heinrich. *Der sogenannte Jahwist: Beobachtungen und Fragen zur Pentateuchforschung.* Zürich: Theologischer Verlag, 1976.

Schmid, Konrad. See Gertz, Jan Christian.

Schmidt, Brian B. "Canaanite Magic vs. Israelite Religion: Deuteronomy 18 and the Taxonomy of Taboo." Pages 179–94 in *Magic and Ritual in the Ancient World.* Edited by Paul Mirecki and Marvin Miller. Religions in the Graeco-Roman World 141. Leiden: Brill, 2002.

———. *Israel's Beneficent Dead: Ancestor Cult and Necromancy in Ancient Israelite Religion and Tradition.* Winona Lake, Ind.: Eisenbrauns, 1996.

———. "The 'Witch' of En-Dor, 1 Samuel 28, and Ancient Near Eastern Necromancy." Pages 111–29 in *Ancient Magic and Ritual Power.* Edited by Marvin Meyer and Paul Mirecki. Leiden: Brill, 2001.

Schmitt, Rüdiger. "Kultinventare aus Wohnhäusern als materielle Elemente familiärer Religion im Alten Israel." Pages 441–77 in *Berührungspunkte Studien zur Sozial- und Religionsgeschichte Israels und seiner Umwelt. Festschrift für Rainer Albertz zu seinem 65. Geburtstag.* Edited by Ruth Ebach, with Ingo Kottsieper, Rüdiger Schmitt, and Jakob Wöhrle. AOAT 350. Münster: Ugarit-Verlag, 2008.

———. *Magie im Alten Testament.* AOAT 313. Münster: Ugarit-Verlag, 2004.

———. "The Problem of Magic and Monotheism in the Book of Leviticus." *JHS* 8 (2008): 2–12.

———. "Theories Regarding Witchcraft Accusations and the Hebrew Bible." Pages 181–94 in *Social Theory and the Study of Israelite Religion: Essays in Retrospect and Prospect.* Edited by Saul M. Olyan. RBS 71. Atlanta: Society of Biblical Literature, 2012.

———. See also Albertz, Rainer.

Schneider, Tammi J. *Judges.* Berit Olam: Studies in Hebrew Narrative and Poetry. Collegeville, Minn.: Liturgical Press, 2000.

Schniedewind, William M. "The Search for Gibeah: Notes on the Historical Geography of Central Benjamin." Pages 711–22 in *"I Will Speak the Riddles of Ancient Times": Archaeological and Historical Studies in Honor of Amihai Mazar on the Occasion of His Sixtieth Birthday* 2. Edited by Aren M. Maeir and Pierre de Miroschedji. Winona Lake, Ind.: Eisenbrauns, 2006.

Schroer, Silvia. "Ancient Near Eastern Pictures as Keys to Biblical Texts." Pages 31–60 in *The Bible and Women: An Encyclopaedia of Exegesis and Cultural History.* Edited by Irmtraud Fischer and Mercedes Navarro Puerto, with Andrea Taschl-Erber. Leiden: Brill, 2011.

———. "Frauenkörper als architektonische Elemente: Zum Hintergrund von Ps 144, 12." Pages 425–50 in *Bilder als Quellen/Images as Sources: Studies on Ancient Near Eastern Artifacts and the Bible Inspired by the Work of Othmar Keel.* Edited by Susanne Bickel, Silvia Schroer, Renee Schurte, and Christoph Uehlinger. OBO. Fribourg: Academic Press; Göttingen: Vandenhoeck & Ruprecht, 2007.

———. "Die Göttin auf den Stempelsiegeln aus Palästina." Pages 89–207 in *Studien zu den Stempelsiegeln aus Palästina/Israel* 2. Edited by Othmar Keel, Hildi Keel-Leu, and Silvia Schroer. OBO 88. Freiburg: Universitätsverlag; Göttingen: Vandenhoeck & Ruprecht, 1989.

———. "The Iconography of the Shrine Models of Khirbet Qeiyafa." Pages 137–58 in *Khirbet Qeiyafa in the Shephelah. Papers Presented at a Colloquium of the Swiss Society for Ancient Near Eastern Studies Held at the University of Bern, September 6, 2014.* Edited by Silvia Schroer and Stefan Münger. OBO 282. Fribourg: Academic Press; Göttingen: Vandenhoeck & Ruprecht, 2017.

Schunck, Klaus D. "Zentralheiligtum, Grenzheiligtum und 'Hohenheiligtum' in Israel." *Numen* 18 (1971): 132–40.

Schwartz, Baruch J. *The Holiness Legislation: Studies in the Priestly Code.* Jerusalem: Magnes, 1999 (Hebrew).

———. "Israel's Holiness: The Torah Traditions." Pages 47–59 in *Purity and Holiness: The Heritage of Leviticus.* Edited by M. J. H. M. Poorthuis and J. Schwartz. Jewish and Christian Perspectives Series 2. Leiden: Brill, 2000.

———. "The Sabbath in the Torah Sources." Paper presented in the Biblical Law Section of the Annual Meeting of the Society of Biblical Literature, San Diego, Calif., November 19, 2007.

Schwartz, Joshua. See Poorthuis, Marcel.

Scott, R. B. Y. "Introduction and Exegesis: The Book of Isaiah, Chapters 1–39." Pages 151–381 in *The Interpreter's Bible* 5. Nashville: Abingdon, 1956.

Scurlock, Jo Ann. "Baby-Snatching Demons, Restless Souls and the Dangers of Childbirth: Medico-Magical Means of Dealing with Some of the Perils of Motherhood in Ancient Mesopotamia." *Incognita* 2 (1991): 137–85.

———. "Magic (ANE)." Pages 464–68 in *ABD* 4.

———. "Physician, Exorcist, Conjurer, Magician: A Tale of Two Healing Professionals." Pages 69–79 in *Mesopotamian Magic: Textual, Historical, and Interpretative Perspectives.* Edited by Tzvi Abusch and Karel van der Toorn. Groningen: Styx, 1999.

Seaford, Richard. "The Tragic Wedding." *Journal of Hellenic Studies* 107 (1987): 106–30.

Seeden, Helga. "A Small Clay Shrine in the AUB Museum." *Berytus* 27 (1979): 7–26.

Segal, J. B. *The Hebrew Passover: From the Earliest Times to A.D. 70.* London Oriental Series 12. London: Oxford University Press, 1963.

Seifert, Elke. See Jost, Renate.

Seow, Choon-Leong. "Linguistic Evidence and the Dating of Qoheleth." *JBL* 115 (1996): 643–66.

Sered, Susan Starr. *Women as Ritual Experts: The Religious Lives of Elderly Jewish Women in Jerusalem.* Oxford: Oxford University Press, 1992.

Shafer-Elliott, Cynthia. "'He Shall Eat Curds and Honey' (Isa 7:15): Food and Feasting in Late Eighth-Century Judah." Pages 279–98 in *Archaeology and History of Eighth-Century Judah.* Edited by Zev I. Farber and Jacob L. Wright. ANEM 23. Atlanta: SBL Press, 2018.

Shai, Itzhaq. See Uziel, Joe.

Shectman, Sarah. "Women in the Priestly Laws: A Reassessment." Paper presented in the Biblical Law Section of the Annual Meeting of the Society of Biblical Literature, Boston, Mass., November 25, 2008. Posted online at https://biblicallaw.files.wordpress.com/2013/07/shectman.pdf.

Sheppard, Gerald T. "More on Isaiah 5:1–7 as a Juridical Parable." *CBQ* 44 (1982): 45–47.

Shiloh, Yigael. "Iron Age Sanctuaries and Cult Elements in Palestine." Pages 147–57 in *Symposia Celebrating the Seventy-Fifth Anniversary of the Founding of the American Schools of Oriental Research (1900–1975).* Edited by Frank Moore Cross. Zion Research Foundation Occasional Publications 1–2. Cambridge, Mass.: American Schools of Oriental Research, 1979.

———. "Megiddo." Pages 1003–24 in *The New Encyclopaedia of Archaeological Excavations in the Holy Land* 3. Edited by Ephraim Stern. New York: Simon & Schuster, 1993.

Sims, Rebecca H. See Oakley, John H.

Sinclair, Lawrence A. "Archaeological Study of Gibeah (Tell el-Fûl)." *BA* 27 (1964): 52–64.

Sinclair, Lawrence A., and Ray L. Cleveland. *Archaeological Study of Gibeah (Tell El-Ful): The Excavation of the Conway High Place (Petra) and Soundings at Khirbet Ader.* New Haven: American Schools of Oriental Research, 1960.

Singer, Itamar. *Hittite Prayers.* SBLWAW 11. Atlanta: Society of Biblical Literature, 2002.

Singer-Avitz, Lily. "Household Activities." Pages 1430–51 in Ze'ev Herzog and Lily Singer-Avitz, *Beer-Sheba* III: *The Early Iron IIA Enclosed Settlement and the Late Iron IIA–Iron IIB Cities.* Monograph Series of the Sonia and Marco Nadler Institute of Archaeology, Tel Aviv University 34. Tel Aviv: Emery and Claire Yass Publications in Archaeology; Winona Lake, Ind.: Eisenbrauns, 2016.

Smelik, Klaas A. D. *Writings from Ancient Israel: A Handbook of Historical and Religious Documents.* Louisville: Westminster/John Knox, 1991.

Smith, Henry Preserved. *A Critical and Exegetical Commentary on the Books of Samuel.* ICC. Edinburgh: T&T Clark, 1899.

Smith, Mark S. "The Baal Cycle." Pages 81–180 in *Ugaritic Narrative Poetry.* Edited by Simon B. Parker. SBLWAW 9. Atlanta: Scholars Press, 1997.

———. *The Early History of God: Yahweh and the Other Deities in Israel.* San Francisco: Harper & Row, 1990; 2nd ed. Grand Rapids: Eerdmans, 2002.

———. "Is Genesis 1 a Creation Myth? Yes and No." Pages 71–102 in *Myth and Scripture: Contemporary Perspectives on Religion, Language, and Imagination.* Edited by Dexter E. Callender, Jr. RBS 78. Atlanta: Society of Biblical Literature, 2014.

———. *The Origins of Biblical Monotheism: Israel's Polytheistic Background and the Ugaritic Texts.* Oxford: Oxford University Press, 2001.

———. *The Rituals and Myths of the Feast of the Goodly Gods of KTU/CAT 1.23: Royal Constructions of Opposition, Intersection, Integration, and Domination.* RBS 51. Atlanta: Society of Biblical Literature, 2006.

———. *The Ugaritic Baal Cycle I: Introduction with Text, Translation and Commentary of KTU 1.1–1.2.* VTSup 55. Leiden: Brill, 1994.

———. *Where the Gods Are: Spatial Dimensions of Anthropomorphism in the Biblical World.* AYBRL. New Haven: Yale University Press, 2016.

Smith, Mark S., with contributions by Elizabeth Bloch-Smith. *The Pilgrimage Pattern in Exodus.* JSOTSup 239. Sheffield: Sheffield Academic, 1997.

Smith, William Robertson. *Lectures on the Religion of the Semites: Their Fundamental Institutions.* 3rd ed. London: A. & C. Black, 1927.

Soggin, J. Alberto. *Israel in the Biblical Period: Institutions, Festivals, Ceremonies, Rituals.* Edinburgh: T&T Clark, 2001.

———. *Judges: A Commentary.* OTL. Philadelphia: Westminster, 1981.

Speiser, E. A. *Genesis: A New Translation with Introduction and Commentary.* 3rd ed. AYB 1. Garden City, N.Y.: Doubleday, 1983.

Spencer, John R. "The Tasks of the Levites: *šmr* and *ṣbʾ*." *ZAW* 96 (1984): 267–71.

Sprinkle, Joe M. "Deuteronomic 'Just War' (Deut. 20, 10–20) and 2 Kings 3, 27." *Zeitschrift für altorientalische und biblische Rechtgeschichte* 6 (2000): 285–301.

Spronk, Klaas. *Beatific Afterlife in Ancient Israel and in the Ancient Near East.* AOAT 219. Kevelaer: Butzon & Bercker; Neukirchen-Vluyn: Neukirchener, 1986.

———. "Deborah, a Prophetess: The Meaning and Background of Judges 4:4–5." Pages 232–42 in *The Elusive Prophet: The Prophet as a Historical Person, Literary Character and Anonymous Artist.* Edited by Johannes C. de Moor. OtSt 45. Leiden: Brill, 2001.

Stackert, Jeffery. "Compositional Strata in the Priestly Sabbath: Exodus 31:12–17 and 35:1–3." *JHS* 11 (2011): 2–21.

———. *A Prophet like Moses: Prophecy, Law, and Israelite Religion.* Oxford: Oxford University Press, 2014.

———. *Rewriting the Torah: Literary Revision in Deuteronomy and the Holiness Legislation.* FAT 52. Tübingen: Mohr Siebeck, 2007.

Stager, Lawrence E. "The Archaeology of the Family in Ancient Israel." *BASOR* 260 (1985): 1–35.

———. "The Canaanite Silver Calf." Pages 577–80 in *Ashkelon 1: Introduction and Overview (1985–2006).* Edited by Lawrence E. Stager, J. David Schloen, and

Daniel M. Master. Harvard Semitic Museum Publications: Final Reports of the Leon Levy Expedition to Ashkelon. Winona Lake, Ind.: Eisenbrauns, 2008.

———. "Forging an Identity: The Emergence of Ancient Israel." Pages 90–131 in *The Oxford History of the Biblical World.* Edited by Michael D. Coogan. Oxford: Oxford University Press, 1998.

———. "The Fortress-Temple at Shechem and the 'House of El, Lord of the Covenant.'" Pages 228–49 in *Realia Dei: Essays in Archaeology and Biblical Interpretation in Honor of Edward F. Campbell, Jr., at His Retirement.* Edited by Prescott H. Williams, Jr., and Theodore Hiebert. Atlanta: Scholars Press, 1999.

———. See also Garnand, Brien K., and King, Philip J.

Stavrakopoulou, Francesca. "'Popular' Religion and 'Official' Religion: Practice, Perception, Portrayal." Pages 37–58 in *Religious Diversity in Ancient Israel and Judah.* Edited by Francesca Stavrakopoulou and John Barton. London: T&T Clark, 2010.

Stavrakopoulou, Francesca, and John Barton. "Introduction: Religious Diversity in Ancient Israel and Judah." Pages 1–8 in *Religious Diversity in Ancient Israel and Judah.* Edited by Francesca Stavrakopoulou and John Barton. London: T&T Clark, 2010.

Stern, Ephraim. *Archaeology of the Land of the Bible 2: The Assyrian, Babylonian, and Persian Periods, 732–332 BCE.* AYBRL. New York: Doubleday, 2001.

———. "The Eastern Border of the Kingdom of Judah in Its Last Days." Pages 399–409 in *Scripture and Other Artifacts: Essays on the Bible and Archaeology in Honor of Philip J. King.* Edited by Michael D. Coogan, J. Cheryl Exum, and Lawrence E. Stager. Louisville: Westminster/John Knox, 1994.

———. "From Many Gods to One God: The Archaeological Evidence." Pages 395–403 in *One God—One Cult—One Nation: Archaeological and Biblical Perspectives.* Edited by Reinhard G. Kratz and Hermann Spieckermann. BZAW 405. Berlin: de Gruyter, 2010.

———. "The Phoenician Source of Palestinian Cults at the End of the Iron Age." Pages 309–22 in *Symbiosis, Symbolism, and the Power of the Past: Canaan, Ancient Israel, and Their Neighbors from the Late Bronze Age Through Roman Palaestina.* Edited by William G. Dever and Seymour Gitin. Winona Lake, Ind.: Eisenbrauns, 2003.

———. "Schumacher's Shrine in Building 338 at Megiddo: A Rejoinder." *IEJ* 40 (1990): 102–7.

Stökl, Jonathan. "Ištar's Women, YHWH's Men? A Curious Gender-Bias in Neo-Assyrian and Biblical Prophecy." *ZAW* 121 (2009): 87–100.

———. "The *mtnb'wt* in Ezekiel 13 Reconsidered." *JBL* 132 (2013): 61–76.

———. *Prophecy in the Ancient Near East: A Philological and Sociological Comparison.* CHANE 56. Leiden: Brill, 2012.

Stol, Marten. *Birth in Babylonia and the Bible: Its Mediterranean Setting.* Groningen: Styx, 2000.

———. *Women in the Ancient Near East.* Berlin: de Gruyter, 2016.

Stowers, Stanley K. "Greeks Who Sacrifice and Those Who Do Not: Toward an Anthropology of Greek Religion." Pages 293–333 in *The Social World of the First Christians: Essays in Honor of Wayne A. Meeks.* Edited by L. Michael White and O. Larry Yarbrough. Minneapolis: Fortress, 1995.

———. "On the Comparison of Blood in Greek and Israelite Ritual." Pages 179–94 in *Hesed ve-Emet: Studies in Honor of Ernest S. Frerichs.* Edited by Jodi Magness and Seymour Gitin. BJS 320. Atlanta: Scholars Press, 1998.

Strawn, Brent A. *What Is Stronger Than a Lion? Leonine Image and Metaphor in the Hebrew Bible and the Ancient Near East.* OBO 212. Fribourg: Academic Press; Göttingen: Vandenhoeck & Ruprecht, 2005.

———. "A Woman at Prayer (Psalm 131, 2b) and Arguments 'from Parallelism.'" *ZAW* 124 (2012): 421–26.

Tadmor, Hayim. See Cogan, Mordechai.

Talmon, Shemaryahu. "The 'Desert Motif' in the Bible and in Qumran Literature." Pages 31–63 in *Biblical Motifs: Origins and Transformations.* Edited by Alexander Altmann. Philip W. Lown Institute of Advanced Judaic Studies, Brandeis University, Studies and Texts 3. Cambridge, Mass.: Harvard University Press, 1966.

Thiel, Winfried. *Die deuteronomische Redaktion von Jeremia 1–25.* WMANT 41. Neukirchen-Vluyn: Neukirchener, 1973.

———. *Die deuteronomische Redaktion von Jeremia 26–45: mit einer Gesamtbeurteilung der deuteronomistschen Redaktion des Buches Jeremia.* WMANT 52. Neukirchen-Vluyn: Neukirchener, 1981.

Thomsen, Ole. *Ritual and Desire: Catullus 61 and 62 and Other Ancient Documents on Wedding and Marriage.* Aarhus: Aarhus University Press, 1992.

Tigay, Jeffrey H. *Deuteronomy.* JPS Torah Commentary. Philadelphia: Jewish Publication Society 1996.

Tita, Hubert. *Gelübde als Bekenntnis: Eine Studie zu den Gelübden im Alten Testament.* OBO 181. Fribourg: Universitätsverlag; Göttingen: Vandenhoeck & Ruprecht, 2001.

Toorn, Karel van der. "Ancestors and Anthroponyms: Kinship Terms as Theophoric Elements in Hebrew Names." *ZAW* 108 (1996): 1–11.

———. "Cultic Prostitution." Pages 510–13 in *ABD* 5.

———. *Family Religion in Babylonia, Syria, and Israel: Continuity and Change in the Forms of Religious Life.* Studies in the History and Culture of the Ancient Near East 7. Leiden: Brill, 1996.

———. "Family Religion in Second Millennium West Asia (Mesopotamia, Emar, Nuzi)." Pages 127–58 in *Household and Family Religion in Antiquity.* Edited by John Bodel and Saul M. Olyan. Oxford: Blackwell, 2008.

———. "Female Prostitution in Payment of Vows in Ancient Israel." *JBL* 108 (1989): 193–205.

———. *From Her Cradle to Her Grave: The Role of Religion in the Life of the Israelite and the Babylonian Woman.* Biblical Seminar 23. Sheffield: JSOT Press, 1994.

———. "Gods and Ancestors in Emar and Nuzi." *ZA* 84 (1994): 38–59.

———. "Introduction: Religious Practices of the Individual and Family." Pages 423–24 in *Religions of the Ancient World: A Guide.* Edited by Sarah Iles Johnston. Cambridge, Mass.: Harvard University Press, 2004.

———. "Israelite Figurines: A View from the Texts." Pages 45–62 in *Sacred Time, Sacred Place: Archaeology and the Religion of Israel.* Edited by Barry M. Gittlen. Winona Lake, Ind.: Eisenbrauns, 2002.

———. "The Nature of the Biblical Teraphim in the Light of the Cuneiform Evidence." *CBQ* 52 (1990): 203–22.

———. "Nine Months Among the Peasants in the Palestinian Highlands: An Anthropological Perspective on Local Religion in the Early Iron Age." Pages 393–410 in *Symbiosis, Symbolism, and the Power of the Past: Canaan, Ancient Israel, and Their Neighbors from the Late Bronze Age Through Roman Palaestina.* Edited by William G. Dever and Seymour Gitin. Winona Lake, Ind.: Eisenbrauns, 2003.

———. "Saul and the Rise of Israelite State Religion." *VT* 43 (1993): 519–42.

———. "Theology, Priests, and Worship in Canaan and Ancient Israel." Pages 2043–58 in *CANE* 3–4.

Toorn, Karel van der, and Cees Houtman. "David and the Ark." *JBL* 113 (1994): 209–31.

Toorn, Karel van der, and T. J. Lewis. *"tĕrāpîm."* Pages 777–89 in *TDOT* 15.

Tov, Emanuel. "Different Editions of the Song of Hannah and of Its Narrative Framework." Pages 149–70 in *Tehillah le-Moshe: Biblical and Judaic Studies in Honor of Moshe Greenberg.* Edited by Mordechai Cogan, Barry L. Eichler, and Jeffrey H. Tigay. Winona Lake, Ind.: Eisenbrauns, 1997.

———. *Textual Criticism of the Hebrew Bible.* 3rd ed., revised and expanded. Minneapolis: Fortress, 2012.

Trible, Phyllis. "Bringing Miriam out of the Shadows." *BRev* 5/1 (February 1989): 14–25, 34.

———. "Eve and Miriam: From the Margins to the Center." Pages 15–24 in *Feminist Approaches to the Bible.* Edited by H. Shanks. Washington, D.C.: Biblical Archaeology Society, 1995.

Tropper, Josef. *Nekromantie: Totenbefragung im Alten Orient und im Alten Testament.* AOAT 223. Kevelaer: Butzon & Bercker; Neukirchen-Vluyn: Neukirchener, 1989.

Tsumura, David Toshio. *The First Book of Samuel.* New International Commentary on the Old Testament. Grand Rapids: Eerdmans, 2007.

———. "'New Moon' and 'Sabbath' in Samuel." *Exegetica* 6 (1995): 77–99 (Japanese).

Tuell, Steven S. *The Law of the Temple in Ezekiel 40–48.* HSM 49. Atlanta: Scholars Press, 1992.

Turner, Edith. See Myerhoff, Barbara G.

Turner, Victor. *The Forest of Symbols: Aspects of Ndembu Ritual.* Ithaca, N.Y.: Cornell University Press, 1967.

———. "Pilgrimages as Social Processes." Pages 166–230 in Victor Turner, *Dramas, Fields, and Metaphors: Symbolic Action in Human Society.* Symbol, Myth, and Ritual. Ithaca, N.Y.: Cornell University Press, 1974.

———. *Process, Performance, and Pilgrimage: A Study in Comparative Symbology.* Ranchi Anthropology Series 1. New Delhi: Concept, 1979.

———. *The Ritual Process: Structure and Anti-Structure.* Ithaca, N.Y.: Cornell University Press, 1969, 1977.

Twiss, Katheryn C. "Home Is Where the Hearth Is: Food and Identity in the Neolithic Levant." Pages 50–68 in *The Archaeology of Food and Identity.* Edited by Katheryn C. Twiss. Occasional Papers 34. Carbondale: Southern Illinois University Press, 2007.

Uehlinger, Christoph. See Keel, Othmar.

Ulrich, Eugene, ed. *The Biblical Qumran Scrolls: Transcriptions and Textual Variants.* VTSup 134. Leiden: Brill, 2010.

Ussishkin, David. "The Date of Building 338 at Megiddo: Additional Comments." *IEJ* 68 (2018): 232–36.

———. "The Date of the Judean Shrine at Arad." *IEJ* 38 (1988): 142–57.

———. "Fresh Examination of Old Excavations: Sanctuaries in the First Temple Period." Pages 67–85 in *Biblical Archaeology Today, 1990: Proceedings of the Second International Congress on Biblical Archaeology, Jerusalem, June–July 1990.* Edited by Avraham Biran and Joseph Aviram, with Alan Paris-Shadur. Jerusalem: Israel Exploration Society, 1993.

———. "Schumacher's Shrine in Building 338 at Megiddo." *IEJ* 39 (1989): 149–72.

Uziel, Joe, and Itzhaq Shai. "Iron Age Jerusalem: Temple-Palace, Capital City." *JAOS* 127 (2007): 161–70.

van den Boorn, G. P. F. See Boorn, G. P. F. van den.

van der Toorn, Karel. See Toorn, Karel van der.

van Dijk-Hemmes, Fokkelein. See Dijk-Hemmes, Fokkelein van.

van Gennep, Arnold. See Gennep, Arnold van.

Van Seters, John. *Abraham in History and Tradition.* New Haven: Yale University Press, 1975.

———. "The Place of the Yahwist in the History of Passover and Massot." *ZAW* 95 (1983): 167–82.

———. *The Yahwist. A Historian of Israelite Origins.* Winona Lake, Ind.: Eisenbrauns, 2013.

Vaughan, Patrick H. *The Meaning of "bāmâ" in the Old Testament: A Study of Etymological, Textual and Archaeological Evidence.* Society for Old Testament Studies Monograph Series 3. Cambridge: Cambridge University Press, 1974.

Vaux, Roland de. *Ancient Israel: Its Life and Institutions.* Grand Rapids: Eerdmans; Livonia, Mich.: Dove, 1997.

von Rad, Gerhard. See Rad, Gerhard von.

Vos, Clarence J. *Woman in Old Testament Worship.* Delft: Judels & Brinkman, 1968.

Vriezen, Karel J. H. "Archaeological Traces of Cult in Ancient Israel." Pages 45–80 in Bob Becking, Meindert Dijkstra, Marjo C. A. Korpel, and Karel J. H. Vriezen,

Only One God? Monotheism in Ancient Israel and the Veneration of the Goddess Asherah. Biblical Seminar 77. London: Sheffield Academic, 2001.

———. "Cakes and Figurines: Related Women's Cultic Offerings in Ancient Israel?" Pages 251–63 in *On Reading Prophetic Texts: Gender-Specific and Related Studies in Memory of Fokkelien van Dijk-Hemmes.* Edited by Bob Becking and Meindert Dijkstra. Leiden: Brill, 1996.

Wacker, Marie-Theres. "Hosea: The God-Identified Man and the Woman/Women of Israel." Pages 371–85 in *Feminist Biblical Interpretation: A Compendium of Critical Commentary on the Books of the Bible and Related Literature.* Edited by Luise Schottroff and Marie-Theres Wacker. Grand Rapids: Eerdmans, 2012.

———. "'Kultprostitution' im Alten Israel? Forschungsmythen, Spuren, Thesen." Pages 55–84 in *Tempelprostitution im Altertum: Fakten und Fiktionen.* Edited by Tanja S. Scheer. Oikumene Studien zur antiken Weltgeschichte 6. Berlin: Verlag Antike, 2009.

———. "Die Spiegel der Frauen (Ex 38, 8)—ein Beispiel." Pages 142–55 in Marie-Theres Wacker, "'Religionsgeschichte Israels' oder 'Theologie des Alten Testaments'—(k)eine Alternative?" *Jahrbuch für Biblische Theologie* 10 (1995).

Wagenaar, Jan A. *Origin and Transformation of the Ancient Israelite Festival Calendar.* Beihefte zur Zeitschrift fur Altorientalische und Biblische Rechtsgeschichte 6. Wiesbaden: Harrassowitz, 2005.

———. "Passover and the First Day of the Festival of Unleavened Bread in the Priestly Festival Calendar." *VT* 54 (2004): 250–68.

———. "The Priestly Festival Calendar and the Babylonian New Year Festivals: Origin and Transformation of the Ancient Israelite Festival Year." Pages 218–52 in *The Old Testament in Its World: Papers Read at the Winter Meeting, January 2003, the Society for Old Testament Study, and at the Joint Meeting, July 2003, the Society for Old Testament Study and Het Oudtestamentisch Werkgezelschap in Nederland en België.* Edited by Robert P. Gordon and Johannes C. de Moor. OtSt/OTS 52. Leiden: Brill, 2005.

Wagner, S. "*biqqēš.*" Pages 229–41 in *TDOT* 2.

———. "*dāraš.*" Pages 293–307 in *TDOT* 3.

Walsh, Carey Ellen. *The Fruit of the Vine: Viticulture in Ancient Israel.* HSM 60. Atlanta: Scholars Press, 2000.

Walters, Stanley D. "After Drinking (1 Sam 1:9)." Pages 527–46 in *Crossing Boundaries and Linking Horizons: Studies in Honor of Michael C. Astour on His 80th Birthday.* Edited by Gordon D. Young, Mark W. Chavalas, and Richard E. Averbeck. Bethesda, Md.: CDL, 1997.

———. "Hannah and Anna: The Greek and Hebrew Texts of 1 Samuel 1." *JBL* 107 (1988): 385–412.

Weber, Max. *Ancient Judaism.* Translated and edited by Hans H. Gerth and Don Martindale. Glencoe, Ill.: Free Press, 1952.

Wegner, Judith Romney. "*'Coming Before the Lord':* The Exclusion of Women from the Public Domain of the Israelite Priestly Cult." Pages 451–65 in *The Book of*

Leviticus: Composition and Reception. Edited by Rolf Rendtorff and Robert A. Kugler. VTSup 93. Leiden: Brill, 2003.

———. "'Coming Before the LORD': *lpny yhwh* and the Exclusion of Women from the Divine Presence." Pages 81–91 in *Hesed ve-Emet: Studies in Honor of Ernest S. Frerichs.* Edited by Jodi Magness and Seymour Gitin. BJS 320. Atlanta: Scholars Press, 1998.

Weinberg, Saul S. "A Moabite Shrine Group." *MUSE* 12 (1978): 30–48.

Weinfeld, Moshe. *Deuteronomy and the Deuteronomic School.* Oxford: Clarendon, 1972.

———. *Deuteronomy 1–11: A New Translation with Introduction and Commentary.* AYB 5. New York: Doubleday, 1991.

Weippert, Manfred. *Jahwe und die anderen Götte: Studien zur Religionsgeschichte des antiken Israel in ihrem syrisch-palästinischen Kontext.* FAT 18. Tübingen: Mohr Siebeck, 1997.

Wellhausen, Julius. *Prolegomena zur Geschichte Israel.* Berlin: G. Reimer, 1883. Originally published as *Geschichte Israels.* Berlin: G. Reimer, 1878.

———. *Reste arabischen Heidentums.* 2nd ed. Berlin: de Gruyter, 1927.

———. *Der Text der Bücher Samuelis untersucht.* Göttingen: Vandenhoeck & Ruprecht, 1871.

Welton, Rebekah. "Ritual and the Agency of Food in Ancient Israel and Judah: Food Futures in Biblical Studies." *Biblical Interpretation* 25 (2017): 609–24.

Wenham, Gordon J. "*Betûlāh* 'A Girl of Marriageable Age.'" *VT* 22 (1972): 326–48.

———. "Deuteronomy and the Central Sanctuary." Pages 94–108 in *A Song of Power and the Power of Song: Essays on the Book of Deuteronomy.* Edited by Duane L. Christensen. Sources for Biblical and Theological Study 3. Winona Lake, Ind.: Eisenbrauns, 1993.

Werline, Rodney A. "Prayer, Politics, and Power in the Hebrew Bible." *Interpretation* 68 (2014): 5–16.

Werner, Eric. "Jewish Music, Liturgical." Pages 614–34 in *The New Grove Dictionary of Music and Musicians* 9. Edited by Stanley Sadie. London: Macmillan, 1980.

Westbrook, Raymond. "Elisha's True Prophecy in 2 Kings 3." *JBL* 124 (2005): 530–32.

Westenholz, Joan Goodnick. "Religious Personnel: Mesopotamia." Pages 292–95 in *Religions of the Ancient World: A Guide.* Edited by Sarah Iles Johnston. Cambridge, Mass.: Harvard University Press, 2004.

———. "Tamar, *Qĕdēšā, Qadištu,* and Sacred Prostitution in Mesopotamia." *HTR* 82 (1989): 245–66.

Weyde, Karl William. *The Appointed Festivals of YHWH: The Festival Calendar in Leviticus 23 and the* sukkôt *Festival in Other Biblical Texts.* FAT 2/4. Tübingen: Mohr Siebeck, 2004.

White, Ellen. "Review of Carol Meyers, *Households and Holiness: The Religious Culture of Israelite Women.*" *JHS* 5 (2005). http://www.jhsonline.org/reviews/review195.htm.

Whitekettle, Richard. "Leviticus 12 and the Israelite Women: Ritual Process, Liminality, and the Womb." *ZAW* 107 (1995): 393–408.

Whitney, J. T. "'Bamoth' in the Old Testament." *Tyndale Bulletin* 30 (1979): 125–47.

Wiggins, Steven A. "The Myth of Asherah: Lion Lady and Serpent Goddess." *UF* 23 (1991): 383–94.

Wildberger, Hans. *Isaiah 1–12: A Commentary.* Continental Commentaries. Minneapolis: Fortress, 1990.

Wilhelm, Gernot. "Marginalien zu Herodot, Klio 199." Pages 505–24 in *Lingering over Words: Studies in Ancient Near Eastern Literature in Honor of William L. Moran.* Edited by Tzvi Abusch, John Huehnergard, and Piotr Steinkeller. Atlanta: Scholars Press, 1990.

Willett, Elizabeth A. "Women and Household Shrines in Ancient Israel." PhD diss., University of Arizona, 1999.

Williams, Gary R. "Frustrated Expectations in Isaiah V 1–7: A Literary Interpretation." *VT* 35 (1985): 459–65.

Williamson, H. G. M. *The Book Called Isaiah: Deutero-Isaiah's Role in Composition and Redaction.* Oxford: Clarendon, 1994.

———. "The Death of Josiah and the Continuing Development of the Deuteronomistic History." *VT* 32 (1982): 242–48.

———. *1 and 2 Chronicles.* New Century Bible Commentary. Grand Rapids: Eerdmans; London: Marshall Morgan & Scott, 1982.

———. "Prophetesses in the Hebrew Bible." Pages 65–80 in *Prophecy and Prophets in Ancient Israel: Proceedings of the Oxford Old Testament Seminar.* Edited by John Day. LHBOTS 531. New York: T&T Clark, 2010.

———. "Reliving the Death of Josiah: A Reply to C. T. Begg." *VT* 37 (1987): 9–15.

Willis, John T. "An Anti-Elide Narrative Tradition from a Prophetic Circle at the Ramah Sanctuary." *JBL* 90 (1971): 288–308.

———. "Cultic Elements in the Story of Samuel's Birth and Dedication." *ST* 26 (1972): 33–61.

———. "The Genre of Isa 5:1–7." *JBL* 96 (1977): 337–62.

———. "The Song of Hannah and Psalm 113." *CBQ* 35 (1973): 139–54.

Wills, Lawrence M. *Judith: A Commentary on the Book of Judith.* Hermeneia. Minneapolis: Fortress, 2019.

Wilson, Michael K. "'As You Like It': The Idolatry of Micah and the Danites (Judges 17–18)." *Reformed Theological Review* 54 (May–August 1995): 73–85.

Wilson, Robert R. "The Hardening of Pharaoh's Heart." *CBQ* 41 (1979): 18–36.

Winckler, Hugo. *Sammlung von Keilinschrifttexten.* Leipzig: Eduard Pfeiffer, 1893–1895.

Winter, Urs. *Frau und Göttin: Exegetische und ikonographische Studien zum weiblichen Gottesbild im Alten Israel und in dessen Umwelt.* OBO 53. Freiburg: Universitätsverlag; Göttingen: Vandenhoeck & Ruprecht, 1983.

Witte, Marcus. See Gertz, Jan Christian.

Wood, Bryant G. *The Sociology of Pottery in Ancient Palestine: The Ceramic Industry and the Diffusion of Ceramic Style in the Bronze and Iron Ages.* JSOTSup 103. Sheffield: JSOT Press, 1990.

Wright, David P. "David Autem Remansit in Hierusalem: Felix Coniunctio!" Pages 215–30 in *Pomegranates and Golden Bells: Studies in Biblical, Jewish, and Near Eastern Ritual, Law, and Literature in Honor of Jacob Milgrom.* Edited by David P. Wright, David Noel Freedman, and Avi Hurvitz. Winona Lake, Ind.: Eisenbrauns, 1995.

———. *The Disposal of Impurity: Elimination Rites in the Bible and in Hittite and Mesopotamian Literature.* SBLDS 101. Atlanta: Scholars Press, 1987.

———. "Ritual Theory, Ritual Texts, and the Priestly-Holiness Writings of the Pentateuch." Pages 195–216 in *Social Theory and the Study of Israelite Religion: Essays in Retrospect and Prospect.* Edited by Saul M. Olyan. RBS 71. Atlanta: Society of Biblical Literature, 2012.

———. "The Spectrum of Priestly Impurity." Pages 150–81 in *Priesthood and Cult in Ancient Israel.* Edited by Gary A. Anderson and Saul M. Olyan. JSOTSup 125. Sheffield: JSOT Press, 1991.

———. "Two Types of Impurity in the Priestly Writings of the Bible." Pages 180–93 in *Proceedings of the Third International Symposium on Medicine in Bible and Talmud, Jerusalem, December 7–9, 1987* (= *Koroth* 9, 1988).

———. "Unclean and Clean (OT)." Pages 729–41 in *ABD* 6.

Wright, David P., and Richard N. Jones. "Discharge." Pages 204–7 in *ABD* 2.

Wright, Jacob L. "How and When the Seventh Day Became Shabbat." TheTorah .com (2015). https://thetorah.com/article/how-and-when-the-seventh-day-became-shabbat.

———. "Shabbat of the Full Moon." TheTorah.com (2015). https://thetorah.com/article/shabbat-of-the-full-moon.

Wright, Richard M. *Linguistic Evidence for the Pre-Exilic Date of the Yahwistic Source.* New York: T&T Clark, 2005.

Wyatt, Nicolas. *Religious Texts from Ugarit: The Words of Ilimilku and His Colleagues.* Biblical Seminar 23. Sheffield: Sheffield Academic, 1998.

Yamauchi, Edwin M. "Cultic Prostitution: A Case Study in Cultural Diffusion." Pages 213–22 in *Orient and Occident: Essays Presented to Cyrus H. Gordon on the Occasion of His Sixty-Fifth Birthday.* Edited by Harry A. Hoffner. AOAT 22. Neukirchen-Vluyn: Neukirchener; Kevelaer: Butzon & Bercker, 1973.

Yee, Gale A. "The Form Critical Study of Isaiah 5:1–7 as a Song and a Juridical Parable." *CBQ* 43 (1981): 30–40.

———. "Ideological Criticism: Judges 17–21 and the Dismembered Body." Pages 138–60 in *Judges and Method: New Approaches in Biblical Studies.* 2nd ed. Edited by Gale A. Yee. Minneapolis: Fortress, 2007.

———. *Poor Banished Children of Eve: Women as Evil in the Hebrew Bible.* Minneapolis: Fortress, 2003.

———. "Recovering Marginalized Groups in Ancient Israel: Methodological Considerations." Pages 10–27 in *To Break Every Yoke: Essays in Honor of Marvin L. Chaney.* Edited by Robert B. Coote and Norman K. Gottwald. SWBA 2/3. Sheffield: Sheffield Phoenix, 2007.

Yoder, Christine Roy. *Wisdom as a Woman of Substance: A Socioeconomic Reading of Proverbs 1–9 and 31:10–31.* BZAW 304. Berlin: de Gruyter, 2001.

Zayadine, Fawzi. "Sculpture in Ancient Jordan." Pages 31–61 in *Treasures from an Ancient Land: The Art of Jordan.* Edited by Piotr Bienkowski. Stroud, Gloucestershire: Alan Sutton; Liverpool: National Museums and Galleries of Merseyside, 1991.

Zborowski, Mark, and Elizabeth Herzog. *Life Is with People: The Culture of the Shtetl.* New York: Schocken, 1952.

Zenger, Erich, et al. *Einleitung in das Alte Testament.* 7th ed. Kohlhammer Studienbücher Theologie 1,1. Stuttgart: Kohlhammer, 2008.

Zevit, Ziony. "Converging Lines of Evidence Bearing on the Date of P." *ZAW* 94 (1982): 481–511.

———. *The Religions of Ancient Israel: A Synthesis of Parallactic Approaches.* New York: Continuum, 2001.

Zias, Joseph. "Lust and Leprosy: Confusion or Correlation?" *BASOR* 275 (1989): 27–31.

Zilberg, Peter. "A Simple Clay Portable Shrine." Pages 73–81 in Yosef Garfinkel, Saar Ganor, and Michael G. Hasel, *Khirbet Qeiyafa Vol. 4. Excavation Report 2007–2013: Art, Cult, and Epigraphy.* Edited by Martin G. Klingbeil. Jerusalem: Israel Exploration Society, 2018.

———. See also Garfinkel, Yosef.

Zimmerli, Walther. *Ezekiel 1: A Commentary on the Book of the Prophet Ezekiel, Chapters 1–24.* Hermeneia. Philadelphia: Fortress, 1979.

———. *Ezekiel 2: A Commentary on the Book of the Prophet Ezekiel, Chapters 25–48.* Hermeneia. Philadelphia: Fortress, 1983.

Zorn, Jeffrey R. "Naṣbeh, Tell en-." Pages 101–3 in *OEANE* 4.

Index of Subjects

Index of Modern Authors

Index of Ancient Sources